Praise for *Encyclopedia of Goddesses and Heroines*

"Patricia Monaghan is deeply missed by her colleagues, friends, and students; this new edition of her marvelous *Encyclopedia of Goddesses and Heroines* is a fitting memorial to her lifelong contribution in the field of women's spirituality and goddess scholarship. This book is a rich resource and a valuable asset for investigators looking into the ancient worldwide tradition of goddess veneration. Who knew She had so many names?"
—**Vicki Noble**, cocreator of the *Motherpeace* Tarot deck and author of *Shakti Woman*

"This introductory overview of historical goddesses worldwide is a much-needed correction to the androcentric biases that still skew our sense of religion. I'm grateful to Patricia Monaghan for researching and composing this rich history of spiritual abundance."
—**Charlene Spretnak**, author of *Lost Goddesses of Early Greece*

"I count Patricia Monaghan as one of the illustrious ancestors of the global women's spirituality movement. The *Encyclopedia of Goddesses and Heroines* first came onto the literary scene at a time when most people knew little about the feminine face of the divine and almost nothing about the myths and rituals of African people. Patricia's book gives us the names and definitions that make it possible to embrace goddesses from cultures around the world. A new generation of students and artists will reap the benefit of her legacy."
—**Yeye Luisah Teish**, author of
Jambalaya: The Natural Woman's Book of Personal Charms and Practical Rituals

Praise for Patricia Monaghan's *The Red-Haired Girl from the Bog*

"A rich, beautiful story of a nearly forgotten world…Myth, tale, and tradition are brought to light and burnished in an engaging style. The world of w͏ ͏
nine power all shine through."
author of *T.*

"Few stories are as fascinating as this story of a return to Irel͏ ͏ ͏ ͏ ͏ ͏ ͏ ͏ ͏ ͏ ͏
enchantment. It's amazing to find someone who presents so wcn the people and places, the myths, realities, and history of this country."
—**Thomas Berry**, author of *The Dream of the Earth* and *The Great Work*

"Patricia Monaghan daringly braids past and present together on her inspirational pilgrimage to Ireland's mythic sites."   —**Caitlín Matthews**, author of *The Celtic Spirit*

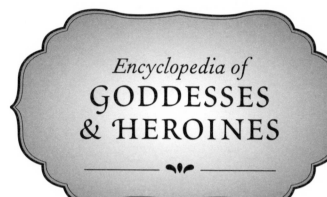

Encyclopedia of
GODDESSES
& HEROINES

ALSO BY PATRICIA MONAGHAN

Dancing with Chaos

Encyclopedia of Celtic Myth and Folklore

Meditation — The Complete Guide (with Eleanor G. Viereck)

The Goddess Companion

Goddesses in World Culture

The Goddess Path

Grace of Ancient Land

Homefront

Magical Gardens: Cultivating Soil and Spirit

The Red-Haired Girl from the Bog: The Landscape of Celtic Myth and Spirit

Seasons of the Witch

Encyclopedia of
GODDESSES
& HEROINES

PATRICIA MONAGHAN, PhD

REVISED EDITION

New World Library
Novato, California

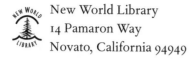 New World Library
14 Pamaron Way
Novato, California 94949

Encyclopedia of Goddesses and Heroines, 2 Volumes, by Patricia Monaghan, was originally published in hardcover by Greenwood, an imprint of ABC-CLIO, LLC, Santa Barbara, CA. Copyright © 2009 by Patricia Monaghan. Condensed ebook edition by arrangement with ABC-CLIO, LLC, Santa Barbara, CA. All rights reserved.

Text design by Tona Pearce Myers

Library of Congress Cataloging-in-Publication Data
Monaghan, Patricia.
Encyclopedia of goddesses and heroines / Patricia Monaghan. — Revised Edition.
    pages   cm
Includes bibliographical references and index.
ISBN 978-1-60868-217-1 (pbk. : alk. paper) — ISBN 978-1-60868-218-8 (ebook)
1. Goddesses—Encyclopedias. 2. Women heroes—Encyclopedias. I. Title.
BL473.5.M663 2014
202'.11403—dc23   2013045131

First printing, April 2014
ISBN 978-1-60868-217-1
Printed in Canada on 100% postconsumer-waste recycled paper

 New World Library is proud to be a Gold Certified Environmentally Responsible Publisher. Publisher certification awarded by Green Press Initiative. www.greenpressinitiative.org

10 9 8 7 6 5 4 3 2 1

CONTENTS

THE AMERICAS

INTRODUCTION

In 2008, archaeologists in Germany made a startling discovery. In Swabian Jura, where caves in limestone cliffs sheltered ancient humans, a figurine was unearthed from rubble. Carved from mammoth ivory, the figure showed a naked woman. Such figures have been found before where this "Venus" emerged, for the figure found in Hohle Fels Cave was named for a Roman goddess, as has been common since these figures were first discovered more than a century ago. In Austria (Willendorf and Galgenberg), France (Brassempouy, Laussel), and other European sites (Dolní Vûstonice in the Czech Republic, Moravany in Slovakia, Monruz in Switzerland, Mal'ta in Russia), archaeologists have found tiny figures of naked women. They are among the most ancient artworks of humanity, carved from stone or bone or molded from clay between twenty and thirty thousand years ago.

That long ago, during the Paleolithic Era, humans lived in small groups hunting and gathering foods. Recent studies suggest a large proportion, up to 80 percent, of their diet came from plant foods like berries, fruits, and roots, which scholars assume were gathered by women. Meat, while providing necessary nutrients, was less readily available and required significant strength and skill to acquire, and it is presumed hunting was a predominantly male occupation, although women may have trapped small mammals and caught fish. What distinguishes this period of human history from earlier ones is that for the first time humans began to use stone tools. This revolution led to others, such as the establishment of year-round villages and the invention of art.

What knowledge we have of these ancestors comes from scanty traces of their daily lives. Only material resistant to decay survives the millennia: bone, stone, fired clay. We have no way of knowing how ancient humans dressed or what footwear they favored. We have no Paleolithic fishing nets or traps, no spears, no baskets. We do not know how they organized their societies or traced their descent lines. We have no idea what languages they used. But because they carved bone and painted on stone, we can see and appreciate their art.

The cave paintings at Lascaux and Pech-Merle in France show that these ancient humans had a sophisticated sense of beauty and a command of painterly techniques. In Lascaux, animals leap and prance around the walls and roof of a series of interlocking caves. At Pech-Merle, spotted horses and woolly mammoths adorn the walls, and the outline of a hand suggests the presence of the artist. In addition to such painted galleries, we have dozens of examples of Paleolithic portable art in the form of expressive incised drawings of animals on bone and delicate carvings of "Venus" figurines.

Before 2008, experts dated these figures to between 28,000 and 24,000 years ago. Despite the span of time involved and despite the stylistic diversity in the figures, the Venuses share an emphasis on female sexual characteristics. Breasts and pubic triangle are always exaggerated; thighs and buttocks can be disproportionately large as well. This emphasis seems to have been so important that many Venuses have no facial features and only sketchy arms and legs. They are never clothed, although some wear what appear to be woven belts, and most have elaborate hairstyles. Contemporaneous cave paintings, with their highly realistic depiction of prey animals, show that these artists did not lack pictoral ability. Rather, the artists appear to have selectively exaggerated certain aspects of female anatomy.

Although we cannot know whether men or women (or both) made the carvings, or what they meant, interpretations abound. Among these is the idea the images represent the first known deity: a goddess. This theory is supported by the fact that virtually the only human images found in such ancient art are these full-bodied naked females, with the artists otherwise focusing their energies on animals. But this idea is a controversial one, especially among male scholars, some of whom prefer to label the figures as "Paleolithic pornography," projecting today's sexual behavior into the distant past. Because for nearly 2,000 years, male monotheism has been the dominant religious pattern, the idea that ancient humans honored a goddess as their primary divinity is unsettling to many, scholars and nonscholars alike.

Whether a goddess or not, the figure at Hohle Fels Cave created a sensation. Finds of Paleolithic Venuses, while never commonplace, are frequent enough that archaeologists were not surprised to unearth another. But stone figures like the Venus of Willendorf have been found with other objects suggesting an age of no more than 30,000 years. Because the Hohle Fels figure

was carved of bone, scientists were able to carbon-date it. This showed the figure to be 35,000 to 40,000 years old, 10,000 years older than similar finds. The Venus of Hohle Fels is the oldest depiction of the human form ever found. And she is indisputably female.

What does this Venus look like? Like other such works, she is naked and robust, corpulent or possibly pregnant. Her breasts are huge and her pubic triangle exaggerated. Her arms and legs are tiny in proportion to her body, and she has no face. Where the head should be, Venus has a ring, suggesting she was worn as a pendant or amulet. She is only 2½ inches long and weighs less than an ounce.

Is this the image of humanity's primal divinity? We cannot know what people believed in prehistory, as by definition they left no written records. We do know that since recorded history began, humans have honored goddesses, for among the earliest written documents are hymns to the Babylonian goddess Inanna. But the Hohle Fels figure is ten times older than the oldest religious writing.

We cannot know whether those who carved the Hohle Fels Venus intended to represent a divinity in female form. But we do know that almost every culture since the dawn of time has honored goddesses as well as gods. Then, somewhere around 2,500 years ago, monotheism emerged in the eastern Mediterranean, first in the form of Hebrew tribal religion (which became Judaism), then as Christianity, and finally as Islam. These related religions center their worship on a single male divinity. In doing so, they eliminate age-old reverence for the divine female.

By contrast, no goddess has ever occupied the solitary position in a religion. The difference between monotheism and goddess religion cannot be clearer: No monotheistic goddess religion has ever been found. Every religion that honors a goddess honors a god as well.

Debate rages over whether the honoring of goddesses makes any difference to the lives of real women, with critics pointing out the practice of widow burning in Hindu India, for instance, as proof that placing a goddess on the altar does not necessarily free women from oppression. Similarly, Greek and Roman religion created magnificent images of the feminine divine, yet denied basic rights to women. Patriarchy and monotheism are not identical. One can exist without the other.

There is no question monotheism limits women in religious situations. Only recently have some Christian denominations permitted women to serve as priests, with others holding up the presumed "sex of god" as a reason to deny the pulpit to women. Whether such bias extends beyond the church is a matter of debate, but there is little question that boys who are taught that god looks like them, but not like their mothers and sisters, grow up differently than girls who are taught the opposite. It is probably not surprising that those raised with such an orientation find it difficult to believe that our forebears may have honored divinity in female form and captured her image in forms such as the Hohle Fels Venus. Although it is certainly possible men carved big-breasted women as fantasy sexual objects 35,000 years ago, the greater likelihood is that this faceless woman represents what we call "Mother Nature," the embodiment in female form of the forces to which human life is subject.

Whether or not prehistoric figures represent goddesses, there is no doubt that once written history begins, we find goddesses sharing the religious stage with gods. Throughout the world, people pictured divinity in female form. Often, divine women acted like human women, especially when they performed the one activity biologically limited to women: bearing children. Goddesses often conceive without a male partner. They are impregnated by wind or ocean waves, by snakes or fiery flames, or simply by their own desire. When they have a mate, the relationship need not replicate those of humans. The goddess may have intercourse with her father or her brother, with a stranger, or with several deities at once. She may be promiscuous. Or she may have one mate with whom she forms a model of the ideal human couple.

Not all female divinities are "mother goddesses."

Goddesses can appear as young nymphs, self-reliant workers, aged sages. They can be athletes or huntresses, dancers or acrobats, herbalists or midwives. We find goddesses as teachers, inventors, bartenders, potters, surfers, magicians, warriors, and queens. Virtually any social role women have played or are capable of playing appears in a goddess myth.

This volume shows the breadth of possibilities associated with the feminine through many ages and cultures. Some figures will be familiar to the general reader, especially those from classical European sources. Others are obscure, recorded only in a single source as, for instance, some native North American stories transcribed from the last speaker of a dying language. Not all would be called "goddesses" by the people who told their stories, for that word generally refers to divine or supernatural beings. Between such figures and mortal women exists a category this work calls "heroines." Some were originally human women who attained to legendary status: clan ancestors, extraordinarily faithful lovers, self-sacrificing saviors, remarkable queens, bold adventurers, wonder workers. Others represent a halfway category between human and divine. These include women with superhuman powers, spirits of nature, personified abstractions, bodhisattvas, ogres, cannibals, and saints. Finally, monotheistic religions often have female figures who function in goddess-like ways, giving birth to gods or saving humanity from peril. Although monotheisms deny the existence of goddesses, these figures are listed in this work, because such figures are sometimes submerged goddesses or powerful goddess-like beings. Where such figures are included, the view of worshippers from that religion is clearly stated.

No encyclopedia, no matter its length, could list all the goddesses the world has known. Due to colonization and forced conversion, innumerable goddesses and their stories have been lost. But an impressive amount of information remains, although scattered in sacred texts, literary epics and drama, story collections, ethnographies, and many other works. This encyclopedia brings together thousands of such sources to offer an entry point for further research. Casual and curious readers will find the legends and myths the most compelling part of this work, but researchers will be able to trace each figure to additional writers, who in turn will provide further reference points.

All the works referenced in this book are in English. This excludes many works available in other languages, especially those of the cultures in question. In some areas, as with the former Soviet Union, little is available in translation. Were all published material in multiple languages to be included in this encyclopedia, it would be volumes longer. But the sources listed typically offer bibliographical references in the languages of cultural origin for each figure, so scholars should be able to access information where available.

Sources are not limited to scholarly ones, because much goddess material appears in literature and in children's storybooks. The Roman poet Ovid, for instance, wrote goddess narratives that are among the classics of ancient literature. In other cultures, such literary treatments are not available in English, but the myths and legends appear as narrations for children and young adults. Where traditional religion was subjugated, goddess narratives often were sustained by becoming "old wives' tales," told orally to children and as entertainment to adults. Thus folklore as well as literature provides a source of information about ancient goddess figures.

Due to the occasional inconsistency of electronic sources, only material published in paper format has been used. Scholarly material continually becomes more readily available electronically, and many of these sources can be accessed that way. However, some materials available only on the Internet are of questionable validity and/or offer an uncritical analysis of the material. Thus Internet-only sources have been excluded.

The encyclopedia's sections are based on geographical and cultural divisions. Each section offers an introduction describing the role of women therein.

Any specific questions contemporary researchers address are also covered in these introductory sections. Finally, modern revivals of ancient goddess religions are mentioned as well as ethical or other concerns about such revivals. Each section provides individual entries for important goddesses and heroines from that culture. Rather than full footnotes for each entry, the source of the story is noted, for which readers may refer to the bibliography.

Despite this book's length, there is no question that some goddesses are missing. In some cases, their stories have not yet been published in English. In other cases, the narratives do not specify their names. A figure might be called "the earth goddess," while in the same story a male divinity is given a personal name. The quest to reclaim lost goddesses is never ending, for as with the Venus of Hohle Fels Cave, information continually comes to light. Such new information can only add to the great richness of images of female potency and power offered in these pages.

NOTE ON SPELLING AND PRONUNCIATION

Hundreds of languages and thousands of sources are found in this book. Because languages undergo changes, especially when transliterated (changed from one alphabet to another), varying spellings make consistency difficult when so many sources are involved. Therefore, the following rules have been used: where possible, the best-attested modern spelling is employed; otherwise, the spelling from the most recent source is offered. In a few cases, where a figure has become widely known under a spelling now considered inexact, the common spelling is used, with the more modern spelling included. Pronunciation guides are not offered, due to the number of languages involved. For pronunciation, see sources and bibliographies.

AFRICA

Among continents, Africa ranks second after Asia in size and population. Africa's size challenges researchers into religion and spirituality, as does the depth of its history. Most scientists agree the human race emerged in Africa approximately 200,000 years ago. All humans descend from "Eve," who lived some 140,000 years ago in eastern or central Africa. Other prehistoric women have descendants today, but "Eve" supplied the DNA of all human mitochondria.

Rivers, deserts, mountain ranges, and rain forests divide Africa into regions reflected in the continent's cultures. Speakers of Bantu languages predominate along the Niger and Congo Rivers, and in some parts of central and eastern Africa. Nilotic groups live in east Africa. In southern Africa's Kalahari Desert live the Bushmen (San), while Pygmy peoples live nearby and in central Africa. In most of eastern Africa, Arabic influence and language are dominant.

Today, most of Africa is Christian or Islamic; thus this section does not represent the spiritual views of a majority of contemporary Africans. Approximately 10 percent of Africans practice traditional religions; although a statistical minority, these practitioners number in the millions. Traditional religions include the Ifá rituals of the Yoruba in western Africa, the most popularly held indigenous religion in Africa today.

Smaller numbers follow the religions of the Fon of Benin and the Ewe of southern Ghana. Small numbers practice traditions of the Bushmen and other groups. In North Africa, despite the intense pressure of Islam, some indigenous religious ways can be found among the Berbers of Morocco and Algeria and seminomadic people such as the Tuareg of the Sahara.

Researchers in goddess religion face challenges in Africa because of the influence of monotheistic religions, which arrived with European and Arab colonization. In the nineteenth and twentieth centuries, missionaries recorded some myths, possibly misinterpreting information provided by African people. For instance, sources describe a "high god" who withdrew from humanity to control life on earth from afar; this god resembles the male god of Abrahamic religions. Yet sources suggest such divinities were originally not only male but female, dual sexed or bisexual, or without gender.

African religions often describe twin primal ancestors, usually a sister and brother. Scholars have written about the importance of twins in African cosmology, but little attention has been paid to specific roles of the male and female twins, who may embody an ideal of cosmic balance. Some cultures show evidence of matrilineality in tandem with patrilineality, although scholars typically elevate the latter.

Most African religions have multiple beings, ranked below gods but above humans. Such a being might be called a "spirit" or an orisha (the latter a Yoruba term). Spirits can be harmful, as with a murdered, and thereafter murderous, ghost. Benevolent spirits include ancestors, who become helpers to descendants. Devotion to ancestors is prominent in many African religions. Because ancestors are both male and female, female ancestral spirits are celebrated with equal rites.

Using "goddess" to describe figures from traditional African religion presents difficulties. Because the Abrahamic concept of divinity is typically abstracted from nature, African religions have been dismissed as "animistic," as though finding divinity in nature is less developed than abstraction. Such attitudes diminish the roles natural powers, including the earth, play in traditional African religions. Additionally, the role of ancestors is not well described with the term "goddess," which can imply an immortal and nonhuman figure. Finally, the distinction between a folkloric or semihistorical figure and a divine one can be difficult to discern; early recorders may have wrongly demoted such female figures, whereas African religion often sees ancestors as becoming godlike figures after death.

African traditional religions are based in ritual and orally conveyed story. Rituals require the artistic efforts of community members. Both women and men typically take part, although the common practice of having secret societies means men and women may not participate in, or know of, each other's rituals. As traditional religions have given way to Christianity and Islam, many women's traditions have been lost.

Traditional religions are not the only ones native to Africa, for Egyptian religion has deep roots and still-thriving branches. Since approximately 10,000 BCE, people have lived along the banks of the Nile. By approximately 6000 BCE, two large civilizations thrived, the Upper and Lower Kingdoms; although they traded with each other, the kingdoms remained

separate for almost 2,000 years. Divinities included many goddesses, especially bovine divinities who represented an important resource among cattle-herding peoples.

Egypt was unified around 3000 BCE as the Old Kingdom. The pyramids of Giza were built, indicative of a well-developed religious tradition of caring for the dead. An unsettled period, called the First Intermediate Period, followed but stability returned with the Middle Kingdom (2040 BCE). Around 1650 BCE, an invasion briefly disrupted Egyptian life, but establishment of the New Kingdom (1550–1070 BCE) returned Egypt to Egyptian rule. During the fourteenth century BCE, King Akhenaton declared the land would honor only a male sun god, Aten, creating what was arguably the world's first monotheism. Upon Akhenaton's death, Egyptian polytheism was restored. Although politically Egypt went into decline in 343 BCE, Egypt continued to have religious influence on the lands around the Mediterranean. Under Greek rulership and under the Roman Empire, non-Egyptian followers embraced Egyptian goddesses, including divinities such as Isis. After Christianization, some goddess images survived in a Christian context, so the influence of Egyptian goddesses remains active today. Finally, revivals of Egyptian religion have been prominent in European occultism for centuries.

Consideration of African religions would be incomplete without discussion of the African diaspora. The Arabic slave trade was established before the arrival of Europeans, with attendant forcible conversion to Islam. There are no known Afro-Arabic syncretic religions, as there are Afro-Brazilian and Afro-Caribbean religious paths.

With the enslavement of millions of Africans in the fifteenth through the nineteenth century, people ripped from their religious roots retained and revived their traditions in the New World. Slavery brought Africans into connection with indigenous Americans, some also enslaved, as well as enslaved and indentured Europeans, usually rural poor who sustained pagan traditions. Melded or syncretized African religions are attested as early as the 1500s.

In Brazil, where almost half the population has African heritage, several syncretic religions emerged, followed by millions. Afro-Brazilian religions include Candomblé or Macumba/Quimbanda, both based in Yoruba religion, the latter including European witchcraft practices. In Cuba and Puerto Rico, Yoruba orishas are honored through the practices of Santeria; in Haiti, Voudoun derives from the religion of Benin and from Nigeria. Congo rites are also known. These religions are practiced as well in the United States. Two lesser-known traditions, the West Indian/Jamaican Obeah and the southern U.S. Hoodoo, derive from traditions of African sorcery and magic. In all these traditions, female figures hold power and prestige.

Today, African traditional religions retain the devotion of a significant minority of Africans on the home continent and an increasing number of adherents in diasporic lands. In addition, African spirituality imbues the Womanist movement, which also draws upon Christianity's social gospel. While distinct from feminist spirituality, Womanist theology similarly seeks to empower women through use of female images of divinity.

AFRICAN PANTHEON

Abenaa An Akan river goddess, Abenaa ("Tuesday") is associated with gold, brass, and other symbols of wealth. Abenaa protects children and, because she views her worshippers as her children, defends them as adults. (Bádejo 1998)

Abrewa This Akan goddess, possibly identical to **Asase Yaa**, lived on earth with her children, where they were cramped because the sky was so close. She hit the sky god with her pestle, which forced him to move away. Then god was too far away, so Abrewa had everyone gather mortars, which she piled atop each other. When only one mortar was needed to reach

god, the supply ran out. Abrewa moved the bottom one to the top, but the structure collapsed, isolating people on earth. Abrewa disappeared after founding a matrilineal line of rulers from her eldest daughter, **Asona**. (Ephirim-Donkor)

Abuk Born tiny, Abuk was put in a pot, where she swelled like a bean. When she was grown, the creator god gave Abuk and her mate, Garang, one grain of corn to eat each day. The human race would have starved had Abuk not stolen what people needed. Deng, the rain god, joined with Abuk to bring abundance. They had three children, two sons and a daughter, Ai-Yak; some narratives offer two daughters for the goddess, Candit and Nyaliep, both of whom became divine after drowning.

The frightening Lwal Durrajok appears in a tale wherein Abuk created people from fat she softened over fire. She molded individual people and, after they dried and hardened, sent them across the road that connected heaven and earth. But when she went to gather more wood for her fire, Lwal Durrajok made crippled humans he pledged to fix. Then he boiled a pot of fat, into which he plunged the cripples, who met horrible deaths.

The Dinka, Nuer, and Atuot envision Abuk as the primal woman and divinity of fertility. Her symbols include the moon, snakes, and sheep. In some myths, the name of this goddess is given as Acol. (Burton 1981, 1982a, 1982b; Cummings; Evans-Pritchard; Lienhardt; Ray 2000)

Adoma In Cameroon, this folkloric heroine was an exemplary daughter except she refused to marry. This angered her parents and she became something of an outcast. During a festival across the Mbam River, all the young people set off to enjoy themselves, so Adoma went along. But when they reached the banks of the river, no one would let Adoma ride in their boats.

As she sat there glumly, a crocodile urged her to take his hand and step onto his back. The crocodile took her below the waves and decked her in finery before taking her to the festival. Elegantly attired, Adoma caught everyone's eye, and men competed for her attentions. She refused until she felt like dancing, then took a flute from a bag the crocodile had given her. When she played it, people stuffed money into her bag. As soon as it was full, it disappeared, then reappeared, empty and ready for more offerings. Back in the river, the crocodile counted the money, which had been transmitted to him.

When the party was over, more than one suitor wanted to take Adoma home, but she went back to the crocodile, who once more took her beneath the waves and dressed her splendidly. When the girl returned home, her older sister decided she, too, would gain a fortune, so she went to the riverbank. When the crocodile appeared, she said he was smelly, so he ate her. (Matateyou)

Agbanli In Benin, when a hunter saw the antelope girl Agbanli take off her hide, revealing herself as a young woman, he stole the skin so he could claim her as his wife. Agbanli agreed, demanding only that he keep the secret of her animal identity. The hunter agreed, and Agbanli went home with him.

The hunter's primary wife did not take kindly to the stranger. Every day they argued, and every day the woman said something that showed the hunter had not kept his promise. Finally she revealed to Agbanli where her antelope skin was hidden. The girl reclaimed it and returned to the forest.

Later, the same hunter tried to shoot Agbanli in her antelope form. She gestured until he recognized her. Having overheard birds talking about how their excrement, mixed with water, could turn an animal permanently into a woman, the hunter used that magic on Agbanli. Now a woman forever, Agbanli returned to the hunter's home, after she had extracted a promise she would no longer be tormented by the senior wife. (Feldmann 1963)

Aje The Yoruba goddess of wealth often appears in the form of money. At time's beginning, she was a

five-toed chicken, scratching the earth's hard surface until it became rich soil. In her honor, women leaders are called Aje, a word sometimes translated as "witch," which indicates womanly power, especially in market economics or trade. (Beier 1980; Olupona; Sekoni)

Ala The most popular divinity of Nigeria's Igbo people is earth mother Ala, creatrix of the living and queen of the dead, provider of communal loyalty and lawgiver of society. She is guardian of morality, on whom oaths are sworn and in whose name courts of law are held. Among her powers is fecundity; she is a benevolent deity, celebrated in the New Yam festival. Ala's shrine is at the center of a village, where people offer sacrifices at planting, first fruits, and harvest.

As part of Ala's role as maintainer of order, she is the goddess who punishes misdeeds and transgressions against custom. Army ants, who serve the goddess, attack those who break such rules. But first they appear in nightmares, so the wrongdoer might rectify his or her behavior. (Jell-Bahlsen 2008; Cole; Ford; Iloanusi; Jones; Mbon; Parringer 1967, 1970; McCall)

Alyett The Nuer ancestral mother was born from a tree near the Guoal River, called the "river of smallpox" due to the nearby prevalence of the disease. At the beginning of every rainy season, cattle and other animals were sacrificed to Alyett at her sacred tree. (Burton 1981)

Amokye Among the Ashanti, Amokye guards the entrance to the otherworld. As she welcomes recently deceased women, she demands payment from the beads bedecking their burial garments. She is variously imagined as a genial old woman, sympathetic to the newly dead, and as a crone who sets obstacles in the way of arrivals. (Ford)

Andriana The mythology of Madagascar has much in common with that of Indonesia, despite the island's location beside Africa and the presence of many

Africans there. The islands were settled relatively late, between 350 BCE and 500 CE, by seafarers from Indonesia. At around the same period that Indonesians were settling the island, Africans speaking a Bantu language arrived. Later, Arabs moved there from the north. The mythology of Madagascar is thus richly derived from multiple sources.

Among important mythic figures are the Vazimba or Andrianas, water spirits who lurked around marshes and streams. One of the most prominent was Andriambavirano, "Princess of the Water," who originally lived in the sky. Curious about humanity, she turned herself into a leaf and dropped into a lake. A prince locked the leaf in prison until Andriambavirano reappeared as a goddess. The children of the prince and the goddess became heroes and heroines.

Ranoro is the most renowned spirit woman today because of her connection with the important Antehiroka clan. When their ancestral father happened upon Ranoro, he immediately proposed marriage to her. She demanded her new husband never use salt or even speak the word. When he forgot, Ranoro leaped into the water, never to be seen again.

Another Andriana was beautiful long-haired Rasoalavavolo, who lived underwater and answered prayers for children if offered smooth stones and silver jewelry. Some Andrianas bore the name Ra-mitovi-aman-dreniny, "the likeness or equal of her mother." They also went by the name of "green princesses" for their long green hair, light-green skin, and mirror-like eyes. (Graeber; Ottino; Radimilahy; Silbree)

Ara The Ekoi sky maiden Ara was given to the earthly god Obassi Nsi, while that god's son went to heaven to live with Ara's family. Ara arrived on earth with many slaves, for she was not used to working hard. But Obassi Nsi demanded she carry jars of water long into the night and otherwise perform menial labor. He starved her, he humiliated her in front of his people, and he made her sleep with goats. Ara rebelled. Sent to gather water, she sat down by the side of the stream and refused to return. When she saw a rope hanging from the tree, she climbed it back to heaven. Furious, her father, Obassi Osaw, sent her to her mother, Akun, who tended her wounds and dressed her in finery. Then Obassi Osaw sent for the son of Obassi Nsi and cut off his ears in punishment for what Ara had suffered. Weeping, his tears mixing with those of the wronged maiden Ara, the boy ran back to earth. Their tears were the first rain to fall. (Radin)

Asase Yaa This Ashanti goddess of agriculture and human fecundity appears as Asase Efua among the Fante and Akan. The two names indicate Thursday (Yaa) and Friday (Efua), the "birthdays" of the two goddesses, on which farmers allow the earth to rest. When Christianity came to western Africa, a difficulty was that this supreme divinity lives and is worshipped in plowed fields, not in heaven or in temples like the Christian divinity. Asase reclaims people at death, and everyone who works a field becomes a co-power of fertility after death. (Ephirim-Donkor; Feldmann; Manyoni; Mbon; Parringer 1967, 1970; Pobee; Radin)

Asona Eldest daughter of the Akan primal woman **Abrewa**, Asona was so beautiful that the back of her head was more beautiful than another woman's face. When the first gold was found, protected by a venomous snake, Asona said she would rather die and leave her children with a rich inheritance than live and have them poor. She took the gold but was fatally bitten. She left her descendants wealthy, and her ambition remains within her family. (Ephirim-Donkor)

Atage The goddess of a hill in southwestern Nigeria, Atage has breasts like large water-storage pots, suggesting this goddess is connected with fertility, as does the tradition of women praying at her shrine for healthy children. At the end of the dry season, in March, the goddess's priest sets the time of Atage's festival by consulting the Ifa, after which he spends the night naked on the goddess's mountain. Any child born on the day of the festival is named for the goddess and considered her favorite.

Also honored on that day is the goddess Alafo-fūnfūn, "owner of white clothes," who has a temple devoted to fertility near a stream where women pray for children. In her honor, women dress in white and bathe in the stream. Throughout the festival, people act with abandon, holding images and shouting phrases that evoke Alafo-fūnfūn's sexuality. (Parringer 1951)

Atete Ethiopian Atete guarded married women, who left their families to move to their husbands' villages, but once pregnant the women returned to their home villages. Women from the home village sing and dance, addressing Atete, whose creativity the birth-giving mother recreates. At Atete's feast day in September, a goat is offered as a symbol of her reproductive prowess. (Bartels; Jaenen)

Ayirol During a drought, the Atuot people of the southern Sudan were forced to desperate measures. Their only well was filled with blood but, when the young woman Ayirol was sacrificed to it, clear water began to gush out, forming a lake that bears her name. When the sun rose, Ayirol's spirit hovered on the shore. But when people reached where she had stood, they could not find her. Instead, they found a boat and a spear, as well as edible fish that had never been caught there before. (Burton 1982)

Bayanni This Yoruba orisha, sister of the thunder god Shango, is called his "crown." She is embodied in the cowrie-shell crowns worn in ceremonies. Little myth is known of her, although one narrative says she committed suicide after Shango was driven away because of his troublemaking ways. She has been identified with the better-known **Ọba**. (Gleason)

Butan Among the Batammaliba, the earth goddess Butan created people. The first women, Kuiyecoke and Puka Puka, never went hungry because Kuiye fulfilled all their needs. But they grew bored. Their complaints

reached Kuiye, who made rivers and created plants, after which people had to draw water and grow food. They work hard but are no longer bored. (Ray 2000)

Chichinguane A heroine of Mozambique, Chichinguane was the oldest daughter of the chief's favorite wife. The other wives were envious of the love she received from her father, so they encouraged their children to persecute her. When the village girls went to gather clay for pottery, her sisters made Chichinguane stand in the pit, from which she handed out baskets filled with clay. When they had filled their baskets, the girls ran away, leaving Chichinguane unable to climb out.

One side of the pit was low enough to allow escape, but it led into the waters of a lake. As night began to near, the desperate girl took that route—only to find herself facing the jaws of a great fish. The fish did not swallow her, but carried her to a beautiful land beneath the lake, where everyone was kind to her.

There Chichinguane lived for months. But one day, as she was swimming near shore, she saw the same bullying village girls tormenting her sister. The girl was trying to draw water but was too small to carry the jug properly. She sat by the lakeside, weeping helplessly. When her missing sister suddenly appeared, the younger daughter looked up in surprise and delight. Chichinguane walked the girl back to the village, carrying her water jug, then made her promise to say nothing about the visit.

Thereafter, Chichinguane appeared every day to help her sister. Finally, their mother became suspicious and extracted the truth from the girl. The next time Chichinguane assumed human form, she was greeted by her mother, who begged her to return to human life. She declined, explaining she was a fish now and well treated by her people. When she returned under the waves, Chichinguane could not shake her homesickness. The fish who had brought her to the lake world gave her a magic wand and delivered her to her village. There, he told her, she should wave the wand over her body. When she did, the scales fell off, transforming themselves into silver coins. Chichinguane then lived in wealth and comfort. (Knappert 1986)

Darāwīsh Spirits of fertility to Muslims of the northern Sudan, the Darāwīsh are offered white clothing and white rams as sacrifices. They include Sitti Khuḍara ("green lady"), who wears green clothing. Similar figures, the Ḥabish, take possession of humans, making them dance wildly. They include Dodo, "lady of coffee"; Hamāma-t-al-Bhar, "river pigeon," a beautiful prostitute; noble and flirtatious Maray; Sitt am-Mandil, "lady of the handkerchief"; Zâar LulÂiya, the guide for newly wedded women; and Janāt Jozay, a double spirit. (Boddy)

Eka-Abasi The Nigerian Annang and Ibibio honor this goddess, whose name means "God Mother" and who places souls in wombs. Each woman of childbearing age has her own Eka-Abasi to protect her unborn children. (Mbon)

Fatna A heroine of the Sudanese Muslims, Fatna the Beautiful was a young woman whose parents promised her in marriage, against her will, to her brother. Fatna led seven other young women to escape this betrothal. On their journey, they encountered an old man whose skin could be removed if acacia thorns were put on his head. Fatna did so, then used his withered hide as a disguise so no men would approach her.

After many adventures, Fatna became aide to a prince, who did not discern the beautiful woman under the old man's skin. But when she bathed, she was forced to remove the skin. When the prince saw Fatna, he fell in love with her. Challenging her to a game of chance with their hides as the prize, the prince lost twice. Each time, Fatna refused the prize. On the third try, the prince won, and Fatna gave up her disguise to become his wife. (Boddy)

Gbadu This sixteen-eyed spirit, born male and female, lived atop the palm tree that divided earth and sky. When she closed her eyes, she could not open them without help, so her brother Legba climbed the tree each day and helped her rise. Sometimes he opened the eyes on the back of her head; sometimes, he opened the eyes in front. Gbadu had two daughters, the oldest being Minona, the women's goddess. When Legba slept with Minona, Gbadu grew angry, because he was her lover as well. She demanded Legba go with her to see **Mawu**, who cursed Legba with a perpetually erect penis. (Herskovits and Herskovits)

Idemili A primary goddess of the Nnobi Igbo, Idemili lived in lake waters, where she appeared as a mermaid. She and her husband formed an image of the perfect couple. Together, they were invoked for children and other blessings. She was a healing goddess, whose priests and priestesses served as doctors and herbalists. (Amadiume 1987)

Idris A king's least-favored wife, Idris worked hard but was tormented by her co-wives and never protected by her husband. No matter how many wives he had, the man had no children, because he was sterile. So he found a magician who mixed a potion that would cause all his wives to bear. All the wives were greedy to be the first to bear a child, so they fought each other as the medicine was passed around. Idris timidly took the small bit that was left over, which was enough to make her round with child.

The other wives came to labor before she did; all bore monsters as punishment for their greed. When the time came for Idris to go into labor, she hid in the forest to give birth to a perfect little girl. She knew the baby would be at risk from the jealous co-wives, so she gave her daughter, Adesuwa, to a forester.

When she had grown into a young woman, Adesuwa was so beautiful she attracted the lustful gaze of her father. But when he tried to make her his wife, she told him the truth. He was shocked. A test was set up to see if Adesuwa could recognize her mother, who would then be lauded above all other wives. The wives were each to prepare a dish, from which Adesuwa would select one, thus revealing her mother's identity. The favored wives cooked magnificent dishes, while Idris could only cook a poor dish and serve it in a broken pot. Without hesitation, Adesuwa went to that dish, recognizing her mother, who was brought into prominence as the mother of the king's only child. (Osoba)

Igbaghon The Benin river goddess was once a woman who frightened men with her intelligence. When her parents gave her to a nearby ruler as a junior wife, she suffered from her husband's cruelty. He set the household against her. Then one night, sneaking back from a forbidden solitary walk, Igbaghon overheard her husband plotting to have her killed as a sacrifice. She prayed to her ancestors, who turned her into an eagle. She flew away and, as her talons touched earth, she was transformed into a river. (Osoba)

Ilâmbe A heroine of the west African Mpongwe people, Ilâmbe was the daughter of the least-favored wife of a wealthy man. Ra-Mborakinda neglected Ilâmbe's mother, Ngwe-ĭĕg, while favoring his senior wife, Ngwekonde. But no matter what riches she had, Ngwekonde wanted more. When Ra-Mborakinda left for a trip, putting Ilâmbe in charge of sharing his goods with his family, Ngwekonde saw her chance to punish the girl for gaining her father's favor.

Ilâmbe's father had warned her not to go far from home, but one day she went for a walk. As she left the village, no one noticed, because Ngwekonde had enchanted them into unawareness. When the girl was far enough into the forest, Ngwekonde attacked, beating her horribly and leaving her tied to a tree. Ilâmbe survived, but when she managed to wriggle out of her bonds, she had no idea where she was.

She soon found herself at a cozy home in the forest. Not knowing any other way to live, she set to work making supper and tidying the place. Then she hid. When the owners arrived, they were amazed to find a warm meal awaiting them. The home was occupied by a group of woodsmen who called out, hoping to lure their benefactor from hiding. But Ilâmbe remained hidden. The next morning, she started work again, only to be surprised by one of the men. He assured her they would treat her as a sister but warned her about

a dangerous bird that flew in every noon looking for someone to kill. For a while, Ilâmbe lived happily with the woodsmen, but one day the bird surprised and killed Ilâmbe. The men, sorrowful at losing their companion, put her in a tree where they could look at her undecaying body. (Nassau)

Inkosazane The Zulu primal being was "the princess," a goddess of abundance. She invented rites that should be performed by women to ensure the fertility of crops, cattle, and women. (Ngubane)

Isong This tortoise-shell goddess of the earth's fertility was one of the primary Ibibio and Ekoi divinities. Her alternate name, Abassi Isu Ma, has been variously translated as "Goddess of the Face of Love" and "Goddess of the Face of Mother." (Jones)

Iya Nla Among the Yoruba, Iya Nla stands at the center of religious rituals related to fecundity and death, conducted by women initiates whose prayers are potent in the danced rituals of Gelede. Like her followers, Iya Nla has magical powers. Despite those powers, Iya Nla could not have a child with her mate, Oluweri, although she had born many children previously, including the magical orishas. An oracle told her to sacrifice corn and clay dishes, then to deck herself with a carved wooden hat and metal anklets. The goddess was soon pregnant with the joker Efe. Then the goddess had another child, the chubby dancer Gelede. These children, once grown, could not reproduce until they enacted the ritual dances their mother had performed before their conception. (Lawal)

Lueji Among the Lunda and Bemba, Bantu-speaking peoples of central Africa, this moon goddess is embodied in a black stork whose white underbelly looks like the moon when it flies during the night. She represents the dry season and sterility, for in her stork embodiment she controls the seasons, drying ponds by flapping her wings. She is also connected with the rainbow. (Bonnefoy)

Mammywata A relatively new goddess, Mammywata is a form of the water goddess honored across coastal and western Africa. Her worship especially thrives in areas of cultural exchange, as in ports and cities. She is typically depicted as of foreign origin, and her name is a version of the English for "mother of waters." She has been described as a hybridized goddess, connecting indigenous with imported or foreign influences.

Evidence of Mammywata devotion appears as early as the fifteenth century, when she was credited with freeing captives from slave ships. This tendency to resist oppression of personal freedom is a theme in Mammywata legend. Ethnographers observe that contemporary devotees of Mammywata are often nonconforming women. In public ritual, Mammywata appears as a woman who loves technology and Westernized foods. In private observances, she is honored at shrines erected in bedrooms. Many Christians regard her as demonic, although a few make room for her as a "saint." In Islam, she has been defined as one of the nonhuman race called *jinn*. (Jell-Bahlsen 2008; Kaplan; Houlberg; Ray 2000; Olupona)

Marwe The Wachanga and Chaga of Kenya say Marwe and her sister were set to guard the family bean garden. Thirsty Marwe walked to a nearby pond for a drink, leaving her sister to watch the beans. While Marwe was gone, a baboon troop descended and devoured the entire crop.

Marwe, ashamed of losing her family's food supply, threw herself into the pond. Sinking to the bottom, she found a village where she was given hospitality. Wise in the ways of spirit people, Marwe refused to eat their food, claiming people above the waters lived on bitter foods, unlike the tasty meals served beneath.

The old woman with whom Marwe was staying gave her instructions, which she disobeyed. This drew out a little girl who told Marwe to ask to go home, then to obey the old woman's orders. The old woman told Marwe to jump into a pile of manure. She did, and instantly she found herself at home, covered with silver chains and expensive beads.

An envious village girl tried to imitate Marwe's actions. When she arrived beneath the waters, she followed the old woman's orders to the letter—including leaving all the housework to Marwe's helper, the little underwater girl. This child told the visitor to ask to go home, but reversed the advice she'd given Marwe. The girl returned home full of poisonous fire that drove her to drown herself.

In Cameroon, a similar story appears, centered on the heroine Mbango. She lived with her aunt and cousin, Milango, who abused her mightily. One day, while fetching water, Mbango dropped her calabash in the stream. When she returned, her aunt beat her until she ran out the door and back to the stream.

There she saw the calabash floating and followed it until she was swirled up by a whirlpool, within which she found an old woman's home. The woman invited her in and offered her pig excrement. Mbango accepted the generosity and found the meal transformed into delicious dainties. She spent three days with the woman and, when she was leaving, accepted the gift of three eggs with instructions that she should break them when she returned home. She did, and riches poured out.

The lazy, ill-tempered cousin was certain she deserved as much as Mbango. So Milango threw a calabash into the stream, followed it through the whirlpool, and then sat around the old woman's house refusing to do anything but complain. Nonetheless, the woman gave her three eggs as she was leaving. But when the girl broke them, scorpions and wild cats came out and attacked her and her mother, killing them. Mbango married a young man and lived richly thereafter. (Matateyou; Parringer 1967)

Massasi The Wahungwe of Zimbabwe say this primal woman was the mate of the first man, who did not know how to have intercourse. Putting oil on his finger, he inserted it into Massasi, whereupon she conceived and bore plants, then died. The man, Mwuetsi, grieved so long the creator god made another woman, Morongo, the evening star. This woman showed the man how to make love, so she was able to bear animals rather than plants. In this way, she populated the world. Morongo fell in love with one of her sons, but Mwuetsi refused to leave her alone, finally raping her. Chaos reigned until his children strangled Mwuetsi. (Ford)

Mawu With the huge snake Aido-Hwedo, the Fon goddess Mawu created the earth. Because of the snake's shape, the earth has sinuous hills and valleys; mountains, with their veins of metal, came from the serpent's excrement. When she finished her creation, Mawu decided it was too heavy, so she instructed Aido-Hwedo to coil underneath it and float with it on the cosmic sea. To this day, the snake's movement creates earthquakes. Then Mawu created human beings, using clay mixed with water. When she ran short of materials, Mawu re-enlivened the dead, which explains why people sometimes look like their forebears. Her first children were twins, Nyohwé Ananu and her brother, Da Zodji; her third child was a dual-sexed being like herself, called So. The first were sent to the earth, to become spirits of water, while So remained in the sky.

When humanity grew arrogant, Mawu retreated to the sky, becoming an unreachable force. Some myths say her trickster son Legba caused her departure. Someone was stealing from her garden, and Mawu demanded to know the culprit. Legba stole Mawu's sandals and walked through the garden at night. The next day, Legba accused his mother of stealing her own yams. Furious and humiliated, Mawu departed.

Later Mawu sent her son (or twin-lover) Lisa to teach useful arts to humanity. Because Lisa was sometimes identified with the sun, Mawu was sometimes interpreted as a moon spirit. Other scholars consider Mawu the supreme deity. Sometimes she is described as bisexual, with two joined bodies able to self-impregnate; occasionally, Mawu is described as entirely male. Where only female, Mawu is envisioned as wise, old, and large breasted. (Booth; Herskovits and Herskovits; Parringer 1967)

Mbokomu The primal woman of the Ngombe lived in the sky. Because she bothered the sky-folk, she was placed on earth with her two children. Mbokomu made the first gardens. As she began to age, she recognized that the world needed more people. She instructed her children to have sex with each other, and soon a child was expected. But one day, Mbokomu's daughter met a hairy being in the forest. This creature seemed friendly, so she shaved his body until he looked human. But he was a sorcerer, so when the first human was born, witchcraft came to earth as well. (Feldmann)

Miseke From Rwanda comes the tale of magical Miseke, who was born after her mother prayed for help when her soldier husband abandoned her. Thunder and lightning answered her prayer, saying that she would be delivered safely, but that she must give the child to thunder as a wife. The woman agreed, and the child was born healthy and with the miraculous talent of dropping jewels from her lips when she laughed. But when the father returned, he swore he would never give his daughter to thunder, so when she came of age, he locked her inside, hoping that she would never be seen.

Miseke grew tired of being indoors, so she slipped away and ran down to the river, where she found other girls playing. Day turned to night, and before the girls could run home, thunder appeared to demand his bride. One after another, he made them laugh, then rejected them because they did not produce jewels. Miseke could not disguise her identity, so she went with him to his home in the sky. There she bore several children, but finally, because she was so homesick, thunder sent her back to earth, laden with wealth and surrounded by her children. She never made it, because she was set upon by malicious spirits and, sending her youngest child for help, was rescued and taken back up into the sky forever. (Ford)

Moombi Among the Kenyan Kikuyu (Gihuyu) people, this woman was ancestral mother, wife of the son of god, Gikuyu, the first agriculturalist. His brothers

Masai and Kamba were the first herdsman and first hunter, respectively. Moombi ("molder" or "creator") had nine daughters but no sons, but after preparing a sacrifice, Gikuyu found nine young men to be his daughters' husbands. They were welcomed, provided they were willing to live under Moombi's roof and consider all their children as her descendants. They agreed, and this matrilineal descent continued when the nine daughters moved into their own homes, bringing their children with them and founding nine Kikuyu clans. Among that group, the women took several husbands, until the men revolted. Secretly, they agreed to impregnate all the women at once so that six months later, the women would have difficulty resisting their seizure of power. The men changed the name of the primary clan from Moombi to Giyuku, but the nine clans descended from Moombi's daughters retained their names. (Parringer 1967)

Moremi In early times, when the Yoruba city of Ife was thriving, another town called Ile-Igbo was doing poorly. Neither town knew of the other's existence until a hunter from Ile-Igbo stumbled from the forest into the rich fields of Ife. He returned to his village with reports of Ife's wealth, whereupon the leader of Ile-Igbo came up with a plan. His men of Ile-Igbo would dress as spirits of ancestors and raid Ife, stealing food and terrifying the people.

The first raid went smoothly. The people of Ife, frightened at the appearance of the ghosts, ran, and the Ile-Igbo men looted their homes. This happened at intervals until Moremi, an intelligent and courageous woman, realized that their invasions made no sense. Why would ghosts need food? She made a vow at a nearby stream that she would sacrifice her only son if she could save her people, then went to the leader and asked permission to stay behind during the next raid. Reluctantly, he granted it.

The next time ghosts appeared, everyone but Moremi ran away. When the men of Ile-Igbo found her, they did not know what to do, so they brought her back as a captive. Their leader made her one of his wives, so Moremi learned how Ile-Igbo men had been stealing Ife's riches. Then, when the household had forgotten about her, she dressed herself in rags and escaped as a beggar woman.

It took her many days to traverse the forest, but she was welcomed back to Ife with great celebration. There she revealed what she had learned, and the village prepared itself for the next assault. When the Ile-Igbo men overran the village, the Ife people were ready. Turning on them with torches, they set them ablaze. Some died, but others escaped back to their village with the news that their raids on Ife were at an end.

Moremi did not forget her vow. She prepared her beloved son for sacrifice, then with the rest of her people, she led him to the stream where he would meet his death. When they reached the water, a chain came down from the heavens and lifted him up, to live as a heavenly being thereafter. Some people refer to Moremi as an orisha. (Courlander)

Muhongo This queen of the Mbundu in northern Angola was married to King Kitamba, who mourned her incessantly after she died. He sent a shaman to find her. But when the shaman reached Muhongo, she was sitting peacefully weaving a basket. The queen told her visitor that the dead join another kingdom and cannot return to earth's surface. The story was carried to the New World during the slave trade, appearing in Haiti, where it was a voudon priest who found the dead queen selling coffee beans in the afterlife. (Rosenberg)

Mujaji The Rain Queens of the Lovedu bore the name of their primary goddess, whose incarnations they were. These women, highly regarded for political prowess as well as military might, kept their people safe first from the Zulu and later from the European Boers. A weather goddess, Mujaji controlled storms and floods; those who worshipped her were rewarded with gentle rain. (Parringer 1967)

Mweel The moon goddess Mweel of the southern African Kuba people was the lover of her brother,

Woot, who left to travel to the east, causing the first eclipse. Only when Mweel begged Woot to bring back the light did the eclipse end and normal daylight return. (Bonnefoy)

Nagoro The Masai and Myot heroine Nagoro lived in a primal time. But, even then, people had fallen away from proper rituals for the divine forces. Men drank too much and ignored the children, who were kidnapped by slave traders. Disabled people were cast away to be killed by wild beasts. The elders, who predicted punishment for such sins, were ignored.

Then an immense rainstorm began, one so fierce that it seemed it would never end. When the rain eased, a drought began. A year or so passed. Everything was dying: plants, animals, people. The rivers were dry. And so the elders determined only one thing could be done: the sacrifice of a human being. Because the people knew they could never sacrifice one of their own children, they determined to send one to a sacred place, where, if the heavenly powers wanted a sacrifice, they would take her.

There were rigorous demands for a sacrifice. She had to be pure, with living parents and siblings, and of a hardworking family. The mother of the girl Cherop knew, because her daughter's given name meant "the sacrificed one," that the girl was fated to perform this role. But Cherop did not fully understand what was demanded of her. Other girls had walked in the sacrificial procession but had not been killed, so she understood the honor of her selection but not the deadly outcome.

With her friend Langok, she ran to tell her boyfriend. When the girls could not find Sigilai, they went off searching, risking their lives as hyenas, lions, and other animals threatened them. When they found Sigilai and told him the news, he determined to protect Cherop by eloping with her. Because she had not yet been initiated into womanhood, they lived as brother and sister until the villagers, realizing where they were hiding, came to get them.

Cherop was attired in white ostrich plumes and beautiful clothing and renamed Nagoro, "the sacrificed girl." She held her head high so that her family would suffer no embarrassment. Even when she was left on the shores of a former lake, to be taken by a man-eating bird, she showed no fear. But before the bird could reach her, Sigilai leaped out. He fought the bird. As he did, rain began to fall. Thus balance was restored to the world and Cherop lived to bear him strong children. (Koech)

Nalubaale The goddess of Lake Victoria in east central Africa is the motherly Nalubaale, whose name means "female deity" in the Luganda language. In that region, bodies of water are often gendered as feminine. (Burton 1982)

Nambi The Baganda first woman lived in the sky but desired an earthly man, Kintu, who had only one cow. She descended to make love with him. When Nambi returned to the sky, her family was appalled that she would love a poor earthling. Nambi's father, Ggulu, stole Kintu's cow, taking it to the sky so that Kintu would starve. But Nambi told Kintu where to find his cow. Kintu traveled to heaven, where Ggulu presented him with herds of identical cattle, demanding that he find his own. With Nambi's help he identified the beast, but the sky father subjected Kintu to other tests: cut firewood from rock, eat a whole houseful of food, collect enough dew to fill a pot. Kintu passed each test, so Ggulu allowed the marriage.

The sky father also warned Nambi that her brother Walumbe (death) might follow them to earth. The couple left in haste, taking the first animals with them. Halfway down, Nambi realized they had no seeds for edible plants; she stole back to get some. Walumbe saw her and followed her to earth. Now, although humans have food, they also have the unwelcome presence of death. (Feldmann; Ford; Parringer 1967; Radin; Ray 1991, 2000)

Nanamburucú To the Fon people, the creatrix Nanamburucú was mother of **Mawu** and her brother-lover Lisa. Her worship was so widely known that it is difficult to pinpoint its source; in some places she was the preeminent deity, while in others she is less important. In Nigeria, she appears as a world creator; throughout Yoruba territory, she is the supreme deity. She is also known in Brazil, where she is called Nanan. (Bastide; Barnet; Ford)

Ngomba The Bakongo girl Ngomba was fishing one day with three other girls, who pushed her away because she was covered with sores. So she went fishing by herself, not realizing that a man with murderous intent followed her. He captured her and took her to his home, where he kept many other prisoners. She promised to be an excellent servant if he would cure her sores. When he did so, she was revealed as a lovely young woman, so he made her his concubine. But she was determined to escape from him, so, with the other prisoners, she fashioned a flying boat. Distracting the murderer every time he thought about killing her, Ngomba loaded all his riches and the other prisoners onto the boat and flew away. Infuriated, he followed her to her village, where he claimed her as his bride. She pretended to be glad to see him, and her relatives went along with the deceit until they could trick him into falling into a hole, where they killed him. (Radin)

Nsia The mother of the Ashanti trickster, Ananse the spider, Nsia was offered in partial trade for the stories of the sky god Nyankonpon. Ananse told Nsia about the bargain, but before it could be concluded, he had to capture five other beings, including hornets and pythons. With the help of his wife Aso, Ananse did so and was rewarded with the stories that were henceforth called spider-stories. (Radin)

Nunde The wife of the Benin trickster god Legba took a lover. When Legba discovered this, he demanded the reason. Nunde told him that it was because his penis was too small. So he ate a great deal, which made his penis grow, and had intercourse with her while everyone in the village played drums and

sang about how large he was. Afterward, when he traveled, he took her along, so that she could not have other lovers.

Although Konikoni is said to be another name for Nunde, in some narratives she appears as another character, Legba's first wife, with whom Nunde as second wife did not get along. She complained to Rabbit, who went to seek an oracle. When he returned, he told Nunde that she had to sacrifice a goat, a chicken, corn flower, and palm oil, all seasoned with salt and pepper. She also needed a gourd filled with water. When the sacrifice was complete, the women were best friends. (Herskovits and Herskovits)

Nyakae The crocodile goddess Nyakae was the spouse of the high god Okwa and, because people depended upon fish for their livelihood, the source of abundance. A similar goddess, the python Nalwanga, was the divine spouse of the king of Buganda. (Burton 1982)

Nyalé In the upper Niger valley, this goddess was the sister of the better-known **Ọya**. By touching the four directions, Nyalé brought the four elements into being. Within her creation was the spirit of moisture, which she fanned until it congealed into earth. Later, Nyalé became the earth goddess Mousso Koroni of the Bambera. She was the color of rich earth, sometimes appearing as a panther or leopard. An ancestral mother, she gave birth to all life, after the god Pemba took the form of a tree and penetrated her with his roots. She was goddess of life's passages, who caused girls to menstruate and oversaw initiations. (Gleason)

Nyame Among the Ashanti, this supreme goddess was connected with the moon. Early scholars described the divinity as male, but now she is considered female; Nyame may have been a double-sexed divinity. (Parringer 1970)

Nyamugondho This Atuot magical woman lived in a lake, where a fisherman hooked her and married her. Immediately he became rich, as cattle appeared from nowhere. But the man undid his own good luck. Because he got drunk and abusive, Nyamugondho left him, walking into the lake with all her cattle. The man rushed to stop her but was turned into a tree. Nyamugondho was reborn as Simbi, but when she was again abused, she caused an explosion that killed everyone who had injured her. Ultimately, returning to humanity, she became a rainmaker. (Burton 1982)

Nzambi Selfish women ignored Nzambi, an old woman with a thirsty child, but a man brought her a water-filled gourd. In gratitude, she asked him to join her at the same spot the next day. When he did, he found a lake where there had been fields the previous day. The "old woman," in reality the Bakongo creatrix Nzambi, told him the selfish women had been turned into fish. No women could eat the fish, which provided food for men and children. After giving the man gifts, Nzambi went away.

She moved through the land until she came to a village, where she called at each home asking for a place to rest. Because she was a dusty stranger, she was turned away until some poor people took her in. She told them to leave immediately and cursed the others to be drowned under the waters of a huge lake.

Nzambi had one daughter, a beautiful girl whom everyone wanted to marry. Nzambi announced that whoever brought fire from heaven would win the girl. The animals cooperated, but spider delivered the speck of fire to Nzambi. She was ready to award the girl's hand to spider, but the other animals complained that they had all helped. Nzambi retracted her offer and kept her daughter with her. (Feldmann)

Ọba Goddess of the African river that bears her name, Ọba is an important Yoruba orisha. Her myth centers on her rivalry with coquettish **Oshun**, Ọba's co-wife and her rival. Oshun desired Ọba's mate Shango and would stoop to anything to get her way. One day, Oshun told Ọba that Shango preferred her recipe for his favorite dish, because she cut off her ears and put them in the dishes. It was only ear-shaped mushrooms floating in the soup, but Ọba was fooled.

The next time Ọba cooked for Shango, she mixed a whole ear with the food. It gave Shango immense strength, but when Ọba took off her headscarf and Shango saw her mutilated head, he ran away to live with Oshun. When Oshun arrived to gloat, Ọba attacked her, and both goddesses turned into rivers. (Bascom; Gleason)

Oddudua The primary Yoruba mother goddess is the orisha of earth as well as its creator. Her mate is the god Orishanla, younger than she and possibly her son; she is typically depicted nursing a child from elongated breasts. The spot where she descended from the sky is still identified in Yoruba territory. Her religion, Ogoni, devotes itself to maintaining social order. In some myths, Oddudua appears as male or as two gendered, like **Mawu**, to whom she may be related. (Bastide; Booth; Manyoni)

Ogboinba Before this heroine of the Nigerian Ijaw was born, she and another woman, about to be born as Ogboinba's best friend, asked the primal goddess Woyengi for gifts. Ogboinba wanted psychic powers; her friend, many children. Both had their prayers answered, although by the time they received their results, they had forgotten what they wished for.

Ogboinba had psychic powers but no children, and she envied her friend's large family. So she set off to ask the goddess to make her over as fertile. As she traveled, she grew in power, but she could not command Woyengi. The goddess, stripped of much of her power, returned to earth, where she hid in the eyes of a pregnant woman, where she can sometimes still be seen. (Beier; Okpewho)

Ogbuide The Igbo honor a goddess of fresh waters called Nne Msiri, who in southwestern Nigeria bears the name Ogbuide. Oguta Lake, at the confluence of the river Niger with the Urashi River, is the home of this goddess, whose multiple names (see also **Idemili**) attest to her continuing prominence and importance. She is a generous divinity who provides sustenance and good luck. Should a hungry person come to the lakeshore, Ogbuide provides food. Mother ancestor of the region's people, she controls the fecundity of the land and water. She is beautiful and fecund; she has a big head, crowned with dreadlocks that show her unbounded nature. Because she can take life as well as give it, a python appears as her symbol. (Jell-Bahlsen 2008)

Olókun The ocean goddess in the Yoruba Ifá religion, Olókun, whose name is also used as an epithet of **Yemaja**, appeared at the beginning of time, ruling the waters and marshlands; the other orishas lived in the heavens, above a chaos of water and mist. The god Obatala descended to Olókun's realm and created land. Olókun grew angry that this was occurring without her permission, so she flooded everything, killing many people. People performed sacrifices to the heavenly orishas, and one descended to dry up the flooded areas.

But Olókun was not easily conquered. She challenged Olorum, the supreme god, saying that she could best him at weaving. Olorum was concerned, because everyone knew that the ocean's colors were beyond compare. So he sent as his messenger Agemo, the chameleon, who changed color with every piece of fabric Olókun showed him, forcing the goddess to retire to her limited domain. (Courlander; McClelland)

Omelumma With her sister Omelukpagham, this Igbo folkloric heroine was captured and the two were sold into servitude in different villages. But their fates were different. Omelumma's owner saw her worth and made her his wife, while Omelukpagham was sold to an oppressive master. When Omelumma gave birth to a son, her husband bought her a slave to care for it—her own sister. Because of the length of their separation, neither sister recognized the other. Indeed, Omelumma had forgotten the difficulties of her past and was abusive to her servant sister. But one day when the baby was restless, Omelukpagham sang a

song about her life. A neighbor, hearing the song and realizing its import, told Omelumma. The sisters were reunited, and Omelumma vowed to be kind to her servants ever after. (Abrahams)

Oshun Oshun is the Yoruba goddess of the river bearing her name, and her domain includes not only the human concerns of family, health and fecundity but also the land's fertility and the demands of the spirit world. She animates all other orishas; without her, they have no power. As controller of destiny, Oshun rules divination, especially that using cowrie shells. Her connection with the cowries came to her from the important god Obatala. Oshun wanted to know how to use the shells, which Obatala wished to keep secret. When the god of mischief stole Obatala's sacred clothing, Oshun promised she would get it back. She traded sex with Eshu for the clothes, then demanded Obatala teach her divination.

Oshun is honored with an annual ceremony called Ibo-Osun. A feast of yams begins the evening, then women dance for the goddess, hoping to be chosen as her favorite. Once selected, the woman serves her community by assisting with family problems and illnesses. Those who wish to have children especially consult Oshun, for she had many descendants, who live along her river's waters. Oshun is the primary divinity of the region of Oshogbo, where she is honored with brass objects, jewels, and yellow copper. She is a healer, invoked as the one who cures when medicine fails. (Abiodum; Bádejo 1996, 1998; Bastide; Beier; Courlander; Gleason; Murphy and Sandford 2001; Ogunwale; Ray 2000)

Ọya This Yoruba goddess rules storms on the Niger River. Her name means "she tore," for her winds tear up the river's surface. She is also called "mother of nine," for the nine estuaries of the Niger. Ọya is a warrior goddess as well as patron of female leadership.

Her first husband was the blacksmith Ogun, but she took a second, the warrior–thunder god Shango.

She made off with the gourd that held his power, and Shango chased Qya as she fled to where sky and water meet. He caught her, but she ran to her sister Oloso, goddess of lagoons. Through the world they ran, Qya always hiding from Shango, until she reached a shrine built for her. Shango forgave Qya, but she still fears him.

Qya was not Shango's only lover. The voluptuous **Oshun** also shared his bed. Qya was reduced to begging Oshun to share the secret of her appeal, whereupon Oshun played a nasty trick. She told the senior wife that she used erotic magic, feeding Shango parts of her body so that he would be forever bound to her. Qya tried this, cutting off her ears and hiding her ravaged head with scarves. But Shango was disgusted with the flavor of his food and even more disgusted to see what Qya had done to herself.

The rivals turned into rivers. Where their waters meet, there is always turbulence. When one is crossing the river Qya, one must never mention Oshun, or the river will swamp the boat; the same is true of Oshun, who drowns anyone who speaks of her rival. The story of the amputated ear is also told of **Qba**. Oshun, Qba, and Qya change places in various versions of the myth.

Buffalo horns are placed on her altar, for Qya is a water buffalo when not in human form. Once a hunter saw a buffalo shed its skin. When the beautiful woman who emerged hid the skin and went to market, the hunter stole her skin and forced her to become his mate. But his other wives teased her about being a buffalo, and in anger, she killed them. She stormed out to the fields to find the man who had betrayed her, but he bought his life with bean fritters, Qya's favorite food.

Those who honor Qya also offer her palm wine, goat meat, and yams. Wednesday is her holy day, when her followers wear dark-red beads to please her. When she enters a dancer, the dance becomes frenzied as Qya swings a sword. Sometimes she dances with arms outstretched to hold off ghosts, for she is the only goddess who can control them. (Beier 1980; Courlander; Ford; Gleason 1987)

Sanene The Yoruba huntress goddess lived in the bush, far from human settlement. She was brave, strong, and self-creating. Good hunters are related to her, having been initiated by her daughter Komifolo, a bird deity. (Gleason)

Sela In Kenya, the Luyia people say the first woman, Sela, lived in a house on wooden stilts because the earth, in primordial times, was infested with crawling monsters. Her children, the human race, were bold enough to descend from her hut and live in houses built on the ground. (Parringer 1967)

Wanjiru The Akiyuku tell of a girl who was sacrificed to bring rain, and a young man who sacrificed himself to bring her back. During a drought, diviners, asked to determine what the spirits wanted, said the girl Wanjiru had to be bought from her parents with payment of goats at a specific place. The next day, everyone who had a goat brought it to the place, where her family stood with Wanjiru. As people began to offer goats to the family, Wanjiru began to sink into the ground. But no rain came, so people came forward with more goats.

When she was in up to her neck, rain began, coming down in sheets. But the family, which stood around her, did nothing to help her, instead taking more goats from the people. Because of their greed, Wanjiru sank out of sight.

One young man among the crowd loved Wanjiru. He determined he would retrieve her from the otherworld, so he went to the place where she descended and let himself sink into the ground. When he had reached the underworld, he found a naked, sorrowing Wanjiru, whom he carried back to earth. For some time he hid her in his home, feeding her so she grew splendidly fat and happy. He let her family see her and, when they called out in remorse, paid the full brideprice for her and made her his wife. (Feldmann; Radin)

Woyengi The Ijaw creatrix came to earth where a huge tree grew. First thunder sounded, and a table and chair fell from the sky, together with a stone.

Soil appeared on top of the table. Then Woyengi descended. She sat in the chair with her feet on the stone, forming humans out of clay and bringing them to life by embracing them. Woyengi let them choose if they were to be male or female, rich or wise or fertile, long-lived or not. Each person made the choice, and thus the lives that people lead are chosen before they are born. (Beier 1966; Ford; Mbon; Okpewho)

Yasigui Among the Mande, this primal mother was the twin of Ogo, born from a seed that contained all the elements of the universe. Ogo detached himself and, stealing some of the placenta, set off to create the world. Because he had broken the primal unity, his creation was flawed. Ogo thought that Yasigui was with him, so he returned to the sky, where he found his twin had been given to another god. He then became a creature called the "pale fox."

Creation began anew. From the egg's shell, a new earth was created, as well as four pairs of twins and all animals and plants. This new earth attached itself to the earlier one, and light burst into the universe. On the fourth day, Yasigui descended during the first solar eclipse. Yasigui married a twin, and after the marriage of a solo person to a twin, single births became the norm, and the previously natural twin birth the exception. In turn, Yasigui married each of the twin men, until the earth's current order was firmly established. But the universe's mythic order entailed twin births, which remained spiritually powerful. (Dieterlen 1989)

Yemaja The Yoruba goddess of the Ogun River, daughter of the primary god Olodumare, Yemaja married her brother Agangyu. They had a son named Orungan, so handsome his father died of envy. The young man raped his mother, who climbed a nearby mountain and died. As she did, fourteen gods burst forth from her, including **Oshun** and **Ọya**.

Depictions of Yemaja show her with large breasts, because she was the mother of so many gods; yet at times, she is described as having only one breast, for which reason she feared marriage. The orisha Ogun overheard her worrying about the problem and proposed to her. She agreed, on the understanding that he would never touch her breast. But when Ogun tried to prepare a meal for her, he dropped a pot on the floor. When she came into the kitchen and berated him, he struck her and then, in an attempt to comfort her, stroked her breast. Immediately she turned into water.

Yemaja gave birth to the world's waters and endlessly creates new springs and water sources. At her main temple, she is offered rams, yams, and corn. In the Ifá religion, where Yemaja is goddess of witchcraft, priests carry bell-topped staffs to frighten away Yemaja's servants, who can appear as red-beaked birds. Similar ocean goddesses of western Africa are Dandalunda from Angola and Kaiala from the Congo. (Bastide; Beier; Gleason; Gordon)

EGYPTIAN PANTHEON

Ament The "westerner," Ament lived in a tree on the desert's edge, welcoming the newly deceased with bread and water. Those who took her offerings could never return to the land of the living. (Ellis; Müller; Wiedemann; Wilkinson)

Ammut An underworld goddess who was part hippopotamus, part lion, and part crocodile, Ammut ate the souls of the unworthy dead, who were judged by what they did during life and what they left undone. She was feared, but magic could avert her actions. She has been interpreted as a form of **Ma'at**. (Ellis; Faulkner; Wilkinson)

Anuket At Aswan, this water goddess was honored as part of a triad with her mother, **Satis**, and father, Khnum. Predynastic but forgotten, she was rediscovered during the Third Dynasty. During a drought, the king sent a courtier upriver to the point of the Nile's emergence, where Anuket ruled with Satis and Sothis. When the king established a priesthood in Anuket's honor, the drought ended.

Anuket's name, meaning the "embracer," may refer to the Nile's two tributaries, imagined as her arms. She was goddess of the river's annual inundation and as such was connected with fertility. The Nile floods have been virtually eliminated by the building of dams, including one at Aswan that drowned many goddess temples there.

Anuket's feast changed, because the Nile's rising was dependent upon weather. Her festival involved public rituals; less formally, people ate fish in her honor. Typically fish was forbidden, because a fish had eaten the missing phallus of Osiris (see **Isis**), but on Anuket's feast, eating fish was required. (Ellis; Müller)

Bast Domesticated between the Old and Middle Kingdoms, cats kept down the rodent population, thus protecting each household's store of grain. Thankful Egyptians cherished cats, decking them with golden jewelry. When they died, cats were mummified and buried in the vast cemetery at Bubastis or other temples of Bast.

At first Bast was a lion goddess who symbolized the sun's fertilizing force. Later she became a cat carrying the sun, or a cat-headed woman with a lion breastplate. Bast ruled pleasure and joy. In Bubastis, as throughout Egypt, celebrations in her honor were filled with drinking, dancing, singing, and jesting. Hundreds of thousands attended the annual festival in Bubastis, at Bast's temple on an island in the Nile. Worshippers rode ferryboats to the festival, singing and feasting. As the boats passed villages, women revealed themselves and shouted suggestively to those on shore, a custom derived from the story of Bast's self-exposure to the sun god Ra, who smiled when he saw the goddess's privates. (Ellis; Lesko; Scott; Wilkinson)

Bat This very early goddess lost importance in later times, becoming virtually unknown. But she was a predynastic cow (or perhaps buffalo) divinity of great power. Unlike with later cow goddesses, her horns were shown growing from her temples, like true cow's horns, rather than sitting on top of her head.

The cow goddess was a primary divinity among prehistoric and predynastic Egyptians, who relied upon cattle. The cow was connected with the moon, whose crescent can be seen as cow horns. Bat was especially honored in Upper Egypt, near the source of the Nile River, but with the joining of the Two Lands, she became guardian over both parts of Egypt. (Lesko; Wilkinson)

Bês This goddess appeared as a female corollary to the dwarf earth god Bês. She was depicted nude or wearing a cat skin to match her cat ears and killing a snake. (Müller)

Ennead The nine gods of the ancient Egyptians were personified as a goddess, single or double, who became mother of all the gods. (Troy)

Hathor Egypt's most popular goddess, Hathor was worshipped for more than 3,000 years. Because of the length of her prominence, a profusion of legends surrounded her, and she was depicted in many different guises: mother and daughter of the sun, lioness and cow, sycamore and date palm. Goddess of the underworld, she ruled the sky. Patron of foreigners, she was mother of the Egyptians.

Her name is often translated as "house of Horus" but may mean "lady of the house." The first suggests her connection to the celestial god Horus, while the second suggests domesticity and sovereignty. Her festivals were carnivals of intoxication, especially that held on New Year's Day, when Hathor's image was brought from her temple to catch the rays of the newborn sun. Revels broke out, appropriate because Hathor was the patron of bodily pleasures. These included music and song; art, cosmetics, the weaving of garlands; dance and lovemaking. Many love poems address her as "the golden one," the goddess who strengthens bonds of affection. She was beloved by her people, who held fast to her rites.

One of Hathor's most familiar forms was the winged cow of creation that gave birth to the universe;

she was also depicted as a suckling human mother. The image of goddess as mother connects Hathor with fertility of land and people; in some temples, phallic images and figurines of nude nubile women have been found. Because of her connection with cows, Hathor was honored in ritual with bowls of milk, offered as libations.

Hathor ruled birth and death. She appeared as seven Hathors who foretold each newborn's destiny. She also received the dead, for which she was called Queen of the West, the direction associated with death. She accompanied worshippers on their final journeys, so rituals to her were part of funerals.

Hathor had several important symbols. One was the sistrum, a rattle in the shape of the ankh, indicating the union of masculine and feminine, shaken to welcome the goddess and to drive away evil. Hathor's other major symbol was the mirror. Grave paintings show dancers bearing mirrors, performing in Hathor's honor. Mirrors were given as offerings at her shrines.

Hathor's solar connections were emphasized by her title "eye of the sun." She was originally the sun's eye but grew angry and went to live in the desert as a lioness. Gods went to bring her back, but she was slow returning. When she did, she was greeted with music and dancing. Some texts suggest that Hathor was not involved; rather, her anger split off to become the goddess **Sekhmet**, who was pacified with red beer after killing many people. Others suggest Hathor did the killing, stopping only when she was drunk. (Bleeker; Buhl; Ellis; Faulkner; Lesko; Shafer; Lichtheim 1976; Müller; Parkinson; Pinch 1982, 1993; Springborg; Traunecker; Wiedemann)

Hekt Frog-headed Hekt represented the embryonic grain that seems to die, then revives. An ancient divinity, Hekt was midwife at the birth of the sun. At creation she touched lifeless humans with the ankh, causing them to breathe and move. Like other birth goddesses, she was considered a prophet because she foresaw the newborn's life. In addition, the croaking of her frogs predicted the rising of the Nile. (Müller; Wiedemann)

Heret-Kau The name of this obscure goddess seems to refer to her as ruler of the spirit world, suggesting a connection with the afterlife. (Wilkinson)

Hesat One of Egypt's numerous cow goddesses, Hesat bears a name meaning "wild cow" and was the mother of a golden calf. (Wilkinson)

Ipat A minor hippopotamus goddess, Ipet was nurturing and protective. Although shown as a hippo, she had the feet of a lion; sometimes she had human breasts, engorged with milk. Mostly worshipped in the area of Thebes, she may have been the city goddess there. (Ellis; Wilkinson)

Isis Greek rulers pronounced the name of Au-set ("throne") as Isis, and so she was known throughout the ancient word. The winged goddess was associated with the sky, while her brother/lover Osiris represented the Nile. First daughter of **Nut**, Isis turned a kind eye on the people of earth, teaching women to grind corn, spin flax, and weave cloth.

The goddess lived with Osiris until their evil brother Set killed him. Isis cut her hair and tore her robes, then set out in search of her brother's body. In Phoenicia, Queen Astarte hired the pitiable widow as nursemaid. Isis placed the infant prince in the fire, where his mother found him smoldering. When she pulled him out, the queen undid the magic of immortality Isis had been working, and the goddess was forced to reveal her identity. The queen pointed out a tamarisk tree that contained the body of Osiris, which Isis carried back to Egypt. But Set found the body and dismembered it.

Isis's search began anew. She found most of the pieces of her beloved, but because she could not find his penis, Isis substituted a piece of shaped gold. She invented the rites of embalming and applied them to the body. Osiris rose, and Isis conceived a child through the golden phallus. Festivals told this story as a symbol of the agricultural cycle, from Nile flooding, which brought fertility to the land, through harvest and fallow winter. Because of Isis's power in reviving Osiris, she became associated with funerary rites.

In another myth, Isis gained magical power after she fashioned a poisonous snake to bite the god Ra. Sickened by the bite, he called for Isis. The goddess claimed to be powerless unless she knew the god's secret name. Ra hesitated, growing weaker. In desperation, he was forced to whisper the secret word to her. Isis cured him, but Ra had given her power over him. From this myth, Isis became connected with magic.

The religion of Isis outlasted the Egyptian empire. She became the Lady of Ten Thousand Names or Isis Panthea ("Isis All-Goddess"), identified with many other goddesses. Yet she continued to be honored as a local goddess in Egypt, where many of her shrines were under the control of priestesses. Thus Isis was simultaneously local and universal.

Having attained such prominence, Isis continued to have religious power after the rise of the Roman Empire; she was one of the most important imported goddesses in multiethnic Rome. A characteristic image of Isis showed her as a nursing mother. This image, popular in Rome in the early Christian era, was adopted by Christians to show the virgin mother, **Mary**. Although Isis has not been part of any official religion for more than 1,500 years, she has become the center of several revivalist goddess organizations in the past century. (Brandon; Cott; De Horrack; Donalson 2003; Ellis; Faulkner 1968; Frankfurter; Lesko; Lichtheim 1976, 1980; Magness; Meyer; Müller; Tacheva-Hitova; Brenner; Wiedemann; Žabkar 1988)

Ma'at Goddess of truth, Ma'at took the form of an ostrich feather balanced on the underworld's scales, opposite someone's heart. If the dishes balanced, the heart was light with justice, and the soul would live on. If the dishes did not balance, the monstrous goddess Ahemait destroyed the person. Sometimes divided into two goddesses indicating natural and moral law, Ma'at has been described as a personified abstraction.

But some scholars point to her temples, the priesthood dedicated to her, and the herds of cattle tended in her name to argue that she was an ancient goddess. (Ellis; Faulkner 1990; Müller; Wiedemann)

Mafdet The "Lady of the Castle of Life," an early goddess whose symbolic animal has been interpreted as both a cat and a mongoose, was invoked against snakebite. (Müller; Wilkinson)

Mehet-Weret One form of the goddess **Neith**, Mehet-Weret also appears as a separate goddess whose name means "great flood," connecting her with the fertilizing waters of the Nile flood. She was a cosmic goddess who took the shape of the cow who raised the sun into the sky each day. She was shown as a pregnant woman with huge breasts or a cow-headed woman holding a lotus. (Lesko; Müller; Troy; Wilkinson)

Meret This water goddess was often described as a double goddess named Merti ("two Merets") or as southern and northern Merets, both celestial musicians. She created the cosmic order through music. (Lesko; Müller)

Meretseger Benevolent and punishing by turns, Meretseger was shown as a coiled snake with three heads (snake, human, and vulture) or as a snake with a human head. (Lesko; Müller; Wilkinson)

Meskhoni A human-headed brick or a woman with a brick headdress symbolized this birth goddess, a household divinity. During labor, women rested their heads on brick pillows, awaiting Meskhoni and the obscure goddess Ermutu. When contractions began, they appeared and remained through delivery to predict the future of the newborn. Meskhoni's name means "omen," and her role included setting the course of a person's life. In Egyptian art, Meskhoni appears as a woman wearing palm shoots on her head; these have also been interpreted as insect antennae. (Müller; Wilkinson)

Mut This creatrix, depicted variously as vulture, lioness, and crowned woman, was a punitive goddess in whose temple traitors were burned to death. She was associated with the period preceding the Nile's annual flooding, when harvest had left the fields empty and the people relied upon stored foods. Some have theorized that she was an invented goddess, designed as a corollary to the important god Amun, but evidence shows her to be an early divinity of Thebes. (Ellis; Lesko; Müller; Wilkinson)

Neḥem-ʿauit This goddess of wisdom, originally a distinct divinity, was absorbed into **Hathor**. Her name has been interpreted as "she who removes violence" and "she who delivers us from violence," suggesting a protective divinity. (Müller)

Neith One of Egypt's most ancient goddesses, Neith was historically connected with the Nile delta but had her origin in Libya. Her symbols were a pair of crossed arrows or bows tied together, so Neith appears to have been a warrior. Later, wearing the double crown of unified Egypt, Neith commanded reverence from her temple city of Sais. In her most important festival, an image of the goddess as a sacred cow bearing the sun was carried through the streets, while lamps were lit in every home. Later, Neith assumed attributes of other goddesses, becoming a complex figure associated with handicrafts and industry because, at the beginning of time, Neith took up the shuttle, strung the sky on her loom, and wove the world. She wove nets and from the primordial waters pulled up living creatures, including men and women.

Like other goddesses, Neith was connected with fertility. She invented childbirth by bringing forth Ra. Neith was a midwife and a healer, during and after life. During her worshippers' lives, she was responsible for their health, for her priests were healers. After death, she guarded their remains while welcoming their souls. (Ellis; Lesko; Müller; Brenner; Wiedemann)

Nekhbet The vulture-headed goddess of the Nile's source, she was creatrix of the region around the city of Nekheb; her original temple has been found at the rich archaeological site of El Kab. After unification of the two lands, Nekhbet became the king's protector. As goddess of the Upper Nile, she was called the "twin" of **Wadjet**, goddess of the Lower Nile; together they formed the Neb-Ti, the "two mistresses." (Lesko; Lichtheim 1976; Müller; Parkinson; Wiedemann)

Nephthys This Greek version of her name is more commonly used than her original Egyptian name, Nebthet. She was Isis's sister and opposite: Isis was the force of life and rebirth; Nephthys, the tomb-dwelling goddess of death and sunset, invoked as queen of night. They had similarly opposite mates. Isis's consort was the fertility god Osiris, while her sister's mate was the evil god Set.

Set was not only wicked but sterile. So Nephthys, who wanted children, plied Osiris with liquor until he tumbled into bed with her. That night she conceived the god Anubis. Set killed and dismembered Osiris. This proved too much for Nephthys, who left Set to join her sister's lamentations and restore Osiris to life. (*EL*; Faulkner; Lichtheim 1980; Müller; Brenner)

Nut First daughter of **Tefnut**, the sky goddess Nut lay across the body of her brother, Geb the earth, holding him in constant intercourse. But the god Ra disapproved and commanded Shu, their father, to separate his children. Shu hoisted Nut into a great arch, but he was forced to remain forever holding them apart, supporting Nut's belly.

Ra cursed Nut, forbidding her to bear children during any month of the year. But the god Thoth outwitted the curse, gambling with the moon and winning from him five days that float between the years. In these five days, from her brother's seed already within her, Nut produced five children: the sister goddesses **Isis** and **Nephthys**, their mates Osiris and Set, and the sun god Horus.

Sometimes Nut took the form of a cow, as she did when Ra decided to abandon the earth because of human insolence. She knelt so he could climb on her. She leaped into the air, bearing the god until she became dizzy from the weight. Four gods rushed to hold up Nut's body, remaining as the world's pillars. (Brandon; Buhl; Ellis; Lesko; Müller; Piankoff; Troy; Wiedemann)

Ogdoad The Egyptians called primordial beings that emerged from the abyss of pretemporal waters the chaos divinities. They included four female snakes (or snake-headed women) named Naunet, Kauket, Hauket, and Amaunet. Their companions were four male frogs. From their random movements a pattern emerged, which grew increasingly regular until they had brought order out of chaos. (Shafer; Müller; Brenner)

Pakhet This early lioness goddess bears a name that means "the one who tears" or "the scratcher." Although the Egyptians had many lion divinities, Pakhet was one of the most aggressive and fearsome. She was especially honored in the desert land of Speos Artemidos (cave of **Artemis**), a Greco-Egyptian name that points to the identification of Pakhet with that wilderness goddess. There, a cemetery like that of **Bast** at Bubastis provided a location for the burial of sacred cats. (Ellis; Lesko; Müller; Wilkinson)

Qebhsnuf With **Selkhet**, she was guardian of the embalmed dead, who stood in the sky behind the Great Bear (Big Dipper). (Faulkner)

Raet This sun goddess was the corollary of the sun god Ra. She is frequently conflated with **Hathor**, for both wore the solar disc between cow horns with the uraeus snake, and with the minor goddess **Pakhet**, a lioness-sun divinity. She was celebrated with a festival after the end of harvest. (Ellis; Wiedemann; Wilkinson)

Renenutet Invoked as the "mistress of provisions," Renenutet was a cobra goddess to whom offerings were made for agricultural success. A motherly woman with a snake's head, she protected vineyards; altars were

erected to her during wine pressing. After Christianity arrived, she was honored as Saint Thermuthis. (Ellis; Leibovitch; Lesko; Müller; Wilkinson)

Saosis This Egyptian goddess took the form of an acacia tree in which both life and death were entrapped. She was considered the female sun, counterpart to the sun god Atum or described as his right hand. (Buhl)

Satis "She who runs like an arrow" was an archer goddess who personified the waterfalls of the Nile; she also had cosmic connections, identified with the star Sothis (Sirius), whose annual rising coincided with the Nile's flooding. (Ellis; Faulkner; Müller; Wiedemann)

Sekhmet Once, the lion-headed sun goddess became so disgusted with humanity that she decided to slaughter the race. Her fury terrified the gods, who deputized Ra to calm Sekhmet. But she refused to be restrained. Attempting to save the remnant of humanity, Ra mixed beer with pomegranate juice. He set the jugs in Sekhmet's path, hoping she would mistake them for human blood. She drank herself into a stupor and, when she awoke, had no rage left.

The red drink was thereafter consumed on feast days of **Hathor**. Some interpret Sekhmet as the terrifying side of that pleasure-ruling goddess. Others say she was the opposite of **Bast**, who embodied the sun's nurturing rays, while the lion Sekhmet represented her destructive drought-bringing potential. Sekhmet represented the desert winds as well, for which reason she was described as breathing fire. She was a martial goddess under whose protection armies marched. Occasionally, she caused plagues, but she was also a healing goddess. Her main center was Memphis, but temples to her were built in many areas. The minor goddess Shesmetet could be related. (Ellis; Faulkner; Lichtheim 1976; Lesko; Müller; Parkinson; Wiedemann; Wilkinson)

Selkhet In pyramid tombs, mourners placed golden figures of guardian goddesses. One was Selkhet, a scorpion goddess of great antiquity who, with Qebhsnuf, protected the vessels that held the corpses' intestines. Selkhet offered instructions for the afterlife. Shown with a scorpion headdress, she symbolized rebirth. (Lesko; Müller)

Seshat This goddess was the "mistress of the house of books," inventor of writing and secretary of heaven. She was also "mistress of the house of architects," studying the stars to determine the axes of new buildings. Seshat invented mathematics; she measured the length of human lives with palm branches. Accompanied by a duplicate named Sefkhet-abwy, Seshat wore the leopard skin of a priest, with two inkstands slung over her shoulder. (Müller; Wilkinson)

Sothis The star now called Sirius (the "Dog Star") was the goddess Sopdet or Sept to the Egyptians, better known under her Greek name of Sothis ("soul of **Isis**"). Her mate was Sah (the nearby constellation of Orion) or the obscure god Khnum, with whom she was consort together with **Anuket** and **Satis**. In predynastic times, she was a cosmic cow goddess. Later, she was connected to the Nile's annual inundation, which occurred when Sothis appeared at dawn on the eastern horizon. Because Osiris was connected to the Nile flooding, Sothis became connected to that god's sister-lover Isis.

Openings once described as air vents in the Great Pyramid have been shown to be alignment points that bring the light of Sothis into the pyramid's interior. Sothis was envisioned as assisting in the rebirth of the dead, as Isis did when she resurrected her brother Osiris. The goddess was depicted as a horned girl wearing a five-pointed star. (Ellis; Wilkinson)

Taweret This early mother goddess was a pregnant hippopotamus with human breasts and a woman's wig, standing on her hind legs and carrying the scrolls of protection. She carried a crocodile on her back or in her arms; she bared her teeth, a signal of protective

maternity. Taweret was popular during the Ptolemaic period and Roman occupation. Her worship endured until the fifth century CE. (Ellis; Müller; Springborg; Frankfurter; Wiedemann; Wilkinson)

Tayet The Old Kingdom goddess of weaving, Tayet was considered the king's mother because she wove his clothes as well as the bandages in which his body was mummified. (Lesko; Wilkinson)

Tefnut Named for the dew, this goddess was associated with the mountains of the dawn. She was the first female being, one of a pair of twins spat out by the male god Atum. As a divinity of death, she represented the moist atmosphere of the lower world. (Müller; Brenner; Wilkinson)

Wadjet The vulture goddess of lower Egypt and the Nile delta, she joined with **Nekhbet** to form the "two mistresses" of the land, the Neb-Ti (Nebty), a symbol of Egyptian unification. Inscriptions called her the "great enchantress"; she was associated with the snake crown, symbol of sovereignty. As Weret-Hekaw, "great of magic," she had oracular powers; thus she figured in funeral scenes and prayers. The Greeks called her Buto, after one of her shrines. (Boss; Faulkner; Johnson 1990; Lesko; Müller; Wiedemann)

AFRICAN DIASPORA PANTHEON

Adja This Haitian *lwa* deals with herbs and drugs. She appears to have descended from a Yoruba goddess who kidnapped people whom she wished to endow with medicinal knowledge. When she possesses a worshipper, the person eats broken glass from medicine bottles. (Courlander 1944)

Agwe This ocean goddess, originally from Benin, is prominent in African diaspora religions, appearing in Brazilian religion as Abe and in Haiti as Agwe. In Haiti, when Agwe dances, she moves her hands as though swimming. (Bastide; Dunham; Herskovits; Simpson)

Aida Wedo The African primal snake is honored in Haiti as Aida-Wedo, the companion of the most popular god, Damballah-Wedo, also a serpent. She rules fire, water, wind, and rainbows. When she appears in ritual, she slithers across the ground wearing a jeweled headdress and a white dress. The *lwa* Domici Wedo is her daughter or co-wife. (Courlander)

Calunga Originally a Bakongo sea goddess, Calunga is well known in the New World, especially in Brazil, where an image of her is carried in carnival processions. As a spirit of death, she is called Our Lady of the Rosary. Her symbol, the cross, indicates her ability to pass between worlds. (Bastide; Kiddy)

Ezili The Haitian *lwa* of sensuality, Ezili is generous to the point of extravagance with worshippers and expects the same in return, so they bestow costly gifts on her: gowns, perfumes, and powders. She is a beautiful yellow-skinned woman, flirtatious and charming. When she appears in ritual, she has unbound hair; her altar bears a comb and lipstick. One of her symbols, the pierced heart, points to the pain of separation that lovers endure. Dancers who embody her often weep copiously. Called Our Lady of Sorrows (Mater Dolorosa), Ezili can be a triple divinity or a trinity of sisters. The distinction between Ezili and **Oshun** is unclear. (Bastide; Bellegarde-Smith; Courlander; Houlberg; Marks; Brown)

Icú Frightening Cuban goddess of death, Icú guarded Shango, lover of **Oya**. But **Oshun** determined to free him, luring Icú into a night of drinking that ended with the death goddess proposing a sexual encounter with Oya, who used the occasion to attack Icú. But Oshun was not rewarded with intercourse. Shango remained true to Oya. Icú lives in bottles, which is why they must remain capped. (Lachantañeré)

Kouzinn The Haitian *lwa* of commerce and finances, Kouzinn is honored with her consort, Azaka, but has importance herself as a representative of women's commerce. (Brown)

Maman Brigitte A Haitian spirit of death, she owns all cemeteries, particularly those in which the first body interred was a woman. Her children are the spirits who outline, dig, and mark graves. She is the mother of many important *lwa*. (Courlander; Mettraux)

Nanan Buluku In the African diaspora, the important African goddess **Nanamburucú** continued to exert influence. In Cuba, she corresponds to the Virgin of Mount Carmel or to Saint Emilius. In Brazil, she became St. Anne, honored by followers wearing red, white, and blue beads. She is the senior wife to the primary god, Oshala, whose other wife is **Ymoja**. Oldest of the water orishas, she is celebrated on Saturdays, when she dances carrying a broom. (Bastide; Courlander; Lachantañeré; Landes)

Oba The African goddess **Ọba** migrated to Cuba. When Oba possesses a dancer, she wears a scarf that hides one ear and must be kept from any dancer who embodies **Oshun** because of rivalry between the two. Oba is syncretized with saints Catherine and Rita. (Barnet; De La Torre; Lachantañeré)

Obatallah This hermaphroditic creatrix is among the four great divinities of Brazil, the others being **Oshun**, **Oya**, and **Ymoja**. She is also found in Cuba as the most powerful of feminine spirits, a warrior-lover connected with rivers and their fertilizing power; she is called Our Lady of Mercy or of the Blessed Sacrament. Her color is white, her domain everything pure and unsullied. Yet she was earthy as well as celestial. She once slept with a boatman in exchange for his services, thus conceiving her son, the god of fire and chaos, Shango. (Barnet; Lachantañeré)

Ochumare The Yoruba goddess of the rainbow was Catholicized into Our Lady of Hope in Cuba. She appears in Brazil as an increasingly popular divinity sometimes transformed into a male saint, Bartholomew or Patrick, but often into a form of the Virgin **Mary** (see Eastern Mediterranean). (Bastide)

Oddudúa This Cuban *lwa* was created after the world began, to be the mate of the primary divinity, Obatalá. The pair immediately began to conceive orishas. Traditions say this divinity was the male part of Obatalá, while the female part was known as Yemmú; or that Oddudúa was the younger brother of Obatalá. She is not greatly honored in ritual today. (De La Torre)

Oshun The African river goddess Oshun is one of the most important Afro-Caribbean goddesses, her devotees numbering in the tens of thousands. She is a spirit of sensuality and passion. When she possesses dancers, their movements are those of a woman who loves to swim, who makes her arm bracelets jangle, and who admires herself in a mirror.

Wife of the old diviner Orúmbila, Oshun suffered because her sexual appetite outstripped her husband's. Finally she found herself in the presence of Ogún, a god with a wide reputation as a seducer. But just one night with Oshun changed him. He wished to enjoy her forever, but she returned to her husband, continuing her affair with Ogún. Her husband set parrots to watch her, but Oshun fed them, so the birds lied about her whereabouts. The diviner suspected the truth and undid the drug, so the parrots told the truth and her affair was ended.

Oshun also had an affair with turbulent Shango. It began because Oshun always attracted attention with her sensual dancing. Sometimes she selected a man to take home. One night she conceived a passion for Shango, the best drummer a dancer could desire, but he refused her. When finally he succumbed, he still verbally rejected her. But when he fell from popularity, she was the one who accompanied him, giving up riches to do so.

In Brazil, Oxun is goddess of waters; she is depicted wearing jewels, holding a mirror, and waving a fan. Her altars hold copper bracelets and fans, as well as dishes of Omuluku (onions, beans, and salt). She rules love, beauty, and flirtation.

In Cuba, Oshun is Our Lady of La Caridad del Cobre, patron of the island and special goddess of Havana. Cuban worshippers see her as a beautiful mulatto woman, sensuous and graceful, affectionate and charming. Honey and gold are among her attributes; yellow is her color, the peacock her bird, and a small brass bell the sound that summons her. Oshun rules pregnancy and protects women and unborn children. She is patroness of prostitutes, especially in her identity as Panchágara, who dances to lure money from men.

In Trinidad, Oshun appears dancing, often balancing a full jug of water on her head. She can also demand rituals beside a river, where she will offer food that is shared with the attendants. Her symbols are the anchor and wineglass; she wears blue and white; she is connected with St. Philomena. (Olmos; Barnet; Bastide; De La Torre; Lachantañeré; Murphy and Sandford 2001)

Oya Oya, a stern mistress of the realm of the dead, is one of the most powerful African diaspora goddesses. On her holy day of Wednesday, her followers wear dark-red beads and offer her palm wine, goat meat, and yams. When she dances, the dance becomes frenzied as Oya swings a sword or a flyswatter. Sometimes she dances with arms outstretched to discourage ghosts, which she controls. In Brazil, where she is one of the primary divinities, she is called Yansan, patron of bisexual men because she is a "man-woman." Wife and possibly sister of the thunder orisha, Shango, Yansan is a fierce warrior; some scholars see them as a single two-sexed being. When a powerful enemy brought Shango near death, Oya revived him with her energies, so he would become her mate. He agreed, but she posted the death spirit Icú at their bedroom door so he would be too frightened to think of seeing other women. Finally **Oshun** freed Shango by seducing Icú, but Shango still preferred Oya. A storm goddess who also rules fire and lightning, she is served by wild spirits. She is identified with St. Barbara.

Patron of justice and memory, she is pictured holding a flame. She is a heavenly being, ruling the lightning and wind (whence her name Centella, "lightning") and the rainbow. She corresponds to the Virgin of Candlemas or of Mount Carmel. In Trinidad, Oya lives in the breeze; when she possesses worshippers, she dances vigorously, holding her left ear to hear the wind. Green and red are her colors; her day is Friday; corn is her offering. She is assimilated to St. Catherine. (Olmos; Barnet; Bellegarde-Smith; De La Torre; Gleason 1987; Houlberg; Lachantañeré; Landes; Mettraux; Mischel)

Yegguá In Cuba, this *lwa* appears in pink and white. But her appearances are few, for not many women open themselves to her. If they do, they must lead a celibate life; should they try to marry, they are miserable. Yegguá is connected with Our Lady of Montserrat and deals primarily with death. (Barnet)

Ymoja When Ymoja lived on earth, she caught a spark falling from the heavens in her outstretched apron and found it to be Shango, god of fire, whom she raised as her son. He was a demanding child, always wanting food or drink or entertainment and even a secret divination tool that belonged to **Obatallah**. Ymoja tried to steal it but failed, and Obatallah forced her into servitude. Later, Ymoja found herself aroused by her adoptive son and, when he rejected her, began to masturbate publicly until he satisfied her. This was the world's first incest.

In Cuba she is Yemayá, appearing in a skirt with seven flounces; her colors are blue and white, symbols of the seawater she controls. She wears beads: seven blue ones alternating with seven white ones; her blue and white skirts represent the ocean's waters and its foam of waves. When she dances, she can be wild or calm; sometimes she rolls her body like waves. Goddess of intelligence and motherliness, of reason and intellect, she is syncretized with Our Lady of Regla and Mary, Star of the Sea.

In Brazil, she is called Yemanja or Our Lady of the Immaculate Conception. She is ocean goddess of the crescent moon; her followers wear crystal beads. On February 2, crowds gather on ocean beaches to offer her soap, perfume, jewelry, and fabric, which, together with letters bearing requests to the goddess, are thrown out to sea. She often appears as a mermaid, for which reason she is conflated with **Ezili**.

In Trinidad, Yemanja is benevolent. When she appears in ritual, she seems to be rowing a boat while sitting on the ground and sliding forward. Her symbols are a gourd full of water and an oar; her feast day is Thursday; and her colors are watery blue and white. She is assimilated to St. Anne. (Olmos; Barnet; Bastide; De La Torre; Gordon; Lachantañeré; Omari; Landes; Mischel; Gates)

EASTERN MEDITERRANEAN

No area holds more significance to the question of women and religion than the eastern Mediterranean, where the world's three monotheisms were born. Judaism, Christianity, and Islam are called Abrahamic religions because all claim descent from the patriarch Abraham. All honor a single, male god. No other world religions have so thoroughly denied the possibility of goddesses. No parallel religion based on a single goddess, exclusive of a male divine figure, has been found.

In addition to the region's Abrahamic traditions, Zoroastrianism influenced Western religious thought. While monotheistic, it acknowledged semi-divine females. Finally, the dualistic philosophy called Manichaeism originated in this area and gave rise to Gnosticism, with its feminine matter and masculine spirit. Although giving primacy to spirit, and thus by implication to the masculine, the Gnostic worldview does acknowledge the power of the feminine. Finally, a short-lived monotheism devoted to the god Aten is considered in the section on Africa.

Disinterested scholarship about this region is rare, with many scholars serving as apologists for religious orthodoxy, especially when texts are considered the literal word of God. Challengers often find themselves under attack by conservative scholars. Given the masculinist bias of the region's religions, this especially affects those researching suppressed goddess traditions. It also affects those exploring alternative views of, and roles for, women in monotheistic religions.

The region offers a plethora of texts and monuments. Because writing was invented here in the fourth millennium BCE, multiple texts can be compared and contrasted. Many, inscribed on clay tablets, suffered breaks at important places; presumptive renderings can be influenced by scholarly bias. Varying translations can yield dramatically different myths and names. Taken together, the depth of history, number of texts, and bias among interpreters make this a challenging region of study for those interested in goddess religion.

Standing between the continents of Africa and Asia, the eastern Mediterranean has been a cultural crossroads since the beginning of civilization. As empires rose and fell, their religions gained and lost power, with some divinities surviving in altered form. Urban culture began early in the region, with centralized governments supporting temples and other religious institutions. These civilizations are typically named for their most important city. Yet rural populations worshipped in ways that sustained different myths and rituals, some of which entered into the mainstream. For these reasons, the eastern

Mediterranean presents a complex picture to the scholar of religions.

The region, shaped like a backward letter "C," is called the Fertile Crescent. The northern portion, once known as Asia Minor, was homeland to the Hittite and later the Persian Empire. To the southeast was Mesopotamia, where cultures flourished along the Tigris and Euphrates Rivers. Along the southeastern shores of the Mediterranean stretched lands known from the Bible. Farther south, along the Persian Gulf, was the source of the Islamic religion. In Anatolia, in approximately 7000 BCE, a city was established significant to goddess studies. Çatal Hüyük reveals human occupation almost 9,000 years ago. Among the finds, statues of stout female figures suggest religious meaning. The theory offered by early excavators, that Çatal Hüyük was a pacifist agricultural community, has been challenged, as has the presumption that female images reveal a religion centered around a goddess. But the importance of that goddess in the region remains unquestioned.

No one knows when, why, or how early Anatolian civilizations declined. By 2500 BCE, the Hurrian culture had grown to prominence. Hurrians were aggressively expansive, controlling land as far away as Egypt and Iran. One of their major outposts was the city of Mitanni, in what later became Mesopotamia. The empire declined by 1300 BCE. Some texts name Hurrian goddesses, but information is minimal.

The next important power was the Hittites, an Indo-European group that entered the region around 2000 BCE. Moving from the north, possibly from Bulgaria and the Ukraine, the Hittites settled in Anatolia among the Hattian people. The Hittites organized their religion around a sun goddess whose earthly embodiment was the queen. Within a few hundred years, the Hittites had established themselves around Hattusa (Boğazköy, Turkey) and began to conquer surrounding lands. At its greatest extent, the Hittite empire reached to Egypt. For five centuries, Hittite fortunes advanced and declined, until by 1200 BCE they had virtually disappeared.

South of Anatolia was Mesopotamia, the land between the waters of the Tigris and Euphrates Rivers (today's Iran, Iraq, Kuwait, and eastern Syria). In prehistoric times, the area was settled by agriculturalists who settled in water-rich areas that include the supposed biblical Garden of Eden, just east of Baghdad. Near Baghdad was Babylon, an empire divided between Akkad to the north (which included Babylon, Nippur, and Kish) and Sumer to the south (which included Ur and Uruk). Akkadian and Sumerian religion had much in common, but different names were given to divinities, who over time developed significant differences in myth and ritual. The Sumerian culture later evolved into what is known as Chaldean, centered near today's city of Basra.

From Mesopotamia came some of the most impressive ancient religious texts, including the *Epic of Gilgamesh* (ca. 2000 BCE), as well as the poems of the first known poet, the priestess Enheduanna. Many texts, written in a wedge-shaped alphabet called cuneiform, survived. European scholars of the eighteenth and nineteenth centuries often compared Mesopotamian texts with the Bible. The presence of goddesses in the Babylonian pantheon, as well as the extent of available texts, has led to significant literature on this subject.

Also located in Mesopotamia was the Assyrian civilization, not to be confused with present-day Syria. Emerging as a regional power in the fourteenth century BCE, the Assyrians expanded their empire for almost 800 years. Among the goddesses of this culture, Ishtar of Nineveh stands out, not only because of the significance of her temple but also because of her appearance in many texts and inscriptions. Like earlier empires, the Assyrians could not hold their large territory, and the united Medes and Babylonians defeated the Assyrians in 612 BCE at Nineveh (today's Mosul). The Babylonians did not enjoy power for long. In 539 BCE, the Babylonian empire was defeated by the Persians under the control of Cyrus.

The Medes retained power longer. In the second millennium BCE, an Indo-European people had migrated into Mesopotamia, dividing soon into Persians and Medes. The first soon became subject to the Medes, who controlled today's Iran, known as Media to the Greeks, and later established an empire (modern Azerbaijan and parts of Afghanistan); they are among the ancestors of today's Kurdish people. The Medes and Persians joined again to form the Achaemenid Persian empire. Although Persian expansion ended at the battle of Marathon, the empire remained a regional power.

During this period, reorganization of native religion into Zoroastrianism began. Once the predominant religion of what is now Iran, Zoroastrianism has declined to minority status since the rise of Islam. According to the tenth–sixth-century BCE prophet Zoroaster, the sole god was Ahura Mazda, the uncreated creator known through seven emanations, of which several are feminine. Ahura Mazda's creation includes only what is orderly, with the rest being the work of Angra Mainyu, the force of evil whose domain includes such natural processes as decay. The sacred texts form the Avesta, oral texts transcribed in the early centuries CE. The most sacred texts are called the Garthas, claimed as the words of Zoroaster himself. An anionic religion based on a male supreme deity, Zoroastrianism leaves little space for the feminine.

The Achaemenid Persian empire came to an end in 331 BCE, when Alexander the Great swept through the land. Alexander's vast empire could not be sustained, and within a few hundred years another Persian culture, the Parthian, arose. During this period the sage Mani articulated his philosophy. Born in Babylon in the third century CE, Mani claimed to bring together diverse religions into complete truth. That truth was based in monotheism, which Manichaeism transformed into a dualistic vision of spirit in endless struggle against matter, gendered respectively as masculine and feminine.

The empires of Mesopotamia extended into lands now occupied by Palestine, Israel, Jordan, Lebanon, and Syria. There, Judaism and Christianity were born. In this "Holy Land," archaeology finds evidence of settlement as early as the seventh millennium BCE. But whereas the books of the Jewish Bible describe a religion monotheistic from the start, archaeology unveils a different history. Digs at Jericho and other sites, often centering upon "tells," or earthen hills above settlements, show a religion involving a primary goddess. Hundreds of images of her, sculpted in clay, have been found.

This region, the homeland of the Israelites, was also home to the Canaanites, a term that is never clearly defined. Ancient sources use it to refer to non-Israelites. The Hebrew scriptures describe all goddesses as foreign or "Canaanite," but archaeological finds suggest goddesses existed in the earliest Israelite religion. Although evidence for a consort to the high god YHWH has recently become more widely known, conservative Jewish and Christian theologians argue that monotheism was a cornerstone of the religions.

Part of conservative reluctance to accept archaeological testimony for an Israelite goddess stems from a belief that the Bible is the revealed "word of God." This leads to belief in the historicity of every detail of the scriptures. But contemporary biblical scholarship has found evidence of different authors of the primary books, the Pentateuch. When archaeological finds are compared with scripture, the historicity of scripture is called into question. Especially important are finds from Ugarit, a city whose domain lasted from the fourteenth to the twelfth century BCE. In 1928, the hill that covered the ancient city center, now called Ras Shamra, was excavated and texts were found that provided information about goddesses previously known only from biblical sources. The Ras Shamra texts changed the scholarly view on the role of goddesses in the area's religion.

The Ugaritic culture was not the only one considered "Canaanite" in the Bible. That label also referred to Phoenicians, who spoke a Semitic language like those of Israelites and Ugaritic peoples. From 1200–900 BCE, these navigators established trading centers in today's Lebanon and Syria. Their sailing prowess made them wealthy, and they created distant settlements to support their enterprise. The most famous, Carthage, was known for its war with the Roman Empire. Goddesses are known both in the Phoenician homeland and in Carthage.

The final culture represented in this region is that of the Arabian deserts. In early times, a minority of Arabs converted to monotheistic religions such as Zoroastrianism, but most continued traditional ways, including goddess worship, until the coming of the prophet Mohammed in the seventh century CE. The youngest of the Abrahamic religions, Islam is most rigorous in excluding the feminine divine.

Recently, feminist scholars and the faithful have sought ways of accommodating Abrahamic religions to women's desires for more inclusion. In Jewish tradition, midrash, or commentary, reinterprets scripture to connect it with changing times. Alternative liturgies acknowledge the feminine divine. Christian women seek ways to include the feminine, including honoring the Virgin Mary in controversial ways.

Fundamentalist worshippers often deplore such efforts. For some, finding room for feminine divinity means leaving monotheistic religion. Some become secularists, but others search for new religious affiliations. Because of the large number of former adherents to Abrahamic religions in new religious movements, figures such as Asheah and Mary have been claimed as goddesses by heterodox worshippers.

EASTERN MEDITERRANEAN PANTHEON

Àisha Qandisha Arabic people in coastal northern Morocco pictured this *djinniya* (female spirit) with a beautiful face, pendulous breasts, and goat legs. She was wanton and free, seducing young men, despite having a *djinn* consort named Hammu Qaiyu. She may have been a water goddess; a possible translation of her name may be "loving to be watered," although the "water" in question may have been semen. This figure has been connected with **Astarte**, who had a consort, Haman. The transmission route to North Africa was

likely through Carthage, where Astarte had a temple, to Carthaginian colonies in Morocco. The bedouins of the Beni Ahsen, living on the sites of Carthaginian colonies, were especially prone to visitations by Àisha. (Fernea and Malarkey)

Aktab-Kutbâ Until the middle of the twentieth century, this goddess's name was lost, but the "divine scribe" was rediscovered through inscriptions and texts found in the Nabataean city of Petra in southwestern Jordan, famous for its stone-cut buildings. Little but her name, which hints at her role, survives. She has been connected with the better-known **Uzza**. (Milik and Teixidor; Strugnell)

Allani This Hurrian goddess was sun goddess of the netherworld. When gods visited her, they feasted on cattle and fat-tailed sheep, while long-fingered Allani served them wine. In the Ugaritic pantheon, a similar goddess named Arşay was daughter of the god Ba'al and consort of Nergal, god of the underworld. (Albright 1968; Gurney; Hoffman)

Al-Lat This word appears as a title for several goddesses, including **Asherah** and **Athirat**. More importantly, it is the name of the pre-Islamic Arabic goddess who formed a divine trinity with **Uzza** and **Manāt**. Al-Lat is "the goddess," a name grammatically parallel to Allah, "the god." Some have theorized that she was his consort, as divinities of this area typically had consorts.

With her companions, Al-Lat appears in the "satanic verses" cast out of the Qur'an. According to a legend considered heretical by devout Muslims, Mohammed attempted to convert the people of Mecca, where his family, the Quraysh, controlled a shrine. But the people of Mecca were devoted to their female trinity, the "daughters of Allah." The prophet spoke a verse, included in the Qur'an, that reads: "Have you considered al-Lāt and al-'Uzzā, and Manāt, the third, the other?" But then the satanic one tempted him to utter a strange second sentence that includes a word that defies translation: *Gharānīq*, a word that appears nowhere else but has been translated as "cranes" and "swans." The "satanic verse" says: "These are the exalted cranes whose intersession is to be hoped for."

Legend says the Meccans understood this to mean their religion would be respected. Later, the angel Gabriel showed Mohammed that the verse was satanically inspired, and it was replaced by a command to ignore the goddesses: "They are but names you have named, you and your fathers. God has sent no authority for them." The insult understood by some Muslims when the "satanic verses" are discussed arises from the belief that the Qur'an is the literal word of god, revealed through his prophet; by contrast, the Bible is understood to have been written by men.

Most of what is known about early Arabic divinities derives from inscriptions, rock art, and reports from outsiders. All reveal the prominence of Al-Lat from the sixth century BCE to the rise of Islam. She was the central goddess of Petra in southwestern Jordan, as well as at Mecca, where 360 goddesses were worshipped at the sacred stone, the Ka'aba. Her religion was strong among nonurban people, especially shepherds, who associated Al-Lat with Venus, the morning star. Whether she was the "eye goddess" associated with images of staring eyes is not established.

Al-Lat was worshiped at Ta'if near Mecca in the form of an uncut block of white granite addressed as "My Lady." The Quraysh circled the stone chanting verses that, according to the medieval Book of Idols, were almost identical to the "satanic verses." Some sources contend that the stones were retained at Mecca and still form part of Islamic reverence. Medieval Jewish sources speak of the Black Stone, carved with ancient symbols, that was set backward into the Ka'aba so the writing was not visible.

In South Arabia, this goddess's name survived Islamicization to indicate the sun, suggesting Al-Lat was a solar goddess. Under the influence of other religions, she became identified with the earth. As an earth goddess, Al-Lat was considered unshakable and immovable. Al-Lat's connection to **Astarte** has been examined by some scholars but the issue is unsettled.

Similarly, the connection to the Chaldean goddess of death Allat is not established. (Qur'an 53:20; al-Kalbi; Bodington; Jobling; Langdon 1931; Lichtenstadter; Rabinowitz; Petty; Steptimus; Stuckey 1998)

Anāhitā Arēdvī Sūrā Anāhitā ("humid, strong, immaculate one") was a ruling deity of the pre-Zoroastrian Persians. She embodied the physical and metaphoric qualities of water, the fertilizing force that flowed from her supernatural fountain in the stars, formed at the beginning of time after Ahura Mazda had subdued the powers of evil. By extension she ruled semen, thus human generation. She was a protective mother to her people, nurturing them while defending them from enemies.

In statuary, Anāhitā was the "golden mother," arrayed in a golden kerchief, square gold earrings, and a jeweled diadem, wrapped in a gold-embroidered cloak adorned with otter skins. She drove in a chariot drawn by four white horses that signified wind, rain, clouds, and hail.

In Armenia, she was Anahit, "golden mother," the only female figure in Zoroastrianism and representative of womanliness. Two annual festivals celebrated her, one requiring the sacrifice of a heifer, a parade to a nearby river, and a feast at which the goddess's golden image was crowned. Cows may have been sacred to her; ancient writers record seeing untended cows branded with her crescent moon. (Ananikian; Carnoy 1916; Dexter; Hanaway; Malandra)

Anat This Ugaritic goddess appeared under four aspects: warrior, mother, virgin, and wanton woman. The final category has led to her being dismissed as goddess of fertility, but her domain was more far-reaching. A contradictory figure, "Mistress of All Gods" yet a virgin, Anat was both creatrix and bloodthirsty killer.

For centuries, Anat was paid little attention by scholars, perhaps because she appears infrequently in the Bible (where she is confused with **Asherah**), and few other texts were devoted to her. This changed in

1928 with the finding of the Ras Shamra texts, a group of early ritual poems centered on Anat. The goddess's origin is debated. She was not known in Babylonia. Most likely, Anat was a Semitic goddess whose worship extended across the region.

As goddess of desire, Anat appears as the favored sex partner of her brother Baal. Their appetite for each other was prodigious; in one case Anat found Baal hunting, after which they copulated seventy-seven times. For this occasion, she took the form of a cow, and the progeny she bore were oxen and buffalo. Recently, feminist scholars have challenged the conventional understanding of Anat's incestuous relationship with Baal, interpreting this famous narrative as referring to Anat's power over animal reproduction.

Anat's rage for blood was noteworthy. When her brother waged a victorious battle, Anat ordered a feast on the heavenly mountain and invited the defeated. Anat painted herself with rouge and henna, entered the hall, and closed the doors. She slew everyone in sight, wading in knee-deep blood and strapping dismembered bodies to her waist.

Anat once coveted a magnificent bow owned by the hunter Aqhat. When he refused her gifts, Anat pledged to take the bow by force. First she pretended to have forgotten her dispute and offered to teach Aqhat her hunting secrets. Anat then apparently took Aqhat's bow, with his life. As hunting was associated with males in Ugaritic culture, Anat crosses gender boundaries in this story.

Anat later fused with Asherah, a less contradictory goddess who was originally her mother. Her worship had already traveled from Ugarit to Egypt, where she was honored by the Israelites (see **Anat-Yahu**). There she was honored both in public observance, in temples dedicated to Anat and Baal, and in private, as names like Bent-Anat, "daughter of Anat," suggest. She was especially worshipped in Memphis, where she was identified with **Isis** (see Egypt). (Albright 1941, 1968; Cassuto; Cornelius; Cross; Day P 1992; Freedman; Gibson; Hooke; Kapelru; Langdon 1931; Petty; Oden; Pritchard 1943, 1969; Stuckey 1993; Van der Toorn 1992)

Araru A story parallel to the Hebrew creation narrative was found on an Akkadian cuneiform tablet with a Semitic translation, but the goddess Araru appears as creator. It describes a time before the sky and earth existed, when a stream ran down the center of the universe. A god, Meridug, created dust, out of which the human race was formed. Then Araru brought life to the new beings. She was depicted bearing shafts of lightning. The same goddess appears as creator in the *Epic of Gilgamesh*, forming the image of the universe in her mind to create it. (Bodington; Graves and Patai; Pritchard; Temple; Ward)

Ārmaiti In pre-Zoroastrian Iran, Ārmaiti was preeminent, an earth goddess who ruled reproduction, fructification, and destiny; later, she was demoted to a daughter of Ahura Mazda, the Zoroastrian high god, as Spendta Ārmaiti, "holy devotion," Spendarmat, or Spendarmad. Of the seven aspects of Ahura Mazda, three were feminine: Ārmaiti and the sister divinities Haurvatat ("integrity") and Ameretat ("immortality'), who ruled the physical as well as the spiritual manifestations of these qualities. In some myths, Ārmaiti created the first humans, suggesting derivation from an early creatrix. (Ananikian; Azarpay; Dexter; Hinnells)

Ashi The Zoroastrian goddess of life's pleasures was Ashi, whose name means "reward," for such pleasures were believed a reward for moral action. Daughter of the high god Ahura Mazda and **Ārmaiti**, Ashi was goddess of a happy domestic life. (Malandra)

Ashnan The Sumerian goddess of grain and her friend **Lahar**, goddess of cattle, had to provide food and drink for the gods. But they got drunk instead, so humanity was created to take up the slack. Some texts tell of a time before Ashnan and Lahar had descended to earth, when naked humans grazed on grass and drank from streams. When the goddesses brought food and the civilizing power of clothing, people were saved from their barbarism. (Hooke; Kramer 1961, 1979; Pritchard 1969)

Ashtart In several texts from this region, including the Ras Shamra texts, a goddess of this name is mentioned, connected with the consort of **Anat**, Baal. She is described as a fertility goddess, to whom propitiatory offerings were made. The name also was known in Egypt, where she appeared mounted or bearing weapons. The plural form, **Ashtoreth**, is better known. (Pritchard 1943)

Astarte Astarte is a Greek transliteration of the name of a Semitic goddess whose worship appears to have been widespread, although confusions between Astarte and the similarly named **Anat**, **Asherah**, and **Atargatis** have led scholars to question the extent of this goddess's power. In addition, Astarte has so many similarities to **Ishtar** that it is difficult to distinguish them.

As the morning star, Astarte was robed in flames, armed with a sword and bearing quivers of death-dealing arrows. But as the evening star, Astarte descended to the underworld to reclaim a lost lover, causing human and animal copulation to cease until she returned. Her colors were red and white; in her honor the acacia tree produced flowers in these colors. She loved the cypresses of her country, the stallions that she rode, the first fruits of the harvest, the firstborn of the womb, and bloodless sacrifices. In some images, Astarte stands small breasted and naked on the back of a lioness, with a lotus and a mirror in one hand and two snakes in the other. Other goddesses of the region, however, are also seen astride lions, so some "Astarte" figures may represent others. Her temples were typically situated in high places, where stones were anointed during ceremonies.

Inscriptions and texts with Astarte's name have been found in Egypt, Sidon, Philistia, Cyprus, and Phoenicia. She has been identified as an antecedent of **Tanit**; she may have developed into **Aphrodite** (see Greece). Whether Astarte is connected to **Al-Lat** is debated. Whether she is the "Queen of Heaven" warned against by Jeremiah is similarly an unsettled question; generally, she appears in the Bible as **Ashtoreth**.

Of the important goddesses of the eastern Mediterranean, Astarte is paradoxically both well known and obscure. (Albright 1968; Binger; Cornelius; Day J 2000; Gibson; Brenner and Fontaine; Heimpel; Kapelru; Patai 1990; Petty; Pritchard 1969; Oden; Stuckey 1993)

Atargatis No one is certain of the original name of this Syrian or Aramaic goddess. She was called Derceto, a Greek translation of her name. Ceto appears as another variant. In Rome, the term "Dea Syria" ("the Syrian Goddess") described Atargatis. Some philologists suggest that the goddess's original name (which appears to mean "divine Ata") was related to **Ishtar** and **Astarte**. Finally, a later cult of Atargatis associates her with **Aphrodite** under the name **Hagne** (see Greece).

The Nabataeans, who built the city of Petra in today's Jordan, especially honored Atargatis. They were a wealthy and cosmopolitan people whose domain stretched along the trade routes between Arabia and Syria. Modern commentators consider them to be Arabic. Like other pre-Islamic Arabs, they centered their religion on the feminine divine.

The spirit of fertilizing moisture, Atargatis descended from heaven in the form of an egg, from which she emerged as a mermaid. Beautiful and wise, she aroused the jealousy of a rival, who cursed her to love a beautiful youth. She bore **Semiramis**, placed her in the wilderness with doves to feed her, then threw herself into a lake to become the omnipotent fish mother. In honor of her, the Syrians refused to eat fish or doves. Atargatis appeared in other guises as well: as a vegetation goddess who protected cities; as a sky goddess with eagles around her head; as a dolphin-crowned sea goddess. Her sanctuaries were centered on fish-filled ponds, where doves roosted in sacred trees.

During the Roman era, eunuch priests worshipped Atargatis. At the shrine in Hieropolis founded by Semiramis, eunuch priests served the image of a fish-tailed woman, according to Lucian. An Assyrian queen, Stratonice, dreamed she must rebuild Derceto's temple and set off with a man named Combabus to execute the task. Knowing the queen's reputation, Combabus castrated himself and left his genitals, in a sealed box preserved in honey, with the king. When the queen fell in love with Combabus, he revealed his mutilation, which did not dissuade her from desiring his constant companionship. When the jealous king sentenced the eunuch to death, Combabus called for the sealed box to prove his innocence, then returned to the goddess's shrine to become its priest. (Bikerman; Hinnells; Langdon 1931; Lucian; Oden; Petty; Smith)

Athirat The primary goddess in the Ras Shamra texts was Athirat, also known as **Al-Lat** (perhaps the Arabic goddess of the same name); occasionally she was called Qadeshu ("holy woman"). Ruler of Tyre, Sidon, and Elath, to some Athirat is considered the Canaanite form of **Asherah**. Athirat was depicted as a naked, curly-haired goddess riding a sacred lion, holding lilies and serpents in upraised hands. Because of her title "Lady of the Sea," early scholars described her as a goddess of water. Her connection with the ocean is suggested by the location of her shrines at coastal towns. But contemporary scholars question that assumption, as texts connect her with the land, especially the steppes and mountains.

Athirat was preeminently a spouse goddess, connected to human and animal reproduction. The Ras Shamra texts show her as consort of the primary god, El, and head of a pantheon that included their seventy children. Some texts suggest estrangement between El and Athirat, which may record a period when the main god was changing but the primary goddess remained the same. Later, she appeared as a protector of her children, who were threatened by Baal and his sister **Anat**.

A Mesopotamian goddess, similar or identical to Athirat, was Ashratu, who appears in a narrative in which she attempted to lure the storm god into her bed; he refused and reported the matter to Ashratu's consort, who killed dozens of her children. This story

does not appear in the Ugaritic material. It has been argued that Ashratu is a different goddess from Athirat, or a goddess descended from the same source who developed differently. (Becking et al; Lipinsky; Mastin; Petty; Pritchard 1943)

Aya This obscure early goddess is known from Akkadian texts as a star goddess connected with sexuality. Because she was described as spouse to the sun, she may be a consort goddess; she is also invoked as "the bride." (Pritchard 1969; Roberts)

Ba'alat Her name meant "Lady" or "Our Lady" and is equivalent to that of the god Baal ("Lord"). Chief Phoenician deity of the city of Byblos, she was sculpted as a heavily built naked woman whose hands supported her mature breasts. When dressed, she was a stylish matron in a shoulder-strapped tight robe and an elaborate Egyptian hairstyle. The Sumerians called her the "wise old lady" of the trees; this connection of goddess and tree was common in the ancient Near East. (Albright 1920; Pritchard 1969)

Banit Banit was as an obscure Babylonian goddess whose name is translated as "creatrix" and "beautiful one." Biblical authors said she gave her name to Babylon, but that is linguistically unlikely. She is known from inscriptions from the city of Syrene but does not seem to have been a Syrian goddess. As a consort goddess of an unnamed god, Banit parallels the little-known goddess Tashmetu, who had a similar relationship. Banit may be an honorific title of Tashmetu. (Kings 17, 30; Van der Toorn)

Bau This Babylonian goddess gave her name to the king of Lagash; upon taking the throne he became Ur-Bau, "man of Bau." Her name has been interpreted as "giver of vegetables," showing power over the fertility of the fields. She also ruled human reproduction. Later texts merged Bau with **Gatamdug**, then **Gula**. (Barton; Prince 1907)

Belit-Ilani A Babylonian title meaning "mistress of the gods," Belit-Ilani was the name of the evening star of desire. Some consider it a title of **Astarte**, some of **Ninlil**, some of Nintud. The title is inscribed on portraits of a woman who bears a baby whom she suckles while blessing the child with her right hand. (Barton)

Belit-Seri In Babylonian theology, she was the scribe of the afterlife who recorded all human activities. Lady of underworld wilderness, she squatted in front of the queen of the dead to call out judgments on the lives of the newly deceased. The name is sometimes given as a title to **Geštinanna**. (Barton; Day J; Pritchard 1969; Sandars)

Damkina In Akkadian, this name means "lady of earth." An early divinity of the Mesopotamian pantheon, she was consort of the heaven god Ea and mother of the hero Marduk (see **Ti'âmat**). (Jacobsen; Pritchard 1969)

Dido A Carthaginian queen seduced and abandoned by the wandering Trojan Aeneas, Dido killed herself rather than face public dishonor as a ruler whose wishes could be flouted. But behind this legendary figure is another, for Dido was also the founder of Carthage, who killed herself rather than being taken captive. Did Dido live for many centuries and commit suicide twice? That would be necessary to incorporate all the events of "Dido's" life into one story. More likely, the name was a title held by several queens.

The first Dido, originally Elissa ("goddess") of Tyre, discovered her brother had murdered her husband, so she quit her homeland with a retinue of eighty women. Dido traveled to North Africa and purchased a hide's worth of land, then cut the hide into strips and claimed all the land they surrounded. Her city, Cartha-Elissa, flourished, but she killed herself when a neighboring king threatened war unless she slept with him. The sacred grove of Elissa remained in Carthage until the Romans obliterated the city. The most famous Dido was Carthage's queen when the Trojan hero

Aeneas arrived in search of land; she entertained him, became his lover, and killed herself when he abandoned her. (Virgil; Honeyman)

Ēni Mahanahi This was the Anatolian name for a goddess known to the Greeks as **Leto**, mother of **Artemis**. As Artemis was also a goddess of human and animal birth, her "divine mother," Ēni Mahanahi, would presumably have had more cosmic duties. She may thus be described either as goddess of the land and its produce or as ruler of the universal force of life. She is connected with a little-known warrior goddess, Malinya. (Bryce)

Ereshkegal In Sumerian and Babylonian theology, a huge black-haired woman slept naked in a palace of lapis lazuli, drawing the dead to herself. Ereshkegal ruled the wilderness at the world's end, surrounded by rainbow gardens. Those who came to her had to divest themselves of all that pertained to earthly life. In art, Ereshkegal appeared as a lion-headed woman suckling cubs. She was also shown in a boat, kneeling on the horse of death and traversing the boundary river between her world and ours, gazing toward offerings the living placed on its shores. She appears famously in the myth of **Inanna**. (Dalley; Harris 2000; Hooke; Jacobsen 1976; Langdon 1931; McCall; Sandars; Walls; Wolkstein and Kramer)

Fatima The daughter of Mohammed is not a goddess in Islam, any more than **Mary** is a goddess in Christianity. However, each of these women occupies a unique position in their religions, as figures to whom the power granted is similar to that held by goddesses in polytheistic cultures.

Fatima ("shining one") was married to Ali, a cousin of the Prophet and one of his early followers. The marriage was not a happy one, and Ali threatened to take other wives, but Mohammed discouraged it because he loved his daughter deeply. She returned the love, staying close to him despite her marriage and taking care of him after he was wounded in the battle of Uhud.

Fatima and Ali had two sons, Hassan and Hussayn. When her father died, he told her she would be the first to join him in paradise. Ali expected to succeed the Prophet as leader, but conflict broke out almost immediately with Abu Bakr. Fatima sided with her husband but died soon thereafter, leaving orders that upon her breast should be placed a tiny box holding a contract, written in green ink, that gives directions for the salvation of all Shi'ites. Thus green is an emblematic color of Shi'ite Islam, whose people honor Fatima more actively than do the Sunnis.

Fatima holds quasi-mythic status as mistress of waters (thus the Qur'anic verse "Water is the source of all life" is held to refer to her) as well as mistress of salt. She is known as the Eternal Weeper, for she deeply mourned her father's death as well as those of her sons, killed in internecine battles. In paradise, Fatima's tears gain the attention of Allah, who grows angry at her suffering. For this reason, she is called Mistress of the House of Sorrows.

Shi'ite Muslims believe Fatima will have a role during the day of judgment, when she will hold her sons' bloody garments as she judges women. Although they will hold on to her cloak as they attempt to pass from the desert to eternal life, only those who wept for Fatima's sons will pass, while their enemies will fall to everlasting death. (Sered 1991; Young)

Gatamdug Goddess of the city of Lagash, where she was counselor to kings and interpreter of dreams, Gatamdug was assimilated into the healing goddess **Gula**. As an independent goddess, she controlled the entrance of semen into the womb. (Barton; Frymer-Kensey)

Geštinanna Around the dying god Dumuzi hovers the trinity of **Inanna**, **Ninsûna**, and Geštinanna, the god's lover, mother, and sister, respectively. Tortured by nightmares, Dumuzi brought the dreams for interpretation to Geštinanna, who realized her brother was under attack by demons. Dumuzi fled, swearing Geštinanna to secrecy. Demons arrived, attacking Geštinanna, who remained silent. Nevertheless, the demons found Dumuzi, hiding in his sister's sheepfold. He was carried to the underworld; Geštinanna set off in pursuit, and the siblings were reunited. Whether the pair returned to life is an unsettled question. Sources prior to the late twentieth century agree that Dumuzi returned to life, but some later scholarship claims his resurrection was a false projection from Christian material. However, other scholars find evidence of rebirth for Dumuzi, if not Geštinanna, in the literature. (Barton; Frymer-Kensey; Jacobsen 1976; Pritchard 1969; Sandars; Yamauchi)

Gubarru A Sumerian goddess associated with the mountain god Amurru, Gubarru appears to be the same goddess found in the Akkadian language as Ašratum; that name, in turn, has been argued to be the same as **Athirat**. Gubarru was known as **Belit-Seri**, "lady of the steppes," a term used for several other goddesses. Thus, while Gubarru's name is known, her identity is not established. (Binger; Livingstone)

Gula The Akkadian and Babylonian "great physician," Gula could inflict and cure disease; she was shown with the eight-rayed orb representing the body's heat, which sustains and can destroy life. She took over attributes of lesser goddesses **Bau** and **Gatamdug**, whose worship faded; sometimes she was called Gula-Bau.

Gula lived in a garden at the world's center, where she watered the tree that forms its axis. The moon-man, her consort, stood in the sky over the tree, from which Gula plucked fruit to offer her worshippers. A dog accompanied her, symbol of her control over health and death. Dog skeletons have been found in her temples, suggesting they lived on the temple grounds. In some carvings, Gula was depicted raising both hands into the air in an attitude of worship. (Frymer-Kensey; Gurney; Langdon 1931; Livingstone; Pritchard 1969)

Hannahanna An important Hittite myth says the fertility god Telipinu once disappeared. Water ceased to flow; animals ceased to bear; the milk of human mothers dried up. Gods and humans searched, but even the wind god could not find Telipinu. Food became scarce. Then Hannahanna, queen of heaven and mother of all, had an idea. While other gods mocked, she instructed a bee to find Telipinu, then sting the god awake, for it was clear that he must be asleep to have missed the commotion of the searchers.

The bee flew until exhausted, but in a village so tiny that previous searchers had overlooked it, she found Telipinu asleep. She stung him mightily. Telipinu awoke in a rage, destroying everything within reach. But Hannahanna was ready. She sent an eagle to fetch the god and, with the help of maidens bearing sesame and nectar and accompanied by the enchantments of **Kamrusepa**, removed the god's fury, and fertility returned to the world.

Several texts suggest it was Hannahanna herself who disappeared, leaving the earth in distress and the crops threatened. When she was gone, logs would not light on the hearths, cows did not tend their calves, and mothers ignored their children. When the goddess returned, all was restored to order. (Deighton; Gurney; Hoffman; Hooke)

Hebat Originally the presiding goddess of the Hurrian pantheon, Hebat later merged with the Hittite sun goddess **Wurusemu**. She was named in one text that invokes "the sun goddess of Arinna, my lady…In the Hatti country thou bearest the name of the sun goddess of Arinna, but in the land which thou madest, the cedar land, thou bearest the name Hebat." She was depicted as a distinguished, well-dressed matron, wearing a crown, jewelry, and fancy shoes, standing on a lion. Little is known of her mythology except a fragmentary narrative in which she hid from a monster that threatened her. (Akurgal; Gurney; Hoffman; Laroche)

Hutena With her twin sister Hutellura, this Hittite goddess of fate derived her name from the verb for "writing." The twins appeared at birth to forecast an infant's life; they may have been seen as creating the

child's life. In Hattian, their counterparts were the goddesses Istustaya and Papaya. (Gurney)

Inanna The greatest goddess of Sumer, the southern part of Babylonia, was Inanna; in the northern region, the figure became **Ishtar**. While similar, these goddesses differ in some aspects and are thus separately discussed. Some scholars refer to this figure as Inanna-Ishtar to emphasize their dual identity.

Inanna's most famous myth began with her entertaining two suitors, the farmer Enkidu and the shepherd Dumuzi. Both brought her gifts; both wooed her with flattery. Her brother urged the farmer's suit, but Dumuzi's soft woolens tipped the scales, and he became the goddess's favorite. But soon Dumuzi grew arrogant, for which he would ultimately pay.

Inanna decided to visit the underworld. She arranged for her prime minister, Ninshuba, if she did not return within three days and nights, to stage mourning ceremonies and appeal to the highest deities to rescue her. Then Inanna descended. At the first of the underworld's seven gates, the gatekeeper demanded part of Inanna's attire. So it was at each gate. Piece by piece, Inanna gave up her jewelry and clothing until she stood naked before **Ereshkegal**, who turned eyes of stone on the goddess from the upper world.

Inanna lost all life and hung as a corpse in the realm of death. When Inanna failed to return, Ninshuba did as instructed. Enki, the goddess's father, came to her aid. Fashioning two strange creatures, Kurgurra and Kalaturra, from the dirt beneath his fingernails, he sent them into the afterlife with food and water to revive Inanna.

But no one could leave the underworld unless a substitute was found. So demons followed the goddess as she ascended to her kingdom, grabbing each god they met. Each in turn Inanna freed, remembering good deeds they had performed. But when Inanna reached her holy city, Erech, she found Dumuzi had set himself up as ruler in her stead. Angered at his presumption, the goddess commanded that he become her substitute. Luckily for Dumuzi, **Geštinanna** won back his life from Ereshkegal for half of each year.

Dumuzi was not Inanna's only lover. She had an affair with the hero Enmerkar, who took her to his city of Erech, later to become her most important shrine. But Inanna proved fickle, abandoning Enmerkar in his time of need and returning only after he begged her to do so. Mesopotamia's most famous epic begins with the goddess walking along the banks of the Euphrates River. There she noticed an uprooted tree. She rescued the tree and brought it to Erech, where she replanted it with the intention of making a throne from its wood. But the demon goddess **Lilith** had taken up residence in the tree's roots, as had a snake and a magical bird. Inanna called upon the hero Gilgamesh for help. He killed the snake and frightened away both the bird and Lilith. Then Gilgamesh grew haughty and began to suppress the city dwellers, for which reason his magical implements fell into the underworld, beginning the epic that bears the hero's name.

Gilgamesh further insulted the goddess when she saw him arrayed in fine clothes and proposed that he marry her. He not only refused but reminded her that her earlier lovers had come to grief. The offended goddess begged her father to give her the bull of heaven to use against Gilgamesh. Despite its size and strength, the hero killed it, shocking the goddess and her women worshippers. Gloating over his strength, Gilgamesh failed to realize that his offenses against the gods would cause his downfall, which took the form of the death of his companion, the wild man Enkidu. Afterward, Gilgamesh went on a quest to find the herb of immortality, a quest that led him to **Siduri**.

While Inanna's loves constitute an important part of her mythology, some myths show her active in other ways. She brought civilization to this world by stealing the Tablets of Destiny from their original owner, the god Enki, who kept them to himself. But Inanna took pity on humanity and traveled to her father's hall, where she was welcomed with food and wine. Enki loved his daughter's company so much that he took cup after cup of wine from her and then promised her

anything she desired. Instantly Inanna asked for the Tablets of Destiny. Too intoxicated to object, Enki agreed.

Inanna immediately set sail for Erech. Awakening the next day, Enki regretted his action. By the time he caught up with her, Inanna had gained the safety of her kingdom, and even seven tricks Enki played on her did not regain his treasures.

Some of the most important Sumerian literature was devoted to Inanna or created for her rituals. The earliest poet known by name, Enheduanna, daughter of king Sargon of Akkad, wrote of Inanna as both a loving and destructive goddess. The works of this poet were lost for millennia, but a cache of three long poems to the goddess and forty-two temple hymns was found in excavations of Ur in the 1920s, providing scholars with important information as to Inanna's character and worship.

Inanna represented fertility and the abundance of grain in the storehouse; she also represented war, as the protection of assets from potential invaders. She was embodied in the star Venus, which appears with the sun at morning and evening; as goddess of lovers, Inanna was especially connected with the evening star. (Barton; Dexter; Enheduanna; Frymer-Kensey; Hallo and Van Dijk; Harris 1991; Heimpel; Jacobsen 1976; Kramer 1961, 1969, 1979; Langdon 1914, 1931; Pritchard; Sandars; Stuckey 2001; Wolkstein and Kramer)

Inara In Hittite myths, inherited from the culture's Hattian predecessors, this goddess rescued humanity, which was threatened by the dragon Illuyuksa. The goddess filled vessel after vessel with liquor, inviting a man named Hupasiyato to set them as bait for the dragon. That night Inara rewarded the human's industry by sleeping with him. The next morning the pair found the dragon and her children unconscious from intoxication, easy to slay.

As a reward, Inara installed the man in a splendid house on a cliff, where they lived in pleasure until the goddess was called on a journey. Inara instructed her paramour not to gaze out the window while she was away, but after twenty days he disobeyed. Spotting his human wife and children, the man grew homesick for mortal company. His complaints angered Inara when she returned, and she dispatched him to the underworld for his disobedience.

The story of the destruction of the dragon of darkness was celebrated each new year by Inara's worshippers at the feast of Purulli. A man enacting the part of the goddess's human helper may have met his death after spending the night with a priestess, although this common early interpretation of the texts is now debated. Inara appears to have been similar to Greek **Artemis**, a huntress who lived in wilderness areas, although she has also been interpreted as a goddess of sovereignty. (Gurney; Hoffman)

Išhara This Hurrian goddess gave her name to a mountain; she was also the source of a disease that bore her name (perhaps indicating a tumor or raised area of skin). A tablet from Carthage may identify her with **Hebat**. The name was also borne by Babylonian **Inanna** in her rarely seen motherly aspect.

The name appears in various Mesopotamian texts invoking the goddess as guarantor of oaths and mistress of oracles. (Levi Della Vida; Enheduanna; Roberts)

Ishtar In the northern Babylonian kingdom of Akkad, Ishtar stood at the head of the pantheon. Because the Akkadians took over the lands and traditions of earlier Semitic people, Ishtar acquired attributes of earlier goddesses after conquest of their peoples. Among the nearby Assyrians, who also honored her, Ishtar was important, though less prominent. The goddess may have originally been paired with a similarly named consort, Ashtar, later absorbed into the goddess.

Ishtar grew mightier as lesser goddesses were assimilated into her, becoming only titles: Aja, a dawn goddess associated with eastern mountains; Anatu, a cosmic divinity, possibly Ishtar's mother; the Akkadian light goddess Anunitu; the war goddess Agašayam;

Irnini, goddess of Lebanon's cedar-forested mountains; Kilili or Kulili, the desirable woman symbolized by windows and birds; Sahirtu, sender of messages between lovers; Kir-gu-lu, the rain giver; and Sarbanda, force of sovereignty.

Ishtar was a complex, sometimes contradictory goddess. She was depicted as a fertile mother holding out her massive breasts, yet she was also violent and destructive. She was the ever-virgin warrior, but also a wanton lover. Like **Inanna**, Ishtar loved a vegetation god who died and was reborn. Like Inanna, Ishtar descended to the underworld. Texts imply, but do not clearly state, that Ishtar was inspired by her desire to free her lover Dumuzi. But Dumuzi (also transliterated as Tammuz) remained in the land of death, and the goddess took a new consort each spring.

Ishtar ruled the moon. She also owned the morning and evening stars, symbols of the warlike and lustful energies of the feminine. As the morning star Dilbat, Ishtar hitched her chariot to seven lions before setting off to hunt animals or humans. As Zib, the evening star, she was adored by women as "glad-eyed Ishtar of desire, the goddess of sighing." She was called Harimtu, "harlot of heaven," and was depicted dressed like a prostitute. Because goddesses in this region were typically provided with consorts, the Assyrians linked Ishtar with their primary god, Assur. (Ananikian; Craig; Dalley 1991; Frymer-Kensey; Harris 1991; Heimpel; Jacobsen 1976; Kapelru; Langdon 1914, 1931; McCall; Petty; Prince 1910; Pritchard 1969; Rodney; Sandars; Temple; Walls; Yamauchi)

Jahi According to Iranian mythology, this demonic woman roused from sleep the spirit of conflict, Angra Mainyu, ending the primordial peace. She had to shout three times, so fearful was Angra Mainyu of the powerful Ahura Mazda. Finally he rose and kissed her, changing his form from a lizard to a handsome man. Energized, he set about making evil in the world. The Persian menstruation spirit, she was perceived as a *drujs*, or demon, who urged men to evil deeds. (Carnoy 1931, Boyce)

Jēh The Indo-Iranian first woman, called the "queen of all whores" because she arrived at the creation with the devil already in tow and had intercourse with him immediately, she represented not only women's sexuality, in an obviously derogatory fashion, but the temptation of religions other than Zoroastrianism. Because of her lust, Jēh was cursed with menstruation, which she transmitted to her descendants. (Boyce)

Kamrusepa This Hittite goddess of magic assisted **Hannahanna** in restoring the earth's fertility. When the god Telipinu arrived raging in heaven, she used her magical powers to tame him. Several texts about Kamrusepa contain magical formulas that employed such obscure items as the fire of the steppe and the wheat of irrigation. She ruled chanting, healing, and ritual purification. Her name in Hattian was Kattahziwuri. (Deighton; Gurney; Hoffman; Hooke)

Ki The Sumerian earth goddess was the original female principal of matter, twin to An, the heaven god; both were born of the primal goddess, **Ti'âmat**. Ki lost stature as her son Enlil took power from her. Even her name was stripped from her when she was identified with **Ninhursag**. (Kramer 1979; Langdon 1931; Sandars)

Kotharat The goddesses of this name appear in Canaanite scripture as daughters of the new moon and prophetic forces. Through their efforts, they brought fertility to young couples. They may also have been guardians of nubile young girls. Called the "wise goddesses," they set the bride price for every woman, including **Ishtar**. (Gibson)

Kubaba An ancient Hattian goddess, Kubaba was the mountain mother from whom **Cybele** (see Southeastern Europe) derived her name. Later writings called her Queen of Kargamis, after a Hittite metropolis; there she was called Khipa or Khebe, then Kubabas, and finally Kubaba. Mounted on or between two lions, Kubaba links the unnamed mother goddess

of Çatal Hüyük with Cybele. (Gurney; Mellart 1989; Vieyra; Garstang)

Lelwani The Hittite (possibly originally Hurrian) earth goddess, at whose shrine near Babylon the festival of Inara was celebrated, was identified in Hittite treaties with **Ereshkegal**. (Deighton; Macqueen)

Manāt With **Al-Lat** and **Uzza**, this goddess of fate and time formed the ancient Arabian religious trinity. Her worship stretched across Arabia; she may have been the eldest of the Arabic goddesses. Her principal sanctuary, the shrine of Qudayd, stood between Mecca and Medina. Her ritual entailed a pilgrimage to places of spiritual significance, at the end of which pilgrims shaved their heads and worshipped at **Manāt**'s shrine, an uncut black stone demolished by Mohammed's son Ali under his father's orders. Mohammed also gave Ali the shrine's treasures, including two jewel-studded swords, one of which later became famous as "the Sword of Ali." (al-Kalbi; Langdon; Rubin)

Mylitta The name of this goddess, Mulitta or Mu'Allidtu, was Hellenized by the Greek historian Herodotus when he described how her Babylonian priestesses, burning incense and wearing wreaths around their heads, awaited strangers with whom to perform sacred rites of love. Mylitta's worshippers bobbed their hair at puberty and offered up their youthful locks, following that by offering their bodies in sexual rituals with others. At her shrine beside the sacred spring of Afka, these women set up booths or camped in the green groves, enjoying intercourse with those who came to them.

Among the most controversial questions about religion in the eastern Mediterranean is that of so-called sacred prostitution. Ancient authors claimed to have witnessed women offering their bodies to strangers in goddess temples; the Hebrew Bible refers to male prostitution as part of the non-Israelite religion. Many contemporary scholars find little evidence for sex as a religious practice in the region, describing earlier writers as engaging in fantasy rather than proper interpretation and, especially, claiming that the theory of "cultic prostitution" is demeaning to women. Yet others continue to find evidence of sexual rituals in honor of goddesses and interpret them as honoring women's sexuality. (Herodotus; Lerner; Qualls-Corbetter)

Nammu The earliest Sumerian goddess, Nammu was embodied in the abyss from which the universe emerged. She gave birth to gods, including **Ki**, and then assisted **Ninmah** in forming the human race. When **Ashnan** failed to provide food for the deities because she was drunk, Nammu's son Enki created mankind to serve the immortals. Nammu lost status as her powers were transferred to Enki. She may be the original of **Ti'âmat**. (Brandon; Kramer 1979; Hooke; O'Brien; Pritchard 1969)

Nanâ This early Arabic goddess was associated with the planet Venus. In the city of Uruk, she was honored together with **Inanna**, also associated with Venus. Unlike other goddesses, she appears to have retained her own identity rather than being absorbed into Inanna, but little is known of her independent worship. Nanâ was also an old Babylonian name for **Ishtar**. Ishtar's worship as Nanâ was long-lived. Assyrian conqueror Assurbanipal, sacking the Elamite capital of Susa in 636 BC, discovered an image of the goddess that the Elamites had carried off 1,635 years earlier. Taking on the aspects of the Iranian goddess **Ārmaiti**, Nanâ survived even later, appearing as a funerary goddess. (Azarpay; Barton; Gurney; Heimpel; Pritchard 1969)

Nanshe This Babylonian water goddess was honored each year with a flotilla of boats. In Lagash, the flotilla joined a sacred barge bearing the goddess's image, and the procession floated about as Nanshe's worshippers reveled. A wise goddess, she was an interpreter of dreams and omens. She served each New Year's Day as the judge of each person's activities during the preceding year; she ensured that widows and orphans received the care they needed. (Kramer 1979; Pritchard 1969; Roberts)

Nikkal In Canaanite scripture, this lunar goddess ("clear lady") was betrothed to the moon god Yarikh through the efforts of the god of summer, Khirkhib. Yarikh offered a bride-price of gold and silver, as well as jewels, for the hand of the goddess. When Khirkhib suggested other available goddesses, two daughters of Baal named Pidray and Ybrdmy, the moon god rejected them and said his heart lay only with Nikkal, after which the couple were wed. (Gibson)

Ningal This Sumerian goddess, daughter of the reed goddess Ningikuga, was courted by the moon god, Nanna, who brought necklaces of lapis lazuli and turned the deserts into orchards. He gathered birds' eggs and promised to milk all her cows. Their marriage was fruitful, with **Inanna** being their eldest daughter. The high priestess of Nanna incarnated the goddess, sharing the title Zirru with her. Her duties included attending to the goddess through daily offerings of food and beer. (Jacobsen 1976; Wolkstein and Kramer)

Ninhursag The Mesopotamian goddess of birth lived with the god of wisdom, Enki, with whom she had a tempestuous relationship. In Dilmun, where Ninhursag and Enki lived, there was no age or death, no sickness, and no barrenness. But the land was dry until Ninhursag pleaded with Enki for something to drink. He answered her prayers with an abundance of sweet water that made the land prosperous and its residents comfortable.

Once this was done, the primal deities turned to reproducing themselves. One day Ninhursag's belly swelled up. Nine days later the goddess Ninsar ("plant woman") was born. Enki seduced his daughter, who bore Ninhurra ("mountain woman"). Enki slept with his granddaughter, who bore **Uttu**, the spider goddess of weaving. Enki wanted her too, but her mother said she must demand a bride-price of cucumbers, apples, and grapes. Lustful Enki granted it, and Uttu agreed to occupy his bed.

From their affair sprang eight varieties of plants. But Enki ate his offspring as quickly as they appeared. Furious Ninhursag leveled so terrible a curse at him that he fell down, stricken in eight parts of his body with eight diseases. The other gods grew concerned as Enki weakened, but the goddess refused to heal him. Finally, when Enki was a breathing corpse, the deities prevailed on Ninhursag to cure him.

The goddess agreed to a compromise: she would create eight tiny goddesses who would control the health of Enki's afflicted parts. If they chose to, they could do the healing. The little goddesses set to work, and Enki was soon well again. Some texts differ on the means of curing, saying that Ninhursag cured Enki by placing him in her vagina, whence he could be reborn, together with the plants that had sickened him.

Ninhursag gained her name, which means "lady of foothills," from her son, the storm god Ninuta, who built a mountain in her honor and named her for it. Because of the abundance of wildlife in the hills, she was a goddess of animals, both wild and tame. Ninhursag has been interpreted as a later form of **Ki**. (Barton; Brandon; Carnoy 1916; Frymer-Kensey; Hooke; Jacobsen 1976; Kramer 1961, 1979; Langdon 1931; Pritchard 1969; Young)

Ninkasi The Sumerian goddess of intoxicating fruit, especially grapes, had as her consort a god whose name meant "good vinestalk." Their seven children included Sirîs, goddess of beer, called the "drink of the mountains" because it was believed to be the preferred intoxicant of less-civilized hill dwellers. Ninkasi lived on a mythical mountain, Sâbu ("drink wine"), from which she dispensed her gifts to humanity. Ninkasi has been described as another form of **Siduri**. (Albright 1920; Pritchard 1969)

Ninlil Represented by serpents, mountains, and stars, Ninlil was the city goddess of Nippur, whose prince ruled as her consort. She was a goddess of grain and the wealth it provides; her mother was the goddess of barley, Ninshebargunu. As **Ishtar**'s worship spread across Babylonia, Ninlil became associated with her, ultimately losing her identity. Some texts describe Ninlil as the mother of the god Ninurta, who built a levee to control the flow of the Tigris River and bestowed the name of **Ninhursag** on his mother; other sources consider them separate.

Various texts describe Ninlil's mating and maternity. In one, Ninlil was bathing in a lonely spot. The god Enlil took advantage of the solitude to rape the virgin goddess. (In another version of this myth, Ninlil's mother, Ninshebargunu, told her daughter how to conceive by the god: to walk along the river until she found a place to bathe, knowing that she would attract Enlil.) The other deities banished Enlil to the underworld. But Ninlil, having conceived, followed Enlil.

The child in Ninlil's belly was the moon. If born in the underworld, he would remain there for eternity. When her time came, Ninlil performed magic: She bore three shadow children, one each for herself and Enlil and one for their child, each to remain perpetual hostages to Ereshkegal. Then, still pregnant, she climbed to earth with Enlil. Thus was the moon god Sin born. (Barton; Frymer-Kensey; Jacobsen 1976; Kramer 1961; Pritchard 1969)

Ninmah The creator of humanity was the lapis-crowned Sumerian goddess Ninmah. A potter, she mixed clay to form images of herself, placing seven on her right hand and seven on her left. She uttered life-giving incantations over the clay images, and they sprang to life, those on her right hand as men, those on her left as women. Delighted with her creations, Ninmah called the gods to celebrate. Soon the goddess began drunkenly playing with remnant clay, creating barren women, eunuchs, and four other unrecorded human types. This excited Enki, her consort, who decided to display his creativity. He too was drunk: Up from the ground wobbled a crippled, retarded man.

Horrified, Enki begged Ninmah to correct him, but the creatrix could not change what already existed.

Sumerian women evoked Ninmah's name during childbirth; she was especially kind to those birthing second children, hence her titles Mami ("mother goddess") and, in Sumerian, Ninmah ("lady mother"; also an early goddess of birth or an epithet of **Ki**). It has been argued she is the same goddess as **Ninhursag**.

As Ninmah's worship traveled across the Mediterranean, she became less a gentle earth mother, more a warrior goddess. As owner of the earth, she demanded that a corner of every field be left wild; if this was done, she would protect against bad crops and covetous neighbors. In later times, Ninmah was portrayed standing or riding on lions, bejeweled with the riches of her people. When she reached Rome, she was the image of the warrior **Bellona** and was transformed into Mah-Bellona. (Brandon; Dalley 1991; Jacobsen 1976; Kramer 1961, 1979; Livingstone; Pritchard 1969; Roberts)

Ninsûna The "lady of wild cows," this goddess gave birth to two important figures: the hero Dumuzi, beloved of **Inanna**; and Gilgamesh, who spurned Inanna and was punished for it. She bore several kings as well, sometimes assuming human form to do so. In the *Epic of Gilgamesh*, she appears as Rimat-Ninsun, the "revered cow" and "wise custodian of knowledge," who interpreted her son's dreams and offered sacrifices to assist him. (Jacobsen; McCall; Temple)

Ninurra The Sumerian goddess of pottery making, Ninurra, clearly a goddess in early texts, was later transformed into a male god. A similar transformation happened to the goddess of magic, Ningirim; she had domain over magical incantations in earliest times, but this power was transferred to male gods and Ningirim faded away. (Frymer-Kensey)

Nisaba "She who teaches the decrees" of divinity to humans, this goddess brought literacy, accounting, and astrology to a Sumerian king on a tablet inscribed with the names of the beneficent stars. An architect as well, she drew up temple plans for her people; she was also an oracle and dream interpreter. The most learned of deities, this snake goddess also controlled the fertility of her people's fields. She was called "great knowledgeable perceptive one" and "woman who knows everything." (Frymer-Kensey; Horowitz; Kramer 1979; Pritchard 1969)

Nungal The Sumerian goddess of prisons had domain over those who failed water ordeals designed to determine guilt on the final day of judgment. If, after having been thrown in water, the accused floated, he was released as innocent; if he sank, he was pulled into shore and handed to Nungal, who put him in her prison until his heart was clear and pure, whereupon he was released to the gods. (Frymer-Kensey)

Paghat Little is known about this Ugaritic heroine except that she figures in narratives concerning **Anat**, who had Paghat's brother Aqhat killed because she coveted his prize bow. Her father, Danel, tired to dissuade her from taking vengeance, but she would not be stopped. The end of the story is missing; apparently Paghat succeeded not only in avenging her brother but also in restoring him to life. (Cassuto; Pritchard 1969)

Qudšu "Holy one" was used in Ugaritic texts to refer to **Athirat**, although in other texts the goddess in question was **Anat**. Under this title, the goddess was depicted as riding a lion; the position of her outstretched hands suggests that she was offering something. A goddess of this name was known in Egypt, where she was depicted nude, astride a lion, carrying snakes and flowers; she has been identified as a Hittite goddess, despite her non-Hittite name. Qudšu appears to have been an independent goddess in some places, a goddess title in others. (Ackerman 1993; Binger; Brooks; Cornelius; Day J 1986; Lerner; Petty; Pritchard 1943)

Rūdābah In the *Sha-Nameh*, a compilation of Persian poetry on mythological themes, Rūdābah was an exquisitely beautiful heroine—more beautiful than the sun, her body like rubies, her hair like amber. Falling in love with a man named Zal, she wandered to his camp, pretending to gather roses. Captivated by her, Zal agreed to a night of love. She prepared by decorating her palace with brocade hangings, placing vats of fragrant flowers throughout it, and perfuming it with amber. Rūdābah made him pledge he would never raise a hand to her before she welcomed him to her bed. (Carnoy)

Sauska A Hurrian divinity, Sauska seduced even monsters with her winged beauty. When the sea monster Hedammu threatened the world, she arrayed herself in finery and went to do battle. Sedating the monster with a love potion, Sauska may have killed him, although the text is unclear. The kings of Anatolia served her, and she commanded them through dreams, oracles, and the augury of female soothsayers. Sauska may be a form of **Hannahanna**. (Gurney; Hoffman)

Semiramis Whether this legendary figure represents a goddess or a human has long been in dispute. One of the earliest Western writers to record the Semiramis legend, Ctesias, assumed she was a disguised form of a historical queen, Sammuramat, who ruled from 812 to 783 BCE in Babylon or Syria. It has also been argued that Semiramis was merely an Assyrian noblewoman.

There is evidence of an early Semitic goddess, Shemiram (possibly "famous one"), who developed into Semiramis. Lucian supports the likelihood that this is the name of a goddess, saying she was worshipped at a temple where water was brought twice annually from a distant source and poured into a channel. This goddess may have once been named Simi. Some have argued that she was originally a Semitic goddess named Shemira whose shrines were called Shemiramoth.

Her legend says she was the daughter of the Syrian goddess **Atargatis**, who left her in the desert to be raised by doves. When she grew up, she attracted the attentions of Prince Omnes. After they married, he

remained so infatuated with her that, when Semiramis decided to become queen of Babylon with a second husband, Ninus, Omnes committed suicide. He was not the only man destroyed by love of Semiramis. Unwilling to share her life with a man, she took handsome soldiers to bed and had them killed afterward. Across western Asia, "mounds of Semiramis" are said to be her lovers' graves.

Semiramis was a great builder, especially of earthworks; many towns were named for her. She was said to have built several important structures throughout Iran and Iraq. In Armenia, Semiramis fell in love with the sun. When he did not return her affection, Semiramis attacked him with a huge army. The queen took the day, and Er, the sun, was killed in the battle. But then Semiramis repented her fury and begged the other gods to restore the sun to life. (Dalley 2005; Lucian; Sayce; Smith)

Sertapsuruhi The daughter of the ocean in Hurrian myth, Sertapsuruhi gave birth to a monster serpent, Hedammu, who was discovered by the goddess **Sauska**. She told her brother, the hero Tessub, about her discovery, but he became withdrawn with fear, so Sauska took action, seducing the monster and defeating him. (Hoffman)

Shamaili Heroine of an Afghan folktale, Shamaili was the daughter of an oppressive king who confined her in a labyrinthine house, intending to kill any suitor who could not locate her within the maze. Seven sons of a neighboring king wanted to marry Shamaili. The first six lost their lives trying. Finally Jallad Khan hid himself in a sculpture that was taken to the princess's bedroom. As she slept, he slipped out and exchanged rings with her. When Shamaili found the new ring, she was both excited and frightened. Speaking to the statue, she asked it to become her husband. At that, Jallad Khan came forth and slept for ten nights with Shamaili, after which he demanded her hand from her father. (Kraft)

Shamhat A hero of the *Epic of Gilgamesh* was the wild man Enkidu, an animal-like being who ate grass with the gazelles and bathed with the herds. Created by the goddess **Araru** as a warrior, Enkidu seemed untamable. But the prostitute Shamhat initiated him into sexual pleasure, mating with him for six days and seven nights. At the end, the wild man was so tame that animals ran away from him and Enkidu, fully human, sat at Shamhat's feet to gain instruction in civilization. (Harris 2000; Walls)

Shapash In the ancient Near East, the sun was more often female than male. Shapash was her name in Ugaritic mythology; whether this was a title of **Asherah** has not been determined. In the Ugaritic *Epic of Baal*, Shapash retrieved the fertility god's plaything from the underworld and seems associated with that realm. Shapash served as a messenger of the gods because she traveled easily across the face of the earth. Although it has been established for a half century that Shapash was a goddess, the assumption that solar deities are always male leads even recent scholars to call Shapash a god. (Ackerman 1992; Binger; Gibson; Pritchard 1969; Roberts)

Shataquat In Ugaritic mythology, this goddess of healing saved King Keret from an illness brought on by his betrayal of promises to **Athirat**. The text begins and ends with the illness of the king. At the beginning, he was ill with grief over losing his family. But the high god, El, appeared to him in a dream and told him to threaten a neighboring town. Making vows to Athirat for success, Keret followed El's instructions and, when offered riches to deter the invasion, demanded instead the princess Huriya. Their marriage ceremony was blessed with good omens, but Keret failed to fulfill his vows and fell desperately ill. The land, too, fell ill; rain failed to come and the harvest was threatened. Keret sent for his sister, Thitmanat, who made sacrifices for the health of the land and its ruler. From this effort, Shataquat came flying over a hundred towns to get to Keret's side. Her presence drove away death, and the king was cured. (Hooke)

Siduri When the hero Gilgamesh sought treasure at the world's end, he found this veiled woman in a bejeweled vineyard, watered by four streams. There, Siduri sang of the fleetness of time and the pleasures of life, telling Gilgamesh to dance and play. He refused, demanding instead directions to death's ferryman. Siduri told him, but Gilgamesh's search did not end well. (Albright 1920; Harris 2000; Jacobsen 1976; Pritchard 1969)

Tanit The seagoing Phoenicians made much of their wealth transporting tin, used in making bronze, from Cornwall in England to the smelters of the eastern Mediterranean. Because they needed a refueling base for the long journey, they established the city of Carthage. There, the primary divinity was Tanit, whose name may have been a title of **Astarte**, although the identification is debated; some scholars maintain that the original of Tanit was **Anat**. Tanit may also have been an indigenous goddess of the Berbers whose identity meshed with that of an immigrant goddess.

The winged goddess with a zodiac around her head, holding the sun and moon, was a sky goddess; she was also depicted with doves and holding a scepter. Her image was the triangle, the "sign of Tanit." According to the Christian writer Tertullian, Tanit especially ruled rains; prayers to her relieved droughts. That her worship remained after the fall of Carthage to Rome in 146 BCE can be assumed because the fourth-century Christian apologist Augustine speaks of her declining power. (Cross; Day J 1986; Ogden; Petty)

Ti'âmat Before our world was created, there was Ti'âmat, dragon woman of bitter waters, and her mate Apsu, god of fresh water. Some early texts say Ti'âmat gave birth to two divinities, Lahmu and the goddess Lahāmu, whose names refer to silt, the first bits of created matter. These twins mated to produce the horizon, heavens, earth, and finally winds and storms.

The Babylonian epic *Enuna Elish* says Ti'âmat gave birth to monsters and storms. Finally, gods came forth from the womb of Ti'âmat, including the heaven god, An, and his consort **Ki**. The gods set up housekeeping in another part of the universe, where their noise disturbed Apsu. He approached Ti'âmat with the suggestion that because she had created them, she could do away with the gods. Ti'âmat refused.

The gods got wind of the conversation and killed Apsu. At that, Ti'âmat exploded and, with Kingu, her firstborn son, attacked the gods. They waged a battle that goes on to this day, with the hero Marduk each year swallowed by an enormous dragon. In some stories, Ti'âmat became a civilizing fish mother. Other myths say Marduk killed his mother in the battle. Her body fell into the lower universe, one half becoming the dome of heaven, the other half a wall to contain the waters. Her right eye became the Tigris River, her left the Euphrates. Her ghost wanders the world as a camel. (Brandon 1963; Horowitz; Harris 2000; Jacobsen 1968, 1976; Langdon 1931; Livingstone; McCall; Sandars)

Uttu The Sumerian goddess of weaving was the descendant of **Ninhursag**. Advised to demand bridal gifts before sleeping with her ancestor Enki (as her mother, grandmother, and great-grandmother had done), Uttu did so, becoming the first "married" woman in the pantheon. But she had difficulty bearing a child, which Ninhursag had to remove from her womb. Afterward, Enki gave her domain over women's crafts. In her role as goddess of weaving, Uttu was the weaver of the world. (Frymer-Kensey; Pritchard 1969)

Uzza One of a trinity of goddesses worshipped in pre-Islamic Mecca, Uzza ("the mighty") was goddess of the morning star. Early in Islamic history, Mohammed's soldiers destroyed Uzza's sanctuary of acacia trees, centered on a sacred stone representing her, south of Mecca. The Prophet himself had honored this goddess in his youth, offering her a sheep. His family, the Quraysh, practiced ritual circumambulation to the goddess.

With **Al-Lat** and **Manāt**, this goddess was one of the "daughters of Allah." She was considered the most recent of the three, associated with oracular pronouncements. But monotheistic writers connected her, as they did other goddesses, with evil; the early Christian writer Jerome specifically described Uzza as a form of the fallen angel Lucifer.

Uzza's name was borne by the prophet Mohammed's paternal uncle, 'Abd al-'Uzzā, also known as Abū Lahab. As a member of the Quraysh clan, he, like Mohammed, had roots near Mecca and Uzza's sanctuary. According to Islamic tradition, Aflah b. al-Naḍr al-Shaybanī, who tended Uzza's shrine, despaired it might go unattended after his death. Mohammed's uncle 'Abd al-'Uzzā promised to tend the shrine but changed his loyalty to Allah when Mohammed conquered the land. The sanctuary of Uzza was destroyed shortly after the fall of Mecca in 629 CE.

Two sons of 'Abd al-'Uzzā had married Mohammed's daughters Ruqayya and Umm Kulthūm. But 'Abd al-'Uzzā ended those marriages because of Mohammed's rejection of the three Arab goddesses when the "satanic verses" were replaced by verses that specifically denounced them. In retaliation Mohammed prayed a lion would kill one son, and shortly thereafter the young man was mauled. Abū Lahab died soon after, and his wife, a high-ranking noblewoman, was condemned as a "wood carrier," apparently a reference to part of Uzza's rituals.

The campaign against Uzza included a raid upon her sacred trees, which were cut down one after another. When the third was cut, a woman with disheveled hair appeared and was cut in half by one of Mohammed's warriors. (al-Kalbi; Heimpel; Rubin; Septimus)

Vashti A minor Elamite goddess appears in the book of **Esther** as a queen of the Persians and the state's high priestess. A diplomat and daughter of a king,

Vashti married a fool who drunkenly demanded she appear before his friends naked. She refused. But an Israelite adviser, intent upon replacing Vashti with a woman of his tribe, urged the king to sentence her to death, and the king followed his advice. The uprising that followed was only put down when Esther ascended the throne. (Esther 1:10; Clay; Ginsberg 6)

Wurusemu This Hittite goddess was better known as the sun goddess of Arinna after a city that may have been the location of a solar shrine. She was called Estan (later a god's name), or Wurusemu, an untranslated name; she is identified in one text as identical with the Hurrian goddess **Hebat**. Her shrines were carved on rock outcroppings with sun signs engraved on upright stones in her honor. At Yazilikaya, near Boghazkoy, an impressive shrine shows a parade of divinities headed by Wurusemu astride a lioness and crowned with solar rays. Two identical smaller female figures follow her, perhaps her daughter Mezulla and granddaughter Zuntehis. Metal statues show the goddess in a gracious open posture, a winged sun as headdress.

As fate goddess, she allotted each person what he or she deserved. The gods received their power from her, in return for which they opened and closed the door of heaven as she passed. Her servants were the fortunetellers Istustaya and Papaya, who divined the length of a king's reign or a worker's hard life using their magic mirrors and spindles.

The sun was queen of the dead, to whom funeral services were offered. Conducted by old women, funerals started with sacrifices of oxen and goats; fiery offerings went on overnight. Then, at dawn, women quenched the fires and drank to the souls of the dead. A human figure made of fruits was placed on the pyre and filled with food and drink. The priestess balanced gold and silver with mud, calling out to Wurusemu to offer salvation to the deceased.

Her consort was the weather god; her rituals were performed by a high priestess, who also ruled the country as queen. The sun goddess was ruler of the heavens. Reflecting her status, the early Hittite queens were substantial rulers. (Gurney; Macqueen)

Yimāk Iranian legend says this primal woman mated with her brother, Yima. Yima gave Yimāk to a demon and married one of that devilish breed, creating races of monsters. In Zoroastrianism, the legend was connected with the human twins Mashya and Mashyōi, who resisted the need to populate the earth for fifty years, after which they had intercourse and created the human race. Alternatively, they were joined to become a plant, from which ten fruits were born, becoming the ten kinds of humans. (Carnoy 1916, 1931)

Zarpandit "Silver shining" or "seed creator" was a Babylonian pregnant goddess who was worshipped each night as the moon rose. She was the consort of the hero god Marduk. (Mastin; Pritchard 96)

CHRISTIAN AND JEWISH PANTHEON

Agrath Bath Maḥalath This queen of 180,000 demons drove her chariot on Wednesdays and Fridays, hunting anything that moved. On other days, rabbis were able to constrain the wanderings of this "spirit of uncleanness." (Ginsberg 5; Patai 1990)

Anat-Yahu In the Egyptian city of Elephantine, texts describe worship of the goddess Anat-Yahu, or "Anat consort of Yahu" (YHWH), who may be the same as the "Anat of Bethel" named in the same text. Scholars theorize that in northern Syria, powerful YHWH was absorbed into the pantheon. As gods required consorts, he was provided with similarly powerful **Anat**, who moved with her worshippers to Egypt. (Brooks; Kapelru)

Asherah The name of this goddess, found in inscriptions and scriptures, appears as Asherah and as **Athirat** (both with variants). This section deals with the appearance of the goddess in Hebrew scripture; see Athirat for her Ugaritic form.

Whether the Israelites worshipped a goddess is a much-debated question; whether that goddess was named Asherah is similarly debatable. For centuries, scholars argued that Asherah was a term (found more than three dozen times in Hebrew scripture) indicating a cultic object. But in 1929, Ugaritic texts were discovered that proved the existence of a goddess of this name.

The name probably derives from a root word meaning "straight," referring to posts and trees, which were her image. Another proposed meaning is "spouse," pointing to her preeminent role as consort goddess. The character and powers of Asherah are vague, coming down through Hebrew writings documenting suppression of Canaanite religion. Some texts, perhaps deliberately, confused Asherah with **Astarte**. Asherah's religion proved difficult to eradicate. Often banished, it reemerged just as often, giving rise to waves of reform. Nor was her worship restricted to the margins of society. Even King Solomon sacrificed to Asherah "on the high places," as well as building temples for other divinities.

Solomon was not the only early Hebrew ruler to honor Asherah. Manassah erected an image of Asherah in a temple, and **Ma'acah** made an image of the goddess. Zealots took the life of **Jezebel** on the charge of "harlotry" during religious festivals. Hebrew scriptures describe the removal of Asherah's image from the temple, suggesting it was normally kept there. Thus Asherah has been connected with kingly sovereignty, perhaps as an image of the queen mother. Other scholars believe Asherah was as a household goddess, worshipped by women seeking healthy children; inscriptions to the goddess from men seem to argue against that limitation.

Asherah was unquestionably revered among the Canaanites. Whether she can be considered part of early Hebrew religion is debated. Scholars who believe inscriptions indicate Asherah was YHWH's consort date Hebrew polytheism to as late as the eighth century BCE. Those who refute this claim interpret the inscriptions as referring to poles erected in Hebrew temples, a Canaanite ritual for the goddess unexplained as a way of honoring an otherwise aniconic male divinity. In her temples, worshippers erected pieces of wood called *asherim* (plural of *asherah*); this ritual may derive from an ancient cult of tree worship.

In homes, a legless woman-shaped clay figurine, with a base for insertion into an earthen floor, represented the goddess. As Asherah is typically shown with full breasts, sometimes holding them out to the viewer, she may be the divinity called El Shadday, "the one with breasts," a term usually translated as "the Almighty" and said to refer to YHWH. It is not clear whether Asherah is the "Queen of Heaven" referred to by Jeremiah, declaiming against rituals in which women "bake cakes for the Queen of Heaven." Cakes were known in Mesopotamia as offerings for **Ishtar**. Along the Euphrates, molds, which may have been used in making ritual cakes,have been found of an ample-figured goddess. (1 Kings, 2 Kings, Jeremiah; Ackerman 1992, 1993; Day P 1989; Albright 1968; Becking et al; Binger; Cassuto; Cornelius; Day J 1986, 2000; Dever 1984; Freedman 1987; Frymer-Kensey; Gibson; Hadley; Brenner and Fontaine; Kirsch; Kletter 1976; Lutzky; Maier; Margalit; Mastin; Ogden; Olyan; Patai 1965, 1990; Petty; Skipwith; Pritchard 1943; Stuckey 1993; Oden)

Ashtoreth This word from Hebrew scripture has given rise to considerable scholarship. While not clearly a proper name, *'ashtaroth* appears in contexts suggesting a goddess. She has been described as a divine ancestor of early Semitic peoples; the Phoenicians used her name as a generic goddess title. The likely name of the primary Israelite goddess was **Asherah**, of which this word is a variant, with the insinuation of the word "shame." The name has also been interpreted as a reference to **Astarte**. (Day J 1986; Frothingham; Brenner and Fontaine; Kapelru; Patai 1990; Pritchard 1943; Skipwith)

Bilqis The legendary queen of Sheba appears in Hebrew scripture, the Qur'an, and the folklore of Arabia and Africa. In the first, she arrived in Jerusalem, having heard of the wisdom of King Solomon. After testing him with riddles, she declared herself satisfied and returned to her own land. In the Qur'an and in Islamic legend, Bilqis's mother was Umayra, of the *jinn* race. Raised among her mother's people, Bilqis joined humanity as a young woman. A nearby king made a habit of raping a new maiden each week and, hearing of Bilqis's beauty, arranged to have her. But when he came, she cut off his head, then convinced his followers they should revolt against him. When they agreed, she went into her palace and returned with the king's head, which she held up as proof of loyalty to their cause.

Solomon learned of the queen's amazing wealth, which intrigued him enough to invite her to his court. She sent him a present instead. Three times this happened, but finally she came to Solomon's court, where she converted to Islam and became his consort. Solomon tested the queen with magic tricks, forcing her to reveal her *jinn* descent by lifting her skirts to reveal hairy feet. (1 Kings, 2 Chronicles; Qur'an; Brenner 1994; Stowasser; Toy)

Deborah A prophet, Deborah selected the unlikely Barak, "the ignoramus," to lead the Israelites in battle. He refused until she agreed to accompany him. A poet and a judge, she sat in the open air dispensing judgments and composing poems. The verse attributed to her is one of the oldest in the Bible. (Judges; Kirsch; Camp and Fontaine)

Dinah Mother of the last matrilineal Israelite tribe, the daughter of Leah was changed from male to female in her mother's womb when her mother, pitying her childless sister, prayed that her child be female. Her father, Jacob, kept Dinah in a chest whenever possible suitors were in sight, so she could not meet an uncircumcised man. Nonetheless, while out with friends Dinah stumbled upon a group of dancers. One of

them, Prince Shechem, won her heart and slept with her. The Israelites objected to Dinah's marriage to a man from an uncircumcised tribe, so Shechem's people agreed to forfeit their foreskins. While the men were recovering, the Israelites massacred the tribe, taking away Dinah, pregnant with a daughter. Interpreters vary in their sympathies, some finding Dinah a self-assured woman whose independence was thwarted after she chose the wrong lover, others seeing her as a victim of rape rightfully avenged by her kinfolk. (Genesis; Camp and Fontaine; Kirsch; Sheres)

Esther Many scholars believe this Israelite heroine was **Ishtar** in thin disguise. Whether the book of Esther, recorded in the third or second century BCE, should be part of scripture has been argued since the early years of the Common Era. The only book in which YHWH's name does not appear, it also does not include references to prayers, the law, or the covenant. Instead, the book relates the story that a Persian queen, **Vashti**, and her prime minister, Haman (an Elamite god), were replaced by a pair of Israelite cousins, Esther and Mordecai (a name that resembles that of the Babylonian hero Marduk, cousin of **Ishtar**). The story, used to support the celebration of the Jewish feast of Purim, describes how Esther replaced Vashti as queen of Persia. (Esther; Hoschander; Day P 1989)

Eve Eve was created simultaneously with Adam, says one biblical verse, although a later one says she was created from his rib. Some scholars contend that the conflicting stories represent a hidden tradition of Adam's earlier wife (see **Lilith**), while others find evidence of two differing creation stories.

Eve lived in paradise with Adam until, tempted by a serpent, she broke YHWH's commandment, eating fruit from the Tree of Life, which she offered to Adam. With one bite, they realized they were naked and clothed themselves with leaves. Knowing their sin, YHWH cast them into the outer world, where they had to toil for food. Eve was cursed with pains of childbirth; Eve and her children were condemned to die.

Behind this disobedient temptress stands another figure. Genesis calls Eve the first man's *'ezer*, a word usually translated as "helpmeet." But the masculine word is read, in other biblical contexts, as "instructor," suggesting an earlier, more prominent role for this wifely figure. Eve has many traits in common with goddesses of the region; some parts of her story echo myths of the Israelites' neighbors.

In documents from Nag Hammâdi in Egypt, hidden during the early years of the Christian era and rediscovered in 1945, Eve was created from the earth by the god Ialdaboath at the same time that Adam was created. Eve knew a secret, a word of knowledge that gave the couple power threatening to god. Punishment for this knowledge was separation from each other spiritually. But a new and androgynous Eve was born from **Hokmah**; called "life's teacher," she was sent to save the lost world.

In Jewish legend and Kabbalistic writings, unorthodox images of Eve appear. In one story, paradise was divided, with Eve serving as mistress of west, south, and female animals, while Adam ruled north, east, and males; another text says Adam consorted with animals until Eve was created. The serpent put poison in the forbidden fruit, which caused Eve to menstruate for the first time. After Adam's fall, she promised to stand up to God for him, but he spoke first and blamed her.

Jewish folklore says Adam did not trust Eve with the truth about YHWH's prohibition; instead, he told Eve YHWH had forbidden them to touch the Tree of Life, which would kill them. The serpent shoved Eve against the tree; when she did not die, Satan argued that YHWH had lied. Seduced by reason, Eve ate the fruit.

The scriptures tell little about the life of Adam and Eve after paradise, but Jewish legend describes the couple engaging in seven days of lamenting before they were forced into their new world. Legend claims Cain and Abel were conceived by Eve in intercourse with the serpent, whom she believed an angel. Eve, a prophetess, foresaw the death of her younger son. Some legends say the brothers argued because both wished to mate with Eve, there being no other women at the time; other tales say that Adam decided which sisters the boys would marry, giving Cain the less beautiful one. When Cain killed Abel, Adam withdrew from Eve, leaving himself open to the wiles of Lilith, who slept with him and conceived demon children. Only being shamed by his daughters-in-law drove Adam back to Eve's bed. Ultimately the couple conceived thirty pairs of twins. After almost a thousand years, Adam lay near death, and Eve prayed that half his illness would come upon her. She traveled to heaven, winning YHWH's pity. Although Adam still had to die, YHWH promised Eve he would be reborn.

In Islam, Eve (Hawwa') appears as primal mother, wife of the prophet Adam. Formed from Adam's crooked rib, Eve was auburn haired and black eyed, pale, and very plump. But she did not tempt Adam to eat the apple. Rather, the Qur'an suggests that Adam was the first to bite the fateful fruit after being tempted by Iblis (Satan). Later interpretation emphasized the sexual nature of the fall, with the first humans' genitals becoming visible to them after eating of the tree. (Genesis; Qur'an; Arthur; Bird; Brandon 1963; Ginsberg 1, 5; Hooke; Meyers; O'Brien; Otwell; Patai 1990; Stowasser; Young)

Gomer The words of the late Israelite prophet Hosea attract considerable attention from feminist scholars. The prophet married Gomer, whom he beat and rejected. Although traditionally read as an allegory of YHWH's relationship to his chosen people, who "whored after false gods" (see **Asherah**), the human story describes domestic violence. Gomer, often described as a prostitute, may have been a woman who believed in other divinities, a belief considered equivalent to harlotry. After Gomer bore children to Hosea, he withheld food and water. Broken by abuse, Gomer gave up her "harlotries." Then, in a passage of disputed meaning, YHWH told Hosea to buy a woman who had no other lovers; whether that woman is different from Gomer, or whether Gomer recovered from his attack and their relationship recommenced, is unclear. (Hosea; Brenner 1995; Weems)

Hagar Hagar was an Egyptian woman given to **Sarah** as a slave, then to her husband, Abraham, as a sexual companion, because Sarah had passed the age of childbearing. Hagar grew disrespectful to Sarah once pregnant with the patriarch's heir. Hagar fled into the desert, but an angel told her to return, promising her that her descendants would be numberless. Years after Hagar had borne Ishmael, Sarah gave birth to Isaac. When Ishmael was fifteen, Sarah saw him playing with Isaac and, for unclear reasons, cast out Hagar and Ishmael forever. Abraham agreed to the banishment when YHWH said Hagar and Ishmael would survive their second wilderness sentence. In some traditions, Abraham married Hagar, under the name Keturah, after Sarah's death. In other legends, Keturah was a different woman, whose six sons were entrusted with magical secrets, including the names of demons who served them.

Despite the tradition that Hagar was the mother of the Arabic people, the Qur'an says little about her. Islamic legend fleshes out the picture of a young mother exiled to the desert, where she had to fight for survival and, succeeding, made it possible for her son Ishmael to become the ancestor of the prophet Mohammed. Ishmael rebuilt the Ka'aba, Islam's holiest place (see **Al-Lat**), with his father, Abraham. Some Islamic tradition claims female genital removal began with Hagar as a way of eluding Sarah's jealousy about her relationship with Abraham. Originally Hagar may have been a mountain goddess; her son's name means the "goddess's favorite." The Christian Paul linked her with Mount Sinai in Arabia. (Genesis; Qur'an; Ginsberg 1; Day P 1989; Kirsch; Stowasser)

Hokmah YHWH had Hokmah ("wisdom") from the first, and almost from the first this quality became a functional goddess, perhaps taking over the attributes of early Israelite goddesses like **Asherah**. Some contend Hokmah was always allegorical, but in Proverbs and Ecclesiasticus, she makes strong claims to an identity separate from YHWH. Her separateness was clear in the eleventh century CE, when the Spanish Arab scholar Ibn Hazm noted she had the powers of a goddess. Recently, many scholars have agreed with that insight. The earliest creation of YHWH, Hokmah was also his favorite. Hokmah cast her shadow on the primeval waters, stilling them. Hokmah gave consciousness to humankind, for humans crawled like worms until she endowed them with spirit. Hokmah even called herself YHWH's playmate. This figure and that of the **Shekinah** softened the patriarchal religion of the Jews with a semidivine femininity.

Some scholars find Egyptian influence in Hokmah's iconography, especially when she is envisioned as winged (see **Isis**). By the time of Hellenistic Judaism (first century BCE), Hokmah appeared as a figure in her own right. She became more and more clearly personified, even splitting into positive ("wisdom") and negative ("folly") aspects. In Christianity, where she is known as Sophia, Wisdom's femininity remained palpable. Early church father Justinian built an enormous church dedicated to Hagia Sophia, "divine wisdom," in the capital of the eastern Roman Empire, Constantinople (Istanbul). She appears as a powerful woman, hands upraised, glowing with light, throughout the Greek Orthodox world. (Proverbs, Ben Sirach, Enoch, Wisdom of Solomon; Arthur; Camp; Brenner and Fontaine; Meyendorff; Pagels)

Idith The story of Sodom and Gomorrah does not provide a name for Lot's wife, but Jewish legend calls her Idith, while Islamic traditions give her name as Waliha. When YHWH sent angels to Lot's home to warn him of coming destruction, the depraved residents demanded sexual access to them. Lot offered his virgin daughters. The offer was refused, and Lot and his family set off for safety. One married daughter was not warned, and Idith looked back for her; she was turned into a pillar of salt. Later, believing themselves alone in the destroyed world, Lot's daughters gave him enough wine to make him delirious and then had intercourse with him to become pregnant. (Genesis; Stowasser)

Jezebel Her name appears today as a synonym for "harlot," but the Jezebel of scripture was never accused of selling sexual favors. Rather, she was a powerful queen who worshipped a goddess, possibly **Asherah**, in the face of an increasingly patriarchal religious establishment.

In her native Phoenician tongue, Jezebel was Itha-Baal, "woman of Baal"; her father, king of the Sidonians, was a priest of Baal. (Some sources consider Jezebel an ancestor of **Dido**, queen of Carthage.) In the scriptures, Itha-Baal was changed to I-zeval, "woman of excrement," by writers intent upon defaming her; this became Jezebel in Greek.

Jezebel married Israelite king Ahab, who built temples to Baal and erected an Asherah pole, offenses the Bible claims were worse than an earlier king's use of his children's bodies as foundation sacrifices. Ahab called for a contest between Elijah, prophet of YHWH, and 450 prophets of Baal and 400 of Asherah. When the prophet of YHWH won, those of Baal were murdered, but nothing is said about Asherah's prophets, leading some interpreters to believe the contest was between male gods only.

Jezebel's death came because she forged letters that led to the murder of an Israelite whose vineyard Ahab coveted. For this, Ahab and Jezebel were murdered. Jezebel "painted her eyes, adorned her head, and looked out the window," a typical pose of the goddesses of love. From that window, she was thrown to her death. The common vision of Jezebel as a promiscuous woman has no basis in scripture. (1 Kings, 2 Kings, Revelation; Ackroyd; Bronner; Patai 1990; Brenner 1994)

Jocebed Despite Pharaoh's command that Israelite children be killed, Jocebed, the mother of Moses, hid her child in a rush boat, where he was found by Pharaoh's daughter. When she could not nurse it,

the baby's sister **Miriam** brought forth the midwife Jocebed, who was thus able to nurse her own son. When Moses led his people to Palestine, Jocebed accompanied him, entering the promised land at the age of 250. (Exodus; Ginsberg 2, 3)

Laïlah According to Jewish legend, this "angel of night" gathered sperm from a woman about to conceive and brought it to YHWH, asking for its fate to be determined. After God decided whether the person was to be rich or poor, gifted or dull, he commanded a soul to enter the sperm, which Laïla then carried to the womb. (Ginsberg 1)

Leviathan According to Jewish legend, Leviathans ruled over creatures of the sea. But because the combined strength of two Leviathans was so immense, YHWH killed the female. The remaining beast became God's companion. The Leviathan's ultimate end will be at the last hour, when he will be killed and served as a delicious treat; the female Leviathan, preserved in brine, will be simultaneously placed on the table. Other legends say this snake-shaped monster was the daughter of **Lilith**. (Ginsberg 5)

Lilith Although Lilith is never mentioned in the Bible, the Israelites and other Eastern Mediterranean people recognized her for millennia. She was first mentioned in Sumerian texts of the mid–third millennium BCE, including the *Epic of Gilgamesh*, where she appears occupying a tree planted by kindly **Inanna**. Banished, she lived in deserts and other desolate places.

Her name, from the Sumerian Lilîtu, refers to a wind spirit; she appears in Babylonian myth as one of a group of storm spirits that also included Ardat Lilî (Lilith's handmaid, mother of demons) and the male Irdu Lili. Lilith may have connections with Babylonian Labartu, a child-killing spirit who spread plague as she suckled dogs and pigs. She infected children but attacked adults as well, drinking their blood and consuming their flesh. To avoid her, parents hung plaques or amulets bearing Labartu's name. The demon, thinking them signs of reverence, went elsewhere.

Jewish legend held that Lilith was Adam's first wife, created simultaneously with him. (Variants say she was created before him; or after him, from the slime of the earth; or much later, as the twin of the evil Samael.) When Adam suggested they make love, Lilith enthusiastically agreed. But when he instructed her to lie beneath, she refused, pointing out that they had been created equally and should mate so.

Lilith went to YHWH and tricked him into revealing his secret name. Once she had power over YHWH, Lilith demanded wings, on which she flew to the western deserts. There she had orgies with elemental spirits, producing demon children. Adam was provided with a new mate, but he and **Eve** soon fell from YHWH's favor. As penance, Adam vowed to avoid the pleasures of marriage for a century. Then Lilith took her revenge. Each night she came to Adam and had dream intercourse, capturing his emissions to form demon babies. One of these was the evil Samael, whom Lilith took as her playmate and companion.

Lilith had luxurious hair and arching wings, with talons instead of feet. Her unearthly beauty was dangerous to young men, who lusted after her, never aroused by mortal women. Lilith threatened children as well, for she had power over all infants in their first week, all babies on the first of the month and on Sabbath evenings, and all children born of unmarried people. Mothers protected their young by hanging an amulet marked "Sen Sam San"—for the protective angels Sensenoi, Samangelof, and Sanoi—around the child's neck.

When Lilith came to steal a child, it was usually at night, when the babe was tucked in crib or cradle. Because she liked her victims smiling, she tickled the infant's feet. When it giggled, Lilith strangled it. Mothers hearing their children laughing in dreams, or noticing them smiling as they slept, hit the babies' nose three times to drive Lilith away. When not stealing children, Lilith lived in Shinar, often defined as Babylonia, probably a mythic wilderness. Although

typically described as a solitary being, Lilith sometimes appears as multiple being, the Lillin.

In Kabbalah, Lilith was the mate of Samael, who continually attempts to debase the pure **Matronit**. Samael and Lilith were sexually awakened when Eve bit into the apple and caused strife on earth thereafter. Other sources declare Lilith's consort was the demon Asmodeus. The confusion about the name of Lilith's mate may stem from there being more than one figure of this name.

Each year, Lilith spends the Day of Atonement in the desert screaming with **Maḥalath**. Yet despite her depraved nature, she became the mate of YHWH, who was forced to take her as bride when the temple of Jerusalem was destroyed. At the same time, Lilith's demon mate Samael was able to sexually degrade the pure Shekinah. But at the end of time, order will be restored and Lilith will die as the divine YHWH and Shekinah are reunited. (Dan; Ginsberg 1; Kramer 1979; Langdon 1931; Patai 1964; Shearman and Curtis; Wolkstein and Kramer)

Ma'acah Two royal women of Judah, both mothers of kings, bore this name. Biblical lineage lists provide not only the names of kings but also those of their mothers, indicating the importance of this role. Queens, as wives of kings, had little power, but as a king's mother, a woman achieved influence and privileges.

The first Ma'acah was a wife of King David. The second, her namesake, brought the worship of **Asherah** back to Jerusalem. Her fanatic son Asa cast out the images, including burning one made by his mother, whom he deposed at the same time. Asa's son Jehoshaphat continued the purge, but the Asherah religion would not die. Upon Jehoshaphat's death, his successor restored Asherah to the temple, where it remained for fifty years. (2 Chronicles, 1 Kings; Patai 1965; Brenner 1994)

Maḥalath In Jewish legend, Queen **Maḥalath** commanded 478 bands of dancing demons. On the day of judgment, she will march them into the desert to meet her rival **Lilith** in combat. **Maḥalath**, a compulsive dancer, will whirl and gyrate in an attempt to terrify her enemy. Legend does not predict the outcome of the conflict. Her daughter was **Agrath Bath Maḥalath**. (Ginsberg 1)

Mary Never considered divine, the Virgin Mary nonetheless served in a goddess-like capacity within Christianity until the Reformation; she is still revered by Catholics. Although barely mentioned in scripture, Mary became a popular figure in early centuries, when extrascriptural legends grew around her. Some became so much a part of Marian imagery that many of the devout would be surprised to learn that there is no biblical basis for them; these include the story that Mary's childless mother was told by God that she would bear a child and that Mary remained a virgin after giving birth. Even the now-doctrinal belief that Mary was assumed bodily into heaven has no biblical basis. Legends, some directly traceable to goddess myths, helped Mary grow in power.

If the scriptures did not provide a full biography for Mary, later writers filled in the gaps. Born of an aged, pious, but infertile couple, Anna and Joachim, Mary was sent at the age of three to live in the temple; at the time of her dedication, she danced with joy and was fed by angels. At puberty, Mary vowed perpetual virginity, so her parents betrothed her to an elderly widower, Joseph in Nazareth. Yet Mary became pregnant after an angel visited her and gained her assent (*fiat*, or "let it be"). Joseph, suspecting another man had impregnated her, withdrew but was visited by an angel who attested to Mary's innocence.

When the Roman rulers called for a census of the residents of the empire (not attested in any Roman documents), Mary and Joseph set out for his ancestral home of Bethlehem. There, unable to find lodging, Joseph installed Mary in a stable, where she gave birth; her hymen remained undamaged, so she lived thereafter as a virgin. Three wise men found them by following astrological indications, bringing gifts of gold, frankincense, and myrrh. When the violent Roman puppet ruler Herod learned the king of the Jews had been born, he killed all male babies under the age of two; angels warned Mary and Joseph, who fled to Egypt with the newborn. After Jesus's ministry began, Mary interceded at a wedding in Cana, asking him to help the host, who had run out of wine; this provided the occasion for Jesus's first public miracle. Mary appeared at the Crucifixion, one of the few to remain faithful to Jesus until his death. She lived in Ephesus afterward. When she died there, her body was taken to heaven, so, like her son, she never decomposed.

Such legends have many sources. Some scholars contend that early Christianity contained female-oriented rituals that used iconography derived from ancient goddess religions. The excesses of Mary's followers brought warnings from church officials that she was not a goddess. The Kollyridians, deemed heretical by the early church fathers, honored Mary as divine. In addition, the Montanists believed Mary was an image of the feminine divine, also pictured as the Holy Spirit. With prophetesses Maximilla and Priscilla, Montanus conducted worship services that resembled ancient goddess rites. The Montanists were declared heretics in 177 CE.

As Christianity spread, Mary took on the identity of regional goddesses. In Europe, Mary appears as the Black Madonna. Usually found in churches, these images are sometimes said to have been altered by fire. As black is connected with the soil, the darkness of these madonnas suggests an ancient heritage in emblems of fertility.

Because she was the mother of Jesus, recognized as a prophet in Islam, the Qur'an mentions Mary. Several verses focus on her relationship with her guardian, the prophet Zachariah, of the line of Solomon. He was married to Elizabeth, Mary's maternal aunt (sometimes described as Mary's sister). Elizabeth's unborn child jumped when Mary appeared to tell Elizabeth the news that she was bearing Jesus. Later verses describe the birth of Jesus to the still-chaste Mary and uphold Mary's virginity as an example of faithfulness to God's will. Islamic tradition offers additional details about

Mary's life. She was born of an aged woman, Anna, who saw a vision of a dove nursing its young and was inspired to sleep with her similarly aged husband, Amram, at which time she conceived. Because he assumed the child would be male, Amram dedicated it to God, who accepted the dedication even though the child was female. When Amram died, Zachariah became the young woman's guardian. Under his tuition, she grew up in the temple, praying constantly in a locked room to which only Zachariah had a key. When he visited her, she gave him fruit out of season, whereupon he conceived John "the baptist" upon his wife Elizabeth. Later traditions name the angel who accompanied Mohammed, Gabriel, as the one who brought the news of her pregnancy to Mary.

Today, Mary is honored on important feast days that replaced earlier pagan festivals. She is omnipresent at Christmas, December 25, when the Madonna is a common image; the feast replaced winter solstice festivals, including Roman Saturnalia. The Purification, celebrating the ritual by which Mary was "made pure" after birth, was fixed on February 2, an important Celtic feast; Mary is honored as "Queen of the May" on May 1, another Celtic feast. The Assumption is celebrated on August 15, taking the place of earlier harvest festivals. (Matthew, Mark, Luke, John; Qur'an; Corrington; Harrington; Taylor; Sered 1991; Stowasser; Weigle; Young; Warner)

Mary Magdalen Christian scripture describes a prostitute who washed the feet of Jesus; it also describes a woman named Mary Magdalen who was among Christ's disciples. Her name appears to refer to a town called Magdala, but no such place existed. Some consider her the same as Mary of Bethany, although that is a minority view. Magdalen was a witness to two important moments in the Christian scripture: she stood at the foot of the cross, and she was the first person to see the empty tomb and to know Jesus had risen from the dead. Thus she is both important and elusive in the Christian story.

The figures of prostitute and Magdalen were conflated early. Soon, Mary Magdalen was imagined retiring to the desert to become a hermit, praying ceaselessly for forgiveness. This Magdalen was honored as St. Mary Magdalen, patron of contemplatives, converts, druggists, and reformed prostitutes. Church sources disagree about her life after the Resurrection, some saying she traveled to Ephesus with **Mary** and died there, others claiming she converted southern France, where her head rests as a sanctified relic in La Sainte-Baume.

Other versions of the Magdalen's life appear in apocryphal writings. The Gospel of Macian describes Jesus casting out seven demons from Mary Magdalen, while the Gospel of Peter describes her as a "myrrh-bearer" who went to Christ's tomb after his burial and discovered the absence of his body. Mary Magdalen is especially important in the writings of the Gnostics, an early Christian sect who described the world as a battle between light and darkness. The apocryphal Gospel of Philip called the Magdalen the "companion" of Jesus. Such texts have led to an unorthodox tradition that Mary Magdalen was the wife of Jesus. This has been joined to the Provençal legend that Mary Magdalen escaped to southern France after Jesus's execution and bore his child there.

Arguably the most important Magdalen text is the Gospel of Mary, found in 1896 in Egypt. This text describes Mary Magdalen as a bearer of secret knowledge that parallels the Gnostic vision of the soul entrapped in flesh. Little evidence shows how widely known the Gospel of Mary was in early Christian times, and the views it contains are unorthodox in today's Christianity.

Recent feminist interpretations of Mary Magdalen depict her as a priestess of the Canaanite religion, ritually "wedded" to Jesus but actually serving ancient goddesses; or as the "Holy Grail" of British legend, interpreted as the Magdalen's body. Both extrapolations from minimal scriptural sources emphasize the Magdalen as a sexual woman, thus balancing the motherly but sexless Virgin Mary. (De Boer; Fiorenza; Haskins; Jansen; Marjanen; Meyer; Pagels; Warner)

Matronit In the Kabbalah's esoteric Judaism, we find two demigoddesses formed by analyzing the mystic name of god, YHWH. The "Y" of YHWH became the Father, and the first "H" the Mother. These two produced "W," the Son, and finally a second "H," the blameless Daughter, Makhut or the Matronit. These children were born attached back-to-back but were separated soon after birth.

However abstract the analysis that produced her, the Matronit soon became a lively personage. Lowest of the ten mystic emanations of the male godhead, she was the only one human senses could perceive. Jacob married her, although the marriage remained unconsummated until he joined her in the afterlife. Moses mated with the Matronit in physical form after separating from **Zipporah**. After his death, the Matronit flew his body to a secret burial place. But her usual lover was her brother, with whom she cohabited in the temple on Friday nights and for whom Solomon built a special bedchamber in the temple at Jerusalem. Jewish couples were encouraged to have intercourse on Fridays in emulation of the sacred couple. In this way, the Matronit is conflated with **Shekinah** as the Sabbath bride.

Whenever the children of Israel fell into sin, the king mated with **Lilith** while the demon king Samael had intercourse with the Matronit, taking the form of a snake to do so. This rape continues until the Day of Atonement, when a scapegoat hurled off a cliff attracts Samael's attention as it falls to its death, burdened by the people's sins. Thereupon the Matronit reunites with her husband. This figure may derive from **Ishtar**, **Inanna**, or **Anat**. (Patai 1964)

Miriam The greatest woman prophet of Jewish tradition, she began to foretell the future at five, when she began working with **Jocebed** as a midwife. She foresaw the birth of her brother Moses and knew he could be saved if placed in a reedy basket in a river. Her prophetic gift matched her genius for poetry; Miriam's song celebrated her people's escape from Egypt's pharaoh. Like many prophetic females, Miriam was associated with water. Her name seems to be derived from *marah*, "bitter water," and she sang her most famous poem after crossing the Red Sea. She gave her name to the spring that burst forth from the desert rock struck by Moses. But Miriam sided with **Zipporah** when the latter complained that Moses's divine revelations had led to his abandoning conjugal duties. A furious YHWH spit in her face, and Miriam grew leprous for seven days, during which time the Israelite people would not leave the spot of Miriam's confinement. (Exodus, Numbers, Deuteronomy, 1 Chronicles, Micah; Ginsberg 2 250–269)

Naamah In ancient times this word, which means "pleasant," was used for **Astarte**. But Jewish legend gives the name to a demon queen so beautiful angels could not resist her. She seduced them with her cymbal music; once they became aroused, she stole their semen to form demon children. In some interpretations, she was Noah's wife; other writers say she was the wife of a demon, Shamdan, and mother of devils. Like **Lilith**, Naamah strangled sleeping babies, but she much preferred to lure men from their appropriate mates. In the Kabbalah, she lived in the sea, where monsters, infatuated with her beauty, pursued her constantly. (Ginsberg 5; Patai 1990)

Rachel The Canaanite Rachel brought her family's teraphim (household gods) when she joined the household of Jacob. Jacob had loved her for many years but was forced to marry her older sister Leah first. Rachel became Jacob's second wife, sharing him not only with Leah but also with the servants Zilpah and Bilhah. The four women are considered the matriarchs of Israel; although Jewish law defines heritage matrilineally, none of these foremothers was Israelite.

As befitted her status as favored spouse, Rachel gave birth to favored sons, Joseph and Benjamin. Rachel prophesied the birth of her second son but was cursed for pridefully saying, "I will bear another son," rather than praying that it might occur. She bore one son more but died in labor. Because her own childbearing history was so difficult, Rachel aided barren, pregnant, and birthing mothers. Today, her tomb is a site of pilgrimage. (Patai 1965; Sered 1986; Brenner and Fontaine)

Rebecca The counterpart of **Sarah** was the mother of Jacob and Esau. Like Sarah, she was prescient, had an unearthly beauty, and lived under a magical cloud that never left her tent. Like Sarah, she lived with a man who, in times of danger, pretended she was his sister. A shrewd mother who favored her younger son over her older one, Rebecca engineered the famous birthright-stealing episode whereby Jacob snatched Isaac's blessing from Esau. (Ginsberg 1)

Ruth One of the greatest matriarchs of Jewish tradition is Ruth, a Moabite woman married to a Israelite man, Boaz. Her story appears to have been written in approximately 400 BCE, during a period when intermarriage with neighboring peoples was discouraged; as such, the heroic Ruth stands in opposition to contemporary regulations. Her story may have originally been a folktale, absorbed into scripture; it parallels to a great extent the narrative of another matriarch, Tamar, and deals with fertility, sex, and death.

Ruth's story begins with a famine that forced the family of Israelite Elimelech to move to the barren land of Moab. There the sons, Machlon and Lilion, married women of the region. Machlon's wife was Ruth ("friend"), who was soon widowed; Machlon's father and brother also died, although the texts provide no reason. Ruth's mother-in-law, Naomi ("gracious"), wished to return home but was concerned for her young daughters-in-law. Ruth refused to leave Naomi, uttering the famous words often used in marriage vows, "whither thou goest, I will go." She promised Naomi they would stay together until death and "Where you die, I will die. That is where I will be buried."

So the women returned to Bethlehem, Naomi's home, where they found the barley harvest in progress. Ruth set to work picking up bits missed by the reapers. There she was noticed by an elderly, childless landowner, Boaz. Naomi, noticing Boaz's interest, urged Ruth to seduce the wealthy but elderly Boaz ("strength"). So she dressed alluringly and went to Boaz's bed during the festival of harvest. The next day, Boaz took Ruth in a levirate marriage (marriage to a widow of childbearing age by a relative, although there is no evidence that Boaz and Naomi were related). He then went to the city gate and proclaimed that Naomi's husband's property was for sale; when a relative came forward, Boaz said impregnating Ruth to assure continuance of the family was required, and the interested party withdrew. Boaz thus took Ruth as his wife, and they became the great-grandparents of King David. (Bal; Shearman and Curtis)

Sarah The first and greatest Israelite matriarch, Sarah was a Chaldean princess who bestowed wealth on Abraham by marrying him. Sarai, as she was originally named, was beautiful and ageless. Her loveliness was such that, when she and Abraham moved to Egypt, Pharaoh sent armed men to steal her. Sarah lied to Pharaoh, describing Abraham as her brother, so the king appointed Abraham to a position of honor and wealth. The king even gave Sarah his own daughter, **Hagar**, as a slave. But when the king tried to sleep with Sarah, an angel crippled him with leprosy. To free himself from the disease, he gave Sarah back to Abraham.

Sarah did not bear a child until she had lived nearly a century. Sarah laughed in disbelief when YHWH told Abraham she would bear a child. Rather than exhausting her, the birth of Isaac rejuvenated her. Unearthly radiance shone from her face; a miraculous cloud marked her tent. She held conversations with YHWH.

A minor figure named Sara appears in the noncanonical book of Tobit as a woman married seven times. On each wedding night, a demon killed the bridegroom. Tobias, who desired Sara, learned from an angel to burn the innards of a fish, the odor of which would drive away the demon, then to pray to

YHWH before making love to Sara. These precautions proved successful, and Sara was freed from the demon. (Genesis, Tobit; Ginsberg 1; Kirsch; Teubals; Van der Toorn 1994)

Seila Daughter of the careless warrior Jephthah, this Israelite maiden was sacrificed because her father promised to kill the first thing he met upon returning home from a battle. To celebrate her father's success, Seila met him on the road, dancing to the sound of her timbrel. Rather than break his vow, Jephthah decided to kill his daughter. Seila uttered a famous lament, weeping that she would die a virgin. Her death did not go unavenged: Jephthah was cursed by YHWH and died by dismemberment.

Her name is not recorded in the Bible, where she appears only as "Jephthah's daughter," but comes from an anonymous first-century commentator known as Pseudo-Philo. A passing biblical reference tells of an annual festival celebrated by the Israelite women in honor of this heroine, but nothing more is known of the ritual. (Judges; Day P 1989; Fuchs; Kirsch)

Shekinah The Talmud tells us human senses cannot perceive YHWH, but we can see, hear, and touch his Shekinah. This word, meaning "emanation," is feminine in gender and, like **Hokmah**, took on a feminine personality as a disputative but compassionate demigoddess who argued with God in support of his creatures. The Kabbalah describes the loving marriage between YHWH and Shekinah as culminating in a mystical sexual union, replicated when devout followers enacted that union on Sabbath eve. She is often conflated with another important Kabbalistic female figure, the **Matronit**. (Kirsch; Patai 1990)

Tamar Three Biblical figures bear this name. One was a Canaanite woman who outlived several Israelite husbands. Her first, Er, was born of a Canaanite mother and a Israelite father, Judah; he offended YHWH and lost his life. Under the law of levirate marriage, it was the duty of the next brother, Onan, to impregnate

her, but he "spilled his seed upon the ground," which denied to Tamar offspring who might threaten Onan's inheritance. Because of this offense against custom, YHWH saw to it that Onan died.

The next-oldest son was too young for intercourse, so Tamar remained a marginalized widow. When this seemed likely to become permanent, Tamar wrapped herself in a veil worn by prostitutes. She positioned herself at a crossroads where she knew Judah would pass. Judah desired the disguised Tamar, but she withheld her favors until he offered her his signet ring and staff, promising he could redeem them for a kid from his herds. Conceiving a child, Tamar returned to her father's household, where she arrayed herself again in widow's garments.

Judah sent the promised kid to the crossroads, but no harlot could be found. Soon, however, news came that Tamar was pregnant. He demanded she be returned to his household for execution. When she came, Tamar bore the signet and staff of Judah, which shamed him into accepting her offspring as legitimate. Tamar is named as one of the four female ancestors of Jesus, along with **Ruth**, Bathsheba, and Rehab.

Another Tamar was the sister of King David's son, Absalom, and half sister to Amnon, who lusted after her. Pretending to be ill, Amnon called for her to bring him food and drink, but once they were alone, he raped her. When David did nothing to punish the crime, Absalom tricked Amnon into attending a banquet, where Absalom's men killed the rapist. Finally, another Tamar was Absalom's daughter. (2 Samuel, 1 Chronicles, Genesis, Matthew, 2 Samuel; Binger; Bird; Brooks; Kirsch; Brenner and Fontaine)

Torah In the Hebrew language, the word for "law" is feminine. As a result, Torah grew to have a mythic presence. Although never deified, she sometimes functioned as a goddess. Her temperament was judicious and fair. Early in the Creation, she admonished YHWH not to create humanity for a short, woeful life. After YHWH convinced Torah repentance was possible, she ceased her protest. (Ginsberg 1)

Zipporah The Midianite Zipporah could only wed a man who could touch a man-eating tree. Moses survived the tree's attack, but Zipporah's father, Jethro, threw him into a deep pit. The girl secretly fed him for seven years, then suggested to her father that if Moses survived, he was a man of miracles. Moses, emerging hale and well fed, became Zipporah's husband.

Later, she had to save him from death again. A power (possibly YHWH, or an angel in his service) tried to kill Moses while the family slept. Suspecting Moses was threatened because their first-born son, Gershom, had not been circumcised, Zipporah grabbed a stone and performed the operation, thus freeing Moses from YHWH's attack. (Exodus; Kirsch; Shearman and Curtis)

Zuleika This passionate woman is referred to as "Potiphar's wife" in scripture, although her own name is given as Zuleika in Jewish and Islamic legend. She desired the Israelite prince Joseph. To show her friends how unnerving Joseph's beauty was, she threw a banquet. At each place, she set knives and oranges. When Joseph entered, the guests lost awareness of anything but him; the table ran with blood and orange juice while the guests were entranced by Joseph's presence. Afterward they sympathized with the woman's passion. Zuleika tied Joseph down while she fondled herself; he still rejected her advances. Zuleika then accused Joseph of attempted rape, and Joseph was thrown into prison and whipped. (Genesis; Qur'an; Ginsberg 1; Stowasser)

ASIA AND OCEANIA

CHINA *and* KOREA

China reaches from desert to tropics, from mountainous west to coastal east. Its culture represents an equally diverse ethnic background. China's earliest civilizations were not the highly centralized bureaucracies of later Chinese life, nor were their mythologies the highly structured regimes of later centuries. Rather, eastern continental Asia was home to indigenous peoples whose mythologies were absorbed into developing religions.

Among these ethnic groups, women held considerably higher status than in later times. Women shamans mediated between this world and worlds beyond. Commentators note connections between the word for "shaman" and those for "mother," "dance," "fertility," and "egg." Thus the woman religious practitioner may be symbolically implied in myths where she does not appear. The role of women as religious leaders did not survive in China, although it did in Korea. China and Korea are discussed separately here.

Aboriginal Chinese religion forms the basis for Taoism and Confucianism, both properly called philosophies rather than religions. Taoism reached back to China's shamanic roots with its emphasis on the balance of feminine (*yin*) and masculine (*yang*). Taoism's founder was the sage Lao-Tzu of the sixth century BCE, author of the important *Tao-te Ching*. As Taoism became the religion of choice for imperial China, its pantheon began to reflect social organization of earthly life, resembling a bureaucracy complete with monthly reports to superior gods and annual performance reviews.

The ideas of Confucius, a sage of the fifth century BCE, became the basis for an ethically sophisticated life. The abstractness of the Confucian way gave rise to few myths, although it provided rituals celebrating seasons and ancestral powers. Rather, Confucian ideas were appended to extant myths, sometimes producing a disjuncture between mythic action and its interpretation, or ancient myth was recast as history.

In the third century CE, Buddhism arrived from India by way of Tibet and Afghanistan, bringing many vivid mythic figures. Few were feminine, but the most powerful female figure in China, Guanyin, derives from this religious tradition. Originally male, Guanyin continued China's tradition of balancing masculine and feminine energies, for although she was the singular female figure among Buddhist divinities, her power exceeded that of most male figures.

Despite the imperial strength of China, evident in public works like the Great Wall, the court did not dictate all religious ways. Messages alternative to the mainstream religion were found in two places: in the residue of indigenous religions, as in the folktales and folkways of ethnic groups like the Miao; and in the religious myths of neighboring peoples, the Turks and Manchus as well as the Mongols.

In addition, the nearby kingdom of Korea has kept its women's shamanic tradition alive into the present. Such shamans come from two traditions. Southern-tradition shamans derive their powers from matrilineally inherited access to spirits. Northern shamans are self-selected by "spirit sickness" before being initiated by a practitioner. Located historically in territory that is now North Korea, this tradition is now predominant in Seoul, to which many northern shamans fled to escape Communist suppression.

Persecution of shamans is not new in Korea. Its strategic location between China and Japan led to invasion and occupation by both. When the Chinese brought Confucianism and later Buddhism, they tried to eliminate the native religion. Shamans survived marginally as healers, because no provision had been made to train doctors. But in 1409 CE, all shamanic books were burned; in 1472, the shamans were driven from Seoul.

The *mudang* survived, going underground until the end of colonial rulership. In the North, dictator Kim Il-sung made it his mission to end all religious practices save a token Buddhism. Shamanism in Communist Korea ended with the flight of *mudang* to Seoul, where they formed the basis of South Korean shamanism. The new Korean democracy did not welcome the refugee shamans. But the Fifth Republic, dedicated under its 1980 constitution to preserving Korean cultural heritage, permits public announcement of rituals; dedicatory rituals led by *mudang* have

opened several skyscrapers in Seoul. Yet like Native American tribal dances, these public performances do not mean the new government supports the old religion.

CHINESE, MONGOL, AND TAIWANESE PANTHEON

Alan Qo'a The ancestress of the Mongol hero Činggis Khan was visited nightly by a yellow man who descended through the smoke hole, rubbed his stomach, then turned into a yellow dog. This visitor fathered five sons. One day their mother gave them arrows to break. Although they could break single arrows, none could break five held together. Thus Alan Qo'a showed her sons the necessity of cooperation. Another Mongol ancestral mother, Ala Nur, gave birth after encountering a lion. (Bonnefoy; *SH*)

Billkis The Uighur, a Chinese minority, tell of the princess Billkis, who began at the age of eight to embroider a veil for her wedding. It took eight years, so when Billkis turned sixteen, the veil was finished. She told her father that the man who could understand her veil would become her husband, for he would be able to read her innermost thoughts. One after another, princes came and looked at the veil, but all they saw was embroidered silk. They could not interpret Billkis's designs.

Finally, a raggedy young man discerned the veil's meaning. In the swirls of color, he saw a mountain, on which a witch stood guard over a green bird. His interpretation was correct, but Billkis wanted him to get the bird for her. Asking only for the pearl she wore in her right ear, he set off.

Finding the mountain, he climbed to the top, where he discovered the bird and the witch. Calling for the pearl to help him, he threw it into the air. There it glittered so strongly that the witch had to cover her eyes, allowing the hero to capture the bird and escape with it. This heroic action satisfied Billkis that the young man was her intended mate, but her father was horrified that she would not marry wealth. The king set impossible tasks for Billkis's beloved, saying he would cut off the lad's head if anything went awry. Instead, Billkis and her lover escaped on the bird and lived happily together. (He Liyi)

Bixia Yuanjun This mountain goddess, honored by women through the early part of the twentieth century, represented untamed femininity, sometimes perceived as dangerous. Midwives and healers were devoted to her, as were young wives. Both rich and poor worshipped her, with as many as forty-seven festivals offered in her honor, most significantly her birthday, celebrated with a month of drumming and chanting. (Ferguson; Pomeranz)

Ch'ang O The Chinese moon goddess originally lived on earth, where her husband was the archer Yi. Yi killed her brother and shot an arrow into her hair to show that her life was in his control. Because of his skill, the gods gave Yi the elixir of immortality, which Ch'ang O found and drank. Then she fled to the moon, where she begged the moon hare for protection. The hare breathed out a strong wind, and the pursuing Yi was unable to mount to the sky. Ch'ang O remained in the moon, transformed into a toad. (Birrell 1993; Saso; *CCM*)

Changxi Changxi was distinct from Ch'ang O, although the two moon goddesses may have originally been the same. Changxi was mother of the twelve moons, each a different shape, that daily crossed the sky. She was an important early goddess demoted to a minor position. (Birrell 2000; Bonnefoy; *CMS*)

Chhit-niu-ma In Taiwan, this collective of birth goddesses protected children. Their festival was celebrated on the seventh day of the seventh month, when people vowed to do good works. On a child's sixteenth birthday, prayers thanked the Old Maids' protection through childhood. The weaving goddess **Chih Nu**

shared the festival. Some stories say she lived with her six unmarried sisters, connecting her with this collective. (Saso)

Chhng-Bú This Taiwanese spirit kept babies from crying at night or contracting childhood illnesses. To invoke Chhng-Bú's aid, parents filled bowls with rice and unsalted fried pork. The offerings were placed in the crib to nourish the bed spirit. (Saso)

Chih Nu One of China's most beloved goddesses wove the iridescent seamless robes of the divinities. Every year, she came to earth on the seventh day of the seventh month. On one descent, Chih Nu fell in love with the cowherd god; she spent so much time with him that heavenly robes began to tatter. The chief god moved Chih Nu to one side of the heavens, her lover to the other, allowing them one night together each year. That evening, magpies built a footbridge for the reunion. If it rained, the magpies were stranded on earth, and the lovers remained separated. Their annual mating was celebrated by women who floated dolls down streams while praying for healthy children, and by girls who played divination games. (Birrell 1993; Bonnefoy)

Ehé Tazar The Mongol primal goddess Ehé Ureng Ibi existed from primordial times as the mate of the creator god, but little is said of her role in creation. Another goddess, Ehé Tazar, appears in myth as the earth mother, who asked the high god Esege Malan for the sun and moon. Although he agreed, he could not get the luminaries down to the earth's surface. But he convinced the hedgehog god Esh to come with him to heaven to discuss the matter. When Esh arrived, however, the high god's swan-shaped daughters laughed at him, whereupon he grew furious and withdrew to wreak havoc on earth. As he was doing so, some of the high god's servants overheard him speculate about why Esege Malan did not ask the earth goddess for something equally impossible, like an echo and the warm air of summer. They returned to heaven with this information, whereupon Esege Malan descended and asked for the two items in return for the sun and moon. Ehé Tazar could not capture them, and so the sun and moon remained hers, although separate, and Esege Malan retained the echo and summer breeze. (Curtin)

Ehuang This daughter of a river god shared a husband with her sister, Nüying. When he died, Ehuang drowned herself in sorrow. The story may descend from a tradition of human sacrifice in which women shamans sacrificed themselves to prevent famine from drought or other natural disaster. (Strassberg; Yüan)

Emegelǰi Eǰi The earliest Mongolian shaman offered his deceased mother sacrifices; she became "oldest grandmother" and had charge of the dead. She could be protective or destructive, depending on circumstances. She was also known as Niduyan, "shaman woman." (Heissig)

Etugen The Mongol earth goddess derived her name from the holy mountain Otuken. Her people honored her by eating clay obtained from sites called "earths of strength." Etugen, who may have been a collective of seventy-seven goddesses, caused earthquakes by shaking to eliminate impurities. Her connection to the earth goddess Altan-Telgey is unclear. (Heissig; Bonnefoy)

Feng Pho-Pho Riding herd on the winds, the old woman Feng Pho-Pho had a tiger for a steed and clouds for her road. She brought calm days when she rounded up the winds and stuffed them into the bag she carried. Sometimes described as a male divinity, she may have been bisexual or hermaphroditic. (Werner)

Fubao Many cultures ascribe a miraculous conception to heroes, and China's Yellow Emperor was no exception. His mother, an intellectual, sat outdoors one spring night watching an unearthly light play across the sky. Soon Fubao found herself pregnant. Her child Huang-Ti gestated for two years—another common

phenomenon among heroes, who often spend more time than usual in their mother's wombs. (Bonnefoy)

Gaomei Originally a Chinese goddess whose name ("first mother") suggests a creatrix, Gaomei was transformed into a male divinity. Her name is sometimes translated as "Great Matchmaker," suggesting involvement with human fecundity. Her spring festival was dedicated to rituals for healthy offspring. As she was connected with a magical mountain also associated with **Nüwa**, these figures may be the same. (Bonnefoy)

Guanyin (Kuan Yin) Buddhism came to China in approximately the first century CE, via Tibet, bringing the merciful male bodhisattva Avalokiteśvara, who had become feminized by the twelfth century, perhaps because mercy was typically connected not with the masculine (*yang*) force but with the feminine (*ying*). Guanyin may have absorbed the iconography of an earlier goddess, perhaps Tibetan **Tārā** or the indigenous holy girl Miao Shan.

Guanyin originally lived on earth as Princess Miao Shan. Her father had prayed for a son, and Miao Shan's birth disappointed him. She yearned to become a Buddhist nun, but her father wanted her to marry a wealthy man, so he imprisoned her. But she meditated and prayed, becoming yet more saintly. Next, her father put her in a convent, where he instructed the nuns to humiliate her with menial work. Again, Miao Shan seemed unaware of discomfort. Furious, the king ordered his daughter killed, but a tiger took her to the underworld, where she saw condemned souls weeping. When she begged the king of the dead for mercy, many souls were freed.

After a lifetime of helping others, Miao Shan performed one final act of forgiveness. Her father fell ill and was told by a Buddhist monk to find his daughter. When he sent servants to her, she cut off one hand and one eye, and instructed that they be taken to the king. But the king was only half cured. So the servants came back, and Miao Shan offered up her other hand and eye. The king fell in remorse for all he had done, and Miao Shan was restored to health. After that she received illumination.

But Miao Shan refused to become a near-divine bodhisattva. Instead she retained human form, promising to stay on earth until everyone attained enlightenment. Simply to utter her name assured salvation from physical and spiritual harm. Even better was the observance of Guanyin's testimony of peace and mercy. Her worshippers eat no flesh and do no violence to other beings. Guanyin's birthday is celebrated in midsummer, when offerings of flowers and fruit decorate her altars.

Statues show her dressed in flowing garments with golden necklaces, attended by the dragon girl Lung Nu. Often she holds willows or jewels; she makes symbolic gestures of generosity and the banishment of fear. She also appears as a temple guardian, with a thousand arms or a thousand eyes, always alert. Such statues were designed as guides to meditation, but the most effective meditation was repetition of Guanyin's name.

Guanyin has for centuries been a symbol of compassion, honored in China and Japan (where, as Kwannon, she is often pictured as male) and Southeast Asia. In Vietnam, where she is called Quan Am, she lived on earth as the girl **Thi Kinh** (see Southeast Asia and Indonesia). Outside her homeland, Guanyin is honored in immigrant communities who bring her images and traditions to their new homes. This diaspora has led to an increase in non-Asian worshippers of Guanyin, including Americans drawn to Buddhist philosophy and practice. (Blofeld; Chamberlayne; Dudbridge; Kinsley; Liu; Paper; Overmyer; Palmer and Ramsay; Shahar and Weller; Sommer; Tay; Waley)

Ho Hsien-Ku The hairless maiden Ho Hsien-Ku, one of Taoism's Eight Immortals, dreamed she could gain eternal life by eating mother-of-pearl. When she did, she passed through solid objects and traveled at impossible speeds. She wandered about gathering flowers and herbs, especially mugwort. Ho Hsien-Ku never died but lived in the heavens with **Xiwang Mu**.

Another of the Eight Immortals, Lan Tstai-Ho, had indeterminate gender. Variously described as a woman and as a hermaphrodite, Lan Tstai-Ho dressed as a woman but had a male voice. She became a street musician who dressed in blue and wore one shoe. One night, intoxicated, she threw away her clothing and was lifted to heaven on a stork's wings or a cloud. Afterward, she brought delight to heavenly gatherings, carrying her flute and a basket of fruit. (Liu)

Hou Ji The Chinese goddess of millet was one of the primordial deities, the one who taught humans how to recognize food plants and to prepare them, as well as how to prepare them for sacrifices of gratitude for the earth's abundance. Although her name can indicate either a male or female divinity, Hou Ji was typically shown as a goddess, as women were connected with the fecundity she symbolized. In the late Chinese pantheon, Hou Ji was minister for agriculture. (Birrell 2000)

Hou-T'su Like most other recorded cultures, the Chinese saw earth as a female divinity ("Empress Earth"), patron of fertility, worshipped until modern times on a square marble altar in the Forbidden City, whereon the ruler offered sacrifices each summer solstice. (Birrell 1993)

Hsiao Ming Goddess of the north, "bright evening" was the daughter of the obscure goddess Teng Pi Shih and sister of Chu Kuang ("torch glare"). The two sisters may be early goddesses of moon and sun. (*CMS*)

Hsi Shih A Taoist story tells of the greatest spy of her time, a noblewoman called Hsi Shih who conspired with the minister Fan Li to free her country from oppressive rule. The noble ruler Yu Chien succumbed to arrogance and challenged a nearby lord, thereby losing his own kingdom. Held hostage, Yu Chien began to give way to despair and lures of luxury. But Fan Li helped him remember he was a king, even in captivity, and between them they plotted to escape. Their plans were helped when the beautiful Hsi Shih volunteered to become a courtesan and to seduce Yu Chien's captor. In this way, she learned about the army's strength and its strategies. After Hsi Shih negotiated the release of Yu Chien, the three traveled safely back to their country and won back the lost territories. Then Hsi Shih and Fan Li left the dangerous world of the court to go into business, with such success they are considered the patrons of entrepreneurship. (Wong)

Huang Chü chih shih The "corpse of the giant yellow woman" appears briefly in the *Classic of Mountains and Seas*, an early Chinese text, although little is said except that she lived in the wild lands to the west. She was connected to **Ch'ang O**, the moon goddess. (*CMS*)

Huaxu This heroine was one of many legendary women who became pregnant under unusual circumstances. Huaxu found a giant footprint in a marsh, home of the dragon-shaped thunder god, who fertilized her through the footprint. Huaxu gave birth to the serpent-bodied god of the heavens, Fuxi, mate of the creator goddess **Nüwa**. The same story is told of the ancestral mother of the Zhou clan, **Jiangyuan**. (Yüan; Bonnefoy)

Jiandi Chinese ancestral mothers found unusual ways to get pregnant, and Jiandi ("bamboo-slip maiden"), ancestral mother of the Yin clan, was no exception. Walking with two companions, she felt a need to bathe. She and the other maidens found a pool and, descending into it, refreshed themselves. While bathing, Jiandi saw a swallow lay an egg, which she picked up and swallowed whole. Shortly afterward, she found herself pregnant, and the child she bore was the heroic ancestor of the Yin family, one of whose clan names (Zi, "swallow") recalls the myth of Jiandi's conception. Some legends say Jiandi shared her husband, King Gao Xin, with her sister Jian Pi. (Birrell 2000, Bonnefoy; Yüan)

Jiangyuan Like other Chinese ancestral mothers, Jiangyuan ("Jiang the Originator") was a virgin mother impregnated by stepping into the toe of a giant footprint. She painlessly and bloodlessly bore a child who was the ancestor of the Zhou clan. (The same story was told of **Huaxu**, mother of the heaven god Fuxi, who stepped in the footprint of the thunder god.) Thinking the child would be unlucky due to its conception, Jiangyuan exposed him on a roadway, but cows came and gave him milk. She then tried to leave him in a forest, but woodcutters rescued him. She put her child on an icy lake, but birds nested nearby and kept him warm. Finally she accepted him as her son. Several texts describe Jiangyuan as on her way to sacrifice to the Great Matchmaker, **Gaomei**, when she found herself with child. (*CCM*; Birrell 1993, 2000; Bonnefoy; Mackenzie; Sommer)

Kang-kys The father of this Mongolian warrior was dissatisfied when a mere girl was born. In retaliation against Kang-kys's mother, he set off to seduce Saiyn-Uran, the wife of his greatest enemy. But Saiyn-Uran served Abak-Möge strong drink. While he lay passed out, his enemies raided his home, enslaving Kang-kys's mother, Angyr-Ala. A serving woman, Karbyn, hid the infant, then brought her up as a warrior.

The girl hunted, while the old woman kept house. Kang-kys turned away men, until she gained a reputation as a spirit woman. One day, horsemen kidnapped Karbyn. Kang-kys dedicated herself to finding the woman who had raised her. Magical helpers provided her with arms and a horse so she could gather her father's people and drive out the invaders.

Her enemy turned into a fox, which Kang-kys pursued. Just as she shot, an eagle swooped down, and the arrow pierced it. The eagle turned into a handsome man, who married Kang-kys. One last adventure awaited her: to find her mother and father and return with them to lead a happy life in their homeland. (Van Deusen 2000)

Lao-mu In the White Lotus tradition of Buddhism, Lao-mu was the great mother, honored with chants that call her "oh great Buddha" and "venerable mother." Ignorance caused those on earth to believe themselves separated from her, so she sent masters to teach them how to attain unity with her. Through the middle of the past century, Chinese residents in Singapore honored Lao-mu by practicing vegetarianism and sexual abstinence. Called Wu-sheng lao-mu ("venerable mother who was never begotten"), she was the mother of **Nüwa**, who with her brother gave birth to millions of children. (Overmyer)

Linshui The powerful goddess Linshui was reputedly born in either 766 CE or 904 CE and declared a goddess in the thirteenth century. She was originally the shaman Chen Jinggu, conceived when her barren mother, Lady Ge, swallowed the blood of **Guanyin**, splashed onto a leaf. When she gave birth, perfume and music filled the air. The child showed clairvoyant abilities at age four and learned to read at seven. From birth, she was devoted to Guanyin.

The girl was fated to marry Liu Qi, the reincarnation of a man who had attempted to gain Guanyin in marriage by throwing silver dust at her. Most of the dust struck her hair, turning it white, but some fell into a river, where it became a destructive serpent. This serpent was Chen Jinggu's enemy throughout her life. As a teenager, Chen Jinggu learned shamanism from a magician, after which she became more famous than her teacher. With her sister shamans Lin Jiuniang and Li Sanniang, she worked for healing and order. She was also a warrior who mastered the martial arts. The stars of Ursa Major formed her sword, and she bore a serpent-headed whip when she rode into combat.

Chen Jinggu fought the magical serpent three times. The first time, the serpent transformed itself into the semblance of the queen and threatened the king. Chen Jinggu cut it into three pieces and hid them in separate locations. One part escaped, so Chen

Jinggu had to fight it again. Finally the snake's head, disguised as a beautiful woman, forced Lui Qi into sex.

Chen Jinggu decided to marry Lui Qi, something she had refused to consider. When she was pregnant, drought struck the land. Because a pregnant woman could not shamanize, she performed an abortion on herself. She hid the fetus, intending to re-impregnate herself after rain had come. But while she was ritually dancing, the snake attacked her child and ate it. In retaliation, Chen Jinggu killed the serpent, but she herself died of a hemorrhage. In the afterlife, she retrieved her child's soul and made him a god.

Chen Jinggu is worshipped in the town of Daqiao, where her mummified body rests, together with the remains of the serpent. Her worship continues in Taiwan, brought there by migrants. In both places she is regarded as a protector of women and children. (Shahar and Weller)

Mah Ku The original figure of this name was a goddess of the east, associated with time's passage. Later, the name was used for a Taoist sage, daughter of a corrupt official who stole his people's food, demanding they work all night. Skilled in imitating animals, Mah Ku crowed like a cock at midnight, and the soldiers ended the day's work at that point, giving the exhausted workers several hours of sleep. This went on until Mah Ku's father realized the project was falling behind. Lying in wait, he discovered his daughter giving the signal, captured her, and tied her up in her room. But before he could punish her, she escaped. Hiding in the wilderness, she met a sage who taught her the secrets of immortality. (Cahill 1993)

Ma-tsu The Taiwanese island of Ma-tsu was named after this goddess of land and sea. She was holy from her earliest days, reading scripture by the age of eight and having clairvoyant visions. Once she dreamed her fishermen brothers were drowning. But they returned home safely, because as her brothers reported, Ma-tsu had appeared from nowhere to calm the waters. When she was sixteen, a spirit taught her magical incantations, permitting her to control the weather. Before being taken up to heaven, she performed miracles, including subduing demons and feeding her starving parents from the flesh of her leg.

Seafaring people cherished her, calling her Tien Fei and Tien Hou. The second name may refer to a separate figure, associated with the Buddhist dawn goddess Zhunti and the Taoist North Star goddess Doumu. Ma-tsu is honored on the mainland, but less devoutly than on Taiwan, where she remains one of the most popular divinities. (Boltz; Irwin; Ruitenbeek; Sagren; Saso)

Meng-Jiang Jyu This Chinese heroine was born miraculously. Two neighboring families, both childless, found a watermelon halfway between their homes. Within it was a magical girl, whom the families decided to raise jointly, bearing the names of both families, Meng and Jiang. Meng-Jiang, a good girl, made both sets of parents happy. When she came to marry, she found a young man from the village who cherished her. All went well until one summer day, when the emperor's soldiers came and conscripted Meng-Jiang's husband to build the Great Wall.

Months passed and, worried her husband would be cold without winter clothes, Meng-Jiang set off to find him. She walked, asking everyone for her lover, but each village sent her farther on. She almost drowned crossing the Yellow River, but the river god became sympathetic to her cause and saved her. Finally, she reached her destination, only to find that her beloved husband had died and his bones had been interred somewhere in the Wall. She cried out to heaven, and the Wall collapsed—revealing thousands of bones. How could she find her husband's? Recalling their vow to be blood of each other's blood, she bit herself and, bleeding, walked among the bones. Her husband's bones recognized and absorbed her blood, so she was able to give them a proper burial. (Chin et al; Sanders; Thompson)

Mifei Daughter of the god of the east, Mifei drowned in the Lo River, of which she was then made tutelary goddess. She had been gathering mushrooms and feathers on the riverbanks with her attendants when the river god saw her and fell in love. In order to keep her to himself, he drowned her. But he was a fickle lover who soon left the girl to seduce others.

Mifei appeared through historical times on riverbanks, luring men and causing them to fall in love with her. A famous poem of the third century BCE, by Qu Yuan, addressed her as the "bright fairy" who always turned away from her suitors, no matter how rich their offerings. Whether this fairy woman represents a vestigial early goddess or a late allegory is not clear. (Cahill 1985; Liu; Schafer; Yüan)

Moye Threatened with death unless they forged a perfect sword, the smith Moye and her husband Ganjiang set to work. Ganjiang gathered iron and gold from five mountains and ten directions but was unable to use the metals until Moye remembered transformation requires sacrifice. She ordered 300 young people to operate a bellows while she leaped into the furnace. Ganjiang cast a famous sword bearing her name from the resulting metal. (Bonnefoy)

Mulan When Mulan was a girl, the imperial army took away one man from every family. Because Mulan's elderly father was the family's only male, the forces planned to take him, until Mulan appeared dressed as a boy. She became a renowned warrior, later, a general. After she defeated the empire's foes, she returned to her family home, where, as her men celebrated, she withdrew and dressed herself again as a woman. Her men-at-arms were stunned to realize that their brilliant general was a woman. (Liu)

Na Bo Nok'o A confusing tale of the Ch'uan Miao, ethnic people of southern Szechuan, tells of a woman of this name who sewed up the sky, then brought out the "sister sun," a goddess who had to go through a cave before coming out in the sky. (Graham)

Ntse Among the Miao, this ancestral goddess gave birth to the first people when, after a flood, only a brother and sister were left. They entered a drum and were carried up to the sky. When they returned to earth, they had to mate in order to repopulate it. (Overmyer)

Nü Ch'i The priestess Nü Ch'i guarded sacred places between two rivers. She was connected to several obscure figures: Nü Mieh, the girl destroyer who lived in the western wilderness; and the blazingly hot Nü Chi'en. Although only a vestigial myth describes her significance, Nü Chi was an important early creatrix. (*CMS*; Yüan)

Nü Chou The old woman Nü Chou periodically sacrificed herself so that waters would never rise above the land. Her crab-like body resulted from these self-immolations, from which she returned with deformed hands. She wore green, to signify the rebirth that occurred from her sacrifice. (Birrell 1993; Strassberg; *CMS*)

Nü Pa This goddess dried up rivers, sending famine and disease to the people of the watershed. When her father fought the war god, Nü Pa was his secret weapon, for she destroyed the rain god. The effort trapped her on earth, where her anger brought pain to humans. She could be sent away with rituals and prayers that asked, "Goddess, go north." (Birrell 2000; Yüan)

Nü Shih "Girl corpse" has little place in Chinese mythology except as the source of an aphrodisiac plant called the dodder, a parasitic plant in the morning glory family, into which she was transformed when she died. Anyone who ate the dodder plant became immediately sexually irresistible. Nü Shih was said to live in the central part of the world. (*CMS*)

Nüwa Nüwa, and her mate and brother, the heavenly god Fuxi, were depicted as snakes whose tails entwined. Because of the depth of her marriage bond, Nüwa was hailed as the Divine Matchmaker Shenmei. She was a force of reproduction, able to create the universe through self-transformation, with ten gods being born from her intestines.

Nüwa made the first human beings in her image from Yellow River clay. At first, she carefully molded them to look like her, but with legs instead of a dragon's tail. Finding this tedious, Nüwa dipped a rope into clay and shook it so that drops splattered onto the ground. Thus two types of beings were born: from the molded figures, nobles; from the clay drops, peasants.

When a dragon shook heaven out of alignment, Nüwa restored order by melting multicolored stones to rebuild the sky. She found pebbles from the Yellow and Yangtze Rivers in five primary colors, so heaven's arch would include all necessary elements. She melted these pebbles together, then mended the sky so that the damage cannot be seen. Finding other problems caused by the dragon's rebellion, Nüwa set about correcting them. She cut off the toes of a giant tortoise and used them to mark the compass's points; she burned reeds to ashes, using them to dam the flooding rivers. She also established marriage rites so children would be raised well. She invented the flute, for which she is considered goddess of music. Order restored, Nüwa retreated to the sky, or perhaps disintegrated into a thousand sprites that remain on earth. Among Chinese immigrants to Japan, Nüwa was known as Jokwa. (Birrell 1993, 2000; Ferguson; Irwin; Jungsheng; Bonnefoy; Yüan; *CCM*; Overmyer; Schafer; *CMS*)

Nuxiu The ancestral mother of the Chin people, who gave their name to China, she became pregnant miraculously when she ate an egg dropped from the sky by a black bird. The child born from this pregnancy was the first ruler of the Qin dynasty. The story is almost identical to that told of another ancestral mother, **Jiandi**, except the latter conceived in a magical mulberry forest, while Nuxiu was weaving when she was granted the magical impregnating egg. (Bonnefoy)

O Nü An early goddess described in the Chinese text *Classic of Mountains and Seas*, O Nü was the daughter of Lei Zu, the thunder goddess. Her name means "lovely girl," and she was the mother of a hero. Another figure with this name also goes by Yüan-fu ("liaison wife") and was the mother of culture-bringing gods. (*CMS*)

Pao Sze This dragon maiden was born when a box of dragon foam fell open at the king's court and a black lizard crept out, impregnating a local girl by the touch of its skin. When the girl exposed her strangely conceived infant, a childless couple found her and were delighted to have a child to rear. But they heard that the court magicians had discerned the existence of the dragon's daughter, so they escaped with her to the nearby kingdom of Pao, where they offered the child to the king, who reared her to become his consort. In doing so, he set aside his first queen, Chen, and their son, installing Pao Sze's son as crown prince instead.

Pao Sze was beautiful but strangely sad. The king tried everything to bring a smile to her lips, although she constantly warned him not to do so. With a practical joke, he forced her to laugh, but the joke turned serious when an enemy invaded the unprepared palace and killed the king, taking Pao Sze prisoner. They could not hold her; she turned into a dragon and escaped. (Visser; Liu; Mackenzie)

Ren A Chinese folktale tells of a girl named Ren who met a handsome but poor boy named Zheng. She invited him into her home at the edge of town and then into her bed. The next day, he tried to find out more about her, but the shopkeepers told him there were no houses where he had been, just a wilderness filled with foxes. When he saw her again in the market, she hid from him, for she was ashamed that he knew her secret. But he was persistent in courting her, and so they married. He prospered and became rich. Years later, Zheng wanted Ren to travel to the capital with him, but she refused, saying it would be bad luck. He teased her into going against her instincts, but along the way hounds set upon the two. Instantly Ren turned back into a fox and tried to outrun the dogs, but they caught her and ripped her to shreds. Zheng spent the rest of his years grieving for his beautiful fox wife. (Liu; Sanders)

Shui-mu Niang-Niang Although most river divinities in China were male, there are exceptions, including Shui-mu Niang-Niang, "old woman of the waters," who ruled the region around the old city of Ssu-chou, which sank beneath her waters in 1574 CE. She had threatened it for years and regularly flooded it, but the people did not move. Even a request by the Lord of Heaven did not change her mind. He tried to trick her out of her attempts to flood the city, by sending a magical donkey to drink her pails of water, but she saw through the ruse and knocked over one bucket, which was filled with the water of several lakes. The lake that now covers the city is called Hung-tse. (Werner)

Sun Pu-erh Called a goddess in some Taoist texts, Sun Pu-erh was the only woman among the seven most renowned Taoist masters. She was wed to Ma Tan-yang (sometimes called her brother), with whom she lived a celibate life so both could attain immortality through the secret alchemy of desire. When even that nonsexual relationship stood in her way, she threw cold water into a wok full of hot oil and did not step back when the oil flew everywhere. Her beauty thus defaced, she was accepted into the highest ranks of alchemical students and learned to unite yin and yang within her.

Disguised as a madwoman, she then traveled the countryside, begging for food and sleeping in caves. Despite her disguise, she attracted the attention of two rapists, who tried to assault her. As they moved toward her, the heavens opened and huge hailstones fell, incapacitating the instigator while leaving his more reluctant companion untouched. News of the heavenly protection spread, and from then on Pu-erh lived peacefully and safely, concentrating on her spiritual practices. (Sommer)

T'ai-hsüan Nü A woman of magical powers, this Taoist sage decided to study magic after it was predicted she would have a short life. A widow with one son, she devoted herself to occult arts until her son was old enough to have his own family. Then she went into the wilderness to refine her craft. She was able to melt snow with a glance, to cause avalanches with a wave of her hand, and to blow out forest fires with her breath. She lived for 200 years before flying into the sky and becoming a heavenly immortal. (Wong)

T'ai-yin Nü Because she could not find a teacher of the arts of immortality, T'ai-yin Nü set out to learn them for herself. She worked in a wineshop while she studied and watched for a teacher. Finally she met a man who spoke mystic riddles. She closed her shop and went to his hermitage, where he shared the secrets she had hoped to learn. It took many years before she could make the elixir of immortality. Although she was over 200 years old when she drank it, she still looked like a young woman. (Wong)

T'ai Yuan This Chinese saint lived on clouds in the mountains and remained celibate until the age of forty, by which time she had become androgynous as well as ethereal, living only on the nourishment provided by cloud vapor. A beam of light, wandering by, saw the shining "Great Original" and penetrated her uterus. Twelve years later T'ai Yuan gave birth, through her spinal cord, to a heroic child who became ruler of the underworld. (Colegrave)

T'ang Kuang-chen When T'ang Kuang-chen was small, she attracted the attention of the immortals. They offered her the chance to live in the heavens, but she declined because she had to care for her mother. With magical pills provided by the immortals, she lived for years without feeling heat or cold, hunger or thirst. When her mother died, T'ang Kuang-chen mounted a giant toad and rode to heaven. (Wong)

Tien-Hou She was born Mei Chou, the sister of four sailors. One day she fell into a trance, frightening her parents. They tried everything to break the spell and at last succeeded, much to Mei Chou's anger. Soon afterward, three brothers returned home with the news that the fourth had been lost at sea. They too would have drowned, they said, had not their sister walked across the water to save them. Mei Chou was elevated to heaven as Tien-Hou, Empress of Heaven. Not to be confused with **Xiwang Mu**, Tien-Hou was an ocean goddess who rode across the sky on clouds, consulting wind servants to find sailors in danger and hastening to their rescue. Her associate Chun T'i, all-knowing Taoist goddess of light, was depicted with eight hands, two of which held the sun and the moon. (Ferguson; Irwin)

Tien-Mu To make lightning, this Chinese goddess flashed mirrors at each other; from their intersecting rays, lightning shot out. She was depicted wearing bright robes of blue and green, red and white. Her companion, the thunder goddess Lei Zu, brought silk cultivation to China. (Birrell 2000)

Tou-Mou The Chinese goddess of the polestar, the "Bushel Mother," was the judge of all peoples, keeping records of their lives and deaths. In addition, she was heaven's scribe, keeping a tally of all the divinities, their duties, and their various estates in the nine heavens. Both Buddhists and Taoists honored her. She is the Taoist parallel to the Buddhist divinity of mercy, **Guanyin**, and looked upon human failings with a sympathetic heart. She was depicted seated on a lotus throne, with three eyes to see everything and eighteen arms to offer aid. (Werner)

Ts'an Nü A family whose father had been missing for a year promised a young daughter to whoever could bring him home. A horse did so, and the parents felt that they should keep their vow, but the girl refused. When the horse demanded payment, the father shot and skinned it. But as the girl walked past the horse's hide, it spirited her away. Days later, the hide was found beneath a mulberry tree; the girl, turned into a silkworm, was spinning silk threads. Shortly thereafter the parents saw their daughter flying on the horse through the sky, having become a goddess for her invention. Another tale says that a legendary empress, Hsi-Ling Shih, invented silk and the culture of silkworms, which she taught to her people. (Miller)

Tushan This earth goddess plays a lesser part in Chinese mythology than does her daughter, whose name is not recorded. Tushan's daughter was an eager wife to Yu, a great human leader; she was the first poet to compose love songs. Tushan and her daughter are sometimes confused in the texts, which refer to Yu having relations with Tushan herself. (Birrell 1993; Bonnefoy)

Wa According to Chinese writings from the first century CE, this was the name of a divine woman who, in ancient times, "produced the ten thousand beings through metamorphosis." It is difficult to tell exactly how this creator goddess populated the world— whether she transformed parts of herself into other beings, or transformed rocks, clay, or other substances, as mother goddesses in other cultures did. Her name appears as a syllable in **Nüwa**, the name of another creator goddess. She may also be the same as the goddess sometimes called **Gaomei**. (Bonnefoy)

Wengu The beautiful Bai woman Wengu was as hard-working as she was pretty. Many young men in her region looked at her with thoughts of marriage, but one poor but loyal man, the woodcutter Xianga, won her heart with his beautiful singing. Whenever he passed her home, carrying wood to market, he would sing the most lovely songs, and soon Wengu arranged to meet him near the place called the Bottomless Pond,

a clear deep pool. There they exchanged words of love and pledges to marry.

But a tyrannical ruler, hearing of the beautiful girl, decided to take Wengu as his concubine. He found her and murdered her father, who tried to protect her. Wengu fled to the Bottomless Pond, where she met her assailant with firm resolve. Despite his attempt to win her, first with bribes, then with torture, she refused to go with him. Nonetheless, the tyrant took her prisoner and dragged her to his palace.

Xianga heard of the kidnapping and bravely found his way to the tyrant's palace, where he freed Wengu. They ran for safety, but soon the tyrant's soldiers were in pursuit. Capturing the couple on the edge of the Bottomless Pond, the soldiers prepared to take them back, Wengu to be raped, Xianga to be executed. But the couple turned and leaped into the pond and drowned. The people, finally enraged by the tyrant's abuse, rose up and killed him. And the next day, from the center of the Bottomless Pond, two butterflies flew out, then hundreds more. Afterward, the pond was called the Spring of Butterflies; to this day, it is always surrounded by the flashing wings of butterflies. (He Liyi)

Wu Lo This goddess, who looked like a cat wearing earrings, offered fertility to women who approached her. Most girls conceived after visiting her. She also endowed visitors with sexual charisma so they became irresistible to lovers. (*CMS*)

Xihe There were once ten suns that appeared, one after the other, in a ten-day cycle. Each day, Xihe bathed one of them, then hung him in a mulberry tree to dry. It was difficult to remember in which order to bathe the suns, so Xihe established the calendar. But the multiple suns broiled the earth. The archer Yi brought down nine of the suns, leaving only the one whose chariot was driven by Xihe herself. Late Chinese mythology turned this goddess into two male gods, Xi and He, and put them in charge of the Board of Astronomy. Another goddess, whose connection with Xihe is unclear, is the similarly named

Hsü ("exhalation"), who lived in the west, where she received the setting sun. (Birrell 2000; Bonnefoy; *CCM*; *CMS*)

Xiwang Mu In 1986, an archaeological find exposed figures from Liaoning province that looked like a goddess described in old Chinese texts, pregnant and surrounded by dragons, birds, and tortoises. The figurines have been dated to 3000 BCE. Since that find, scholars have examined early writings to find suggestions that Xiwang Mu may descend from ancient cultures of China, although her period of greatest fame was the T'ang dynasty (618–907), when she was the most significant Taoist goddess.

In her most ancient form, Xiwang Mu was a wild-haired human-faced female with tiger's teeth and a leopard's tail. She lived in a cave where three-footed birds fed her and from which she sent disease and death. She controlled the world's water, withholding or loosing floods. This early form of Xiwang Mu has been interpreted as a goddess of wilderness. She has also been called a goddess of shamans, because of the headdress and tiger's teeth she wore, both associated with shamanic costume.

Later, Xiwang Mu appeared as an ageless woman dispensing peaches that, mixed with ashes of mulberry trees, cured human disease. She lived with her sister, attended upon by the deities of immortality. On remote Jade Mountain, Xiwang Mu lived in a golden palace where, every 3,000 years, she threw herself a birthday party. On that occasion a peach tree ripened, providing the fruit of immortality. Three green birds and a nine-tailed fox served her. Her messenger was the bluebird and her familiar, the long-lived tortoise. Depictions of Xiwang Mu from the fourth century CE show her acting like human royalty.

Xiwang Mu was goddess of female energy, the essence of *yin* and the ruler of individual female beings. As goddess of the west, she was associated with the setting sun, the waning moon, autumn, the death of a soul into afterlife. Imported to Japan, this goddess was called Sieobo. (Cahill 1986, 1993; Dubs; Ferguson; Irwin; Bonnefoy; Ching and Guisso; *CMS*; Wu)

Yaoji (Yao-Ji, Yao-chi.) This goddess, "Jasper Lady" or "Turquoise Concubine," was a happy girl who died young and, rather than descend to the underworld, reincarnated herself in a tree that bore fruit that made beautiful anyone who ate it. She was worshipped in the form of a sacred rock at the summit of the Mount of the Sorceress (Mount Wushan), where she was seen as the mist rising at dawn. Rain on Mount Wushan was said to be Yaoji's tears, as she wept for her brief life. According to legend, a king encountered her in a dream, revealing not only her name but also the location of a plant to be used in love magic. She was also called Yunhua Furen, "Blossoming Lady of the Clouds." She was probably a Taoist invention rather than an indigenous goddess. (Birrell 1993; Schafer; Yüan; Kaltenmark)

Yin Wu-Ch'ang If you died after the age of fifty, your name was recorded on the heavenly rolls by this goddess or ghost; her consort wrote down the names of those who died before that age. (Katz)

KOREAN PANTHEON

Arirang Beautiful Arirang, daughter of a magistrate, attracted the obsessive interest of her father's servant Hong Ki Sam. He lured her to a secluded spot, where he sprang upon her. When Arirang fought him, Hong Ki Sam stabbed her to death and hid her body in a bamboo grove. Her grieving parents, unable to find their daughter and unaware that she had been murdered, left the area.

The new magistrate died on the first night in Arirang's old home. Rumors spread that her ghost had frightened him to death. The post stood vacant until a young man agreed to take it on. His first night he encountered a ghost with a knife protruding from her breast. Although frightened, the young magistrate noticed Arirang carried three red flags with her. The next morning, he asked whether there was anyone in the village named Hong Ki Sam, which means "three red flags." He was summoned, and Arirang's still-bleeding body was discovered in the bamboo grove. The story, altered to disguise the original rape theme, became a popular folk song. (Tae-Hung Ha)

Aryong-Jong "Lady of Dragon Palace" controlled the rainfall. In times of drought, shamans poured water through a sieve on the parched soil so Aryong-Jong would open the clouds. (Grayson 2001)

Hae-Soon This sun goddess lived with her mother and two sisters in an isolated valley. One morning the mother went to market, warning the girls not to open the door, for the land was full of tigers. But the woman was eaten by a tigress, who then tried to pass herself off to the children as their mother. The girls ran out the back door and climbed a tree. The tigress followed, discovering them when they giggled. She demanded that they come down, but they refused. She tried to climb the tree but could not.

So she got an axe to carve steps into the tree. Terrified, the children called to heaven. As the tigress reached the treetop, the girls grabbed a heavenly golden chain. The tigress called for help, and a rotten straw rope descended. She grabbed hold, only to be smashed to death when the rope broke. In heaven the girls were given duties: Hae-Soon, to ride the sun, Dae-Soon, the moon, and Byul-Soon, a star. (Zong In-Sob; Kim Yol-gyn)

Huang Jini The daughter of a dancer and a nobleman, Huang Jini was raised to be artistic and cultured. Engaged to a young nobleman, she was heartbroken when his parents objected to a half noble. So she became a renowned entertainer, taking her former fiancé as her first lover. She lived a long and illustrious life, writing poetry and composing songs about her triumphs and tragedies. (Tae-Hung Ha)

MaGo One of the oldest Korean texts, the *BuDoZhi* (City of Heaven's Ordinance), describes the world as created by MaGo, mother earth. Dating to the fourth century CE, the *BuDoZhi* was written by Bak-Zhe Sang, a scholar and librarian of the Silla dynasty, as part of an encyclopedia of scientific and cultural knowledge. The book was hidden for centuries, until it was discovered in the early twentieth century by a descendant of the author, Bak-Gum. After thirty years of effort, he was in the process of publishing it when war broke out. In a refugee camp, Bak-Gum wrote down what he had memorized and published it by mimeograph. Most of the copies disappeared, but one was retranslated into modern Korean in 1986.

It tells how, in the time before time, only music existed. From this sound came forth MaGo and the City of Heaven's Ordinance, her material essence, of which human cities are but a pale echo. MaGo was beyond all dualities. She gave birth parthenogenetically to GungHee ("vault lady") and SoHee ("nest lady"), who each gave birth to four children, two sons and two daughters. These divinities were charged with maintaining order through musical tones. MaGo then pulled her city into the water beneath the heavens, where it spread through the clouds and created matter. The city began to rotate, and through the combination of motion and music, the earth came into being.

This universe was not stable; it disappeared suddenly and just as suddenly reappeared. To stabilize the universe, MaGo ordered her grandchildren to give birth to humans. The children of GungHee and SoHee paired up and each created six children, in pairs of male and female. Within a few generations, 3,000 descendants lived in the goddess's city, all sages who could hear the tones of heaven. They lived on pure water of MaGo's streams, until a man named ZhiSo ate grapes that hung over his balcony. After that, the people ate the beautiful fruits of the city and, as a result, grew teeth and developed poisonous saliva. Death came to the city from ZhiSo's action, for shame of which he departed with the other flesh eaters and hid in the wild world outside.

But some of the outcasts came back and, trying to find a way back into the city, diverted the streams that fed its residents. The city's leader taught the people how to live on kudzu and sent them away. MaGo set to work with her two daughters to repair the damage. But as they diverted heavenly streams to cleanse the city, the overflow fell to earth and caused a flood that destroyed many of the city's former inhabitants. After this, MaGo retreated from humanity. Whether this text indicates a goddess-centered ancient religion in Korea is a subject of scholarly dispute. (Yun 2003)

Mama The smallpox goddess left spirit footprints, which appeared as pimples, on the bodies of those she visited. If children talked while in the grip of fever, it was her voice. The ritual to send away Mama began five days after infection, when poxes appeared. Clean drinking water was employed to ritually welcome her spirit. Conducted by a woman shaman, the preventive ceremony continued through the twelfth day, when the patient was no longer in danger; then Mama was sent away on a mugwort mount. (Covell 1983)

Pali Kongju This princess was the ancestor of all shamans. Her father, King Upbi, had decided to marry despite predictions of misfortune. When she was born, seventh in a steady line of daughters, he demanded she be thrown into the ocean—whence her name, "princess thrown away." The queen put her in a jewel box, which soldiers threw into the sea, where golden turtles rose to carry it away. The princess was brought to shore, where she was adopted by a peasant couple. She grew to be a happy, loving daughter.

Meanwhile, the king and queen were stricken with a wasting illness from which diviners said they could recover only if Pali Kongju brought medicinal water from the Western Sky. Dutiful Pali Kongju set out and found the ugly guardian of the well of heaven, who told her he would release the water in return for money. The princess had no money, so she married the god and bore him seven sons. He gave her the water, and she set off for home.

She arrived too late, for her parents' funeral was under way. She sprinkled them, which brought them back to life. They wished to shower her with gifts and love, but she realized duty demanded that she return to the world beyond so she could help others in need. Taking her seven sons, she disappeared. This story is found in parts of China where there was an ancient tradition of women shamans, as well as in Korea. Alternate versions describe Pali Kongju's first shamanic journey as to the underworld in search of her dead brother, whom she brought back to life. (Carpenter; Covell 1983; Tai-Dong Lee)

Ryuhwa Her jealous father, the god of waters, held Ryuhwa captive so that no man would have access to her. But sunlight entered her room and impregnated her. From this intercourse, she laid an egg, which her father threw to a dog. The dog would not eat it, so the man gave it to a pig, which refused it. He tossed it onto a road, but horses walked around it rather than crush it. He abandoned it in a field, but birds sheltered it with their wings. Giving up, he gave it back to his daughter, who hatched it into the archer god Cumong. (Grayson 2001)

Samshin Halmoni Three goddesses of birth were celebrated at birthday parties with offerings of rice, wine, and soy sauce, laid out like a dinner. When a woman wished to conceive, she shared rice with a recently delivered mother or wore a piece of cloth that had been placed on a coffin. At times, these grandmothers were converted to male "buddhas" in paintings, but oral tradition said they were born triplets from one mother, T'ang Kum Agassi, a shaman descended from the heavens. Seduced by a monk, she was threatened by her brothers with death for dishonoring the family. She gave birth in a cave and was freed by her mother. (Covell 1984; *KF*)

Ungnyeo The bear woman Ungnyeo lived in the mountains with a tiger. Both prayed to become human and were answered by a voice instructing them to eat twenty-one garlic cloves and stay out of the sun for twenty-one days. Eating the garlic was easy, but staying in a cave for three weeks was not. The tiger did not even make it to the halfway mark before he bolted into the sun. But the bear remained in the cave and, when she walked out, she had become a beautiful woman. Because she was not born human, she could find no husband. Finally she caught the attention of Han Woon, the king of spirits. His breath caused her to conceive, and she gave birth to the first king of Korea. (Carpenter; Grayson 2001; Olmstead)

Yŏ-sansin These mountain spirits guarded specific hills and mountains, which bore their names. Few Korean mountains carry male names, suggesting that such eminences were understood as female. Mount Unje was ruled by the spirit of the same name, to whom prayers were offered during droughts, so clouds would gather on her heights. Some stories say Lady Unje was a queen who, after giving birth on the mountain, was transmogrified into a spirit; women seeking aid in conceiving a son prayed to her. (Grayson 2001, 1996)

CIRCUMPOLAR NORTH

The vast circumpolar north is home to many distinct cultures. While rich with food during the brief summers, the land is harsh in winter, when animals must be hunted under an omnipresent threat of severe weather. Circumpolar cultures center on the need for a strong relationship with nature, often embodied in a divine "food dish," a goddess who provides nourishment for humanity.

The circumpolar people also share a tradition known by the Siberian Tungus word "shaman." Shamanism is found in many cultures, but the circumpolar lands are home to the unique form whereby shamans are called by an initiatory experience. As part of initiation, the shaman-to-be encounters and often "marries" spirits that agree to be guides. Thereafter, the shaman serves as healer and visionary leader.

Women as well as men have historically gone through the challenging initiation. However, many modern commentators discount women practitioners as anomalous. Male shamans often practice wearing women's attire, while women shamans rarely engage in similar cross-dressing. In addition, shamanism emphasizes the importance of goddesses or female powers. Shamans visit the food-giving goddess, appeasing her when humans break spiritual laws. She especially needs to be propitiated when animals have been needlessly or cruelly killed.

In the tripartite shamanic world, humans live in the middle world, from which a river descends to a lower world inhabited by immortal women. From the middle world rises a tree whose branches reach the upper world. Souls perch there until time for rebirth, when they drop through smoke holes into tents, enter the hearth fire, and find a womb. Shamans rise into the upper world to reclaim lost souls, travel through the middle world to see distant events, and descend to the lower world to reaffirm the order of creation. The lower world is home to goddesses and ancestral mothers, which causes Russian theorists to hypothesize that ancient Siberian culture was mother centered.

Given the vast geographical areas in question and the many different languages spoken, the circumpolar people should not be considered as having a single culture or religion. Northern Asia is home to five distinct cultures: Finno-Ugric, Altaic, Turkic, Tungus-Manchu, and Paleo-Arctic. The influence of Buddhism, Manichaeism, and Islam on these peoples has meant the loss of some goddess traditions, but a number remain accessible in folklore and ritual.

In North America, the common term "Eskimo" covers many cultures, including Inupiaq (northern Alaska), Yu'pik (southwestern Alaska), Siberian Yu'pik or Yuik (Gambell Island, Russian far east), and Inuit (Canada); the last is sometimes incorrectly used as a generic term, in the way "Eskimo" used to be. Most groups traditionally earned their living from the sea, for while the land is barren, the seas teem with fish and mammals. Thus the food goddess was envisioned as living below the ocean.

Arctic life was ruled by a series of taboos that have, in recent years, been typically forgotten or ignored. No longer are women required to live separately after giving birth or to abstain from meat for a year afterward. But while Christianization resulted in persecution and suppression of native religions, recent years have brought some recovery.

CIRCUMPOLAR NORTH PANTHEON

Aakuluujjusi The Inuit creatrix made animals from her clothes. First she set her trousers on the ground, creating caribou, and gave them tusks. When she threw her jacket down, it turned into a walrus; she placed antlers on its head. The animals kept attacking people who tried to hunt them, so Aakuluujjusi made some revisions, swapping horns and tusks. The walrus were then perfect, but the caribou were too quick for hunters. So Aakuluujjusi turned their belly hair around. Afterward, those hairs caught on the wind and slowed the creatures. (Bonnefoy)

Ajysyt Among the Siberian Yakuts, this birth goddess kept laboring women safe and breathed souls into the newborn. Women held secret ceremonies glorifying Ajysyt after a birth. For three days the birthing woman remained sequestered with women friends; a man's presence would have been sacrilege. Then the midwife tied straw from the birthing bed atop a tree. Ajysyt was also divinity of domestic animals. (Levin and Potapov; Motz)

Albys This fearsome spirit of the Tuvan, a Turkic Siberian people, appeared as a long-haired woman with no back. She lurked in lonely places, singing to attract people, after which she drove them mad. (Van Deusen)

Anoritoq The only son of this Eskimo woman used to cut off the hands of members of his own hunting party, to keep them from catching game. In retaliation, they killed him. This left Anoritoq with no hunter in the family, so she asked the hunters to bring her the fetus of the next pregnant bear they killed. They did so, and Anoritoq raised it as her own child. When the bear was ready to hunt, the village hunters killed it. Anoritoq turned to stone with grief. A variant tale says Anoritoq asked the bear people for a stepchild, which they gave her. When the bear was grown, she marked it with soot so hunters would not mistake it for another bear, but they killed it anyway. She sang "a bear, a bear, a bear," over and over until she turned to stone. People rubbed animal fat on that stone when they wished to hunt bears successfully. (Holtved)

Apasinasee Once, the Inuit of Hudson Bay say, a haughty young woman refused all the men in her village until her father angrily suggested, considering her behavior, that the family dog was a proper mate. The next day the dog disappeared, and a handsome young man dressed in dog-skin clothing arrived and slept with Apasinasee. Soon the young woman gave birth to a litter of puppies, so noisy that Apasinasee's father carried parents and children across the river.

Apasinasee's father provided for them, sending meat tied around the dog's neck until, tired of the effort, he substituted rocks and the dog drowned. Left without support, Apasinasee sent her children away. One group traveled inland, where they became giants; another, living on the coast, became dwarfs. Some she put into a ship; they disappeared. A few stayed, becoming the Inuit.

Another story says that ancestral mother Uinigumasuittuq bore puppies to the family dog and, when her father drowned him, instructed her half-dog children to kill their grandfather; then she sent them away so they would not be killed in retaliation. She packed the first puppies into a boot and sent them south, where they became the white people. The others became ancestors of the native peoples. She stayed in the area, refusing human suitors but finding a second husband among the seabirds. Some scholars connect this story with **Sedna**. (Kroeber; Motz)

Arnakuak This shaman woman could change her shape at will, so she became a man in order to seduce her daughter-in-law, Ukuamak. When the two ran off together, Arnakuak's son followed them and killed his mother. (Rink)

Asiaq In Greenland, this mother of weather determined when and how much snow would fall. Shamans called upon her in spring, for if ice did not break up in a timely fashion, migrating sea mammals could not return. If she was happy, Asiaq sent rains to melt the spring ice. (Osterman 1938)

Bugady Enintyn Her name, to the Siberian Evenks, combines "sky" with "universe" and "homeland." Mother of the clan, Bugady Enintyn lived beneath sacred rocks or in the roots of sacred trees, sometimes in the shape of an elderly woman, sometimes as a reindeer or elk. Another goddess, Bugady Mušun, was the mother of animals, envisioned as a very old, strong woman or as a huge female elk or reindeer. She was worshipped at rocks shaped like petrified animals. (Bonnefoy; Malandra; Nahodil)

Chiti khys This mountain spirit of the southern Siberian Khakass people was once a mountain who fell in love with another mountain, named Mindir ("hail"). A larger mountain, Ir taskhyl ("man mountain"), wanted her for himself. She refused, and in retaliation Ir taskhyl hit her so hard that she broke into seven pieces. The mountain now has seven peaks. (Kazachinova and Van Deusen)

Chuginadak The Aleuts said that Mount Cleveland was once a woman who refused to marry any man except one who shot rosy finches. Chuginadak walked across water until she came to a village where she saw the man she wanted. She called to him, and they embraced. When they parted, the man lay dead.

Chuginadak retreated to a cave to mourn. When the village chief found the body of his son, he enlisted several old women to divine the murderer. Then he sent armies of warriors and magical spirits against Chuginadak, but no one could conquer her. Finally, a fox spirit convinced her to explain her deed. When Chuginadak did so, the chief realized that she loved his son. He danced and sang until the body rose. Then the old chief passed leadership to his son, and Chuginadak became his wife. (Jochelson)

Dja minju The Enet earth goddess turned so fast that people were dizzy. During a council, Dja minju suggested dropping heavy stones around the world. The rocks became mountains, which slowed the earth. After this, Dja minju created genitals for the first man and woman. As such, she was the goddess of childbirth; women carried egg-shaped stones that represented her. (Dioszegi and Hoppal)

Dunne Enin To the Siberian Tungus and Evenks, Dunne Enin ruled clan territory. Whenever camp was broken, she received an offering of old cloth, a bit of ribbon, or a broken bowl. Women asked her permission when a new camp was established, a new tent erected, or a new fire lit. She set rules of community behavior and enforced them by withholding game. Should that occur, an individual offered black and white ribbons on trees near the tent. If this offering did not satisfy Dunne Enin, a shaman traveled to her, begging that she look kindly on her children. At first she resisted, but she released the food animals if **Bugady Enintyn** agreed. (Michael; Bonnefoy; Malandra)

Emengender Among Altaic peoples, limbless images of Emengender were made from everyday materials such as cloth or wood, with a face and eyes made from beads. Women kept these figures near them when they gave birth, for children were stillborn or blind without Emengender's help. People also prayed to the figures in cases of illness or danger. Among Yakuts, the dolls appeared on shamans' costumes. (Motz; Dioszegi)

Irdlirvirisissong The crazy cousin of the sun goddess **Malina**, this clownish dancer lived in the sky with the moon. She kept dogs who waited for people to die so they could eat the intestines. When shamans came to visit the moon in trance, she tried to make them laugh until they dried up inside, after which she ate them. (Kroeber)

Irt A mountain spirit of the Siberian Khakass people, Irt had red-brown hair, which she wore in two braids. In place of legs, she had snakes, so she was considered the protector of reptiles as well as of rivers. (Kazachinova and Van Deusen)

Ja-Neb'a To Siberian Samoyeds, Ja-Neb'a was mother of animals and of humanity. Among the nearby Udegeis, the same goddess was Sangia-Mama; among the Nasnai, Sengi-Mama. Statues of these goddesses were covered with the blood of animals to encourage her to provide more game. (Dioszegi)

Kadlu When she was a girl, the Eskimo thunder goddess played so noisily that her parents told her and her sisters to go outside. There they invented a game in which Kadlu jumped on hollow ice, causing thunder; Kweetoo rubbed flint stones together to create lightning, and another sister urinated so profusely that she created rain. Transported to the sky, the girls lived in a whalebone house, wearing no clothing but blackening their faces with soot. In some areas, women averted thunderstorms, or created them, by leaving offerings for the trinity of weather goddesses: needles, bits of ivory, old pieces of sealskin. (Holtved; Rasmussen 1921)

Kaja é The sun goddess of the Siberian Enets and Nenets was a maternal force who retreated every winter to a home beyond the horizon. White reindeer with spots on their sides, sacred to the goddess, were permitted to graze freely until they died. If someone grew ill, a reindeer was sacrificed and its head hung across the room from the sickbed. (Dioszegi and Hoppal)

Kasum Naj-Ekva The ancestral goddess of the Siberian Mansi wore pendants in the form of birds, which jingled as she walked. Massively powerful, she could kill six opponents at once; she was also a magician known for the strength of her curses. Two suitors wooed her. She lived with one for a time, then abandoned him and their daughter, whom she turned into a mountain. Then she lived with the other, but discovering that they were siblings, left him. She was honored as a bird goddess, and her image was embroidered on pillows for protection. (Motz; Dioszegi and Hoppal)

Kigvalu'uutchik Among the Inupiaq of Alaska's Kobuk River, Kigvalu'uutchik was a girl who, watching migrating geese, yearned to follow them to their southern home in autumn. When she grew into a lovely young woman, Kigvalu'uutchik was kidnapped by two male geese who had seen her watching them. She traveled with the geese but was never one of them, for she missed her human family. A kindly old goose told her the secret of escape: she had to find a piece of driftwood that water had hollowed out and use it as a boat to float home. He warned her to stay in the hollow log for four days after she reached her village, for she would still be under the power of the geese.

She followed the old goose's instructions, escaping when she saw the geese turning themselves into people near a big ice floe. It took her a long time to find the hollowed-out driftwood, and a long time to float home. Once there, she warned her elderly parents not to touch her, or she would not be able to return. Although they cried and cried, they followed her instructions, so she was able to return to human form. (Swann)

Koko Wild hairy people called *kelye* lived in the mountains, said the Siberian Chukchi, and one of them kidnapped the young widow Koko. Koko was forced to live with the woman *kelye*, who went naked despite the cold. Kept in a rock cave, Koko murmured her name to herself to keep a sense of her humanity. After some time, the *kelye* told Koko that she had once been human and had been held captive until she became covered with hair. Taking pity on Koko, the *kelye* let her return to her village, where she found her baby son grown into an elderly man. (Van Deusen)

Kunananguaq In Greenland, this little orphan girl lived with a foster mother who disliked her. When the villagers were moving to their summer home, the woman told Kunananguaq that some skin stretchers had been left behind. When the obedient girl ran to get them, her foster mother jumped into her skin boat and rushed away. When Kunananguaq came back to the seashore, there was no one left to carry her to the summer village.

She built herself a little hut but began to starve because there was little to eat except rotten food from the village dump. One day a seabird came ashore and called to her. When she walked to the water's edge, it transformed itself into a kayak and took her away. The bird took her to her villagers' new home, where it left her with the advice not to immediately rush into town but to stand on the hill above, shading her eyes and looking down. The little girl did so, and after a time the villagers came to bring her down the hill and make a home for her. (Osterman)

Malina In Greenland, the sun goddess as a young woman, Malina, lived with her brother Aningak. Once, when playing a game in darkness with other young people, Aningak grew aroused by his sister and had sex with her. This happened again, and Malina became curious about her lover's identity. She darkened her fingers with soot and, the next time Aningak seized her, covered his face with stains. Then Malina lit a handful of moss and recognized her stained brother.

He also lit a tuft of moss, but there was no flame. Still aroused, he chased her. When he had almost caught her, Malina cut off a breast and threw it at his feet. Then she rose into the sky, becoming the sun. Her brother, the moon, continued to pursue her, but the sun always rose higher than he could reach.

Malina raced through the sky dressed in white reindeer leather, chasing seals on the Arctic Sea. Aningak ran after the sun, making himself thin from exertion in the process. Once a month he disappeared, traveling from the sky to hunt enough seals to grow fat again. Malina shared a house with her brother at midsky, but because summer is always full of light and winter without it, she never had to see him.

The sun goddess was, together with **Sedna**, one of the most common figures in circumpolar mythology. Her myth varies slightly but always includes incest. In Canada, the incest was deliberate and the couple fled out of shame when discovered. Along Alaska's Kobuk River, the sun was seduced while secluded with her first menstrual blood, while in another story the incest occurred between a foster mother and son. In Barrow, Alaska, the sun woman appeared as a beautiful woman with a skeletal back. In some instances, both partners knew the other's identity and moved to the sky to

continue their relationship. Along the Bering Strait, the sister rose to the sky in order to nurse her brother. But typically the relationship was based on ignorance on the one hand, deceit on the other, with the sun woman enjoying her partner while ignorant of his identity. The story contains a cosmic myth, for it was to the moon man that shamans traveled when they ventured to the upper world. (Chapman; Irimoto and Yamada; Holtved; Kroeber; Osterman 1938; Weyer; Giddings; Rink; Sonne; Thompson)

Miti Among the Siberian Chukchi, Miti created people by tossing stones on the earth where her husband, Raven, had thrown twigs to make reindeer. When she had made herders, she gave them shelter by making huts from moss, placing fire within them, and throwing them to earth. (Van Deusen)

Mou-Njami Among Siberian Uralic speakers, this earth goddess carried an uncountable number of eyes within her. When females became pregnant, Mou-Njami provided eyes for the offspring. Because of the sacredness of eyes, hunters were forbidden to injure those of their prey, whose eyes had to be cut out and buried as an offering to Mou-Njami. She looked like a huge green animal, for grass was her fur. Because soil was her skin, her people never cut into it with knives. Needless digging and even driving of fence posts was forbidden. (Dioszegi and Hoppal)

Navarana This Polar Eskimo woman married the wrong man. As soon as they moved in together, he began to torment her. He constantly poked and prodded her, deeply enough to cause pain. She complained, but he would not cease injuring her. Finally she walked away, back to her parents' village. There she told her brothers how she had suffered, and they went to teach her husband a lesson.

When they got to his home, the husband was shorter than they remembered. He would not talk to them, so they beat him to death, only to find that they had beaten a dog. The husband crept from the house and attacked the brothers and killed them. A variant version of the story says the man had stolen his wife by killing her kin, then cut off the woman's arms to keep her from attracting another mate. Such violent stories may have been related as cautionary tales that helped young women realize the possibilities of violence in intimate relationships.

In a similar story, a woman named Navaranaāluk left her cannibal relatives to marry a man whose family did not eat human flesh. She was never comfortable in her new home and decided to set a war in motion. Visiting her native village, she wore mittens on her feet instead of boots, so her relatives would believe she was being treated with disrespect. As she had hoped, they launched a raid on the other village and killed all the women except three, who escaped. When the men of the village returned to discover the carnage, the surviving women told the sorry tale. To prepare for a return raid, the women sewed so many stone-headed arrows that they wore the flesh off their fingers. But their weapons proved successful, as the men killed all the men of the invaders' village and took their women as wives, killing only the destructive Navaranaāluk. (Holtved; Rasmussen 1921)

Pinga Although the most widespread Inuit food goddess was envisioned as living beneath the sea (see **Sedna**), the inland Eskimo said the goddess Pinga created and controlled land animals, especially caribou. She has been described as identical to **Sila**. (Merkur 1983; Motz)

Poza-Mama Among Siberian peoples, this goddess lived in the hearth fire, keeping the family intact and, through her warmth, alive. The Ulchi spit the first mouthful of every meal into the fire as a prayer for food; the Khakass used the same ritual to honor the goddess. The Negidals kept pictures of the fire goddess Kutug-a next to the hearth, revering the spot. Among the Shors, fire was Otuz Pastu Ot Ana, "thirty-headed Mother Fire," and Altyn Tondu Ot Ana, "Mother Fire in her golden coat." The Altai called her Ot Ana, "Mother Fire," and Kyz Ana, "Virgin Mother," because she perpetuated herself without a male. She was responsible for all family members, living and dead, for she lit the way to the afterlife.

Ot Ana was envisioned as a very old woman hunching protectively over the hearth. Not only did Ot Ana give life; she sustained it, as goddess of animals. The hearth fire led hunters to game by creating maps of their location in the coals or by sputtering significantly. Fire also was used to purify traps and hunters' clothing. (Bonnefoy; Dioszegi)

Qiporquat Although her husband, Qissuk, was a great hunter, he was also a violent man who beat Qiporquat regularly. She ran away each time, but each time he lured her back with gifts and sweet talk. He began to sleep with her clothing as a pillow, so that she could not run away from him. But she hanged herself to escape. When he found her body, two walruses came after him and killed him. (Holtved)

Sedna Beside the Arctic Ocean, a widower lived with his daughter, Sedna, a young woman so beautiful that all men sought her. She found none to her liking. One day, a seabird came to her and promised her a soft life in a warm hut full of bear skins and fish. Sedna flew away with him but, finding her home a stinking nest, regretted her rejection of humanity. That was what she told her father. Anguta put his daughter in his kayak to bring her home. Perhaps he killed the bird husband first, perhaps he just stole the bird's wife, but in either case the vengeance of the bird people followed him. The rising sea threatened death.

As they struggled, Anguta realized that flight was hopeless. He shoved Sedna overboard. Desperate, she grabbed the kayak. Her father cut off her fingers. She flung her mutilated arms over the skin boat's sides. Anguta cut them off, shoving his oar into Sedna's eye before she sank into the icy water.

At the bottom of the sea, she lived as queen of the deep, mistress of death and life, "old food dish." Her amputated fingers and arms became fish and marine mammals, which she offered to people if they accepted her rules. For three days after their death, the souls of her animals remained with their bodies, watching for violations of Sedna's demands. Then they returned to the goddess, bearing information about the conduct of her people.

This myth has many variants. On the western coast of Hudson Bay, her name was Nuliayoq, and she was an orphan whose villagers moved to another place. They were leaving her behind when she jumped onto one of the departing boats. But she missed her footing and drowned, becoming the controlling spirit of marine life. Nuliayoq made her home in a heavenly land, where souls of good people and of suicides traveled to play ball with a talking walrus skull; these games were visible as the aurora borealis. When not in her heavenly home, Nuliayoq guarded animals and fish, waiting at the entrances to inlets and rivers to punish anyone who flouted her regulations. She was not especially friendly to humans, who had rejected her when she lived on earth. But she could be generous when humans showed appropriate behavior.

Sedna was concerned with taboos, the breaking of which created disunity between the cosmos and humanity. She was especially concerned with the ritual demands of each gender. For men, this had to do with reverence toward animals they killed for food. For women, keeping secrets about menarche or abortion was outlawed. Breaking such taboos meant that Sedna's hair grew full of parasites. Because she had no hands, she could not comb them out. When the pain grew too terrible to endure, she stopped permitting sea animals and fish to swim close enough to be captured. If Sedna's stumps began to ache, she punished humans by sending sickness, starvation, and storms.

The sea mammals returned only if a shaman traveled to Sedna's home, crossing an abyss in which an ice wheel turned slowly. Then a cauldron of boiling seals blocked the way. Finally, a narrow ledge led to a house of stone and whale ribs, where Sedna dragged along the ground with one leg bent beneath her. A horrible dog guarded her, said by some to be her husband. Should

the shaman pass all these dangers and ease Sedna's pain, the goddess permitted him to return, bearing the news that Old Woman had forgiven her people.

Although the figure of a supreme food-providing goddess might seem to indicate individual women were revered, this was not always the case. A male shaman might return from his trance with word that a member of the community, often a woman, had to be punished for an infraction. This could include hiding a stillbirth or an abortion, touching meat while menstruating, or other infringements of strictures about women's reproductive functions. Such scapegoating positioned male hunters as successful unless interfered with by women or marginalized members of the group. As in other cases, the existence of a preeminent female divinity did not necessarily mean that religion did not sometimes oppress women.

Although Sedna was often described as a pan-Eskimo divinity, there was less evidence about her in Asia and Alaska than in eastern Greenland and Canada, although the story of the woman with an animal husband appears widely. Some theorists assert that Sedna's original homeland was the area around Hudson Bay, where the name Sedna and its immediate variants are found. (Boas 1887, 1894; Bierhorst; Burland; Holtved; Hultkrantz; Lantis; Paper; Porterfield; Rasmussen 1921, 1930; Smith; Sonne; Thompson; Wardle)

Siġvana Among the people of Tikiġaq village (now known as Point Hope, Alaska), this woman refused to marry a monster spirit (*anatkuq*). The monster stalked her, but she always stayed one step ahead of him. Finally he put a spell on her so that overnight she became a toothless old woman with white hair. Her parents, horrified at the transformation, begged her to marry the spirit, who would then take the spell off her and make her young again. They called to the *antakuq*, who came into the house and watched as a seal rose from the woman's ancient flesh, then merged with her again. Only after that did he free her from his curse and marry her. (Swann)

Sila The force of nature's laws, Sila is imagined as feminine although no myths personifying her are extant, only verbal formulas such as "Sila will keep her eye on you." She created the world when rocks fell from the heavens and humans grew up like plants. The people lived in darkness but did not die naturally. Finally a flood came and drowned most of them. Two women among the survivors argued, one saying that people should remain in darkness but live forever, the other saying that people needed both light and death. They buried the dead people, but they kept coming back as ghosts until a woman told them to stay dead. Then light came to earth, brought by the presence of death. The old women who created the world order may be personifications of Sila, otherwise known only through her creation.

Several theorists position Sila as the supreme divinity in Inuit religion. Others argue that evidence for a supreme being comes after colonization and is therefore suspect. Similarly, the question of whether Sila is masculine or feminine presents difficulties, for evidence is found of both genders. On Nunivak Island, Alaska, Sila is definitely female. Among the Caribou Eskimo, she is envisioned as mistress of the animals and has a maternal quality.

Although the word "Sila" can be interpreted to mean "air," the meaning extends to all that supports life. Sila is important to the shaman, for once she recognizes the shaman, Sila becomes a conduit for prophecies and visions. Sila has been described as identical to **Pinga**. Alternatively, Sila has been seen as a form of **Malina**, whose connection to the shaman's role is well established. (Merkur 1982; Sonne; Rasmussen 1929, 1927)

Sklúmyoa The "spirit of the universe" to the people of Nunivak Island, off the western Alaska coast, created the world from the lining of her fish-skin parka. Two boys were lost on the Arctic Ocean and, when Sklúmyoa heard the younger one crying, she came to rescue them. She tossed bits from inside her parka into the ocean, where they grew into Nunivak. She threw down more frayed bits, which turned into plants and animals. Then Sklúmyoa turned the crying boy into a girl, so she could bear children. Sklúmyoa may be the same figure as **Sila**. (Bierhorst)

Sug Eezi This Khakass mermaid emerged from water, naked and combing her golden hair with a golden comb. Riverbanks and the banks of lakes were good locations to leave offerings to her, because they form the boundary between her world and ours. (Van Deusen)

Tayune Among the Canadian Inuit, this folkloric heroine escaped from a brutal husband by walking away across the tundra, determined to die in the snow rather than endure his abuse. She was saved by a strange circumstance. Finding some caribou meat stashed by hunters, she ate enough to continue her journey and found herself walking onto a foot-shaped hill with five toe mounds. Unknown to her, this was the body of the giant Kinak, who, when he awoke and found her sleeping on him, took pity on Tayune and invited her to live in his huge nose, in a little hut built from hairs plucked from his beard. There she was kept warm by his breath and recovered her strength. Homesick for human company, she decided to return to her village, strengthened by the giant's promise of continued protection and made wealthy by the fur he gave her.

Upon her return, Tayune's husband soon fell into his old ways. As he beat Tayune, she screamed for help. Immediately it began to snow; then a whirlwind came down and swept the husband away. Kinak, who had caused the storm, did not intend to kill the husband. He gave him shelter in his nose, as he had with Tayune, and asked only that the husband not enter his giant mouth. But the man refused to respect the giant, so Kinak spit him all the way to the stars. Then the giant disappeared from view, although he can sometimes be sensed when his warm breath melts the snow in the middle of winter. (Riordan)

Tu-Njami The Siberian "Mother Fire" looked like a small naked girl but was strong enough to protect the whole family. She was a goddess of purification and healing whose special concern was the removal of disease and filth. Tu-Njami also ruled birth, giving birth to daughters on every twig in the fire. (Bonnefoy; Dioszegi and Hoppal)

Umaj Almost all cultures in Russian Siberia worshipped a birth goddess. The Khakass believed Umaj lived in the placenta; among the Shors, she was the protector of newborns. As Umay, the Mongol earth goddess controlled human fertility from the placenta. As Qatum, or "empress," Umaj was embodied in human queens. Umaj may be the same goddess as Ötükan, "female shaman." (Dioszegi; Bonnefoy; Van Deusen)

Yiä-il Among the Altaic Buryats and Dolgans, every shaman had a Yiä-il, or "animal mother," who appeared at significant times. First she appeared when the potential shaman was an infant, nursing the child from her breasts. She appeared at the point of initiation and finally at death. She might look like a caribou, or an unknown species. Without Yiä-il, no one could gain shamanic power. (Motz)

Yiniangawgut Among the Koryak of Kamchatka, this powerful primeval woman was the object of competition between Raven and Little-Bird, both of whom sought her in marriage. To find out the better mate, she challenged her suitors with the task of mending a break in the sky. Raven was terrified by the heights, but Little-Bird mended the tear with some fat and won Yiniangawgut's hand. Raven then chewed up the sun, leaving the earth in darkness.

Yiniangawgut's sister Chanyai created the world's rivers through singing, so there was enough water to drink, but the people still suffered from darkness.

Yiniangawgut went to Raven's house to trick him into letting the sun out. She tickled him until he was roaring with laughter, then had intercourse with him. When he awoke, she pointed out that his home was missing important utensils, like plates, which she had at her home. Then she stuck his head on a roof so that it became a new sun. (Swann)

Ylynda Kota The Selkup old woman of heaven sent souls to earth, wearing the form of birds, to incarnate as humans. She was one of several important Selkup goddesses, including the ruler of snakes, Selči Šÿt Emysyt, and the goddesses of sun and fire. (Dioszegi)

Yumima Because this Chukchi woman had an impatient husband, she lived in misery, always fearing ill treatment. But one day as she was walking on the tundra, she saw a beautiful home. Finding its door open, she went inside and was overwhelmed by its cleanliness and beauty. In a corner, a lamp was burning, but it was a magical lamp, burning beads rather than oil. She popped a bead into her mouth but, hearing footsteps, was forced to hide. Someone entered, and seeing the light flickering because it was missing a bead, spoke to the lamp, which replied that Yumima was hiding in the house.

Yumima discovered that the home belonged to a helpful woman magician who, after she had replaced the stolen bead in her magic lamp, told Yumima that as long as she was very slow in responding to her husband, he would be happy with her. Yumima went home and followed the magician's instructions. She moved very slowly whenever her husband made demands, and as a result, he grew very happy with her and she lived in peace with him thereafter. (Van Duesen 1999)

INDIA

India and the surrounding region attract scholars of goddess religion because it is home to today's only major polytheistic religion. Hinduism offers a complex pantheon of goddesses found in ancient literature and still honored by millions of people. Yet the prominence of goddesses in Indian religion has not led to similar status for women. Although one of every six of the world's women lives in India, poverty and lack of education limit their opportunities. Hindu beliefs offer empowering images of goddesses, but the region's myths, rituals, and customs can also be oppressive to women.

This section deals with female figures of India and neighboring regions whose indigenous goddesses were subsumed into Hinduism. Buddhism is discussed despite being non-theocentric, for Buddhism includes regional goddesses who have survived in disguised form. The same is true of Jainism. Finally, goddesses never absorbed into the Hindu pantheon are examined. As the region is home to over a hundred spoken languages, the complexity of the region's religion cannot be overstated.

An early civilization, centered on the cities of Harrapa and Mohenjo-Daro in Pakistan, ended in approximately 1700 BCE. The cities, lost for millennia, were discovered and excavated in the 1920s. Statues of powerful female figures led scholars to theorize that the civilization recognized a powerful goddess and to question whether a substrata of imagery from this period was carried forward. Evidence for survival includes styles of jewelry and attire, found on Indus Valley figures, still worn by Indian women.

Indo-Europeans, who moved into the Indian subcontinent in 1500–1200 BCE, brought a religion that was strongly patriarchal despite the presence of goddesses. As their arrival coincided with the decline of the Indus Valley culture, scholars debate whether the two were connected. Until recently, Indo-Europeans were described as invading the Indian subcontinent, but contemporary thought suggests a gradual migration with assimilation of earlier peoples. Earlier worship may have continued, as deposits of goddess figurines in rivers from this era suggest.

The first written records of Hinduism date from this time. Called the Vedas ("knowledge"), they were written in Sanskrit, one of the oldest Indo-European languages. The world's oldest known religious text, the *Rig Veda*, collects hymns and liturgical verses, including some to goddesses. Three other texts constitute Vedic literature, two consisting of verses from the *Rig Veda* arranged for specific purposes, while the last, the *Artharvana-Veda*, offers spells and curses. Few goddesses appear in these texts, leading scholars to theorize that Hinduism's goddesses derive from non-Vedic or indigenous sources.

Later texts include the Upanishads (eighth century BCE), philosophical texts that form the basis of what is known as Vedānta, an orthodox form of Hinduism, as well as of Buddhism and Jainism. Goddesses are rare in this literature. But the *Puranās* offer considerable information. There is no exact Western equivalent to this nonliturgical literature that includes myths of non-Indo-European people as well as folktales and genealogies. By the time of composition (late BCE to early CE), indigenous goddesses were gaining significance in the Hindu pantheon. Although most of the *Puranās* are dedicated to male divinities, their consorts play important roles. Important Puranic narratives for goddess scholars are the *Baāgavata*, which tell stories of the god Vishnu's consorts; the *Devī-bhagavata*, which tells of Durgā; the *Devī Mahatmya*, which describes Devī and her aspects; and *Padma Puranā*, devoted to Manasā. Evidence from artifacts similarly attests to increasing public importance of goddesses who had previously been honored privately, even secretly. Although some appear as generic "earth goddesses," specific features of later-known divinities are discernable. Thereafter, goddess imagery in art became more clearly developed. Finally, two epics are notable: the *Ramayana*, relating the tale of Rama and his love for Sītā; and the *Mahābhārata*, devoted to Draupadī and her five husbands. Various minor texts describe aspects of various Hindu goddesses or offer instructions for their worship.

The joining of indigenous goddesses with patriarchal religion resulted in the division of Vedic religion, connected to ritual and sacrifice, from non-Vedic, devoted to private practice and ritual. Called India's "great" and "little" traditions, they may be practiced simultaneously by the same worshipper. Both traditions find expression in the arts. Innumerable sculptures of goddesses show the diverse imagery. Paintings served as a form of worship and as a means of encouraging it, and poets dedicated themselves to praising the goddess. In addition to textual and artistic evidence, a wealth of practice offers information about Hindu goddesses. These range from private *bhakti* (honoring rituals) to seasonal festivals that bring together communities.

From the seventh century onward, Islam had an effect on Indian and Southeast Asian religion. The religion arrived through trade and, later, through Syrian and Persian invasion. The arrival of monotheism meant exclusion of the goddess. In a few cases, traditional rituals continued, with their basis in goddess religion ignored or disguised.

From 1858 to 1947, much of the Indian subcontinent was under English control. This had less effect on religion than did earlier invasions, for British colonialism generally focused on economic exploitation rather than religious conversion. The coincidence of this with the rise of the folklore movement in Europe meant that tribal material was recorded and published. In addition, British occultists found India fascinating, predominantly studying Brahmanic traditions. Later, some Indian patriots connected Hinduism with national identity, which led to the division of the country into Muslim Pakistan/Bangladesh and Hindu India, and to continuing sectarian conflict.

Outside India, Hindu goddesses are found in Bali and Java, where Hinduism melded with indigenous religion. In addition, two religious descendants found widespread adherence within and outside India. The first to emerge was Jainism, a radically pacifist, egalitarian, ascetic sect founded in the first millennium BCE. Although there are no goddesses in Jainism, there are important female *devas*, or celestial beings.

Buddhism, another descendant of Hinduism, arose in the fifth century BCE, possibly in Nepal, spreading over India and adjoining regions. Despite being formally nontheistic, Buddhism can be called functionally patriarchal, for male figures predominate in religious art, and leaders are traditionally male. In Tibet, where Buddhism melded with the native *bon-po* religion, female figures remain important. In Burma, rituals involving recognition of *nats*, or spirits, survive; in Thailand, domestic cults related to matrilineal spirits continue.

Hinduism as exported beyond India tends to be of the "great" tradition, connected with India's upper castes, who have greater social and even physical mobility than do lower-caste people. As a result, traditions of Vedānta and Yoga are known throughout the West. However, some goddesses with roots outside the Vedic tradition, such as Kālī, have found distant adherents. Employment of Hindu goddesses as archetypes for psychological states has given rise to controversy among scholars and practitioners, some of whom decry the practice as dishonoring the original religion, while others welcome the connection of ancient goddesses with contemporary worshippers.

Finally, a form of worship known as Tantra finds expression in Hindu, Jain, and Buddhist traditions. Often misunderstood as a sexual practice in the West, Tantra envisions the world as balanced between Śakti (feminine power) and Shiva (masculine essence). Although early scholars claimed Tantra debased women, recent feminist work has called those assumptions into question.

HINDU AND BUDDHIST PANTHEON OF INDIA, NEPAL, AND TIBET

Abhramū The original female elephant could change shape at will. But Abhramū's tribe lost its wings when, flying across the sky, the elephants grew weary. When they alighted in a tree, their weight broke the branches. An ascetic meditating beneath was unharmed, but falling branches crushed his students. When the sage cursed the elephants, their wings dropped off. Elephants have been earthbound ever since, trapped in the shapes they were wearing during the encounter. (Zimmer 1946)

Adītī An early Indian goddess, Adītī embodies whatever transcends measurement. Her mother, **Shatarupa**, divided herself into thirteen bodies so that the world might become quickly populated. Adītī, first of these forms, gave birth to twelve Adityas, one for each month. Or she may have had one son, Varuna, so splendid his presence hurt her eyes; she divided him into twelve parts. Or she had seven normal sons, then gave birth to an egg that rose into the sky to become the sun. She also gave birth to Vishnu (occasionally said to be her consort), Indra, and others. (Berkson; Daniélou; Dexter; Dimmitt and van Buitenen; Ions; Jamison; Kinsley 1986; Pattanaik)

Alakṣmī Sister and opposite of **Lakṣmī**, Alakṣmī represents all that is difficult about human life. Depicted as an old woman accompanied by crows, Alakṣmī travels with hunger, pain, and privation. During her sister's festival of Dīvalī, Alakṣmī appears with bands of evil spirits; for three days, people light lamps to exorcise them. Annually in Bengal, a straw image of Alakṣmī is

created and destroyed, and an image of **Lakṣmī** put in its place. (Kinsley 1997; Pattanaik; Sharma)

Ali This warrior woman had no time for assignations with men, but the hero Arjuna desired her. Disguised as a swan, he sneaked into her tent, but she recognized the deceit and cast him out. Then he took the form of a serpent and raped her while she slept. The result of the rape was a forced marriage. (Pattanaik)

Amba In southern India, Amba is "Mother Earth." Possibly pre-Indo-European, this mother goddess was assimilated into other Hindu divinities, among them **Durgā**, **Pārvatī**, and **Umā**. Into modern times she was honored near Jaipur with dawn sacrifices of black goats. A temple to Amba Bhai, one form of this goddess, stands in Kolhapur, in the southwest of Maharashtra province. Built in the tenth century, it was badly damaged by Muslim invaders in the fourteenth century and has never been completely restored, although it was substantially repaired in the 1700s. Images of dancing celestial maidens (see **Apsarās**) deck the temple, which has separate sections dedicated to the goddess as **Lakṣmī**, **Kālī**, and **Sarasvatī**. (Berkson; Daniélou 1964; Dehejia; Gupta S; Moor; Narasimhan; Pattanaik)

Ambikā After **Durgā** destroyed the buffalo demon who threatened the world, devils still lurked. So the goddess **Pārvatī** sent her feminine power, which appeared as Ambikā, "Little Mother," a beautiful woman who lured demons to their death. First she told them she had made a vow never to sleep with anyone who could not defeat her in battle. When the demons approached, she killed them with a supersonic hum. Then she transformed herself into **Kālī**.

Jainism, despite being originally a religion without personalized gods, accepted goddesses as *sasanadevatas*, guardians of the faith. Among these, Ambikā (under the name of Kushmandi) was one of the most popular. Women who wish to bear sons invoke this goddess because of her association with fertility. (Cort; Dehejia; Dimmitt and van Buitenen; O'Flaherty)

Ammavaru This creatrix produced three eggs at the dawn of time, each holding one of the great gods (Adya has a similar myth; she may be the same goddess as Ammavaru). To populate the earth, she intended to have intercourse with her three sons, but two refused. The third agreed, naming as his price the goddess's third eye, wherein her power rested. When the goddess gave up that eye, her son killed her. She returned in shattered form as the multiple village goddesses called the **Grāmadevatā**. The same story is told of **Pedammā-Mariammā**. (Foulston; Kinsley 1986; Whitehead)

Ankamma In the region of Telugu-speaking people in Andhra Pradesh, central India, this goddess was the central mythic figure. Conveyed through an oral tradition only recently transcribed, her tales constitute an important part of the region's heritage. Her major temple is found in Kārempūḍi, where a pierced wall allows the goddess to look out at passersby. (Roghair)

Annadai The earth goddess of the Bagai tribe of central India descended from the heavens to make the land fertile. When she arrived, she took root like a plant. When shaken, she produced grains that were sown and grew into food crops. She grew fat until cut down by twelve men who offered some of her body, the kernels of grain, back to the goddess. (Jayakar)

Annapurṇā This goddess may be an Indian version of the rice goddess found throughout Asia (see Southeast Asia, **Dewi Shri**). A common household deity, often depicted enthroned and feeding a child from a full ladle, Annapurṇā is especially significant in Benares, where a harvest festival honoring her is called Annakuta, "food mountain," because a mountain of rice and sweets fills her temple. A form of **Durgā** or **Devī**, Annapurṇā is a mountain goddess, with four

mountains bearing her name in central Nepal. (Bernbaum; Larson et al; Hamilton)

Apsarās When the Hindu gods churned the primordial ocean, the famously wanton dancers called Apsarās emerged, large hipped and languid, with soft inviting eyes. As forces of desire, they could be tempting or threatening. One famous Apsarās, Motini, was imprisoned by a demon who convinced her she was his daughter; when a human hero appeared, she escaped her erstwhile father and, transforming herself into a warrior, protected her beloved in battle. Another Apsarās, Rambha, offered a garland of flowers (symbol of her readiness to have intercourse) to a sage, who passed it along to the god Indra. Indra, playfully drunk, put it on the trunk of an elephant, which dropped it in the road, where a horse walked on it. The sage put a curse on Indra that caused **Lakṣmī** to return to the primordial ocean of milk, which had to be rechurned to bring the universe back into being.

The Apsarās Pramlocha was sent by Indra to seduce a sage who had kept his semen within his body for years, thus being close to escaping from the wheel of reincarnation. She brought him such pleasure that he felt he had lived a century in one night. But, when the night was over, he grew furious at losing his spiritual power. As the pregnant Pramlocha ascended into heaven, her perspiration impregnated the trees, which gave birth to a beautiful woman named Mariṣa, whose son established human civilization. (Dimmitt and van Buitenen; Jayakar; Pattanaik; Pintchman 1994; Whitehead)

Aranyāni In the *Rig Veda*, this invisible goddess can be heard by travelers passing through her forests, who think they hear either screaming or bells tinkling. Although generally kind, she can kill if provoked. Aranyāni is a goddess of earth's abundance, offering nuts and berries to those who come near. She may be related to the nature goddesses called **Yakṣī**. (Kinsley 1986)

Ardhanarīnara This name, which means "half goddess, half god," is especially used of **Pārvatī** with her consort Shiva, but may also be used of **Prakṛti** and her mate Puruṣa. Sometimes the divinities are depicted as two bodies joined in sexual intercourse, while at other times there is a single body, male on one side, female on the other. The *Puranās* say the divinity came into being when the primary god, Brahma, meditated upon the image of Shiva mating with his female half, at which moment Ardhanarīnara burst into being. From this time onward, humans and other animals have reproduced through sexual intercourse. (Dimmitt and van Buitenen)

Astangi Devi Among the Dewar of central India, the wind impregnated virginal Astangi Devi with the sun god Suraj and the moon goddess Chandra. At that time, humans ate only twigs. Astangi invented rice, bamboo, and other plants to feed her twins something more nourishing. But an envious man set fire to her fields. Putting out the fires, Astangi let sparks fly into the heavens, which became the stars. She sent her children to live in the sky, patting her daughter on the cheek and leaving marks visible on the moon's face. (Elwin 1949)

Avidya This obscure goddess hides within herself a hermaphroditic god who created the world by dancing. Bedecked in a skull necklace, she is said to rule the throat chakra, one of the points of energy on the human body. Representing ignorance, she is distinct from illusion (**Māyā**), the latter being a more cosmic force. (Daniélou 1964, 2007)

Bagalāmukhī This Tantric goddess was born when Vishnu undertook austerities to save the universe from destruction. When he prayed to **Tripura-sundarī**, she brought forth Bagalāmukhī, who frolicked in a lake of turmeric until the storm died down, thus preserving the world. Another myth says she protected the world from a demon. Although she intended to kill him, he fell down in worship, an action that saved his life. A final narrative says she was formed when **Pārvatī** tired of waiting for her consort, Shiva, to feed her. She ate him, but he forced her to regurgitate him and transformed her into Bagalāmukhī. Bagalāmukhī grants magical powers to her worshippers, who experience them as skills. These include the power to paralyze others, whether through force or immobilizing them with love. (Kinsley 1997)

Bahucharā In an attempt to save herself from rape, this heroine cut off her breasts and, bleeding to death, cursed her attacker with impotence. Terrified, the rapist begged for mercy, so Bahucharā mitigated the curse: he would thereafter dress in women's clothing and serve as her priestess. She remains the special goddess of homosexual men and transgendered people in the state of Gujarat, including male priests called *hijrās*. Worshipped in a shrine where her only representation is a vulval triangle, she is sometimes seen as part of a trinity, with her two sisters who also killed themselves rather than submit to rape. (Jayakar; Pattanaik; Young)

Bai Tanki Disease, say the Agaria of central India, came into the world because men tried to rape a girl. Bai Tanki, a hardworking and pretty virgin, was gathering wood when men threw her to the ground. As each tried to rape her, a disease struck. The penis of one discharged a foul fluid, another found himself covered with itching sores, another could not maintain an erection. But one young man managed to rape the girl despite her magical protection. She dissolved into a stream of water that spread disease all around the world. (Elwin 1949)

Baṇḍamma This regional goddess of Andhra Pradesh is celebrated in a great festival just before the monsoons cool the land, when her worshippers offer tribute to the goddess in hopes that she will protect them from disease. The weeklong festival offers the goddess entertainment in homes, then leads her to the fields, where sacrifice is offered. The goddess is embodied in a square-headed armless statue. (Tapper)

Basmoti Among the Parenga of Orissa, this earth goddess ate so much at a feast she vomited. From her vomit, seven girls and five boys sprang forth. The girls were every kind of rice and millet, which now bear their names, just as their mother gave her name to a kind of rice. With their brothers, the seven sisters descended to the earth and brought abundance. (Elwin 1954)

Behmata Goddess of fate in northern India, she sat by the side of the sea making marriages by twisting rope and tossing the ropes into the waves. When two ropes sank, the marriage was doomed to be short and unhappy, but if they floated across the waves, the marriage would be long and happy. (Wadley)

Bhagavati Kerala's most important goddess, Bhagavati may have developed from the Tamil war goddess Korravai (see **Koṭavī**). A benevolent virgin mother, Bhagavati has little mythology except the story that, as the warrior Bhadrakāḷi, she banished a demon king. Thousands of temples are devoted to Bhagavati as an earth goddess. As such, she reincarnates as a lower-caste man, who lives in the temple and serves as an oracle. In ritual reenactments of the goddess's victory over the demon, men enact the goddess's role, dressed in artificial scarlet breasts. In Cochin, pilgrims annually desecrate the goddess's shrine with stones and curses, which provides immunity from disease for a year. In her Chengannur temple, Bhagavati is depicted as a young woman dressed in a white cotton shift and a silk sari. The image irregularly menstruates; red stains appear on its shift, whereupon the temple is closed for three days, after which the goddess's image is bathed. The stained petticoat is an object of devotion. (Caldwell; Pintchman 2001; Hawley and Wulff; Dehejia; Gentes)

Bhārat Mātā "Mother India" was the creation of Sarala Devī, who in 1903 organized the first festival to this neo-goddess. A nationalist artist depicted the subcontinent as a four-armed goddess dancing on lotus flowers. The image became an icon in the struggle for independence from the British Empire. The power of the new goddess sustained itself after independence. Pilgrims to her temple in Hardwar find a huge map of India and an image of Bhārat Mātā holding milk and grain. She remains a popular goddess to whom temples are still built, including a temple complex erected after the 1983 All-India Sacrifice for Unity. In some cases, devotion to Bhārat Mātā has been connected with anti-Muslim agitation. (Hawley and Wulff; Subramaniam; Dehejia; McDaniel 2004; Ramaswamy)

Bhavani "Bestower of existence" is a wilderness goddess from the Osmanabad desert. Without consort or children, she represents that area's stark earth as well as being the primary goddess of the warrior people Marathas. As Tulja Bhavani, she was important in the seventeenth century, when she presented a sword to the local ruler with instructions that he treat invading Muslims the way the goddess **Durgā** had treated the buffalo demon. The king succeeded in driving the invaders from the land, after which many temples were built to Bhavani. (Daniélou 1964; Dehejia; Gupta S; Kinsley 1986; Moor)

Bhogavati According to Puranic literature, this princess unwittingly married a prince who happened to be a snake. Learning the truth, she did not turn away from him but remained his loyal wife. When her husband later learned that his form came from a curse that could be undone should a virtuous woman bathe him in a sacred lake, he asked Bhogavati to perform the service. When she did, her husband revealed himself as a handsome prince. (Pattanaik)

Bhudevī A form of **Lakṣmī**, Bhudevī is also associated with **Pārvatī**. Her myth tells how, floating on the cosmic sea, she was attacked by a demon. Vishnu, hearing her cries, leaped into the ocean in the form of a wild boar, goring the demon into releasing Bhudevī.

As the couple rose together into the light, they embraced, and Bhudevī's womb swelled with life, for the god had impregnated her. Into the earth Vishnu plunged his tusks, filling it with seed. As a result of this mating, Vishnu was named guardian of the earth.

Vishnu also wed Lakṣmī, but the two wives fought constantly. Once, he was given a magical tree that both wives wanted. When Bhudevī received the tree, she used the gift to taunt Lakṣmī. So Vishnu decreed that the tree would bloom only on the side facing Lakṣmī's home. When Lakṣmī teased Bhudevī about the beautiful flowers, Vishnu further decreed that the flowers would bloom only when he was making love with Bhudevī.

At one point, Bhudevī grew angry at humanity for being ungrateful to her. Seeds became sterile, and no plants bore fruit. Famine struck. Vishnu demanded that Bhudevī return fruitfulness to the earth, but she turned herself into a cow and ran away. He pursued her, but when captured she remained adamant in her refusal. To bring back the goddess's affections, Vishnu promised to protect her from greed. He agreed to teach proper techniques of agricultural economy to the people. With that pledge, Bhudevī returned. (Ngaranjan; Pattanaik)

Bhuvanésvarī The Tantric goddess Bhuvanésvarī was born as the world was created from **Tripurasundarī**. Bhuvanésvarī represents the tangible world. The universe arises from her, rests on her, and disintegrates into her. Crimson faced and three eyed, crowned with the lunar crescent and with jewels, her hair black, Bhuvanésvarī is so beautiful that Shiva created his third eye so that he would have more enjoyment in viewing her. She too has three eyes, to watch over her world. One of her major symbols is the yonic triangle, for she is the essence of feminine reproductive power. She controls all phases of creation, from emergence through maintenance to final destruction. (Pintchman 2001; Kinsley 1997)

Bijaldai Kaniya Among the Baiga of central India, this lightning spirit was held captive by a young man.

Escaping, she became lightning flashing across the sky, while he, shooting his arrows at her, made the sound of thunder. The Dhanwar of the same region say Bijaldai Kaniya was born from a lovely fat woman named Panbijiya Rani, a virgin, who was impregnated by the wind and who, burned black as her daughter exploded out of her, became the leaf scorpion.

In another version of her tale, told among the Dewar people, Bijaldai Kaniya was born from a virgin, Beti Bidyarsin, who was impregnated by the seed of a king who masturbated while admiring her bathing in a river. She shone so brightly at birth that she was enclosed in a bamboo reed so her brilliance would not blind potential husbands. When a man had married her, however, he ignored the instructions not to open the bamboo reed until he was safely at home. Tearing it open along the way, he freed Bijaldai Kaniya, who ran away from him into a bamboo grove, where she continues to live, always hunted by her thwarted husband. (Elwin 1949)

Bisal-Mariamna A brass pot full of water, called an "eye-mirror," symbolizes this Mysore goddess of sunlight. Into the pot worshippers put pepper leaves and coconut flowers; a small metal mirror leans against it. One of seven sister goddesses, Bisal-Mariamna is worshipped in an unroofed shrine filled with sunlight. (Whitehead)

Bomong The cosmic goddesses of the Minyong were Bong and Bomong. Daughters of earth and sky, they glowed from birth, growing brighter under the care of a treasured nurse. They loved her so much that when she died, they died too. In the darkness that followed, earth's creatures grew afraid. Thinking the nurse had stolen the light, they dug up her body. But it had rotted away except for the eyes, which held images of Bong and Bomong. The people, thinking they had the goddesses back, took the eyes to a stream and washed them. A carpenter carefully cut the images from the reflecting eyes, and the two girls jumped back to life.

The people did all they could to keep the goddesses. But Bomong ran away into the sky. Her brilliance made the earth crack. Bong followed her, shining brightly but not unbearably. People fainted from the heat, so they sent a frog to kill Bong. He shot her twice, and she fell dead. Her body lay until a rat dragged it to Bomong, who covered herself with a rock in sorrow. A rat, a bird, and a cock went to find Bomong, who said she would never return until her sister was revived. In animating the goddess, a carpenter made her smaller so that she could become a moon. (Elwin 1958, 1955)

Brag-srin-mo The Tibetan ancestral goddess encountered a monkey in yogic meditation. Becoming sexually aroused, she encouraged him to mate with her. He claimed a vow of chastity, but **Tārā** explained that his cooperation was necessary for people to be born. Thereafter, Brag-srin-mo bore six little monkeys. When she fed them special food, they lost their tails and fur and became human. (Bonnefoy)

Budi Ma This name or title means "ancestress" or "old woman" and refers to many goddesses of Bengal: Vana Durgā, tree goddess; Rupasi, the sheora tree; Hathi-Dhara-Buri, the elephant-catching old woman; and the ancestral goddesses Jatra Budi, Buri Thakurani, and Burhi Mai. As Ghaghrabudi, this goddess was discovered in 1956 in the form of a group of egg-shaped stones revealed when floods uprooted a tree. She is also called Vriddheshvari, "aged goddess," in the Brahmanical cult, where she is honored as the smiling, bejeweled nurse of the universe.

She is often worshipped in aniconic form, embodied in a stone or a tree, to which offerings are made of flowers and animal meat. Her rituals entail dancing and, occasionally, ascetic practices like body piercing. Where her worship is active, villagers mark New Year's Day by donning formal clothes to perform their daily tasks. As an aged and revered old woman, she is distinct from the brahmanic goddesses, who tend to be young and beautiful. Although often shown singly, she is also worshipped together with her consort, the old man. (McDaniel 2003, 2004)

Butani-butki The chili pepper, according to the legends of the Gadaba of Orissa, was originally a girl with a very bad temper. She cursed at anyone who tried to be friendly to her. After she died and was cremated, a bit of bone was left over from the pyre. A shaman planted the shard, from which the first chili plant grew. (Elwin 1954)

Caṇḍī In ancient India, the moon was a male divinity named Chandra. But **Durgā** had a similar name, Caṇḍī. The similarity gave rise to the idea that the moon was a goddess, or a god one month, a goddess the next. The goddess lodged herself in rocks, which are displayed on wooden thrones. Hunters carried a rock sacred to Caṇḍī in order to find game. Caṇḍī had multiple aspects, being connected with forests, rivers, and humans under different titles. (Dehejia; Gupta S; Kinsley 1986, 1975; Manna; McDaniel 2003, 2004; Zimmer 1946)

Chinnamastā Hindu images show a naked dancing woman cutting off her own head with a sword. Spouts of blood pour from her severed neck into her three-eyed head, which she holds in one hand, and into the mouths of two dancers near her. Sometimes she is shown having intercourse with a god (usually Shiva) while she self-decapitates, or standing on the love god Kāmā as he satisfies Rati. Devotees of Tantra display this image to represent both the control of sexuality and its active celebration.

Chinnamastā came into being when **Pārvatī** grew sexually aroused while bathing, a moment of impurity that turned her skin black. Her handmaids, Jayā and Vijayā, grew hungry as they waited for her, so she tore off her head to feed them. Other versions of the story say she was engaged in intercourse with Shiva, producing the two attendants Dākiī and Vāriṇī as he ejaculated into her. She later fed them by cutting off her head. Yet another version has her excited by battle

93

and cutting off her own head when there was nothing else left to attack.

Chinnamastā is associated with yoga. The subjugation of the instinct for survival, implied in her self-decapitation, has also been connected with war. Finally, she has been connected with ancient unnamed headless sculptures showing squatting women. Worship of Chinnamastā is relatively rare as she has few temples or shrines and is considered a dangerous goddess. In Buddhism, this goddess (as Chinnamuṇḍā) is the fully enlightened Buddha; as such, she is a form of **Vajrayoginī**. (Kinsley 1997; Shaw 2006)

Churalin A woman who dies in childbirth melts into the repository of frustrated maternity called Churalin, a monster that roams the countryside looking for infants to kill. But a Churalin can be tamed into a submissive wife, if a man can find an attractive one, for most are terrible to look at. Distinguishing between the types can be difficult, as they are invisible. One man tricked a Churalin into revealing herself by playing sweet music. He married her and, for twenty years, she was an ideal wife, but on the day of the marriage of their last child she disappeared. (Elwin 1980)

Cundā Once a very powerful Buddhist goddess, Cundā has become less prominent since her heyday in the ninth through twelfth century CE. As a goddess who purified negative karma, she was invoked by believers throughout India and, to a lesser extent, in Tibet and Nepal. Literary sources provide evidence that she was envisioned as a protective goddess whose powers included elimination of epidemics and other diseases. She inspires practices that help her devotees toward enlightenment. (Shaw 2006)

Daini-Api The Abors of the Siang Valley believe this spirit causes sterility among human women. She was once human herself, but when she offended a water spirit (see **Nippong**) while she was having her first menstrual period, she was cursed never to bear a child.

In sorrow, she haunts streams and rivers, hoping to meet girls who have come to do their laundry after the end of their first menses; Daini-Api has the power to make them barren. (Elwin 1955)

Dakadidi Among the Khond of Middle India, she was the primal mother, who with her brother Daspajka conceived the first people while the world was covered with water. Later, when their grandchildren were born and there was still no land, the couple sacrificed one of their granddaughters to dry up the earth so it could be cultivated. Various other versions say it was the children, not the grandchildren, of the primal woman who were sacrificed. (Elwin 1949)

Ḍākinī These powerful female beings, attendants on **Kālī**, reveal themselves in terrifying aspect, sometimes fish bodied, sometimes huge as an ogre, often eating raw flesh or drinking blood (from which they are called Asrapas, "blood sippers"). In Nepal, they are guardians of greater goddesses; two principal ones are lion-maned Singhini and tiger-headed Baghini.

In Tibet, the Ḍākinī have another aspect, for beneath their horrific guise they grant supernormal powers and insights to practitioners of yoga. Called Khadoma, or "sky walkers," these beings appear as beautiful maidens or withered hags. They can be kindly or horrifying, depending on their spiritual mission. These spirits may derive from indigenous goddesses of the Bön pantheon, where Ma Namkha ("mother sky") is among the chief divinities. Although generally described as a collective, some Ḍākinī have individual names. Simhavaktra has the head of a lion and attends **Lha-mo**, while Makaravaktra has a crocodile head. (Campbell; Daniélou 1964; Dehejia; Beyer; Atkinson et al; Shaw 2006)

Dānu This goddess figure appears in early Vedic literature as the mother of the the *asuras*, a divine race, called the Dānavas after her. Their name, "children of Danu," recalls names from other Indo-European peoples, especially the **Danaids** (see **Danae**, Greece) and the Irish Tuatha Dé Danann ("people of goddess **Danu**"; see Celtic World). It has been hypothesized that such figures descend from an ancient Indo-European goddess (*Danu) whose name survives in Europe in the river name Danube; the Vedic Dānu may similarly represent primordial waters. She is also described as the mother of a reptilian demon whom the gods defeated. (Dexter; Kinsley 1986)

Depum The creator mother of the Shimong people of northeastern India, Depum was confined with her brother deep in the earth. There, they fell in love and mated, and Depum conceived. She gave birth to earth's creatures in succession: first fish, then frogs, then other beings. After each delivery, she released her offspring to the earth's surface. Because of the taint of incestuous love, such creatures lived apart from human beings. (Bhattacharya)

Devaki Devaki's father was Devaka, uncle of the evil Kansa, who opposed the gods and who was born following the rape of his mother, Pavanarekha. Her husband, who had already wed Devaki's six older sisters, was Vasudeva. At her wedding, the god Vishnu picked hairs from his head and from the body of the serpent on which he reclined, prophesying that the hairs would become Devaki's seventh and eighth sons, respectively. But Kansa threatened Devaki, agreeing to spare her only if her sons were killed the moment they were born. Thus Devaki's first six sons were killed, but when she was pregnant with the seventh, Vishnu transferred her child to the womb of the kindly **Rohinī** and pretended Devaki had miscarried. Imprisoned while pregnant with Krishna, Devaki gave birth safely and saw her son spirited away to be raised by the herdswoman **Yasoda**. An alternative story says Devaki's fetus was transferred into a surrogate's womb while a goddess, **Nidrā** or **Durgā**, entered Devaki's womb. When Devaki gave birth and the enemy seized the child, the goddess revealed herself and escaped. (Ions; Pattanaik)

Deval Devī This legendary princess of the Rajput culture tended her herds of cattle while mounted on a black mare named Kesar Kālīni. When a neighboring king wanted the mare, Deval refused to let him take her but then, fearful of the consequences, hid in another kingdom. There she was protected by a foster brother, to whom, in gratitude, she gave the magical horse. He in turn promised to protect Deval and her cattle forever. When, later, the young man married, the cattle were attacked during his wedding ceremony. Deval turned into a bird and whispered into his ear that he had pledged to protect her cattle, and so the young man and his bride rode off to the herd's rescue. The prince was killed in the attempt, as was the magical horse. (Jayakar)

Devasmitā When Devasmitā was about to be separated from her husband, she asked a boon of Shiva, to whom she was devoted. He gave her two red lotus flowers, telling her that as long as the couple remained true to the marriage vows, their flowers would remain fresh. With this guarantee of chastity in hand, the husband set off on a business trip, but in a distant city he was set upon by some wily and corrupt men. Learning of the magical flower, they traveled to Devasmitā's town intent upon seducing her, for no other reason than to test the efficacy of Shiva's boon.

The chaste wife realized what was happening and tricked them into drinking drugged wine, after which she took all their clothing and branded them on the forehead with a dog's paw print. Once she finished with them, she took them to their own city, where she sold them to their fathers as slaves. Then, with her husband, she returned home richer for her experience. (Ghosh 1965)

Devayānī This voluptuous young woman was seduced by Kaca, a young man who wished to use her affections to learn secrets held by her father, a sage. Kaca had taken a vow of celibacy, so he only flirted promisingly with her, causing her to fall in love with him. Weak with desire for him and not realizing that he did not intend to satisfy her, Devayānī was on the verge of revealing her father's secrets, which protected the powers of nearby demons.

But when those demons realized that Kaca was about to learn secrets that protected them, they killed him and pulverized his body. Devayānī's father, to satisfy his desperate daughter, spoke magical words that brought Kaca back to life. Over and over, the same actions occurred: the demons pulverized the hero, and the heroine's father brought him back to life. Finally, the demons ground him to a powder that they put in wine, which was drunk by Devayānī's father. The clever girl made her father promise to share the secret of bringing back the dead. When Kaca was reborn, in the process killing Devayānī's father, Kaca spoke the magical words and brought the father back as well. But then Kaca refused to marry Devayānī, because, having occupied her father's body, he was equivalent to her brother. (Ghosh 1965; O'Flaherty 1975)

Devī All Hindu goddesses are aspects of the powerful Devī. This understanding dates to approximately the sixth century CE, when the text called the *Devī Mahatmya*, "glorification of the great goddess," appeared. This and similar texts posit a single goddess whose reality underlies all individual goddesses. This belief obscures ethnic and cultural divisions among worshippers of goddesses subsumed under her name.

Devī transcends categories, including the visible and invisible world. She was born at the beginning of time from the combined anger of the gods, so she might battle a demon (in this guise, she is the same as **Durgā**). Her first action was to laugh; her second, to slay the demon. After this action, she became a natural force animating other goddesses. She can be a natural object such as a water-filled cleft in rock, a living girl dressed in bright red, or a high-breasted young mother with a girlish face. Her worship often includes decking her images in silk, flowers, and jewelry. It can be difficult to distinguish her images from those of other goddesses or to distinguish them definitively in mythic narrative. (Beane; Brown; Chandola; Hawley and Wulff; Dehejia; Gatwood; Hiltebeitel and Erndl; Gupta S; Ions; Kinsley 1986; O'Flaherty 1975; Pintchman 2001; Spivak; Zimmer 1946)

Dhūmāvatī A little-known Tantric goddess, Dhūmāvatī is depicted as scarred and dirty, with long breasts and a long nose, black skinned as a crow. Fierce and unfriendly, fond of blood, Dhūmāvatī eats bones and chews on corpse meat. Born from the smoke of self-immolating **Satī**, Dhūmāvatī has been described as a form of that loyal wife. One legend says that when Satī grew hungry and her mate refused to feed her, she ate him and, when he forced her to vomit, was turned into the frightening Dhūmāvatī.

Dhūmāvatī has been connected with **Nirṛti**; both may descend from ancient times, for Nirṛti appears in the earliest Vedic texts. In Tantra, Dhūmāvatī represents the condition of absolute freedom that comes from having given up or lost everything. She offers worshippers happiness, provided they renounce worldly ambitions and possessions. She has few temples, and most of her worshippers are unmarried. Yet a heterodox tradition holds that Dhūmāvatī is a sensual goddess who loves to dance and have wild sexual adventures. (Kinsley 1997)

Dīrghajihvī The demon Dīrghajihvī ("long-tongue") licked up the gods' liqueur, *soma*, whenever it was offered in sacrifice. When the god Indra failed to stop her depredations, he instructed a handsome god named Sumitra ("good friend") to seduce her. But Dīrghajihvī refused him; the god had only one penis, while she had vaginas all over her body. Sumitra returned to Indra with the information, and Indra magically endowed the handsome god with penises all over his body. When he made love to Dīrghajihvī, they stuck within her, immobilizing her, until Indra came and killed the demon queen. (O'Flaherty 1985)

Dītī If **Adītī** is "boundless," her counterpart Dītī is "the bounded one." Both come from a non-Indo-European source, for their children, though supernatural, were never part of the official pantheon. Dītī's children were *asuras,* called after her the Daityas. They were powerful beings, especially the warrior Maruts. Dītī, whose earlier children had been killed by Indra, practiced magic while pregnant again. Indra watched her constantly. When Dītī fell asleep, Indra entered her vagina, traveled to her womb, and dismembered the fetus. Cut to pieces, the fetus was so powerful it re-formed into forty-nine separate warriors. (Berkson; Daniélou 1964; Dimmitt and van Buitenen; Ions; Kinsley 1986; Pattanaik)

Draupadī The heroine of the epic *Mahābhārata,* Draupadī was brought to life by a king who organized a sacrifice to create an improbably strong warrior. From the fire emerged a man strong enough to meet the king's needs. At the same time a ravishing young woman emerged, dark skinned and with blue-black hair, from whose body poured forth the fragrance of lotus blossoms. From the moment of her birth, the king hoped she would wed the hero Arjuna.

When she was old enough to wed, the king organized a contest for her hand. The winner had to string a rigid bow and then, using a pond as a mirror, shoot in the opposite direction, hitting the eye of a wooden fish turning on a wheel. Only one could perform such a feat. Arjuna won but had to fight the other contestants in order to leave with Draupadī.

When they arrived home, Arjuna's mother, Kuntī, called out, "whatever you won, you must share equally." Thus Draupadī became polyandrous, sleeping in turn with each of five husbands, the Pāṇḍavas. Several alternative stories describe why she had five husbands. In one, she was so eager to marry that she invoked Shiva five times, receiving a husband for each invocation. In another, Draupadī was the incarnation of **Lakṣmī** (or **Indrāṇī**), married to five incarnations of her consort, Vishnu (or Indra), at once.

When her oldest husband gambled her away,

Draupadī's virtue protected her. As her attackers attempted to drag her sari from her, it lengthened into hundreds of yards of material, so Draupadī was never naked. Humiliated nonetheless, she pledged to wash her hair in her enemies' blood.

Many adventures lay ahead for Draupadī and her husbands. They spent years in exile, far from the cities to which they were accustomed. While the Pāṇḍavas and Draupadī lived in the wilderness, she was unable to give hospitality as a queen should. She pleaded with the goddess of abundance, and Lakṣmī gave Draupadī a cooking pot that could never be emptied.

Although she appears as a romantic heroine in the *Mahābhārata,* Draupadī is worshipped as a goddess in southern India, where festivals for her are held and temples erected. A major festival near Puducherry features fire walking in honor of Draupadī, because she was born as a result of her father's sacrificial fire. (Dehejia; Whitehead; Hiltebeitel 1988, 1999; Hiltebeitel and Erndl; Gupta Ś 1991; Narasimhan; Pattanaik; Zimmer 1946)

Durgā Durgā, a golden-skinned, ten-armed woman, holds a spear and wears a blood-red sari. She was born during the primordial war between gods and demons, which dragged on until the gods concentrated their energies. Flames sprang from their mouths in the shape of a beautiful woman. Although produced by gods, the goddess was stronger than all of them, and was eager to fight. The gods handed weapons to Durgā, who rode a lion toward the enemy chief, Mahiṣa. He used his powers to assume one fearsome form after another. Still Durgā advanced until, as Mahiṣa assumed the form of a buffalo, the goddess slaughtered him, freeing the earth for the gods to inhabit.

The goddess also had to defeat Durgā, whose name she took. Durgā marched against the demon's army. Durgā grew a thousand arms and used them to throw flaming brands. When she reached her enemy, Durgā tore herself into nine million pieces and destroyed the army, then strangled its leader.

Other myths provide alternative versions of

Durgā's birth. In one, she was the emanation of the creative force of Vishnu, summoned to protect the endangered Krishna. Then she hid herself in the womb of Krishna's mother, Devaki, allowing herself to be killed at birth so Krishna would live. For that, she was granted perpetual sacrifices. Although Durgā's maternal nature is rarely emphasized in myth, she was the mother of **Lakṣmī** and **Sarasvatī** by her consort Shiva.

Durgā is celebrated as part of a nine-day autumn ritual to aspects of **Devī**; five days are devoted to Durgā. The rite is popular in Bengal, where a lion-mounted Durgā, crafted of straw and wood, is paraded through villages and installed in her temples. Domestic rituals, using smaller images, are part of this holy period.

Durgā temples on the outskirts of settlements are often dedicated to Vana Durgās, or "forest Durgās," for Hinduism never fully assimilated these local goddesses. In Java, Durgā is associated with graveyards and black magic, although she was in earlier times a beneficent goddess and protector. In Bali, as Betari Durgā, she rules destruction, although in her association with **Ibu Pretiwi**, she is a cosmic goddess of birth and death.

In Nepal, the goddess is embodied in priestesses called Kumaris ("virgins"), of whom the chief (Raj-Kumari, or "royal virgin") emerges annually from her residence in Kathmandu to renew the state. The chief Kumari abdicates her position when she begins to menstruate, when it is believed the goddess leaves her body. The name Kumari has been known for at least two millennia as indicating a daughter divinity. She was long ago absorbed into Durgā and is infrequently worshipped as a separate divinity. (Allen 1975, 1976; Berkson; Dehejia; Gupta Ś 1972, 1991; Harle; Ions; Kinsley 1986, 1989; McDaniel 2004; Pattanaik; Rodrigues; Santiko; Schnepel; Sharma; Whitehead; Young 1994; Zimmer 1946)

Eling-Llitung-Tune The earth goddess of the Minyong of northeastern India was made of rock. She gave birth parthenogenetically to another rock called Peddong-Nane, who in turn gave birth to earth's creatures. (Elwin 1958)

Erukamma Once she was a woman, accused of stealing children and hiding them beyond the boundaries of the village, where she would cut off their heads and eat them. After she died, she was deified so that her fearsome energies would protect rather than assault the village. The same story is told of the goddess **Hārītī**, who may have been a similar local goddess of earth and sky transmuted via Buddhism into the Hindu pantheon.

Erukamma is a village goddess (see **Grāma-devatā**) who has become absorbed into the larger Hindu pantheon as the coastal Bengalese city of Visakhapatnam has expanded into one of the subcontinent's most populous areas. Originally a lower-caste goddess, she is now honored by people of all castes. Other village goddesses of the area are the protective Pyḍamma, credited with helping the village attract commercial investment; Durgālamma, a snake goddess who attracts wealth; Pollamma, a powerful ocean goddess joined by the snake goddess Nīlamma (Nīlamāmba) and by Kunchamma (Kunchamāmba); Kanaka Durgā (Kannakamma), an agricultural divinity; Mariḍamma, goddess of low-caste people honored in the form of a healing neem tree; and Kanaka Mahālakṣmī, a goddess worshipped only in the open air. (Pintchman 2001)

Gaṇgā The mother of rivers lived in heaven with her younger sister **Umā**. Gaṇgā flowed three times around the heavenly city that rose on the summit of sacred Mount Meru. When sea-dwelling demons harassed the earth, the sage Agastya swallowed the ocean where they hid. Agastya got rid of the demons, but the earth was left parched and dry. Life on earth would have died, but Gaṇgā threw herself down. Unbroken, Gaṇgā's power could have washed away the world, but Shiva received her torrent on his head. Thereafter the goddess, embodied in the river Ganges, made the land fertile and sacred as she flowed across it.

Part of Gaṅgā remained in heaven as the Milky Way. Another part flowed under the earth. The intersection of the three at Benares is sacred. An important pilgrimage involves walking the Ganges from source to sea and back again, marking shrines to the goddess along the way. At sites along the river, people wash themselves in its purifying waters. Annually, hundreds of thousands travel to avail themselves of Gaṅgā's promise to wash away ten sins from each of a bather's past ten lives. Devout Hindus seek to die immersed in Gaṅgā, for the goddess ensures instant freedom from punishment and reincarnation.

Gaṅgā Daśaharā, celebrated throughout India, marks the moment when the river descended from the heavens. Those unable to travel to the river bless themselves with some of her water from a vial. Calling out the goddess's name is a powerful form of worship, rewarded with goodwill and blessings. (Bonnefoy; Daniélou 1964; Dehejia; Hawley and Wulff 1982; Ions; Gupta L; Gupta Ś; Kinsley 1986; Narayan; Narasimhan; Sharma; Whitehead; Zimmer 1946)

Gaurī Before she made her reputation as a warrior, **Durgā** was Gaurī, the golden sky virgin. Sometimes Gaurī is called **Pārvatī**, Shiva's dark lover, after she underwent magical skin-lightening beauty treatments. Yet again, some say Gaurī is another name for Varunī. In any case, Gaurī is the name used for the goddess worshipped in August festivals. Gaurī's particular day is August's new moon, when bedtime sweets are eaten to bring Gaurī's honeyed grace into the soul for the year.

In northern India, women celebrate Gaurī at an eighteen-day festival called Gaṅgāur. Unmarried maidens pray for a good husband, while wives celebrate in hopes of making their unions happy. Images of the goddess are decked with flowers and grass, then plunged into water in replication of Gaurī's austerities undertaken to achieve union with the god Shiva. Her practices were so effective that Kāmā, god of

love, shot an arrow that caused the whole world to blossom, at which the god fell in love with Gaurī. As Gaurī-Sankar, the goddess is embodied in the world's highest peak, Mount Everest. (Daniélou 1964; Dehejia; Gupta S, Gupta Ś 1991; Ions; Kinsley 1986; Jayakar; Zimmer 1946)

Gāyatrī Because some rituals could not be performed without a wife to accompany the celebrant, Gāyatrī was installed as the wife of Brahma when his first wife, **Sarasvatī**, could not be found. Gāyatrī was the mother of the four Vedic scriptures; her name refers to a Vedic meter. (O'Flaherty 1975; Pattanaik)

Girdoli The sacred milk cobra was the primal entity upon which the earth rested, according to the Lohaar of central India. When the gods sought a place for the earth, they came to Girdoli's mother-in-law, the cobra Dudh Nang, who had Girdoli's husband gather all the old rags in the world and build a pad for Girdoli's head, upon which the earth was placed. Girdoli still loves her husband, so every thirteen years she puts the earth down so she can make love with him. When she does, earthquakes occur. (Elwin 1949)

Goda A South Indian legend says the girl Goda, a reincarnation or avatar of the goddess **Devī**, was born in the town of Srivilliputtur, south of Madurai, and intended from birth to become a bride of Krishna. She composed many lovely hymns still used in the daily rituals of the goddess in that area, then disappeared into a black stone that embodied the god's phallus. Every year her marriage to the god is celebrated in her temple, with the icon of the goddess placed on a swing like a bride. (Dehejia)

Gōpīs These "cowherds" play an important role in myths about Krishna. Because his mother, **Devaki**, was threatened with Krishna's murder, he was brought up as the son of the cowherd **Yasoda**. As a child, he saved the Gōpīs when they drank the waters of a lake poisoned by the serpent Kāliya. Krishna wept, and his tears revived the Gōpīs. Later, when the Gōpīs were playing on the lakeshore, their ball went into the waves, and Krishna went in after it. When an evil serpent attacked, Krishna swelled up until he was a giant, saving both himself and the cowherds' ball.

Krishna grew into a charming young man with whom all the cowgirls fell in love. One day he stole their clothes while they were bathing, extracting from them a promise that they would dance with him every full moon. Thereafter, the sound of Krishna's flute brought the Gōpīs to the forests, where each one felt he was dancing with her alone. When Krishna chose **Rādhā** as his beloved, the other Gōpīs ostracized the girl, bringing about Krishna's illness and near death. But when Rādhā passed a test of loyalty, the Gōpīs accepted Krishna's love for her. The story of the Gōpīs is enacted by dance troupes that perform the *ras lila* ("play of love") in ritual settings during monsoon season. During this ritual, one woman serves as a living representative of the beloved Rādhā. (Beswick; Dehejia; Dimmitt and van Buitenen)

Grāmadevatā In addition to divinities of orthodox Hinduism, India is home to myriads of goddesses unknown outside their individual villages. Often no temple or shrine exists, for the goddesses are honored in the form of an unusual rock or large tree. These "village goddesses" are guardians of boundaries that they keep safe from aggressors. Their simple festivals honor the abundance of the earth and the goddess who provides it. In the south, the name Amman ("lady" or "mistress," a root word found in **Māriyamman** and similar names) indicates the goddess is a Grāmadevatā.

When a village grows into a city, its matron goddess grows in stature. Myths describe the goddess as the reason for the city's foundation. At times, the city goddess is the ancestral divinity of the ruler's family. Such a goddess is Danteshvari, goddess of the region around Jagdalpur in Orissa. Although the ruler was an invader who conquered the indigenous tribal people, they did not discontinue their own village goddess

worship, simply adopting the new name. Meanwhile, old regional goddesses were assimilated into the newcomer by being declared her thirty-two sisters. Although these goddesses are technically Hindu, they are non-Vedic and have little connection with Vedic divinities. Most do not appear in textual sources; they are known through prayer and practice in their immediate localities. (Crooke; Dehejia; Foulston; Jayakar; Sharma; Whitehead)

Halia The lightning goddess of the Bugun of northeastern India is a young girl who constantly attempts to avoid being assaulted by her brother. She hides in clouds, but he finds her whenever she has to wash her hair, which falls down and turns the sky black. When he sneaks up on her, she pulls out a hairpin that flashes as lightning. He runs away, making the sound of thunder. When Halia drops the hairpin, it strikes trees and burns them up. (Elwin 1958)

Hanai The sun goddess of the Buguns and Khowas of northwestern India was Hanai, whose husband was the moon, Habia. Their daughter was Lomi and their son, Jomi. When Lomi and Jomi consummated an incestuous love and conceived a child, they ran away out of terror at what their mother would do. Lomi gave birth in the sky, then threw the monstrous child down to earth, where it still lives on an oceanic rock. (Elwin 1955)

Hārītī This ogress had 500 children, whom she loved passionately. When the Buddha hid one of her children until she accepted his faith, she converted and, in the process, became tenderhearted toward women who had lost children. The devourer and bestower of children, she enjoyed wide popularity that hints at a cosmic goddess demoted into demonic form. (Pintchman 2001; Shaw 2006; Young 2004)

Hathay In Parañganad in South India, this goddess ("grandmother") was originally a girl who refused to marry the man selected for her. She drowned herself in the pool in the center of the village. When she appeared to people in dreams, announcing she had been an incarnation of **Parvatī**, her worship was assured. (Gupta S; Whitehead)

Holikā The demon queen Holikā is worshipped on one of India's major national holidays, Holī, which marks winter's end. She was originally a princess who bathed in fire every day, but one day her magic disappeared, and Holikā burned up. Another story says Holikā was a demon of fire who attempted to kill the young Krishna by offering him her breasts, but he sucked so hard that he killed her. Her myth is reenacted in the burning of an effigy decorated with cow dung by dancing women. Small household fires clear away piles of discards from spring-cleaning. (Patton; Gupta Ś 1991)

Ilā With an apparently ancient name for the Indian earth goddess, Ilā appears in contradictory stories that leave unanswered questions about her original identity and form. Some stories call her male, or say she changed sex several times. In the *Rig Veda*, Ilā was the goddess progenitrix of humanity who invented food and milk to feed her children. When invoked, she is often mentioned together with lesser-known earth goddesses, Bhāratī, Mahī, and Hotrā. (Dimmitt and van Buitenen; Kinsley 1986)

Indrāṇī Indra, the tempestuous storm god, raped Indrāṇī ("divine grace"), who became his consort and bore three sons. One of her names, Śacī, denotes "power," from which this goddess has been interpreted as her consort's personified might. (Ions; Pintchman 1994)

Jaṅgulī This three-mouthed, six-handed golden Buddhist snake goddess is shown holding a sword, a thunderbolt, and an arrow with her right hands, while her left hold a noose, a blue lotus, and a bow. She was invoked as a protector against poisonous snakes. Because Buddhism did not permit killing such creatures, magical invocations to Jaṅgulī ("snake charmer") were popular among those fearing snake-bite. She was herself a snake goddess, one of a type common in India (see **Manasā**). (Shaw 2006)

Jayamālā At the foot of the Bhutan hills, Jayamālā and her husband, the priest Jayanath, lived frugally but happily together—or so thought Jayamālā. But her husband had a streak of greediness. When he was offered the chance for a second wife, the only daughter of a wealthy man, he succumbed to greed. No sooner had the new wife moved in than she built a new home for herself and husband, barring Jayamālā from entering or from seeing their husband. Only once each day, when she brought water from the river, would Jayamālā see the man she had loved. Then she would sit by the river and weep, making the waters salty with her tears. It was this salt that the king of elephants tasted, a taste that led him to find the lovely abandoned wife. He proposed marriage to her but Jayamālā was true to her first love, until a wave rushed in, tearing down the palace the rich girl had built and carrying away all its occupants. With that, Jayamālā went willingly into the land of elephants, where a waterfall of magic colors turned her into a queen elephant. Since then, legend says, all elephant herds are headed by a queen in honor of Jayamālā. (Pakrasi)

Jyeṣṭhā Jyeṣṭhā is rarely worshipped now, but this was not the case during the seventh and eighth centuries, when she was an extraordinarily popular divinity. Early images show her as a stout woman with firm breasts and an abundant belly. She stands in relaxed posture, holding a lotus flower and a water pot, making a protective gesture. She wears an elaborate hairstyle and fine jewelry. Crows surround her, as do small children. Born when the cosmic ocean was churned, sister of **Lakṣmī** (thus sometimes identified as **Alakṣmī**), Jyeṣṭhā was dark and unattractive, with breasts that hung to her stomach and a huge stomach. She married a hermit, who was not a good husband. When he abandoned her, the gods decreed that she be supported by women's offerings and that she appear whenever married couples argued. (Kinsley 1997; Leslie)

Kadrū One-eyed Kadrū was born at the beginning of time, when **Shatarupa** divided herself into thirteen parts. Best known as the mother of **Manasā**, Kadrū wagered with her sister Vinatā about who could see farthest. But she attempted to cheat and, as a result, forfeited one of her eyes. Kadrū prayed to become the mother of a thousand snakes, while her sister prayed for two children more powerful than all her sister's.

Kadrū laid a thousand eggs, Vinatā two. For 500 years they rested together in a jar of water. Then Kadrū's eggs hatched into a thousand snakes. Anxious, Vinatā broke open one of her own eggs to see if anything was alive. She found a son, but the lower half of his body was malformed from hatching too early. He cursed his mother to serve her sister for another 500 years, at the end of which time the second egg hatched into the giant snake-eating bird Garuda, who avenged his mother by eating Kadrū's offspring. (Dange; Kinsley 1986; Pattanaik; Zimmer 1955)

Ka Iam She and her sister Ka Ngot, water divinities of the Khasi people of Assam, had a race in which they took on the forms of the rivers Umiam and Umngot, each river reflecting the personality of the girl who submerged herself into it: Umngot took an easy path and slid along, and Umiam made her way energetically through ravines and gorges. Despite her slow progress Umngot won, reaching the coast and spreading out into a lovely semicircle. When she arrived, Umiam, shamed by her loss, broke into five small rivers. (Pakrasi)

Kaikeyi Passionate and beautiful, this warrior wife joined her kingly husband in battle. One day, she saw his chariot wheel about to fly off. So she put her thumb into the bolt-hole and held the chariot steady despite intense pain. When he learned how her effort had saved him, the king promised her two gifts, which she said she would choose later. Many years passed before she claimed her boon: that he pass over his oldest son by another woman to crown her own son king. The king was forced to comply, leading to the exile of his favored son, Rama, the consort of **Sītā**. When the king died of a broken heart, Kaikeyi blamed herself. Her son also blamed her, never again referring to her as his mother. (Narayan; Pattanaik)

Kaitab Among the Raja Muria of central India, this was the name of the earth's mother. In order for the earth to be born, men stoned Kaitab to death. From her flesh the earth was formed, from her bones the rocks. (Elwin 1949)

Kālī Her tongue juts out of her black face. Her four hands hold weapons. Her necklace and earrings are strung with dismembered bodies. Kālī wears snakes all about her body, writhing on her head and around her neck. She was born at time's beginning, manifesting herself when the demon Dāruka threatened the gods. **Pārvatī** entered the body of Shiva and gathered poison stored in his throat, bursting forth as three-eyed Kālī, armed with a trident. This emanation dispatched the demon, but her battle fury was uncontained, and Kālī threatened the world until Shiva restrained her. Stories of Kālī as a demon destroyer connect her with **Durgā**, as does her name Chamunda (see **Matrikas**), formed from demons Chanda and Munda, whom she killed.

Several myths speak of Kālī's uncontrollable energy. Once, Kālī and Shiva danced together, growing more competitive, until it seemed the world would shake to pieces; and so it will, for beneath appearances that dance continues. Another time, Kālī killed two demons, which required that she strip because they were invulnerable to all but a naked woman. This enraged her, so she killed them, then celebrated her victory by draining their blood. Her wrath unappeased, Kālī danced wildly, until she realized Shiva was underneath her. The god's tactic slowed Kālī's wildness, but only for the moment, for she will resume the dance that ends the world.

During the world's first age, the Satya Yuga, Kālī lived with Shiva. Shiva abandoned Kālī but could not escape her, for wherever he turned, one of her forms appeared, teaching him that Kālī is all-pervasive and inescapable. So he returned to her and they watched the four eras unfold. By Hindu calculations, we are currently enduring the age of Kālī, the 432,000-year-long Kālī Yuga, which began on Friday, February 18, 3102 BCE. Creation's final stage before its destruction and rebirth, the Kālī Yuga is a period when kings lack tranquility, women and cows are recklessly killed, and money is the basis for nobility. At the end of this desperate age, humanity will be destroyed after a hundred-year drought followed by fire and flood, until the entire universe dissolves into **Prakṛti**. Then the cycle of creation will begin again.

Several attributes are important in Kālī's iconography: her blackness, her jutting tongue, and her wild, snake-like hair. Kālī is described as the cast-off black skin of Pārvatī, who underwent austerities to gain beauty that would attract Shiva. After she had purified herself, her skin whitened, with its blackness consolidating itself as Kālī. The myth, which refers to attitudes toward skin color in caste-conscious India, may point to an indigenous or non-Indo-European origin for the goddess. Another myth describes Kālī as having a pockmarked face, connecting her with **Sītāla**. The rest of her body is unmarked, because her brother licked her all over to remove the scars, but modesty forbade him to lick her face.

Images show Kālī with tongue distended. Often her lips are bright red, suggesting she has been drinking blood. Some texts say the gesture indicates Kālī's sudden mortification at finding herself dancing on her consort, Shiva, but it is more likely that the tongue indicates sexuality and/or consumption of forbidden foods, with which Kālī is connected.

Images also emphasize Kālī's wild, disheveled hair. Well-dressed hair is an important part of the Hindu woman's self-presentation, so Kālī's hairdressing (or lack thereof) breaks social norms and taboos. It also connects her to the forbidden parts of women's lives, for they traditionally unbound their hair when "polluted" by menstruation or death.

Although her maternal nature is not evident from her iconography, the goddess is known as Kālī-Mā, "mother Kālī." Bloodthirsty Kālī grows tender-hearted toward anyone who adores her as mother. Such a vision of Kālī animated the work of Indian poets Rāmprasād and Ramakrishna. In addition, the kindly side of the goddess was visible to devotees in the Yugoslavian Catholic nun Mother Teresa, who was seen as an avatar of the goddess.

Kālī is one of India's most popular goddesses, second only to abundance-granting **Lakṣmī**. Her picture hangs in homes, and her name is familiar in Calcutta, home to the temple where her skull is kept. Preeminent among Tantric divinities, Kālī is primary in both right- and left-handed paths but is especially important in the latter, for she represents the fearful and the forbidden. Dancing in cemeteries, drinking blood, she shows the way to enlightenment through confronting fear and death. (Beane; Caldwell; Dehejia; Daniélou 1964; Dimmitt and van Buitenen; Gombrich and Obeyesekere; Gupta S; Hixon; Ions; Kinsley 1975; Hawley and Wulff; Kripal; McDermott; McDaniel 2004; McDermott and Kripal; Larson et al; Mookerjee; Pintchman 2001; Sen R; Thadani; Whitehead; Zimmer 1946)

Kāmadhenu This name is commonly used of the sacred cow that symbolizes prosperity in India (see **Lakṣmī**). She is also called Śabalā and Kapilā, depending on whether she is spotted or reddish. In Sanskrit, the words "cow" and "earth" are synonyms, indicating the connection between this figure and the earth goddess. As a divine "wish cow," or granter of abundance, she was born of Surabhi ("fragrance") and was the mother of the bull who accompanied Shiva. (Bonnefoy; Daniélou 1964; Gupta S; Zimmer 1946.)

Kāma-Kalā Goddess of sexuality, Kāma-Kalā is depicted as a series of three dots or circles representing erotic parts of the female body, the breasts and mouth. (Jayakar)

Kamakhsya Among the Koch people of central Assam, this was the name of the high goddess, a form of the great Hindu goddess Durgā. She appeared in her temple annually in human form, as a naked girl who danced all night. One night when she was dancing, the king fell in love with her. She agreed to marry but required that he build stairs into her temple from the valley below, the entire project to be completed in one night. The workers came close to finishing, but a cock crowed just before dawn, saving the goddess from marriage to a human. The king then attempted to rape her, after which the goddess cursed him and his family and disappeared into her statue, never to return in the form of a living woman.

Another version of her legend has it that the tribal Garos people were driven out of their original homeland by invaders. A woman named Nunui Nanokhi (Noini Mechik) carried an image of their ancestral goddess, Phojou. When the woman set down the image of the goddess, it thereafter refused to move. Realizing that this was the place the goddess had selected as her own, the people built a shrine to her and changed her name to Kamakhya. (Ghosh and Ghosh; Pakrasi)

Ka Nam Among the Khasis (Hynniew trep), an ethnic group in northern India and Bangladesh, Ka Nam was born, so beautiful that her mother feared she would be kidnapped. So she imprisoned the child in a secluded part of the village. The girl's father finally convinced his wife that their child should lead a more normal life, which was to prove her undoing.

One day, as Ka Nam was drawing water from a well, a huge tiger dragged her off to its lair. When the tiger, U Khla, realized what a tiny morsel the girl was, he decided to fatten her up. He brought her little candies and made her feel at home. Ka Nam forgot to be afraid and grew into a young woman with perfect trust in tigers.

Her host, however, had not lost sight of his objective in rearing the girl. When Ka Nam had reached full growth, U Khla invited all his tiger friends for a feast. A mouse warned Ka Nam and she ran away, following the mouse's directions to the cave of the magician toad U Hynroh. He said he would protect her, but in fact he only intended to make her a slave. Telling her he was going to make sure she would be safe from the tiger, he turned her into a truly hideous toad.

The tiger, returning to his den, found his captive had escaped. He grew furious and called down curses on whoever had stolen his prey. The other tigers, when they realized they wouldn't get anything to eat, turned on U Khla and tore him apart.

Back at U Hynroh's, the mouse had witnessed Ka Nam's transformation. Taking pity on the girl, she led Ka Nam to a magical tree that led to the sky. The maiden climbed into the tree and spoke the mouse's magic words: "Grow tall, dear tree, the sky is near, expand and grow." The tree grew until it reached the sky, and there the maiden entered the Blue Realm.

Ka Nam, looking like a toad, went from palace to palace begging for help, but the heavenly folk were so repulsed by her ugliness that they threw her out. Finally she approached the palace of **Ka Sgni**, the sun mother, who gave her an outhouse to live in.

There she sat one day, toadskin off, combing her hair. And there the son of Ka Sgni saw her and fell in love with her. He ran to his mother and asked her to move the maiden indoors so he could be near her. Ka Sgni, a wise mother, waited to see if the infatuation would pass. She also went to spy on the toad in the outhouse and saw the maiden without her toad disguise shining with loveliness.

Realizing that the maiden had been bewitched, Ka Sgni knew she would have to find the maiden asleep and then burn the toadskin. She did so, releasing the maiden but incurring the fury of the magician toad. For days he tried to devour Ka Sgni, causing the world's first eclipse. Below on earth, the people stood in fear, watching the goddess fighting for her life. They screamed and they cried, they beat drums and cymbals.

When he heard the commotion, U Hynroh thought an army was about to advance on him. He released the sun goddess but continues to attack her periodically, hoping humans will be too busy to help. For this reason, the Khasis say, it is important always to make a lot of noise during an eclipse. (Pakrasi)

Kansa Nagin The salt goddess of the Chikanput people of Orissa came from the underworld, where she lived with her mother, the ancestral goddess Dhuli Nagin. When the time came to marry, the girl cleansed herself using turmeric and river sand. The dirt from her bath was carried away by cobra girls and hidden where neither men nor cattle could find it. But somehow a rat found its way to the hidden dirt and carried it to the world of men, where it was found to be tasty. This was the world's first salt. (Elwin 1954)

Kantarupi In the city of Mysore, the goddess **Bisal-Mariamna** and her six sisters stole the husband of a young woman, Kantarupi, for their pleasure. They held him captive, but after growing weary of him, decided to let him return briefly to his wife. Mischievously, they hypnotized Kantarupi, so she was ignorant of the night they spent together. A few months later the apparent widow, Kantarupi, realized she was pregnant but could not explain how. Certain she'd been unfaithful with a secret lover, Kantarupi's father cast her into the woods. There a prostitute adopted her and exposed the baby boy in a snake temple, where his grandfather found him and raised him. Kantarupi, having no other recourse for keeping herself alive, joined her hostess in prostitution.

Years later, the grown son passed through the prostitute's quarters and, seeing Kantarupi, fell in love and arranged a meeting. But on the way, he stumbled over a calf whose mother soothed him by saying, "What can you expect of someone about to sleep with his own mother?" The young man was baffled. He was even more baffled when he approached Kantarupi, and all the mother's milk she had never given him to drink exploded from her breasts. All ended happily, however,

when Bisal-Mariamna released the stolen husband, and the family was reunited. (Shulman 1980)

Karni This minor goddess was said to have asked the god of death, Yama, to restore a woman's son to life. When Yama refused, Karni vowed that none of her devotees would ever die. When they pass from life, they are reborn as the mice that live in her temple in Rajasthan. When the mice die, they are reborn as Karni's devotees. (Pattanaik)

Ka Sgni The sun goddess of the Khasis lived on earth with two sisters, Ka Um (water) and Ka Ding (fire), and their brother U Bynai, the moon. U Bynai was as bright as Ka Sgni. But he was a spoiled and self-centered young man who spent many nights away from home, drinking and gambling.

Then he began to desire his sister. When she realized what he was planning, she grew furious. Scorching his face with ashes, she refused to consort with him. U Bynai was so ashamed he left home to wander through the heavens. His sisters stayed home with their mother until she died. Then they formed the earth from her body.

Another story says the civet cat, U Kui, cut the line holding earth and heaven together. Those below were plunged into darkness because the sun hid in shame over her brother's propositions. Many animals went in search of the sun—the elephant, the horse, the rhinoceros, the buffalo—but none could find her. Finally, the cock saved the day, by convincing the divinity who removes the curse of incestuous love to do so for the sun goddess. Then he crowed three times, and the sun goddess reappeared. (Rafy)

Kayum In the Indian northeast, this great ancestral mother plays little part in human history except to give birth to important beings, including the earth goddess **Sedi**. She is honored in genealogical songs but has little religious role. (Elwin 1955)

Khupning-Knam Born of clouds and mist, this primal woman of the Singpho floated in primeval mist until she gave birth to snow children, a boy and a girl. Because they had no one else to marry, they married each other and produced the earth, the goddess Inga, and the sky, the god Mu. At first the earth was only mud and the sky was only cloud, but the siblings' son, the wind Imbung, blew so hard that Inga dried up and Mu flew upward. (Elwin 1958)

Klu-mo Part of the tradition of *bon-po*, the religion which preceded Buddhism in Tibet, Klu-mo was the first being to emerge from the void of creation. From the top of her head, the sky erupted. Then the moon burst from her right eye, the sun from her left, and the stars from her teeth. Her voice created thunder and her tongue lightning. Her breath formed the clouds, her tears the rain. Her flesh formed the earth, and the rivers that run across it are her veins. When her eyes open, it is day; when she closes them to sleep, night descends. (Bonnefoy)

Koṭavī Wild naked Koṭavī appears on battlefields, where she opposes the forces of the gods while protecting her demon offspring. A similar goddess, found in South India and called Korravai, haunts battlefields and grants victory to her favorites. She is shown nude, with deranged hair. Sometimes armor covers her upper body. She is a special goddess of the women drummers who accompany warriors into battle. (Caldwell; Kinsley 1986, 1997; Pattanaik)

Kubjā This hunchbacked girl worked as a masseuse, for despite the twist in her spine she was strong and agile. She was beautiful, too, although her deformity kept people from realizing that. Nonetheless, she attained renown for the oils she mixed and applied. One day, she met Krishna and, smitten with love for the handsome god, gave him some of her unguents. This so pleased Krishna that he picked her up and, hanging her for a few moments like a fish on a scale, straightened her spine and made her into a desirable woman. (Dimmitt and van Buitenen)

Kuhrami Among the Maria of central India, this primal woman was set afloat in a gourd with her brother. When the gourd ran aground on a rock, the couple found no food or water, and the earth was so hot it burned their feet. But when the high god sent animal messengers to check on the children, they reported that the boy and girl were fine, because the animals wanted to eat them. Finally a monkey told the truth, and the high god sent help, so they were able to plant and harvest. But they could not reproduce, because they were sister and brother. So Budi Matal, the mother goddess, inflicted smallpox upon them, so they became too scarred to recognize each other. From them, all people of the region descend. (Elwin 1949)

Kujum-Chantu The Apa Tanis say this giant woman formed the earth when, noticing that creatures were walking about on her fat stomach and realizing that if she rose they would fall to their deaths, willed herself to die. Her body turned into the earth, with the soil being richer where she was fattest; her eyes became the sun and moon. (Elwin 1958)

Kundalinī Devī A goddess who incarnates herself within human bodies, Kundalinī Devī lives for union with her consort, Shiva, brought about by yogic practices. Kundalinī lives in the lowest of ten chakras, where she appears as a snake coiled around a phallus with her head resting on its top. Through discipline, the snake can be encouraged to unwind herself and stretch up the entire spinal cord, bringing illumination. (McDaniel 2004)

Kuntī An ancient mother goddess, Kuntī was the ever-virginal lover of the gods. Although replaced in Hindu worship by later goddesses, Kuntī figured in the epic *Mahābhārata* as a king's daughter so devout that a sage gave her a magic formula to seduce any god. Kuntī had a son by the sun god but, because she was unmarried, cast the child away. Found by a charioteer, he was raised as such, but his kingly nature kept appearing, so he led a miserable, confused life. Later, Kuntī bore the husbands of polyandrous **Draupadī** by several gods. Kuntī is honored with a fair in north India, where a temple is dedicated to her. (Daniélou 1964; Hawley and Wulff; Gupta Ś 1991; Narasimhan 1965; Pattanaik)

Kurumba Celebrated at the popular Cock Festival in central Kerala, Kurumba is honored by the singing of sexual songs and the ceremonial pollution of her shrine when a lower-caste man circumambulates it. Possessed men dance and cut themselves with swords as they utter oracles from the goddess, and chickens are offered to the goddess, who keeps the region free from smallpox. As the festival site has Jain connections, Kurumba has been described as a form of the Jaina goddess Kannaki; her name is etymologically connected with the word for "anklet," the most important symbol of that goddess. (Gentes)

Lakṣmī India's most popular goddess, golden-skinned Lakṣmī represents abundance and wealth, not only in the form of money but as children, jewelry, and cows. She is the primary goddess of the home, honored with flowers, leaves, and vines. Peacocks and elephants also draw her approving eye.

Early myths describe Lakṣmī floating before creation in the milk ocean. Later myths describe Lakṣmī as rising from the ocean when it was churned by the gods, covered with necklaces and pearls, crowned and braceleted. Every god wanted her as wife, but she preferred Vishnu, being reborn with him in several incarnations. She was Padmā or Kamalā when he was the dwarf Vamana; she was Dharani, the earth, when he was Parasurama; she was faithful **Sītā** when he was Rama. Finally, when Vishnu was born as Krishna, Lakṣmī accompanied him as the cowgirl **Rādhā**, and later as his wife Rukminī.

Once Vishnu cursed Lakṣmī and turned her into a mare, in which form she lived in the underworld. There she centered her mind on the wild god Shiva. After thousands of years, the god was moved by her austerities and came to her, riding on a bull. When he asked her why she prayed to him, rather than to Vishnu, she revealed that she knew their secret: they were the same divinity. Impressed by her awareness, Shiva predicted that Vishnu would reunite with her.

Many interpreters suggest that Lakṣmī was preeminent in pre-Vedic India as goddess of the earth and its fructifying moisture; she was incorporated into Vedic theology when her worshippers would not abandon her. Once established, Lakṣmī grew to symbolize the wealth of the soul, becoming a symbol of spiritual prosperity. Lakṣmī's other name is Śri, "great one," under which she is associated with the lotus (symbol of enlightenment and fecundity) and the elephant (rain and royal power).

Hindu reverence for cows is based on worship of Lakṣmī. Hinduism defines male godhead as passive unless activated by the goddess, so Vishnu's power to enrich life only functions when Lakṣmī inspires it. Therefore it is thought good policy to revere embodiments of wealth, the cows who are called "Lakṣmī" after the goddess. At the festival of Pongal, cows' horns are painted brightly, their necks garlanded with flowers, and their food specially prepared. The festival draws its name from the raisin-filled rice fed to cattle on that day.

Another embodiment of Lakṣmī is rice, used to create wall paintings (*chita*) in honor of the goddess. In Orissa, during the Kaumunī-pūrṇimā festival, women invoke the goddess in a mound of grain and tell how she once disappeared, taking the world's food with her. Her connection with rice led to her adoption in Bali and Java as the goddess Dewi Shri.

As an embodiment of the goddess's reproductive power, brides are called "Lakṣmī" during their wedding festivities. At her *puja* (festival) in Tamil Nadu, Lakṣmī is honored as goddess of happily married women, because of the myth that she honored the god Shiva with a daily offering of a thousand lotus buds. When, one day, she found herself short two buds, she began to cut off her breasts because Vishnu compared them to lotus buds. Shiva, stopping the sacrifice when she had only cut off one breast, turned it into the sacred bael tree, under which he thereafter lived.

Although Lakṣmī is known as a consort goddess, she appears as the dominant partner in some myths. In Purī, she was said to roam the countryside alone, checking into the homes of her worshippers to see that they were performing rituals correctly. She found that they were sloppy in their worship, except for one outcaste woman who created a perfect ritual. Lakṣmī accepted food from the woman, but when she returned, her consort and his brother said she was ritually polluted. The goddess cursed them to wander for a dozen years until they were offered food by a *dalit* ("untouchable"), who would be Lakṣmī in disguise.

Many festivals are dedicated to Lakṣmī, the most important being Dīvalī, the festival of wealth and light. During Dīvalī, lamps are lighted to attract Lakṣmī's bounty. She is drawn to the best-lit homes and spurns dim ones, while her sister **Alakṣmī** prefers to visit dirty places. Devotees also offer Lakṣmī silver coins and light fireworks in her honor; they leave windows open all night, so the goddess has easy access. Businesspeople put their account books on an altar to Lakṣmī. (Daniélou 1964; Dimmitt and van Buitenen; Gupta S; Gupta Ś 1971; Ions; Kinsley 1986, 1989; Kumar; Leslie; Atkinson et al; Hawley and Wulff; Pattanaik; Hamilton; Sharma; Shaw 2006; Warrier; Young 1994; Zimmer 1946)

Lalitā A form of **Devī** or of **Tripura-sundarī**, Lalitā represents universal consciousness embodied as a desirable and desiring young woman. (Brooks; Gupta S)

Lha-mo Tibetan Lha-mo rules life, death, and regeneration. She is depicted as enveloped in flame, riding across a lake of blood. She was so fierce that, when her son refused to convert to Buddhism, she killed him and made a saddle blanket for her mule from his skin. Her companions are goddesses of the seasons, the jewel goddesses and the goddesses of long life. Derived from **Devī**, Lha-mo is the sole female figure among the Eight Terrible Ones who protect the land and its Buddhist believers. Originally a minor figure, she is now one of Tibet's greatest divinities. (Dehejia 1999; Shaw 2006)

Madhighariani Goddess of the city of Rayagada in Orissa, Madhighariani is honored in the form of six small white stones and one large one painted in the form of Madhighariani's head, with huge dark eyes and a golden mouth with protruding silver tongue. Assimilated to **Durgā**, Madhighariani ("in the middle of the fort") was originally a tribal goddess later patronized by the region's kings. A similar goddess, Markama, was the **Grāmadevatā** of the village of Bissamcuttack, adopted by local rulers. She was worshipped in the shape of a red-painted stone that represented her head, while an unpainted stone nearby represented her body. (Schnepel)

Mahi Goddess of the river that bears her name in the state of Gujarat, Mahi was a headstrong girl. She wanted to marry the sea, but her father refused to approve the match. So she set out alone from home to reach her goal. Wandering west, she found jungles filled with tigers. So she turned east, crossing rocky regions until she reached her objective. But the sea, seeing the dark-skinned woman, rejected her. Furious, she returned home and raised an army of stones, with which she assailed the sea. Overwhelmed with her strength and power, the sea married her, burying the stony army at their point of union. (Beck et al)

Mahiṣa Three goddesses incarnated together as the voluptuous and seductive Lila, while three gods incarnated together as her spouse. When the gods grew tired of life's challenges and wanted to enter a hermitage, Lila was not satisfied to go without intimacy. For this, the triple goddess was cursed to be reborn as Mahiṣa. Sister of the demon Mahisa destroyed by Durgā, Mahiṣa engaged in austerities in order to gain spiritual power over the gods. She grew so powerful that she received a blessing from Brahma that no one born of a man and a woman could kill her. But the god Vishnu incarnated as a temptress, the **Apsarā** Mohinī, and seduced the god Shiva, giving birth to the sage Ayyappa. He was so pure, he resisted gorgeous Lila, reborn once again from the ashes of the demon queen. So she took the form of a goddess, Malikapuruthamma, who in turn may be the same as the goddess Kadhiravati, goddess of the acacia tree. (Subramaniam)

Mainakini Once this princess of Sinhala saw a spirit, flying across the sky, lose his garments in the wind. As a result, she could see how small his penis was, and she laughed. In punishment, he stranded her in an all-women's land where she could not become pregnant. The women, desiring offspring, prayed to **Devī**. Although she could not break the curse, the goddess arranged for a god to stand just beyond the limits of the Amazonian world and sing, causing the women to conceive. When a celibate monk was sent to live among the women, he spent many years pleasuring the women and forgetting his spiritual disciplines. After decades, a student of the yogi happened along and brought the sage back to the outer world and yogic practice. (Pattanaik)

Maitreya This divinity of Indian and Tibetan Buddhism appears sometimes as male, sometimes female. Sex changes in divinities may indicate that a force is seen as essentially nonsexual, with the changing sexual identity alerting the viewer not to limit the divine essence to its human form. In other cases, sex change comes with political or social change. A powerful goddess transmuted into a god can indicate that the power represented by that divinity has been transferred from human women to men. It is unclear in which of these categories Maitreya should be placed. (Daniélou 1964; Overmyer)

Manasā The worship of **Manasā**, daughter of **Kadrū**, remains strong in Bengal, where she is honored as a goddess of prosperity and a protector against

snakebite. Her connection to wealth may derive from the reemergence of snakes at the beginning of the growing season. She has the power to bring the dead back to life, as snakes apparently revivify when they shed their skin.

Manasā emerged when Shiva, meditating by a pond, saw a lotus blossom. This caused him to ejaculate. His semen slithered down the stalks of the plant until it reached the king of the *nagas* (snake people), whose mother fashioned the seed into a beautiful goddess of snakes and poisons. She rose to the surface where Shiva sat, frightening him. He called for help in eradicating the snakes, but lovely Manasā pleaded for them. Struck by her beauty, Shiva attempted to make love to her, but she refused him, reminding him that she was his daughter. She did agree to go home with him, for which purpose she turned herself into a spider and hid among the lotus flowers. But Shiva's wife **Caṇḍī** rejected Manasā and, believing her to be Shiva's mistress, put out Manasā's eye with a hot poker. Her remaining eye flung out poison, and Caṇḍī fell down dead. After Shiva pleaded with Manasā to return his wife to life, Manasā restored her.

Manasā also saved Shiva's life after he had drunk poison produced by the churning of the cosmic sea. Because she had power over poisons, she was called upon to save her father. But she demurred because she was naked except for a tiger skin and could not appear before the gods. Caṇḍī gave Manasā some rags to wear and, insulted, Manasā struck her dead. But she went to the dying Shiva and sucked out all the poisons, half of which she shared with snakes and scorpions, the other half of which she kept in her single eye. Again, upon Shiva's request, she revived the dead Caṇḍī.

As part of his fatherly duties, Shiva had to find a husband for his fierce daughter, and he married her to a sage, by whom she had a son. Then she decided humans should worship her. The first people she encountered were cowherds who beat her bloody. She set her snakes upon them, but they still did not acknowledge her divinity. She milked a cow into a leaky basket and, turning it upside down, sipped milk from it, but this did not impress the cowherds. So she made their cattle disappear and refused to return them until they had agreed to festivals in her honor. As she traveled, she had many such encounters with people who, refusing to worship her, were brought into her devotion through threats of death and loss of livelihood.

In Bengal, a man refused to honor her, so Manasā killed each of his sons. Finally only Lakhindar, husband-to-be of Behulā, was left, and he was cursed to die on his wedding night. Local people knew the curse, so no girl would wed Lakhindar. But Behulā came from a distant town and did not know her likely fate as a despised widow. Lakhindar's father tried to thwart the goddess by building a snake-proof iron house, but Manasā threatened the architect, who left a small opening. Soon Lakhindar was no more.

Behulā would not leave the corpse, launching it onto the river with the intention of confronting the goddess. Behulā found her way to the hall of heaven, where she presented evidence against Manasā, who was ordered to restore Lakhindar's life. Through dancing, Behulā gained back the lives of her brothers-in-law, returning to the family as a heroine.

Manasā's most important festival is Naga-pachami, during monsoon season. On that day, the race of serpents that includes the **Nāginīs** was said to have been born. As the rainy season forces serpents from underground hiding, pots of milk are put out for them to feed upon, in hopes of deterring them from biting people. (Daniélou 1964; Dehejia; Gupta S; Ions; Kinsley 1986; McDaniel 2004; Sharma)

Manōdari One of India's smallpox goddesses comes from the region around Malabar. Once she was the wife of a demon whom **Kālī** was sent to kill. In an attempt to save her husband, Manōdari began a series of extreme austerities that finally forced Shiva to give her a boon. He told her that her sweat would thereafter be extraordinarily powerful. So when Manōdari met Kālī, returning triumphant from killing her husband, she hit the goddess with beads of her sweat, which turned into smallpox pimples. As Kālī

lay excruciatingly ill, Shiva grew angry, and his anger formed a hero who licked Kālī all over to remove the pox. But when he came to her face, he demurred out of modesty, for he was her brother and could not lick her face, so the otherwise-lovely goddess has visible pockmarks. The revived Kālī sent for Manōdari and had her arms and legs cut off, forcing her to serve thereafter as a figure to whom people pray under the name Vasūrimāla ("garland of poxes") for relief from the disease. (Aiyappan)

Mari Although women are devoted to this goddess, she is served by transvestite priests called *potarāja*. Legend has it that a lower-caste man, in love with a higher-caste woman, had to bury her when she died, because her family would have nothing to do with the process. In his grief he dressed in her clothing and ran through the town, invoking her as the goddess **Lakṣmī**. Another story says that the goddess, then called Ādimāi, granted the boon of a son to a good but barren man, but demanded that the son be brought up as a transvestite. The goddess has both benevolent and dangerous aspects, the latter connected (see also **Sītāla**) with the affliction of smallpox. As such, she can appear either as a beautiful, healthy woman or as an impoverished, pox-ridden one with mad eyes. It is likely that this goddess is a local version of **Māriyamman**. (Vetschera)

Mārīcī Buddhist goddess of dawn, invoked as the sun rises, Mārīcī was the consort of the Buddha Vairocana. Usually seen with three heads, at least one of which is a pig, she is also shown in a chariot drawn by seven wild boars. She is a protective divinity, endowing her worshippers with assurance that thieves and enemies cannot harm them. As such, she is sometimes depicted as a warrior. Mārīcī was masculinized into a god in China and Japan. (Dehejia; Shaw 2006)

Māriyamman This smallpox goddess is honored in southern India, where her temples must be built far from residences. Pox is understood as a visitation from the goddess and as a reminder of the importance of maintaining devotion to her. Now that smallpox is rare due to inoculations, the goddess functions as a maternal goddess who loves and disciplines her children. Her images show her as a fierce weapon-wielding goddess.

The goddess was originally a girl of the Brahman class who was courted by a disguised *dalit* ("untouchable"). Furious at being tricked, she killed herself and, becoming a goddess, burned the *dalit* alive. Another story says she was a pure wife, so chaste that she could boil water on her head. But she encountered two people making love and, feeling envy, lost her powers. Her husband, suspecting that she had been impure, had her beheaded. When she was restored to life, her body was mixed up with that of another woman, creating a half-Brahman, half-outcaste goddess.

Māriyamman has been connected with the **Matrikas** as both inflicting and healing disease. Her preferred offering is human hair, so her devotees shave their heads. She regularly possesses her followers (usually male) in ecstatic worship, provided they are chaste and strictly vegetarian. (Pintchman 2001; Kapadia; Kinsley 1986; Younger)

Matrikas The "seven mothers" may descend from the ancient Indus Valley civilization, where sculptures of seven goddesses have been found from Mohenjo-daro. In Hinduism, the Matrikas are said to have been the consorts of important gods: Brahmanī (female aspect of Brahma), Maheśvarî (Shiva), Kaumārī (Skanda), Vaiṣnavî (Vishnu), sow-faced Vārāhī (Varaha-Vishnu), **Indrāṇī** (Indra), and skeletal Cāmuṇda (with no consort, a form of **Devī** sometimes called Kālīka). Their worship is common throughout India, especially in Orissa. Honored with life-size images, they may have their own temples or be lodged in those of other divinities. Occasionally a temple is devoted to a single Matrika, commonly Vārāhī or Cāmuṇda. The latter is found in Nepal, where images of an emaciated goddess seated on a corpse are called Mahakālī, "great black one."

This collective is seen as benevolent and protective, although occasionally danger is associated with them. Stories exist of Matrikas attacking newborns or pregnant women, with the first ten days of a child's life said to be especially dangerous. Fierce Matrikas include Jarā, who stole two miscarriages to eat but accidentally formed a whole baby out of them; Pūtanā, an ogress who tried to kill the young Krishna by poisoning her breasts; and the husbandless **Jyeṣthā**. The dangerous Matrikas are offset by benevolent ones to whom offerings were left on crossroads and to whom barren women made sacrifice in hopes of a healthy pregnancy. (Dehejia; Kinsley 1986)

Matsya This goddess was conceived when a king accidentally ejaculated on a leaf he gave to a parrot to take to his queen. Attacked by a hawk, the parrot dropped the semen-containing leaf, which was eaten by the water nymph Adrika, who took the form of a fish for the occasion. When caught in a net, the fish was found to have twins in her belly: Matsya ("fish born") and her brother, who was adopted by the king while the girl was abandoned to the fisherfolk.

The fisherwoman Matsya was so smelly, from constantly handling dead fish, that she was called Gandhavati, or "stinky." But she was a good-hearted woman who wished to marry someday. To attract divine attention, she offered her boat to anyone who needed to cross the river. One passenger was a sage, who in the midst of the journey decided he had to have sex with the woman. Although frightened, Matsya agreed. The sage covered them with clouds so that they could not be seen. The sage was so powerful that Matsya lost her virginity, got pregnant, carried her child, delivered her baby, and was restored to virginity within a few moments. In recompense for providing him with offspring, the sage turned Matsya's odor into an intoxicating fragrance that attracted a king, who married Matsya and made her queen.

Because she had been betrayed by her own father, Matsya demanded that only her sons be allowed to inherit, thus forcing the king to disenfranchise the son he already had. To further ensure that there would be no contenders to the throne, Matsya demanded that the son, Devavrata, take a vow to remain childless; he did so, becoming known as Bhisma, "terrible vow." But Matsya's sons were unable to find brides, so Devavrata found a woman named **Amba**, at whose reincarnated hands he eventually died. The name Matsya is also used of an avatar of the god Vishnu. (Narasimhan; Pattanaik)

Māyā Māyā is a philosophic concept embodied in female form. Her role in the universe is important in Vedānta philosophy, which describes her as the creative force within Brahma. Because she endlessly creates new forms, Māyā disguises the ultimate oneness of all beings. Often called "delusion," she is more properly "illusion." There is no existence without Māyā, but we mistake her for reality. For this reason, Māyā is referred to as the veil of illusion, the distracting dance of multiplicity. Māyā's illusion is not falsehood or error; she is the basis of the universe, as well as being that universe.

In Buddhism, Māyā incarnated as a queen, mother of the bodhisattva Shakyamuni. It was his final rebirth, after having been born of the same mother for many lifetimes. Asleep and alone, Māyā dreamed that a white elephant with golden tusks entered her womb through her right side, impregnating her. From that moment, the bodhisattva was fully conscious in Māyā's womb. The pregnancy was pleasurable, for divine nymphs ceaselessly massaged Māyā. Anyone whom Māyā touched was instantly healed of disease and unhappiness. When her time was at hand, Māyā gave birth effortlessly. But seven days later, she died, her life's purpose fulfilled. She went to heaven to watch over her son, descending to learn from him after he had attained enlightenment. A number of sites of pilgrimage are devoted to Queen Māyā, especially around Kapilavastu, where the Buddha was born. (Daniélou 1964; Dehejia; Gupta S; Kinsley 1986; O'Flaherty 1980; Paul; Pintchman 1994; Shaw 2006; Whitehead; Young 2004; Zimmer 1946)

Menā Queen of the world's highest mountains, Menā lives in the peaks in a golden palace, tended by magical birds and maidens. Her consort, the airy Himavat (Himālaya), was the father of **Pārvatī**. According to West Bengali myth, Menaka was a devotee of **Satī**, to whom Menaka offered rituals for twenty-seven years. For such devotion, the goddess offered a boon, and Menaka asked for 101 children, all boys except for one girl. Satī agreed, adding that she herself would incarnate as Menaka's daughter. As the goddess reincarnated as a child with blue-black skin, flowers fell from the sky like rain. She was named **Kālī**, and she wished to have Shiva as her husband. But her father disagreed, claiming that Shiva was a homeless drunk. He was correct, for Kālī lived a miserable life with Shiva (see **Pārvatī** for another version of this myth). (Daniélou 1964; Dimmitt and van Buitenen; McDaniel 2004)

Mīnāchīamman A local goddess (see **Grāmadevatā**) of Madura, she incarnated as a girl to revenge herself on a king who dared close her temples. She appeared miraculously in the palace, wearing a bracelet that duplicated a favorite of the queen's. Astrologers warned the king not to adopt the babe, so he cast Mīnāchīamman into the river, from which a merchant plucked her. He raised her to be a fine young woman, who attracted the eye of Shiva, incarnated as a poor man in a village on the river Kaveri. They were so poor that Shiva took the bracelet from his wife's arm and attempted to sell it. Accused of stealing the queen's jewel, he was put to death. The goddess, taking her demon form, under which she was called Thurgai, killed the king in retaliation. (Whitehead)

Mīnakṣī Born from a sacrificial fire, Mīnakṣī had three breasts at birth, but her royal parents were warned by a heavenly voice that the third breast should remain until she met her intended husband. Mīnakṣī grew up to become queen of Madurai, from which she set out to conquer the world. City after city fell, until she reached the home of Shiva in the wild Himalayas. Even Shiva's army could not withstand Mīnakṣī, and as disaster loomed, the god took to the battlefield. There

Mīnakṣī's third breast disappeared, and the girl realized that Shiva would become her husband.

They were wed in Mīnakṣī's city, where Shiva took the name of Sundaresvara. When their son, Skanda, was old enough to rule, the couple entered the temple dedicated to them and disappeared. They continue to be worshipped in the center of an industrial city of a million residents. One of the largest in India, the temple receives daily visitors in the tens of thousands. The goddess is envisioned as the preeminent member of the couple, such that female-dominant marriages are sometimes called Madurai marriages. (Berkson; Hiltebeitel and Erndl; Fuller 1980, 1984; Gupta Ś 1991; Harman)

Mitki In Madhya Pradesh, this goddess was once a young woman who lived with her husband and her brothers. When a dam broke and threatened the area, Mitki's brothers sacrificed her husband by burying him inside the dam. Mitki, seeing her husband's hand stretching forth from the earth, drowned herself in the canal and has since been worshipped on Fridays. She possesses people who act as her mediums. (Dehejia)

Miyolangsangma The goddess of the world's highest mountain, Everest, was one of five Tibetan goddesses known as the Sisters of Long Life. The other sisters reside on peaks that are part of Everest or near it. Their leader is Tashi Tseringma (goddess of Gaurī Shankar, west of Everest, and Chomolhair in western Bhutan). Golden Miyolangsangma, astride a tiger, carries a bowl of barley, while her companion, a mongoose, spits out jewels. Her main festival, Mani Rimdu, climaxes in the release of a yak. When international interest in the mountain grew, the region around it was renamed without a goddess reference as Sagarmatha ("Forehead of the Sky"), a title of the god Vishnu. (Bernbaum 1990)

Mohinī Once Vishnu assumed a voluptuous female body and sat beside the milk river, intending to seduce Shiva, dancing god of destruction. In the shade of a tree on the ocean's edge, Shiva and Mohinī united in sexual joy. Their flowing juices formed the river Ganges, and from their union the hermaphroditic divinity Ariharaputiran was born. (Daniélou 2007)

Mrityu Goddess of death, she was unhappy from the moment she was born from the scowl of the high god Brahma and assigned the task of destroying life. She wept until her eyes were as red as her sari, but Brahma convinced her that because humans would fear her, they would be captured once again on the wheel of desire, ensuring that they would be reborn. Mrityu grew into her job, becoming a goddess who killed children in the womb and grooms on their wedding nights. She lived in the cremation grounds outside the village, where food was offered in hopes that she would stay on the periphery and not wander into the village homes. (Pattanaik)

Muthumāriamman This regional agricultural goddess of Puducherry in the Tamil region is celebrated in a ten-day summer festival in which the goddess's image is paraded through the streets. She is believed to have the power to protect people against diseases prevalent at that time of year, including smallpox and measles (see also **Sītāla**). Those who are cured of such diseases often offer homage to the goddess by piercing their tongues. (Gupta Ś)

Naddidai Daughter of the Parenga goddess Gongadai, Naddidai was washing her clothing at the end of her first menses when a god attempted to rape her. She ran away, her necklaces breaking. The red and black beads turned into red and black ants, which attacked the rapist god. But he continued, so she took her hairstring and tossed it to the ground, where it turned into a snake that bit the god. This discouraged him, and he begged the goddess to forgive her. She agreed, but ants and snakes have remained in the world. (Elwin 1954)

Nāginīs These semidivine snake women now appear as background figures in myths but may have had greater religious importance in the past. Sculptures of snake-girdled women found in eastern India suggest that goddesses like **Manasā** may derive from an ancient cult. Indian mythology associates snakes with water, perhaps because the monsoon season brings them out into the open. Although all snakes are revered in India, the most sacred is the cobra, which Indians will not kill. If left alone, the cobra does not strike, for which it is seen as a protective being. During festivals marking the monsoon month, images of Nāginīs are decorated with silk and ribbons, and food is offered to them. (Dehejia)

Naina Devī The Bilaspur eye goddess was brought to earth by a supernatural cow, who gave great floods of milk at a place to which pilgrims travel regularly. Most are Sikh, although attendance by followers of that religion at a Hindu shrine is otherwise unusual. Thus the goddess has been seen as a folk divinity of Sikhism as well as Hinduism. Her sacred lake was formed when the eyes of **Satī**, whose charred body was being carried around the world by her grieving husband, Shiva, fell to earth. (Bhardwaj; Gupta Ś)

Nandā-devī An aspect of **Pārvatī,** Nandā-devī is "goddess of bliss." Near the border with Nepal, her mountain rises 25,645 feet near peaks called Nandā Ghunti (Nandā's Veil) and Nandā Kot (Nandā's fortress). The region around Nandā-devī is intensely sacred, visited by tens of thousands annually to honor the goddess at her temples and shrines. Every dozen years, a pilgrimage brings an image of Nandā-devī to the mountain, at which time a decorated four-horned ram is released into the snowy wilderness. The goddess was said to have offered solace to humans when, at the dawn of time, the world was flooded. Only the sage Manu and his family were saved, when Vishnu took the form of a fish and towed their boat to the peak of Nandā Devī, from which Manu and his wife descended to repopulate the earth.

The American mountaineer Willi Unsoeld was so enraptured with the beauty of Nandā Devī that he vowed to name his first daughter after it. In 1977, at the age of twenty-one, Nandā Devī Unsoeld and her father set out to climb the mountain. The young woman died at the summit, where her body remains buried in the snows. Local people believed the girl was the incarnation of Nandā-devī, and her death was the return of the goddess to her mountain home. (Bernbaum; Gupta Ś 1991; Sax)

Narmadā The holy river Narmadā is the embodiment of this goddess, who like **Gaṇgā** removes the sins of those who bathe in her waters. Even Gaṇgā bathes in Narmadā's waters, in the shape of a black cow. So holy is Narmadā that, to remove all sins of all lifetimes, one must bathe three years in the Saraswati, seven days in the Yamuna, or one day in the Ganges—or merely glance at the Narmadā. Narmadā's waters are held effective against snakebite, for which reason she is sometimes considered related to the **Nāginīs**. (Gupta Ś 1991)

Nidrā Nidrā, the sleep of time, is a black-skinned goddess clothed in yellow and dark blue silk, who practices ascetic rites. When the evil Kaṃsa attempted to destroy the world, Nidrā descended into the womb of **Yasoda** while her brother Vishnu incarnated through the womb of Devaki. At birth, the two babies were exchanged, and Kaṃsa kidnapped the baby he thought was Vishnu and smashed its head against a rock. But the goddess arose and flew to heaven, leaving Vishnu alive, as Krishna, to combat the demon. Nidrā is called Yoganidra for her ascetic practices, and Vindhyavasini for the village in which her cult is practiced; sometimes she is viewed as a form of **Māyā**. (Hiltebeitel and Erndl; Ions)

Nimibatapa Among the Sherdukpens, this goddess creates lightning when she argues with her husband. He pursues her across the sky, but she runs away. Her genitals flash lightning, while her husband's heavy steps are the sound of thunder. Other tribes in northwest India tell similar stories. The Miri waterfall goddess Chigum-Erum creates lightning when she lifts her skirt to show her vulva, while her husband creates hail when he spits at her. Another goddess, Dorak, lives with her husband in a water tank in the sky, which sometimes overflows to cause rain. When it is dry, she lifts her cane belt, causing lightning from the revelation of her genitals. Meanwhile, her husband clashes armor together, causing thunder. (Elwin 1955)

Nippong Among the Abors, these water spirits bring harm to women by causing excessive menstruation or miscarriages. Because the Nippong keep their fingers clenched together, the best way to drive one away is to set fire to her hair, because she finds it hard to put out the flames with joined hands. They appear in men's dreams, bring them to orgasm, and attempt to wed them after death. (Elwin 1955)

Nirantali The creator goddess of Orissa gave turbans to the world's most important people, but she forgot the moon goddess. So Nirantali promised that she would give the moon a turban in return for a feast. The moon held the party, and the goddess gave her a lovely turban. She also gave the moon a baby hare, with instructions to carry it always. When the moon grows full, those on earth can see the ornament on the moon's face and the hare in her lap. When the sun came wanting a turban too, Nirantali had none left, so she offered a crown, which emits golden rays.

Nirantali made humans by breaking a metal pot, making powder of the metal and adding wax. Because of the wax, the first man's color was black. He was big, with a soft body and buttocks so large they dragged. He was endlessly hungry, so Nirantali gave him rice, which the pregnant moon goddess stole. In revenge, he ate her, but Nirantali made him vomit her back up. For this reason, whenever there was an eclipse, the people threw rice at the moon so her captor would be distracted and let her go. (Elwin 1954)

Niṛrti Humanity's misfortunes are embodied in this goddess, a weary old woman, starved and leprous, begging for alms. She protects those born into poverty and crime who attempt to live righteously. Those wishing for a change of luck pray to her as the goddess who endures earth's misfortunes. Wearing black garments and ornaments that imitate Niṛrti's attire, priests offer sacrifice, then put a stone into water and toss it to the southwest, transferring more disease and ill fortune to Niṛrti's heavy shoulders.

An ancient goddess, she was born before **Lakṣmī**. Thus misery came into the world before luxury and beauty. Niṛrti, who appears in early Vedic literature, has been seen as a precursor to the later development of **Kālī**. She has also been described as the negative aspect of **Adītī**. (Dexter; Kinsley 1986, 1975)

Padmāvatī This Jaina snake goddess protected the founder of a dynasty when, as the king was fleeing from his cannibal father's army, she created a phantom army to frighten away the soldiers. She instructed the king to touch the vulva of her statue with an iron bar, which turned to gold, sufficient for him to establish a city, over which he ruled. Rituals to Padmāvatī connect her with riches and with transformation. (Cort)

Parṇásavarī "Leaf-clothed tribal woman" is the name of this Buddhist goddess, a beautiful nature divinity who wears clothing made of leaves and flowers. She provides healing through herbs and magic. She also bears a noose she used to capture diseases as though they were cattle. Other weapons like arrows and swords are also part of her regalia, to be used to destroy negative energies that affect health. She is thus connected with the protective village goddesses (see **Grāmadevatā**), divine mothers who can either bring or ward off epidemics of dire illnesses. (Shaw 2006)

Pārvatī Whereas the union of Vishnu with **Lakṣmī** exemplified the idealized image of Hindu marriage, a different relationship is pictured in the tempestuous marriage of the mountain goddess Pārvatī and the wild god Shiva. This may arise from the fact that, among ancient goddesses, Pārvatī is unusual in being both a consort goddess, in which legends emphasize her role as a married woman, and a supreme goddess who holds power without needing a mate.

She gained Shiva's attention by practicing asceticism until he could not resist her. Thereafter he spent his time pleasing the goddess. Once she demanded that he provide jewels for her. It took years for him to respond, but finally he showered her with seeds of the rudrakasha ("bead tree"), which she strung into necklaces.

Once, interrupted during sex before she was satisfied, Pārvatī cursed the gods so that their consorts were barren but pregnant. They were miserable until Shiva allowed them to vomit up the semen that had impregnated them. Another version of the story says that when Shiva and Pārvatī were interrupted, he was turned into a phallus, while the goddess covered her face with a flower, becoming thereafter known as Lajja-Gaurī. Barren women wishing to conceive employ figures with this name, painting the vulva and breasts of the figures with butter and red paint.

Pārvatī is connected to maternity, but never in an ordinary way. Once, she offered her breasts to the gods, but they suckled so hard on her right breast that they drew blood. Undeterred, they continued to suck until the breast shriveled up; Pārvatī's blood made these divinities uncontrollable.

Pārvatī had one son of her own. Shiva did not want to be bothered with children, but Pārvatī wanted a child to caress. Shiva ripped a piece from her skirt and told her to fondle it. Pārvatī grasped the red cloth and, as it touched the goddess's nipples, the cloth began to nurse. Thus was benevolent Ganesha born. But Shiva, angry and jealous, beheaded the child, saying that he slept in a ritually incorrect way. Pārvatī was desperate with grief, and Shiva, ashamed, told her he would find the boy another head. The only one he could locate was an elephant's, so Ganesha was reborn half human, half elephant.

Another myth says the hero Kartikeya was born when, interrupted while he made love to Pārvatī, Shiva spurted sperm into the mouth of the fire god Angi.

Kartikeya became leader of heaven's armies, but he became so lust filled when he killed that he raped any women he encountered. Pārvatī put a curse on him so that every time he tried to rape a woman, she would turn into the likeness of Pārvatī. Kartikeya stopped his aggressive behavior.

Pārvatī could function without Shiva, but the reverse was not true. When a sage attempted to trace sacred circles around the god, Pārvatī told him that he had to circumambulate her as well. The sage refused, so Pārvatī mounted Shiva, but the sage turned himself into a bee to irritate Shiva into dislodging Pārvatī. The goddess melded herself into Shiva. The sage turned himself into a worm, intending to burrow between the two fused sides of the divinity, but the goddess struck him with such weakness that he could no longer stand. When the sage begged for mercy, Pārvatī gave him a third leg so that he could hobble around the couple and acknowledge their equality.

The consort of Shiva is also called **Kālī** and **Durgā**. One legend explains how the goddess divided herself. Originally, she had dark skin, about which Shiva teased her. Furious, she set off for the mountains, intending to practice asceticism until she gained her desire. With Ganesha accompanying her, she left Viraka, Shiva's attendant, to guard his bedroom so that he didn't enjoy other women's company. But a demon disguised as Pārvatī attempted to kill Shiva. He lured the god to bed after loading his illusory vagina with nails. Shiva, recognizing the deceit, put a sword on his penis and dispatched the demon.

Pārvatī's informants spread the word that a woman had been seen entering Shiva's bedroom, and Pārvatī exploded in anger. Her anger shot out of her mouth in the form of a lion. Then she continued practicing yoga until Brahma took pity on her and asked her what she wished. When she said she wanted a golden skin, he blessed her. From her body sprang another goddess: black **Kālī**. Now golden and beautiful, Pārvatī started home.

Pārvatī resides in the sacred mountain Kailas, a major pilgrimage destination. The mountain rises near the source of four great rivers. Although the Ganges does not arise there, Kailas is mythically connected with the descent of that river goddess from heaven. As with many primary goddesses, Pārvatī bears many names, many of which are identical to those of other goddesses, who may be aspects of Pārvatī or assimilated to her. She is **Umā**, **Gaurī**, **Śakti**, and **Bhudevī**. As daughter of the god of the Himalayas, Himavan, and the woman Mena, she bore the name of Haimavati. (Beck et al; Bennett; Bernbaum; Caughran; Daniélou 1964; Dimmitt and van Buitenen; Gupta S; Handelman; Ions; Kinsley 1986, 1997; O'Flaherty 1980; Hawley and Wulff; Pattanaik; Young 1994; Whitehead; Zimmer 1946)

Pedammā-Mariammā The virgin goddess saw jasmine blooming near an anthill. Transforming herself into a bird, she sat on the flower until she conceived, then laid three eggs, one of which was sterile, while the other two contained the universe and the gods. When the gods were old enough, she taught them how to pray and then decided to make them her consorts. Brahma and Vishnu refused her, but Shiva agreed, in return for the third eye he wore in her forehead. When she agreed, she was turned into an old woman, with no desire for sex. Full of vengeance, she began to kill demons. But every time demon blood fell to earth, more demons were conceived, so she began to lick the earth with her enormous tongue. Thus she captured the blood as it fell, except for the bit that formed a buffalo demon, which the goddess fought and killed. At her festivals, a buffalo sprinkled with turmeric is sacrificed in commemoration of her heroic deed, and her image is carried from the temple to the town's boundary to protect it. (Jayakar; Whitehead)

Phoureima This Indian rice goddess is personified in a round black stone sitting in a pot upon a bed of rice grains (never directly on the ground) within the granary. So long as the goddess is honored in this way, it is believed that there will be no shortage of rice. (Bahadur)

Pidari This South Indian snake goddess was depicted with flaming hair and three eyes; she held a noose and a drum to frighten away evil spirits from the villages she guarded. Her worship has been traced to the first millennium of the common era. (Whitehead)

Ponniyammān The "rice mother" of Tamil Nadu, Ponniyammān is one of the Sapta Kannimaars ("seven virgin sisters"), represented by rock heads placed in fields, the earth forming the goddess's body. She is honored in rituals, where she is offered rice cakes and other food that is then ceremoniously consumed. (Hamilton)

Prajñāpāramitā This figure, a golden-skinned woman who emits rays of light, was the mother of space and of secrets hidden at time's beginning, to be revealed when humankind is sufficiently advanced. She was especially prominent in Sri Lanka, where Buddhism has been dominant since the third century CE. Honored by Buddhists, she may have been Hindu in origin. (Dehejia; Shaw 2006; Zimmer 1946, 1955)

Prakṛti Hindu philosophy gives divine feminine form to three philosophical concepts: **Māyā**, **Śakti**, and Prakṛti. These three concepts are closely connected and difficult to separate, as each is identified with one or another of the triad. As articulated early, Prakṛti stands for feminine energy as the universal creative principle. Prakṛti's male counterpart is Puruṣa, consciousness, who took the form of Brahma. Prakṛti is the active part of the dyad, for without her, the god is inactive and uncreative. The goddess has three major qualities: purity, activity, and lethargy, combinations of which form everything in the tangible universe.

Early in creation, Prakṛti laid an egg, then surrounded it with seven layers of herself. Within the egg grew Brahma, together with other divine and semi-divine beings. When they were born, the afterbirth formed the mountains, while the water of Prakṛti's womb became the ocean.

Self-knowing and endless, Prakṛti exists

everywhere in various forms. She is therefore paradoxical, divinely alone but with uncountable forms. (Hiltebeitel and Erndl; Dimmitt and van Buitenen; Daniélou 1964; Gupta S; Kinsley 1986; Pattanaik; Pintchman 1994)

Prapañcésvarī "Mistress of the fivefold world," this early Tantric goddess may be the same as the world mistress **Bhuvanésvarī**. Sun colored and brilliant, she ruled the five elements of earth, air, fire, water, and ether. As such, she was embodied in mountains, winds, stars, and oceans. Other names for this goddess were Pradhāna ("receptacle of matter") and **Prakṛti**. (Kinsley 1997)

Pṛthivī The feminine earth in both Hinduism and Buddhism is Pṛthivī, a cosmic cow full of milk. A pre-Vedic divinity, she lost power as Hinduism spread. Many prayers are offered to her, but she figures in few myths. In one, Pṛthivī hid treasures until threatened with death by a king whom she had married. She could find no refuge among the gods, so she returned to her husband, who beat her, which is why farmers use sharp tools to cut into the earth.

Although generally a benevolent goddess, she shows her fierce side during earthquakes, when she evinces displeasure at human behavior. In Buddhism, she was depicted wringing out her wet hair, thus connecting earth and water. This goddess is difficult to distinguish from **Prakṛti**. (Gupta S; Ions; Kinsley 1986; Pintchman 1994; Shaw 2006.)

Rādhā Each time **Lakṣmī** became human, so did her consort, Vishnu. When he was born as Krishna, she was reborn as Rādhā, one of the **Gōpīs**. Although married to his uncle, Rādhā could not resist the beautiful Krishna. Like the other Gōpīs, she danced with him at night, offering love, which he finally returned. Every night Rādhā stole from her home to make love on the banks of a river. Gossip caused Rādhā to become a pariah and Krishna to grow ill with fever, for which the lustful Gōpīs blamed Rādhā. But a sage predicted that water carried in a sieve would cure the god.

Every woman tried, but the water ran out the holes. Finally, Rādhā successfully carried the curative water, proving that her love was chaste despite defying social convention.

Rādhā is still honored in rituals and shrines in northern India, where she inhabits a woman's body for the occasion. Naked except for jewelry and flowers, the woman is revered by groups of male and female worshippers. Love-tormented poems in the voice of Rādhā form part of the canon of Indian literature. (Dehejia; Dimmitt and van Buitenen; Gupta S; Hawley and Wulff 1982, 1986; Ions; Kinsley 1986; Pattanaik; Sharma; King)

Rangada This maiden was brought up dressed as a boy. She learned all the manly arts, from riding and hunting to fighting like a warrior. One day, when she was hunting, she stumbled upon the sleeping hero Arjuna. Finding him attractive, she sat on her heels watching him until he woke, then told him frankly that she wished to enjoy his body. Shocked at her frankness, Arjuna said that he had taken a vow of celibacy—and he would never be tempted by such an aggressive woman.

So Rangada went home. She dressed herself in womanly silks, perfumed herself, and went back to Arjuna's tent. It did not take him long to break his vow, and he did so frequently for the next thirteen months. But Rangada's people came looking for her, bemoaning the loss of their protector. As they sang her praises Arjuna began to wonder aloud what it would be like to love such a strong woman. Finally Rangada came from the tent to see her former comrades; they were overjoyed to see her, and Arjuna was thrilled to ride into battle beside his bedmate. (Ghosh; Pattanaik)

Rātri Kindly goddess of passionate night, Rātri is sister of **Uṣas**, the dawn. Each night she walks the earth, wearing dark robes set with stars. Her devotees pray for safety from robbers, wolves, and other predators. She is also goddess of sexual passion. Rātri was not born beautiful, but through her devotion to **Lakṣmī**, she obtained accessories that made her look so beautiful that Kāma, god of love, fell for her. Rātri was an embodiment of **Kālī**. But while Kālī was the perpetual night that ends creation, Rātri was the earthly night in which all beings rest. In esoteric tradition, Rātri symbolized enlightenment, for if **Māyā**'s dance of creation confuses the senses, Rātri's darkness permits less confusion. (Daniélou 1964; Dehejia; Ions; Kinsley 1986, 1997; O'Flaherty 1980; Pattanaik)

Reṇukā Reṇukā was the wife of a sage, so dutiful that she went out every day when her husband practiced archery and picked up every arrow. But one day she did not return and her husband, suspecting her of infidelity, demanded to know where she had been. She was overwhelmed, she said, by the heat and had sought shelter under a tree. The next day, the sage threatened to shoot the sun out of the sky in order to protect his wife. But the sun god offered a parasol and sandals to protect Reṇukā.

Reṇukā is a model of the perfect wife. She was said to be so holy that she could carry water in sieves. But she was not so pure that she did not occasionally entertain a lascivious thought. This happened when she saw a handsome man frolicking in the river. Instantly the impurity caused her to lose her magical power, which revealed her adulterous fantasy to her husband when suddenly water ran out the holes in her sieve. Furious, he had his son behead Reṇukā. Because of his son's obedience, the father granted him a boon, and he asked that Reṇukā be brought back to life with no memory of her death. Because she had hidden among lower-caste people beheaded for sheltering her, Reṇukā's head was placed accidentally on the body of an outcaste woman, after which she was called Elammā (or Embikā-Elammā). The same story is told of the village goddess **Māriyamman**.

Near Puducherry, Reṇukā is honored as a goddess who cured diseases, especially those involving the eyes. At a temple dedicated to her, three major festivals invoke her curative powers. At all three, the image of the goddess is dressed in silk and led in procession through the town, with devotees feeding the poor in the goddess's honor. (Pintchman 2001; Dehejia; Gupta Ś 1991; Jayakar; Pattanaik)

Rohinī The sage Daksha had twenty-seven daughters, all married to the moon god Chandra. Although the moon promised to spend his favors equally, he fell in love with Rohinī. Daksha cursed the moon with consumption, but his daughters prevailed on him to lighten his curse, so he allowed the disease to be chronic rather than fatal. Whenever Chandra leaves Rohinī at the full moon, he wanes and grows thin. (O'Flaherty 1975; Pattanaik; Zimmer 1946)

Śakti In Hinduism, goddess energy animates male divine energy. Thus religious artists show a goddess having intercourse atop a god, activating his languid body. Like **Prakṛti** and **Māyā**, Śakti refers to an abstract understanding—in this case, power and potency. Śakti can also refer to the essence of femaleness. Each member of the Vedic trinity was provided with his Śakti: Māyā enlivening creative Brahma; **Lakṣmī** empowering nurturing Vishnu; and **Pārvatī** or **Kālī** as the consort of destructive Shiva. Śakti is sometimes used as a name for Shiva's energy alone.

Little myth describes this goddess. When the genderless god Bhagavān uttered the primal sound ("om"), Śakti emerged. She immediately wished to have intercourse with the god, who divided into Brahma, Vishnu, and Shiva. She was so powerful that Brahma, looking at her, grew old and gray, and Vishnu grew afraid and called her "mother," but Shiva united with her and satisfied her. When Śakti realized that Vishnu was mocking her in his heart, she cursed him to have ten incarnations, in each of which he would be threatened by demons and have to call on the goddess to save him.

The Hinduism in which the goddess is most prominent is called Śaktism. Although goddesses are found in all forms of Hinduism, the goddess is not central in other forms. Some forms of Śaktism see all goddesses as unitary, while others envision the many goddesses as separate. Sometimes Śaktism centers on the goddess, other times including worship of her consort. Typically honored in rural villages (see **Grāmadevatā**) and lacking any written tradition, Śaktism is based in experience rather than study, for its teachings are transmitted orally from guru to student. Śakti is also significant in Tantric philosophy. While Shakta Hinduism emphasizes the role of the goddess, Tantric schools talk about the polarity of being, with Śakti being the necessary equivalent of every god. (Beane; Brown; Gupta S; Hiltebeitel and Erndl; Gupta and Gombrich; Kinsley 1986; Koppers; McDaniel 2004; Pintchman 2001, 1994; Warrier; Zimmer 1946)

Samjñā The sun's wife Samjñā hid in the wilderness disguised as a mare when her husband's intense brilliance tired her, leaving her disguised handmaiden Chhaya in her place. But the sun discovered her ruse and transformed himself into a stallion to have intercourse with her. Samjñā turned her face to him; he breathed upon her and she conceived through her nose. From their union came the horse-headed Aswins, as well as the god of death Yama and his sister **Yamī**. Samjñā agreed to return to the sky, but first she had her father trim away some of the sun's rays to diminish his brightness.

The goddess Saranyū, sometimes identified with **Uṣas**, had a similar marriage. She bore the sun twin children, Yama and Yami, but she grew weary of her husband's brilliance and left a maid in her place, upon whom her husband fathered a child. She was able to remain away for years, until Yama annoyed the substitute, who kicked him so hard that the child was wounded. This alerted Surya to the deception, and he found his true wife. (Daniélou 1964; Hawley and Wulff 1996; Ions; Kramrisch; Pattanaik; O'Flaherty 1979)

Saramā Mother of dogs and wild animals, she was one of the primal goddesses formed when the god Brahma's only daughter, **Shatarupa**, divided herself in order to quickly populate the world. As Saramā (possibly "to speed"), she was sent to find missing divine

cows, performing miracles as she went. When she found the cows with the demons that had stolen them, the demons tempted Saramā to side with them. She refused, returning to the gods with the location of their precious cattle. (Another version claims she, acting as a typical dog, ate up the milk and then skulked back to heaven, where she was forced to vomit up the milk. She fled back to the demons, with the gods following the trail of her vomit to locate the missing cattle.) For this deed, Saramā was given the boon that her descendants would all be able to kill anything that attacked them, even tigers. (O'Flaherty 1985; Kramrisch; Pattanaik)

Sarada Devī During her lifetime, Sarada Devī became known as an incarnation of **Kālī** or **Durgā**. Wife of the poet and spiritual leader Ramakrishna Paramahamsa, she is honored as the primary goddess of the tradition he founded. She was partially crippled from rheumatism and spent much of her time caring for a mentally handicapped adoptive daughter, yet during her lifetime she attracted many followers and since then has continued to attract attention. Born on December 22, 1853, she was married at the age of five to Ramakrishna, believed by his family to be mad and in need of marriage, but she did not live with her husband until she was sixteen.

With her father, she walked sixty miles to meet her husband, who immediately began to worship her as an incarnation of the goddess. They lived together in a sexless marriage, with recent work finding a reason in Ramakrishna's homosexuality. Widowed when she was thirty-two, Sarada went through a period of poverty and isolation until her women followers began to describe the ecstasies she experienced. After being derided for her unwillingness to give up her bright saris and bangles, a requirement of widowhood, Sarada had a vision of Ramakrishna that emphasized that he was not dead; thus she could not be a widow and was, like him, divine. Thereafter, until her death on July 20, 1920, Sarada wore the bangles to emphasize her status as goddess. (Kripal; Pintchman 2001; McDaniel 1989, 2004)

Sarasvatī For the world to come into being, Brahma required the power of his consort Sarasvatī. As such, she is called Viraj, the female part of primordial chaos. She is also called Sāvitri or **Shatarupa**, first-born of Brahma and incestuously desired by him, mother by him of sacred texts, musical rhythms, and inner knowledge.

Sarasvatī's portraits show a sinuous, light-skinned woman wearing a lunar headdress as she sits astride a swan or peacock. In four arms she holds a book, a musical instrument, a rosary, and a ritual pot, to indicate her connection with the arts and the sacred. Her colors are white and yellow, sometimes with a touch of watery blue, for she is one of a trinity of water goddesses that includes **Gaṅgā** and Yamuna (see **Yamī**). Inventor of arts and sciences, patron of intellectual endeavors, Sarasvatī is honored by students and artists. She is **Lakṣmī**'s rival, for if someone has the favor of one goddess, the other turns away. In her identity as **Vāc**, she invented the sacred language, Sanskrit.

Sarasvatī was consort of both Brahma and Vishnu. At first, Sarasvatī was co-wife to Vishnu with Lakṣmī and Gaṅgā. But she was jealous of Gaṅgā, accusing her of stealing Vishnu's affections. The other wives drove her away because of her outbursts, whereupon she became Brahma's consort. She remained somewhat haughty in her new role. Once she refused to hurry to meet Brahma for a sacrifice, so the god married **Gāyatrī** as an immediate stand-in. In retaliation, Sarasvatī cursed Brahma that he would be worshipped only once a year, a curse that remains in effect.

Sarasvatī is celebrated at the spring festival of Vasanta Pachami, when people dress in yellow clothes to mimic the mustard blooming in the fields. Sarasvatī is a special goddess of the Jains, a religion that began in the late centuries BCE and emphasizes not divinity but transcendent *jinas*, highly evolved souls. Even this nontheistic religion could not entirely eliminate devotion to the goddess, of whom Sarasvatī was the favorite form. (Daniélou 1964; Dehejia; Gupta S; Gupta Ś 1991; Ions; Kinsley 1986; Kramrisch; Sharma; Shaw 2006; Subramaniam; Warrier)

Satī Anglicized, her name becomes *suttee*, for Satī was the first woman to dare the flames of death. An incarnation of **Devī**, she was married against her father's will to an incarnation of Shiva named Rudra. She immolated herself when Rudra's honor was threatened and he, in grief, began to dance with her corpse. (Some stories say anger transformed Satī into **Kālī**, and she destroyed the integrity of the sacrifice by her suicide, whereupon Shiva began dancing with her charred corpse.) But Vishnu hacked her body apart, and as the pieces fell to earth, they sanctified each place. This began the Tantric practice of honoring the *yoni*, the genitals of the goddess fallen to earth; it also began the practice of yoga, which Shiva inaugurated as a way of distancing himself from the wildness of his emotions upon Satī's death.

In Tantra, Satī is the source of the ten goddesses known as the Mahāvidyās, which include **Kālī** and **Tārā**. The goddesses were created when Satī and Shiva were not invited to the home of Satī's father, who disapproved of Shiva's going about naked and meditating in cremation grounds. Satī, infuriated by this slight, decided to confront her father. Shiva forbade her, so Satī transformed herself into a terrifying but beautiful goddess with a lolling tongue and necklace of skulls. When Shiva attempted to run away, Satī surrounded him with ten different forms of herself, the Mahāvidyās. Thereupon Shiva acknowledged her wish, and the goddesses disappeared. Satī went to her father's home and immolated herself in protest of his actions. She was reborn as **Umā** or **Pārvatī**.

The practice of suttee can be dated to as early as 400 BCE. Although praised as an act of loyalty to the deceased husband, suttee may have been the only option for a woman who faced a life of poverty as a widow. Drugs may have been used to induce women into fiery oblivion, allowing property to pass to male relatives. Outlawed in 1829, the practice has continued to the present despite the ban. While the practice attracts a great deal of attention from lay readers as well as scholars, some argue that it has always been the exception rather than the rule.

In Rajasthan in 1987, Roop Kanwar was immolated with her husband at the age of eighteen after a brief arranged marriage, igniting an outcry against wife murder and attempts to deify the girl. Evidence that she was drugged, stumbling on her way to her death, convinced many that her death was at least partially unwilling, as do reports that she attempted to escape the flames. Her death, celebrated by as many as a quarter million people, resulted in the trial of her father-in-law and others, but all were acquitted of her murder. As a result of Roop Kanwar's death, a law outlawing the glorification of suttee was passed.

In most areas of India, a widow faces a difficult life. She lives in almost complete isolation and often receives little food. She cannot participate in any social events or eat with others. Some have argued that some women indeed embrace death over such a life. But not all "bride murders" involve immolation or the death of a husband. In 2000, a young woman was beaten to death for carrying an empty water jar, an inauspicious action. Women who survive "bride burning," often horribly disfigured, are said to have accidentally burned themselves. The number of victims is difficult to ascertain, although figures in the thousands or even tens of thousands are offered. Objections to the practice of suttee and other forms of violence against women are the subject of feminist activity in India today. (Dimmitt and van Buitenen; Hawley and Wulff 1996; Cormack; Hawley 1994; Ions; Kinsley 1986, 1989, 1997; Leslie; Sen M; Sharma; Zimmer 1946)

Śedi-Bakup Among the Komkar people of Pakistan, Śedi-Bakup is the earth goddess, married to Melo-Baloat, the sky man. At the beginning of time, they lived so close that there was no room for the people and animals to lift their heads. So they joined together with the spirits to determine what could be done. A brave spirit, Sid-Diyor, grabbed the sky man and beat him so furiously that he ran away. As he rose, space opened between the sky and earth, revealing that Śedi-Bakup was pregnant. She gave birth to two daughters, Bong and **Bomong**, but was so sad at the loss of her husband that she could not look at them. They later became the sun and the moon. (Elwin 1955)

Shatarupa On the cosmic ocean slept Vishnu, from whose navel rose a lotus carrying Brahma. Brahma created sons by thinking, but sons alone cannot populate the universe. So he knitted his brow, from which sprang forth two-sexed Shiva. Brahma divided him into two parts, the left becoming Shatarupa, who could take any form. As soon as she was born, Shatarupa so excited Brahma that he grew four new heads with more eyes to watch her. Shatarupa saw her father's eyes shining with lust. She transformed herself into a cow, whereupon he became a bull; she turned into a mare, he a stallion; she became a doe, and he turned into a buck. She created new beings more quickly than he could respond. All creation rises from Shatarupa's attempt to avoid her father; she is usually considered identical to **Sarasvatī**.

A similar figure is found in Sandhya, created by the god Prajapati when he discovered that his thought-generated sons could not propagate. But he became lustful toward his daughter, who ran to her brothers for help. They asked a monkey for help, who shot an arrow into Prajapati, whose ejaculate formed a lake from which all animals were born.

This goddess also appears as Sāvitri. The name is given to a beautiful brilliant woman who remained unmarried because men found her intimidating. So she traveled the world, looking for a husband. She had no luck, but when she returned home she met a woodcutter. Despite her father's objections, Sāvitri decided to marry him; he was secretly a king, driven from his throne by corrupt officials. The couple wed despite predictions that he would live only one year.

When four days remained of the allotted life span, Sāvitri began fasting. When the fated day came, she begged to accompany her husband. Sāvitri encountered the god of death and, when Satyavān's soul was taken, followed it to the otherworld. Yama, god of death, offered her any boon but her husband's life. She asked for a hundred sons, which was granted. Then Sāvitri demanded her husband, for she had already been pledged a hundred sons and needed him to make that happen. Impressed with her cleverness, Yama released her husband.

Sāvitri is honored in a festival during which women fast and pray that their husbands will live long lives. Offerings of rice, wheat, millet, lentils, chickpeas, and sorghum are left at the base of a long-living banyan tree, around which married women dance. (Babb; Beswick; Daniélou 1964; Dimmitt and van Buitenen; Gupta S; Gupta Ś 1991; Kinsley 1986; Pattanaik; Sharma; Zimmer 1946)

Sichi The earth goddess of the Singpho, Tagin, and Minyon peoples of Pakistan quarreled with her husband, the sky, when he threatened her with an army of stars. She retaliated by threatening him with the poisonous snakes that lived in her waters, which so frightened him that he surrendered. Still, he intended to kill Sichi, so he began to lower himself until it seemed that he would kill everything on the earth's surface. Birds and animals gathered, discussing what they could do to make the sky move back up. A bird finally served as ambassador between the warring spouses, setting up a treaty specifying that both would remain indoors for ten days or risk becoming deformed. Sichi could not endure the captivity and exited her home after three days, for which reason the earth has bumps and ridges on it. But the sky stayed indoors, for which reason it is smooth all over. The similarly named primal goddess of the Minyong, Sedi-Nane, created thunder when she wept over the death of her children, while lightning came from her flashing eyes. (Elwin 1958)

Sītā Sītā, born from the earth when it was cut with a plow, was reincarnated from the woman Vedavati, whom the demon Rāvaṇa threatened with rape. She burned herself to death rather than endure his assault. Nine months later, she was reborn to Rāvaṇa's wife.

But the demon heard a prophecy that the child would be his death, so she was thrown into the ocean. The sea would not kill her but gave her to the earth, who assured her safe rebirth.

The moment she saw Rama, she fell in love with him. But her father had set a condition for a suitor: a huge bow that belonged to Shiva had to be lifted, strung, and shot by the bridegroom. Many came, eyed the bow, and left without even trying. But Rama, with one swift movement, met the required challenge, and the destined couple were united in marriage.

Then the couple faced their first challenge together, because Rama's mother's co-wife, Kaikeyi, denied his claim to his father's throne. She was within reason, for she had extracted a promise that her own son would inherit the throne. Kaikeyi forced Rama into exile, charged with ridding the land of demons. Loving Sītā accompanied him, but while in that forest exile, Sītā was kidnapped by Rāvaṇa. A golden deer with jewel-covered legs came from the forest. Enraptured with the creature, Sita begged Rama to capture it. While Rama chased the improbable animal, Rāvaṇa captured Sītā.

Rama destroyed Rāvaṇa, fulfilling their destiny. But even divine incarnations are imperfect, and Rama doubted Sītā's chastity during her imprisonment. Though Sītā underwent a test of fire, Rama continued to doubt. Sītā, pregnant, retreated to the wilderness to bear twin sons, who, recognized as adolescents by Rama, brought about the couple's reunion. Still Rama doubted. Sītā called for a final test: earth, which gave her birth, should take her back if she were innocent. The earth opened and Sītā disappeared, leaving Rama convinced of her purity and heartbroken at her loss.

As Rama was an avatar of Vishnu, Sītā is connected with **Lakṣmī**. Like other consort goddesses, she reincarnated with her husband, becoming his partner in life after life. In each lifetime, she was loyal and modest. In one, Vishnu incarnated as a leper, but Sītā (here named Anasūyā) treated him with respect, even taking him to a prostitute when he demanded it. As he rode on her back to the brothel, the leper kicked a demon, who cursed Vishnu with death at sunrise. Sītā kept light from returning until the gods removed both curses. (Daniélou 1964; Dehejia; Dimmitt and van Buitenen; Hawley and Wulff 1982; Ions; Kinsley 1986, 1997; Narayan; Pattanaik; Sharma; Whitehead; Warrier)

Sītāla This goddess possesses those stricken with smallpox. Born after other goddesses, Sītāla had difficulty getting humans to pay attention to her, so she invented smallpox to force them to her altars. Now Sītāla is one of the most worshipped goddesses of India, called the Mata ("mother") of each village.

Another version of her birth says a prince who wanted a male heir offered a sacrificial fire, from which a woman emerged. Brahma told her to carry lentils always, to ensure that humans would honor her. When she desired a mate, she was given a demon born from the sweat of Shiva's austerities. Then she and her mate visited the gods in disguise, changing the lentils into poxes. The gods implored her to set her lentils loose on earth, promising that this would encourage people to worship her.

Pictured as a red-clad, golden-skinned goddess carrying rods to strike her victims, Sītāla is honored by menstruating women. The ritual involves placing a pan of water in front of her image, with a prayer that pox will pass over the home. On her feast days, children were taken to her temples and blessed with flowers and water; if they were not stricken, the parents offered thanksgiving gifts to the goddess.

Sometimes said to be **Kālī** or **Devī**, Sītāla is worshipped annually in the festival called Thadari, when cooking fires must go out and cooling buttermilk porridge is served. In northern India, the late-winter Shitala Ashtami festival celebrates Sītāla as Vasanta, who wears yellow, the color of the season's blossoms. The goddess is honored by housecleaning, for she hates dirt and disorder. The cleaning doubtless has a prophylactic effect, especially in seasons when disease threatens. (Babb; Hawley and Wulff 1982; Gatwood; Patton; Gupta Ś 1991; Ions; Kinsley 1986; McDaniel 2003; Misra; Pattanaik; Sharma)

Sitātapatrā This Buddhist goddess protects devotees from black magic and astrological disasters. She carries a silken parasol, indicating the umbrella of protection she casts around her children. The goddess's emergence is described by her full name of Uṣṇīṣasitātaptrā, "lady of white parasol who emerged from Buddha's crown of light." She has a thousand legs so she can rush to her worshippers' aid, and her body is covered with eyes so she may better watch over them. (Shaw 2006)

Sonwari Among the Kerba people of Orissa, this was the name of the woman who brought light to the world. She lived alone in darkness until she was married, at which time she moved in with her husband. While single and later married, she wore great golden earrings. One day, as she was drawing water, a huge bird came from the sky and snatched one of the beautiful earrings and tossed it into the spider's web that stretched across the sky. There it fixed itself and became the sun that afterward lit the world. Through her tears over her lost ornament, Sonwari was grateful for the light and warmth. (Elwin 1954)

Srid-Icamphrul-mo-che Tibet's ancestral goddess lived in heaven with her parents and only brother. When a human man asked for her in marriage, she accepted. But before she departed the heavens, she asked for half of the world as her inheritance. But she was told that, as a girl, she only got one-third, as well as a spindle from her mother and an arrow from her father. These dowry gifts were sufficient for Srid-Icam to create a comfortable world for her descendants. In northwestern Tibet, this goddess's name is rNam-rgyal. (Bonnefoy)

Śrīmati Two sages both fell in love with this princess, and both asked her father for her hand, but neither sought the opinion of the girl herself. Śrīmati's father told the sages that choice of a husband was the girl's, not his, and they could present themselves to her at court. Both then prayed to the god Vishnu that the other would be given the face of a monkey, and when they turned up to present their suits to the princess, she was confronted by men with identical monkey faces. She turned to a beautiful young man standing nearby and put a garland around his neck, indicating her desire to wed him. The young man was the god Vishnu in disguise. (Pattanaik)

Subbu-Khai-Thung The Dhammai people gave this name to the earth goddess, born from primal mother Zumiang-Nui. Right after her birth, Subbu-Khai-Thung disappeared into the mouth of a worm, but her mother killed the worm and found her alive within its belly, from which the earth was formed for the goddess to rule over. Subbu-Khai-Thung bore a series of children in twin pairs, boy and girl; each of them mated to give birth to earth's creatures. (Elwin 1958)

Sujātā Buddhist legend tells of this woman, daughter of a village chief, who was inspired by a vision to offer food to the future Buddha. Her vision instructed her to wish for his enlightenment as she offered him a dish of the freshest rice cooked in the cream of a thousand cows. She prepared the meal, then strewed flowers about and sent for the Buddha. She offered the sweet rice in a golden bowl, and gave it to him, despite the fact that as an ascetic he had no need of such an object. Shortly afterward, he attained enlightenment. (Young 2004; Zimmer 1955)

Sukanyā When this princess accidentally blinded a sage by poking a twig into the ants' nest where he was performing austerities, her father bore the brunt of the resultant curse. To avoid his fate, the king gave Sukanyā ("lovely maiden") to the sage. The man was not a good husband for a princess, but she was a loyal wife. When twin trickster gods tried to seduce her, she refused; when they transformed her husband into their likeness, she was still able to see his identity and

avoid being compromised. Impressed with her loyalty, the gods left Sukanyā's husband with his new youthful beauty so that the couple could enjoy true marital pleasure. (O'Flaherty 1985; Pattanaik)

Surabhi One of the beings who emerged from the ocean as it was churned in primordial times was the cow Surabhi, goddess of plenty, called the "fragrant one." She produced all luxury—and a daughter, **Nṛrti** ("misery"). She was also one of the multiple forms of the god Brahma's only daughter, **Shatarupa**, and the ancestral mother of all domesticated animals. (Daniélou 1964; Kinsley 1986; Pattanaik)

Sūryā The feminine sun has a name almost identical to that of her father, Surya. Little myth exists about her, although she is referred to as the consort of twin gods, the Aśvins. Her father intended to marry her to the moon god, Soma. A race was held, with Sūryā as the prize, and the twins were the winners. Thereafter, she rode with them in their chariots through the sky. Some texts describe her as the consort of Soma and embodiment of sacrifices to him. (Kinsley 1986)

Swasthānī In Nepal, this goddess is widely honored as a representative of ideal womanhood and a protector of the home. A form of **Devī**, she is described in the *Swasthānī Vrata Katha*, a sacred text that may have come from India. Invoked through fasting by women only, Swasthānī concerns herself with women's marital happiness. (Bennett)

Taleju The Nepalese guardian goddess was a virgin who, insulted when the king cast lustful eyes at her, left his borders unguarded to teach him a lesson. He sued for mercy, and she agreed to return if he worshipped her thereafter in the form of a girl who had not yet menstruated, in the belief that this would keep him from having lascivious thoughts. Such girls, called Kumari, are said as well to incarnate the goddess **Durgā**. (Pattanaik)

Tambaku The spirit of the tobacco plant was once a yearning young woman who was so unattractive that she could not attract the attention of a lover. Her father offered a huge dowry, but no one came forward to marry Tambaku, who died of loneliness. She was reincarnated as the tobacco plant, which all men love. (Pattanaik)

Tansirjo The sun goddess of the Bondo of Orissa was the sister of the moon goddess, Jonmati. They shared a house with their children, giving equally to all even though Tansirjo had more children. But one day Jonmati grew angry that she was feeding more of her sister's children than her own, and so she hid hers in her hair. When Tansirjo came in and asked where the children were, Jonmati said they had been bothering her so she ate them. This made Tansirjo aware of how annoying her own children were, so she ate them too. When Jonmati's children came out of their mother's hair, Tansirjo wished she could have her own back. But she could not bring them out of her stomach. Furious, she cast Jonmati out and remains hot with anger. But Jonmati, though she has her children with her, misses her sister and is very cold for that reason. (Elwin 1954)

Tārā Tārā is one of the ten Mahāvidyās connected to Tantric practice. She is second only in importance to **Kālī**, although tradition stresses that all goddesses are ultimately one. She is more important in Buddhism than in Hinduism, where the "Green Tārā" predominates. Blue skinned and wearing bone jewelry, she sits on a corpse, blazing like a pyre. This frightening Tārā can show her kindly side, for she carries the dead on a ghostly boat rowed by beautiful singing boatwomen. She aids her devotees when they are in need. Even to this kindly goddess, blood sacrifices of goats are offered daily.

Tārā is more fully a Buddhist figure. Although Buddhist cosmology is nontheistic, most figures of devotion are male, with Tārā an important exception. Because of the multiplicity of her images, she can be seen as a collective figure, some aspects of which may originate in indigenous religions such as *bon-po*. The earliest textual references refer to her as "lady twilight," a bodhisattva second only to Avalokiteśvara, of whom she is sometimes said to be the female aspect. She came into being when Avalokiteśvara, about to reach nirvana, heard the cries of humans to be left behind. He shed a single tear, and that tear was Tārā.

In Tibet, where she is honored among all classes and sects, Tārā appears as an ancestral mother. In her incarnation as a sexually eager rock ogress, she mated with a monkey (Avalokiteśvara in disguise), from whom the royal family was born. This "White Tārā," or Cintachakra, is a generous maternal figure with a personal relationship with each worshipper. She offers relief from life's difficulties, for she is the epitome of compassion. Calling out to Tārā or reciting her mantra provides protection from enemies and dangers.

This Tārā has a fierce side, called Tārā Kurukullā, who wears a crown of skulls and a necklace of decapitated heads. She dances, attired in a tiger's skin and baring her fangs, to drive away a devotee's enemies or to conquer evil spirits. Dressed in red garments, devotees can embody the powerful energy of the goddess after reciting her mantra 10,000 times. (Beyer; Bühnemann; Galland; Kinsley 1997; Shaw 2006)

Tārāka This woman's father was a Yakṣa (see **Yakṣī**); as befits a nature spirit, she was wild and energetic. When a sage killed the father of her sons, Tārāka and her children demanded retribution. Instead, they were turned into demons who devoured everything with fire. The sons abandoned their mother, who created deserts out of fertile land until killed by Rama, an incarnation of Vishnu.

Tārāka was also the name of a woman who attracted the eye of the moon god Soma. He kidnapped her from her husband, a sage, and refused to release her. During the war that followed, Soma was vanquished and Tārāka returned to her husband. She was found to be pregnant, with the father of the child unknown. When the child was born, the humiliated

Tārāka hid him in a clump of grass and only under threat of a curse presented him to Soma; the child became the planet Mercury. (Gupta Ś 1991; Narayan)

Tārī In Bengal, the sun god propositioned this earth goddess. She refused him, so he created human women. But they took up the worship of the goddess, and the struggle between Tārī and the sun continues to this day. In the early twentieth century it was estimated that as many as 150 people annually were sacrificed to this goddess. Brought in or captured from another village, the victim was treated with respect and kept well fed, often for years, before being sacrificed. Victims were drugged and told how the goddess required blood in order to be fruitful. Then they were attacked by the entire village, armed with sharp knives. The body parts and blood were used for rituals of restoration of the goddess's fertility. When human sacrifices were outlawed, animals were substituted. (Berkson; Zimmer 1968)

Thabaton In Manipur, there was a beautiful girl whose seven brothers went in search of fortune, leaving her unprotected. A tiger demon heard about her lonely situation and came to abduct and eat her. As Thabaton was dragged through the jungle, she ripped tiny pieces off her garments and left them to mark her trail. Many years later the brothers finally returned and, finding the house empty, set off in search of her. Following her fabric trail, they located and freed her. But she wanted to wreak revenge on the tiger, who had made her his sexual slave, and she asked the brothers to wait until she did so. She pretended that all was as usual but asked the tiger for the skin of an old woman, which he brought from his next killing expedition. The next time he was due home, Thabaton set the hut on fire and made the burning skin clearly visible. When the tiger came home, he thought the skin was Thabaton and leaped into the fire and died. (Beck et al)

Trikalā When Brahma noticed Shiva making love with **Pārvatī**, he imagined Vishnu and, from the unified power of three gods, Trikalā burst forth. She had

three distinct bodies, one beautiful and creative, known as Brahmī; one red and abundant, called Vaiṣṇavī; and one black destroyer named Raudrī. This goddess was later assimilated to **Prakṛti**. (Pintchman 1994)

Tripura-sundarī Third in importance among Tantric goddesses (after **Kālī** and **Tārā**), Tripura-sundarī is depicted as a shining goddess holding weapons in her four hands, covered with jewels and crowned with the moon, seated on a throne composed of the corpses of gods. She lives high in the Himalayas, where sages and heavenly women worship her. There she decks her crystal body with tigers' skins and drapes snakes around her neck.

Tripura-sundarī serves as a protective goddess; her myth describes how she helped the gods when the demon Bhaṇḍa attacked. She led an army of goddesses against the demon, who laughed at the sight of female warriors under the banner of the goddess, here called Lalitā. But the demon judged wrongly, for Tripura-sundarī cast forth innumerable deities from her body (including **Durgā**), who fought the demons Bhaṇḍa produced. The goddess prevailed, in the process re-enlivening the god of love, Kāmā, who had been killed before the battle.

In addition to being a protector, Tripura-sundarī is also associated with passion; she is the wife of Kāmā or a form of Rāti. Many titles describe her as passionate and beautiful, filled with erotic desire. Even heavenly beings were aroused by her, for which reason a young woman often stood for the goddess in ceremonies, receiving honors to each part of her body.

Her voluptuous nature notwithstanding, Tripura-sundarī has a fierce side, in which she wears skulls and has a long, protruding tongue. A myth explains this contradiction: Kālī was once insulted by Shiva and withdrew to practice asceticism. When a sage convinced Kālī to return, she did not realize her austerities had turned her complexion white and, seeing her own reflection in Shiva's heart, thought it was another goddess and became enraged. Shiva told her she was now light and beautiful and would henceforth be known under the name Tripura-sundarī, "beautiful in three worlds." A temple in Varanasi, dedicated to Tripura-sundarī under the name of Rājarājeśvarī, is so suffused with her presence no one can spend a night there without going mad. (Dempsey; Kinsley 1997; Warrier)

Tushu This Bengali agricultural goddess is honored in public and private worship. Her popular annual festival marks the completion of harvest. Songs are sung each night asking the goddess to be generous with her gifts during the following year. Some songs describe Tushu as a village woman who protects fields against invaders, although more typically she is a divine woman whose domain includes rivers as well as the fertile fields. (McDaniel 2003)

Umā When **Pārvatī** mastered the ascetic arts, her skin became golden, after which she was called Umā, "light" or "beauty." (This form of Pārvatī is also associated with the golden **Gaurī**.) She was the reincarnation of **Satī** and awaited marriage with her intended mate, Shiva. It had been predicted that their child would kill the demon who threatened the gods. Shiva did not wish to marry, so Kāma, god of love, was sent to inspire him. But when he shot his arrow toward the god, Shiva deflected it, so Kāma was killed by his own darts. Umā, stricken with guilt, collapsed. Dressed as a hermit, she began to meditate upon Shiva, thus attracting his attentions. As part of his courtship, Shiva restored Kāma to life. As prophesied, the child of Shiva and Umā grew up to free the gods from the demon. (Beswick; Sharma; Daniélou 1964, 2007; Ions; Kinsley 1986; McDermott 2001; O'Flaherty 1975; Zimmer 1946)

Urvaśī Most famous of the **Apsarās** was Urvaśī (a name sometimes used of **Uṣas**). She was born when a sage surrounded by tempting Apsarās slapped his thigh, causing energy to fly out in female form. Like others of her kind, she was both lustful and loving. Once she consented to live with a human king but told him human nakedness disgusted her. He promised she would never see him unclothed. But he broke his promise, and when Urvaśī caught one glimpse of his naked body, she fled. Unhappy without her, the king grew more and more wicked until his subjects revolted and killed him. Other tales about the couple say that when he promised to become an erotic singer-dancer, Urvaśī agreed to return; that Urvaśī either complained or bragged about his making love to her three times a day; and that Urvaśī taught him the secrets of immortality. Occasionally, Urvaśī appears in animal form, as a waterbird or a mare. (Daniélou 1964; Dimmitt and van Buitenen; Ions; O'Flaherty 1980; Zimmer 1946)

Uṣas The dawn goddess, popular in Vedic times, stayed eternally young but made men grow older. She appeared each morning, driving a chariot drawn by red horses and throwing off her bright-red blouse to reveal shining breasts that filled the heavens with splendor. The sun relentlessly pursues Uṣas across the sky, intent upon ravishing her. Another myth says Brahma, her father, turned the beautiful Uṣas into a deer and raped her in that form.

Uṣas can appear as singular, dual, or multiple, and her name ("burning") emphasizes her solar connections. She is said to be the sister of Rāti, both daughters of the sky. Her connection with the chief of the **Apsarās**, **Urvaśī**, is unclear. (Beswick; Daniélou 1964; Ions; Kinsley 1986; Thadani; Zimmer 1955)

Uṣṇīṣavijayā Buddhist goddess of long life, Uṣṇīṣavijayā assures worshippers that they will not be reborn in a lower form of existence. She emerged when the Buddha, asked by Indra to have mercy upon a carefree prince who would be reborn as a dog, promised that those who honored Uṣṇīṣavijayā would not be subjected to such difficulties. She extends life by purifying karma and bringing the devotee to a state of blissful surrender. She also permits entrance to paradise, where residents can move toward enlightenment without descending into the human realm. (Shaw 2006)

Uyugsum Among the mountain people called the Koraput, this mythic woman cut her daughter's throat in order to have something to eat. But the child's soul blazed out through the wound and threatened the world with a holocaust. To avoid the destruction, Uyugsum swallowed her daughter. She then rose from the earth into the sky, where, lit from within by her daughter, she is now the sun. (Obeyesekere 1984)

Vāc Goddess of eloquence, Vāc can appear as a form of **Sarasvatī** or a separate divinity. Called the mother of the Vedas, she is associated with the important symbol of abundance, the cow. One text says she is present in all worship. She is also the mother of the celestial nymphs, the **Apsarās**. She is envisioned as a queenly woman, wearing gold, graceful of movement, benevolent, and generous. (Daniélou 1964; Kinsley 1986)

Vaiṣṇo Devī This Kashmiri goddess is honored with pilgrimages to a vagina-like cave at the end of a nine-mile trail up a 6,000-foot peak called Trikuta. Attested to a millennium ago, the pilgrimages draw as many as five million people each year. Manifest in three rounded boulders, she is **Devī**, who was reincarnated in a young girl in order to vanquish demons. (Pintchman 2001)

Vajrayoginī The supreme goddess in Tantric Buddhism, Vajrayoginī offers an image of highest enlightenment. With bright-red skin, she holds a bowl made from a skull and brandishes a crescent-bladed knife. Like other **Ḍākinīs**, Vajrayoginī represents liberation from human life. As an instructor in Tantric mysteries, Vajrayoginī ("indestructible practitioner of yoga") asks male adepts to serve women as embodiments of herself, offering food, flowers, and sexual satisfaction. Although early writers on Tantra envisioned sexual practices as debasing to women, recent feminist scholarship points to figures like Vajrayoginī as evidence of a contrary tendency.

Because of her Buddha nature, Vajrayoginī is three bodied: the "truth body" is pure radiance, while a "bliss body" allows her to frolic through time and space, and the "transformation body" is tangible to gross human senses. She mostly stays in her bliss body, enjoying the pleasures of her paradisiacal home. The rainbow is her signature, for her adepts dissolve into rainbows at death. (Dehejia; Gupta S; Hiltebeitel and Erndl; Shaw 2006)

Vaḷḷi In Tamil-speaking areas of southern India, the romance of Vaḷḷi and her consort, the god Murugan, has been a popular part of religious life for more than a century. Vaḷḷi's mother was a doe who was raped by a male hermit. The baby was rejected by her deer mother, who nonetheless made a hole to protect the infant, who was shortly found by a group of hunters. Brought up as the adoptive child of the hunters' king, Vaḷḷi attracted the eye of a wandering god, who drew her picture and took it to his lord, Murugan. Infatuated with the wild woman, Murugan approached her directly, inviting her to have sex with him, but to no avail. So he came in the form of a merchant, offering bangles, only to be rejected again. Finally, he came disguised as a sage and, when Vaḷḷi once again spurned him, created the illusion of a stampeding elephant to drive the girl into his arms. Then he turned into the handsome god he truly was and won her love. Though Vaḷḷi's family resisted, they were ultimately won over by the god, and the wedding was celebrated. (Hawley and Wulff 1982; Handelman; Jayakar)

Vasudhārā The Buddhist goddess of wealth is similar to Hindu **Lakṣmī**, with whom she shares many traits. Her name is also sometimes used as a title of **Lakṣmī**. In Nepal, Vasudhārā ("stream of good fortune" or "fortune giver") is a popular goddess invoked for riches, including healthy children as well as productive fields. (Dehejia; Larson et al; Shaw 2006)

Vindhyavāsini In the mountains that bear her name and in a village named for her, the local goddess Vindhyavāsini has her temple complex. Although brought into the Hindu pantheon through the story of how she saved the baby Krishna from death by incarnating herself as a substitute victim (see **Nidrā** and **Yasoda** for more of this story), she existed earlier as a local goddess, perhaps one of the most ancient divinities of the region. Pilgrimages to her temple remain popular, as does Tantric meditation upon her sacred image. (Hawley and Wulff 1996)

Virāj This name for the great creatrix appears in Vedic literature, including the *Rig Veda*, where she and her consort simultaneously gave birth to each other. In other texts she is described as a hermaphrodite, while yet others give her a masculine gender. In all cases, she appears as the creative power of the universe and the foundation upon which the material world depends. (Pintchman 1994)

Vrinda The wife of a demon king, Vrinda, through her virtue, protected her husband from the gods' attempts to slay him. To negate her power, the gods sent Vishnu to her, disguised as her husband. When Vindra was unable to see that she was not making love chastely to her husband, she left him unprotected, and he was killed by Shiva. Another story told of Vrinda is that she was such a loyal wife that she performed intense austerities in order to gain the boon of immortality for her husband, but he only grew arrogant with her protection and went to war against the gods themselves, even lusting after the goddess **Pārvatī** in the presence of Vrinda. Vrinda, however, remained loyal and prayed to Vishnu to aid her husband. The god, more loyal to the other gods than to his devotee, sent her a corpse disguised to look like her husband, over which she began to mourn. Thus tricked into revealing that she was not perfect in her wifely devotion, Vrinda learned that her mistake had cost her husband his life. Furious, she cursed the gods, who turned her into the plant called tulsi ("the incomparable one," Indian basil), still revered as a holy plant in India today. (Babb; Gupta Ś 1971; McDaniel 2003; Pattanaik)

Yakṣī These voluptuous figures, found in third to first-century BCE sculptures, may descend from indigenous woodland love goddesses, as they are not part of the Vedic pantheon. Associated with trees and water, thus known as nature spirits, the heavy-breasted Yakṣī are depicted surrounded by animals and, occasionally, male figures called Yakṣa. The Yakṣī were irresistibly beautiful, so much so that the love god never bothered to use his arrows when they were around. Their bodies were a perfect blend of slenderness and plumpness, for they had massive breasts, hips, and thighs but girlish waists. Artists' representations of them show them scantily attired but wearing magnificent jewelry. To emphasize their connection with nature, a Yakṣī may stand beneath a tree, fondling its branches. She may also point to her barely covered genitals, emphasizing her connection with fertility.

Occasionally the Yakṣī appear terrifying, luring men to their deaths with unearthly beauty. Such Yakṣī enjoy men's sexual favors before eating them, but even demonic Yakṣī could be converted. Although the figures are well attested in Hindu contexts, they also appear in Buddhism, where the Yakṣīṇī appear on temples and shrines as sculpted maidens who protect the inner sanctum. The figure of **Hārītī** has been categorized as a Yakṣī. Finally, the Yakṣī are honored with devotional practices as Jaina goddesses. (Cort; Dehejia; Subramaniam; Ions; Shaw 2006; Young 2004)

Yamī This primal goddess asked her brother, Yama, to inseminate her so that the world might be populated. He refused, preferring to die childless than to engage in a befouling sin. He became lord of the dead, while Yamī became the night goddess Yamini. In some versions, Yamini was created to soften the pain of rejection that Yamī felt. Some sources said Yamī mated with her brother, producing the human race before Yama grew doubtful as to the sanctity of their behavior. In Bengal, she is identified with the goddess Yamunā, divinity of the Jumna river. (Bonnefoy; Daniélou 1964; Ions; Pattanaik; Zimmer 1955)

Yasoda Foster mother of Krishna, Yasoda was pregnant with **Nidrā** when the also-pregnant **Devaki** was threatened with the death of her child. The two fetuses were switched, so that imprisoned Devaki gave birth to the goddess, who flew away, while Yasoda gave birth to Krishna, safe from the threatening King Kaṃsa. Thereafter, Yasoda raised Krishna as her own son. A cowherd, or **Gōpī**, Yasoda brought her friends to admire the growing child, and when he was grown they danced to his flute. (Ions)

Yeshey Tsogyal "Bliss Queen" is the title of this Tibetan goddess born in warrior form from a lotus blossom. She is a figure of enlightenment among Tibetan Buddhists, seen as a form of **Tārā** or **Vajrayoginī**. She was incarnated in the eighth century as a Tibetan queen, who was fully enlightened but chose to appear as a young girl. She showed herself to be a spiritual adept from childhood, despite persecution. Once installed as queen, Yeshey Tsogyal taught spiritual discipline through words and extreme asceticism. She is depicted as red and naked, revealing her vulva for her devotees' edification. (Atkinson et al)

Yoginī These spirits play important parts in Tantric practice, whose female adepts are called by this name. Like **Apsarās**, these celestial beings can fly or transform themselves into birds. They are envisioned as full-breasted, small-waisted women; sometimes they have animal heads. Their special role is to protect Tantric practitioners, but they also punish those who are initiated but lapse (as such, they are equated with **Ḍākinīs**). Yoginīs may appear as mother, sister, or wife, or the same yoginī may take these different roles with a practitioner. (McDaniel 2004; Hiltebeitel and Erndl; Stoddard)

Yuk The primal mother Yuk of northeast India was a lightning goddess who helped create life. Because earth was bare, she revealed her genitals, and her sun-bright vulva flashed lightning across the sky. This brought rain, which nourished the earth so that plants burst forth. (Elwin 1958)

SOUTHEAST ASIA *and* INDONESIA

SOUTHEAST ASIAN AND INDONESIAN PANTHEON

Arrang Dibatu Born from rock, this primordial woman of the southern Celebes sent her husband west, looking for gold with which to create the world. From flakes of its ore, he created animals, plants, and humans. (Bonnefoy)

Au-Co In Vietnam, Au-Co was an immortal queen who lived in the mountains, while her consort, the dragon king, lived in the sea. Au-Co gave birth to a sticky pouch from which a hundred eggs emerged. She divided the hatched offspring, leaving half with their father and taking others to land; thus some people live in the highlands, others by the sea. (Bonnefoy; Nguyen Ngoc Bich)

Bimān Chan This Cambodian heroine was taken into the sky by the moon god Chan, who had fallen in love with her. When his other wives grew envious, Bimān Chan begged the moon to lift her higher, but the wind there blew her to pieces. Her head fell to earth, but her body remained aloft. (Bonnefoy)

Buan Buan, moon goddess of the Philippines, had as many children as the sun. Because the sun's were brighter, Buan feared for her duller children. So she convinced the sun god to kill his children, promising that she would kill hers too. But she hid hers behind clouds, from which they occasionally emerge to shine as stars. The grieving sun everlastingly chases Buan across the sky. But she stays far away, guided by her eldest daughter, Tala, the morning and evening star. In a similar story from the Luzon people, in which the moon's name was Mayari, the goddess fought with her brother, the sun god Apolaqui, over who would rule the world. He put out one of her eyes, so her light is fainter than his, and henceforth she ruled the night. (Rahmann)

Bugan The first woman of the Ifugao of the Philippines wanted her daughter Bugan and her son Wigan to populate the world, but they were resistant to leaving home. So she sent them into the forest, then unleashed a flood. Floating on the raging waters, Bugan and her brother found houses, pigs, cats, chickens, dogs, and jars full of food. They soon had a nice homestead, but populating the land was difficult because, as brother and sister, the couple were forbidden to have sexual relations. One night Wigan impregnated his sleeping sister. The taboo against brother-sister incest was reimposed as soon as the earth was populated. (Demetrio; Bonnefoy)

Bundo Kanduang In Sumatra, Bundo Kanduang is the earth goddess, a primary divinity whose worship continues despite Islamic influence. Bundo Kanduang was created simultaneously with the visible world and ruled from the traditional Minangkabau capital, Pagarrujung, with her son Duang Tuanku. An important if complicated legend revolves around the betrothals of Bundo Kanduang's daughter Puti Lenggo Geni and her niece, Puti Bungsu, the latter of whom was kidnapped at her wedding, which resulted in the goddess leaving this world. Bundo Kanduang still inhabits human women and occasionally men. Believers seek the reincarnated goddess's counsel and offer her homage. The goddess's name designates women who hold leadership positions in the region, where inheritance passes through the mother's line. (Abdullah; Blackwood; Frey; Kartomi)

Dayang Raca When a flood exterminated all humanity except for this woman, she was unable to continue the race without divine help. So the spirit of fire impregnated her with a child that had half a body. In despair at his deformity, the boy tried to drown himself but was saved by the spirit woman Indai Jebua, who gave him the world's first rice. (Bonnefoy)

Dewi Nawang Sasih Among the Sundanese, this celestial nymph taught people how to cook rice. The recipe was easy: place one grain in a pot, and wait until it divides into a meal. People lived in comfort for many generations, because the men always obeyed Dewi Nawang's one commandment: Never touch a woman's cooking implement. But a king broke the goddess's rule, and Dewi Nawang Sasih departed from earth. Since that time, it takes a bunch of rice to fill a pot, because the grains no longer divide and reproduce. This goddess may be a form of **Dewi Shri**. (Bonnefoy)

Dewi Shri The rice goddess of Bali and Java, goddess of the underworld and the moon, has both earthly and celestial powers. Although she rules life, through her control of foodstuffs, she also controls death. Most importantly, she controls the monsoons, and thus the time of rice ripening. Under the name of Dewi Danuh, this goddess is a divinity of the ocean. As benevolent Giriputri, she rules the sacred mountain where water is drawn to bless the harvest.

Her myth begins when the god Batārā Guru created a girl named Retna Dumilah. Then, although she was his daughter, he desired her. When the god was unrelenting in his demands for intercourse, Retna agreed that they could wed if he provided her with a gamelan that played itself, a dress that never wore out, and a food that sustained without filling. Batārā Guru sent his messenger, Kula Gumarang, to earth to locate these magical items, but there he met Dewi Shri, with whom he became infatuated. But she would not break her vow to her husband and changed Kula Gumarang into a wild boar because of his insolence.

Meanwhile, in heaven, Batārā Guru grew impatient. He raped Retna Dumilah, who died of shame. Batārā Guru was struck with remorse, but the god of death assured him that he would never see his beloved

again. However, if he buried her with proper ceremonies, a boon would come. Batārā Guru followed these instructions, and Retna's body dissolved into many kinds of food—coconuts, mangos, beets, and, most importantly, rice.

Meanwhile, Dewi Shri, still pursued by the wild boar, begged heaven to let her dissolve into food; she did so, but the rice that came forth from her body required constant irrigation, while that Retna produced could be dry-farmed. Kula Gumarang changed himself into pests that devour rice crops. Dewi Shri, in retaliation, transformed herself into a snake that eats vermin.

In the Sundanese version of the story, Shri was hatched from an egg presented to the god Guru. Suckled by Guru's wife, the child grew to be a beautiful woman upon whom the god's desires became fixated. Because of the threat of incest, the other gods killed the maiden, and when her body decomposed, useful plants including bamboo and rice sprang from it. The gods named her Nji Pohatji Sangjang Sri.

In one of her incarnations, Dewi Shri was the incestuous Sri, who with her brother Sadana created all beings, who emerged from their decaying bodies after they died for their illicit passion. Sadana and Sri fled separately from the palace of their father, who had promised Sri in marriage to an ogre king. The ogre and his demon army pursued her as she tried to reunite with her brother. Finding the devout woman Patani, Sri asked for a room in which to rest and then told ritual secrets to the woman.

In Bali, where Batari Sri Dwi is an important and popular divinity, she is the focus of a wedding ritual at the primary temple, Pura Bessakih. Simpler rituals in rice fields are also part of Balinese religious life. As goddess of the irrigation systems, she is known as Dewi Danu, although that name is also used of a goddess who emerged from an erupting volcano and now rules Mount Batur. Her consort is Dewu Agung, the god who rules another volcano, Mount Agung. Dewi Danu is honored at an important temple where twenty-four priests and a single priestess serve. A high priest, selected by the priestess, incarnates the goddess.

Despite the influences of Islam and Christianity, devotion to Dewi Shri continues. Emerging rice stalks are covered with a fertilizing liquid invented by Dewi Shri, and irrigation water includes bits of chalk as offerings to her. (Headley; Bonnefoy; van der Kroef; Wessing 1990)

Giri Devī In rituals associated with **Pattinī** of Sri Lanka, Giri Devī is invoked in dances and songs. She was the sister of a demon who indulged an illicit desire for her. This grew to be an obsession, until at Giri Devī's wedding, the demon went crazy, ate all the food, then kidnapped her. Taking her to the forest, he had intercourse with her and kept her prisoner. Giri Devī hanged herself from a tree. The demon never recovered from his loss, although Pattini kept him from devastating the world. (Obeyesekere 1984)

Hainuwele On the island of Ceram, this supernatural woman was born when the hunter Ameta pursued a wild pig into a deep pool. The animal drowned, and Ameta tried to drag out the body for meat. What emerged was a fruit stabbed with a boar's tusk. Ameta planted the fruit, which flowered within a week. From one of its leaves, fertilized by Ameta's blood, Hainuwele was born. Like the coconut tree from which she sprang, Hainuwele grew swiftly. She showed miraculous powers, offering people jewels and other treasures that she made of her own excrement.

Less than a week after her birth, she led the world's first ritual dance. Around and around the people spiraled, as Hainuwele began to sink into the ground. The people danced over her head until Hainuwele was buried. Hers was the world's first death. From her place of descent grew food plants, never before seen on earth. Furious at the death of the young girl, the village's woman chief, Mulua Satine, left and became queen of the dead. She and Hainuwele are considered aspects of the goddess whose other aspects are Mulua Dapie Bulane and Tapele, moon and earth goddesses, respectively. (Jenson; Bonnefoy)

Ibu Pretiwi This Balinese goddess of abundance, often assimilated to the better-known **Dewi Shri**, represents birth, fertility, and germination. Flower, fruit, and rice-dough sculptures are offered to her on altars erected in fields or rice paddies. Ibu Pretiwi's boar son was the force of vegetation that sprang from the earth. She is honored at plowing and planting. Dedication of new buildings and naming of children also fall under her power. Her consort is the sky god, with whom she is called upon to witness religious rituals and thus promote their efficacy. (Brinkgreve)

Inada Samadulo Hosi The mother goddess of southern Nias came from rock and produced twin gods with no father, then gave birth to a bisexual sister wife, Silewe Nazarata, who could be both kindly and threatening. (Bonnefoy)

Kaṇṇagi Among the 40 million Tamils in southern India, Sri Lanka, and Malaysia, this is the name of the ancestral mother, symbol of their unity and ruler of the faithfulness of wives, important in patrilineal traditions. This emphasis on monogamous chastity in an ancestral mother is unusual, for such divinities often produce children through parthenogenesis or through multiple matings, so it is possible that Kaṇṇagi's myth once depicted her as engaging in less-than-chaste behavior that was later discouraged. Despite her importance as a symbol, little ritual activity is connected to Kaṇṇagi; temples devoted to her are rare. The epic of Sri Lanka, the *Cilappatikāram*, tells how Kaṇṇagi was transformed into the goddess **Pattinī**. Whether they were originally separate figures is unclear. (Kinsley 1986; Preston; Parthasarathy)

Kinnarī In Thailand, these bird women descend to earth to dance and sing near lakes and in forest clearings. They sometimes meet and mate with humans, but such affairs are usually short-lived. In India, the Kinnarī were nymphs like **Apsarās**. (O'Flaherty 1985; Bonnefoy)

Kiri Amma Her name has several meanings—milk mother, wet nurse, and grandmother—all of which indicate her nurturing interest in the Sri Lankan people. Kiri Amma appears as seven divinities but also in singular form. When a child falls ill, seven women dressed in white impersonate the goddess, arriving at the house with rice and cakes. A blessing from lactating women is especially effective in healing childhood diseases, for in such women the strength of this protective goddess is strongest. She may be an ancient goddess displaced by **Pattinī**, whose worship spread from South India. (Gombrich; Obeyesekere 1984)

Kling Among the tribal Indo-Chinese, this falcon goddess was the mother of many sons, who waged war using kites to which they tied themselves. Flying beneath their drifting kites, they attacked and conquered enemies. (Bonnefoy)

Lieu Hahn This Vietnamese goddess was exiled because she broke a wine cup in the home of her father, the Jade Emperor. She lived an unremarkable life, marrying and bearing a son, then dying when her exile ended. After she returned to heaven, she was haunted by memories of life on earth. So she returned, clothing herself in the form of a flute player. She ran a teahouse that disappeared whenever she left it, then reappeared at her return. Lieu Hahn was often seen at sites of natural beauty. Meanwhile, the husband of her first incarnation reincarnated as a great scholar, whom she married and with whom she lived another happy lifetime.

When she died, she ascended again to heaven but still wished to return to earth. In her third and final incarnation she became a village goddess. There she happily remained, caring for her people, until the seventeenth century, when an emperor ruled she was a demon and destroyed her shrine. Infuriated, she afflicted men and animals with a fatal illness, until the emperor admitted his error and rebuilt her shrine. (Bonnefoy)

Mae Khau This goddess of the Vietnamese Tai helps rice thrive. A planting ritual reinforces the connection of female fertility and food, for only a woman with many children can ceremoniously plant the first rice, from seeds that had been set aside during the previous harvest. (Hamilton)

Mae Phosop Thailand's most important goddess is the source of rice. When rice plants bloom, the goddess is envisioned as a nubile maiden awaiting conception. When rice grains appear, Mae Phosop is said to be pregnant. Offerings are made to her: oranges, for pregnant women like the fruit as an antidote to morning sickness; powder and perfume, because pregnant women like to pamper themselves. Several plants are groomed as though they are women, their leaves combed back like hair.

In some places, the soul of Mae Phosop is bound to the ripening plants with small threads. At the conclusion of the ritual, boundary markers are set in place so that no one disturbs the goddess until her birth time arrives. Only women are permitted to perform Mae Phosop's rituals, for she hates men because she was threatened with rape, so she flew away and took rice with her. Only when people agreed to worship her in rituals in which only women participated did she return.

After the harvest the ritual called "calling the rice mother's soul" is celebrated. Set-aside stalks are ritually struck against the ground, releasing their seeds; these grains are used to bless the harvest before storing. The next morning, flowers and boiled chicken are offered to the goddess, and water is sprinkled on family members and cattle in her honor. (Hamilton)

Maguayean In the Philippines, the goddess of sea breezes fell in love with Captan, god of the winds from the land. Their courtship was fearsome, as each tried to outdo the other. But when Captan proved himself the equal of Maguayean, they swept each other up and dived together into the ocean. Some versions of the

135

story say they had one child, a reed that broke in half to form the first people; the first woman was named Sicauay. Other creation legends name the first woman Dwata; she lived with her twin sister, Saweigh, on an island the size of a hat, on which no trees or grass grew until a bird brought a seed across the waters. Other names for the primal woman include Lakbang and Lakarol. (Demetrio)

Māyāri Among the Luzon of the Philippines, this moon goddess was the beloved daughter of the high god, sister to the sun. When the high god died, the sun took all power. Māyāri opposed this, so he put out one of her eyes. Horrified at his behavior, he offered to share the world. Thus she rules at night with one eye, while he rules the day. (Rahmann)

Mba Kuy The Dyaks of Borneo believe food came to earth due to when Mba Kuy, threatened with marriage to a man she did not choose, tore out her uterus and threw it to earth, making herself barren. But she was so fertile that, even detached from the goddess's body, her womb brought forth rice and other grains for human consumption. (van der Kroef)

Mebū'yan The Bagobo of the Philippines say this death goddess is covered with nipples, so that babies who died unweaned can be nursed. She tends them as though they were her own children and, when they reach the point at which they no longer need her milk, she releases them to their ancestors, who feed them rice. All spirits visit Mebū'yan on their way to the underworld. She washes them free of their bodies; if she did not, bodies would reanimate themselves. (Benedict)

Nachailiavang The matrilineal Ifaluk give this name to a creatrix. When her sister, Nachailiol, began to steal from her, Nachailiavang grew angry. Limes were disappearing from her tree, so Nachailiavang washed herself in her sister's watering hole. Their parents sided with Nachailiol and cut Nachailiavang's hair off.

Furious, Nachailiavang left, taking her son with her. She walked on top of the ocean's waves dropping sand from a coconut, creating islands and atolls. (Spiro)

Nawangwulan This Javanese swan maiden married a mortal. She made one rule: he should not watch her while she made rice, because she had the power to feed her entire family on one grain. Unable to control himself, he observed her. Thereafter she had to hull each grain of rice separately and, finding this odious, Nawangwulan flew away. (Bonnefoy)

Ntsee Tyee Ntsee Tyee, primal woman of the Hmong, rose from a crack in the rocks with her consort, who brought a flower with him. At first they ate seeds from the flower to survive, but finally the seeds were almost gone, so they planted the remaining ones. One stalk grew, but it was miraculous: corn and millet, on the same plant. As each kind of grain ripened, it spoke to Ntsee Tyee and Lou Tou, calling them "mother and father" and giving instructions as to how they were to be preserved. (Livo and Dia Cha)

Nyai Lara Kidul The primordial serpent of west Java, Nyai Lara Kidul lives beneath the waves in a golden palace whose courtyard is paved with jewels. An important indigenous goddess, she has been connected to Hindu **Durgā** and to Buddhist **Tārā**. **Dewi Shri** has been described as this goddess's positive side, while the temptress Nyai Blorong represents her negative aspects; in such interpretations, Nyai Lara Kidul is a multifaceted goddess whose power was divided among more specialized divinities.

On the southern coast of Java, where she is called Roro Kidul or Ratu Kidul, fisher folk avoid wearing green garments near the ocean, so as not to offend this queen of the sea, who might dash their heads against rocks or change her currents to endanger them. Fishermen worship Ratu Kidul, as do those who gather swallows' nests from the sides of sheer sea cliffs. In the 1500s, a king had intercourse with Ratu Kidul; only their descendants can see the goddess now. Festivals dedicated to her survive despite Islamicization of the region. (Brakel; Jordaan; Bonnefoy; Resink; Wessing 1988, 1997)

Nyi Pohaci This Sundanese rice goddess was daughter of the serpent goddess Antaboga. Her mother, afraid to lose her to marriage, gave her fruit from the tree of paradise to eat. It was not enough to sustain her and she wasted away. As her body decomposed, rice sprang from her eyes, bamboo from her thighs, and the coconut palm from her head. (Bonnefoy)

Pattinī The greatest goddess of Sri Lanka and of the Tamil people in Malaysia and southern India, one-breasted Pattinī is served by transvestite priests who enter trances and engage in difficult ascetic practices. She is honored as the mother of all children, although her myth shows her virginally pure. Pattinī is the only goddess known universally, for others are restricted to specific localities. She is described in the epic poem called *Cilappatikāram*, "the epic of the silver anklet" (lost for several centuries and then rediscovered), as well as in rituals and folkways.

Pattinī appears in myth as an exemplary wife. Born miraculously from a mango and known during her lifetime as **Kaṇṇagi**, Pattinī married a merchant with whom she could not have intercourse. Her husband, Kovalan, left her for a prostitute, Madavi, on whom he squandered his fortune, returning home penniless to Pattinī, who was mired in poverty as an abandoned wife. But she gave him her precious silver anklet to sell in the marketplace. Unbeknown to them, the queen's identical bracelet had been stolen. When Pattinī's luckless husband showed the bracelet to the jeweler who was the real thief, he was captured and executed.

Pattinī went to the king to plead for her husband's life. It was too late, for he was already dead. Pattinī tore off her left breast and threatened the king, then threw it at the city. It burst into flame, destroying everything but the body of her husband, whom Pattinī resurrected. Then she rose into the sky, becoming transfigured into a goddess. Summer's heat and drought are caused by her. Cooling ceremonies include drinking sacred water in which an anklet has been dipped. (Gombrich; Obeyesekere 1981, 1984; Parthasarathy; Winslow)

Rangda Associated with **Durgā**, said to have been Rangda's teacher, Rangda is a folk memory of a pre-Hindu goddess of Bali. Her legend says she was the widow of a king who, because no one would marry her daughter because of Rangda's reputation as a sorceress, tried to destroy the land. Her image in Balinese folk drama is almost indistinguishable from Durgā's. (Brinkgreve; Preston)

Royot At the beginning of time, the universe was united and whole, and gods walked on earth. But, say the Jarai, a young man drank a love potion intended for another man, which caused him to fall desperately in love with his sister Royot. She returned his love but died giving birth to their child. The gods were so stricken by this tragedy that they turned the doomed lovers into boulders. Now humans no longer understand the language of animals or birds, for when Royot died, the universe was permanently torn apart. (Bonnefoy)

Si Boru Deak Parujar Among the Batak of Indonesia, this creatrix was born in the heavens with her sister, Sorbayati. Their parents arranged for Sorbayati, the older sister, to marry the lizard god, but at a dance party he revealed that he really preferred Si Boru Deak Parujar. Humiliated, Sorbayati threw herself off heaven's balcony; her body disintegrated into bamboo and rattan. The bereaved sister then descended. Since she could not bring back her sister, Si Boru Deak Parujar created the earth on the back of a snake. Only after doing so would she agree to marry the lizard god, who was transformed into a human. From this union were born the first humans, including the first woman, Si Boro Ihat Manisia, and her twin brother. (Bonnefoy)

Tagbudangan This earth goddess of the Philippines marked the land. Where she urinated, grooves in the rock can be seen. She left her footprints on other rocks when pursued by potential rapists. She dented a rock when she lay her newly shampooed hair on it. Consort of the culture hero Maka-andog, she appears under several names, although it is unclear whether several wives are intended. Because Maka-andog was notoriously unfaithful, his wife left him and returned to her woodland home. (Hart and Hart)

Thi Kinh Although famous for her beauty, the Vietnamese heroine Thi Kinh pledged to sacrifice her happiness to alleviate the pain of others. To further this, she married a poor and ugly man, with whom she had a peaceful if impoverished life. She treated her husband with the utmost tenderness, which led to difficulty, for as he slept one day, she saw a hair on his chin that he had missed while shaving. To spare him the embarrassment of discovering it, she took a scissors to cut it. But at the moment she touched him, he jolted awake and stabbed himself against the scissors. He had been unable to believe his good luck in finding a beautiful wife, and now he imagined she had turned against him. He accused her of attempted murder, and the village turned against her. Recognizing that there was no way to prove her innocence, Thi Kinh disguised herself as a man and entered a monastery.

A young woman worshipper fell in love with her. When Thi Kinh reminded the woman of the monk's vow of chastity, the girl's love turned to fury. When she bore a child to another man, she left it on the temple steps with a letter saying that Thi Kinh had impregnated her. Thi Kinh was called to defend herself. The baby began to cry, and she picked it up. This convinced the abbot that Thi Kinh was guilty, so she was expelled from the monastery. She spent her life supporting the child through begging until, near death from starvation, she returned to the monastery and told the truth to the senior monk. As she died, she left the child to the monastery's care. Thereafter, she was deified as Quan Am Tong Tu, "merciful protector of children," who is still honored in Vietnam, often seen as a form of the Chinese goddess of mercy, **Guanyin**. (Boucher; Do Vang Ly)

Thusandi Among the Palaungs of Thailand, this primal serpent woman was the ancestor of all people. She married a prince, by whom she bore three eggs. Her mate was called away and wrote her an explanation, enclosing a jewel to show his love. He entrusted the letter to parrots, who fell in with other parrots. While the messengers were playing, enemies of the couple found the abandoned letter and replaced the jewel with bird droppings. When the parrots finally delivered the letter, Thusandi was so furious that she threw two of her eggs into the river Irrawaddy; they floated downstream and hatched into royal beings. The third, she smashed against rocks; the bits became rubies, for which the region is still famous. (Scott)

Trung-Trac The rain goddesses of the Tonkin were originally warrior women who led a revolt against a Chinese governor. The uprising was successful, and Trung-Trac, the elder sister, became queen, while Trung-Nhi was honored as a war hero. The women were deified after death. (Scott)

Tuglibung Among the Bagobo, this primal woman was created already old, together with her spouse Tuglay. Because the sun hung too low in the sky, interfering with her housework, she demanded it move to its present height. She also created everything in the world. (Benedict)

Upu Nusa The Molucca goddess Upu Nusa engendered the universe through her union with the sky god. Similar primordial goddesses found in the region are Tana Ekan (Lamaholot, eastern Flores Islands) and Irik (Iban of Borneo). (Bonnefoy)

Ya-hsang Ka-shi The Wa people said the water goddess Ya-hsang Ka-shi conceived after eating a gourd, whose seeds she sowed near a rock. Two enormous plants grew, each bearing one gourd. Eating the gourd brought on a sexual passion for the goddess, and she gave birth to a powerful tiger-eared daughter, Nang Pyek-kha Yek-khi, to whom Ya-hsang Ka-shi gave the gourds, telling her that only the man who could cut them open was worthy to be her husband. Ya-hsang Ka-shi began to age, but she lived long enough to give her consent for her daughter to marry a man who opened the gourds, setting loose animals and human beings. (Scott)

Yang Sri The toad goddess of the Senang people of Vietnam can bring or withhold rain. She was the wife of the thunder god, so, in times of drought, the Senang captured a toad and bound it, believing that the threat to his beloved would cause her husband to let the rains come. Yang Sri is also goddess of rice, because the outer husk of rice resembles a toad's skin. (Dang Nghiem Van)

JAPAN

Only one of the world's major religions is centered on a goddess: Shinto, which grew from myths and rituals of several cultures, indigenous and imported. An important influence on Japanese arts, culture, and philosophy for more than 2,000 years, Shinto has always given prominence to goddesses, embodied in natural forces.

Japan's most ancient culture, the Jōmon, was based on a female divinity. Big-hipped and large-breasted goddess figurines, made from 11,000 to 300 BCE, have been found near or in graves, often broken, suggesting a ritual of release. Connection of the Jōmon culture with other peoples of Japan is unknown. Before 1500 BCE, the Ainu people lived throughout the archipelago, but later settlers drove the Ainu to the northern islands of Honshu and Hokkaido. The beliefs of other early people, such as those found in Okinawa, appear in vestigial form in myths. Both the Ainu and the Okinawans have traditions of female shamanism that can be found as well in the early Shinto era, when entranced priestesses conducted ceremonies and empresses sought counsel through trance before making political decisions.

Such shamanic queens were the norm through the era of the Yayoi (300 BCE–300 CE). Rice farmers, the Yayoi crafted goddess images that were often accompanied by phallic stones. Ceremonial jewels, mirrors, and swords, which play a significant role in the mythology of the sun goddess, were introduced at this time. Then, in approximately the fourth century CE, Japan was overridden by a new culture. Horsemen from central Asia brought religious images of warriors and a peculiar stone tomb for their warlords. How these nomadic warriors were absorbed into Japanese culture is unclear, but two centuries later the ruler was male, although the primary divinity remained female.

After Buddhism became the land's official religion in 592 CE, earlier myths were nearly lost. But in 681,

Heida-no-Are, a court woman of phenomenal memory, was assigned to memorize ancient tales. Thirty years later, Empress Gemmyo assigned a scribe to take down stories from the aging Heida. Called the *Kojiki*, these writings form the basis of Shinto beliefs. A few years later Gemmyo had additional material compiled from other sources. The *Nihongi* is an important source of information on Japanese mythology.

As the court became more Buddhist, some figures from that religion were brought into Japanese culture. Most were male, a change that diminished the role of women. Yet Shinto continued to thrive, influencing Buddhism until a nature-oriented Buddhism called Zen emerged. Even today, the distinction between Shinto and Buddhism in Japan can be unclear, and many people practice both religions.

In 1868, Shinto became a state religion, its rituals and symbols used to enhance imperialism. This status formally ended when the 124th emperor of Japan was forced to renounce his claim of direct descent from the sun goddess, in the treaty that ended World War II. Yet when Hirohito died in 1989, his son Akihito was installed with ceremonies claiming that he was the sun's descendant. For a decade, because the royal family had no sons, there was debate about changing the rules so that princess Aiko would be permitted to inherit the throne. But in 2006, a son was born to the royal house, and discussion ceased.

If the prospect of a restoration of the traditional role of empress has faded, women have once again begun to practice as Shinto priests. While today only a small minority of Shinto priests are women, that number is increasing and represents the first strong female presence in the Shinto hierarchy in centuries. At a lower level, local shrines increasingly permit girls to carry portable shrines during festivals, a privilege formerly limited to boys.

Contemporary Japan is a predominantly secular

land, despite which Shinto beliefs continue to be recognized. However, little attention is paid to the goddess culture of the land. Outside Japan, there is little awareness of the importance of goddesses either in Shinto or in its environmental and ecological aspects, although *miko* ("shrine maidens") appear in anime comics as feisty heroines.

JAPANESE AND AINU PANTHEON

Amaterasu In simple shrines, notable for architectural purity and the central mirror that represents her, Amaterasu ("great shining heaven") is honored as the ruler of all deities, guardian of Japan's people and symbol of Japanese cultural unity. Her emblem, the rising sun, flies on Japan's flag, and the emperor is called her direct descendant.

Japanese scriptures say Amaterasu was brought into being after **Izanami** died giving birth. Her husband Izanagi washed his left eye, from which the sun goddess was born. Giving her a sacred necklace, Izanagi also granted power over land and sea, while to his son Susano-o, Izanagi gave oceans and storms. Not long after, Amaterasu and her brother quarreled. Two reasons are given: either he murdered their sister **Uke-Mochi**, or he engaged in deliberately provocative acts against Amaterasu.

Amaterasu did not trust Susano-o. One day he came to heaven, claiming he meant no harm. Amaterasu was wary, but he promised he would undergo a ritual test to prove his goodwill. They agreed to give birth magically. Amaterasu broke Susano-o's sword with her teeth, spitting out three pieces that became goddesses. They were called Susano-o's children because they were born from his sword. Then Susano-o asked Amaterasu for her jewels. She gave him five, which he cracked open and made into gods, considered Amaterasu's children.

Susano-o grew wild with excitement and tore through the world destroying everything in his path. He piled feces under Amaterasu's throne, then he stole into her quarters and threw a flayed horse through the roof of her weaving room

This was too much for the goddess, who shut herself up in a cave. The world was plunged into blackness. The eight million *kami* pleaded for her return, but no response came forth. Then **Uzume** turned over a washtub, climbed on top, and began dancing and singing. Soon the dance became a striptease. When she had shed her clothes, Uzume began dancing so wildly the gods and goddesses shouted with delight. Amaterasu asked what was going on. Someone answered that they had found a better goddess than the sun. Provoked, Amaterasu opened the door of her cave.

The gods and goddesses had installed a mirror outside the cave. Amaterasu, who had never seen her own beauty, was dazzled. While she stood there, other divinities tied the door open. Thus the sun returned to warm the earth. Mounted again on her heavenly throne, Amaterasu threw Susano-o out of heaven. Then she and her son Oshi-ho-mimi rid the island land of restless spirits, after which they handed over the sacred implements of rulership—the mirror, jewels, and sword—to her grandson, ancestor of the imperial clan.

Amaterasu's shrine is still a center of religious activity. At the Great Shrine at Ise, a complex of buildings rises in the center of a 13,600-acre forest where trees are raised for reconstruction of shrine buildings. The two major buildings are rebuilt every twenty years, the new buildings exactly duplicating the old. Pilgrimage to Ise is the highlight of the Shinto believer's life, with some six million making the journey annually. Favored times are September and April. Other major pilgrimage times are mid-February and mid-June, while minor festivals in January and March draw thousands. (Aston; Blacker 1982; Kirkland; Littleton; Matsumae 1978, 1980; Miller 1984, 1987; Monaghan; Piggot; Phillipi; Takeshi 1978)

Benten Among the seven divinities of good luck, only one was a goddess: Benten, who brought inspiration, talent, wealth, and romance. Benten was a dragon woman who swam with white snakes. She protected her devotees from earthquakes by mating with monstrous snakes that thrashed about beneath the land. She could also appear as a lovely human; in this form she was usually portrayed mounted on a dragon. (Littleton)

Chup-Kamui Among the Ainu, the sun was the highest divinity, greeted each morning as though she were a living being. People were careful not to step into sunbeams flooding toward the stove, for that was the sun's greeting to the hearth goddess **Kamui Fuchi**. Originally Chup-Kamui was the moon, but after watching illicit moonlit trysts, the modest girl asked the male sun to trade places. Thereafter she rose each day from the mouth of a devil who spent the night trying to eat her. A magical helper shoved crows and foxes into the devil's mouth while Chup-Kamui escaped. Hence these animals were sacred to the Ainu. During an eclipse, the Ainu dipped willow branches in water and cast droplets upward while calling out prayers. As soon as the eclipse passed, they drank sake to celebrate their escape from darkness. (Batchelor 1892, 1894, 1971; Kuzono)

Fuji Now the highest mountain in Japan, Fuji was once the same height as nearby Mount Hakusan, wherein a god lived. A dispute arose about which was taller. The Amida Buddha connected the two peaks with a long pipe and poured water in one end. Unfortunately for Fuji, water fell on her head. But her humiliation did not last long, for the proud goddess immediately struck Hakusan eight blows, creating the eight peaks of today's mountain. The name of the mountain may derive from **Kamui Fuchi**. (Batchelor 1892, 1971; Kuzono)

Hani Yama Hine One of the children of the primal goddess **Izanami**, Hani Yama Hine was the "pottery-clay mountain princess," one of the earliest-born of the second generation of divinities. Her sisters, minor

divinities born of the blood and feces of Izanami's birth giving, included Kana-Yama bi me No Kami, the princess of metal mountain; Mi Tsu Ha No me No Kami, the archer–water goddess; and Nitsu Ha No Me, the elephant girl. These deities were connected to the transformation of nature's materials into things useful for humanity. (Fairchild)

Himiko Japan's first ruler was Himiko, who lived in the third century CE. Called "the great child of the sun," this empress never left her palace and governed through messages received in trance. She lived to an advanced age but never married, living in seclusion with thousands of maiden attendants. During her long reign, Japan was at peace, both within itself and with its neighbors. Her name may be a title held by shaman queens who used trance to govern. There is evidence that these women ruled in tandem with their brothers, suggesting a matrilineal social organization. (Blacker 1982; Littleton; Piggot)

Ikutamayorihime From the *Kojiki*—Japanese myths compiled in the seventh century by the noblewoman Hieda-no-Are—comes the story of this woman who conceived a child from a mysterious lover. To discover the man's identity, Ikutamayorihime's parents told her to sew a thin, long hemp thread to him to follow it after his departure. The next morning, the thread was found to go not under the door but through the keyhole, from which it led straight to the snake god's shrine on Mount Miwa. After this miraculous conception, the child in Ikutamayorihime's womb became the ancestor of the shrine's priestly family. In this tale scholars have detected a vestigial matrilineal tradition of an ancestral human mother and an unearthly father. (Blacker 1982)

Inari One-third of all Shinto shrines are dedicated to this goddess of rice. At tens of thousands of Inari shrines, fox sculptures indicate the goddess's animal form, for she appears in the form of a vixen, often in rice fields in spring. Although some Buddhist traditions consider Inari male, Shinto tradition claims her as feminine, and women religious leaders invoke her with groups of women who make pilgrimages to Inari shrines.

The rice goddess was honored on farms because she brought fertility and prosperity, for which reason she has been connected with the food goddess **Toyo-Uke**. Inari took human form to sleep with men, who had excellent crops as a result. One of these men realized he was sleeping with the goddess when he saw a furry red tail sticking out from the blankets. He said nothing, and she rewarded his discretion by causing his rice to grow upside down, thus bearing a full harvest that was exempt from the rice tax. (Blacker 1982; Hamilton; Opler and Hashima)

Ishikore-Dome This smith goddess created the first mirror, which saved the world from darkness. Three times she tried, while **Amaterasu** hid herself in the Sky-Rock-Cave, and twice she failed to create a perfect reflection of the sun's beauty. But she succeeded on the third try, after which her mirror became a sacred relic, held in the Imperial Shrine at Ise. Each of the more than 90,000 Shinto shrines across Japan preserves a mirror in its sanctuary. (Wheeler)

Izanami Before this world, there was only oil and slime, which slowly congealed into Izanami, the inviting woman, and her consort Izanagi, the inviting man. Standing on the rainbow, they stirred chaos with a spear until matter formed. Placing this island on the oily sea, they descended to populate the earth.

They did not know how until they saw two wagtail ducks mating. Then Izanami gave birth to the islands of Japan, water, and animals. Last to be born was fire, which exploded from Izanami's body, leaving her retching and bleeding. From her excretions, new creatures sprang up. The water goddess Mi Tsu Ha No me No Kami was born from her urine; the earth goddess **Hani Yama Hine**, from her excrement.

Izanami died and traveled to the underworld. Desperate without her, Izanagi traveled there to beg her to return. She had already established herself in the world of death and refused, but she suggested he ask the lord of death for her release. Izanami also warned him not to enter the palace.

Izanagi approached the dark building. He took a comb and broke off its last tooth. Lighting it, he looked inside, where the body of Izanami was decomposing. Her spirit attacked him, humiliated at being seen that way; she drove him from the underworld and, as they parted, claimed that his actions constituted divorce. Some say Izanami rules still as queen of death. She is also described as an earth goddess, honored in musical ceremonies and flower offerings. (Aston; Blacker 1982; Holtom; Bonnefoy; Murakami; Phillipi; Wheeler)

Jingu This warrior queen remained pregnant for three years, rather than stop her war on Korea to give birth to her son. Jingu devastated three Korean kingdoms; some credit not her battle prowess but her supernatural control of the tides for the victory. Once, when her consort expressed doubt as to the accuracy of her shamanic predictions, Jingu killed him with a gesture. (Aston; Blacker 1982)

Kaguya-Hime When she incarnated on earth, the spirit-woman Kaguya-Hime was the most beautiful child ever. Despite this, her human parents abandoned her. An old farmer found her and raised her. When she grew into the lovely maiden her early beauty had promised, Kaguya-Hime attracted the emperor's eye. They were married, but after some time she revealed her celestial origin and told him she needed to return home. Before she rose into the sky, Kaguya-Hime gave her love a mirror into which, whenever he wanted to see her, he could gaze, a motif that connects her with the most important Shinto divinity, the sun goddess **Amaterasu**. The emperor pined away, eventually climbing Mount **Fuji** in order to be closer to his heavenly love. He died there of grief. (Katz; McAlpine; Tyler)

Kamui Fuchi The most important Ainu goddess was a matron of great age and stature charged with protecting humans from disease and with judging them after death. Ainu shamans served Kamui Fuchi in a ritual lit by the hearth-fire. The hearth was a microcosm of the universe, the fire a living goddess. To the accompaniment of drums, the shaman placed herbs on the fire to create fragrant smoke, then asked Kamui Fuchi to help sick family members. When the shaman spoke again, it was in Kamui Fuchi's voice, diagnosing the illness and giving instructions for its cure. (Baba; Batchelor 1892, 1971; Munro; Ohnuki-Tierney)

Kono-Hana-Sakuya-Hime The cherry-tree goddess was younger sister of the rock goddess Iha-Naga. Both desired the man Ninigi, who chose the younger goddess; Iha-Naga cursed their children with short lives, while hers would have lived as long as the rocks. Kono-Hana gave birth nine months after marriage. As she swelled, her new husband began to suspect that she had conceived before they met. Insulted, Kono-Hana built a magic house that, when labor began, she set afire, saying that any children born who were not Ninigi's would die in the blaze. Triplets were born, all safe, disproving the man's doubts. As the same story was told of Sengen Sama, a goddess of Mount Fuji, it is probable that Kono-Hana was the same goddess under a different name. (Taryo)

Otohime The adventurer Urashima, rescued by a turtle when his ship sank, was brought to the dragon queen Otohime, who endowed her new lover with valuable gifts. Time passed more quickly than Urashima knew. Finally he grew homesick for his family and for earthly life. Otohime agreed to let him go, giving him a small box with the requirement that he never open it.

When Urashima reached home, he found the faces and names unfamiliar. Puzzled, he found an ancient resident who recognized the name of his family and learned he had been gone for hundreds of years. Sadly, the young man sat down and, forgetting his promise, opened the box. Out swept the years he had lived with

Otohime. Surrounding him like smoke, they withered his body, and he fell into dust.

In recent years, a woman named Fujita Himiko announced herself as the reborn Otohime. From a shrine near Kyoto, she serves as a shaman, bearing the goddess's name. The reborn goddess has announced that humanity suffers from the same delusions as Urashima, because societies fail to recognize the power of women. (Kawai; Shillony)

Sukunabikona This heroine appeared to the creator and hero Okuninushi. From the otherworld of Tokoyo no Kuni, the land beyond the sea, Sukunabikona arrived on a flying boat, wearing wings that made her look like either a bird or a butterfly. She helped the hero create the land, then departed as mysteriously as she had come. (Bonnefoy)

Tamaya-gozen This ancestor guides blind women shamans on the island of Honshu. Tamaya-gozen fell in love with a magical stallion, Sedan-kurige. The two married happily, but Tamaya-gozen's father became enraged that his daughter had made such a marriage. He killed the stallion and flayed it. The flayed hide wrapped itself around Tamaya-gozen and the pair flew off to heaven, dropping silkworms as they ascended. This was the first shamanic ascent to the heavens; thus Tamaya-gozen was adopted as an image of the shaman woman. (Miller 1993)

Tamayorihime Like the similar heroine Seyadatara-hime, Tamayorihime was a young woman who became the ancestor to an important family after mating with an otherworldly creature. He came in darkness, but not seeing her lover did not disturb the girl until she became pregnant. Then, to discover his identity, she sewed a long hemp thread to his hem and, the next morning, followed it to a dark cave. At its mouth she called out for her lover to show his face. "You would burst with fright," a deep voice called. Unafraid, she continued her demand until he appeared, a scaly monster with a needle stuck in its throat.

Tamayorihime fainted but lived to bear the great warrior Daida. The heroine's name, meaning a woman (*hime*) possessed (*yor*) by a god (*tama*), may have been a title borne by the shamans called *miko*. (Blacker 1982)

Toyota-Mahime This goddess married a mortal, setting a condition on their happiness: that he should never look upon her in childbed. Then she hid in a hut thatched with cormorant feathers. Her mate, unable to contain his curiosity, peered inside to see Toyota slithering around in her serpent form. Discovering his betrayal, she retreated to the ocean and forever closed the door joining their realms. (Blacker 1982; Mackenzie; Phillipi)

Toyo-Uke A food goddess whose gold-filigree shrine stands at the Great Shrine of Ise, Toyo-Uke may be an early sun goddess whose worship was made secondary to that of the powerful **Amaterasu**. (Fairchild; Littleton; Ross)

Tsuru When Japan lived under the rule of shaman queens, this woman offered herself as a human sacrifice in the building of a dike against a raging flood in Oita prefecture. Buried alive in the river, she successfully diverted the waters so the village was safe. She may have been a *miko*, or shaman, for there is a tradition—the *hito-bashira* or "human pillar" tales—that only such women could hold back floodwaters, provided they were willing to lay down their lives. In some interpretations, this "death" was metaphoric and meant retirement to life in the shrine. Tsuru was worshipped at Aibara shrine near the site of her sacrifice. (Blacker 1982)

Turesh The Ainu remembered a golden age when humans did not have to work for a living, for the god Okikurumi caught fish in the celestial sea and sent them in baskets with the goddess Turesh. There was a single law in this paradise: no Ainu should ask their benefactress's name or seek to discover her

appearance. One Ainu was curious and grabbed the hand as it set food upon his table, pulling into the house a sea monster. Since then the Ainu have struggled for food. (Chamberlin)

Uke-Mochi Japan's food goddess had a peculiar way of providing for the world: she vomited. When she faced the land, rice poured from her mouth. Facing the sea, she regurgitated fish. Looking to the mountains, she vomited game creatures. She set her table this way when the violent Susano-o was visiting her. It disgusted him, so he killed her. Her body, falling to earth, dissolved into food: cattle from her head, silkworms from her eyebrows, rice plants from her belly. (Phillipi; Aston)

Uzume When **Amaterasu** hid in a cave, Uzume ("sky-frightening woman") lured her out with a merry mockery of shamanic ritual. Tying her sleeves above her elbows with moss cords and fastening bells around her wrists, she danced on an overturned tub before the heavenly Sky-Rock-Cave. Tapping out a rhythm with her feet, she exposed her breasts and then her genitals. Her striptease caused the myriad gods and goddesses to clap and laugh, an uproar that finally brought the curious sun back to warm the earth.

Uzume is credited with being the first shaman, called *miko* or *sarume* in ancient Japan. Early shamans were queens like **Himiko**, but later they were princesses and commoners. Some Japanese women today, especially those in Okinawa and the surrounding islands, practice shamanic divination. These women often practice a combination of verbal and movement magic called *chinkonsai*, of which Uzume's performance before the Sky-Rock-Cave was the original. Such magic was employed during eclipses and at funerals, suggesting a parallel between the sun's disappearance and death. A dance called Kagura, part of Shinto ritual, enacts Uzume's dance. (Averbuch; Miller 1993; Wheeler)

Yachimata-hime The guardian of travelers always traveled with her consort, Yachiamata-hiko, the two being known as Chimata-no-kami, the "road folk spirits." With their help, travelers could avoid ghosts, demons, and other specters that haunted roadways. (Ross)

Yamanokami This shape-shifting mountain goddess can appear as any kind of animal or dragon. She can also double herself into two people. In human form, she is often a friendly young woman. But she can also become an old woman, Yamauba, whose mouth covers her face.

A goddess of wilderness, she brings luck to hunters and woodsmen who attend to her rites and punishes those who do not. One legged and one eyed, she protects women in childbed. As a seasonal goddess, she annually gives birth to twelve children, the year's months, for which she is called Juni-sama. She is also called Yamanoshinbo, "mountain mother."

Devotion to this goddess appears ancient, but as Japan becomes more crowded, little wilderness is left for Yamanokami. Known throughout Japan, her cult is now restricted to mountain areas where woodcutters and hunters honor her. (Blacker 1996; Hori; Kawai; Schattschneider)

THE PACIFIC ISLANDS *and* AUSTRALIA

Scattered across the Pacific Ocean are thousands of islands and atolls that were beacons for early migrants. Beginning 22,000 years ago, people who relied on fishing, hunting, and gathering populated Australia, New Guinea, and parts of Melanesia. Perhaps 17,000 years later came other settlers, bringing a farming culture. Descendants of these two cultures spread across the region, with migration continuing to at least 1000 CE, when New Zealand was settled.

Because of the distance between culture centers, Pacific mythology has no centralized or hierarchical framework. Innumerable divinities, sometimes known only on a single atoll, are found. Despite this complexity, Pacific myths have similarities, including the importance of an ancestral mother creatrix. This goddess moves between earth, underworld, and heaven; she changes from bird or animal, or even vegetable or mineral, to human shape. The earth is typically a goddess; often sun and moon are goddesses as well. Finally, goddesses connected with the realm of the dead are common.

Not all Pacific islands are small; Australia is a continent that presents a different picture than the generally lush Pacific islands. At European contact, some 550 cultural groups existed there, mostly semi-nomadic groups, each occupying a limited region. As few as a million people populated Australia, where the difficult terrain could not support a huge population. By contrast, rain forested New Guinea boasts a large population and impressive cultural density. Almost a quarter of the earth's languages are compressed into the island's territory. The western portion belongs politically to Indonesia (see Southeast Asia), while the eastern part, called Papua New Guinea, is home to some 850 distinct cultural groups.

Less than half the size of New Guinea, the islands of New Zealand were populated a thousand years ago by migrants from central Polynesia. With the arrival of Europeans in 1840, the Maori began transcribing their myths and sacred histories. Through these myths, scholars have learned much about the religion of Polynesia.

The remaining Pacific cultures are divided into Micronesian, Melanesian, and Polynesian. Micronesia ("tiny islands") extends over a vast area of the western Pacific and includes Guam, the Marshall Islands, and the Federated States of Micronesia. In addition to New Guinea, Melanesia ("dark islands," named for its dark-skinned residents) includes the Solomon Islands, Vanuatu, and Fiji. Finally, the "many islands" of Polynesia stretch across the central Pacific and include Samoa, Tahiti, and the Hawaiian islands; the New Zealand Maori descend from Polynesians and are often counted as part of that group.

The Pacific region provides several important religious concepts, especially those of "totem" and "taboo." The first term refers to a belief that human families are descended from other beings—most typically animals, but occasionally reptiles, insects, or plants. Typically, a person would not eat such relatives, although religious ritual might call for such a communion. "Taboo," meaning a religious prohibition, is the Tongan word introduced into English by Captain James Cook in 1777. Both terms are used casually, sometimes with secular connotations, but retain their religious definitions in scholarly writing.

The most significant Australian religious concept is that of "The Dreaming," a space/time reality wherein creation is continuous and divinity still walks the earth. The Dreaming exists simultaneously with our world yet is unreachable in ordinary consciousness. Into this fertile area, powerful Dreaming humans can venture through mystical states and ritual, as well as when unconscious. Religious leaders adept at making the transition from Dreaming to ordinary consciousness use it in healing their communities.

The land actively participates in Dreaming, being a sacred place wherein creative acts occur. It is humanity's duty to be aware of this sacredness and mark those creative acts. Thus "walkabout," the tradition of walking the land and marking its "songlines" with ritual words and prayers, is an important action to traditional Australians. Through these actions, Dreaming is strengthened, and humanity strengthened as a result.

The role of women is vital in this endeavor. When early European researchers wrote about Australian religion, cultural biases became evident. Because traditional Australian society is divided into male and female spheres, male researchers, unable to gather information about women's role in religion, assumed that there was none. Woman was declared "profane," while men were "sacred." But when women researchers began to gather information from aboriginal communities, the existence of women's rituals and their importance to social continuity were realized.

Although much of the blame for this decades-long derogation of the values of women to Australian traditional society must rest with biased researchers, the secrecy in which rituals are conducted was also a factor. Men in a community might be unaware of the ritual workings of the women within it. "Sacred" equals "secret" in Australian religion. The conveyance of spiritual and religious information took place in structured settings at specific locations and times. Nothing was written down; myths and their meanings were conveyed orally, often in songs.

Indigenous religions continue to be practiced across the Pacific, although monotheistic religions discourage native practices, leading to syncretism or secrecy. In addition, the ongoing effects of colonization affect indigenous residents. In some areas, notably in Hawaii, indigenous religions have been connected to movements for native rights and environmental concerns. Practice of indigenous Pacific religions by nonnative people is rare, although the region's art has drawn collectors from around the world. As much of that art, like the complex and evocative paintings of

Australia, is based in religion and myth, such art draws the attention of outsiders.

PACIFIC ISLANDS PANTHEON

Atanua The dawn goddess of the Marquesas and Society Islands was the daughter of the divinity Atea. Some scholars say Atea, cited in most sources as a male deity, was an overarching sky mother. In the Marquesas Atanua created the sea when she miscarried, filling the earth's hollows with amniotic fluid. (Best; Dixon)

Aukam On Nagi (Mt. Ernest Island) off Australia's northern tip, a woman lived with her lazy brother Poapun and their maternal uncle Waw. Every day she went fishing, while her brother never put net in water. He expected Aukam to feed him and wanted the biggest fish she caught. She was generous, so she fed her brother. But their uncle grew envious of the rich fish she gave Poapun and killed Aukam's son, a boy named Tiai. Heartbroken, Aukam made a necklace of her son's bones but, suspecting his soul was not at rest, went through the islands until she found him. Drawing him away from a game with other young men, she told him he was a ghost. Tiai returned to his friends and asked them to beat a drum and then, running toward his mother, disappeared into the ground, to be followed by the loyal Aukam.

On Saibai Island, Aukam was described as a weaver who made mats by moonlight, refusing to do any other work. The moon man, seeing her diligence, came down to earth and took her up to heaven, where she sits weaving in the moon all night. This motif suggests Aukam may have some connection to **Hina**. (Lawrie)

Dogai I On Mabuiag island north of Australia, this bogeywoman was used to frighten children. Once when a mother tried to silence her child, Dogai I stole the girl. But she could not get the girl to stop crying, so Dogai I killed her. When the family realized what had happened, the men set out to hunt Dogai I. They found her near the water, rocking the child's body. Although she tried to screw herself into a rock wall, the men pulled off one of her arms before she escaped. They brought it back to the village, where they used it for target practice. That night, Dogai I was drawn back to her arm. As she approached, it reattached itself.

The term "dógai," or "ghost woman," is also used of the following figures on Dauan island of Torres Strait: Mekélpal, Samúnu, Kepáde, Gíze, Kowára, Táugin, Butailfáde, Wenalalfáde, Ketaunapíti, and Pítan. These women would pursue hunters and fishermen, hiding in trees until they came near and could be captured. (Lawrie; Wirz)

Enda Semangko A goddess of earthly and human fertility in the western highlands of New Guinea, Enda Semangko was represented by a stone honored with a five-year cycle of ceremonies that culminated in the sacrifice of hundreds of pigs and a dance. (Lawrence and Meggitt)

Fu'uña Among the Chamorro people of the Marianas Islands, this girl ruled the primal world with her brother, Puntan. There was no food or water, no earth or ocean, only death. Puntan, dying, told Fu'uña he imagined a world with land and sea, animals and plants, and people. Grieving, Fu'uña tore out his eyes, which she flung into the air, making the sun and moon. She dismembered him and built the universe, then threw herself into the sea, where she became a rock. After eons, the rock shattered into sand, each grain of which bears a portion of Fu'uña's spirit. These grains are the many people of the world. (Flood)

Haumapuhia The abusive father of this Maori girl turned his other children to stone. Nonetheless, she did not fear him. When her father demanded she draw him water, she refused. To punish her, he held her head down in a stream until she drowned. She transformed

herself into the huge lake of Waikaremoana. (Te Awekotuku)

Haumea Originally, Hawaiian myth says, human women swelled with pregnancy but had to be cut open to deliver. Haumea taught women how to push children out between their legs. As a result, she was honored as goddess of birth. She lived among humans, sleeping with men who were her descendants. One was Wakea, chosen as a sacrificial victim by his people. But Haumea refused to let him die, carrying her lover to safety through tree trunks and leaving shreds of her skirt blooming as morning glories.

Because she owned all wild plants, Haumea could withdraw her energy when angry, leaving people to starve. More often Haumea was a kindly goddess. Found throughout Polynesia, Haumea was a goddess of fertility and sovereignty. The Maori called her Haumia-tiketike, a term that also referred to edible roots and other wild foods. (Alpers; Diab; Dixon; Kame'eleihiwa; Poignant)

Hi'iaka This primary Hawaiian goddess was the opposite of her sister **Pele**. Hi'iaka ruled the clouds, while Pele ruled the fiery volcano. Some sources say that there was not a single Hi'iaka but many goddesses of the same name. They may represent different kinds of clouds: Hi'iaka-wawahi-lani, "heaven-rending cloud holder"; Hi'iaka-noho-lani, "heaven-dwelling cloud holder"; Hi'iaka-kaalawa-maka, "quick-glancing cloud holder"; and Hi'iaka-ka-pu-enaena, "red-hot-mountain-lifting clouds."

One myth tells how a drowned man came back to haunt his daughters, who appealed to Hi'iaka. Through magic and a seawater bath, she coaxed the man's soul into his body, which washed up on the shore, returning the man to his daughters. The major myth of Hi'iaka is the same as her sister's: she was sent to bring back a man for whom Pele lusted and, betrayed by Pele, in turn betrayed her sister. (Beckwith 1970; Handy; Kalahaua; Kame'eleihiwa; Luomala)

Hikuleʻo The Tongan underworld goddess has been described as female, male, and of both sexes. The confusion suggests missionary discomfort with "god" being female, as images of Hikuleʻo show her as obviously female. Born of brother-sister incest from her mother, Havealolofonua, Hikuleʻo owned a land called Pulotu, to which men traveled to seek food. There they had to engage in drinking, diving, and surfing contests. The men performed superlatively, but the gods still refused to share. Hikuleʻo chased the humans away, but they had hidden the seeds of yam and taro in their clothing. (Collocott; Herda)

Hina The greatest goddess of the Pacific was a complex figure. Hina was associated with many aspects of life and had many symbols. She was the tapa-beating woman who lived in the moon; she was the death mother; she was a warrior queen of the Island of Women. In varying guises, Hina appeared in the myths of many cultures.

In Tahiti, Hina was the primordial goddess for whose pleasure the first man was created. From her fertile womb fell innumerable offspring, many bearing her name, so the number of women named Hina grew endlessly. In the Society Islands, Hina was daughter of the high god Taneroa, with whom she created the heavens and earth. Together, they created humanity.

In Hawaii, Hina populated the world with her mate Ku. She lived at the bottom of the sea but came to land to marry a chief. She sent a diver to gather her belongings, from which the moon flew out and began circling the sky. Using this as their guide, her brothers turned into fish and created a flood that people escaped by climbing the island's high mountains.

Among the Maori, Hine-ahu-one was formed when **Papa** died, leaving her all-male descendants no way to reproduce. Papa's last instructions were that Tane should sculpt a woman from red clay. He followed Papa's instructions, and Hina came to life. The Maori also describe Hina as the dawn maiden, a girl seduced by her father through deceit. Ashamed, Hina ran away to the underworld, where she planned to live with Papa, from whose dust she had been formed; this was the first death. Hina transformed herself into the goddess of the underworld. She announced her intention to kill any children begotten by her father, thereby assuring that death would remain a force on earth. Her daughter, Hine-atauira, was taken sexually by her father, Tane, and hid herself and her children in the underworld as well.

Once the hero Maui wagered he could crawl into the goddess's vagina, through her body, to her heart. He boasted that he would eat her heart and conquer death. Maui turned himself into a lizard and prepared to enter the goddess. But his bird companion laughed at the sight of the shrunken hero crawling into Hine-titama's pubic hair. The laughter woke the goddess, who crushed Maui between her legs. The name of the goddess in this myth is sometimes Mahuika.

Living on earth as a mortal woman, Hina bathed in a pool, where she had intercourse with an eel. Her people killed him, only to find that he was a god. Hina buried the eel's head and, five nights later, the first coconut sprang up. Another version of the story, from the Cook Islands, said Hina's eel lover warned of a flood and instructed her to cut off his head. She followed his instructions and planted the head on the highest cliff, whereupon the floodwaters abated. From the amputated head grew the first coconut tree.

Numerous myths tell how Hina found a home in the moon. In Tahiti, Hina was a canoeist who paddled to the moon, which proved to be such a good boat she stayed, guarding earthly sailors. Others said Hina's brother, hungover from indulgence in kava, became infuriated at the noise Hina made beating tapa cloth. When she would not cease her labors, he hit her so hard she sailed into the sky. A Hawaiian variant said Hina, a married woman, grew tired of picking up after her family and left the earth to become the moon's cloth maker. (Alpers; Anderson; Dixon; Kalahaua; Kameʻeleihiwa; Orbell; Poignant; Reed; Williamson)

Hinauri Sister of the Maori hero Maui, Hinauri married the man Irawaru over her brother's objections.

Although his sister's husband was unobjectionable to others, Maui found everything about Irawaru annoying. This reached a crisis when Hinauri's husband went fishing with Maui. Maui failed to catch anything, but Irawaru pulled in fish after fish. Finally Maui realized that Irawaru was using a barbed hook, while Maui used a smooth one. This cleverness drove Maui into a rage, and he turned Irawaru into a dog.

When Maui returned to the village, he lied to Hinauri, telling her that Irawaru was on the shore awaiting her. But Hinauri found the dog, her transformed husband. In grief, she put on a magical belt and threw herself into the sea. The belt kept her afloat, and she remained in the sea for so long that she became covered with barnacles. In this ruined fashion, she washed up on shore, where she was found by two brothers who cleaned her to reveal her beauty, then fell in love with her. She stayed with the brothers for a time but, having heard of a handsome chief nearby, decided to make him her husband.

Vain, chief Tinirau liked to admire himself in clear water, so much that he had several pools fenced for his personal use. It was to one of these that Hinauri went to float naked. Instantly he became enamored of her, and she kept him beside her through magic, calling down food from the sky to nourish them. When she conceived his child, she agreed to return to his village, where he stopped loving her. When she craved fish while pregnant, he locked her up behind a fence of nettles.

Her brother Maui missed Hinauri and traveled to heaven to ask the high god where he could find her. Maui arrived just as Hinauri was about to give birth and, disguised as a bird, took her into the sky with him, her newborn in her arms. Seeing the child's father and realizing the boy would need human companionship, Hinauri let the boy drop into Tinirau's arms. Despite the beauty and gentleness of his mother, Tinirau's son brought evil into the world, including wars and cannibalism, until they were all killed by other Maori. (Alpers; Reed 1963)

Hine-Marama This Maori woman lived with two brothers, one of whom was her husband. Hine-Marama was a kindly, hardworking young woman who kept her family well fed and happy. She fell ill suddenly and died, leaving her husband, Rangi-rua, desolate. He went to the land of ghosts to reclaim her. His brother Kaeo, seeing that the bereaved husband could not be dissuaded, went along. The pair tricked their way into the otherworld and, finding Hine-Marama had not eaten there, stole her back to earth. When she arrived, she realized she was in spirit form and instructed the brothers to dig up her body. When they did, she reentered it and returned to life. (Reed 1963)

Hine-pokohu-rangi The Maori mist maiden fell in love with a human man, Uenuku, from whom she extracted a promise that he would not reveal their love until she had conceived a child. He forgot and she, singing a soft farewell song, disappeared into a column of mist. Her disconsolate lover wandered the world in the form of a rainbow. (Best)

Hit In the Caroline Islands in Micronesia, this name was given to an octopus goddess. Hit's daughter started an affair with a god who already had a wife. The sky woman followed her husband, trying to drag him away from his mistress, but Hit began dancing lewdly. So erotic was her performance that the sky woman fainted from excitement and had to be carried back to heaven. Each time the wife tried to stop her husband from making love to his mistress, Hit began dancing again, allowing for the conception of the culture hero Olifat. (Poignant)

Honabe The primal deity of the Huli of New Guinea, Honabe was so hot she could cook by placing food near her vulva. All gods were born from her, as well as the first birds and animals, who emerged from her menstrual blood. She had one daughter, the moon goddess Hana, who lived on earth until violated by her brother. Hana liked to wrap herself around a tree. When her brother saw this, he inserted a sharp rock to cut Hana and, when he saw her bleeding, raped her. She rose into the sky; he followed her, becoming the sun as she turned into the moon. (Lawrence and Meggitt; Swain and Trompf)

Ho'ohoku-i-ka-lani Hawaiian mythology tells of this primordial woman who was raped by her father, Wakea. Although wedded to **Papa**, Wakea plotted to sleep with his daughter. He initiated nights when spouses were to sleep separately, then entered his daughter's bed. But one day he overslept; Papa found his crime and left him. Ho'ohoku-i-ka-lani bore a child to her father, a deformed stillborn shaped like a root. Wakea buried its body, and from the tiny grave grew the first taro plant. Then Ho'ohoku-i-ka-lani bore a child named Haloa; the boy grew up to be the ancestor of all Hawaiians, who were related to the taro plant. (Hopkins)

Hopoe Hopoe was a hula dancer who taught the art to other goddesses. Hopoe also knew the art of making leis. The cloud goddess **Hi'iaka** fell in love with her, covering the forests with red-and-white lehua flowers in her honor. When **Pele**, believing herself betrayed by Hi'iaka, erupted in anger, Hopoe was at the seashore, unable to escape the fiery lava. She began to dance, and when the lava reached her, she was transformed into a pillar that resembles a dancer. (Beckwith; Emerson 1906)

Jari A heroine of New Guinea, the snake woman Jari inaugurated the institution of marriage. Her husband did not know her real form because she never allowed her snake-bodied mother to visit except while he was fishing. But one day he came home early and, finding their child in the clutches of a snake, killed the viper grandmother. When she discovered her mother's death, Jari departed. Filling her vulva with everything she needed to set up housekeeping elsewhere, she walked until she encountered another man. Because he was uncivilized, she brought out the treasures from her vulva and created a home. But she would not mate with him until she figured out why he smelled so bad. He had been born without an anus and defecated through his mouth. So Jari asked him to turn around and, stabbing him with a piece of bamboo, made him an anus, after which she was able to live happily. As the world's first married couple, Jari and her husband were the ancestors of all people. (Hogbin)

Jina Jina lived with her sister, Kasuara, in their mother's home, from which she was sent to get fire when their cooking flame went out. Encountering two young brothers, she attracted their interest. They decided to marry the sisters but argued over who should get which girl. Jina settled the argument by saying that, as eldest, she would marry first, and took the elder boy as her husband. But the envious old woman Vina blinded Jina on her way to the wedding and, donning the bridal attire, wed the older brother. While hunting the next day, the younger brother found Jina and cured her with herbs, then wed her despite his brother's fury at being tricked. Vina's trickery led to the world's first murders, because the older brother killed Jina's husband. After Jina's son grew up, he killed the murderer, then escaped to another island with his bereaved mother. (Hogbin)

Jugumishanta Ancestral mother of the people of Papua New Guinea, Jugumishanta liked privacy. Although married, she built herself a hut away from her village and told everyone to leave her alone. Around her place she planted wild ginger, and within the wild ginger she hid a flute, wherein she placed one of her pubic hairs, which cried out if touched.

Often Jugumishanta took out her flute to play plaintively. Her husband heard the sad sound and sought to discover what caused it. Watching Jugumishanta, he saw not only how she made the sounds but also where she hid the instrument. He stole it. The flute raised the alarm, and Jugumishanta demanded its return. In the ensuing fight, the flute fell onto the ground—and a forest of bamboo sprang up, where Jugumishanta's people could gather material for flutes.

With her consort, Jugumishanta set down rules for

human behavior and established rituals. She now sits at the base of the world tree, holding the planet steady. Red croton plants represent her blood, and salt her body. (Berndt C 1966; Lawrence and Meggitt)

Kaahu-pahua In Hawaiian mythology, Kaahu-pahua, an enormous shark, was queen of the ocean. She guarded the entrance to Pearl Harbor with her brother, Ka-hi'u-ka. Born human and later transfigured, they remained friendly to humans. In the early twentieth century, belief in this goddess was so strong that, when a newly built dock collapsed at Pearl Harbor, an offense to her was presumed. (Beckwith)

Kalaipahoa The Hawaiian goddess of poison, Kalaipahoa and her sisters Kapo and Pua migrated from an unknown land. On Molokai, Kalaipahoa imbued the trees with a poison so deadly that birds fell dead from the sky. An evil king demanded a sculpture made from the trees, killing scores of workers. The king used the sculpture to threaten his opponents. (Kalahaua)

Kelea This Hawaiian girl was the world's best surfer. She spent all her time on the waves, thrilling those who watched. She had little interest in marriage, but she was the daughter of the king of Maui, so it was expected that she would make an alliance with an important family. She married the chief of Oahu, Lo-Lale, who had sought her hand by sending the handsome Kalamakua to arrange the match. Although Kalamakua fell in love with her as they traveled back to Oahu, he was too loyal to his cousin, Lo-Lale, to interfere with the marriage.

Years later, however, Kelea found that she could not remain a passive queen. She yearned for the freedom of riding the waves and for the man who had brought her to Oahu. Her husband released her to pursue her dreams. She lived out her days with her lover, surfing in the Hawaiian waves. (Anderson)

Kio This spirit woman appears in legends of the Tuamotu islands, west of Tahiti. The human woman

Roi, fishing with her husband Tu, gathered a fine catch of clams. Tu wanted to go home, but Roi wanted one more dive. As she swam below the surface, she was captured by Kio, who shoved Roi's hair under a rock to keep her captive, then rose to the surface having transformed herself into an exact likeness of Roi. Tu, not realizing the deception, began to row home, but Roi freed herself and called out from the water. In the boat, Kio said the voice they heard was a water spirit and convinced Tu to resume rowing.

Once home, Kio defecated in a bowl and tried to feed her feces to Roi's children, who went to their father to tell them of her disgusting offering. Realizing what he had done, Tu set fire to the hut where Kio was pretending to weave, and she exploded, leaving a litter of shells she had stuffed into her belly in order to appear pregnant. But Roi was still missing. In variant versions of the tale, she bore her twin sons on a distant island and was eventually rescued by her older children; or the twin boys grew up and, asking for their father, learned the truth and reunited their parents. (Emory)

Koevasi Although suffering from a cold, this Melanesian creatrix walked through the world making humans. Because her speech was so difficult to understand, people did their best to approximate it, which is why they speak in different dialects. (Codrington 1881)

Kura In the Cook Islands, among the Mangaia people, this woman was gathering flowers when she fell from a tree. The earth swallowed her, pitching her into a land where she was held captive, tied to a post and guarded by a blind old man. Kura's husband, desolate, followed her to the underworld and freed her by throwing food where rats would scuttle around to get it. Covered by their noise, he slipped in and freed Kura, then fled to the upper world. (Dixon)

La'ila'a Among the Hawaiians, this was the name of the first woman born after chaos settled into form. By mating with the sky, she produced humanity. She is sometimes identified with the primal mother **Haumea**. (Poignant)

Laka Patron of hula dancers, this Hawaiian goddess ruled the islands' uncultivated areas, while her dancers represented the untamed element of human nature. Originally, hula troupers were satirists and puppeteers as well as dancers. They worshipped Laka in a piece of wood covered with yellow cloth and decked with wildflowers. She was close to her sister Kapo, so close that sometimes they are considered aspects of the same goddess. Kapo had a useful anatomical feature: a detachable vagina, which can still be seen in the rocks and mountains of Hawaii. (Diab; Beckwith; Poignant; Robertson)

Latmikaik This Micronesian clam mother grew from an ancient volcano where it touched the sky. She took up the whole mountainside, for she held within herself the souls of all beings. But her clamshell stayed closed, so that the beings could not be released. When a great wave crashed against her, her shell was forced open, and life was born. (Flood et al)

Leutogi A Samoan princess sent to Tonga to become the second wife of its king, Leutogi found herself disrespected. When she took pity on a baby bat and nursed it back to health, she was derided for her kindness. But the bats did not forget. Made a scapegoat by the Tongans when misfortune befell the king's family, Leutogi was sentenced to die by fire. But thousands of bats urinated on the flames, saving Leutogi. So she was placed on a barren island, where the Tongans expected her to starve to death. But she lived there happily in the company of bats who brought her fruit for every meal. (Flood et al)

Lilavatu In Tonga, this goddess was the highest female divinity and the source of healing, but she could also cause disease, especially swollen necks. She spoke in a high squeaky voice and turned vindictive toward people who failed to make offerings. (Poignant)

Lorop The creatrix goddess from the island of Yap, Lorop was the daughter of an earlier creator goddess named Liomarar, who tossed sand into the ocean to form islands, then squatted on one to bear her daughter. Lorop had three sons, whom she fed miraculous food. They did not know where Lorop got the rations, and two did not care. But the youngest was curious to see where his mother gathered dinner. Seeing Lorop dive into the sea, chanting a spell, he followed her to the underworld, where she filled baskets with food. Being discovered at her task meant she had to remain below the earth, but Lorop provided for her offspring, sending fish. A similar goddess was called Nomoi or Mortlock in other parts of Micronesia. (Poignant)

Mahora-nui-a-rangi In New Zealand, this was the name of the formless but feminine primordial heaven who, with her mate Maku ("wetness"), gave birth to the first divinities. An alternative name, which means "spreading forth of light," suggests that she was envisioned as a goddess of heavenly light. (Dixon)

Mahui-iki The underworld, according to many Pacific Islanders, was a fiery realm whose queen was Mahui-iki. Her grandson Maui decided to extinguish her power. Maui traveled to Mahui-iki's domain, where he found her stirring a cooking pot. Maui said he needed fire to cook food. When Mahui-iki pulled out a fingernail for him, he secretly quenched it. Maui asked for another, then another, until Mahui-iki had given all her fingernails and nine of her toenails. As Maui was asking for her last toenail, Mahui-iki realized what was happening and, pulling out the nail, set the earth on fire. Maui called down rain to extinguish the blaze, but what landed in the trees remained there, so that humans could thereafter kindle fire from wood. (Alpers; Dixon)

Meanderi This primal woman of New Guinea invented taro and sugarcane, then hid them under her skin while she sought humans with whom to share it. She traced through the land, offering food where she was dealt with respectfully but moving on when insulted. (Lawrence and Meggitt)

Miru Throughout the Pacific, the queen of the last three circles of the underworld was a goddess, with Miru being one of her common names. The soul upon death went to a cliff facing the setting sun, where a wave appeared. The soul took a leap, hoping to land in the arms of ancestors. But Miru stood nearby with a net to catch weaklings and evildoers, whom she threw into her oven after stupefying them with an intoxicating juice. They were instantly consumed, while better souls lived calmly in an eternal world that was otherwise identical to earth. (Gill; Handy)

Mo-o-inanea This dragon goddess of Hawaii migrated, with her brothers, from a hidden land to the visible world. Her brothers wandered about, but she stayed in beds of wet clay people used for hairdressing. Such places had large stones within them, which were considered goddesses (Aku-wahines), to whom prayers and flower offerings were made. One of Mo-o-inanea's favorite claypits was declared taboo by Queen Kaahumanu, Hawaii's last traditional queen. Other dragon goddesses, who may derive from Mo-o-inanea or be entirely separate, were Ha-puu, Mau-ola, Ala-muki, and Kihawahine. (MacKenzie)

Muriranaga The jawbone of this primal Maori cannibal goddess bestowed wisdom and sorcery, so the demigod Maui wanted it for humanity. He traveled to Muriranaga's home on the world's farthest edge and kept her from eating until, half starved, she took her jawbone from her head and gave it to him. With it, she gave humanity gifts that have been with us ever since. (Grace; Orbell)

Nevinbimbaau The cannibal ogress of southern Malekula, Nevinbimbaau created the earth by hauling soil in a giant clamshell on her back to form the island on which her people lived. She was never seen but could be heard during ceremonies in the voice of the bullroarer. (Poignant)

Niwareka Mata, a Māori warrior, fell in love with Niwareka, daughter of the underworld. They wed and were happy for a time, before the man's impatience caused him to strike Niwareka. She disappeared, returning to the world of death, where no violence occurred. Mata traveled to the underworld, where he underwent a ritual tattooing before Niwareka would agree to return with him. Her father, the tattooist of the underworld, gave him a cloak of night, warning him that at the boundary of light he had to reveal that he had it. But, happy to be with his beloved again, Mata forgot, for which offense humans cannot travel to the underworld except after death. (Flood et al)

Opiira In several areas of the Pacific region, this goddess was known as the ancestral mother of humankind. She was the child of the high god Tangeroa, as was her mate, the god Tiki (Ti'i); through their incestuous love, the human race was established. In Tahiti, the goddess's name was spelled Opeera. (Williamson)

Pani This Maori plant goddess was impregnated by a man who had stolen yam seeds from heaven and hidden them in his testicles. Pani gave birth to a plant beside a stream, then retreated to the underworld, where she tended a magical yam patch. (Poignant)

Papa This earth goddess, found in many Pacific cultures, existed from the beginning in perpetual intercourse with her lover, the sky god Rangi. There were ten layers of heaven, suffocating the earth and keeping light from its surface. Finally, the gods decided to separate their parents. Although apart, the pair remained lovers; the earth's damp heat rose to the sky, and the rain fell to fertilize Papa.

The Maori said a god tried to keep food away from people, but Papa hid yams and fern roots for them. She is sometimes considered the mother of **Hina**, who was formed out of red dust. Several of her names refer to coral, indicating the connection of earth to this reef-building animal. (Alpers; Buck; Dixon; Orbell; Poignant; Reed 1963; Williamson; Wohlers)

Pare Among the Maori, Pare was said to have been a flirtatious woman who led on, and then rejected, a young man named Hutu. He exploded in fury at her; ashamed of toying with his desires, she hanged herself. Hutu was so anguished at the news of Pare's death that he decided to convince her to return to life. He traveled to the underworld but found no traces of her. Hoping to lure her from hiding, Hutu began to play Pare's favorite sports. Secretly she began to draw near. Then Hutu pulled saplings down, soaring with them as they snapped upward. Pare found this new sport irresistible. As soon as she joined Hutu, he swung a tree so high that he dragged Pare back into the light. This name is also found as that of a volcano goddess on several Pacific islands. (Anderson; Dixon)

Pele Daughter of **Haumea**, Pele always had a fiery temperament. She spent her girlhood setting things aflame, displeasing her sister, the sea goddess Namaka. After Pele caused a conflagration by toying with underworld fires, Haumea realized there would be no peace while fire and water lived in the same household. She convinced Pele to move. Pele set off in a canoe with several siblings, including the cloud goddess **Hiʻiaka**. For many days at sea, the family found only atolls too tiny to support life. So Pele used a divining rod to locate places to build islands, then caused them to be born in eruptions from volcanoes.

But Pele found no peace, for Namaka soon arrived. Ocean and fire met in a tremendous brawl, of which Pele got the worst, dissolving into a plume of steam above Maui. She disappeared into the Hawaiian volcanoes, where she still lives. Her people honor her as creator and destroyer. Into her craters, they cast offerings: cut hair, sugarcane, white birds, money, strawberries, and hibiscus flowers. Some legends claim human beings were once tossed into the lava, but few scholars find evidence for such rites.

Pele sometimes dozed in her crater, sending her spirit wandering. One night, hearing flute music, she followed the sound until she came upon a group of hula dancers. Among them was the graceful Lohiau, whom Pele seduced. They spent three days making love before she decided to return to her mountain. Promising to send for him, Pele disappeared.

Pele sent her sister Hiʻiaka to fetch Lohiau. Hiʻiaka was a kindly goddess, given to singing with **Hopoe** and to picking tropical flowers. She asked Pele to tend her gardens, then left. Passing through many trials, often relying on magic to defeat monsters, Hiʻiaka reached Lohiau's home just as he died of longing for Pele. Hiʻiaka caught his soul and pushed it back into his body. Then they went to Kilauea.

Hiʻiaka intended to fulfill her task, despite the man's beauty and his expressions of love for her. But Pele burned, imagining Hiʻiaka in Lohiau's arms. Her crater spit lava. Hiʻiaka, recognizing the warning signs, hastened along. But when she reached Pele's crater, Hiʻiaka found her sister had not kept her promise. In her jealous fury, the volcano goddess had killed the dancer Hopoe and scorched Hiʻiaka's gardens.

On the rim of the crater, Hiʻiaka made love to Lohiau. Furious Pele burned the man to death but could not destroy her sister. Hiʻiaka followed Lohiau into the underworld and freed his soul. Pele was unwilling to give up the beautiful man, but Lohiau's comrade Paoa arrived to distract the goddess. Then Pele found her match in the combative hog god Kamapuaʻa, inventor of agriculture, whose idea of courting a goddess included dousing her flames with heavy rain and stampeding pigs across her craters. To this day, their turbulent affair continues on Kilauea.

Pele remains a living goddess on her islands, despite an attempt in 1824 by a converted Christian woman to show that Pele had no power by breaking her taboos (picking sacred berries without making offerings, throwing stones into the volcano) and remaining unharmed. But Pele's power was unbroken, especially after Princess Ruth Keelikoani stopped a lava flow in 1881 by offering silk scarves and brandy to the goddess. Pele is reputed to appear on volcanic slopes as an old woman who asks for a cigarette, lights it with a snap of her fingers, then disappears; or as a red-robed woman dancing on the crater's rim. Sometimes accompanied by a white dog, Pele tests the generosity of those who meet her. Her temper erupts when visitors are disrespectful; she punishes those who steal lava rocks from her volcanoes.

Offerings are still made to Pele when eruptions threaten, but more modern measures are viewed with suspicion. In 1935, a river of lava was diverted from Hilo when the U.S. Army bombed the lava flow. Shortly after, six of the airmen who flew the planes were killed in a midair collision. The story is cited as evidence of Pele's power.

Recently, the goddess's name has been given to an ecological movement. The Pele Defense Fund opposes drilling and building geothermal power plants in volcanoes, because development threatens the last significant tropical rain forest in the United States and because it involves sacrilege toward the goddess. (Anderson; Beckwith; Diab; Emerson 1906, 1978; Kalahaua; Kame'eleihiwa; Poignant; Skinner)

Pokoharua-te-po The Maori grandmother of winds, Pokoharua-te-po gave birth to the storm god and, through him, became ancestor to all weather divinities. Similar minor goddesses of the early period of creation were Hekeheke-i-papa, mother of earth and grandmother of food plants, and Hotu-papa, mother of war. These divinities preceded the major goddess, **Papa**. (Reed 1963)

Poliahu Snowcapped Hawaiian volcanoes are envisioned as goddesses lounging in the sunshine. Lilinoe, goddess of extinct Haleakala, was invoked as a power of desolation. Waiau was goddess of Mauna Kea, who bathed in a pool at the summit. But the best-known snow maiden was Poliahu, goddess of Mauna Kea. She revealed herself to Chief Aiwohikupua, and he proposed marriage. The chief went to prepare, while Poliahu gathered her sisters. When he returned, the goddesses wore gorgeous white robes that caused the humans to shake with cold. So the goddesses took off their mantles and showed themselves in garments made of sunshine. A woman appeared, accusing Aiwohikupua of betraying a promise to wed her. Poliahu covered the woman with her robe, freezing her, then threw a garment of fire over her. The woman retreated, but so did the goddess and her sisters, who returned to their mountains. (Laieikawai)

Poutini According to the Taranaki people of New Zealand, this goddess lived on Tuhua (now Mayor Island) with her brother Tama. It was rich in jade, about which Poutini argued with the residents, finally leaving in a canoe to travel to jade-rich Kotore-pi. She traveled onward, leaving other deposits of jade wherever she tied her canoe. Her brother traveled after her, but his wife Hine-tangiwai ("woman of bowenite") was turned to bowenite, which appears to have drops of water within it, described as Tama's tears. (MacKenzie)

Putawi In a Maori legend, this woman's lover Wetenga was kidnapped in the forest and tied up by a cannibal who intended to use him as bait to lure a firm-fleshed human woman. The ruse worked, for loyal Putawi soon came into the forest in search of Wetenga, and the cannibal captured her. Taking her to the secret world of such beings, he left to gather wood. While he was away, a spirit named Manoa told Putawi that, if she would become his wife, he would save her. Although she loved Wetenga, Putawi saw no other way to survive. She became Manoa's wife but soon escaped, returning to her first love. Not long after their reunion, a child crying in the night awakened Wetenga. In the dimness, he saw Putawi nursing a child. She explained that he was Manoa's spirit child and could never be seen in the daylight. When the child was weaned, he disappeared back to his father's people. Afterward, Putawi and Wetenga became parents of a large family. (Reed 1963)

Qatgoro This Melanesian primal mother was originally a stone, which grew larger until it burst and produced a son. This god, Qat, created the first woman, Iro Vigale, from bits of twigs; when completed, she began to smile. Then Qat took a spirit wife, Iro Lei, who drew the attention of Qat's brothers. They came to Qat's camp to steal her, but Iro Lei disguised herself as an old woman, and they left without recognizing her. (Codrington 1891)

Raukata-uri With her sister Raukata-mea ("red Raukata"), Raukata-uri ("dark Raukata") introduced dancing, music, and games to humanity. The Maori said these sisters lived in the forest, where they were visible in the shapes of leaves, and audible in the sounds of insects. (Orbell)

Riina The great warrior woman of the Solomon Islands was called when cannibal ghosts stole two women, Raronaia and Araanaia, from a village. The women feared for their lives, but the flying cannibals kept them as pets, feeding them fish when the women refused to dine on human flesh. Rescue parties were mounted, but none were successful, with many men dying in the attempts.

Riina set out to free the prisoners, easily finding the island on which they were held. As they approached, Riina's warriors crouched so it seemed only a single woman was rowing toward shore. When one of the ghosts swooped down, thinking to make a meal of Riina, she grabbed him by the hair while the other women clubbed him into submission. In fear of his life, the ghost admitted that his power resided in three objects, which Riina found and disempowered. Then she led her women to shore, to hunt the other ghost, whom she found cowering in a cave full of human skeletons. With her boomerang, she dispatched the second ghost and freed the women. (Flood et al)

Rona To the Maori, the moon was a teasing man. One night when Rona was going to draw water, the moon covered himself with a cloud so she could not see, and Rona stubbed her toe. Annoyed, she cursed him. He came to argue with her. When the moon reached earth,

Rona was so angry that he took her back to the sky, where she clings to the moon's face. Other legends say Rona was the moon's sister or the daughter of the god of fishes. (Anderson; Best; Te Awekotuku)

Sina This Polynesian goddess may be connected to **Hina**, for similar legends are told of them, including the Samoan story of the woman in the moon, ceaselessly beating tapa cloth. When she saw the moon rising, Sina joked that it looked like a breadfruit. The moon, angry at this impertinence, snatched Sina, her tapa-making equipment, and her child, holding them captive in the moon. (Anderson; Chadwick; Flood et al; Orbell; Williamson)

Tahia This heroine of the Marquesas Islands smelled of flowers. She was also beautiful, and many men wished to marry her, but one man decided she would be his. Taking advantage of a time when her relatives were gathering wild foods, he seduced her. When her mother returned, she recognized Tahia's own father, who had abandoned them when Tahia was a baby.

Grief-stricken Tahia refused to eat. Her brothers and uncles knew what would cure her: a beautiful man for a husband. They found one on a nearby island, and the young man agreed to marry Tahia. The couple was blissfully happy until the new husband said he wished to visit his family. Tahia warned him that she could not endure his absence for more than a month and, when he did not return, hanged herself in sorrow. Her ghost visited her husband, who was ashamed of what his lengthy absence had caused. When he begged Tahia to return, she told him a secret ritual that would bring her back. With berries and wild ginger and coconut, he prepared a brew he left behind a curtain for three days. At the end of that time, Tahia walked back into her lover's arms. (Flood et al)

Taranga The mother of the Polynesian hero Maui gave birth prematurely, then wrapped the fetus in her magical hair and tossed him into the sea, offering prayers to protect the child from turning into a demon, the usual fate of such children. In the sea's womb, the child was carried to term and then raised by gods until he was old enough to see Taranga's home. Happy to see her miscarried babe, Taranga welcomed Maui, who became her favorite son.

Taranga spent each day far from home. One day Maui followed her to where she tended the miraculous underworld gardens from which all food on this earth derives. Because of his daring, Taranga allowed Maui to go through the manhood rituals earlier than others. This name is also used for the fire goddess **Mahui-iki**, who may be the same figure. (Grace)

Taua The guardian of women in Pukapuka, an island north of Samoa, Taua punished any man who hit a woman by afflicting him with cancer of the armpit. She protected women's possessions by causing thieves to lose their balance. She protected human corpses by making taboo the use of any part of them. This goddess could make entire islands invisible if danger threatened. (Beaglehold)

Touiafutuna The creator goddess of Tonga was made of stone. When she gave birth, the earth shook and thundered. Every time she went into labor, Touiafutuna gave birth to two children, male and female twins named Piki and Kele, who had no father. (Collocott; Williamson)

Tuli As the Samoan father god Tangeroa watched over watery chaos, the bird goddess Tuli flew across it. As she tired, he threw stones, giving her temporary perches; these became the Pacific islands. While resting on a rock, Tuli grew weary of the sun, so she flew to heaven and brought back a fresh vine as an umbrella. She left the vine behind, and from it swarmed maggots that became the first human beings. Some versions of the myth say Tuli was Tangeroa's daughter and because she yearned for company, he instructed her to plant vines and harvest them; from the decaying vines crawled the first humans. (Anderson; Williamson)

Ubu The owner of fire to the people of Mabuiag (Jervis Island) north of Australia was a woman who kept fire between her fingers. There was no fire in that land until the lizard man Walek went to his sister Ubu, who gave him a coal to take back to his people. But it went out. So Walek stole the fire from his sister's hand, then ran away as she yelled at him that the fire was meant for her daughter, Surka. To swim back to the island, Walek had to put the fire in his mouth, so lizards have red scars on their tongues to this day. (Lawrie)

Var-ma-te-takere On the Hervey Islands, the Mangaian people said the universe was a coconut, at the bottom of which lived this woman who sat doubled up, knees to chest. Taking pieces of her flesh, she formed a fish man from her right side, and another fish man from her left side. Then she created several sons and two daughters, Tumuteanoao, a woman of stone, and Tu-metua, who never left her mother. (Anderson; Williamson)

Waliporlimia The New Guinean goddess Waliporlimia hid inside human women, causing them to become sexually aroused. When men attempted to mate with these women, they were injured or killed by Waliporlimia's force. Women occupied by the goddesses used their sensuality to attract men to their deaths. (Lawrence and Meggitt)

Walutahanga The eightfold snake goddess of the Solomon Islands was born to a human mother who, afraid of her husband, hid the girl. He discovered the deception and cut Walutahanga into eight pieces. After eight days of rain, the girl's body rejoined into a whole; she traveled through the islands, tormenting humans in retaliation. Captured, she was chopped into eight pieces and her bones thrown into the sea. Then everyone except a woman and her daughter ate the flesh of the goddess's body. After another eight rainy days, the bones under the sea formed themselves into the goddess. To punish her attackers, Walutahanga covered the islands with eight waves, which killed everyone but the woman and her child who had not eaten her flesh. The goddess gave them gifts, including coconut and clear-water streams, before retreating to the ocean. (Fox and Drew; Poignant)

Whaitiri Common to the mythologies of many Pacific people was a powerful cannibal goddess who owned thunder. Once she descended to earth to marry a warrior chief, thinking his title "man killer" suggested compatibility. But Whaitiri found that he did not share her affection for eating humans. He also complained about the smell of their children's excrement. So she invented the latrine and showed humans how to use it, then returned to the sky. To the Maori, this figure was the powerful force who separated **Papa** from her lover; her daughter was Hema, goddess of procreation. (Dixon; Orbell; Poignant; Reed 1963)

Wutmara This heroine from New Guinea was co-wife with a ghost from the underworld, whom she resented because visiting her kept the shared husband away from the human world for long periods. She brought about the discovery of the coconut palm, because she convinced her husband to bring the ghost wife to the surface world so they might all live together. She intended to murder her rival, not realizing that ghosts are immortal. Wutmara killed the woman and left the body in the jungle, but the ghost transposed the genitals of Wutmara and her husband, then killed Wutmara and turned herself into a hair on the husband's groin. The husband tricked the ghost into revealing herself and killed her. But she reemerged shortly thereafter as the coconut palm, on which to this day you can see the face of the angry ghost. (Hogbin)

AUSTRALIAN PANTHEON

Abobi The Ngulugwongga (Mulluk Mulluk) people of northern Australia say this woman grew tired of her husband and turned herself into a star. But she left her seven daughters, the Yogamada, with her husband

and he soon began to desire them. He detached his penis and sent it after one girl. As it began to penetrate her daughter, Abobi saw what was happening from her home in the sky. She dropped a rope and the girls climbed to safety. Their father tried to climb after them, so Abobi cut the rope. Still lusting after his daughters, he turned himself into the moon and chases them through the sky. Clustered together as the Seven Sisters, they protect each other from him. (Bozic)

Bila On the Flinders Range, this cannibalistic sun goddess lit the world by cooking victims over an open fire. When lizard man Kudnu wounded her with his boomerang, she disappeared, plunging the world into darkness. Kudnu sent his boomerang to the north to recover the sun, but to no avail. Then he shot it to the west, and the south, but still no light came forth. Finally, the lizard man threw his boomerang east, where it carried the sun goddess high above the horizon, then down again in the west. Because the lizard man saved the world, the Flinders Range people never killed a goanna or a gecko. (Eliade 1973; McLeod et al)

Dinewan The people of the Murray River say that in the Dreaming, the now-flightless emu had enormous wings, until the female emu Dinewan encountered the evil crane Brolga. Dinewan was fascinated with the crane's dances. Hiding her wings behind her back, Brolga told Dinewan that she had to amputate her wings, which would otherwise be in the way when she tried to dance. The emu chopped off her wings. Immediately, Brolga unfolded her own wings. In a nearby tree a kookabura laughed. This is why the emu cannot fly, and why the kookabura laughs.

Dinewan recovered slowly. She began to explore her earthly home, to taste its fruits. She built a nest and laid her first brood. Then she sat to hatch them. Seeing the vast number of emu eggs, the crane played a trick. Hiding all but one of her own offspring, she sang the praises of few children until she convinced the emu to break all her eggs but one. Then she flaunted her substantial brood before the emu.

The next breeding season, troublesome Brolga came back to Dinewan, where she sat proudly on a nestful of eggs. Although the emu told the crane to leave, Brolga tormented Dinewan with cruel names until she lured the emu off her nest. Brolga rushed forward and smashed the emu's eggs. Dinewan tried to save her brood, but all but one of the eggs had been crushed. Carrying the last emu egg, Brolga rose into the air and threw it as hard as she could into the sky. It struck a pile of wood in the sky, which caught fire and became the sun. (Dixon; Flood et al; McLeod et al; Parker 1898, 1993)

Djanggawul Sisters The elder daughter of the Yirrkalla sun goddess was Bildjiwuraroiju; her younger sister was Miralaidj; together they were the Djanggawul Sisters. In the Dreaming, they traveled with their brother Djanggawul, carrying sacred objects that made women powerful: carvings of parrot, goanna, porpoise, and ant, together with a uterus-shaped mat in a sacred pouch. With these totems and with sacred songs only they knew, the Djanggawul Sisters could raise power.

Djanggawul begged to be taught the songs, but his sisters told them that their sacred objects protected women from men's violence. But the brother found a way to own the totems. First he seduced the older sister and gathered their belongings to move to this world, saying it would be best for their child. But the younger sister, Miralaidj, was afraid of being left alone, so she made love with her brother and, conceiving a child, demanded the right to continue traveling.

When they reached this world, it was dry and infertile. The sisters drew water with their digging sticks and created plants from their poles. They sanctified the land with songs and totems. The women grew heavier, but they kept traveling to make fertile their new world. The women had to stop and give birth. Through them, the land was populated.

When their children began to argue, the sisters invented laws and rituals. Even in the new land their brother plotted to steal their sacred objects. When

he succeeded, the women decided that the power of the womb was sufficient and they would not attempt to gain back the sacred objects. (Berndt R 1951, 1952, 1974; Berndt and Berndt; Eliade 1973)

Erathipa In central Australia, a huge boulder in the shape of a pregnant woman bears this name. Down the side runs an opening, where the souls of children are imprisoned. They watch until a woman of suitable age walks by, then slip into her womb to be reborn. Women of childbearing age who do not wish to become pregnant stoop as they walk past Erathipa's rock, pretending to be too old to conceive. (Powdermaker)

Gambil Gambil Among the Weilwan people of New South Wales, this star woman was originally a cannibal. A shapeshifter, she pretended to be a kind old woman to tempt an old man. But he came prepared, for he carried a rope made of the hair of all the women in his village. When she came close, he leaped upon her, intending to strangle her. But she leapt into the air and became a falling star. (McLeod et al)

Gnowee Among the Wotjobaluk of southeastern Australia, the sun mother's name was Gnowee. She lived on earth, where there was no light, so she always carried a torch. In such a dark world, Gnowee found it difficult to find food for her child. She wandered far, but no food was to be found. Finally, concerned that she had walked too far, she turned to go back, but she no longer knew her way. She walked and walked, until she rose into the sky, across which she walks still, searching for her lost child. (Massola; Reed 1993)

Goolagaya An envious barren woman, Goolagaya lived alone with a white dingo, both of them shunned by her people. But Goolagaya made friends with some children by giving them treats. Her intention was not innocent, however. When a woman angered her, Goolagaya stole her baby and hid it under a shrub near a pond. The baby slid into the pond and drowned,

161

and in retaliation the people killed Goolagaya and her dingo, burying them deep in hopes that their spirits would be contained. But the two managed to escape every evening, walking among humans and trying to steal children who wander away from the campfire. (Ellis; Mountford and Roberts 1965)

Julunggul The rainbow snake goddess could transform herself into male, neuter, or androgynous form. She was embodied in the ocean and waterfalls, in pearls and crystals, and in deep pools. As goddess of initiations, Julunggul was the primary spirit when boys became men. The boys approached her in ritual, to be symbolically swallowed and regurgitated as men. Her voice was heard in the bullroarer, the ritual instrument used in initiations. (Berndt R 1951, 1974; Eliade 1967; Poignant; Reed 1993)

Kalwadi An old woman with the human name of Mujingga, this goddess worked as a babysitter. Because she craved infant flesh, occasionally one of her charges would disappear. Her children were upset, because Kalwadi took care of their offspring. Then Kalwadi disappeared. They tracked the goddess to an underwater lair where they killed her and released the children from Kalwadi's womb, where they awaited rebirth. Australian people celebrated this second birth in initiation rituals. Some scholars say Kalwadi was identical to **Kunapipi**. (Berndt R 1951, 1974; Eliade 1968; Poignant)

Karakarook Aboriginal Australians from near Melbourne said two women were set upon by snakes and, while protecting herself, one broke her staff. Flames flew out of it, attracting the attention of a bird, who caught it. When two men ran after the bird, it dropped the flame and started the earth on fire. People hid in fear, and when the fire burned itself out, they were without fire. Without fire to frighten them, snakes began to reproduce wildly. But Karakarook came from the sky to guard the women, bringing a flaming brand with her, which she shared with women so they could be safe. (Dixon)

Krubi According to the people of the Illawarra region, the red-flowering Waratah tree was originally the girl Krubi, beloved of the handsome Bahmai. She watched for him whenever he was away, sitting high on a hill. Always, she wore her bright-red cloak, so he could see her and wave as he returned. But one day, she saw the village's men coming back from a raid. Bahmai was not with them. Stricken with grief, Krubi faded away. Where she died watching, the first red flowers of the Waratah tree were seen. (McLeod et al)

Kuggun According to the Ngulugwongga (Mulluk Mulluk) people, the mother of bees was Kuggun, who was married to Vamar, the fly. But she disliked the rotting flesh Vamar fed her, preferring nectar. When he killed all the flowers so she would have to eat his food, she made sure their children were like her. As they were born, they flew away to find food in the hearts of flowers. (Bozic)

Kultana In southeastern Australia, this Dreamtime woman lives with her husband far to the west, where they light fires to attract spirits of the dead. She controlled cold winds called *jiridja*. (Berndt R 1974)

Kunapipi Eternally pregnant, the mother goddess of northern Australia created every living being. Sometimes represented (like **Julunggul**) as a rainbow snake, Kunapipi is the overseer of initiations and puberty rituals. She came from a sinking land to establish her worship. The goddess and the rituals connected with her go by the name of Kunapipi.

Along the Roper River, people say Kunapipi used her daughters as bait for her favorite meal: human men. Kunapipi ate so many men it attracted the attention of a hero who, catching her in the act, destroyed her. The moans she made while dying struck into all the trees in the world and can be heard if the wood is carved into bullroarers, which cry out "Mumuna," Kunapipi's ritual name. (Eliade 1973; Poignant)

Lumerai The rainbow serpent Lumerai slept in the earth's center for immeasurable eons, then crawled to the surface and across the empty land. Where she passed, earth's features show her track: rivers, lakes, and water holes. She pressed her nose into the earth, forming mountains, and watered the land with milk, causing it to flower. She awakened the earth's creatures. Then she went below the earth to awaken a man and woman, who became the ancestors of all people. (McLeod et al)

Makara This collective name describes seven primordial emus, all sisters, who were hounded by the Wanjin, the dingoes. The women kept flying away, so the dingoes set a fire around the rocks where the emus nested, thinking to burn off the women's wings. The trap worked, but the dingoes injured their own legs trying to run over the burning grasses, so now emus are flightless and dingoes have short legs. When the Makara found that the Wanjin continued to follow them, the women rose into the air, becoming the Seven Sisters, who watch over other preyed-upon women. (Mountford and Roberts 1965)

Meamei The stars of the Seven Sisters once lived on earth as a bevy of beautiful sisters notable for their long hair and icicles that covered their bodies. They hunted alone, never joining with other families. Some young men, the Berai-Berai, began to follow them and leave love offerings of honey. The girls took the honey but ignored the boys. An old man captured the girls and tried to melt their ice, whereupon the girls escaped to the sky and became stars. The Berai-Berai pined away until they, too, were translated to the sky, where they shine as the constellation Orion. Once a year, the girls throw ice down to earth to remind those who remained behind of their presence. In response, people take ice particles and use them to pierce the noses of children, which endows them with the gift of song. (Parker 1898)

Memembel Among the Ngulugwongga (Mulluk Mulluk) of northern Australia, the primal porpoise Memembel lived by the sea avoiding everyone but her own children. She had many, but none were very attractive, so she set out to find a prettier one. The sweetest child was the son of Manark, the kangaroo. She crept along behind the pair until she caught them in an unguarded moment, then lured Manark's son away and ran toward the sea.

Manark, desperate to save her child, grabbed a pole and hit Memembel on her head. The porpoise dropped the child, who ran crying back to Manark. Memembel was so angry at losing the child that she hit Manark with a stick, breaking her arms. Since then, the kangaroo has kept its children hidden away in a belly pouch and has shrunken arms where Memembel broke them. The porpoise also shows the results of the fight; it has a deep cleft in its head where Manark hit Memembel. (Bozic)

Mutjingga Among the Murinbata people, Mutjingga was the all-creating primal mother. She was left babysitting with some children of her village. When the parents returned to find the children missing, they followed suspicious markings leading to a water hole. They speared Mutjingga and retrieved the children from her belly, still breathing. Her voice survived as that of the bullroarer, used in initiation ceremonies. Another creatrix, Imberombera of the Kakadu, walked out of the ocean pregnant and walked around giving birth and planting edible vegetables; she also formed the hills and rivers. (Charlesworth)

Myee Inquisitive Myee was a moth with multicolored wings, according to the people of New South Wales. Despite warnings, she could not resist flying to the mountains to see why they gleamed. Tired from the flight, she fell onto the snow, where she was trapped until spring. When the rains came, they melted her colors, which stained the spring flowers. Myee found herself a dull gray, as her children remain. (McLeod et al)

Nerida The young girl Nerida and her friend Birwain used to play beside a water hole where no one else went for fear of a water monster. Nerida grew into a lovely young woman, and the friendship between her and Birwain grew into love. But the water monster had been watching the girl mature and desired her for his own. One day he caught her alone and, disguising himself as a friendly woman, told Nerida she would have to leap into the pool to save her people from the water monster. To save their people, Nerida did what was asked. Birwain sat by the water weeping until Nerida appeared in the form of a red water lily, then jumped into the pool and was transformed into water reeds, which always grow with water lilies in token of this doomed love. (Parker 1993)

Ngalyod Another form of the great rainbow serpent, the creator goddess Ngalyod of Arnhem Land brings life to creation through her existence in the Dreaming. She appeared as the woman Waramurungundji, traveling with her husband, Wuragog, an importunate man who kept pressing himself sexually upon her. Tired of his insensitivity, she turned herself into a snake, which did not stop Wuragog. She gave birth to the original people and taught them the rules of peaceful society. (Allen)

Numma Moiyuk Ocean goddess of the Yulengor of Arnhem Land, she created herself as a very fat woman, full of unborn children. Though she came from the sea, she created the first pools. Then she gave birth to humankind and taught her descendants crafts, including the weaving of fishnets and the painting of sacred designs. Finally she died, offering her body as food to her children. (Chaseling)

Nurrun The primordial turkey of the Ngulugwongga (Mulluk Mulluk) people was Nurrun, who in the Dreamtime was married to a man named Manor, who knew how to use fire, while Nurrun did not. When he tried to teach her how to bank a fire for the night, she poured sand mixed with hot ashes over him and burned him. Nurrun remained liable to make mistakes. When Manor went to a men's corroborree, she was frightened of the dark and built a fire so huge it escaped, causing a conflagration across the land. In fear, she began to beat her arms until she rose into the air and thus became a turkey. But Manor, because his arms were burned, could not fly; instead he began to run and turned into an emu. (Bozic)

Pirili When an old man desired her for a wife and the other old men agreed, vibrant young Pirili refused to accept her fate. But a man she selected instead tried to rape her. Pirili rose into the heavens, her attacker following her and tearing out stars in his furious pursuit. The women of the Milky Way hid her within the Seven Sisters and, to punish her attacker, sentenced him to remain on earth. Other versions of the myth say the couple, having married happily, were tracked and killed by the jealous old man. Their blood was transformed into myriads of red spring flowers. (Ellis; Mountford and Roberts; Parker 1898, 1993)

Pukwi The sun goddess of the Tiwi people, Pukwi created the world in the Dreaming. She made the ocean from her urine, which is why it tastes salty. She travels the sky in the daytime and goes along the Milky Way to the place of dawn every night. (White)

Quork-Quork In northern Australia, this onomatopoetically named green frog goddess was the mother of the lightning goddess Bumerali, the rain goddess Tomituka, and the man of thunder, Pakadringa. Native Australians were careful not to injure green frogs, for fear that Quork-Quork's children would deluge them with monsoon rains. During the rainy season, Quork-Quork could be seen hopping about and enjoying the noise her children made. During the dry season they retreated to the sky, while their mother hid in rocks and trees. (Mountford and Roberts)

Vena The sun's wife to the people of Tasmania, Vena traveled with Parnuen across the sky. Because he had longer legs, he carried her, dropping seeds of rain as they traveled. When Vena grew tired, she rested on the icebergs of the great southern sea, but her heat melted the ice and she sank, appearing later as the moon. In anger, her husband melted the icebergs that covered Tasmania, revealing the land. (McLeod et al)

Wai-ai This primal goddess of the Tiwi people off Australia's north coast lived in the Dreamtime, when everyone was immortal. There the moon man Tapara seduced Wai-ai, convincing her to leave her baby son Jinaini alone during their assignations. Angry at what she saw, the sun goddess Wyah scorched the child to death. When she found the child, Wai-ai was confused, because she had never seen a corpse. She tried to nurse the child back to life but failed. In grief, the boy's father, Purukapali, created funeral ceremonies and cursed everything on earth to die. After creating the ceremony, Purukapali walked into the sea to his death. (Holms)

Walo The people of Arnhem Land said this sun goddess lived with her daughter Bara and her sister-in-law, the world-mother Madalait, far to the east. Each day Walo journeyed across the sky accompanied by Bara, until one day the sun goddess realized the earth was parched from their heat. She sent her daughter away so the earth could become fertile.

Once, in the Dreaming, Walu slept in an underground cave. When she woke and stretched, light streamed into the sky. Walu climbed over the world's edge. She stroked the soil; trees and plants burst forth. Spirits emerged to help. They dug rivers, piled up hills, sculpted animals and birds. Then Walu sought a place to sleep. On the western horizon she saw the Island of Bralgu, where she rested. The next morning, when she saw the lovely green land, she was pleased.

Spirit people, observing the land's beauty, made it their home. (Berndt 1952)

Waramurungundji The creatrix of Arnhem Land, a figure similar to **Kunapipi**, Waramurungundji gave birth to the earth and fashioned its creatures. She taught her creations to talk and divided each language group from the next. All people were considered relatives through descent from Waramurungundji. (Berndt R 1974; Swain and Trompf)

Wawalag Sisters Two sisters came from the Dreaming. The elder, Gungman, was pregnant by a relative, while Wirlkul was virginal. Carrying stone spears and sporting feather headbands, the women wandered the continent domesticating plants, evolving languages, and naming the land's creatures. As they traveled, Gungman had her child, continuing to bleed and leaving a trail of blood.

They camped next to the pond where **Julunggul** lived, a taboo place where women's blood was prohibited. A heavy rain began, and the women built shelters. As rain ran into the pond, it carried some of Gungman's blood. Julunggul reared out of the water, ready to devour the women. The women began to dance, hypnotizing the snake. Finally, the Wawalag Sisters fell asleep, and Julunggul swallowed them.

But the snake goddess felt ashamed of eating the women and their children. So she vomited them up, and the women were revived by ant bites. But Julunggul could not restrain herself and ate them again. Again she vomited them up, in an endless cycle. According to some versions of the myth, the women remain within the snake, speaking from her belly. (Berndt R 1951, 1974; Caruana and Lendon; Charlesworth; Eliade 1973; Swain and Trompf)

Wuradilagu In Arnhem Land, Wuradilagu wandered across the land, naming its features and endowing them with meaning. Throughout, she kept herself covered with bark so no man could look at her. Carved images often show her pregnant or giving birth; she is honored in a long song cycle. (Berndt R 1966)

Wuriupranili In northern Australia, this sun goddess carried a torch through the sky from east to west. At the western sea, she dipped it into the water, then used the embers to guide her under the earth to reach her eastern starting point. The skies of dawn and dusk came from Wuriupranili's red-ochre body paints misting the sky as she powdered herself. Her companion, the moon man Japara, bore a smaller torch and therefore gave less light. (Mountford and Roberts)

Yhi The goddess of light of the Karraru of southwest Australia, Yhi lay asleep in a world of windless mountains. A whistle startled her. She opened her eyes, flooding the world with light. The earth stirred. Yhi drifted down to this new land, walking north, south, east, west. As she did, plants sprang up from her footprints. She walked the world's surface until she had stepped everywhere. Then the goddess rested on the treeless Nullabor Plain.

As she glanced around, she realized that the new plants could not move, and she desired to see something dance. She descended beneath the earth, where she found evil spirits who tried to sing her to death. But they were not as powerful as Yhi. Her warmth melted the darkness, and tiny forms began to move. The forms turned into insects that swarmed around her. She led them into the sunny world. But there were still caves of ice in which other beings rested. Yhi stared into the caves' interiors until water formed. Fishes and lizards swam forth. Cave after cave she freed from its darkness, and birds and animals poured forth onto the earth.

Then Yhi told her creatures she would return to the Dreaming. Turning into a ball of light, she sank below the horizon. As she disappeared, darkness fell. There was sorrow and mourning, and finally, sleep. Soon, there was the first dawn. A bird chorus greeted Yhi, and the lake and ocean waters that had been rising in mists, trying to reach her, sank calmly.

For eons the animals lived in peace until sadness began to fill them. She had not planned to return, but she slid down to the earth's surface and asked the creatures what was wrong. Wombat wanted to wiggle along the ground. Kangaroo wanted to leap. Bat wanted wings. Lizard wanted legs. Seal wanted to swim. The confused platypus wanted something of every other animal. Yhi gave them what they wanted. From the beautiful regular forms of the early creation came the strange creatures that now walk the earth. Yhi then swept up to the sky.

She had one other task yet to complete: the creation of woman. She had already embodied Thought in male form and set him wandering the earth. But he was lonely. Yhi went to him as he slept near a grass tree. As he woke, he saw a flower stalk shining. He was drawn to it, where Yhi concentrated her power. The flower stalk began to move rhythmically. It changed into the first woman, mother of all people. (McLeod et al; Reed 1993)

Yirbaik-Baik This cannibal woman kept a pack of dingoes with which she hunted humans. She played a trick on her victims, pretending she knew where fat wallabies could be killed easily. But a group of humans surrounded and killed Yirbaik-Baik and her canine companions. The dogs became snakes, and the cannibal woman a small brown bird. Even as a bird, she remained powerful; with her calls she brought forth rain and thunder. (Mountford and Roberts)

EUROPE

THE BALTIC

The Baltic region holds importance in goddess studies because of the significance of the feminine in its mythology and because its pagan culture remained vital into historical times. But because myths were conveyed orally, few religious texts with defined narratives exist. Comparatively little material is available in English, in part because little scholarship was published abroad during the Soviet years. Folk material, when available, remains mostly in its original languages, Lithuanian and Latvian. Despite these limitations, Baltic goddess myths represent a significant resource for scholars of women's spirituality.

The Baltic people share their name with the sea that borders the region. Some fifty million years ago, the forest covering the area sank beneath the sea. Over millennia, salt water petrified the trees into amber, a source of wealth for early Baltic people and a significant factor in their mythology. As amber preserves ancient insects and seeds, Baltic people preserved their myths in songs and rituals. The connection of mythology with an embattled sense of cultural identity resulted in the preservation of mythic material, and because Christianity came late to the Baltic, goddesses were not hidden away as "saints" as in other European areas but were acknowledged as divine into historical times.

The Baltic languages are Indo-European, but we find a substratum of pre-Indo-European religion that derives from the agriculturalists who occupied the region when, in approximately 2500 BCE, Indo-Europeans arrived. Three languages descend from the language they spoke: Old Prussian, now vanished, and Lithuanian and Latvian. Although these Indo-Europeans brought new rituals and deities to the Baltic, the old religion survived in goddesses who shapeshift into animal or bird form.

The Baltic region reaches written history in the work of Roman geographer Tacitus, who in 98 CE wrote of the Aestii, who collected amber and worshipped mother goddesses. Little else was recorded for many years. The region remained independent of Rome and, later, of the Holy Roman Empire. Conversion to Christianity was vigorously resisted. Lithuania did not fall under Christian influence until 1413 and even then was only nominally Christian. Until the eighteenth century, missionaries spoke with frustration of the strength of pagan Baltic culture. Even at the beginning of the twentieth century and despite embracing a devout Christianity, Lithuanians and Latvians performed rituals to goddesses. After Russian occupation in 1940, religious observation was discouraged, but Christian and pagan rituals continued to be celebrated secretly, sometimes melding together.

The linking of pagan religion with the desire to retain regional identity encouraged cultural preservation. In addition, the Baltic remained sparsely settled into contemporary times. Centralized authority had little say over what happened at remote homesites. The continuity of Baltic paganism was also sustained by its importance in women's daily lives, as tending the hearth fire and baking bread ritualized women's connection with feminine divinity.

The greatest expressions of this ancient religion are found in folk songs, primarily a women's art form. Often these songs tell mythic stories or employ mythic images. Women not only composed the songs but were also responsible for their survival. The first song (*dáino*) collected in 1632 was recorded identically 300 years later. But keeping the *dáinos* in the memory was not without danger. In the sixteenth century, women were burned as witches for singing traditional songs. In 1878, Latvians began collecting the songs with an eye to publication. More than two million verses are now recorded.

After the dissolution of the Soviet Union, a resurgence of interest in Baltic religion led to the formation of Romuva, which follows the path of the early-twentieth-century nationalist movement Dievturi. In 1995, the Lithuanian government acknowledged Romuva as a legitimate religion. Romuva celebrates festivals at traditional times and offers outreach to scholars and others interested in Baltic traditional religion.

BALTIC PANTHEON

Aspelenie This household goddess (*žaltys*) was a snake that protected the family's grain from rodents, ruling the corner of the house behind the stove. (Jurgines)

Ausrinė The morning star goddess lived on a sea island, where she tended magical apples that brought love to those who ate them. She also owned iron cows, which gave boiling milk that made anyone who drank it instantly beautiful. Ausrinė's connection to the Baltic goddess **Saulė** is complex, for the former is sometimes described as the sun's rays and at other times as a separate divinity who formed a trinity of star goddesses with Breksta and Zleja. Legends vary as to whether Ausrinė was a victim of incest or was the illicit lover of the moon man Mėnulis (see **Saulės Meita**). An eight-pointed star symbolized the Latvian version of Ausrinė; Auseklis appears occasionally as a male divinity but more commonly as a goddess. (Dexter; Greimas; Landsbergis and Mills)

Austėja Bees were the servants of Austėja, who encouraged abundance, including human fertility. She was an energetic housewife who watched over the safety of the farm and its occupants; a weaver whose bees created honeycombs; and a bride who drank mead or honey wine at her wedding. Austėja was invoked at women's life passages. Her holy day was in August, when bees joined in singing and dancing for Austėja. (Gimbutas; Greimas; Trinkūnas)

Gabija To Gabija, woman offered the first loaf from each baking, marked with dough ornaments. The last loaf was for the baker; no one else could taste it. Gabija's name refers to "covering," for it was the woman's responsibility to cover the fire each evening, praying Gabija would not wander during the night. Before retiring, the woman also put out water in case Gabija felt like cleansing herself. Gabija needed salt, food, and wood to sustain her. She was insulted by refuse being put into her, or by being spat or urinated on. In addition to household fires, the ancient Balts had communal sacred fires tended by priestesses called Vaidiutės; the last Lithuanian sacred fire was extinguished in 1413. (Gimbutas 1963, 1999; Trinkūnas)

Giltinė Sister of **Laimė**, black-clad Giltinė drove a carriage drawn by six black horses; or she was a yellow-clad skeleton carrying a scythe and a bone rattle. She shrouded herself in white when she licked corpses, filling her tongue with poison. White hounds accompanied her into cemeteries. A shapeshifter, she could disguise herself as a snake or a stick of wood. Giltinė ruled healing as well as death. If Giltinė appeared at the foot of a bed, the person would recover, but if she stood at the head, death was imminent. She invented the medical profession, although she ruled doctors could not interfere with her will. (Gimbutas 1989, 1999; Kiskytė)

Juratė This mermaid lived in an ocean castle, roofed in seashells, fish scales, and pearls. Spurning the thunder god Perkunas, Juratė took a human fisherman as her lover. But Perkunas chained him to a rock, then killed the goddess. Amber that washes up on the Baltic shores is her palace, slowly crumbling away. Connection of this figure to Jurasmat, invoked by sailors, is unclear. (Beliajus)

Laimė This fate goddess measured the length and happiness of each person's life. As Muza Mate ("mother of life"), she announced the fate of newborns. A birthing mother offered a sash to Laimė because she was a weaving goddess, sometimes described as three goddesses who spin life's strand, measure it, and cut it. Dekla, a Latvian form of Laimė, wept bitterly when forced to witness the birth of a child for whom a tragic life was destined. As Laimė-Dalia, "happy fate," the goddess ruled good luck, but when she took the form of a cuckoo, her voice warned of misfortune. Humans could gain Laimė's prophetic skill if they found a fern blooming on summer solstice.

Laimė is difficult to distinguish from the sun goddess **Saulė**, also seen as a controller of fate. She appeared in legends of the sun's daughter **Ausrinė**, performing tasks one would expect of a mother, such as arranging the girl's naming ceremony. Similarly Laimė and **Laumė** can be difficult to distinguish, for both had similar powers and resided in woman-shaped stones. Because Laimė is described as "above the other gods," she may derive from the pre-Indo-European strata of Baltic culture. Support for this argument derives from the fact that only Laimė and the high god, Dievs, had the power of creation. (Dexter; Gimbutas 1989, 1999; Greimas; Katzenelenbogen; Landsbergis and Mills; Motz; Rubulis 1970; Trinkūnas)

Laumė Sometimes at night, on footbridges or in thickets, a large-breasted woman with long blond hair appeared, accompanied by a cat. It was best not to laugh, for those who did were changed into animals. Laumė visited homes to judge the industry of their inhabitants. Where people worked hard, she rewarded them, but she devoured lazy people. She loved hardworking children, whom she took away on spirit vacations. Generous but easily angered, Laumė might finish the farm work and then, at a wrong word, undo it and disappear. Sometimes she appeared as a multiple goddess, the Laumės. (Dexter; Trinkūnas; Gimbutas 1999; Greimas; Kiskytė)

Mara This goddess may have evolved as a parallel to the Christian god. The senior Baltic goddess was usually **Saulė**, of whom Mara was a daughter living in the planet Mars. But some Latvian myths describe Mara as supreme. She may have descended from the livestock goddess Lopemat, but she was also described as the goddess of woman's economic contributions.

A force of abundance, she provided nourishment. A proverb says, "God made tables, Mara made bread." Mara was a black cow that represented the fertility of spring; she could also appear as a black insect, a black chicken, or a snake. Until a century ago, fertile black hens and cocks were the first to occupy any new home to bring her power into the house. Mara celebrated her feast on August 15. (Beliajus; Gimbutas 1989, 1999)

Ragana From deep in the forest, Ragana kidnapped human babies. She could not abide salt water, so one could protect a baby by putting it out to sea. She also ate young men after forcing them to have sex with her. Ragana appeared as an elderly woman with long claws and protruding teeth. Accompanied by her totem owl, she could change into a snake or toad so, to protect oneself, it was wise to carry a toad-shaped amulet. She controlled weather, especially storms, which she brewed up with a red wand.

Hunters honored Ragana, offering her their first catch. At stone statues of this goddess, women sacrificed eggs, butter, and hair. Because she opposed **Saulė**, Ragana was celebrated at the winter solstice, when the sun's power was weakest. On that day, assemblies of Raganas gathered on mountaintops to comb ice from their hair. (Gimbutas 1989, 1999; Jaskievicz; Trinkūnas)

Saulė The greatest Baltic goddess was the sun mother who ruled birth, when newborns first saw her light, as well as death, when she welcomed souls into her heavenly tree. She was married to the moon man Mėnulis. Their first child was the earth, and their countless other children were the stars. Hardworking Saulė left the house at dawn and drove her chariot until dusk. Mėnulis, however, was carefree, staying home all day and only occasionally driving his moon chariot.

The light of Saulė's life was her daughter **Saulės Meita**. Each evening, after she had bathed her horses, Saulė looked for the child. But one evening Saulė discovered that Mėnulis had raped their daughter. Saulė slashed the moon's face, leaving marks we see today. Then she banished him, so they are no longer seen together.

Folk songs describe Saulė as a statuesque matron, richly dressed in golden clothing and a golden shawl, with a gold crown on her streaming golden hair. From her castle behind the hill of heaven, she rode forth in a copper-wheeled chariot, bearing a jug from which she poured out light. After her daily ride, she descended into the ocean and began a darker journey, through the land of the dead, back to the point of dawn.

Saulė was worshipped at dawn, when people bowed to the east. She was especially honored on summer solstice, Ligo, when she rose crowned with a braid of red fern blossoms. At that moment, people dived into east-flowing streams. Women donned braided wreaths and walked through the fields singing. Finally, everyone gathered around bonfires and sang. In 1969, the Soviets forbade celebration of the festival, but it survived and has been reestablished.

Another festival, Kaledos, was held when the sun's light was weakest. On winter solstice, solar images were paraded through the fields to bring fertility and abundance in the next season. People dressed as animals danced with the goddess's chariot. An old Baltic myth says a smith, Kalvis, forged the sun, but she was stolen from the sky and freed by the stars, which wielded a giant hammer. This myth echoes in the festival.

Perkuna Tete, "mother of thunder," survives in a myth welcoming Saulė, after her day's work, with a hot bath. She may have had importance obscured in later times. (Balys; Benjamins; Chase; Trinkūnas; Landsbergis and Mills; Machal; Motz; Neuland; Rubulis 1970, 1982; Trinkūnas; Ward; Zobarskas)

Saulės Meita The daughter of **Saulė** was called a "little sun," possibly indicating a star. Myths describe sun daughters who climbed rose trees into the sky to follow their mother. They spent their days spinning and embroidering, as well as helping **Saulė** decorate the heavens, although sometimes they begged to be allowed to play rather than work. When they stayed home, they kept the house clean; sometimes they ran off to Germany to play with the young gods. One daughter, called **Ausrinė**, was raped by her father, the moon man, a story that forms the primary myth of the region.

A pair of twin stars, possibly her brothers, courted Saulės Meita. Such twins appear in other Indo-European myths as companions to the dawn maiden.

Their connection may represent an ancient agricultural cult, for the twins took Saulės Meita across the land on a boat, a common fertility ritual. (Balys; Beliajus; Chase; Katzenelenbogen; Landsbergis and Mills; Neuland; Zobarskas)

Veliona Ruler of the ghostly Vėlė, this goddess watched over the dead, especially those who died in battle. Pigs were sacrificed to her in funeral rituals; the oldest family member killed the pig, which was offered to Veliona, who joined the family for the dinner. Spirits of the dead went through a gate and up a hill, where they lived as though on earth, in homes and families. At a festival in October that honored Veliona, bath-houses and drying houses were set aside for ghostly visitors. (Trinkūnas)

Žemyna No Baltic person spit upon the soil, cursed it, or hit it, for it was the goddess Žemyna. Every celebration began with an invocation and libation to her. Starting with the head of the household, each person thanked the earth, then poured out a ladle of beer. Every spring, a festival celebrated her. Loaves were baked from the last sheaves of the previous harvest, then plowed into the earth. This never happened before the first thunderstorm, which was understood as Žemyna's mate fertilizing her in preparation for a new season of growth.

Even more important was the harvest feast, when a priestess carried twenty-seven pieces of bread to the storehouse, together with a portion of a sacrificed pig. There she prayed for abundance. Because life came from her, Žemyna was honored at every birth, when the soil was kissed and food offerings laid in front of stones, tied to tree boughs, or cast into flow-ing water. (Gimbutas 1989, 1999; Trinkūnas; Jurgines; Landsbergis and Mills)

THE CELTIC WORLD

The term "Celt" is deceptively exact, for there was no centralized Celtic culture. Rather, we find many groups, such as the Belgae, Icini, and Brigantes, who spoke related languages. A Celt was someone who spoke a Celtic language. Beyond that, little can be definitely asserted, especially because we have no early writings from these people, only writings about them from other Europeans. Defining the role of goddess in Celtic cultures requires interpretation of texts by their enemies and descendants, graphic art from invaded lands, and isolated objects and buildings.

Celtic languages are part of the Indo-European language family. Today, six Celtic tongues are known: Irish and Scottish, both called Gaelic; Manx, Welsh, Breton, and Cornish. These languages broke off from an original tongue spoken in central Europe nearly 4,000 years ago, when proto-Celts developed the Hallstatt and La Tène cultures. From central Europe, they settled western Europe (continental Celts) and the islands off the coasts (insular Celts).

Little information exists today about pre-Roman Celtic religion, but far more is known about the products of Roman invasion. Soon, many Celtic divinities bore Latin names, sometimes with the original name added as a title. Most sculptures of Celtic goddesses come from areas once under Roman control, but most written documents come from areas outside the domain of Rome. Because these were oral cultures, documentation of myths did not occur until Irish Christian monks wrote down poems and epics of the old gods. Even where myths were not written down, they survived. In the late nineteenth century, stories were recorded that had been retold for centuries. Goddesses connected with specific festivals or with landscape features were especially likely to have been remembered.

What we know of Celtic religion is thus a combination of archaeology, possibly fallible texts, and the oral tradition. From this we learn of an otherworld, contiguous with our world, where deities dwell. Rather than being arranged in a hierarchical order, the divinities were arranged in families, descendants of a goddess whose fecundity made life possible. Sometimes called a "mother goddess," she was sometimes the ancestor of the tribe, at other times of the gods themselves. Her name in myths is usually Danu or Anu or Dôn, which has been connected with a hypothesized central European goddess *Danu, whose name survives in such rivers as the Danube and the Don. Although she was a goddess of land, the mother goddess also ruled rivers that watered the soil. Thus most rivers in Celtic lands are, even today, named for goddesses.

Whether the primacy of goddesses affected the lives of human women is hotly contested. Evidence suggests that Celtic women fought alongside male warriors, queens led armies into battle, and women were poets and druids. Some scholars dismiss such evidence as describing occasional extraordinary women. This area is one of the most contentious in contemporary scholarship, with some scholars offering evidence of matrilineal succession and others contending that the Celts were entirely patriarchal. In either case, the myths show strong, vital female figures.

Contemporary American goddess religion often claims Celtic heritage, if only through the use of the four Celtic holidays of Samhain (November 1), Imbolc (February 1), Beltane (May 1), and Lughnasa (August 1). In traditional Celtic countries, some revivals of native religions have occurred in recent years, with folk festivals and similar events often including invocations of old gods and/or revivals of religiously based folkways. As many Celtic folkways connected to the culture's goddesses were transferred to saints under Christianity, feminists have also reclaimed some Christian figures and holidays in a quest to revive Celtic spirituality.

CONTINENTAL CELTIC AND BRETON PANTHEON

Abnoba The many rivers Avon bear Abnoba's name. She was associated with the source of the river Danube (see Irish **Danu**) and ruled the watershed of the Black Forest. Images of Abnoba show a woodland goddess accompanied by stags and hunting dogs. The Romans assimilated this goddess to **Diana**. (MacCulloch; Pennick 2000)

Adecina This water goddess was honored in the Celtic region of Spain, near contemporary Castle Túron. Her symbols were the goat and cypress tree. (Bonnefoy 1)

Adsagsona The "weaver of spells" and "she who seeks out" (the latter title perhaps referring to her power to find the object of a spell or curse), this goddess was honored in the Aquitaine. She was invoked in approximately 90 CE on a lead tablet found near the town of Larzac, inscribed by women performing a secret ritual. "Behold: the magic of women, their underworld names, the prophecy of the seer who weaves this magic," the tablet says, calling upon Adsagsona for a binding spell. The tablet has been interpreted as evidence of women who, under magical names, gathered in secret groups to work with a *vidlua* (oracle or prophetess) to perform spells and divination. (Freeman; Koch)

Andarta Tutelary goddess of the Voconces, Andarta is believed to be similar to the war goddess Andraste. However, the syllable *art* is found in the name of several Celtic bear divinities, so Andarta may have been a goddess of wilderness. (MacCulloch)

Arduinna The forest of Ardennes, which once covered a vast area of France, Germany, Belgium, and Luxembourg, was named for this goddess of wilderness, conflated in early times to both Roman **Diana** and Greek **Artemis**. She patrolled her forest on a wild boar, demanding that any hunters who killed animals leave monetary payment for their catch. Arduinna ("height" or "highland") was honored with sacrifices of animal meat at festivals. (Green 1986; Herm; MacCulloch)

Artio The *art* in her name refers to bears; the syllable is often found in names of wilderness divinities. Artio was known in Britain and Gaul, while in Switzerland and France she was called **Andarta**, also known as a goddess of war. In function as well as name, Artio resembles Greek **Artemis**, also depicted as a bear. Bern, where the goddess's image was discovered, continues to host a folk ritual in which bears are raised in pits. (Green 1989)

Aveta Celtic water goddesses took two major forms: as healers and as ancestral mothers whose rivers marked the limits of their children's territory. Aveta combined both aspects, for she was honored at the famous healing spring of Trier in Germany, where her depiction as a nursing mother suggests a tribal ancestress. Clay figures of women bearing fruit, accompanied by dogs or babies, were left at the spring in Aveta's honor. (Green 1986)

Belisama Celtic divinities tended to be local, but Belisama ("brightness") was found in Britain and on the Continent. In the former, she was associated with the river Ribble, which once bore her name (see **Peg O'Nell**). Some see Belisama as a corollary to **Brigit**. (MacCulloch)

Berecynthia Early Christian author Gregory of Tours described this goddess being conveyed, covered with veils, by wagon through fields each spring or whenever the harvest seemed in jeopardy. Images of Berecynthia were among the "pagan idols" smashed by Martin of Tours, who campaigned against Celtic religion. There may have been another Berecynthia. A mountain in Anatolia has this name, which was used as a title of **Cybele** (see Southeastern Europe). (MacCulloch)

Blondine Folktales often hide ancient goddess myths, as with Blondine, a mysterious, powerful figure. A cursed human named Cado had to find Blondine in order to end his misfortune. No one knew the way to Blondine's land, but Cado heard crows discussing the route. Hitching a ride on one, he found Blondine sitting beside a well beneath a tree. Cado wooed Blondine away from her magician father, then proved faithless once they had returned to this world, forgetting her after losing the ring that pledged their love. As he was about to marry another woman, Blondine arrived, bearing the magical ring. When Cado put it on his finger, his memory and his love returned. (Luzel)

Brunissen In legends of Provence, a fairy named the Brown Queen lived in the enchanted forest of Brocéliande. Orphaned and alone, she exhausted herself from weeping, and for seven years only birdsong could ease her sorrow. Finally a hero of the Round Table (Jaufré or Giflet) drew Brunissen away from her grief, after which they lived in her palace at Monbrun. Motifs in this legend suggest Brunissen derives from a bird goddess similar to Welsh **Rhiannon**. (Markale 1986)

Dahut Dahut's father was the Christian king Gradlon, but Dahut was pagan. With the help of the **Korrigans**, Dahut built a city in the sea, Ys, surrounded by immense walls punctuated by sea gates. Opening them would flood the city. Dahut wore the key to these gates around her neck. Her palace was unimaginably wealthy, because Dahut harnessed dragons that brought her riches from shipwrecks. Other homes rose within Ys's golden walls as merchants were attracted to its wealth. But these citizens turned selfish, closing the city against the poor.

The court harbored a secret. Each night, Dahut offered a mask to a handsome visitor so he might slip up to her bedroom. But when the man tried to depart, he found the mask grew tighter until it strangled him. Daily, servants hauled away a body.

Finally Dahut met her match. Dancing at a ball with an unknown prince, she heard him call for a tune on the pipes. She found herself whirling faster, unable to stop. The people around her danced wildly. Her partner, a sea demon, stole the key to the seawalls and opened the gates. As the horrified residents danced, water poured into the city. Gradlon rode to Dahut's rescue, but when she mounted, his horse refused to move. A monk urged him to leave Dahut behind, so Gradlon pushed her into the turbulent sea. Some tales say Dahut lives, a mermaid luring men to doom. (*Breton*; Ellis 1988; Guyot; Markale 2000)

Damona Damona's name, "divine cow," suggests a goddess of domestic animals. The consort of two gods, she may have been polyandrous. Sites dedicated to her are found in Burgundy; a carving shows her crowned with grain and holding a serpent (see **Sirona**). (Billington)

Deae Matres These "Divine Mothers" bear a collective Latin name, their original names having been lost. The Mothers represented land's fertility. Sculptures show two or three goddesses together, holding sacred objects like sacrificial knives and offering plates. They wore round halo-like headdresses. The central goddess stood while the others sat, or sat while they stood. The connection of these goddesses with **Dea Nutrix** ("nourishing goddess") is unclear. The Mothers were occasionally depicted in the form called pseudo-Venus ("false **Venus**"; see Rome), a single woman holding symbols of fertility. (Billington; Buchholtz; MacAnna)

Epona Although most Celtic divinities were known only in one place, scores of altars dedicated to Epona and hundreds of statues have been discovered across Europe and Britain. This devotion may have resulted from Epona's popularity among Roman legionnaires; she was the only Celtic goddess to be granted a festival (December 18) in the Roman calendar. No narrative remains about her, but it is clear that she was connected with horses, as her name ("mare") and sculptures (astride or surrounded by horses) reveal.

Epona's worship reached into homes. Many small altars have been found, showing a maternal Epona surrounded by foals. She carried an offering plate, sheaves of wheat, or a cornucopia, suggesting a goddess of abundance. She was also associated with the end of life. Sculptures show a funerary raven or an otherworldly dog, holding keys to the otherworld. (Brown; Buchholtz; Dexter 1980; Green 1993, 1989; Markale 1997; Ross 1967; Henig; Webster)

Icovellauna Inscriptions to this goddess were found at Metz and Trier, but her legend is lost. As the first syllable (*Ico-*) of her name meant "water," she was presumably a water divinity, probably the healing goddess whose octagonal shrine was excavated at the spring of Sablon. Although she is honored in Germany, her name is Celtic. (Billington and Green)

Januaria Her name may derive from the same source as that of the Roman Janus, god of literal and figurative thresholds. But the goddess shown in the healing shrine in Burgundy, southwestern France, was Celtic. She was depicted playing a pipe, suggesting that musical performance formed part of her ritual. (Billington and Green)

Korrigans In Breton folk belief, lustful women—descendants of women Druids—lived in the water, seducing men and drowning them. Because of their devotion to pagan ways, Korrigans were interested in seducing priests. Less than two feet tall, light skinned and golden haired, the Korrigans had slender translucent wings. While they could live in any water, they preferred running streams. Some Breton legends describe Korrigans as human souls that, because of a tragic death, were doomed to wander the earth. More typically they are seen as nonhuman, with their name used as a synonym for the entire fairy race.

Korrigans were visible less frequently in even-numbered than odd-numbered centuries; they were seen at twilight rather than in the daytime. Some Korrigans guarded treasure, while others tickled horses and caused nightmares. They derived pleasure from circle dances within or near megalithic shrines. (Evans-Wentz)

Marcassa Breton legend says princess Marcassa lived in a distant land, with a magical bird who could cure ills. Even though his two strong older brothers disappeared while trying to find Marcassa, the bumbling prince Luduenn set off in hopes of helping his king back to health. Soon he learned the truth about his brothers: they gave up their quest so they could enjoy a wild life far from home. Although they stole Luduenn's money, he was not deterred. His virtue was rewarded, for he found Marcassa and her magical bird. He stole the bird, but along the way stole a kiss from Marcassa. Miraculously, the kiss made her pregnant. When her son was a year old, the princess set out in search of his father. At his palace, she found that her magical bird had missed her so much he refused to heal the king. In her presence the bird sang joyously and the king was soon well. Soon after, Marcassa and Luduenn were installed as king and queen. (Luzel)

Melusine Goddesses demoted to fairies appear occasionally in continental Celtic legend, most notably in the story of Melusine, daughter of the sea-sprite Pressina and a human male. Typical of fairy wives, Pressina put a taboo on her husband: that he never see her in childbed. But while she was delivering triplets, Pressina's husband rushed into the room. Pressina disappeared, taking the children with her.

The triplets were Melusine, Meliot, and Palatina. Pressina reared them on a fairy island, beautiful and sterile. Melusine was an angry girl who held her father responsible for every discomfort she felt. When she was a young woman, she left the otherworld to entrap her father and his attendants inside a mountain. Far from being grateful, however, Melusine's mother cursed her. Thereafter, Melusine would always be a snake on Sundays. (Variants of the story say Pressina was herself part serpent)

Like her mother, Melusine found love with a human, Raymond (Raimondin) of Poitou. And like her mother, she put limitations on her husband: in this case, that he never enter her room on Sunday. But Raymond could not keep the vow. Melusine disappeared in fury and thereafter haunted his family as a death warner (see Irish, **Banshee**). (Foubister; Sax; Skeat)

Minerva Medica The Romans assimilated the Greek warrior goddess **Athena** to their healer **Minerva**, producing a helmeted goddess concerned with medicine, learning, and crafts. This figure was further assimilated to the healing goddesses whom the Romans encountered in Celtic lands, especially water goddesses whose energy was located in the headwaters of rivers and in thermal springs. The Romans called these goddesses Minerva Medica, the "Minerva of healing." In most cases, the original Celtic name was lost, as with the goddess carved into a quarry near the river Dee in Chester, where she was depicted with owl and **Gorgon**'s head, symbols of Athena. But Minerva Vitrix (a Celtic word meaning "victor" or "victorious") was inscribed on relief carvings of a helmet-crowned female head, while **Belisama**'s name also survives. The most famous Celtic Minerva was **Sul**. (Green 1983; MacAnna 1987)

Morrigain The mermaid who haunted the shores off Brittany, seducing sailors to die on her dangerous rocks by singing sweet songs, descends from an earlier life-and-death sea goddess. Morrigain is especially associated with the Bay of Douaranez, where the pagan princess **Dahut** built her palace and was killed. Sailors were warned to carry a crucifix or other warding amulet when they sailed past Morrigain's rocks. Despite the apparent similarity of name, Morrigain has no known connection with the Irish **Mórrígan**. (MacCulloch; Markale 2000)

Nehalennia Dozens of monuments and inscriptions to this goddess of the Netherlands have been found, but no myths survive. Although her worship was popular among Celts and Romans until late imperial times, Nehalennia vanished for more than a millennium. Then in 1647, a storm hit the island of Walcheren, shifting the dunes to reveal an enormous second- or third-century CE temple to Nehalennia. Unfortunately, 200 years later, the temple was destroyed by fire. Then, on April 4, 1979, a fisherman working the Oosterschelde estuary discovered another shrine to Nehalennia. Since then, almost a hundred artifacts have been found in the area.

Nehalennia may have begun as a local ancestral goddess, later worshipped by sailing crews who prayed to her for safety. Much of her iconography is nautical: boats, oars, rudders, shells, fish, dolphins, and sea monsters. She was typically shown as a strong young woman wearing a cape and a round cap. Usually she was seated, although sometimes she rested her foot on the prow of a ship or hauled a boat by a rope.

Nehalennia was often depicted with a dog, guardian of the dead. Nehalennia (perhaps "woman who steers") steered her devotees home to the otherworld, an island in the western sea. But Nehalennia was also associated with fecundity, depicted with baskets of grain and fruit.

As goddess of commerce, Nehalennia oversaw grain-filled ships. She may have been invoked for heavy, thus profitable, harvests. In addition, Nehalennia may have been envisioned as a goddess of the world's journey through the seasons. (Buchholtz; Green 1995; Hondius-Crone)

Nemetona The Celtic word "nemeton" described a shrine or temple. These were not buildings, for the Celts did not worship indoors, but in the open, often among trees. Nemetona's name has been translated as "goddess of the shrine" and "she of the sacred grove," but it is not clear what her role was, for no myth survives. She may have embodied the holiness of sacred spaces, such as the hallowed springs of Bath, where she was honored. (Green 1986; MacCulloch; Squire)

Rosmerta The "Great Provider," Rosmerta was goddess of abundance in northeastern Gaul and the Rhineland. She may have had a healing aspect, for she resided in springs and wells, locations of healing to the Celts. She was depicted holding a cauldron, a purse, or an offering platter. Her myth and rituals are unknown, although it is clear she was popular, for with **Epona** she was the goddess most frequently mentioned in continental Celtic inscriptions. (Henig; Green 1995; Powell; Sjoestedt; Webster)

Sequana The source of France's great river, the Seine, was called by the Romans Fontes Sequanae ("springs of Sequana") after the river's tutelary goddess. A Roman-era shrine, near Dijon, yielded a trove of coins bearing images of the goddess as a crowned woman, arms aloft, mounted in a boat shaped like a duck holding a berry in its beak. While other Celtic goddesses (see **Rhiannon**, **Mórrígan**) were associated with birds, Sequana was the only one who had a waterbird as her emblem. She may have combined healing qualities of river goddesses with otherworldly aspects of the bird goddess. Another Gaulish river goddess, Nantosuelta, is similarly depicted with a bird, in her case the raven, symbol of death. As river divinities in Celtic lands appear in folklore as devouring spirits (see British **Peg O'Nell**), this imagery may refer to the danger of drowning. Alternatively, river goddesses may have been cosmic life-and-death goddesses, directly connected with the afterlife.

Sequana's healing powers can be recognized from many bronze and silver models of legs, eyes, breasts, and other body parts that were deposited in the river source. Such offerings usually indicated the organ in need of healing. She may have been very important; Romans did not change her name to a Latin one. (Green 1986, 1989; MacAnna)

Sirona Inscriptions throughout France invoke this healing goddess, whose name has been translated as "star." She carried snakes and eggs, suggesting a connection to rebirth and fertility. This goddess may be identical to the similarly named Divona, whose name survives in the river Devon in Britain. (Green 1989; MacAnna; Pennick 2000)

IRISH AND SCOTTISH PANTHEON

Achall A princess of the northern province of Ulster, Achall gave her name to the hill of Skreen near Tara, Ireland's seat of royal power, after she died there. The man who killed Achall's brother brought his head back and, upon seeing it, Achall died of sorrow. (Gwynn 1)

Achtan Mothers of heroes often conceive under unusual circumstances, and such was the case for Achtan. The high king Art stopped to rest on the way to a battle where, it had been prophesied, he would die. He chose the home of Achtan's father, who added a prophecy: Whoever slept with Achtan would have lasting fame. The king went to Achtan's bed, where the couple conceived the hero Cormac. The next day, after arranging fosterage for the child, Art went to die.

Nine months later, Achtan set off to her child's foster home, but she was stopped by a storm. Achtan gave birth in the open, then stumbled away to find help. While she was gone, a mother wolf took the baby away to rear. Years later, a robust man walked out of the forest, Achtan's son, now grown. Reunited mother and child traveled to Tara, seat of the high kings, where Cormac took his father's throne and Achtan lived the remainder of her life in regal splendor. (Colum; Wavle and Burke)

Aeval Ireland's southwestern province, Munster, was associated with the feminine. Among many fairy queens there, Aeval was the most prominent. Her name appears on natural features throughout

County Clare. Ancestral mother or tutelary goddess of the O'Briens, Aeval came to the clan founder, her lover Brian Boru, on the eve of the Battle of Clontarf in 1014, warning he would not survive the battle. Foreknowledge of death made Brian fearless and therefore victorious. Afterward Aeval served as a **Banshee**, chief of Clare's two dozen banshees. In recent years, residents claim to have seen her on Inchiquin Lake, warning of disasters. Aeval's most famous appearance was in "The Midnight Court," a debate between men and women as to which sex least satisfied the other. Serving as judge, Aeval found in the women's favor. (Bourke; Dames 1992; Gregory 1905; Lenihan 1991; Logan 1981; Merriman; Ó hógáin 1991)

Aífe The name Aífe appears several times in Irish legend. One Aífe trained heroes on her island fortress, which she shared with **Scáthách**, her sister or rival. Meeting Cúchulainn, Aífe challenged him. Despite enormous effort, neither could best the other. Realizing she had met her equal, Aífe agreed to help Cúchulainn learn martial arts. Although they had shared a bed, Cúchulainn abandoned Aífe to return to **Emer**. Aífe gave Cúchulainn his greatest weapon, the Gai Bolga. She also bore his son Connla, later killed by his father.

Another Aífe changed **Fionnuala** and her four brothers into swans who lived for 900 years. She may be the same figure as the bewitched woman who became a crane and, upon her death, provided feathered skin for a bag in which the letters of the alphabet lived. (Bourke; Ellis 1988; Gwynn; Gregory 1905; Herm; Hull; Joyce; Kinsella; MacCulloch; Squire.)

Ailinn Ailinn, princess of Leinster, fell in love with Baile, prince of Ulster. Because their lands were far apart, they met midway. A malicious fairy told the prince Ailinn was dead, whereupon he died of grief. Ailinn, hearing the news, fell down dead herself. The lovers were buried together, and from their graves grew trees with entwined branches. From his yew and her apple, poets carved tablets upon which they engraved love stories. When the tablets were finished, the king held them near each other. They clapped together and could never be separated. (Bourke; Hull 1898)

Ailna When the warrior Fionn mac Cumhaill killed Ailna's husband, she vowed revenge. Shape-shifting into the form of a deer, she appeared before the Fianna to tempt them into a hunt. They took the bait and a druidical mist surrounded them so they could not see deer or forest. Separated from his band, Fionn fell into Ailna's power. She held him captive in a dungeon for many days until the Fianna found and freed him, killing Ailna in the process. (Gregory 1905; Joyce)

Áine The fairy queen Áine was a folkloric memory of the region's ancestral goddess, **Anu** (**Danu**). For her feast, celebrated on midsummer night, farmers drove their herds up her hill, Knockainy, waving torches and praying for protection. She was associated with inspiration and madness, for she owned a stone chair near Lough Gur that attracted the insane. If they sat there, they would either recover their wits or be mad forever. If a sane person sat there three times, the result would be insanity or brilliance.

Áine loved the sea god Manannán mac Lir, sometimes described as her father. Among Áine's mortal lovers was Etar, who died of thwarted love, and Maurice, Earl of Desmond, by whom Áine had a son, Gerald. She warned the earl that he must never show surprise at their son's behavior, but when Gerald shrank suddenly, Maurice yelled. Mother and child disappeared, and Gerald now lives in Lough Gur, riding around it every seven years on a white horse. Áine's descendants called themselves Geraldines or Fitzgeralds, claiming sovereignty through connection with the goddess.

In the county of Donegal, another Áine was said to have disappeared to escape a savage father and thereafter spent her time spinning sunbeams. A folk verse from the area has Áine telling discontented wives how to weaken their husbands. Donegal's Áine, like other fairy queens, stole pipers and other musicians to play for her dances.

Finally, a legend in the Fenian Cycle tells of Áine, daughter of a smith, who bore two sons to the hero Fionn mac Cumhaill. Áine and her sister **Milucra** squabbled over who would enjoy the attentions of the hero. Áine spied him first, so Milucra enchanted a lake, then lured Fionn there, claiming she had dropped her ring into the water. Fionn swam out to retrieve it. When he returned, his hair had turned white. Áine had sworn never to sleep with a gray-haired man, so Milucra hoped to win him. But Fionn was now stooped with age, much to the consternation of his warriors, who forced Milucra to restore Fionn's youth. His hair stayed silver. (Dames; Evans-Wentz; Graves; Gregory 1905; Joyce; Logan 1981; MacCulloch; MacNeill; O'Kelly; Rees and Rees; Yeats 1973; Zucchelli.)

Airmid Airmid was an herbalist, a skill she learned from her father, Dian Cécht. When King Nuada lost his arm in battle, Dian Cécht built him a silver prosthesis, while Airmid and her brother Miach made one of flesh. Envious of his children's talent, Dian Cécht killed Miach. Tending her brother's grave, Airmid noticed herbs carpeting it and began to pick them. She would have healed humanity's ailments, but Dian Cécht destroyed Airmid's collection. (Cross and Slover; Squire)

Almu Each of Ireland's ancient provinces had a sacred center; that of the eastern province of Leinster was the low bog-encircled Hill of Allen, where an invisible entrance to the otherworld opened. Almu, goddess of the hill, was called "all white" but is otherwise obscure. (Dames; Gwynn 2; O'Rahilly; Rees and Rees)

Anu Anu has no real mythology, although she is named by the early writer Cormac as "mother of the gods of Ireland." Her name seems to mean "abundance," perhaps indicating an earth goddess. In addition to being connected or confused with **Danu**, Anu has been seen as identical to **Áine**. Welsh mythology has a figure named Ána or Anu who, after Christianization, became conflated with Saint Anne, grandmother of Jesus, to whom holy wells are dedicated. In Britain, Anu gave her name to a river. **Black Annis** may be another form of this goddess. (MacCulloch; Rhŷs; MacNeill; Squire; Westropp)

Badb Badb ("crow") appeared as one of three phantom queens, the others being **Mórrígan** and **Macha**. Badb also appeared with Mórrígan, **Medb**, Fea ("hateful"), and **Nemain** ("venomous"), the entire group bearing Badb's name. Badb screamed over battlefields, inciting soldiers to bring her human meat, for which she was called "red mouthed." She appeared standing with one foot on each side of a stream, washing the bloodied clothing of those who would die. Among continental Celts, the horse-mounted Cathubodua may have been ancestral goddess to the Buduogenos, "people of Bodua." In Britain, Tacitus described black-robed women druids who imitated Badb, screaming to incite warriors during battle. (Dexter; Green 1995; Koch; Ó hÓgáin 1999)

Banba Invading Ireland, the Milesians encountered three goddesses, first Banba, then **Fódla** and **Ériu**. Although the goddesses seem to form a trinity, they may have been unrelated. Banba was a magician, against whom the Milesians sang spells. Her emblem was the pig, symbol of prosperity, suggesting a goddess of abundance. (Cross and Slover; Koch; Hull 1906; MacAlister; MacNeill)

Banshee Although known in several lands, the banshee ("fairy woman") was most widely reported in Ireland. The banshee's wail, predicting a coming death, recalls the ancient practice of wild screaming ("keening") whereby women mourned the loss of a loved one. Occasionally the banshee was seen, usually wearing otherworld colors (green or red) but occasionally swathed in somber gray or unearthly white. Sometimes she was seen combing her hair. She could be either a young woman or an aged hag. But her appearance was less notable than her voice, which rang with sorrow as she bemoaned the dead.

Not all families had banshees. Some sources claim only the oldest families in a region had a banshee. Among those mentioned are the O'Briens, Magraths, Hynes, and Faheys. Other sources claim only five families were entitled to banshee attendance: O'Brien, O'Connor, O'Neill, O'Grady, and Kavanagh. Yet another list claims the banshees served the MacCarthys, Magraths, O'Neills, O'Rileys, O'Sullivans, O'Reardons, and O'Flahertys. A commonly stated idea is that no family lacking a "Mac" or "O" in the name (signs of ancient origin) could have a banshee, but many lists defy that rule. Personal names are given to some family banshees, such as Áine to the O'Briens' and Clídna to the MacCarthys'; in those cases the banshee is also a clan ancestor. Banshees may have originated in divine mothers.

Whether the banshee could be heard only by the family of the doomed, or by others, is disputed. Tales describe multiple banshees wailing at the death of an important person. Sites of great tragedies like battles and shipwrecks may be forever haunted by banshees. While some tales describe the banshee as tied to a specific community, others see her as mobile, able to follow members of an emigrating family. Thus banshee stories are told in Canada, Australia, and America.

Another specialized banshee, the Bean Nighe was a woman who died in childbirth leaving laundry unfinished. From then until the time she would have died of old age, she appeared as a green-cloaked, one-toothed specter washing linens in a stream. Legend has it that if a witness sucked on one of the Bean Nighe's long breasts, she or he would be granted any wish. A prophetic figure, the Bean Nighe would answer three questions of any passerby, provided three questions were answered truthfully in turn. The Bean Nighe is a folkloric version of the goddess **Badb**, prophesying death in battle as she washed the bloodied clothing of those doomed to die.

The Washer was generally prescient, able to see more in the future than just imminent death. Thus if one caught a glimpse of her before she noticed, she had to provide a prophecy. But such fortune-telling could be risky, because the Washer could injure an observer, inflicting broken bones by waving her laundry in the air. (Beck; Colum; Croker 1862; Evans-Wentz; Gregory 1970; Lenihan 1987; Logan 1981; MacDougall; McKay 1969; McNeill; Spence 1972; Westropp; Wilde 1902; Yeats 1973)

Béare The rocky far southwestern peninsula of Béare in Ireland derives its name from this Spanish princess who was probably originally a goddess of the land. She is often conflated with the **Cailleach** Bhéirre or "hag of Béare," a goddess of the pre-Celtic people associated with the area. Her petrified remains can be seen on a roadside on the north side of the peninsula.

She had two forms: Büi ("yellow one") and Duineach ("strong one"), although she also appears in a trinity with two other land hags of nearby peninsulas, the Cailleach Bolus and Celleach Corca Dhuibhne. The same name, and presumably the same character, appears in southern County Armagh, where she was said to have taken the hero Fionn mac Cumhaill as a lover. Stones connected with them, found around the countryside, were traditionally whitewashed each spring. (Ellis 1995; MacNeill; Zucchelli)

Bébinn Several Irish figures bear this name. One, goddess of birth, was the sister of **Bóand**. Another was a giant from Maiden's Land who traveled surrounded by magical birds. She escaped a brutal husband, only to be pursued and killed. (Graves; Gregory 1905; Rolleston)

Bebo A tiny fairy, Bebo traveled with her husband to Ulster, which they believed was populated by giants. Diminutive Bebo caught the king's eye. Despite physical challenges (his phallus was bigger than her body), Bebo became the king's mistress for a year, until her husband offered magical shoes to gain her back. (Rolleston)

Becfhola One of the few heroines to have a significant text devoted to her, Becfhola is the protagonist of the *Tochmarc Becfhola* (The Wooing of Becfhola). As queen of the sacred hill of Tara, Becfhola ("a small fortune") represented sovereignty of land. So when she grew unhappy with the king, Diarmait, and fond of the hero Crimthann, the governance of the land was cast into question. Intent upon an assignation with Crimthann, she met instead the fairy Flann, with whom she had a bliss-filled affair. As time passes faster in fairyland than in our world, she was able to resume her throne without anyone realizing she had been absent. (Bourke et al.; Cross and Slover)

Bé Chuma A member of the Tuatha Dé Danann (see **Danu**), Bé Chuma was renowned for her sexual appetite. She left her powerful husband in the otherworld for a lover, for which she was banished to the surface world. There she married the high king but fell in love with her stepson, whose wife demanded Bé Chuma's ostracism. (Cross and Slover; Rees and Rees; MacCulloch 1996)

Berba In southeastern Ireland, three rivers irrigate the land; together, they are the "three sisters," watery embodiments of goddesses. Longest is the Barrow, named for Berba. Her sisters were Eoryus (the Noir) and Suirus (the Suir). The name also appears as an alternative to **Cesair**, first human resident of Ireland. (Cambrensis)

Bláthnat "Little flower" was the daughter of Midir, high king of the Irish fairies. Bláthnat possessed a magic cauldron hitched to three cows that brought abundance wherever she passed, suggesting she was originally a goddess of abundance. But woman, cauldron, and cows were stolen from the otherworld by competing heroes, one of whom held Bláthnat captive. Her legend is similar to that of Welsh **Blodeuwedd**, for Bláthnat collaborated with her captor's enemy to cause his death. (Cross and Slover; MacCulloch 1911)

Bóand Bóand's name means "woman of white cows" or "radiant cow," yet her myth does not mention cows. She may be related to the goddess of abundance, **Bó Find**, but is best known as a river goddess. The important river Boyne was formed when Bóand visited a forbidden well in search of wisdom. Nine hazel trees that shaded the well bore nuts of wisdom. A salmon swam there, eating nuts and growing wise. When Bóand approached the well, it overflowed and chased her across the land. As she reached the sea, Bóand drowned, leaving the river bearing her name.

Ireland's most famous ancient monument is the Bru na Bóinne, or "palace of Bóand," a tumulus built nearly 6,000 years ago into which the winter solstice sun annually penetrates. There Bóand entertained the god Dagda, who lured her away from her consort, Nechtan. To hide their affair, Dagda caused the sun to stand still for nine months so Bóand could bear their child, the god of poetry, Aongus. In addition to ruling at the Bru na Bóinne, Bóand was connected with another great Irish monument, the hill of Tara, which is replete with sites named for the cow goddess. Her connection with significant sites puts Bóand in the category of **Brigit** and **Medb** as one of Ireland's most important goddesses. (Bourke; Cooney; Cross and Slover; Jackson; Gwynn 2, 3; Koch; Logan 1980; Slavin; Squire)

Bó Find In primordial times, when Ireland was barren, this white cow appeared from the western sea with the red cow Bó Ruadh and the black cow Bó Dhu. Each headed in a different direction: Bó Dhu went south, Bó Ruadh north, and Bó Find to the island's center, where she gave birth to twin calves from whom descended all cattle. (Wilde)

Brigit Because of the local nature of Celtic divinities, few were honored across a wide geographical area. But there is evidence of a widely known goddess with a name or title meaning "high one." In Britain, the Brigantes honored a goddess, Brigantia. In Gaul, we find Brigindo or Brigindu, of whom little is known

181

except that she was invoked to encourage abundant harvests. At a thermal spring in southern France, Brixia was honored.

In Ireland, Scotland, and Wales and on the Isle of Man, Brigit appears as a central goddess. Her symbols were cattle, fire, and water; her holy day, February 1. A member of the Tuatha Dé Danann (see **Danu**), Brigit was daughter of the god of fertility, Dagda, and mother of the hero Rúadán, at whose death she invented keening. She appears in three related forms, as goddess of healing, smithcraft, and poetry. It is unclear whether her worshippers knew three separate goddesses named Brigit, each with her own specific domain, or whether all were one goddess.

Ritual devotion to Brigit, centered on sacred fire and holy wells, continued after the goddess was "converted" to a Christian saint. Documents suggest that a college of priestesses served Saint Brigit. Giraldus Cambrensis reported that nuns in Kildare tended an undying ashless flame, a ritual identical to that offered to **Sul**. Not long after Giraldus made his 1184 report, clergy dowsed the fires. In 1988, the foundation of the ancient temple was rediscovered in Kildare. Not long after, the Brigidine sisters spearheaded an international revival of interest in Saint Brigit.

Both saint and goddess are honored on February 1, the feast of Imbolc, still celebrated in Ireland. The most widespread ritual entails praying at dawn at a holy well. Pilgrims also tie small pieces of cloth to trees nearby. In Kildare, rush crosses are hung on houses to prevent fires. In County Kerry, Biddy Boys dress in white, don straw hats, and go begging; giving to them ensures a good harvest. Other traditions include crafting dolls from rushes, laying fabric outdoors for Brigit to walk upon as the sun rises, and jumping through a circle of straw. In Scotland, Imbolc was celebrated by dressing sheaves in women's clothing and setting a wooden club beside the figure. The next morning, women looked in the ashes for an impression of Brigit's club.

Brigit may have taken on aspects of a pre-Celtic seasonal goddess. In Scotland, stories relate how the Cailleach kept Bride imprisoned in high mountains. Her son fell in love with the girl; at winter's end, they eloped. The hag chased them, causing storms. After she turned to stone, Bride was freed. (Bourke; Brenneman and Brenneman; Carmichael; Condren; Cunliffe; Danaher 1922; Delaney; Cambrensis; Ellis 1995; Koch; Logan 1980; MacAnna; Clancy; MacKinlay; MacNeill; O'Faoláin; Ó hÓgáin 1985, 1999; Wavle and Burke)

Bronach The most famous of Ireland's scenic wonders is connected to this goddess: "hag's head" (Ceann na Cailighe), the highest of the Cliffs of Moher. Local stories say Bronach ("sorrowful" or "dismal one") fell to her death off the cliff in pursuit of a young man. Other tales claim her profile is visible on the rock face. In August 1317, she appeared to local residents as a hag with gray matted hair, ulcers on her face, immense eyebrows and watery eyes over a stubbly beard. She announced herself as a member of the Tuatha Dé Danann (people of **Danu**), but the goddess or Cailleach from whom she descends is probably pre-Celtic. She was seen in the rocky Burren area of County Clare as recently as 1939. (Westropp)

Buan This woman had the power to understand her husband, Mesroeda Mac Dá Thó, even after death, by translating the faint reddening and whitening of his flesh in response to her questions. Thus Buan learned that her beloved had died of treachery. She then died from weeping. Thereafter, a hazel tree called Coll Buana grew from her grave, producing branches used in divination. She may descend from the goddess **Buanann**. Another Buan was a maiden who, desperate with love for the hero Cúchulainn, threw herself after his chariot and was killed. (Cross and Slover; Gwynn 4; Koch; MacCulloch 1996)

Buanann The early Irish glossarist Cormac called Buanann "mother of heroes"; her name has also been translated as "good mother." Little is known about this goddess or her offspring. Some early texts contrast her with **Anu**, whose children were gods, suggesting Buanann was ancestral mother to a human tribe or family. A heroine of this name appears in the Fenian Cycle as a warrior who trained the hero Fionn mac Cumhaill. (MacCulloch 1911)

Cáer Cáer appeared in dreams to Aongus, god of poetry, so he set out to find her. When he did, she was dressed as a swan with 130 golden chains around her neck. Aongus changed into a swan to join her, and the two flew off, singing so sweetly that people fell asleep for three days and three nights. (Gantz 1984; Jackson; Markale 2000; Rolleston; Sax; Squire)

Cailleach The hag goddess found in Ireland and Scotland and on the Isle of Man was probably not Celtic. She created the world by dropping rocks from her apron or by throwing boulders at a neighbor. As settlement in Ireland preceded the Celts by some 4,000 years, the Cailleach may be Ireland's oldest divinity. Her name ("veiled one") appears on some of the land's most prominent mountains, probably named in antiquity.

In Munster, the "Hag of Beare" formed islands by towing them around with a straw rope until it broke. She was a goddess of abundance, as her personal name Bói ("cow"), indicates; cows were symbols of prosperity. She lived on an island, where she rode a white, red-eared cow, colors of divine origin. On the rocky Burren, she had several names, including **Bronach**. A blue-faced woman with one eye, the Cailleach had red teeth and matted white hair. She owned a farm and hired workers with the stipulation that none would be paid who could not outwork her. Many a man died of overwork trying to keep the pace. Finally, the Cailleach's name is found on a small mountain with a prehistoric cairn directed toward the spring and fall equinoxes. Approximately forty minutes after sunrise, the sun's rays penetrate the chamber within the cairn, illuminating petroglyphs with solar or stellar references.

As harvest goddess, her name was given to the last sheaf, which was dressed in women's clothing and kept

as a charm for prosperity. She appeared during harvest as a hare. Harvesters sang or shouted as they went about their work, to "drive the Cailleach" hare forth. In Scotland, Carlin was animating spirit of the harvest; at Samhain, the Carlin sheaf warded off otherworldly visitors. On the Isle of Man, Caillagh ny Groamagh ("gloomy old woman") gathered twigs for her fire every February 1. In fine weather she gathered enough to extend winter, but if weather kept her indoors, spring came earlier. A similar figure in Britain, **Black Annis**, was connected with weather and seasonal changes.

Such legends connect the Cailleach with agriculture, but some suggest an origin in earlier society. In Scotland, a giant Cailleach lived on the milk of deer. She guarded the wilderness and its animal life, punishing hunters who killed pregnant animals by choking them with their hair. She has also been connected with the goddess of sovereignty (see **Flaith**), especially in myths where she makes a man king after he kisses her. In legends of Camelot, the Cailleach appeared as the **Loathy Lady**, who begged a kiss from handsome men; she also appears as Ragnell, alternately as hag and maiden.

The connection of the Cailleach to the **Sheela-na-Gig** is unknown, although many Sheela figures are called "cailleach." The Cailleach who appears in the story of Da Derga's Hostel, cursing a king who had broken his sacred vows, assumed positions similar to Sheela's. In Britain, the squat Grimes Grave Goddess, found in an area of prehistoric flint mines, may represent this hag divinity. Because it is nearly impossible to date rock, the origin of the tiny figure cannot be established. That the Grimes Goddess was deliberately deposited in the mine is argued by offerings found with it. The original name of the figure has been lost, and her meaning can only be the subject of conjecture. (Bourke; Campbell 1973; Danaher 1922; Green 1986; Hyde; Geddes; Long; MacAnna; MacNeill; MacKenzie 1935; McKay 1932; O'Faoláin; Paton; Spence 1972; Kiernan; McMahon and Roberts; Rees and Rees; Zucchelli)

Canola This woman of legend invented the harp, emblem of Ireland. Canola, upset over an argument with her lover, left his side to wander the night and fell asleep on the seashore to the sound of strange sweet music. When she awoke, she discovered that the music came from a natural instrument: the rib bones of a whale with sinew still attached, through which the wind sang. The discovery inspired her to build the first harp. (MacCulloch 1996)

Caolainn A holy well in County Roscommon, in Ireland's western province of Connaught, was historically said to be efficacious against eye diseases. Its powers come from this saint, probably originally a goddess, who healed herself of a self-inflicted wound. A man admired her beautiful eyes, so Caolainn, intent upon remaining celibate, gouged them out and threw them at him. Then she groped her way to the well, blindly tearing the rushes that grew along its banks and rubbing them into her bleeding eye sockets. Her eyes grew back. An almost identical story is told of the goddess **Brigit**, to whom three nearby healing wells are dedicated, suggesting Caolainn was a localized form of that divinity. (Logan 1980)

Caoránach On the important Christian site of Station Island, Saint Patrick fought the serpent Caoránach while both stood submerged in lake waters. Patrick subjugated but did not kill the serpent, who remains alive in Lough Derg. Similar stories are told of other monstrous females and the Christian patriarch. Patrick brought low the stork Corra by throwing his bell at her, after which she fell into Lough Corra. This monster goddess may derive from Celtic times, for legends link her with the hero Fionn mac Cumhaill. When the shinbones of Fionn's dead mother were thrown into Lough Derg, they came alive as Caoránach. (MacNeill)

Carman Powerful Carman was a sorceress whose three sons were Darkness, Wickedness, and Violence. Together, they blighted Ireland until the Tuatha Dé

Danann (see **Danu**) killed them. The mother was a greater challenge, falling to the powers of the sorceress Be Chille, who restored fertility, then established a festival in Carman's honor. (Gwynn 3; MacNeill)

Cathleen ní Houlihan Several folkloric names were applied to the ancient earth goddess who represented the sovereignty of Ireland. Among these were Cathleen ní Houlihan ("Cathleen, daughter of Houlihan," referring to an unknown father), who walked roads of Ireland as an old woman until heroic patriots revealed her as a young girl. As the same story is told of the **Cailleach**, they may be the same figure. Another name used for this figure was Dark Rosaleen (in Irish, Róisín Dubh), referring to the darkness of the fertile earth in spring. When she appears as an old woman she is called the Shan Van Vocht, or "the poor old woman." (Clark)

Cesair Cesair, granddaughter of Noah, escaped the Flood together with fifty women and three men. She sailed to Ireland, beyond the Flood's reach. When they disembarked, Cesair put one man in each of three groups of over a dozen women. The women's demands proved too much for two men, who died of exhaustion. The other, Cesair's mate Fintan, turned into a salmon and fled.

The names of the women who accompanied Cesair represent the world's ancestral mothers, for they included German (Germans), Espa (Spanish), Alba (British), and Gothiam (Goth). In addition to having biblical antecedents, Cesair is described as the daughter of **Banba**, while at other times she is called **Berba** or Heriu, a name similar to **Ériu**. (Cambrensis; Koch; Löffler; MacAlister)

Cethlion Irish myth tells of several invasions by supernatural races, one of which was the Fomorians, who may represent early, non-Celtic people of the island. Cethlion ("crooked tooth" or "bucktoothed") was their queen, a prophet-warrior who foresaw her people's defeat by the **Danu** but who nevertheless fought bravely and wounded one of the Danann chieftains. (MacCulloch 1911; Squire)

Chlaus Haistig In the legends of the warriors called the Fianna is the tale of this witch, who stole sleeping children until she was taken hostage by the hero Fionn mac Cumhaill. The unnamed queen whose children were stolen resembles the Welsh goddess **Rhiannon**, whose child similarly disappeared. (Kennedy)

Clídna The beautiful fairy Clídna lived inside a hill from which she went out on expeditions to kidnap young men. Clídna had affairs with Earl Gerald Fitzgerald and with Caomh, ancestor of the O'Keeffes. She also served as **banshee** to the MacCarthys, to whom she told the secret of the Blarney Stone. Goddess of sea and land, Clídna occupied offshore rocks and the ninth wave in every series, said to be larger than the rest. She ruled Tír Tairngire, the Land of Promise in the western ocean. The feckless warrior Ciabhán charmed her. One day she took him to shore to hunt but decided to stay on her boat. A wave crashed over, drowning Clídna. (Gwynn 3; Gregory 1905; Logan 1981)

Clothra Clothra, sister of **Medb**, **Eithne**, and Mugain (see **Mairenn**), bore her three brothers a son whose body was marked by red stripes, revealing the dividing point between the parts sired by different fathers. Clothra then mated with her son to produce a hero, Crimthan, born posthumously after Clothra was killed by Medb. These incestuous matings suggest an ancestral goddess, as does Clothra's appearance in mythic genealogies. (MacCulloch 1996)

Craebhnat An ash tree near the town of Doneraile in Munster is dedicated to this fairy or saint. She was sitting under the tree when she heard she would be required to marry a man she disdained, whereupon she tore out her eyes, hoping to make herself so ugly that her potential groom would turn away. The same story

is told of **Brigit**, suggesting that Craebhnat might be a localized form of that goddess. A tree near Craebhnat's was said to possess the magical quality of keeping people afloat, so emigrants took a twig with them for good luck on water journeys. (Logan 1980)

Créd Two nipple-shaped cairns cap the breast-shaped hills called the Paps of **Danu** (or **Anu**). There, the fairy queen Créd owned a palace no man had entered. Créd challenged suitors to compose a praise-song to her palace without having seen it. Only Cáel could meet the challenge, winning Créd's heart and the key to her bower. Because Cáel was pledged to fight for his king, Créd crafted a battle dress covered with spells. Her magic was powerful, but even Créd could not protect Cáel from death, whereupon Créd threw herself into her lover's grave.

Another (possibly the same) Créd was married to a king but in love with an impoverished Scottish warrior-poet, Cano. Cano pledged that they would be together when he regained his wealth. Entrusting her with a stone containing his heart, Cano set off to reclaim his kingdom. In his absence, Créd's stepson revealed her adulterous love and caused a scandal. Shamed, Créd killed herself, crushing the stone that held her lover's soul; he died shortly after. (Bourke; Ellis 1995; Gregory 1905; Logan 1981; MacNeill; O'Faoláin)

Crob Derg Little is known of this goddess who ruled an area rich with mythic significance. In the province of Munster, on the flanks of the important site called the Paps of **Danu**, bubbles a holy well dedicated to Crob Derg, "red claw." The nearby hill fort called Cahercrovdarrig ("red claw's palace") was the site of a spring ritual in which cattle were driven past the sites for purification. With two other regional goddesses, **Latiaran** and Inghean Bhuidhe (sometimes **Gobnait**), Crob Derg forms a trinity called "sisters," but the other two were Christianized into "saints," while Crob Derg remained a shadowy figure of legend. (MacNeill)

Crochan Although she appears in legend as serving-maid to the runaway queen **Étain**, Crochan herself derived from a powerful goddess. The woman, whose name means "vessel" and, in its extended form, "blood-red cup," gave birth in the cave of Oweynagat ("cave of the cats") in County Roscommon, beneath the hill fort dedicated to her daughter, the warrior-queen **Medb**. Today the cave appears only as a damp but impressive stalactite-studded chamber, but Crochan saw it as a beautiful palace and lived there after her daughter moved aboveground. The fact that Medb's rath and the surrounding impressive city were named Crúachan suggests Crochan may have originally been goddess of the region. (Gwynn 3)

Danu The most famous of Ireland's mythic races was the Tuatha Dé Danann, "people of the goddess Danu," later diminished to "fairies" called the Daoine Sidhe ("Danu's fairy folk"). Though her children's exploits are well known, less is known about Danu. Many connect Danu with Indo-European goddesses of similar name, perhaps descended from an original named *Dánuv ("flowing one") or *Dan ("knowledge"). Danu may have arrived with the Celts in approximately 400 BCE.

The renowned Paps, two breast-shaped mountains bearing Danu's name, are also called the Paps of **Anu**. The easily confused goddesses may represent different cultural strata. Some texts call Danu the daughter of the god of abundance. She may be the same as Danann, daughter of the wilderness goddess **Flidais**, or identical to the obscure Donand, known as mother of three heroes. (Ellis 1995; Graves; Squire; MacCulloch 1996; Westropp)

Dealgnaid The invader Partholón set off to conquer Ireland, abandoning his wife Dealgnaid to a servant. While Partholón satisfied his territorial urges, Dealgnaid satisfied her sexual ones. Partholón begged his wife to return, which she did, becoming an ancestral mother. (Rolleston)

Dechtire From the Ulster capital at Emain **Macha**, Dechtire and fifty companions vanished. Years later, a horde of birds appeared, devouring everything. Facing famine, warriors attacked the birds, but they flew faster than horses could gallop. The birds, tied together by silver chains and led by a bird in a silver necklace, flew southward. The heroes followed, and two, Briccriu and Fergus, found an abandoned child. Brought to court, he grew up to be the hero Cúchulainn, Dechtire's son.

The swan maiden Dechtire had borne Cúchulainn parthenogenetically. Seeing a worm in a glass of wine, Dechtire recognized the chance to be impregnated with a hero and drank. Other tales say Dechtire was impregnated in bird form by the god Lugh and gave birth by vomiting. (Cross and Slover; Dexter; Hull 1898; Kinsella; Koch; MacCulloch 1996)

Deirdre The birth of this tragic heroine coincided with a feast her parents hosted for King Concobar mac **Nessa**. The king's druid, Cathbad, prophesied that she would be the most beautiful woman ever born and she would bring down the kingdom. The court demanded that the child be killed, but lustful Concobar took Deirdre from her parents and entrusted her to the wise woman Leborcham. Born a slave, Leborcham had such wit and brilliance that she became a bard and druid. She was also strong and agile; she could run the length of Ireland and get back in time for dinner. Leborcham grew as devoted as a mother to her charge.

As a young woman, Deirdre saw a raven drink the blood of a calf. She confided this vision to Leborcham, who recognized Deirdre's fated partner as Noísiu, King Concobar's nephew, who had raven-black hair, pale skin, and red lips. After Leborcham arranged for them to meet, they eloped to Scotland, where they lived contentedly by hunting and trapping. Deirdre remained beautiful, and soon another king desired her. So the group moved to an island, where their life was hard but peaceful.

Concobar sent a deceitful message that he had lost desire for Deirdre but wished to see her safely home. Noísiu was homesick so, despite Deirdre's premonitions, they sailed home, where Noísiu and his brothers were killed and Deirdre put in chains. Reproaching

Concobar bitterly, she refused his attempt at seduction. Humiliated, Concobar gave her to one of Noísiu's murderers. As her captor drove Deirdre away, she leaped from his chariot and was killed. Concobar's kingdom fell, because the king's deceit so disgusted the warriors that many left him to fight with his enemy **Medb**. (Bourke; Cross and Slover; Colum; Dillon 1968; Green 1995; Hull 1906, 1898; Jackson; Kinsella; O'Faoláin.)

Derbforgaill The lustful shape-shifting Derbforgaill tried to seduce the hero Cúchulainn, but he did not recognize her as a woman in swan form and so attempted to kill her for sport. As she fell to earth, Derbforgaill turned back into a woman and Cúchulainn, shocked at the sight, tried to revive her by sucking stones from her body. This healed her but also made the couple blood kin and barred them from mating. Derbforgaill later died at the hands of envious women who challenged her to a contest to see who could shoot urine the farthest. Big-bladdered Derbforgaill won easily but was fatally attacked by the losers. (Hull 1898; MacCulloch 1996)

Dub It is unclear if the capital of the Republic of Ireland was named for a land goddess, as is common in Celtic lands, or the story of the druid poet Dub was invented to explain the name, which can mean "pool of Dub" or simply "dark pool." The pool in the river Liffey, which flows through the city, was Dub's grave. Hers is a tangled tale of deceit and betrayal: after Dub drowned a woman with whom her husband was consorting, he killed her with a slingshot as she stood beside the black pool. (Cross and Slover)

Eachtach This figure appears only briefly in Irish legend, but in a haunting scene wherein she begged for help as her father, Diarmait, lay dying. Although he had the power to do so, Diarmait's lord refused, remembering that he had lost Eachtach's mother, the brilliant **Gráinne**, to the dying man. To revenge herself upon Fionn for his failure to offer aid to her dying father, Eachtach gathered her brothers into a fighting band and harried Fionn for four years, until he was near death from constant battles. She did not, however, manage to kill him. (MacCulloch 1996)

Ébhlinne A range of low hills on the borders of Counties Tipperary and Limerick bears the name of this goddess. Its central peak, Máthair-Shliabh ("mother mountain") was until recent times the site of midsummer festivals in Ébhlinne's honor. Place-poetry describes Ébhlinne as a queen who eloped with her stepson in a love triangle that recalls those involving **Guinevere, Iseult**, and **Gráinne**, all heroines derived from Celtic goddesses of the land's sovereignty. (Gwynn 4; MacNeill)

Echthge Little is now known of this goddess of the tribe of **Danu**, called "the awful one" and "the terrible goddess," except that she killed and ate her children. Such cannibal imagery is often associated with goddesses of the land, which can be abundant or barren. The rolling hills named for her, Sliabh na Echthge (Slieve Aughty, "mountains of Echthge") in east County Clare, were said to have been a gift from her lover. (Gwynn 3; Westropp 2000)

Éis Énchen When her sons were killed by the hero-in-training Cúchulainn, Éis Énchen turned herself into a hag and stalked Cúchulainn. When they met on a path up a mountain, she asked him to step aside. Respecting her age, he did so, hanging by his toes over the abyss beside the path. Éis Énchen stomped on his feet, hoping to send him to his death. But he leapt into the air, spun around, and killed the retributive mother. (Hull 1898)

Eithne Several important figures in Irish mythology bear this name, and it is unclear whether they are related. The most significant Eithne was held captive by her father, the giant Balor, because of a prophecy that her child would kill him. Trapped in a tower, Eithne was safely celibate. But a hero disguised himself as a woman and seduced Eithne. The prophecy was fulfilled when their son killed Balor in battle. Eithne, who could only live on cow's milk, may derive from a cow goddess; her name is also given to the goddess **Bóand**. Several minor figures carry this name, among them Eithne Tháebfhota, or Long-Sides, sister of **Medb**, and the cannibal Eithne Úathach, who became more beautiful the more children she ate. (Cross and Slover; Gregory 1905; MacNeill; Wilde; Squire)

Emer This paragon of womanhood spoke sweetly, possessed wisdom and chastity, and worked magic with her needle. Emer met her match in manly Cúchulainn, who approached her with witty words to which she responded just as wittily. Challenged to become a better warrior to earn Emer's hand, Cúchulainn went to Scotland to study under amazonian **Scáthách** and impregnated **Aífe**, Scáthách's daughter. Thereafter Cúchulainn had affairs, while Emer remained chaste. Only when he fell under the spell of **Fand** did Emer object. The epitome of faithfulness, she died when he did. (Cross and Slover; Ellis 1995; Hull 1906, 1898; Gantz 1984; Koch; Kinsella)

Eri One of the divine Tuatha Dé Danann (see **Danu**), Eri bore a child to her brother Elatha without her knowing their relationship. One day as she sat by the sea, Eri saw a beautiful boat approach. From the silver boat stepped a golden-haired man wearing golden jewelry and carrying weapons of gold, to whom she made love. After their encounter, her mysterious lover left her with a simple band of gold. The couple's son, Bres, became king of Ireland. It is unclear whether this figure is the same as the better-known **Ériu**. (Cross and Slover; MacCulloch 1996)

Ériu In Irish, Ireland is Éire, "land of Ériu." Invading Milesians met three goddesses, each on a mountain throne. To **Banba, Fódla**, and Ériu in turn, the invaders promised they would give the land her name. Because Ériu offered the greatest riches, her name remains. Little else is known of Ériu, who figures in fragmentary tales as daughter of obscure goddess Ernmas, mother of the failed king Bres, wife of the otherwise-unknown Mac Gréine, lover of the alien prince Elatha, and mistress of the god Lugh. Like other members of her tribe (see **Danu**), she was not immortal and was killed in battle by the Milesians. She was buried beneath the Stone of Divisions on Uisneach, which reveals the map of Ireland on its cracked face. (Green 1995; Gregory 1905; MacAlister; Dames 1992; Koch; Sheehan; Rolleston)

Erne The great lake Erne in Ireland, and the river of the same name, was named for this member of the court of **Medb**. Erne and her attendants were frightened by an unearthly voice echoing from a cave beneath the palace at Cruáchan, Medb's capital. Bearing Medb's comb, symbol of female potency, Erne marched forth with her women toward the lake, in which they all drowned. The motif of a woman drowned in a river or lake typically refers to an ancient goddess of the waterway. (Gwynn 3)

Ésa Ésa was daughter of **Étain**, queen of Tara who, while pregnant with Ésa, was surprised by her former lover. One kiss and they fled, later tricking the king into bedding Ésa, whom he imagined to be Étain. Some versions of the story say that Ésa went mad because of their incest. She raved about the countryside, for which she gained the name of Mess Buachalla, "the herdswoman." Another story says Mess Buachalla's father was Cormac, king of Ulster, who wanted a son and demanded his daughter be killed. But the child was so charming that his warriors hid her with a herdsman, whence her name. She wed the king, but not before mating with the bird god Nemglan, by whom she conceived King Conaire. (Cross and Slover; Gwynn 2; Gantz 1984; Koch; Rolleston)

Étain When fairy king Midir brought beautiful Étain home, his first wife, Fuamnach, turned her into a pool of water, then into a mayfly. For seven years, Étain buzzed about, then fell into a cup, was swallowed by a princess of Ulster, and was reborn with no memory. She wed Ireland's high king, but Midir came to win her back. First he disguised himself as the king's brother, claiming illness that could only be cured by sleeping with Étain. Then, ashamed of his treachery, he withdrew from the court. He returned in his own form, to challenge Étain's husband at a game of skill. Each time they played, Midir won. Finally he asked for a kiss from the queen as a final prize. The king granted it, Midir won, and he kissed Étain. Her memory flooding back, she rose into the air. As swans, she and Midir flew through the roof.

The king chased them to Crúachan, where Étain's maid, Crochan, gave birth; her daughter **Medb** is a double of Étain. Étain and Midir fled to his fairy-mound home, where the king caught them. Midir cast a spell over fifty women (including Étain's daughter **Ésa**), so that they looked identical to Étain, then dared the king to find the real Étain. When the king chose their daughter Ésa, Étain remained with Midir.

Several other figures also bear this name. Étain of the Fair Hair is described as a fairy woman who loved a mortal and perished of grief when he was killed. The sea fairy Étain was sister to the renowned **Clídna**. (Clark; Cross and Slover; Dillon 1968; Evans-Wentz; Gantz 1984; Gregory 1905; Gwynn 2; Hull 1906; Jackson; Kiernan; Koch; MacNeill; O'Faoláin; Squire)

Fand Fand, wife of the sea god, was renowned for her dalliance with the mortal hero Cúchulainn. She came to him in a vision on Samhain, after Cúchulainn hunted two birds but failed to bring them down. He sank into a stupor, while Fand and her sister **Lí Ban** drove him into a year-long delirium. The following Samhain, an otherworldly messenger called Cúchulainn to Fand's side. Despite the opposition of **Emer**, Cúchulainn became Fand's lover.

Though he had dallied before, he always returned to Emer. This time Cúchulainn stayed away. Emer went to Fand's land but withdrew when she saw how tenderly Fand treated Cúchulainn. When Fand realized the depth of Emer's love, she turned to her own

husband, who offered a cloak of forgetfulness. Then Emer and Cúchulainn drank a potion that restored their previous happiness. (Cross and Slover; Gantz 1984; Hull 1906; MacCulloch 1996; Markale 2000; O'Faoláin)

Fedelm Several mythic figures bear this name. The most important is the druid Fedelm of Crúachan, who met **Medb** as she departed to invade Ulster. Mounted in a chariot, fully armed, Fedelm foresaw disaster. Medb, unhappy with Fedelm's prophecy, decided to interpret it as promising victory. The name Fedelm may derive from a generic term for a woman prophet. Other figures of this name include the warrior Fedelm Noíchrotach ("nine-times beautiful") or Noíchride ("fresh hearted"); Fedelm of Munster, celebrated in a fire ritual; and Fedelm, princess of Crúachan, who articulated pagan values to Saint Patrick. (Ellis 1988; Kinsella; Koch; Sharkey; Yeats 1973)

Finnabair Daughter of **Medb**, Finnabair arranged a tryst on an island with her lover Fráech. As Fráech was swimming to the isle, a sea monster appeared. Fráech fought the monster and pledged troth with Finnabair. But they were parted when she was kidnapped and held captive in an Alpine castle, from which Fráech freed her. (Gantz 1984; Jackson; Kinsella; Markale 2000; Rolleston)

Fionnghal nam Fiadh Tales of madwomen who seek solace in the wilderness are found in both Ireland and Scotland. In the former, mad **Mis** was driven insane by seeing her father killed in battle. In Scotland, madness came over Fionnghal when her lover betrayed her out of ambition, leaving her for a wealthy woman. The girl ran screaming into the mountains, where she lived naked until she grew enough hair to look like the deer who nursed her. She lived there for so long that most humans, including her own kinfolk, forgot her. But her guilty former lover remembered her and sought her through the Highlands.

It was Fionnghal who found him, tracking him to

his campsite and sleeping there until he awoke. He covered her with his cloak and watched until she opened her eyes to him. Instantly sane again, she spent her last few hours with him, for she was dying when she came to him. Her erstwhile lover carried her body from the mountains and died of sorrow. The two were buried in adjoining graves, from which weeping willows grew. (Carmichael)

Fionnuala King Lir married Áed, daughter of the magician Bodb Derg. Born with her twin brother, Aodh, Fionnuala ("white shoulders") had a happy childhood, until her mother died giving birth to a second set of twins, Fiachra and Conn. Lir then married his wife's foster sister **Aífe**, who hated the children. Convincing Lir she was ill, Aífe set off to Bodb Derg's distant home, accompanied by the children. Along the way, she cursed them to become swans for 900 years.

Although their bodies were feathered, the children had human minds. And they had human voices to sing plaintive songs that moved everyone. When 900 years had nearly ended, Princess Decca heard a rumor about singing swans and found them. But at the instant she saw them, the children dropped their feathers and stood upright. In seconds they aged, then died and turned to dust as the centuries blew through their bodies. (Gantz 1984; Gregory 1905; Joyce; Kennedy 1969; Markale 1986; O'Faoláin; Squire)

Flaith Her name means "sovereignty," and although sometimes personified, Flaith represents a political abstraction. Celtic kings entered into a "marriage" with the goddess, and the success of their reign was judged by how productive the earth was. Should a king fail in his duties, the land withheld food. Flaith, about whom no legends exist, expresses this contract. (Brenneman 1989; Clark; Green 1995)

Flidais Flidais, goddess of wild beasts, traveled in a chariot drawn by deer. She had a huge sexual appetite; her consort, Fergus, needed seven human women when Flidais was elsewhere engaged. Her daughters, the fairy queen **Fand** and the obscure but sensual Bé

Téite, had similar temperaments. Flidais was also goddess of domestic animals, especially those that gave milk. She owned a magical cow whose milk could supply thirty people daily. (Green 1995; Gwynn 4; MacCulloch 1996)

Fódla One of Ireland's three earth goddesses, Fódla extracted a promise from the invading Milesians that they would name the land for her, but they broke their word and named it for the resplendent **Ériu**. The site where the Milesians met Fódla was Sliabh Felim in County Limerick, or the nearby Máthair-Shliabh ("mother mountain"), usually dedicated to Ébhlinne, perhaps a title of Fódla. (Cross and Slover; Green 1986; Koch)

Gablach This gigantic woman was wooed by an equally large Spaniard named Lutur. But another man, Fuither, also set his heart upon her, and he refused to accept her decision to wed Lutur. Fuither attacked the wedding party, but Lutur met violence with violence, killing several dozen soldiers with a roof beam. Gablach, meanwhile, joined the fighting and singlehandedly killed Fuither. (Gwynn 3)

Garravogue Creator goddesses are often dismembered, their body parts forming land, sea, and sky. In County Meath, this hag broke Communion fast by eating blackberries. She turned into a monster who afflicted the area until Saint Patrick threw his staff at her, breaking her into pieces that became water, earth, and sky. In Sligo, an identically named witch fell into a river, which thereafter bore her name. As the same story is told of the drowned girl Gile, hag and maiden may have been aspects of the same divine figure. (MacNeill)

Glaistig Scottish goddess of the hunt, the Glaistig could smile on hunters, but she would hide her wildlife if they killed a doe. A loud-voiced, thin woman with grayish skin and blonde hair, she came near human dwellings with cows but avoided dogs. She was called Luideag, "little shaggy woman," for her mop of shaggy hair. A similar spirit, the Grugach, tended cattle and was honored with libations. (Carmichael; Davidson and Chaudhri; MacGregor; McNeill)

Glas Ghaibhleann This goddess, who never appeared in human form, is found in oral rather than written literature. But her widespread importance is clear from the frequency with which her name is found on the Irish landscape, indicating places she passed by in mythic time. One milking of this cosmic cow fed multitudes; her milk made copious butter. The Glas was connected with rivers, many of which were envisioned to be cow goddesses (see **Bóand**). She appeared with **Brigit**, whose cow filled abbey storehouses with butter. This connection of Glas and Brigit extended to Britain, where she was known as the Dun Cow.

Many legends center on greedy people who wished to steal the Glas for their exclusive enrichment, from whom she invariably escaped. In one story, the Glas was confined in a valley, but she levitated into the sky. Since that time there has been no free milk in Ireland. Other legends claim a wicked woman tried to milk the Glas into a sieve and the great cow disappeared from earth. Another relates how someone tried to milk Glas into an unfillable hole. When she could not fill the cavity, the cow disappeared.

Galvin, a magical smith, took care of the cow, his enchanted sister. But monstrous king Balor coveted the Glas. A man named Cian guarded the cow while Galvin worked at his forge. When Cian fell asleep, Balor loaded the Glas onto a boat. Cian, threatened with death unless the cow was returned, made his way there, where he spied Balor's fair daughter **Eithne**, trapped in a tower because of a prophecy that her child would kill Balor. Cian disguised himself as a woman and sneaked into Eithne's lodgings, where they conceived the hero Lugh. After his affair with Eithne (a title of **Bóand**), Cian brought the Glas back to the smith. (Colum; Curtin 1894; Gregory 1905; Hull 1928; MacNeill, Westropp)

Gobnait A Christian shrine in Balleyvourey in County Cork shows a **Sheela-na-Gig** whose image has been rubbed smooth in the genital area, believed to bring good luck and abundance. The resident spirit of the shrine is said to be Saint Gobnait, a Christianized version of a goddess who formed a trinity with **Crob Derg** (or Lasair) and **Latiaran**. Alternatively, the third sister is said to be not Gobnait but Inghean Bhuidhe, an obscure figure honored in spring. Gobnait's feast in February suggests she was the first of a triad of seasonal goddesses, for her sisters are also linked to significant dates in the agricultural calendar. Her emblem is the bee, which warned her against approaching danger. (Straffon; Kelly)

Gráinne The aging hero Fionn mac Cumhaill staged a footrace, inviting all Ireland's eligible women to run up Slievenamon ("mountain of the women"), with himself as the prize. Princess Gráinne won. Before the wedding celebration ended, Gráinne lost interest in her aging husband. Surrounded by his band of warriors, the Fianna, she saw Diarmait.

Diarmait was unwilling to elope with his king's wife, but Gráinne knew he was under a vow never to refuse a woman who came to him. She came to him veiled in mountain mist, mounted on a goat, at sunset, and forced him to run away with her. (Some tales say Gráinne drugged the court, including her husband, while she convinced Diarmait to elope.) The couple slept separately, for Diarmait feared Fionn's wrath. Again Gráinne prevailed. After a narrow escape from a monster, she mentioned how nice it was that someone found her desirable. Shamed, Diarmait joined Gráinne in her tent.

Fionn tracked the couple, accompanied by his army, but the lovers stayed ahead of him. They never slept two nights in one place or ate a cooked supper; they never slept in a cave with one entrance or landed on an island with one approach. Finally, exhausted, they took refuge with the giant Sharvon the Surly, who allowed them to hide in his magical rowan tree. Sharvon warned them to leave the berries alone, but Gráinne could not resist. Diarmait killed Sharvon, whose dying screams were heard by the pursuing Fionn.

Diarmait and Gráinne hid in the tree, but Fionn suspected their location. He began to play a board game against Diarmait's friend, the bard Oisín. Unable to resist suggesting the next move, Diarmait dropped berries onto the board, revealing himself. So the pursuit began again, until the god of poetry, Aongus, pleaded the lovers' case. The jilted husband gave up his pursuit, and the couple retired to Gráinne's rath.

Fionn had his revenge years later: when Diarmait lay dying from a wound and begged Fionn to bring him water, the old man did so, then let it trickle away as dying Diarmait watched. Gráinne's daughter **Eachtach** begged for her father's life, but Fionn ignored her. (Bourke; Crossley-Holland; Colum; Dillon 1968; Cross and Slover; Gregory 1905; Hull 1906; Joyce; MacCulloch 1911; Slavin; Squire)

Latiaran A monument in Cullen, County Cork, is dedicated to Latiaran: a heart-shaped standing stone near a holy well. Legend describes Latiaran as a woman of such modesty that when she was carrying boulders (or hot coals) in her apron and a blacksmith complimented the shapeliness of her ankles, she dropped her apron. The standing stone fell out of it, wedging itself upright in the ground, and Latiaran disappeared beneath it. The stone, called Latiaran's Heart, can be seen near the graveyard in Cullen.

This curious tale hides an ancient goddess converted into a saint. The motif of rocks falling from an apron is otherwise found in tales of the world-creating **Cailleach**. That Latiaran was a fire goddess is suggested by the hot coals she carried, as well as the names of her two sisters: Lasair ("flame") and Inghean Bhuidhe ("yellow-haired girl"). Conversely, or additionally, the trinity may have been seasonal divinities, for they each ruled a different part of the growing seasons: Lasair, early spring; Inghean Bhuidhe, the beginning of summer; and Latiaran, the harvesttime, connected with that season by the local tradition that

women should curtsey to Latiaran's Heart as they passed during harvest and by the marking of Latiaran's feast day near the old Celtic festival of Lughnasa. Latiaran Sunday is held on or just before July 25, her feast day. It was the first day for eating potatoes in that region, with the weather reputed always to be fine.

Latiaran, whose name is found nowhere else but in Cullen, has been interpreted as a corrupted diminutive form (Laisrian) of Lasair. Both may be variants of the figure of **Brigit**, who like Latiaran was said to have carried hot coals, in Brigit's case in the town of Ardagh, where she dropped them at "the little church of Lasair." As Brigit was a goddess connected with fire, it is possible Lasair and Latiaran were originally titles or local names for her. (MacNeill; Ó hógáin 1985)

Leanan Sidhe A beautiful otherworld woman who stole young men for her pleasure, the Leanan Sidhe first appeared in erotic dreams, then in the earthly world to lead the victim to her fairy palace. There the lovers danced to fairy tunes, ate food more delicious than any known on earth, and drank delectable wine that never made one drunk. They made love until the fairy grew tired of the man, whereupon he awakened on earth, where he swiftly declined and died. Should a man live through his return, food had no taste, music no melody. (Briggs 1967; Jackson; Wallace; Wilde 1902)

Líadan The poet Líadan was born in the province connected with women and song, Munster. As she matured into her craft, she set off on the traditional "poet's circuit" of the land, walking from place to place composing poetry, always keeping her left shoulder to the sea. On her travels she met another poet, Cuirithir, who fell in love with Líadan. But she refused to interrupt her travels for him, although she invited him to visit her upon her return to County Kerry.

She finished her circuit, but Cuirithir did not visit. So Líadan decided that life as a nun would provide her with the economic support she needed to sustain her art. She soon regretted her decision, finding convent life limiting. Then she heard that Cuirithir had become a priest. Confessing her love for Cuirithir to her own priest, she was surprised to hear him suggest the appropriate next step was for them to share quarters, sleeping together but not making love. Líadan followed this advice, but the two were tormented by the experience. Cuirithir went into exile, dying soon after, and Líadan then died of grief. The story, although Christian, has many Celtic echoes, including the position of women as poets and the testing of the virtue of the lovers (also found in the stories of **Gráinne** and **Guinevere**) by having them sleep together without giving in to their passion. (Bourke; O'Faoláin)

Lí Ban Her name means "finest of women," and she was daughter of the king of Tara (and possibly of **Étain**). When someone forgot to put the cover over a sacred well that overflowed to flood the land, Lí Ban's family was killed. She alone was spared and thereafter lived beneath the water in a small bubble, with her lapdog for company. As she watched salmon sport, Lí Ban wished to become one of them. Her wish was granted when she turned into a mermaid. Her dog was changed into an otter.

They lived for 300 years, during which time Christianity arrived. Monks caught the mermaid and baptized her Murgen, "sea born," whereupon she died and was declared a saint. This belated conversion hides a water goddess who may be the same as the fairy queen who ruled Mag Mell ("the honeyed plain") of fairyland. (Bourke; Brenneman; Joyce; Markale 2000)

Lífe Transmuted into "Anna Livia" by James Joyce in *Finnegans Wake*, this goddess originally bore the name of her river, the Liffey, or vice versa. Ireland's place-poetry describes Lífe as a kindly, hardworking peasant woman who died giving birth, after which her husband died of grief. Another story describes Lífe as a woman of the Picts, a non-Celtic group who lived in Ireland and Scotland. When she called the river's plain the most beautiful place she'd ever seen, her husband named the river for her. (Gwynn 2)

Macha Three goddesses bear this name; it is unclear if or how they are related. The first was the wife of Nemed, an early settler, in whose honor the first plains were cleared for agriculture. This first Macha died when she foresaw how war would afflict her land. The second and most famous Macha was a woman of the divine tribe of **Danu** who came to live with a farmer, Crunniuc, creating bountiful harvests and becoming pregnant by him. Macha demanded Crunniuc never brag about her. He followed her rule until, drunk at court, he boasted that she could outrun the king's horses.

The king demanded to see this prodigy. Pregnant, Macha begged for mercy, but the king would not listen. So the goddess set off against the king's team, beating the horses but collapsing at the finish line. The exertion brought on labor and Macha died giving birth to twins, a girl named Fial and a boy named Fail. As she died, she cursed the men of Ulster to suffer labor pains whenever an enemy threatened the land. The curse figures into the Irish epic the *Táin bó Cuailgne*, in which **Medb** invaded Ulster.

The third Macha was a warrior whose father made a compact with two other kings, Dithorba and Cimbaeth, to share rulership of the land, each reigning for seven years. When her father died, Macha attempted to take his place, but her co-rulers objected. Macha killed Dithorba in battle. When Dithorba's sons escaped, she pursued them disguised as a hag, whom they attempted to rape. She overcame them and marched them back to the hill at Emain Macha, where she made them dig the massive earthworks known as Navan Fort in County Armagh (ard Macha, "heights of Macha"). The site includes a large mound, several sacred wells, a racecourse, and other ritual sites that figure in myth. Macha's connection with Ulster leads some to argue that she was goddess of the region's sovereignty. Others interpret Macha as a pre-Celtic goddess who survived the arrival of the Celts. (Benigni; Cross and Slover; Dexter 1980; Hull 1898; Gwynn 4; Gantz 1984; Green 1995; Kinsella; Koch; MacNeill; Raftery; Squire)

Mairenn This queen was never seen without a golden headdress that the king's other wife, Mugain, suspected hid baldness. So Mugain bribed a jester to pull off Mairenn's headdress. As her headdress tumbled to the ground, Mairenn magically grew a full head of hair. Because of her ill will Mugain was forced to bear a sheep and a salmon before she could give birth to a human. (MacNeill)

Máirín Rua A pregnant Irishwoman was visited three times by an old hag. Twice the woman was kindly, and twice the hag blessed the child. But the last time, the woman was in a surly mood and cursed the hag, whereupon the hag cursed her back. The child was born with bright red hair and a little beard, and she was named Máirín Rua, Maureen the Red.

She was so ugly that her parents made a household servant out of her, requiring her to wash and clean and to stay out of sight. But the old traveling woman had predicted that if anyone loved Máirín Rua for herself, she would become beautiful. When her father died and left the family destitute, the other girls—spoiled as they were for their prettiness—could not cope with poverty. Each of the girls was sent, in turn, to find her fortune in the world. Each time, the mother asked if the girl wanted a cake with lots of flour or her mother's blessing. The first two demanded the cake, but Máirín Rua asked for the blessing.

After many adventures, the girls found themselves in a castle, where without Máirín Rua's cleverness, they would have been killed by a giant. When they found their way to the king's court, two of the king's sons fell in love with the beautiful sisters, but the third could not love Máirín Rua because of her red beard. He set three tasks for Máirín Rua: to get the giant's magic cloak, his sword of light, and his bag of gold. She did so, and the prince was delighted with her courage. He married Máirín Rua, who thereafter became more beautiful than both her sisters combined. Many motifs in the story recall tales of the **Cailleach**, who grows young when loved (see also British **Loathy Lady**), suggesting that behind this whimsical tale rests an old goddess myth. (Danaher 1967)

Maoilin When her family demanded she marry a man she did not love, Maoilin flew to a magical rock near Duhallow, County Cork. There she disappeared, leaving behind her handprint, still visible, to show where she had passed. In another version of the story, a fairy lover stole Maoilin from her wedding, taking her to the otherworld through the rock in question. For centuries, girls visited Maoilin's rock on the harvest feast of Lughnasa to deck it with flowers. Maoilin may have been an ancestral earth goddess. (MacNeill)

Medb Although she appears in myth and literature as a queen, Medb was originally goddess of the land's sovereignty. She was first associated with the central region, specifically with the hill of Tara, where she was Medb Lethderg, "Medb Red Sides," who married nine consecutive kings. She may be identical with **Étain**, as their myths overlap significantly. Medb was born of Étain's handmaiden Crochan, who admired the cave where she gave birth so much that Étain made a present of it. Above it, Medb built her great capital, Crúachan. More than seventy ritual and royal sites of the Celtic Iron Age are still visible, including the hill fort on which kings were inaugurated.

Medb's name means "mead" or "intoxication," which may refer either to the cup she offered the king at his inauguration, the intoxication of battle, or both. Medb was fiery and self-willed, sleeping with whomever she chose and never without "one man in the shadow of another." She kept Ailill mac Mata as consort, but her favored lover was the massively endowed Fergus. Fergus played an important role in Medb's cattle raid, which began when Ailill claimed to own more than Medb, a claim that affected Medb's social status. When she found Ailill had in his herds a white bull she could not match, Medb set out to find its equal. The only possibility grazed on the lands of King Dáire.

Medb tried to coax Dáire to lend her the bull. But Dáire overheard Medb's warriors boasting that they intended to take the bull no matter what he said. Insulted, Dáire prepared for war. Medb marshaled her armies, taking advantage of the curse that left the province's men defenseless (see **Macha**). Medb set out in an open cart, dressed in royal finery. Ignoring the warning of the prophet **Fedelm**, Medb moved her armies north.

Medb did not expect Cúchulainn, who single-handedly defended Ulster. While he fought, Medb kidnapped the bull. But the Ulstermen roused to fight off Medb's army, driving them back to her lands. The two bulls also fought, killing each other. Without the white bull, Ailill's possessions matched Medb's, making her equal to her husband.

Medb died on an island sacred to her. There bubbled a well in which Medb bathed each morning, strengthening her power. But her nephew Furbaide Ferbend could not forgive Medb for killing his mother, **Clothra**. Although the island was far from shore, he practiced hurling stones from a slingshot until he was sure of his aim, then flung a ball of dried brains across the water. Medb was buried in the great tumulus of Knocknarea above the town of Sligo. (Bourke; Brenneman 1989; Clark; Colum; Dexter; Ellis 1995; Green 1995, 1993; Gwynn 4; Hull 1898; Kinsella; MacAnna; MacCulloch 1911; Powell; Rees and Rees; Slavin)

Milucra Sister of the lusty goddess **Áine**, Milucra became infatuated with the hero Fionn mac Cumhaill. But her sister had spied the man first, and Milucra knew she would have to outwit Áine to gain possession of the hero. So she enchanted a lake that would turn the hair of any swimmer gray, because Áine had sworn never to sleep with a gray-haired man, then lured Fionn there. Meeting Milucra, who claimed she had dropped her golden ring into the water, Fionn swam out to retrieve it. When he returned, his hair had turned silver-white. But the effects of the magic were stronger than Milucra intended. Fionn was stooped with age, much to the consternation of his band of warriors, the Fianna, who captured Milucra and forced

her to undo the magic and restore Fionn's youth. His hair stayed silver. (Gregory 1905; Joyce)

Mis When the young woman Mis found her father's body after a battle, she lost her wits and drank his blood. Thereafter, she wandered through the mountains, killing animals with her bare hands for food. Mis lived without human contact until a harper attracted her with music. Coming to his camp, she spoke her first human words since her father's death. Mis went to live with her harper. He was killed in battle as her father had been. This time, she did not go mad but became a poet. (Bourke; Ellis 1995; Gwynn 3)

Mongfhinn High king Niall was the son of British princess Cairenn, enslaved by the king of Tara. The king's first wife, Mongfhinn, forced Cairenn to give birth in the open air. Samhain (November 1) was called the Festival of Mongfhinn, for she killed herself that night; women evoked her then. She may have once been an important goddess, for her name includes the divine syllable *fionn*, "light." (Cross and Slover; Koch)

Mór Many earth goddesses bear the name Mór ("great one") including Mór Mumhan, "great one of Munster." Like other territorial goddesses, Mór was demoted to a woman, one who settled with her husband on a promontory, where they lived by scavenging. One day, Mór climbed to the top of the mountain and urinated, forming ravines from the plentitude of her water. Mór's happiness ended when her sons became sailors. As she worried over their fate, her temper grew so bad that her husband left her, settling far away. (MacNeill; Curtin 1894; McKay 1969; Rees and Rees)

Mórrígan One of Ireland's most important goddesses was a winged shape-shifter called Mórrígan, a member of the divine Tuatha Dé Danann (see **Danu**). She appeared in many forms: a white cow with red ears; a giant woman washing clothing near a battlefield; a crow or raven; an eel; a gray-red wolf. This shape-shifting connects her with druids, magician-bards who could change appearance. Legends show her in that role, singing songs that brought her people victory, casting oracles, and foretelling the future.

She assumed bird form to swoop over battlefields, devouring bodies. The Mórrígan was associated with the other goddesses of battle, **Badb**, **Nemain**, and **Macha**. Together they make up the "three Morrigna"; in some texts Mórrígan substitutes for one of the other goddesses. The Mórrígan's appetite for bodies included living ones; she had an immense desire for sex. She had intercourse with a god who came upon her while she was straddling a river and fell upon her lustfully. Desiring a human hero, she ambushed one; when he rejected her, she turned upon him and was injured in their fight. Later Mórrígan protected the same hero in battle, appearing to him in various guises as he held off an invading army. When he went to his death, she attempted, unsuccessfully, to stop him.

Some translate Mórrígan's name as "Phantom Queen" and others, "Death Queen," while others derive it from a presumed early Indo-European goddess, *Rigatona, "great queen." The derivation of her name from the word for "sea" is generally rejected. Rather, she is a land goddess, for like other goddesses of sovereignty she appeared as a hag who could transform herself into a young maiden. (Bourke; Clark; Cross and Slover; Cunliffe; Dexter; Green 1995, 1986; Gregory 1905; Billington; Hull 1898; Kinsella; Koch; MacCulloch 1996; Squire)

Muilearach A seafaring one-eyed hag with a blue-gray face and sharp protruding teeth was known throughout the Scottish Highlands as well as in the islands of Lewis and Harris and in the southern Hebrides. An ancestral goddess, Muilearach lived underwater, healing people with a pot of balm that could also make the healthy grow ill. She had one fast-moving eye and a full head of gray-and-black hair. As Muireartach, the same figure appears in Ireland as a one-eyed hag who lived with a magical smith beneath the ocean waves and caused shipwrecks for their treasure. (Campbell 1862; MacCulloch 1911)

Murna Although she makes only brief appearances in Irish mythology, Murna is important as mother of the hero Fionn mac Cumhaill. Kidnapped by Fionn's father after her father rejected his proposal of marriage, Murna was widowed within nine hours of conceiving her son and raised him with the help of amazonian aunts. (Cross and Slover; Gregory 1905; Gwynn 2; Rolleston)

Nás This obscure Irish goddess had little myth attached to her but remains familiar in Ireland today because Naas, a prosperous town near Dublin, bears her name. She died there, and her husband organized a great assembly at the ritual site of Teltown in her honor, an assembly usually said to honor the goddess **Tailte**. (Gwynn 3; Rees and Rees; MacNeill)

Nemain Least known of Ireland's war goddesses, Nemain formed a trinity with **Badb** and **Mórrígan**. Nemain's name describes her role as rouser of battle panic; she drove warriors insane so that they mistook friends for enemies. Like other war goddesses, she appeared as a crow, waiting to eat carrion. Her name connects with the Celtic word for an outdoor shrine, *nemeton*. She may represent the duty of warriors to protect sacred sites. (Koch; MacAnna; MacCulloch 1911)

Nessa Her name was Assa, "gentle one," when this princess of Ulster first drew the eye of the lustful druid Cathbad. To gain access to the young scholar, Cathbad had her twelve tutors slaughtered. But Assa gathered a company to seek vengeance. She changed her name to Nessa, "ungentle," and battled anyone who did wrong. But she could not find those who had killed her tutors.

Cathbad had not stopped lusting after her. One day, when she was bathing in a pool deep in the woods, the druid assaulted Nessa. Naked and unarmed, the girl saved her life by giving in to Cathbad's demands. He kept her as a hostage, during which time her son Concobar was conceived. He never bore Cathbad's name but was instead called mac Nessa ("son of Nessa"). The name was appropriate because Concobar was not Cathbad's son. Finding two worms in a pail of water, Nessa realized that if she drank them, she would conceive. She did so, and her child was born clutching a worm as proof that Cathbad had no part in his conception. After Cathbad's death, Nessa married the king of Ulster, who died. Fergus assumed the throne and courted her. She agreed to wed, then tricked Fergus into giving up his throne for her son. (Cross and Slover; Hull 1898; Kinsella; Koch; Rolleston)

Niamh The most renowned queen of fairyland, Niamh of the Golden Hair was irresistible to human men. Her favorite was the bard Oisín, son of **Sadb**. They lived happily on her magical island Tír Tairnigiri ("land of promise") until Oisín, homesick, begged to return to Ireland. Niamh loaned him her horse, warning that he must beware of touching the ground. But Oisín fell and, instantly, the years he had lived in fairyland came upon him. He grew old and died, turning to dust and blowing away. Some legends give Niamh a daughter, Plur na mBan, "flower of womanhood." (Cross and Slover; Graves; Gregory 1905; Joyce; Squire)

Nothain Like other madwomen of Irish legend (see **Mis**), Nothain was driven mad by war. She was no innocent bystander, for Nothain was a warrior, well used to the bloodshed. But when an attack left most of her family dead, Nothain buckled from the strain. She lost her wits, wandering the countryside, becoming shaggy and wild. Her father, who survived the assault, searched for a year before he found her, speechless with grief. After a night spent in his comforting presence, she finally spoke, only to ask if anyone else still lived. Hearing that only her father remained, Nothain died of sorrow. (Gwynn 4)

Odras Originally she may have been the tutelary goddess of the lake that bears her name, but she comes into Irish place-poetry as a bold young girl who challenged the phantom queen **Mórrígan** for possession of a cow. When Mórrígan stole Odras's cow to mate with her best bull, Odras refused to accept the robbery and traveled to Mórrígan's cave of Oweynagat to demand restitution. Instead, she was turned into a small lake in County Roscommon. (Gwynn 4; MacCulloch 1996)

Relbeo This minor character plays a significant role in mythic invasions of Ireland. Daughter of a Greek king and practitioner of the druidic arts, she was sent to spy upon the monstrous Fomorians. She became the lover of their king, who confided his battle plans. Through Relbeo's efforts, her people, the mythic Nemedians, gained control over Ireland. (Cross and Slover)

Ruad In County Sligo, a magnificent waterfall at Asseroe (Ess Ruad), flooded by a hydroelectric project in the mid-twentieth century, was named for this otherworldly maiden. She traveled to this world in a bronze boat with tin sails, intending to seduce a human. But once in our world, she heard the sound of mermaids singing and, overcome with passion, leapt into the waterfall. (Gwynn 4)

Sadb Bewitched by her father's enemy, Sadb was turned into a deer. In enchantment, she visited the dreams of Fionn mac Cumhaill, who fell in love with her. These dreams were astonishingly lifelike, for she made love with Fionn and soon was pregnant with his child. Her father's enemy discovered that Sadb had learned to contact others through dreams. So the druid cast another spell, trapping Sabd in her doeskin. When her son was born, Sabd could not resist a flick of her tongue over his fine brow. A tuft of deer hair sprang forth, for which the boy was named Oisín, "little fawn." Some legends say Sadb died of shame after discovering how cruel her lover, Fionn, was in battle. (Almqvist; Gregory 1905; MacCulloch 1996; Rolleston; Squire)

Sampait Ireland's place-poetry tells the story of this strong woman who, tending her flocks one day, was assaulted by a nobleman named Crechmael, who attempted to rape her. But she trussed him up like a pig for slaughter and killed him. (Gwynn 4)

Scáthách On Scotland's Isle of Skye lived Scáthách ("shadowy one"), head of a martial arts academy where she made heroes out of warriors. The exact location of her school was secret, and access was limited to those who could leap across a chasm called the Bridge of the Cliff. Once in Scáthách's domain, the student hero learned secrets such as the thunder feat, the hero's call, and use of the magical Gae Bolga. Scáthách also foretold her students' futures. But she refused to tell Cúchulainn's future, for she knew he would have a son by her daughter **Aífe** and kill him. Cúchulainn tried to win ownership of her island from Scáthách. After days of combat they sat down and together ate hazelnuts of wisdom, which caused Cúchulainn to realize he could never beat the woman. (Gregory 1905; Hull 1898; Kinsella; MacCulloch 1911, 1996)

Scota The people of Ireland were once called "Scoti" or "Scots," a name that followed them to the land previously known as Caledonia, which then became Scotland. This ancestral mother goddess appears in several Irish texts as an early resident of Ireland. In the *Lebor Gabála*, which combines Irish myth with biblical lore, she was called a pharaoh's daughter. (Squire)

Sheela-na-Gig Smiling lewdly from rock carvings, the Sheela-na-Gig's skeletal face rises above huge buttocks, full breasts, bent knees, and a vagina held open by stony hands. The stones have in many cases been incorporated into Christian churches, usually over the entrance, although some are found in other buildings. Her name has been translated as "hag," as "the holy lady," and as a vulgar word for female genitalia. In a few areas, scrapings were taken from the Sheela's vulva to promote fertility. In other places, touching the Sheela enhanced the likelihood of healthy childbearing (see **Gobnait**).

The figures first drew attention in the nineteenth century. The prudery of the era resulted in the figures being misidentified (as a male fool holding his heart open) or misinterpreted (as dirty jokes). In the early twentieth century, researchers described the figures as warnings against expressions of women's sexuality. Today, the figures are generally believed pagan, a goddess brought into churches to co-opt the devotion of her followers. Some scholars date the Sheelas to the twelfth century and argue that they are Christian. More recently, connections have been drawn with folklore concerning a hag descended from a goddess of the land. Celtic sources that describe the evil-dispelling power of women's genital display suggest a source earlier than the Christian era. The source and meaning of the Sheela are not settled.

Several dozen Sheela figures can be seen in situ in Britain and Ireland, while others have been moved to museums. There is evidence that hundreds more once existed and were destroyed, through either prudery or a need to use the stone elsewhere. Whether the Sheela-na-Gig is a Celtic figure, a remnant of the pre-Celtic past, or an apotropaic sculpture meant to represent a Christian conception of the impurity of the female flesh is debated. The Sheela-na-Gig has been used in recent times as an image of women's power by feminist artists. (Anderson; Concannon; McMahon and Roberts; Sheehan)

Silkie Two figures bear this name in Scotland. One was a household guardian named for her silken clothing. At night, she sneaked into houses and cleaned whatever was in disorder. If she found nothing to clean, she messed up the rooms. A better-known figure was the seal woman who could be captured and brought into human society. It was imperative to keep her sealskin cloak hidden; if the Silkie found it, she left behind children and home. The name has been connected to fairy folk called Silly Witches, who may in turn be connected with a harvest goddess, Sele.

On the Orkney isles, people with webbing between toes or fingers were descendants of Brita (or Ursilla), who grew bored with her human mate and made off with a virile male seal. This is an unusual motif, for typically the ancestral mother was a seal. Brita's children's webbed feet and hands had to be clipped into fingers and toes. In the Hebrides, the descendants of seal women are called MacCondrum and MacPhee, while in Ireland, Coneely, MacNamara, O'Flaherty, and O'Sullivan (and sometimes Lee) indicate descent from seal women. (MacGregor)

Sín Although a fairy woman, Sín had the powers of a goddess, able to change water into wine and leaves into pigs, in order to feed battalions of warriors she conjured from thin air. When King Muirchertach mac Erc killed her family, she appeared to him as a seductive woman, then drove him mad and killed him, revealing her identity just before he died. (Bourke; Cross and Slover; Ellis 1988; Markale 2000; Rees and Rees)

Sínann Granddaughter of a sea god, Sínann was warned she should not approach the well wherein wisdom was hidden. But Sínann ignored the prohibition. She caught the salmon of wisdom and, eating its flesh, became the wisest being on earth. The well burst out, drowning Sínann as it carried her to sea. Thereafter the well never returned to its confines. Although often interpreted as a cautionary tale, warning women against seeking wisdom, Sínann's story can be seen as a creation myth in which she sacrifices herself to provide the land's fertility. (Gwynn 3; MacCulloch 1911; Rolleston; Squire)

Tailte The Irish midsummer games were dedicated to this goddess of the Fir Bolg, a group that may represent the pre-Celtic Irish. She was married to the last king of that race, Eochaid mac Eirc, an ideal ruler during whose reign the land bore abundant crops. But when Eochaid was killed, Tailte married a man with a similar name, Eochaid Garbh, from the army that killed her husband. Tailte traveled to the island's center and began to clear fields for planting but died from the exertion. As she died, Tailte asked for a funeral with horse racing and games. Her foster son

Lugh established the August festival of Lughnasa, when the Tailtean Games were celebrated. They took place through medieval times. A smaller-scale festival was held through the nineteenth century. (Cross and Slover; Gwynn 4; Koch; MacNeill; Westropp 1920)

Téa Little is known of the goddess who gave her name to the royal hill of Tara, except that its earthen walls were built at her request and she died there. Called "never unjust," she was one of Tara's early queens. Another figure connected with the site was Tephi, a "daughter of Pharaoh," who laid the framework of the first buildings with her staff; she is sometimes considered the source of Tara's name and is said to be buried there. Yet other theories hold that a woman named Temair ("Tara" in Irish) died tragically on the hill. (Gwynn 1; Koch; Slavin; Rees and Rees)

Tlachtga Tlachtga was a magician who traveled to Italy to learn to build a flying wheel from Simon Magus. His three sons tracked her back to Ireland and raped her on the hill that bears her name. Impregnated with triplets, Tlachtga died on the hill and was buried there. A festival was organized in her honor and held every year thereafter. Now obscure, Tlachtga was once so significant that her hill was the site of the important festival of Samhain. Now called the Hill of Ward, Tlachtga is covered with impressive earthworks. Although archaeologists have paid little attention to Tlachtga's hill, it once held great significance. (Gilroy; Gwynn 4; Raftery; Rees and Rees)

Tuag In Ireland, drowned young women became the great rivers and lakes of the land (see **Bóand, Sínann, Erne, Lí Ban**). Such was the case with Tuag, who was courted by the god of the sea. Manannán mac Lir sent his bard into Tuag's palace, to sing her into a dreamless sleep and carry her away. But the bard was a dwarf, and carrying the young woman exhausted him, so he set her down to rest. The waters of the Bann River rose and drowned her. Its estuary, Tuag Inber, still bears her name; one of the three great waves of Ireland was said to strike its shores. (Gwynn 4)

Uirne A jealous fairy woman, Uchtdealb of the Fair Breast, cast a spell on Uirne, turning her into a dog. She was pregnant when it happened, so her twin boys were born as puppies. The spell dissolved at that point for Uirne, but her children remained dogs. She put them into the care of her brother the hero Fionn mac Cumhaill, and they became his boon companions. (Gregory 1905; Rolleston)

Úna The cairn-capped hill of Knockshegowna rises above the plains of County Tipperary. There Úna lived in a magnificent palace. Once, annoyed by a drunken piper, Úna turned herself into a calf. With the piper clinging to her back, she ran to the shores of the Shannon River. When the piper appeared undismayed by his calf-assisted flight, Úna returned him to the place from which she had stolen him. (Logan 1981; Squire)

BRITISH AND MANX PANTHEON

Albina The Roman author Pliny offers this figure as the chief goddess of Britain. The later British historian Holinshed described Albina as a princess who landed on the island with fifty fugitive women who had killed their husbands (for a similar story, see Irish **Cesair**). Albina's name has been translated as "white," which may refer to the chalky soil of southern Britain. It has also been connected to an ancient word for "high" (as in "Alps"). A famous though controversial statue may represent Albina. Grimes' Grave Goddess, a rotund figure carved from white chalk, has been variously interpreted as a British **Sheela-na-Gig** and as an archaeological fraud. (Bord; Graves)

Andraste The battle queen Boudicca of the Icini invoked this goddess, "invincibility," before her battle with the Roman legions, then released a hare

in Andraste's honor. Although Boudicca failed to drive out the invaders and killed herself rather than submit to rape and torture, she remains a symbol of the island's sovereignty. (Green 1995, 1986; Koch; MacCulloch 1911)

Arnemetia The Celtic word *nemeton* meant "sacred place," and this goddess's name has been translated as "in front of the sacred place." Her shrine at Buxton Spa boasts two mineral springs, which the Romans called Aquae Arnemetiae, "waters of Arnemetia." An excavation of her shrine in 1975 brought forth 232 coins and 2 bronze bracelets. Arnemetia became Saint Anne after Christianization, and her shrine was renamed St. Anne's Well. (Clarke; Green 1986)

Belisama Celtic divinities tended to be local, so finding the same goddess name in several sites is notable. Such is the case with Belisama ("brightness" or "shining"), found both in Britain and on the Continent. In the former, she was associated with the river Ribble, which according to the Egyptian geographer Ptolemy once bore her name; a Romano-Celtic statue found there may represent her, while a murderous folkloric vestige of her is **Peg O'Nell**. On the Continent, Romans renamed her **Minerva Medica**. Some have seen Belisama as a corollary to **Brigit**. (MacCulloch 1911; Spence; Straffon)

Black Annis This blue-faced hag crouched in an old oak growing from a cleft in rock. She scratched children to death, then devoured them. Every spring, a dead cat was dragged past Black Annis's Bower, with a pack of hounds in hot pursuit. Black Annis may have been a weather-witching hag like the **Cailleach**. Whether the origins of Black Annis are Celtic or pre-Celtic is subject to debate. (Campbell 3; Graves; Spence)

Brigantia In Britain, the Brigantes honored an ancestral goddess, Brigantia, whose name hides in the names of the Briant and Brent Rivers. She may have been a form of **Brigit**. (Joliffe; Squire; Pennick 2000)

Coventina Hidden in marshes near Hadrian's Wall, Coventina's well was once a great healing site. Like other Celtic river goddesses, Coventina ruled the waters and adjacent lands, in her case the Carrawburgh. Sculptures show her as a reclining woman pouring water from an urn. Coventina's name has also been found in Spain and France, where the titles Augusta ("high") and Sancta ("holy") emphasized her importance. (Billington; Green 1995)

Cuda A sculpture of this goddess, seated and holding an egg, was found at Daglinworth, near Cirencester, once the capital of the Dobunni tribe. Accompanied by three hooded men making offerings to her, Cuda was a goddess of prosperity. (Green 1986)

Deae Matres Scholars dispute the source of the multiple goddesses found in the Celtic-Germanic borderlands. These "Divine Mothers" bear a collective Latin name, their original names having been lost. Even in German, they are called by a translation of the Latin name (see Scandinavia, **Matronen**). Many sculptures show two or three goddesses together, seated and holding sacred objects like a sacrificial knife and an offering plate. Although often described as representing the three ages of woman (nubile maiden, fertile mother, aging crone), the Mothers were often depicted as identical, their multiplicity providing a visual intensification or representing collectivity. Seated under an archway, they were depicted wearing round halo-like headdresses. The central goddess was distinguished from the others by standing while they sat or by sitting while they stood. Variant names of these goddesses are Matres Coccaae (British "red mothers"), Matres Domesticae (British "mothers of the hearth"), Matres Glanicae (from Provence, France); Matronae Aufaniae (from Bonn, Germany), Matronis Assingenehis (from the Rhine valley), Matronis Mahlinehis (also from the Rhine valley). In Britain, similar mother goddesses are invoked as Campestres, Communes (living everywhere), Domesticae (of the household), Germaniae (of the Germans), Ollototae, Omnium Gentium (of all races), Parcae (of fate), Suleviae (of the sun), Tramarinae (from over the sea), and Tramarinae Patriae (from the overseas homeland).

The connection of the Mothers, who represent the land's fertility, to the singular goddess called **Dea Nutrix** ("nourishing goddess") is unclear. The Mothers were occasionally depicted in the form called pseudo-Venus, a single voluptuous woman holding symbols of fertility. There is no historical indication of ritual practices connected with these goddesses, who seem to have been absorbed into the Roman religious framework in early imperial times. They were probably ancestral goddesses, rulers of the fruitfulness of humanity as well as that of the earth. (Buchholtz; MacAnna; Straffon)

Dea Nutrix (Deae Nutrices, plural.) Archaeological excavations in Britain have produced scores of small Roman-era clay statuettes that show a goddess (or three goddesses) holding symbols of earth's fertility: fruit, eggs, grain, and children. This "nurturing goddess" provided food, through her own body and through the earth. On the Continent, statues of Dea Nutrix have also been found, especially in France and southern Germany, both areas of Celtic influence. Graves and temples are typical locations for these finds, as are sacred springs (including Vichy), into which the images were sacrificially thrown. The connection of this figure with the continental **Deae Matres** is unclear. Both groups are known only by Latin names, their Celtic names having been lost. (Green 1986)

Gillian In Britain, this name was associated with mazes, through which springtime races were run. A young woman was "imprisoned" in the middle of the maze, called a Gillian Bower, then "freed" by a young man. Behind this ritual rests an ancient spring goddess who needed to be released from the grip of winter by heroic human effort. The name Gillian, common in the Middle Ages, came to refer to any flirtatious woman; the word "jilt" derives from her name. (Kraft)

Godiva The legend of Lady Godiva incorporates many Celtic mythological motifs. An eleventh-century woman of Coventry, which celebrated the 900th anniversary of her death in 1967, Godiva was married to Leonfric, Earl of Mercia. While Godiva was renowned for her generosity, Leonfric piled ruinous taxes on his vassals, so peasants starved while the court lived in luxury. Godiva pleaded for justice, but Leonfric refused her with a joking challenge: If she would ride naked through Coventry, he would lower the taxes. Godiva took up the challenge, asking that townspeople stay indoors and that windows be shrouded with fabric. Only one person ignored her request, and his name, Peeping Tom, lives on as a term of approbation. Godiva's bold ride had the desired result. Shamed, Leonfric eased the crippling taxes.

The region around Coventry had been home to the Celtic tribe called the Brigantes, who recognized the horse goddess **Epona**; **Ceridwen** and **Rhiannon** were also connected with white horses. At Southam, a "Godiva festival" took place until the eighteenth century, with two seminude women, one wearing white lace, the other black lace, riding on horseback through town. The purpose of these festivals was to encourage agricultural abundance. Female nakedness as a Celtic ritual to increase fertility of the fields is known from classical sources, including the Roman author Pliny. Thus the quasihistorical Lady Godiva may have religious antecedents. (Davidson 1978; Graves; MacCulloch 1911; Stephens)

Marian The beloved of legendary robber Robin Hood of Sherwood Forest may descend from an early goddess of fertility and abundance. She appears in significant ways in British folklore, most notably in the Abbot's Bromley festival in early fall. There, "deermen" dance in costumes topped with reindeer horns, while a cross-dressed man called Maid Marian accompanies these fertility images. (Long)

Nantosuelta Her name points to one interpretation of this goddess's meaning. "Winding river" should be a typical Celtic goddess of the watershed, in her case the river Trent. But images show Nantosuelta as a goddess of the household, invoked as "protector of the house." Nantosuelta carries a house on a pole, on which a raven (symbol of prosperity) perched; she was depicted holding a cooking pot. She may have represented the prosperity of fertile lands near a river. (Green 1986, 1989; MacAnna)

Peg O'Nell Originally the river Ribble bore the name of **Belisama**. Later folklore created Peg O'Nell, a servant girl who drowned in the river. To punish those who failed to rescue her, Peg returned every seven years on "Peg's Night" to claim a victim, and propitiatory sacrifices of small birds or animals were offered to the river spirit. A similar figure, Jenny Greenteeth, haunted the streams of Lancashire, threatening passersby with drowning. Along the river Tees, Peg Powler wandered about on Sundays; those who drowned in the Tees were said to have been "eaten by Peg Powler." All descend from ancient river divinities. (Briggs 1959; MacKinlay)

Sabrina Originally the divinity of the Severn River, Sabrina was diminished into the daughter of Estrildis, to whom king Humber took a fancy despite being married to Princess Gwendolen. Humber hid Estrildis until she bore their child, Sabrina. When his wife's father died, Humber brought forth Estrildis and Sabrina. Gwendolen was furious; her armies went to war against Humber's, and, when she won, she demanded that Estrildis and her child be drowned in the Severn. (Spence 1972)

Sul Roman Britain's greatest healing shrine was in Bath, where hot springs still bubble forth at the rate of a million gallons a day. Aquae Sulis ("waters of Sul") have been used since Celtic times, possibly earlier. In Roman times, a healing shrine was built there. After the legions were recalled to Rome, the stone baths disappeared under silt deposits. Rediscovered in the seventeenth century, the baths can be visited.

Excavations have yielded information about the goddess to which Bath was dedicated. The Romans equated her to **Minerva**, but she never lost her Celtic name. "Sul" means "sun," and the hot waters of her shrine were connected to solar power. As a healing goddess, Sul is connected to **Brigit**, similarly associated with healing wells. Like Brigit, Sul was served by a college of priestesses who tended an eternal flame. Occasionally Sul appears plural, as the Suleviae, a name also occasionally given to Brigit; Sul may have been a title of Brigit in Bath. (Green 1995, 1986; MacCulloch 1996)

WELSH, CORNISH, AND ARTHURIAN PANTHEON

Arianrhod Arianrhod's niece Goewin was footholder to King Math, whose life depended upon his feet resting always in the lap of a virgin. But Goewin's power was lost when Math's nephew raped her. Math made her queen, and the search began for a new footholder.

Arianrhod's brother Gwydion nominated her for the honor but he, who had collaborated in the rape of Goewin, plotted to hurt his sister. When she stepped over a magical wand to prove her virginity, she gave birth to two unexpected children: Dylan Son-of-Wave, child of the sea, and Lleu Llaw Gyffes, claimed by Gwydion. The humiliated Arianrhod planned to refuse Lleu a name and the right to weapons, two prerogatives of a Welsh mother, but Gwydion tricked her again. The possibility that the children could be parthenogenetic is offered as an argument by those who define Arianrhod as a goddess. Her name, "Silver Wheel," suggests a moon or sky goddess; she lived surrounded by maidens at Caer Arianrhod, the constellation Corona Borealis ("northern crown"). She may

be a goddess of the land, for fruitful soil is often seen as a parthenogenetic mother. Some read the legend as recording a historical change from matriliny to patriliny, pointing out that Arianrhod's only named ancestor is her mother, **Dôn**, and her son depends upon her to grant him a name. (Gantz 1976; Green 1995; MacCulloch 1996; Rees and Rees; Spence 1972)

Asenora In the church in Zennor in Cornwall, a wooden chair boasts a 600-year-old carving of a mermaid. Princess Asenora of Brittany, who founded the church, had been thrown pregnant into the sea in a barrel and drifted to Zennor, where she was honored as Saint Senara. In the same town, a seductive mermaid named Cherry lured the finest singer, Mathew Trewella, from the church to his death. The connection between these similarly named figures is obscure. (Briggs 1959; Straffon)

Blanchefleur Rivalen, king of Lyonesse (a lost land, perhaps the Isles of Scilly), was an ally of neighboring King Mark of Cornwall. To solidify their friendship, Mark arranged for Rivalen to marry his sister Blanchefleur at the castle of Tintagel on the northern Cornish coast. No sooner were they married than Blanchefleur was pregnant; no sooner was she pregnant than Rivalen's land was attacked. The king left Blanchefleur with his most loyal retainer and went to defend his lands. But he never returned. Blanchefleur, hearing of her loss, gave birth and died. The child of her grief was Tristan, himself fated to love and lose his beloved, his uncle Mark's wife, **Iseult**. (Bedier)

Blodeuwedd After **Arianrhod** was tricked into giving birth to Lleu Llaw Gyffes, she withheld from him three maternal gifts: a name, weapons, and a wife. But her trickster brother Gwydion thwarted her, so that her son attained names and arms. The final gift, manufactured by Gwydion and his magician uncle Math, was a woman made of nine kinds of wildflowers and named Blodeuwedd ("flower face"). But when a handsome hunter captured Blodeuwedd's heart, she decided to

203

kill Lleu, who was protected by magic so that he could only be killed when bathing by the side of a river, under a thatched roof over a cauldron, while standing with one foot on a deer. When she dared him to assume that unlikely posture, her lover killed him. For her part in the plot, Blodeuwedd was turned into an owl. (Gantz 1976; Graves; Green 1995; Jackson)

Branwen Branwen was married to an abusive husband who made her into a kitchen slave in Ireland. But she sent a trained crow to her brothers in Wales, and they set off to rescue her, dying in the attempt. Branwen died of sorrow. The epic heroine may hide a goddess, for Branwen has many similarities to the Welsh goddess **Rhiannon**, also exiled and enslaved by her husband's people. An obscure ancestral goddess, Bronwen, may be related to Branwen, though some scholars warn against conflating the two. (Gantz 1976; Green 1995; MacCulloch 1911, 1996; Powell)

Ceridwen One of the most important Welsh goddesses was this sorceress who lived in the middle of a lake with her husband Tegid Foel, a beautiful daughter named Creirwy ("light"), and her ugly brother Afagddu ("dark"). Ceridwen had a plan for Afagddu's future, intending to make him a seer. She gathered the necessary herbs and set them to brew for a year and a day.

The brew had to be stirred constantly. When Ceridwen had other tasks, she left the cauldron to her servant boy Gwion, with the warning that he must never taste the brew. But it boiled, and three drops splattered onto Gwion's hand. He popped it into his mouth, and wisdom and power poured into the boy.

Gwion foresaw Ceridwen's reaction and fled. The furious sorceress started after him. Gwion transformed himself into a hare; Ceridwen turned herself into a greyhound. He became a fish, she an otter; he became a bird, she a hawk. When he transformed himself into a grain of wheat, she became a hen and ate him. Ceridwen, impregnated, bore a boy whom the goddess, still furious, had no intention of nursing. But she could

not bear to kill the infant, so she set him adrift on the sea. A nobleman rescued him, and he grew up to be the great poet Taliesin.

Although these tales show Celtic features, Ceridwen may have derived from a pre-Celtic cosmic goddess of the diurnal cycle, as the names of her children suggest. Her magical cauldron, symbol of abundance, suggests a goddess of prosperity. (Green 1995; Matthews; Straffon; MacCulloch 1996; Trevelyan)

Creiddylad In Wales, a springtime feast was dedicated to this mythic figure, honored with a contest between factions representing contenders for her hand. Such contests between winter and summer are known in other Celtic lands, including Scotland (see **Brigit**) and the Isle of Man. (Gantz 1976; Graves; MacCulloch 1911)

Cymidei Cymeinfoll This Welsh warrior giantess, whose name meant "big-bellied battler," gave birth to innumerable armed warriors, one every six weeks. She also owned the cauldron of regeneration (a symbol of the fruitful womb) that is at the center of the action of the *Mabinogion*. (Gantz 1976; Rolleston)

Dôn While Dôn's powers are difficult to discern, the stories in which her children appear suggest a period of matriliny. Dôn's children bore her name. Succession to the throne of King Math (Dôn's brother) passed to his nephew Gwydion, who was in turn succeeded by his sister's son; her daughter was the virgin mother **Arianrhod**. (Gantz 1976; Robbins; Dexter; MacCulloch 1996; Rhŷs; Spence 1972)

Elaine Cursed to remain forever in her room, Elaine, the Lady of Shalott, saw the world through tapestries she wove. When Lancelot appeared in those tapestries, Elaine fell in love and, undeterred by the curse, set off to Camelot. She died before arriving there, so Lancelot saw only her body. The story, created by Sir Thomas Mallory, derives from the goddess of Scotland's Clyde

River, who possessed a mirror in which she watched the world's activities.

Another Elaine, daughter of the wounded Fisher King, lusted after Lancelot, who refused to sleep with anyone but **Guinevere**. Elaine plied him with liquor until he mistook her for his beloved and conceived with her the fair knight Galahad. Finally, a minor Arthurian figure of this name, half sister to King Arthur, assisted him by marrying one of his enemies. (Spence 1972)

Elen Wales is dotted with churches dedicated to "Saint" Helen, mother of the Roman emperor Constantine, whom folklore claims was a Welsh princess. Behind the name was a woman whose name ("sprite") signifies her origin. Several Elens appear in Welsh folklore; it is unclear how they are related. One was an otherworldly woman, wife of Merlin. Another appeared in the dreams of the hero Maxen. (Evans-Wentz; Jones)

Figgy Dowdy At Cornwall's well of Carn Marth, tradition required that dolls be offered to Figgy Dowdy. Most Cornish holy wells are associated with goddesses (see **Modron**), and Figgy Dowdy's name may mean "reaper goddess." The witch Madgy Figgy may be a forkloric recollection. Madgy, who scrounged debris from wrecked ships, invoked weather spirits to cause wrecks. Once, she found the body of a Portuguese lady and hid the woman's jewels in her house. Every night thereafter, a strange light traveled to Madgy's cottage, then a stranger followed the light. When he left, he took the jewels, and Madgy had a fortune in ransom. "One witch knows another, living or dead," was all she would say. (Hunt)

Goewin As footholder to King Math of Wales, Goewin had a ceremonially important duty to her people, for if the king's feet were ever to touch the ground, he and they would be in danger. Because Goewin's position required that she be virginal, her power was stripped from her when Math's nephew raped her.

Although the rapist was apprehended, Goewin could not resume her duties, so Math made her queen. Other tales in the epic *Mabinogion*, from which we learn of Goewin, contain material known to be mythic, so this figure may be a late version of an early goddess. (Green 1995; Jones)

Goleuddydd The legend of this Welsh princess whose name means "bright day" appears to disguise an ancient goddess of fertility. She married a prince but was unable to conceive, making her people worry over the symbolism of a barren couple on the throne. When she finally became pregnant, Goleuddydd went mad and refused to live indoors, raging through the wilderness instead. When her labor came, her senses returned, and she sought the sty of a swineherd to bear her son, the prince Culhwch, or "pig" (see **Olwen**). Like **Rhiannon**, the Welsh horse goddess who bore a colt, we have here a probable disguise for an ancient goddess of fertility. (Jones)

Guinevere The Matter of Britain centers on the love triangle among old King Arthur, his young queen, Guinevere, and Lancelot, knight of the Round Table. After their wedding, Guinevere lived with Arthur until the arrival of Lancelot, with whom she fell in love. They attempted to restrain themselves but failed. Their affair spoiled the harmony of the Round Table, whose knights set out on quests, including one for the Holy Grail, presumably the chalice from which Jesus drank at the Last Supper.

Finally Guinevere could no longer live with Arthur. One Beltane she arranged to be abducted and, when Lancelot came to her rescue, ran away with him. Arthur recaptured Guinevere and sentenced her to death, but Lancelot rescued her. Camelot was in ruins, for which Guinevere is often blamed, despite the fact that it was Arthur's bastard son, Mordred, who caused the downfall.

What seems like a courtly romance hides a mythic story about the role of the king as sustainer of the earth goddess and his challenge by another man for that role. Some variants of the Arthurian legends show Guinevere as more active than others. In one, Mordred attempted to carry off Guinevere, emphasizing her role as holder of sovereignty. Scholars argue about how much Arthurian legend derives from Celtic mythology and how much is quasihistorical; as there is virtually no source for her historical existence, Guinevere appears to be the goddess of sovereignty in human form.

In some versions of the legend, Arthur had three wives in turn, each named Guinevere. This further strengthens the identification of this figure with the threefold goddess, as does the meaning of her Welsh name (*gwen*, white; *hwyvvar*, spirit). Although she is described as Christian, Guinevere's pagan background is emphasized by the time of her wedding to Arthur, and her departure, on the Celtic feast of Beltane. (MacCulloch 1996; Markale 2000; Squire)

Gwendydd Gwendydd was the twin sister of the great magician Merlin; she may also, or alternatively, have been his lover or wife. She held all Merlin's magical secrets, for after he was trapped by **Nimue** inside a tree, he passed along both his knowledge and his power to Gwendydd. (Ellis 1995)

Gwragedd Annwn Women of the otherworld made notoriously fickle wives, but that was not the case with the Welsh lake maidens called the Gwragedd Annwn, who were dependable, so long as one never lifted a hand against them. Breaking that taboo resulted in disappearance. A lake maiden named Nelferch set a limit of three mistakes. She lived happily except for her husband's tendency to tap her when he wanted attention. She considered it breaking her rule and, after the third incident, disappeared.

Lake maidens are found in many Celtic lands, including Ireland and Scotland, where lakes served as entrances to the otherworld and where fairy palaces could be seen from shore, sometimes beneath the water. Lake maidens could shape-shift into birds (usually swans) and could be captured if a man stole an article of clothing—swanskin robe or comb. The husband had to keep the object hidden, for if the lake maiden found it, she disappeared. (Crossley-Holland; Rhŷs)

Gwyar The story of this ancient Welsh goddess, wife of the god of heaven, is fragmentary. All that is left is the meaning of her name ("gore"); her relationship to King Arthur of Camelot, her brother (at other times the names given for Arthur's sister are **Morgause** and **Morgan**); and the information that she had two sons, one good, the other bad. (Squire)

Igraine Wife of Duke Gorlois of Cornwall, Igraine had several children with him, including two daughters with similar names, **Morgan** and **Morgause**. King Uther Pendragon lusted after Igraine, but she did not respond. So Uther, helped by Merlin, transformed himself into the likeness of Gorlois and spent a night with Igraine. When she discovered that her husband was dead and she was pregnant with Uther's child, she agreed to marry him. (Ellis 1995)

Iseult The greatest myth of Cornwall centered on the fated love of Iseult for Tristan. Mark, king of Cornwall, found a strand of golden hair so gorgeous that he fell in love with its owner. He dispatched his nephew Tristan to find her. When he located Iseult in Ireland, Tristan convinced her father that she should marry King Mark.

Fearing a loveless marriage for her daughter, Iseult's mother made an herbal potion that caused boundless love. She gave it to Iseult's maid Brangien with instructions to save it for the wedding night. But on the way to her wedding, Iseult was becalmed in a boat with Tristan. Desperate with thirst, they shared the potion, which bound them hopelessly together.

Despite her feelings, Iseult became the bride of Tristan's uncle. Brangien, guilt stricken over having served the potion, took her mistress's place in the honeymoon bed, but eventually Iseult had to do her wifely duties. Iseult tried to remain faithful but began to meet Tristan in secret. Iseult's suspicious husband tested her purity, forcing her to cross a stream, where, were she impure in any way, she would drown. Tristan, disguised as a beggar, helped Iseult across, so the queen was able to say that no man had touched her save her husband and the helpful beggar. Ultimately, the pain of deceit caused the lovers to separate. Tristan married a woman who shared Iseult's name, the Breton princess Iseult of the White Hands, but died of a broken heart, and Iseult lived in sorrow until she died. (Bedier; Jackson; Markale 2000)

Lady of the Lake Feminine figures in Arthurian legends are often difficult to distinguish, as sources differ on their roles and even their names. Thus the mysterious woman who gave aspiring king Arthur the sword called Excalibur is described in texts as a fairy; in this form she is compounded or confused with **Nimue**. Later, she was said to be Arthur's magician half sister **Morgause**, a sorceress who created illusions to keep people from entering her lands. Although she was Arthur's original champion, the Lady of the Lake helped bring down his court at Camelot, for she was the foster mother of Lancelot, who stole the affections of Queen **Guinevere**. In some texts, the Lady of the Lake was Lancelot's lover rather than his mother; by him she conceived the pure knight Galahad. Like a goddess of sovereignty, she took Arthur back to her land at the end of his life. (Evans-Wentz; Squire)

Laudine A lengthy Arthurian narrative centers on the mysterious Laudine, who lived within the magical forest of Brocíliande, beside a pool called Barenton. From that pool, great storms could be stirred and sent into the world, so Barenton was guarded by Laudine's husband, Esclados le Rous, called the Black Knight. When one of King Arthur's knights attempted to kill Esclados, only to be defeated, he roused the knight Owein to engage the Black Knight in combat. The tale does not make clear why either man wished to drive the Black Knight from his post.

A maiden named Luned, Laudine's attendant, helped Owein kill the Black Knight, and, further,

win Laudine's love. For a year the couple lived happily, but then King Arthur and his knights arrived. Laudine entertained them with a splendid feast but was heartbroken when they convinced Owein to accompany them on their adventures. Although he pledged to return, in the heat of war and conquest he forgot. A year passed, then Luned appeared at Camelot to challenge Owein on his betrayal. Driven mad by the revelation of his perfidy, Owein roved through the forest until a lion befriended him. Luned again appeared, instructing Owein to sprinkle water around the pool at Barenton. This caused great storms to ravish Laudine's land, which Luned claimed could be stopped by the Knight of the Lion (Owein in disguise), if Laudine would help him reconcile with his lady. When Owein was revealed, Laudine kept her promise. The early medieval narrative employs images of the weather goddess, as well as the theme of marriage between a man and the goddess of sovereignty. (Jones; Markale 2000)

Loathy Lady The Loathy Lady of Arthurian legend, a late form of the goddess of sovereignty, appeared to the pure knight Percival and mocked him because he could not answer questions of the mysterious Fisher King and thus lost the sacred Grail. In one tale, she was an enchanted maiden turned into a hag who won the heart of the knight Gawain. When they married, she told him she could be a lovely woman during the day and a hag at night, or the opposite, and asked him which he preferred. When he gave her the power to make the choice herself, she emerged from her enchantment, revealing that women want to make their own decisions. (Hearne)

Modron In Cornwall, a holy well where healing rituals are still practiced is dedicated to an otherwise unknown "saint" of this name. Trees surrounding the well are hung with offerings of cloth. In British folk history, Modron is called the mother of King Urien and the god Maponus. (Green 1995; MacCulloch 1911; Squire)

Morgan Two Arthurian heroines have frequently confused names: the magician Morgan and the ambitious queen **Morgause**. Both were children of **Igraine** by her first husband and thus were half sisters to King Arthur. Morgan and Morgause are easy to confuse because not only were both ambitious women, but they may both derive from the same original, perhaps a water goddess.

Morgan, a magician who studied with the great Merlin, was proud and imperious. When a knight jilted her, she created the Perilous Valley, where knights who betrayed their ladies became lost. She married a minor king, Urien. When her brother ascended the throne, envious Morgan brought disaster on Arthur by destroying the scabbard that protected the king. Yet it was to Morgan that Arthur was brought at the end of his life.

Morgan's mythic background is hinted at by her identification with the mysterious Morgan le Fay (Morgan the Fairy or Fate). Early texts say she was chief of nine sisters who lived on the Fortune Isles. Goddesses with names similar to Morgan's are found in Ireland (**Mórrígan**, a divinity of death and battle), in Brittany (**Morgan**, a sea fairy who kidnaps sailors), and in Wales (Morgans or **Gwragedd Annwn**). (Graves; Loomis 1945, 1956)

Morgause King Arthur's two half sisters did not make life easy for him. **Morgan** was a magician, Morgause his political enemy. She was also his lover, for through Merlin's meddling, the two conceived a son, Mordred. Arthur, aware that Mordred would kill him, murdered all children born at the time, but Morgause hid her son by moving far to the north on the isles of Orkney, where she married the king. There she taught Mordred to hate Arthur and they plotted the downfall of Camelot. (Squire)

Nevyn Her name resembles the Irish fairy queen **Niamh**, and their stories similarly deal with love and loss. A mermaid, Nevyn loved a Welshman, Ivan Morgan (Ifan Morgan), to whom she bore two children, a son named Nevydd (Nefyd) and a daughter, Eilonwy. Ivan knew Nevyn was a mermaid, but the couple kept it from their children. Nevydd discovered the secret and killed himself in shame. Eilonwy attempted suicide but was rescued by a merrow (merman) prince and lived thereafter with her mother's people. Nevyn came back to land to claim her son's body, then sailed away in a magical boat. (Spence 1972)

Nimue Two important figures in Arthurian material bear this name: the mysterious **Lady of the Lake**; and the lover of the magician Merlin, otherwise said to have been Arthur's half sister **Morgan**. Whether those two were originally the same is unclear. It is also unclear whether Viviane, Merlin's magician-lover, was the same as one or both of them. Nimue was the daughter of the Roman goddess **Diana** and a human man. As offspring of a woodland divinity, she was raised in the forest, where Merlin first met her. Her first request of him was to teach her to make a tower out of thin air; he did so, not realizing his life would end when she fashioned one to be his prison. (Ellis 1995; Markale 1997; Squire)

Olwen Olwen had streaming yellow hair, a red-gold necklace, and dozens of golden rings. As she walked, white flowers sprang up in her footprints. The romance that centers on Olwen begins when her father, Ysbaddaden, opposed her marriage to Culhwch, son of the pig goddess **Goleuddydd**. Because Ysbaddaden believed the match would cause his death, the giant put thirteen obstacles in the young man's way. But Culhwch overcame all to gain Olwen's hand. (Green 1995; Jackson; Jones; Williams)

Rhiannon The distinction between goddess and heroine can be difficult to establish, especially when myths were written after the arrival of monotheism. But in the case of Rhiannon, few deny that the heroine was originally a goddess, possibly descended from an ancient Celtic goddess, *Rigatona, "great queen." In Welsh mythology, Rhiannon appears as an otherworldly woman who raced a white horse around an enchanted spot, where she encountered King Pwyll. He gave chase, but Rhiannon outran him. At last, she stopped to reveal that she was seeking him, for his reputation had spread to the otherworld.

They married, and their first son was born. Shortly after, when the child disappeared, Rhiannon was found with blood on her face. Suspicion was roused that the queen had eaten her son. But Rhiannon was innocent, for when the child's nurses found him missing, they smeared dog's blood on the queen to divert attention from their laxness. Nonetheless, convinced of his wife's guilt, the king made Rhiannon into a horse, forcing her to serve as a mount for visitors. She was released after it was revealed that her son had been stolen by a spectral figure and raised by a nearby herdsman.

After Pwyll's death, Rhiannon remarried, but the kingdom turned barren when her son Pryderi assumed the throne. Rhiannon and her new husband, Manawydan, joined Pryderi and his wife Cigfa in scraping a living from the increasingly empty land. Finally they moved to a distant city, where they eked out a living as artisans, at which they were talented. They incurred the wrath of local craftsmen. Fearing for their safety, the family returned to Dyfed, where Rhiannon and her son disappeared. Manawydan discovered that a former suitor of Rhiannon had stolen them. After a suitable accord was reached, Rhiannon and Pryderi were returned to this world. Several scholars connected Rhiannon with the goddess of sovereignty, for her presence in Dyfed made the land abundant, while her absence made it barren. (Benigni; Dexter 1990; Graves; Green 1995, 1993; Hemming; Jones; MacCulloch 1911; Ross 1967)

FINNO-UGRIC CULTURES

The term "Finno-Ugric" describes not a culture but a group of languages spoken by people of varying racial and cultural backgrounds. We find five related Finno-Ugric languages spread across north-central Europe and western Russia: Ugrian (Hungarians/ Magyars, Mansi, and Khanty); Baltic Finn (Estonians, Finns, Livonians, and Karelians); Saami (Lapps); Finno-Permian (Zerians, Udmurts); and western Finn (Mari, Mordvin). Throughout the region, Finno-Ugric speakers established relationships with indigenous people, creating mythologies with considerable variation. Hungarians share folkways with central European neighbors rather than with distant linguistic cousins among the reindeer-herding Saami. Similarly, myths and rituals from nearby cultures left their mark, so Estonian religion has much in common with that of nearby Lithuania. This conflation makes it difficult for scholars to sort out what was purely Finno-Ugric from what has been absorbed from other influences.

Two religious traditions, however, seem to have been shared: shamanism and a bear-hunting ritual. Shamanism was probably the primary Finno-Ugric religion; words related to the practice reach back into earliest linguistic strata. Finno-Ugric shamanism described a world of many levels, from underworld to upper world, accessed by magicians who traveled while apparently in deep sleep. Such practitioners were spirit chosen and initiated through an arduous psychic process. Throughout Finno-Ugric cultures, women played prominent roles in shamanic practice.

The circumpolar bear cult derives from a belief that the animal was a dangerous ancestor. Despite this, the bear was occasionally sacrificed at a communion feast. Evidence of bear hunts from as early as the Paleolithic has been found in central Europe, so this ritual and totemic belief system may have lasted for millennia. Among the Khanty and the Mari, who held

on to the practice until the early twentieth century, the practices died out only recently.

The Finno-Ugric people rarely appear in early historical texts. Tacitus refers briefly to Finns, but no early writings record Finno-Ugric mythology, which was conveyed orally. Then, in the mid-nineteenth century, folklorist Elias Lönnrot collected tales and songs that he wove into a chronological narrative. The fifty verses of Lönnrot's second edition, published in 1849, make up the *Kalevala*, the major source for Finnish mythology. Not long after, Estonian scholars F. R. Faelmann and Friedrich Reinhold Kreutzwald compiled a similar work, called the *Kalevipoeg*, describing the pantheon of their homeland.

As with other Europeans, the Finno-Ugric peoples experienced a mixed impact from Christianization. While some rituals and rites were sustained by being transferred to saints, persecution or erasure was more common. Similarly, literacy brought some boons but more losses. A few tales and songs were recorded, but many others were lost.

The original power of Finno-Ugric goddesses is difficult to ascertain, although the earth goddess had an unquestionably important religious role. Soviet researchers posit a matriarchal society underlying the later-developing patriarchy. The fact that a creator goddess existed in many Finno-Ugric cultures offers support for this interpretation, typically rejected by European and American researchers. The Finno-Ugric described the earth as feminine, and the feminine was never associated with evil. Indeed, there was no specific concept of "evil" among these peoples, who found their moral imperative in propitiating nature's powers and attending to nature's laws.

In some remote and rural regions of the subarctic, indigenous Finno-Ugric religions are still practiced, in some cases through synthesis with Christianity, in some cases as part of traditional lifestyles. In Finland, a recent resurgence of interest in traditional religion has led to the establishment of a pagan network based in urban Helsinki. Outside the region, some interest has been shown in Finno-Ugric shamanic traditions, but overall the indigenous religions are little known internationally.

FINNO-UGRIC PANTHEON

Aino The first-born son of **Luonnotar** was the poet Väinämöinen. In his dotage, he was offered the hand of young Aino. No one asked Aino what she wanted, and she did not want to marry old Väinämöinen. She dressed herself in her mother's wedding garments, then walked away. Stripping off her clothes and jewels, she walked into the waters of the dead river Tuonela. Väinämöinen tried to reclaim her, but she had turned into a mermaid-salmon. The ballad that tells her story is called *Vellamon neidon onkiminen*, "Fishing for the Daughter of **Vellamo**," goddess of the seas, suggesting Aino was divine. (Comparetti; Lönnrot 1988)

Akanidi The Saami sun maiden noticed that some people smiled when she rose, but some looked downcast. Akanidi decided to help them become merrier and came to earth, disguising herself as the only daughter of an elderly couple who lived alone. There she grew into a lovely young maiden who, when her earthly parents took her to meet them, charmed others with songs and dances. She offered them polished stones and taught them crafts to fill their lives with beauty. But the people fought over her gifts until they set upon Akanidi to kill her. Rather than die, she sang a lovely song and floated skyward, never to descend again. (Riordan)

Ańge-patáj This Mordvin tree goddess may have been related to a Hungarian goddess celebrated on December 6, when people crafted bundles of birch twigs called Nyírfa Kisasszony ("Miss Birch"). Among the Lapps, the newly dead were beaten with birch twigs to protect them in their passage. Ańge-patáj's name means "mother goddess"; she ruled maternity and fecundity. (Hoppál and Pentikäinen)

Annikki Sometimes described as goddess of nightmares, Annikki was the sister of doomed hero Kullervo. Separated as children, they met as adults and had a sexual encounter, after which they discovered they were siblings. Both killed themselves in shame. (Abercromby 1, 2; Lönnrot 1969, 1988)

Aufruvva At appropriate seasons, this Saami mermaid gathered schools of fish and herded them into the mouths of rivers, then led them upstream to spawning grounds. As the people's diet depended upon seasonally replenished fish, Aufruvva can be seen as a goddess of abundance. Her lower body was that of a fish, but she had a woman's head and torso, with long hair that she loved to comb while sitting on rocks in midocean. (Holmerg)

Azer-Ava To Mordvins, the rain-bringing sky goddess made earth ready to bear fruit. As goddess of the ocean, she sent fish into the nets of fisherfolk. Azer-Ava's name, "great mistress," appeared as part of many other goddesses' names. Jurt-Azer-Ava was goddess of the home; Ban-Ava, ruler of the outhouse. Norov-Ava (corn mistress), Paksa-ava (field mother) and Nar-Azer-Ava (meadow spirit) were all invoked for good harvests.

Beyond the settlements were Mor-Ava, sea mother; Varma-Ava, wind woman; and Tol-Ava, spirit of fire. Haughty Cuvto-Ava, tree woman, punished anyone who broke tree branches by striking them with withering diseases. Vir-Azer-Ava, forest mother, assumed a different shape for each part of the forest; hunters prayed to her for luck. Especially significant were Mastor-Ava, earth mother; and the women's goddess, Niski-Ava. Mastor-Ava ruled earth and all its dwellers; at agricultural holidays the community offered sacrifices to her. Women worshipped Niski-Ava in privacy. (Holmberg; Honko et al.)

Barbmo-Akka This Saami goddess controlled migratory paths of birds, whose arrival and departure marked the coming of spring and fall in western Lapland. (Holmerg)

Beiwe With her daughter Beiwe-Neid, this Saami goddess traveled through the sky in an enclosure of reindeer antlers. In the Arctic spring, she brought forth plants so reindeer could prosper and reproduce. At each solstice, her worshippers sacrificed white female animals, the meat of which was threaded on a stick, then bent into rings and tied with bright ribbons. When Beiwe was invoked, a special prayer was said for the insane, for her winter absence caused madness.

On the day winter ended, the Saami smeared their doors with butter so Beiwe could be strengthened. On summer solstice, "sun rings," formed from twists of leafy branches, were hung. On the same day, buttery "sun porridge" was eaten as prayers were offered that Beiwe would "pour her merciful rays over the reindeer, and everything else."

Many Saami folk songs describe the sun goddess and her children. The sun goddess had a daughter, from whom descended a heroic race called the Children of Day, who survive as fairies. These Children included the Kalla-parnek, "famous ones of old," who today are stars but who once lived on earth, where they tamed reindeer and invented snowshoes.

The sun's daughter, named Njavvis-ene, was widowed when her husband was murdered. The same tragedy afflicted Attjis-ene, daughter of the moon. Both women were pregnant and could not hunt or fish, so they captured reindeer and tamed them to provide milk. For this reason, Saami tradition requires that women be given the larger share of reindeer herds.

Like the sun, Njavvis-ene was round and fair, but Attjis-ene was dark and thin. Njavvis-ene had a son; Attjis-ene, a daughter. While picking berries, Njavvis-ene agreed that the one who could pick fastest would take the boy to raise. Attjis-ene stuffed her basket with moss and added a few berries on top, then claimed the prize. When the boy had grown, he came to visit his playmate, Attjis-ene's daughter, and was surprised when Njavvis-ene called him "son." The sun's daughter related how he had been taken through treachery.

Angered, the boy went home and killed Attjis-ene, who, as she died, transformed her reindeer into frogs, toads, and beetles. Other stories say Attjis-ene escaped to become the wife of the north wind, bearing a son who went to live with the moon, his grandfather. Other tales say Attjis-ene was transformed into a beetle for her sins.

The kindly Njavvis-ene lived for a long time and, upon her death, was laid on a bed of *njavvi* (long reindeer hairs) and interred in a mountain that bears her name. Although her body had died, her spirit lived on as an invisible, beautiful reindeer herder. (Billson; Itkonen; Lundmark; Karsten; Paper)

Boszorkány When bad Hungarian fairies (see **Firtos**) had daughters, those children were Boszorkány, witches who looked like old women, frogs, black cats, or horses. To discover witches, one dyed the first egg of a black hen, then took it to church Easter Sunday. This caused witches to turn somersaults to escape the egg's powers. Accusations of witchcraft may have been used, as in other regions, for social control over women. (Jones and Kropf)

Büt aba The Cheremis water mother lived in fresh and salt water. If drought struck, Büt aba was called upon. Gathering on a riverbank, people threw water at each other. Then a sacrificial meal was made of a black animal, whose bones were thrown into the river. In springtime, Büt aba stirred up springs, making their water taste muddy, but offerings of barley calmed her. Fishermen devoted to Büt aba were careful not to pray too loudly, making the goddess aware of how many fish they were taking. Brides sacrificed to her when leaving their mother's homes; coins or beads thrown into water brought Büt aba's blessing and protection. (Sebeok and Ingemann)

Enech This Hungarian goddess appeared to two hunters as a doe. She led them through unknown regions until they came to the land of the Scythians, where she disappeared. In some stories, the young men then married two sisters; in others, the hunters are themselves descended from a doe named Enech. (Róheim)

Firtos Queen of the good Hungarian fairies, Firtos may be a diminished goddess. A castle where she lived with her human lover bears her name. His horse fell as they were mounting the hill beyond the castle and remains petrified. Firtos's opposite was Tartod, queen of the bad fairies. Both good and bad fairies influenced humans through magic, which they worked through words and curses, although folktales also endow them with wands of diamond, whips of copper, and milk that makes the countenance beautiful.

Fairies lived on the tops of mountains. Twenty-three castles in eastern Europe were once fairy palaces, including one built by cats and birds. Occasionally fairies lived in caves, like the one called Almás, from which a cold wind blew forth, causing sickness until blocked with shirts. Occasionally they lived in subterranean palaces of gold and crystal. Dame Rapson's underground castle was lightened by balls of diamonds hung from chains of gold, which reflected light on the treasure heaped there.

When fairies fell in love with humans, their love was fatal to both. Dame Rapson warned her daughter Irma about men, but the girl fell in love with Zelemir. When the lovers fell to their deaths together, Rapson found them and died of a broken heart. The sun petrified another tragic fairy, Helena, when she was returning home from an assignation. A rock is all that is left of her.

Fairy women led carefree lives, dancing and doing needlework. A mountain is named for Tarkö; the rivers running from it are named for her daughters Olt and Marcos. Other Hungarian fairies were Mika, a warrior who served Attila the Hun; Dame Jenö, petrified for saying insulting things about the Christian god; Dame

Vénétur, who defied that deity and was turned into a stone frog; and Dame Hirip, whose sons kidnapped human girls. (Jones and Kropf)

Ganîs The long-haired, long-tailed forest woman of the western Saami was similar to **Luot-Hozjit**. She watched reindeer herds in summer, when they were in wild pasture. Occasionally she seduced young Saami men, but there is no record of her having half-human children. (Holmberg)

Holdja The Estonian house goddess lived in the roof beam, bringing good luck to anyone who greeted her upon entering. Holdja called down curses on a family who destroyed her home to move to a new one. The only way to assure her goodwill was to bring a log from the old house to the new fireplace. Holdja moved in as soon as three logs were crossed and the fire lit. Among Baltic Finns, the goddess was called Haltia ("ruler") or Varjohaltia ("shadow ruler") and predicted the future. (Holmberg)

Hongas In the circumpolar bear-hunting ritual, this goddess guarded bears but occasionally let one be sacrificed. Her name ("fir mistress") may refer to the practice of placing a sacrificed bear's skull on a fir tree. Its body was then brought into the village and feted with beer and a ritual marriage with a human, a girl or boy, depending on the bear's sex. (Honko)

Iden-Kuva This Cheremis harvest goddess haunted the threshing area in early morning to ensure all was in order. She was shy, however, and fled if approached. Harvest ceremonies were dedicated to her. (Holmberg)

Illinti Kota The Selkup "grandmother of life" lived in an iron house beside a birch tree from whose roots human souls emerged. A great river arose there too, from which everything sacred or beneficent flowed, including waterbirds who returned to earth each spring from a sojourn with the goddess. (Hoppál and Pentikäinen)

Ismo The Finnish wind goddess threw foam on burns to cure them. She is among the "daughters of air," who also included Sumutar, daughter of mists, and Suonetar, a weaver who used veins for thread. All air daughters specialized in the healing arts. (Abercromby 1)

Jabmiakka In the chaotic underworld of Jabmiaimo, everyone lived as they did on earth but in a youthful body. Hellish Rotaimo, ruled by the eponymous goddess Rota, derives from Christian beliefs and was not originally part of Saami religion. From Jabmiaimo, Jabmiakka ("old woman of the dead") demanded that black cats be buried alive to appease her ill temper. She also required that beer be served at funerals. Saami shamans traveled to her in trance, for only she could release souls. (Bäckman and Hultkrantz; Karsten; Alhbäck)

Jumala The sun goddess of the Zyrians, Jumala was worshipped until recently. She was known for many centuries; ninth-century Vikings unsuccessfully searched for her solid-gold image. In 1549, a German nobleman found a golden goddess in a Ugrian shrine consisting of three figures enclosing each other, the inmost of which spoke in clanging bell tones. Golden offerings were hung in trees by worshippers and, when enough was accumulated, a new outer figure was forged. Jumala has remained hidden, although as late as 1967, treasure hunters were informed that Jumala was still honored. Jumala's image may have given rise to the Matrioshka dolls that have been popular for at least 200 years.

The vision of the sun as feminine is typical of Finno-Ugric cultures. The Voguls called her Kaltés or Sorńi and considered her the wife of the sky. The Voguls depicted her ruling both sun and moon. The birch was her sacred tree, the hare or goose her sacred animal; she ruled childbirth. She lived with her brother, the world master. Together, they revived their dead

parents by raising them from the seas with the aid of beetles. This goddess was connected with the cuckoo, because seven golden cuckoos lived in a tree behind her house. (Michael; Honko et al.; Hoppál 2000; Hubbs; Róheim; Sadovszky and Hoppál)

Kalma The Finnish death goddess, Kalma's name means "corpse odor" or "grave." Cemeteries are called *kalmisto* after her. Whether or not this figure existed mythologically, or was created from a common noun of feminine gender, is not established. (Abercromby 1, 2)

Keča Aba The Russian Cheremis worshipped the "sun mother" by bowing to the east each morning. Early documents suggest she was their primary divinity, a goddess who bestowed good health and to whom sun-shaped pancakes were offered. In historic times, festivals were held in a sacred grove, in which horses were sacrificed if they signified their desire to die by shuddering at a certain ritual moment. (Sebeok and Ingemann)

Kiputyttö The pockmarked Finnish goddess of pain was one of the daughters of underworld god Tuoni. She lived on a mountain, where she ground pain out of rocks. Her name meant "pain maiden," but she was not a virgin, for she had nine children (pox, gout, and other diseases). The unnamed "small daughter of Tuoni" who appears throughout the *Kalevala* may be Kiputyttö. (Lönnrot 1988)

Kyllikki When the Finnish hero Lemminkäinen sought a wife, he chose the blossom maiden Kyllikki. She had refused all suitors because she preferred the beauty of her land. So Lemminkäinen abducted her and held her until she agreed to be his wife, extracting from him a promise that he would never go to war. She, in return, promised to stop going to parties. But she grew bored with housework and slipped away for some fun, which Lemminkäinen used as an excuse to go back to war. Kyllikki has been interpreted as a double goddess with **Mielikki**. (Abercromby 1; Bonser; Lönnrot 1988)

Linda This "sleek maid" was born miraculously, with her sister Salme, from eggs: Linda from a grouse egg, Salme from a hen's. A lonely Estonian widow found both eggs and, placing them next to her skin, hatched them and raised the girls. When the sun, the moon, and a star came courting, Salme rejected the sun and moon, but the star won her heart. So the moon came courting Linda, who rejected him because of his fickleness. The sun came next, but Linda rejected him because he left the earth cold in winter. Other suitors came: Water, Wind, and the prince, all of whom Linda found reasons to reject. Finally a man came astride a splendid stallion, and Linda's heart was captured. The girls both left their widowed mother to join their new husbands. Linda later appears as the mother of heroes, suggesting a divine origin, as does the creation of a lake from her tears and her eventual transformation into stone. She is described as a bird goddess, sister to Jutta and Siura, also bird women. (Kruetzwald; March)

Loddis-Edne This protective goddess of the western Saami controlled nesting instincts of birds, which brought them back annually to the Arctic, where they provided sustenance in late winter. (Holmerg)

Louhi The fierce Finnish winter queen Louhi was the antagonist of the hero Väinämöinen. The gap-toothed dame had magical powers and great strength, but Väinämöinen was wily enough to outwit her. He stole her *sampo*, the magic mill that brought prosperity. When she realized the theft, Louhi raised a storm and called her son to freeze the sea. But all she managed to do was shatter the *sampo*. Väinämöinen escaped with the fragments still powerful enough to bring abundance and wealth.

Louhi's other great adventure was to steal the sun maiden **Päivätär** from the sky. Again, the hero won, this time with the assistance of the smith Ilmarinen, his brother. The conflict between Louhi and the sons

of **Luonnotar** has been interpreted as a mythic recollection of a change from a period when women had greater social standing to one in which women were more confined within their families. (Abercromby 1, 2; Lönnrot 1969, 1988)

Luonnotar The "daughter of nature" floated in the sky for serene ages, until she grew lonely and threw herself into the ocean, whereupon she floated for seven centuries, growing pregnant although still a virgin. One day, as Luonnotar rested near the water's turbulent surface, a duck appeared. Luonnotar's knee broke the water's surface, so the duck built a nest there and laid eggs. After three days, Luonnotar twitched involuntarily. The eggs fell and were transformed into the universe: lower part into earth, upper part into sky, yolk into sun, white into moon. Luonnotar took a hand in the emerging creation, forming islands and peninsulas, building the earth.

A goddess of birth similar to **Azer-Ava**, Luonnotar was occasionally seen as a triple goddess. She had three sons, all culture heroes (Väinämöinen, Lemminkäinen, and Ilmarinen, representing poetry, magic, and smithcraft, respectively). She was sometimes hermaphroditic, with her alternative name, Ilmater, sometimes described as her masculine name. When part of a goddess trinity, Luonnotar is connected with Udutar and Terhetär, sisters who live together sifting mist through a sieve to cause disease. In some traditions, Luonnotar gave birth to the world's first woman, Kave, who gave birth to humanity, yet at times, Kave is used as a title of Luonnotar. Her connection to the dual goddesses Suvetar, daughter of summer, and Etelätär, daughter of the wind, is unclear, although both are invoked with titles resembling those of Luonnotar. (Abercromby 1, 2; Bonser; Comparetti; Holmberg; Lönnrot 1988)

Luot-Hozjit The Saami reindeer virgin, who lived on a lichen-covered mountain and guarded herds during grazing season, resembled a girl covered in reindeer fur. Prayers were offered to her in spring, when herds were let out to graze, and in autumn, when they returned. (Holmberg)

Madder-Akka This Saami goddess had three daughters: Sar-Akka, Juks-akka, and Uks-Akka, a trinity of fate goddesses. While Madder-Akka controlled fertility, her daughters were directly involved with human reproduction. The goddesses lived beneath the earth's surface or along the Milky Way, which connects earth and heaven. Birds migrated along that starry pathway, which led human souls between the worlds.

Sar-Akka opened the womb. For assistance, wood was chopped outside the birthing tent. The new mother drank brandy in Sar-Akka's honor before giving birth; afterward, her first meal was porridge in which three sticks had been cooked. Whether one found the white one (good luck), the black one (death), or the cleft one (success) revealed how Sar-Akka saw the child's future. Among the Swedish Saami, Sar-Akka was supreme deity and creator of the world. She was painted, together with her mother and sisters, on Saami drums.

Juks-Akka ("old lady of the bow") was also honored in the postbirth ceremony. If the newborn was a boy, she assured him successful hunting, provided a tiny bow was placed in the porridge. The third sister ("old lady of the door"), Uks-Akka, received the newborn into the world of light. Uks-Akka lived just beneath the tent's entry, from which she blessed and protected anyone leaving home. (Bäckman; Billson; Itkonen; Karsten; Hoppál and Pentikäinen; Ränk; Alhbäck)

Ma-Emma The Estonian earth mother was honored wherever a tree stood alone in a meadow or where a pile of stones marked the foundation of an old house. Because Ma-Emma controlled fertility, humans depended on her and offered milk, butter, and wool in thanksgiving. Envisioned as a young woman in spring, she was fed manure in order to bear. When plowing, it was important not to strike the earth and injure her.

At Ma-Emma's midsummer feast, fires celebrated her fruitfulness. Animals were herded into the smoke. Flowers and grasses, carried through the smoke by children, were fed to the cattle. The evening ended when the village's most distinguished woman led processions around the fire, then placed food on the earth. The earth goddess appears under an almost identical name, Maan Emä, among other Finns. (Comparetti; Paulson 1971)

Marjatta This maiden ate a red lingonberry that impregnated her. Cast out by her parents for her pregnancy, she bore a beautiful son in a manger. Due to the stigma of his birth, the boy was unable to find anyone to christen him, but he found a friend in the poetry god Väinämöinen, who predicted he would create a new world. The Christian references are clear, but the story may have roots in a pre-Christian original. (Lönnrot 1988)

Mere-Ama The Finn and Saami water goddess represented the ocean, but she also resided in streams and brooks, which resembled her silver-streaked hair. When a bride moved into a new home, she made acquaintance with the area's "water mother" by offering bread and cheese at the nearest stream. The bride then sprinkled herself with water. Those married in winter, when Mere-Ama was frozen, gathered after the ice broke. All who participated were blessed with healthy children, for Mere-Ama controlled human reproduction. Mere-Ama ruled all creatures of the sea. To woo her good nature, humans poured liquor into the sea. Many fish would bite, for Mere-Ama loved brandy. (Honko et al.)

Metsannetsyt In western Finland, this forest woman exposed herself to passing men. If they took her in their arms, they would find themselves embracing a tree stump. She lived in uncultivated land, where she could be helpful or harmful depending upon how humans treated her. (Holmberg; Lofstedt)

Mielikki Mielikki ("darling") was the Finnish goddess of forests and hunts, as well as the protector of animals.

Her favorite animal was the bear; when she found orphaned cubs, she nurtured them into adulthood. She was also associated with the circumpolar bear cult. The many tender terms for Mielikki ("good mistress") suggest that the speakers saw the goddess as needing to be cajoled. Mielikki may be the same as Tellervo, the forest-mistress. She may also be a more kindly form of the hunters' goddess **Kyllikki**. An alternative name for her, or a separate figure, was Hiiletär ("charcoal woman"), who provided fuel for cooking meat. Other associated figures, or titles of Mielikki, are **Hongas** ("fir mistress"), a hollow-backed woman; Simater ("virgin honey woman"), who wore a silver belt; Nyrkitär, the dejected; and Elina, who snared rabbits.

Mielikki was the wife of the forest god, Tapio, whose daughters were well-known: Tellervo, who wore gold and silver clothing; Lumikki, who kept white-furred animals safe; Ristikko, whose animals had a white cross on their breasts; Päistärys, the weasel goddess; Vitsäri, the game driver; the tree goddesses Tuometer (cherry), Pihlajatar (rowan), and Katajatar (juniper); and Tiuulikki, the wind goddess. Their daughters-in-law were Mikitar, the listening fox; Huijutar and Siiliki, the wasp goddesses; and Kärehetar, who brought foxes to hunters. (Abercromby 1, 2; Bonser; Lönnrot 1988)

Mjer-jema The Livonians of Latvia and Estonia honored the sea mother Mjer-jema. When launching a new boat, the owner poured a glass of liquor into the water for Mjer-jema. She also received sacrifices on the first fishing trip each year, to bring good fortune and keep away bad weather. Mjer-jema was the mother of the Mjer-titard, the "sea daughters," who appear as mermaids (see **Näkinein**) in folktales. (Paulson 1971)

Näkinein The heavy-breasted water spirit of the Estonians, like the Finnish **Aufruvva**, could be seen combing her splendid hair as she sat on a rock in the ocean. A beautiful siren, she was not threatening (see Greek **Sirens**) but rather a force of abundance and herder of the cattle of the deep, the fish and sea mammals. (Holmerg; Paulson)

Ovda Among Russian Finns, this forest spirit looked like a woman with backward feet. She had long breasts, which she threw over her shoulders when she ran. Her home was deep in the forest or in rock caves, where, when annoyed with humans, she caused whirlwinds that spun them around until they died. When threatened by her, people tried to touch the small hole under her left arm, which paralyzed her. (Holmberg)

Päivätär The spinning sun virgin Päivätär wove daylight from a rainbow arch. She held a weaver's batten, a heddle, and a golden shuttle. The cloth she wove was gold, while her moon sister's was silver. **Louhi** captured and hid her, and the metal sun image that replaced her proved unsatisfactory. So the poet Väinämöinen set out to free the sun. He went to Ilmarinen, the smith, and ordered a three-tined hoe, a dozen ice picks, and many keys. Louhi, seeing activity at the forge, disguised herself as a bird and flew over to spy. When she saw it would be impossible to win over the determined heroes, she set the sun free. (Lönnrot 1988)

Pohjan-Akka This Saami goddess was mistress of Pohjan ("northern home"), where anyone who died a violent death lived forever, wearing blood-drenched garments. Witches could visit Pohjan in their living bodies, but no one else could find the place. A river flowed through Pohjan, torn by white-water rapids; after crossing that, the dead passed through a dark gate into Pohjan-Akka's world. (Holmberg)

Port-Kuva The Cheremis said the house goddess Port-Kuva ("house woman") was invisible to human eyes unless disaster was near. Because she controlled such events, causing household accidents when people insulted her, anyone who saw her could repair the breach before ill befell. Sacrifices of black animals were helpful. Bread and pancakes also sufficed, if placed under the floorboards. Boards creaking during the night meant the house goddess was walking about, checking her domain. Should families fail to keep a clean household, she departed, whereupon the house developed problems. (Holmberg; Sebeok and Ingemann)

Puges The Ostian and Vogul goddess of heaven decided who would conceive and what the child's sex would be; she created the new soul, which she rocked until birth. She may have been the same as Vagnegimi, "old woman of seven cradles," who carried a pole on which hung threads representing lives. Her knots determined the length of people's lives. (Holmberg)

Rana Neida Among the southern Saami, this springtime goddess turned south-facing hills green early in the season, giving winter-starved reindeer fresh growth for browsing. To gain her favor, Saami rested a spinning wheel against her altar and covered it with blood. (Dioszegi; Holmberg)

Rauni The Finnish thunder goddess Rauni was incarnated in the rowan tree, whose berries were sacred to her. She brought plant life to the earth's face by having intercourse with the thunder god; she was honored with reindeer sacrifices. (Holmberg; Albäck)

Šundi-Mumi The Wotjakian and Votyak "Sun Mother" was connected with the fertility of fields, as was Gudiri-Mumu, the thunderstorm mother, and the earth goddess Mu-kilšin-Mumi, "mother earth creator." Sacrifices to the earth were appropriate only during summer, because during winter she slept. The earth goddess favored sacrifices of animals with dark skin, the color of rich soil. (Paulson 1965)

Szépasszony Whether flatteringly called Szépasszony ("fair lady") or Kissasszony ("fair maid"), this Hungarian fairy was a figure of fright. She danced with her companions in open areas, leaving raised circles of grass behind. She may have descended from an ancient weather divinity. Her connection with the sky is suggested by such terms for the Milky Way as "linen of Szépasszony" and "fairy way." Like other fairy women, she stole men. (Dömötör; Pocs)

Tündér Ilona The Ugrians, including Hungarians, said the sun was an egg that Tündér Ilona, taking the shape of a swan, laid in the sky. This figure may be the same as fairy queen Helena (see **Firtos**), for Ilona is a Hungarian version of that name; the first part of Tündér Ilona's name refers to a supernatural woman with the power to make things invisible. She is prominent in Transylvanian folktales. (Róheim)

Tuonetar The Finnish queen of death lived in darkness near a black-watered river. It was possible to reach Tuonela, Tuonetar's country, by hiking seven days through underbrush, seven through woodlands, and seven through dense forest. The traveler eventually reached the banks of the river, where Tuonetar's daughters laundered their dark robes. Few survived contact with these goddesses of disease. If one reached the death queen, Tuonetar offered a brew of frogs and worms; drinking it made return to the land of life impossible. (Comparetti; Lönnrot 1988)

Vad-leány The "forest girl" of the Hungarians lived in wild country, where she ran from hunters unless they wore fine boots. If caught, she mourned until reunited with her baby son, but she could be convinced to leave the child with humans. Vad-leány often seduced men; rustling leaves was the sound of the forest girl and her human lovers. (Dömötör)

Vellamo The Finnish "mother of the water" guided fish into nets of the hungry. Vellamo was ancient, her worship having been recorded almost 2,000 years ago. She had many daughters, the sea's waves, who tended cattle and raised crops on the ocean's floor. Fishermen who needed help locating shoals of fish invoked another goddess, Juoleheter. (Abercromby 1; Lönnrot 1988; Honko et al.)

Vitsa-Kuva The Cheremis "cattleyard lady" appeared every night among the flocks, a white-dressed lady who caused animals to mate if she liked their owner, thus increasing family wealth. Woe to the person to whom Vitsa-Kuva took a dislike. She would drive the cattle through the fields all day until, unable to stop long enough to eat, they fell dead. (Holmberg)

Xatel-Ekwa The Hungarian sun goddess rode through the sky mounted simultaneously on three horses. Her daughter Xoli-Kalteš, the dawn, was a hot-blooded young woman who baked men who came to court her. When Xatel-Ekwa saw this, she rescued the young men. Among the Hungarians, moon and sun were female. (Buday; Hoppál 2000; Róheim)

The lasting influence of Greek mythology stems from the region's early development of literacy. By the seventh century BCE the Greeks recorded their myths in epic, lyric, and dramatic poetry that are still read today. But literature can hide as well as reveal. What appears to be a highly structured pantheon, with careful lines of descent among divinities, was originally a complex group of tales from various ethnic groups and eras. Among those myths were those that contradicted or subverted Greek visions of appropriate womanly behavior.

The question of the status of women in ancient Greece is similarly complex. By the historical period, Greek women lived a restricted life, but the goddesses they worshipped showed impressive power, perhaps because they were vestiges of earlier cultures. Archaeology suggests that goddesses figured more significantly in the religion of Crete and its mainland colony, Mycenae, than in Greece after invasion by patriarchal Indo-Europeans. The wealthy Cretan culture flourished around 1600 BCE, only to be destroyed in 1200 BCE, probably by earthquakes and volcanic explosions. Before its destruction, this Minoan culture gave prominence to goddesses. Minoan art shows bare-breasted women worshipping naked goddesses. Cretan myths emphasize a mother goddess but also show vulnerable maiden goddesses.

During the height of Cretan power, a proto-Indo-European group settled on the mainland, where they adopted Minoan culture. These Mycenaean Greeks left inscriptions to Hera, Artemis, and Athena, showing that classical divinities had roots in the earlier culture. Mycenaeans appear in the epics of Homer, recorded around 800 BCE but referring to events of at least 500 years earlier. Helen, Clytemnestra, and other strong female characters existed in oral tradition before appearing in the *Iliad* and the *Odyssey*.

The Indo-Europeans, who based family and religion on father figures, arrived in waves over many centuries. Under the Dorians in 1200 BCE, Mycenaean cities were destroyed and their religious sites sacked. The next 400 years show little cultural development. But earlier religions did not disappear, for the invaders' gods were "married" to indigenous earth goddesses. Thus the thunderer Zeus married the important goddess Hera, as well as raping or seducing innumerable other divine women.

Around 800 BCE, classical Greece emerged with a developed religion and a carefully organized pantheon of divinities that included these earlier goddesses. For the next 200 years, Greek cities held sway over the Mediterranean. Athens, Sparta, Argos, and Thebes were similar in the status afforded to women. Greek women were cloistered in households, where they rarely interacted with men outside their immediate families. Slave women, both Greek and foreign, had few rights and lived lives of dangerous vulnerability. The exceptions were *hetaerae*, educated courtesans who provided entertainment and stimulation for powerful men.

Despite these limitations, Greek women had a place in religious life. In Athens, women offered rituals that showcased their economic contribution through home industries such as weaving. Because the division of "secular" from "spiritual" was not sharp, women holding positions of religious power may have had some secular power as well. The question of the status of Greek women, including their religious rites and duties, is a subject of scholarly debate.

Later, goddesses from other lands migrated with their worshippers. In some cases, room was made for newcomers; such was the case with Aphrodite, an immigrant from the eastern Mediterranean. But other goddesses were too distant from patriarchal values to be welcomed into the divine order. Thus Cybele, great mother of the Thracians to the north, was never accepted into Mount Olympus, though she was honored as Meter, "mother."

As in many lands, ancient Greek religion was not entirely wiped out with the coming of Christianity. Until the early twentieth century, superstitions derived from the older religion were practiced, and place-names reveal old sites of worship. In recent times, revival of Greek paganism has been attempted. In Greece, which by law supports the Greek Orthodox Church, such worship is illegal. In the United States, Hellenic revival paganism, a reconstructed religion, has adherents. Finally, Greek goddesses are invoked in Wiccan rituals, despite the fact that the religion claims descent from western European paganism.

GREEK PANTHEON

Achlys Pale and thin, with long fingernails, bloody cheeks, and dusty shoulders, Achlys wept constantly while her teeth chattered. The shield of **Hera**'s warrior, Heracles, depicted her, as a warning to opponents of the misery he could cause. (Smith)

Adamanthea This obscure figure holds an important place in Greek mythology, for Zeus could not have became the preeminent Greek god without the help of Adamanthea, a **Nymph** or princess. His father, Chronos, intended to swallow the infant god, as he had swallowed Zeus's earlier-born siblings. But earth mother **Rhea** hid the infant in Crete, in the care of Adamanthea. Chronos ruled earth, heavens, and sea; he could see anything that existed in his realm. But Adamanthea hung a cradle from a tree and there—suspended between earth, sea, and sky—Zeus was invisible to his destructive father. In other versions, the nurse of Zeus is named **Aega**, Ida, Adrastea, Neda, Helice, or **Cynosura**. The relation of this figure to the goat **Amalthea** is unclear. (Smith)

Admete This priestess of **Hera** stole the image of the goddess from her home in Argos and carried it to the

island of Samos. When the Argives tried to steal their statue back, the ship carrying it would not move, so the thieves abandoned it onshore. There the Samians found Hera's image, purified it through bathing, and moved it into their temple. They held an annual festival in which the statue was tied to a tree so it could not be moved. Stories like this often recall the transmission of a goddess cult from one area to another, and indeed, Hera is found in both Samos and Argos, although it is unclear which was the original site of worship. The ritual describes the annual spring rite in which Hera was bathed and tied to the sacred lugos tree to transfer her regenerated power to the vegetal world. The name of the priestess, "untamed," connects her with unbroken young horses, symbols of fecundity. (O'Brien 1993)

Aedon The queen of ancient Thebes plotted to murder the eldest son of her sister and rival, the fertile queen **Niobe**, but accidentally killed her own child. Stricken by remorse, Aedon attempted suicide and was transformed into the first nightingale, a bird that haunts the night with its mournful cry. Tales of transformations of humans into animals and birds may derive from a period when totemic ancestry was acknowledged or may derive from "just-so" stories of how animals came to have certain characteristics.

Another myth says Aedon was such a happy wife that she became the object of jealous **Hera**'s ire, perhaps because she boasted of her happiness. The goddess sent **Eris** to destroy Aedon's marriage. Aedon was lured into suggesting a contest to her husband: the first one to finish the projects they were working on (he a carved chair, she a piece of embroidery) would win a female slave. She won the contest but lost her husband, because he dressed her sister Chelidonis as a slave, raped her, threatened her with death should she reveal her identity, and gave her as the promised prize to Aedon. When Chelidonis bemoaned her fate, Aedon overheard her and was horrified at what she learned. The sisters killed Aedon's husband's son and served the flesh to him for dinner, then escaped to their father's home. When the husband came looking for her, Aedon's family covered him with honey and exposed him to ants, but she took pity on him. As she was about to rescue him, Zeus turned the whole family into birds. Aedon became a nightingale, and Chelidonis a swallow. For a similar tale, see **Philomena**. (Graves 2; Homer *Od*)

Aega Like her sisters **Circe** and **Pasiphae**, this daughter of the sun was hypnotically beautiful; when earth-born giants, the Titans, attacked the gods of Olympus, the earth mother **Gaia** placed Aega in a cave to hide her loveliness. It is probable that behind these Greek legends lies a myth in which the three sisters were connected with the sun, for Pasiphae means "she who shines for all," while Circe means "circle." Aega also appears as one of the **Nymphs** who nursed Zeus, slaughtered so her skin might become a shield to protect the baby god, while Aega herself was transported to the sky as a star or as the constellation Capella. Again, solar imagery is involved; the name of Aega's sister was given as Helice, "sunny." (Graves 1; Smith)

Aethilla After the Greeks defeated Troy, they captured the city's women with the intention of keeping them as sexual slaves. The Trojan princess Aethilla refused to live in slavery. When the ship of her captor Protesilaus stopped for supplies, Aethilla organized a mutiny. While their captors were onshore, the princess and her companions set fire to the ship, stranding the Greeks and permitting the captives to escape. They founded the town of Scione. (Smith)

Aethra This princess of Troezen was betrothed to the hero Bellerophon, who tamed **Medusa**'s son, the winged horse Pegasus. But he was mysteriously banished before they could marry. Inspired by a dream, she traveled to the island of Sphaeria, where she was visited by the ocean god Poseidon. She changed the island's name to Hiera and built a temple to **Athena** Apaturia ("the lying one"), to whom brides offered their girdles. Aethra became the mother of the hero Theseus, whose father may have been Poseidon. She

then became a slave of **Helen**, with whom she was taken to Troy during the Trojan War. Her sons were killed in the conflict and, although freed upon the Greek victory, she killed herself in sorrow for her children's deaths. Aethra's story brings together many important goddesses in a confusing narrative. That she was so consistently connected to Poseidon, the original husband of the earth goddess (see **Demeter, Gaia**), suggests that she may have originally been a divinity of some power.

Another Aethra was the mother of the Athenian king Theseus, whose father, Aegeus, had been given advice by the oracle at Dephi (see **Pythia**) about the best way to bear heroic children. The Pythia warned Aegeus not to "loose the jutting neck of the wine-skin...until you have come once again to the city of Athens." Aegeus interpreted this as an instruction not to have intercourse with any woman until he had returned home. But the oracle spoke in riddles. Pittheus of Troezen offered Aegeus an alternative interpretation of the oracle: that he should sleep with Aethra, Pittheus's daughter. Aegeus left Aethra immediately after impregnating her, hiding tokens of his identity under a stone with instructions that the child, upon reaching manhood, claim them and follow his father. After her service in bearing the hero, this Aethra disappears from legend. (Plutarch *Lives*; Smith)

Aglauros Before **Athena** ruled Athens, a trinity of earth goddesses named Aglauros, Herse, and Pandrosos represented the bonds of society. Later, Athena joined them in a complex myth. Athena entrusted the sisters with a box, warning them not to open it. When the curious girls peeked, they discovered Athena's snake son, Erechtheus (sometimes said to have been the child of Aglauros). Variants of the myth say Aglauros and Herse were driven insane; or Aglauros was turned into a stone; or Aglauros threw herself from the Acropolis. Into classical times, girls of noble families served Athena in her temple on the Acropolis and assisted with a secret rite in honor of Aglauros and her sisters. (Larson 1995; Kerényi 1978; Ovid *Met*; Reeder)

Aidos One of the primary attendants of the love goddess **Aphrodite** was the minor goddess Aidos, "modesty." Daughter of **Nyx**, she had huge dark wings to cover the secrets of lovers. She accompanied Aphrodite everywhere, for love thrives most when accompanied by self-respect. Aidos has also been called the goddess of shame, although the Greeks distinguished the proper modesty of Aidos from a sense of disgrace. (Sanford)

Alcestis The Greeks' image of a loyal wife was Alcestis, who died for her husband when he committed sacrilege. She was the daughter of a tyrannical father, Pelias, who refused to let her marry unless a suitor came in a chariot drawn by a lion and a wild boar. The king Admetus did so, with the help of the sun god Apollo, but he forgot to offer thanksgiving sacrifices to the god's sister, **Artemis**. No one else would agree to die for the king, so Alcestis offered her own life. But the queen of the dead, **Persephone**, refused to accept her in Hades and sent her back to life. It is unclear whether Alcestis joined her sisters in murdering their father, Pelias, after being bewitched by **Medea**. (Euripides *Alcestis*)

Alcippe The rape of this daughter of **Aglauros** occasioned the first murder trial. Alcippe ("mighty mare") was assaulted by a son of Poseidon, god of oceans, whereupon her father, the war-god Ares, killed the offender. Called by the gods to account for his actions, Ares was acquitted once he explained. As Poseidon also raped the goddess **Demeter** while they were both in the shape of horses, this may be an altered version of that story. (Graves 1; Kerényi; Apollodorus; Pausinaus)

Alcmene While her husband was away at war, Alcmene was surprised to find him at her doorstep one night. But it was not her husband; it was Zeus, who lusted after her. Their tryst lasted three nights but seemed shorter, because Zeus asked the sun god to lengthen the night in order to better his enjoyment. Zeus left Alcmene unknowingly pregnant. When her husband returned, she expressed delight in the time they had spent together, leaving him baffled and jealous. He consulted an oracle and learned the truth, then never slept with her again for fear of divine jealousy. Her son was the hero Heracles. Alcmene, although described as a mortal woman, may be a goddess. (Euripides *Heracleidae*, *Hippolytus*; Graves 2; Larson; Motz)

Amalthea This magical nanny goat provided such copious milk that the baby god Zeus never went hungry. When he grew up, Zeus turned one of Amalthea's horns into the cornucopia. After providing for humankind, the goat rose into heaven, where she became the constellation Capricorn. She may be the same as the **Nymph** Adamanthea, who hid Zeus from his destructive father. (Smith)

Amazons One of the most powerful female images to emerge from Greek culture is that of the one-breasted warrior woman, the Amazon, who spurned men except for the occasional night needed to produce daughters; sons were either exposed or given to their fathers. To the Greeks, Amazons were warriors bearing ivy-shaped shields and double-bladed axes as they marched under their war queen. Under their peace queen, the Amazons supplied all their own needs and produced coveted artwork. From 1000–600 BCE, Greeks believed their Amazon enemies controlled the shores of the Black Sea.

Did the Amazons exist? Some theorists contend that because northern tribeswomen fought alongside their men, their presence was extrapolated into an entire kingdom. Others argue that the Amazons were projections of the male Greek mind, fearful of what might happen if subjected women were free to do as they pleased.

Many sources claim the word "Amazon" means "breastless." Supposedly, Amazons amputated their right breasts, the better to draw the bow. But Greek art never depicts mutilated women. Rather, artists showed Amazons with two intact breasts, one bared. The false etymology may have arisen to promote the idea of Amazons as unwomanly.

Legends about Amazons connect them with heroes such as Heracles, who, for murdering his children, was sentenced to perform twelve virtually impossible tasks, one of which was to bring back the Amazon's golden belt of queenship. With a huge force, Heracles sailed to the land of women and marched to the palace, surrounded by armed Amazons. Far from resisting, Queen Hippolyta offered him the belt in peace, and her bed with it.

Rumor flew that Hippolyta was under attack, and the Amazons counterattacked. It ended poorly for the Amazons, who were no match for superhuman Heracles. They were forced to surrender their leader Antiope, and Hippolyta lay dead. Antiope was carried back to Athens in chains and given to King Theseus. She became either Theseus's concubine or his legal wife and bore him a son, Hippolytus, named after Hippolyta. But Theseus tired of Antiope, which outraged the Amazons, who attacked Athens, penetrating right to the sacred hill, the Acropolis. There the battle reached an awful pitch, with Antiope dying still captive and many other Amazons losing their lives in the heroic, futile effort. The defeated women retreated, and the trail home was lined with their shield-shaped gravestones.

Many authors related this legend, with variant details. Hippolyta may have wished to follow Amazonian convention by making sure that Heracles was strong enough to father sturdy children, and the Amazon warriors mistook their wrestling match for an attack. She may have died in that first attack, or she may have led the Amazon raid to free Antiope. Theseus, who sometimes substitutes for Heracles in myth, may have been her captor. Some tales say there were three queens, the third being Melanippe, who either was held captive in Athens or led the rescue force. Finally, a queen named Oreithyia appears in some versions, merging sometimes with Hippolyta, sometimes with Antiope. Clearly the story of the attempt to gain the Amazons' symbol of sovereignty,

and their attempt to gain it back, held a powerful place in the Greek mind.

Stories of Amazons distinguish them from typical Greek women. Amazons mated with whom they wished. One Amazon queen, Thalestris, selected only kings and princes for sexual duty. She had borne several children when she cast eyes on Alexander of Macedon and invited him to fertilize her. The Libyan Amazon queen Omphale purchased attractive male concubines because she knew no man could equal a queen. When the hero Heracles came up for sale, Omphale bought him and dressed him in transparent purple dresses.

Amazonian feats in battle were more often described than those of the bedroom. Hiera, a Mysian general, fought in the Trojan War. Lysippe, the first to use cavalry, expanded her empire throughout Asia Minor with her brass-bowed warriors. After Lysippe was killed, her Amazons conquered Thrace and Syria under the leadership of Marpesia. They marched through Ephesus, finally reaching the Aegean Sea.

Myrine subdued Atlantis with 30,000 mounted women supported by 3,000 infantrywomen, armed with bows and protected by snakeskin armor. Myrine executed the Atlantean men and enslaved the women and children. Then she established a city in her name and signed a truce with the Atlantean women to protect them against the fierce neighboring **Gorgons**. The Atlanteans concluded a secret alliance with the Gorgons and overthrew the women warriors.

Myrine escaped and conquered Lesbos, Samothrace, and Lemnos. Caught in a storm, she sacrificed to **Artemis** and was spared, thereafter setting up shrines in the goddess's honor. She died in battle in Thrace, when an alliance of kings invaded Asia Minor; she gave her name to the city of Myrina, as did Amazons who founded Ephesus, Smyrna, and Kyme.

Perhaps the most famous Amazon was Penthesilea, who went to Troy accompanied by a troop that, although outnumbered, nearly turned the tide of battle. Penthesilea engaged the Greek hero Achilles in single combat. The contest was close, but Penthesilea was overcome and killed. Achilles, tearing off her helmet to see his worthy opponent, was surprised to find she was a woman, then raped her corpse and killed a comrade who suggested this was unnatural.

Some Amazon legends may be based in fact. One historical queen was Scythian Tomyris. When Cyrus the Great invaded her country, Tomyris attempted to negotiate a truce. He refused; she sent her son against the invader, who took him prisoner; the young prince committed suicide in shame. In retaliation, Tomyris destroyed Cyrus's army and captured the king. She killed him, then tossed his severed head into a vat of blood, instructing him to drink his fill.

Some sources say the Amazons' ancestral goddess was Otrere, also a title of distinction for women leaders. Mother of famous Amazon queens, Otrere was a daughter of war god Ares or his wife. More typically, the Amazonian goddess was Artemis. Legend says Queen Lysippe built temples to Artemis with the spoils of her victories. Hippo, with Queens Marpesia and Lampado, inaugurated the worship of Artemis at Ephesus. They set up a wooden image of Artemis and performed a shield dance, stamping the ground rhythmically and shaking quivers as pipes played a warlike melody.

Archaeologists have found evidence suggesting mounted nomadic warriors in the region where the Greeks placed the Amazons. Rich graves have revealed remains of women buried with symbols of religion and battlefield. Vestiges of the women's garments, well preserved despite their antiquity, are strikingly similar to garments shown on Amazons in Greek art. (Behan and Davis-Kimball; Bennet; Hawley and Levick; Blundell and Williamson; Lefkowitz; Cameron and Kuhrt; Homer *Iliad*; Ovid *Fasti*; Plutarch *Lives*; Sobol; Suhr 1953)

Amphitrite Amphitrite was a sea goddess whom the invading Greeks "married" to their god Poseidon, demoting her to a **Nymph**. Amphitrite fled to the Atlas Mountains but later, coaxed into marriage, bore several children, among them the island goddess Rhode. When Poseidon began an affair with **Scylla**, Amphitrite turned her into a sea monster. (Hesiod; Smith)

Amymone When she went to fetch water for her father during a drought, Amymone encountered a fine stag. She drew her bow and shot at it but missed and hit a sleeping satyr. Furious, the satyr leapt upon the girl, who was rescued by Poseidon, who then raped her. In another version of the story, Amymone fell asleep from exhaustion while attempting to find water in the drought-stricken land, whereupon she was set upon by a satyr and rescued by Poseidon, who threw his trident at the goat man but missed, embedding it in a rock. After the god raped Amymone, he demanded that she withdraw his trident from the rock and, as she did, water rushed out. The spring was thereafter called by the name of the ravished maiden, who had a son by Poseidon. She is sometimes said to be one of the Danaid sisters (see **Danae**). (Dowden; Graves 2; Smith)

Ananke Plato called her the mother of the **Moirae** (Fates). Ananke was the personification of the abstraction Necessity, the force of destiny perceived in most cultures as female. There was no countermanding Ananke's will, for she ruled all nature and culture. She was also associated with healing, for when a person attends to the demands of necessity, good health follows. (Sanford)

Anaxarete Iphis, a commoner, loved this stony-hearted princess of Cyprus. But she ridiculed him and his affection until, in a fit of depression, he hanged himself. She laughed even then, and for this, **Aphrodite** turned Anaxarete to stone. The statue that was once the girl was displayed for centuries in the temple of Aphrodite at Salamis, where the goddess was called Prospiciens. (Smith)

Andromache Widow of the Trojan hero Hector, Andromache was enslaved by the Greek warrior

Neoptolemus. This was bitter for Andromache, because Neoptolemus had killed her infant son. She was soon pregnant again and gave birth to another son. Despite this bond, Neoptolemus married the daughter of Menelaus and **Helen**, Hermione, who hated her rival and plotted her death. Andromache was saved by the intervention of Peleus, her husband's grandfather. Hermione left the country with her cousin, Orestes (see **Electra**), to whom she had been engaged. (Euripides *Andromache*.)

Andromeda The Ethiopian queen Cassiopeia bragged often of her beauty. In punishment, Poseidon, proud of his own daughters (see **Nymphs**), sent a monster to ravage her land. To calm the god, Cassiopeia exposed her daughter Andromeda on a barren rock, from which the Greek hero Perseus rescued her. They lived together until her death, when **Athena** placed Andromeda among the stars as a constellation; her mother became Cassiopeia's chair. (Garber and Vickers; Ovid *Met*; Smith)

Antigone The loyal daughter of Oedipus of Thebes followed her blinded father into exile and was present at his death. Returning to Thebes, she discovered that her two brothers had been killed fighting each other in a revolt against their uncle Creon. Creon forbade anyone to bury the rebel brother, Polynice, but Antigone knew that unless his body was returned to earth's womb, he could not be reborn. She risked death to spread dust over the corpse. Caught, Antigone was buried alive. (Sophocles *Antigone*; Cameron and Kuhrt)

Aotis An early dawn or sun goddess, she rode through the sky in a chariot drawn by white steeds. She may be a form of the goddess **Helen**; she was honored as a spirit of fertility. (Larson; Lonsdale)

Aphrodite This goddess of sexuality united bodies in passion, rather than families and property in marriage. She was "the Golden," not just because she wore gold jewelry but because under her influence lovers saw each other suffused with radiance. Whether the goddess descends from the Old European or proto-Indo-European strata is unclear; in the first case, Aphrodite could derive from a bird-headed nude goddess, while in the second case, she could descend from water **Nymphs** and sun maidens. Part of Aphrodite's heritage was unquestionably eastern Mediterranean. Scholars claim that Aphrodite is a Greek incarnation of the goddesses of sex, **Inanna** and **Ishtar**. The story of her birth from the sea and arrival at the island of Cyprus traces the route of the sea traders who brought her to the mainland.

The story of Aphrodite's birth is filled with sexual symbolism. At the dawn of time, the children of the old heaven god Uranus castrated him, and his penis, falling into the ocean, ejaculated. The foam gathered itself into long-haired Aphrodite riding a mussel shell. She shook seawater from her locks, its drops turning into pearls. She floated to Cyprus, where the **Horae** greeted her and became her companions. (An alternative story describes Aphrodite as daughter of the sea Titan **Dione** and the sky god Zeus, a tale that provides an Olympian heritage to this imported goddess. An obscure variant offers **Eurynome** as Aphrodite's mother.)

Aphrodite had innumerable lovers. Although her husband was Hephaestus, crippled god of smithcraft, Aphrodite spread her favors liberally among divine and mortal males. Her most famous affairs were with Ares and Adonis. All heaven knew about Aphrodite and Ares, god of war, except Hephaestus, who remained ignorant until someone tattled. Furious at Aphrodite's unfaithfulness, the cuckold fashioned a mesh of gold in which he caught the lovers. Ares and Aphrodite were a laughingstock, naked and damp, their limbs entangled in each other's and the golden web.

As for Adonis, Aphrodite fell in love with his youthful beauty and hid him in a chest she gave to **Persephone** for safekeeping. The queen of the underworld, peeking inside, was smitten with desire and refused to give Adonis back. Zeus ruled that Adonis could live one-third of each year by himself, one-third with Persephone, and the remaining one-third with Aphrodite. Adonis was killed while hunting a wild boar. In his honor, Greek women celebrated the Adonia, filling pots with fast-growing, leafy plants, then weeping for the brevity of life.

Aphrodite not only had affairs herself; she promoted them among others. When the sculptor Pygmalion began to sleep with a statue he had carved of the goddess, Aphrodite made him fall in love with it. Later she pitied his lovesickness, and the statue came alive as **Galatea**.

Perhaps most famous of Aphrodite's myths is recorded in the *Iliad*. Aphrodite started the Trojan War because she desired **Ate**'s golden apple, tossed as a challenge at the wedding of **Thetis**. She kidnapped the world's most beautiful woman, **Helen**, to use as a bribe in a contest with **Hera** and **Athena**. Helen was married to King Menelaus, and war between Greece and Troy was the result.

Although unconcerned with motherhood, Aphrodite had several offspring, most having allegorical meaning, as when Aphrodite (sexuality) mates with Dionysus (wine) to produce Priapus (permanent erection). She was the mother of Phobos, Demos, and Harmonia (fear, population, harmony) by her lover Ares. Most significant was Eros, who appears as a small sprite in statues of the goddess.

Aphrodite's attributes and symbols show her nature as love goddess. She carried arrows or darts to pierce hearts and chains to bind lovers together. She had a magic belt that made everyone desire the wearer; Hera borrowed it to capture the interest of wandering Zeus. Her sacred plants were myrtle, rose, apple, and poppy; her birds, the goose, swan, dove, and sparrow; her animals, tortoise and ram. All had symbolic connections with the act of love—or actual ones, as there is some evidence that aphrodisiacal powers were ascribed to some. (Athanassakis; Barber; Farnell; Flemberg; Friedrich 1978; Grigson; Hesiod; Keuls 1985; Lawson; Lefkowitz and Fant 1982;

Kerényi 1979; Ovid *Met*; Säflund; Sanford; Pomeroy; Sourvinou-Inwood 1978; Suhr 1969)

Arachne This princess of Lydia challenged **Athena** to a weaving contest. Trying to embarrass the goddess into making a mistake, Arachne wove the Greek gods in indelicate poses, while Athena wove pictures of humans being punished for challenging the gods. When Athena saw that Arachne's weaving was superior, she shredded the woman's cloth. Arachne hanged herself in shame. Cutting the weaver down, the goddess transformed her into the first spider (arachnid). (Barber; Ovid *Met*)

Arete The Greek goddess of justice, teacher of the hero Heracles, was a personified abstraction with no real myth. The name was also that of the mother of Nausicaa, the princess who welcomed Odysseus near the end of his journey. Nausicaa instructed the shipwrecked soldier to sue for protection to Arete, not to her father, Alcinous. The poet explains this as respectful of Arete's wisdom, but it probably indicates the queen held power in her own right. (Perandotto and Sullivan; Dexter; Graves 1)

Ariadne In her original Minoan form as goddess of the underworld and germination, only women worshipped Ariadne; she has been connected with girls' initiation rituals. When the Greeks arrived, they demoted the goddess to princess, daughter of **Pasiphae** (or the otherwise unknown Creta) and Minos of Crete. Trapped by Minos in a labyrinth with the Minotaur, Theseus survived because of a spool of thread that Ariadne (infatuated by a wound from **Aphrodite**) slipped to him. As he wandered, Theseus unspooled the thread, so he always knew what corridors he had already walked.

He escaped, but Theseus abandoned Ariadne on the island of Naxos, where the god of wine, Dionysus, discovered her. She became the leader of the Dionysian women, the **Maenads**, before dying in childbed. Another myth says pregnant Ariadne suffered from seasickness, so Theseus left her ashore at Cyprus, where she died. Returning for her, Theseus was stricken with grief and established sacrifices to Ariadne Aphrodite. Finally, a curious legend says there were two Ariadnes; one married Dionysus in Naxos, while the other was abandoned by Theseus. To the first, a joyous festival was dedicated, while to the latter, a ceremony of lamentation was offered. After her death, Ariadne was raised to heaven and given the name of Aridella. (Cantarella; Friedrich; Homer *Iliad*; Lyons; Ovid *Fasti*; Plutarch *Lives*; Sanford; Willetts)

Artemis Two images of Artemis appear in ancient art. In one, she is a lithe maiden, running through the woodland with her company of **Nymphs**. In the other, she is a massive maternal woman, her chest covered with symbols of fecundity. Both figures are called Artemis and, despite their apparent dissimilarity, both are connected to birth and fertility.

As the virgin moon goddess, Artemis roamed the forest, protecting all its creatures. She was an invisible game warden, killing anyone who hunted pregnant beasts or newborns. She not only controlled death; she ruled reproduction as well. She was elder twin of the sun god Apollo and midwife at his birth (see **Leto**). She was the recipient of prayers from mothers in labor, who found comfort in the belief that she nursed them as she did other animals.

Despite her connection with childbirth, Artemis was virginal, avoiding any connection with men. Any man who offended her met death. When Orion boasted that he was better at discus throwing than athletic Artemis, she killed him for the offense (or, according to a variation, for raping her maiden Opis, a name that appears as one of her titles). Other myths say Orion was Artemis's hunting partner before he attempted to rape her, whereupon she killed him. Another claims the virgin goddess returned Orion's love and planned to marry him, but jealous Apollo challenged his sister to hit a moving spot in the sea, which was Orion's head. At his death, Orion became a constellation.

As ruler of virginity, Artemis was the goddess to whom girls were dedicated. From the age of nine to their marriage, girls were under her protection. At her temple at Brauron, girls dressed in yellow shifts and danced like bears in front of Artemis's statue. As her name references the syllable for "bear" and as the girls were called *arktoi* ("bears"), this dance connected the living girls with the goddess. The sanctuary of Artemis in Brauron was established in approximately 1300 BCE and was active through classical times. Nearby was the tomb of **Iphigenia**, who served Artemis after the goddess saved her from the sacrificial knife.

The Nymph of the greenwood has many similarities to Artemis's other most famous form: Artemis Multimammia ("many breasted"), also known as Ephesia from her temple at Ephesus, one of the wonders of the ancient world. There, a massive statue of Artemis still stands. Rising from a legless base into a huge torso ringed with breasts, then up to a head surmounted by the turret crown, the Artemis of Ephesus originally had a stag on either side and hawks on each hand. Lions, bulls, and sphinxes decorated the sides, as well as bees and winged women. She wore a flower wreath, a zodiac necklace, and a lunar hairpiece. For at least 800 years, the statue stood in Artemis's shrine. Hundreds of miniatures of the great image were created; found throughout the ancient world, they were probably sold as sacred souvenirs.

This form of Artemis may have been a local divinity who took on the name of the important Greek goddess. The myth of the goddess's birth on Delos was transported to a grove named Ortygia near the city, where on the spring birthday of the goddess, the mysteries of Artemis were celebrated. The olive tree under which mother Leto rested was pointed out, as well as the mountain where armored boys stood, clashing their armor to distract **Hera** while the goddess was born. In honor of those guardians, young men of Ephesus held feasts in which they competed for the most lavish hospitality.

The image of Artemis of Ephesus is not easy to interpret. What were the protuberances on her chest? Breasts? Eggs? Honeycombs? The genitals of cattle?

Those of castrated men? All have been offered as possibilities, and any could be correct. Most scholars today refute the theory that the swellings represent breasts, for no nipples are present. The suggestion of honeycombs is supported by the name of Artemis's priestesses: Melissae, "bees." Artemis of Ephesus also bore a title of "beekeeper," and Ephesus has been translated as "place of bees." The possibility the goddess wore a necklace of scrota cannot be discounted, for her priests were castrated men.

Although the worship of Artemis died out almost two millennia ago, Greek folklore speaks of the "queen of the mountains" who lives in the forest surrounded by her maiden troupe. Distinguishable from her cohort by her greater height and radiant white skin, she was a dangerous creature who killed those who trespassed upon her haunts. (Athanassakis; Blundell and Williamson; Connelly; Cook; Dexter 1990; Dowden; Elderkin; Farnell; Fontenrose A; Friedrich 1978; Cameron and Kuhrt; Larson 1997; Lawson; Lefkowitz and Fant; Lonsdale; Lyons; Manning; Macurdy; Nilsson; Ovid *Met*; Sourvinou-Inwood 1988; Walbank; Pantel; Cook; Elderkin; Smith)

Asteria Asteria assisted her sister **Leto** in escaping the curse of **Hera** that she could not give birth where sunlight reached. Asteria turned herself into the island of Delos, where Leto gave birth to **Artemis** and Apollo. Afterward, no woman was allowed to give birth on the island, nor was anyone permitted to die there. Pregnant women from Delos traveled to nearby Rheneia to give birth. Other stories say Asteria, assaulted by Zeus, transformed herself into a quail. Asteria may represent a local goddess whose worship was suppressed; she was the mother of **Hecate**. (Smith)

Astraea Daughter of **Themis**, Astraea lived on earth during a peaceful primal age. But as humankind grew more violent, gods retreated to the heavens. Astraea was the last to leave, but finally she abandoned earth to become a star. (Smith)

Atalanta Two divine women of this name, one from Arcadia and the other from Boeotia, have a similar myth. Atalanta's father, disappointed at the birth of a daughter, left her to die. But the baby survived, suckled by a bear. She grew up to become a centaur-killing heroine, the match of any man in Greece. Her father decided to claim fatherhood of the famous warrior and so claimed the right to choose Atalanta's husband. She refused to marry any man she could outrun and demanded the right to kill anyone who lost to her.

Many lost their lives racing for her hand. Finally Meilanion begged **Aphrodite** to help him win Atalanta. The goddess gave him three golden apples to fling down before the speeding woman. Atalanta stopped to scoop them up, losing her advantage. Won by guile, Atalanta nevertheless wed happily. But she and her lover neglected to make proper marital sacrifices, and the couple was punished by being transformed into the lions who drew **Cybele**'s chariot (see Southeastern Europe). (Ovid *Met*)

Ate Daughter of **Eris** and often confused with her, Ate was goddess of folly, moral blindness, and infatuation. She was associated with the Greek concept of hubris, meaning to set oneself against the natural order. Ate represented reckless disregard of consequences. Banished from Olympus for mischief making, Ate moved in among humans. She never touched earth, preferring to walk on the heads of men.

In Ate's most famous myth, she marked a golden apple with the words "To the Fairest" and threw it into a banquet of the gods. **Athena**, **Hera**, and **Aphrodite** claimed the prize, so a contest was arranged. Each offered a bribe to Paris, the judge: Athena offered wisdom, Hera offered power, and Aphrodite offered the world's most beautiful woman, **Helen**. The Trojan War was the result.

Ate was sometimes considered a servant of Aphrodite, who used her to stir up trouble between lovers. She also appeared as a variant of **Nemesis**. Today, many of Ate's attributes have been assigned to her mother, especially the golden apple. (Hesiod; Sanford)

Athena At the founding of Athens, the sea god Poseidon tried to win control of the city over Athena. Because she would not agree, the townspeople were asked to vote. The men voted for the god, the women for the goddess. Because there was one more voter on the women's side, Athena won the day. An alternative story says the Olympian deities judged the dispute. They ruled that because Athena had planted the first olive tree, whereas Poseidon only offered the changeful sea, the goddess was better qualified.

The men bitterly agreed to accept the goddess, but they levied three heavy requirements on the women: that they forgo being called citizens, that they no longer vote, and that their children be called by their fathers' rather than their mothers' names. Afterward, they claimed Athena was a motherless goddess who sprang full grown from the head of Zeus (see **Metis**). This Athena voted on the side of the new patriarchal order against the earlier system of mother right.

Another version of Athena's birth says she was the daughter of Pallas, a winged giant. When he tried to rape her, Athena killed him and tanned his skin to make a shield; she cut off his wings to fasten to her feet. A similar myth says Hephaestus, the smith god, threatened Athena's virginity. When he tried to rape her, he ejaculated on her leg. The semen fell on all-fertile **Gaia**, who bore a half-serpent boy named Erechtheus. Athena gave the boy to **Aglauros** and her sisters to guard, which led to tragedy when the girls peeked inside the box that held the monster child. Horrified, Aglauros threw herself to her death from the Acropolis, where Athena's temple stood.

Hephaestus had no reptile ancestors, so Athena must have provided the serpent blood. **Medusa**, whose snaky visage Athena wore on her cloak, suggests the connection. Athena appears as the snake-haired **Gorgon**'s fiercest opponent, first changing her from a maiden into a monster, then sending Perseus to decapitate her. But Athena placed Medusa's head on her chest, so the two goddess's faces are always seen together. Similarly, the massive snake that reared beside her statue in the Parthenon, her temple on the Acropolis, suggests that the snake was a primary symbol of the virgin goddess.

Athena was originally a Minoan or Mycenaean household goddess, possibly related to the bare-breasted Cretan figures seen holding snakes. This original Athena represented the family bond, symbolized by the serpent that protected the family's food supply against rodents. As household goddess, Athena ruled the implements of domestic crafts: the spindle, the pot, and the loom. By extrapolation, she was the guardian of the ruler's home, goddess of the palace; she was the symbol of the community itself.

When Minoan civilization declined, Athena was not lost. A maiden warrior goddess, **Pallas**, arrived with the Indo-Europeans. This figure was bonded to that of the indigenous tribal symbol to form Pallas Athena. Other goddesses, originally distinct, were assimilated to Athena, as was the Cretan Aphaia, a maiden goddess who swam to safety after being captured by pirates near Crete.

Athena's rituals recalled her origins. Each year at midsummer, Athens' greatest festival, the Panathenaia, was celebrated. The event began months in advance, as four women wove a new yellow-and-purple *peplos* for the life-size statue of Athena. The *peplos* took nine months to weave because it pictured the war between gods and Titans, when Athena saved her city. When the festival began, Athena's image was taken from her temple and borne to the sea. There she was carefully washed and decked in the new robe. Young men accompanied the procession, but when the time came to wash the statue, only women were permitted. The ritual reveals Athena as a woman's deity, mistress of household industry. (Athanassakis; Barber; Bernal; Dexter 1990; Downing; Hall; Hesiod; Homer *Od*; Kerényi 1979; Keuls; Loraux 1993; Motz; Nilsson 1961; Pantel)

Baubo Baubo ("belly") was the sister of Iambe ("abuse"), and a similar story is told of both, in which the weeping **Demeter**, searching for lost **Persephone**, sat down by a well. Baubo came to draw water and tried to console Demeter by offering a cup of wine. The goddess refused, asking for water mixed with barley meal and pennyroyal. Baubo continued to offer sympathy, which Demeter steadfastly refused. So Baubo lifted her skirts and exposed her vulva. Demeter's sorrow was broken by a smile; the sterile earth stirred; Persephone returned.

That such a minor character should have such power over the great Demeter has led some to propose Baubo as a form of **Hecate**, who plays significant roles in Demeter's legend. Baubo's part in the Demetrian mysteries was reenacted at a bridge between Athens and Eleusis, where participants engaged in ribald speech before more serene ceremonies.

Although some sources describe Iambe and Baubo as identical, others separate them. Lame Iambe, daughter of the wilderness god Pan and the **Nymph Echo**, was the originator of the irregular, or "limping," iambic rhythm used in Greek satiric poetry. Iambe is connected more with words than with behavior, the latter being Baubo's preserve.

Ancient writers rarely provide a history for Baubo, but a myth from Asia Minor said Baubo had a single daughter, Mise, who like her mother was oblong. Both had the power of shape-shifting, with the toad their preferred form. Baubo was rarely depicted in Greece, possible exceptions being statuettes that show a woman from the waist down, with a face on her belly. There is dispute as to whether these images are appropriately named for Baubo. (Friedrich; Lubell; Olender; Motz)

Baucis Once a woman and man, Baucis and Philemon, lived together so long that they became inseparable. While Zeus and Hermes were wandering the earth, they stopped at Baucis and Philemon's poor hut and begged a meal. The impoverished couple served what food they had. In recognition of the old couple's kindness, the gods granted a single wish. The pair did not

hesitate: they wished never to be parted. Their hut changed into a temple, where they served the gods for years. One day, as they stood outdoors, their feet took root, and Baucis and Philemon lived on as intertwined linden trees. (Larson 1995; Ovid *Met*)

Bia A warrior maiden, Bia's name means "force." Daughter of the underworld goddess **Styx**, Bia bound the Titan Prometheus to a rocky crag when he was condemned to perpetual torment for stealing heavenly fire for humanity. (Graves 1; Smith)

Britomartis Britomartis, possibly the greatest goddess of Minoan Crete, has been all but lost. Little is known except how she was traditionally depicted: a young, lithe, and strong hunter, carrying arrows. The goddess **Artemis** was said to have loved the Cretan maiden and mourned her death. Artemis took Britomartis's image as a **Nymph**, which remained for 2,000 years her traditional depiction.

King Minos of Crete, intent on rape, chased Britomartis for nine months through the forested island. She finally escaped by flinging herself off a high cliff into the ocean. There she got caught in the fishnets she had invented as a gift to humanity. After this, the goddess was called Dictynna ("netted one"). Some sources say the goddess was Britomartis on the eastern end of the island, Dictynna on the west. Others suggest that Britomartis was Dictynna's daughter. (Elderkin; Larson 2001; Smith; Willetts)

Brizo This goddess, worshipped on Delos, was a prophet and specialist in dream interpretation. She was also a goddess of the sea, invoked to protect ships and their crews, and honored with images of boats. It was bad luck to offer her fish as a sacrifice. (Graves; Smith)

Byblis One of a pair of identical twins, she fell in love with her brother Caunus. They were beautiful beings, grandchildren of the sun, and they grew up together as intimate companions. As she reached womanhood,

Byblis's love changed. She became jealous of other girls and fantasized about her brother. When she finally revealed her love to him, he refused her, horrified, and moved away. Byblis, tormented and ashamed, was transformed into a constantly weeping fountain. (Ovid *Met*; Sourvinou-Inwood 2005)

Caenis Caenis, raped by the sea god Poseidon, appealed to Olympus for revenge: Transform her, she begged, into an invulnerable man so she might murder the sex that had injured her. Her wish was granted, and she became a hero named Caeneus, unstoppable on the battlefield. When she died a heroic death, she resumed her female body and original name and enjoyed a hero's welcome in the afterlife. (Smith; Ovid *Met*)

Callisto Originating in Arcadia, this goddess appeared as a lithe hunter, racing barefoot through the woods. In animal form, she was the powerful and protective mother bear. When worshippers of **Artemis** arrived in the area, the similarity of the goddesses gave rise to the legend that Callisto was a **Nymph**, treasured by Artemis but accidentally killed by her. Saddened, Artemis took on Callisto's name, becoming Artemis Calliste ("Artemis the fairest").

Other versions of the story describe Callisto as a Nymph who attracted Zeus. He disguised himself as Artemis and, seducing Callisto, recovered his male form in time to rape her. Zeus turned Callisto into a bear so that jealous **Hera** would not know of her rival. But Hera arranged to have Artemis kill the girl while hunting. In her years as a bear Callisto bore a son, Arcas; Zeus transformed the pair into stars. Another story says Artemis, bathing with Callisto, noticed her pregnancy and transformed her into a bear. She was transported to the sky, where she became the constellation of the Great Bear. (Borgeaud 1988; Dowden; Johnson; Larson 2001; Ovid *Met*, *Fasti*; Smith)

Calypso Daughter of **Tethys**, Calypso lived on the island of Ogtygia, where the Greek king Odysseus was shipwrecked. Calypso offered Odysseus immortality if he would sleep with her. Odysseus took advantage of Calypso's offer, but after seven years he abandoned his disconsolate lover. Calypso occupies an intermediate status between goddess and **Nymph**, both terms being used to describe her. (Cantarella; Friedrich; Homer *Od*; Larson 2001; Schein; Hesiod)

Campe This female dragon guarded the Cyclops, a monster child of **Gaia**, in its prison deep in her stony womb. Campe was killed by Zeus in order to free the monster to fight against the Titans. (Graves 1; Smith)

Carya In southern Laconia, early residents worshipped trees, in which their goddesses were embodied (see **Helen**). The invading Greeks assimilated most tree divinities to **Artemis**, but the names of individual goddesses remained in legend. This was true of Carya, who was transformed into a walnut tree. Artemis reported on the transformation and was awarded the title of Caryatis ("she of the walnut tree"). She was worshipped under this title in ceremonies where girls danced in her honor. These dances included statuesque poses that inspired the architectural motif called Caryatids. (Smith)

Cassandra The most beautiful of the twelve daughters of Hecuba, Cassandra was doomed from the start, for her mother had a dream while pregnant that she would give birth to a burning log. Although Hecuba had the child exposed, Cassandra survived to become a priestess who caught the eye of Apollo. He promised to grant any wish if she would sleep with him. Cassandra demanded the power of prophecy; Apollo granted her wish. But once she had what she wanted, Cassandra refused the god's advances. Apollo wet Cassandra's lips with his tongue and disappeared.

After that kiss, Cassandra was cursed. Everything she prophesied was true but was received as falsehood. People ignored her when she warned her brother Paris not to go to Greece; they didn't believe there were armed soldiers in the wooden horse; they ridiculed Cassandra for saying Troy would lose the war. When

Troy lost, Cassandra was taken captive by the Greek king Agamemnon and was murdered with him. She was finally respected after death. In Laconia she was worshipped as the goddess Alexandra. (Aeschylus *Oresteia*; Euripides *Electra, Hecuba, The Trojan Women*)

Cerberus A hybrid of lioness, lynx, and sow, Cerberus stood at the entry to Hades, challenging anyone passing to the otherworld. She is sometimes described as a male dog born to the monstrous **Echidna**. Those who passed her could never return the way they had come. (Smith)

Ceto This vague figure in Greek mythology was the Syrian fish mother Derceto (see **Atargatis**, Eastern Mediterranean). She gave birth to fabulous daughters: the three **Graeae**, born with gray hair and with but one eye and one tooth among them; the snake-haired **Gorgons**; the serpent **Echidna**; and the seductive wind demons, the **Sirens**. (Hesiod)

Charilla When the oracle town of Delphi was parching under a terrible drought, a little girl came to the king to beg for food. Thoughtlessly, the king struck Charilla in the face, so she hanged herself in shame. Later, the oracle told the king that he should have been kind to the supplicant, and Delphi must offer propitiatory sacrifices to Charilla's spirit every nine years. Such heroine cults often hide an early goddess. (Harrison 1962; Larson 1995; Sourvinou-Inwood 2005)

Charites The most common English name for these three goddesses, the Graces, comes from the Latin Graciae. In Greek these divinities were called Charites, from a word meaning "to give freely" (cf. "charity"). They ruled movement, manners, and love, the last shared with **Aphrodite**, whose companions they were. The goddesses were Thalia, Aglaia, and Euphrosyne. In early Athens, there were two Charites, Auxo and Hegemone. In Laconia, they were Cleta and Phaenna.

In Rome, there was a single Gratia, the double of Aphrodite and, like that goddess, the mate of smith god Hephaestus.

The Charites represented the delight in living that produces art, dance, music, and love. They were connected with natural beauty, as the force that made plants bud and blossom; their touch caused fruit to ripen. They were older than Aphrodite, whom they met as she rose from the sea; they provided her garments and arranged her hair. The Greeks said the first cup of wine at a banquet was theirs; the second belonged to lustful Aphrodite, while argumentative **Ate** ruled the third. (Farnell; Friedrich; Sanford)

Charybdis This monster daughter of **Gaia** tried to eat one of the heavenly oxen. Zeus tossed her into the sea, where her voracious nature did not change, for she endlessly swallowed the sea and vomited it. She became a whirlpool off the Italian coast, near where **Scylla** trapped sailors. (Homer *Od*; Smith)

Chelone This **Nymph** ridiculed the marriage of Zeus and **Hera** and was changed into a speechless turtle (*chelonia*) in punishment. Another version of the story says Chelone stayed home from the wedding and was punished when Hera appeared and threw her, house and all, into the river. (Smith)

Chimera Part goat, part lion, part dragon, this Greek monster endangered the land of Lycia. She was the daughter of an equally monstrous mother, **Echidna**. Probably she was originally a volcano goddess: there was a volcano of her name in the country she terrorized. (Ovid *Met*; Hesiod)

Circe Daughter of the sun and sister of Cretan queen **Pasiphae**, this illustrious witch gained the rulership of Colchis by marrying its prince. Then she killed him so she could rule alone. When Circe's subjects discovered her crime, they rose against her. The enchantress fled, escaping on her father's rays to the island of Aeaea, a name sometimes used to refer to her.

There Circe lived in a stone house, tended by lions and wolves. She entertained herself by crafting magic potions, which she tried on humans shipwrecked in her vicinity. When Odysseus was shipwrecked on Aeaea, she turned his men into swine. The king escaped Circe's spells, but he could not escape her charms and fathered two sons by her. (Cohen; Friedrich; Hesiod; Homer *Od*; Kerényi 1979; Larson 2001; Marinatos; Ovid *Met*; Schein; Reeder)

Clytemnestra Leda was raped by, or willingly mated with, a huge swan, the disguised Zeus. Shortly afterward, she had intercourse with her husband, the king of Sparta. Nine months later Leda laid two eggs. One hatched to reveal immortal **Helen** and her brother Pollux. The other produced mortal Clytemnestra and her brother Castor.

As she grew, Clytemnestra was overshadowed by her beautiful half sister. Helen became ruler of the city, raising her consort Menelaus to the throne, while Clytemnestra became part of a foreign family by marrying Helen's brother-in-law, Agamemnon of Mycenae. They had three children: two daughters, **Iphigenia** and **Electra**, and a son, Orestes.

Then Agamemnon was called to Troy to regain Helen—and with her, the crown of Sparta—for his brother. At the town of Aulis on the Aegean coast, the navy was stalled by ill winds because Agamemnon had insulted **Artemis** by killing a deer improperly. The brothers needed a human sacrifice, so they sent for Iphigenia, pretending that she would become the hero Achilles's bride. Then they put Iphigenia to death. The sacrifice pleased the wind deities; the Greeks sailed for Troy.

Back in Mycenae, Clytemnestra planned vengeance. She took as consort Agamemnon's cousin Aegisthus. When Agamemnon returned, he brought with him the prophet **Cassandra**, who fruitlessly warned of danger. Clytemnestra and Aegisthus murdered both king and captive. The queen met a violent death when her children avenged their father's death. (Aeschylus *Oresteia*; Euripides *Electra*, *Orestes*)

Coronis The **Nymph** Coronis ("crown") was significant as the mother of the healing god, Asclepius. Another maiden of this name was turned into a crow by virginal **Athena** when the ocean god Poseidon pursued her, intent upon rape. (Ovid *Met*; Smith)

Cynosura The Cretan goddess Cynosura leaves her name in "cynosure," a word that means "center of attraction," and recalls the navigational uses of her constellation, Ursa Minor, the Little Dipper (which some say was the transformed body of the Nymph **Callisto**). Some legends call her the nurse of the Greek god Zeus. (Smith)

Cyrene When Apollo saw this Amazonian woman tear a lion apart with her bare hands, he grew so excited he did not rape her (see **Daphne**, **Dryope**) but decided to marry her. He took her to Libya, whose land he gave her as a bridal gift. Her name was given to a spring where young women bathed before their wedding ceremonies. Cyrene became the mother of the hero Bellerophon, who tamed **Medusa**'s horse son Pegasus. (Lefkowitz 1986; Bonnefoy)

Damia An alternative form of the corn goddess **Demeter**, Damia was paired with a daughter, Auxesia (later used as a title of **Persephone**). In one story, a famine struck the city of Epidaurus. It was prophesied that it would continue until statues of the goddesses were carved of Athenian olive wood. The Athenians gave their neighbors the wood but afterward demanded heavy tribute, including a regular sacrifice to **Athena** and her snake son Erectheus. During a rebellion, the Epidaurians stopped payment of the tribute; the Athenians invaded, intent on carrying home the goddesses's statues. When they would not move, a battle followed. A messenger carrying tidings to Athens of the sacrilege to Damia and Auxesia was murdered by angry Athenian women, and the men of Athens stripped the women of their few remaining rights. In a story in Pausanius, the two goddesses, called "maidens" of Crete, came to Troezen and were killed by stoning. The murder may have been accidental, but the people of the town thereafter paid tribute to them as divine, by creating a festival called Lithobolia. (Larson 1995; Smith)

Danae Danae, a woman of Argos confined to a tower so she could not conceive, was raped by the god Zeus, who came through the window disguised as a shower of gold. Danae bore the hero Perseus. Another myth tells of fifty Danaid sisters married to fifty princes; their father demanded that the brides decapitate the grooms on the wedding night. Forty-nine sisters followed orders but the oldest, Hypermnestra, spared her mate and conceived by him the ruling dynasty of Argos. An alternative legend said the Danaids were threatened with rape by their fiancés, the fifty sons of their uncle Aegyptus, and fled with their father to Argos, where marriage was forced upon them.

Homer refers to the Greek armies as composed of Argives and Danaoi, but whereas the first term clearly refers to the city of Argos, the second term is unclear and may represent a tribal name. The Danaids originated as water goddesses of Argos; Hypermnestra gave her name to a fountain. If the Danaids were connected with Danae, which is unclear, she could be an Argive ancestor goddess. (Aeschylus *The Suppliants*; Dowden; Holland; Homer *Iliad*; Smith)

Daphne A priestess of **Gaia**, this **Nymph** led secret women's rituals to celebrate earth's fertility. But the mortal Leucippus penetrated their rituals in female disguise. When Apollo suggested the women conduct their rituals nude, Leucippus was killed for his sacrilege. When the sun god accosted Daphne, she refused him. Apollo grew violent, and Gaia transformed Daphne into a laurel tree, whose leaves Apollo thereafter wore as a symbol of inspiration. Some sources say this figure is the same as the prophetess Manto. (Dowden; O'Flaherty; Ovid *Met*; Smith)

Dejanira Heracles had affairs before and during his first marriage, which ended when he killed his wife,

Megaera. Despite this, the warrior Dejanira married him and bore him several children. But Heracles brought a mistress into Dejanira's home, a woman named Iole. Dejanira wove a splendid garment and soaked it in what she thought was an infallible charm for the return of love: blood and semen from a dying centaur killed by Heracles. But the centaur had revenge in his heart when he confided the secret potion to Dejanira. His blood burned so terribly that Heracles pleaded for death. The remorseful Dejanira committed suicide. (Ovid *Met*; Sophocles *The Trachiniae*)

Demeter Demeter's daughter **Persephone** disappeared while picking wildflowers, and Demeter could find her nowhere. The weeping goddess searched for days. As she mourned, the goddess withdrew her energy from plants, which wilted and shriveled. She wandered until she came to Eleusis, where she became nursemaid for Queen Metaneira. Demeter tried to make Prince Demophon immortal by smoking him like a log, but the queen pulled him from the fire and demanded an explanation from Demeter, whose divinity was thus revealed. The awed rulers built her a temple and Demeter stayed on in Eleusis, often weeping by a well.

One day the queen's daughter **Baubo** saw the sad goddess and tried to comfort her. Demeter refused her consoling words; so, to make the goddess smile, Baubo exposed her vulva. Demeter chuckled, the first laughter the earth had heard in months. Shortly afterward, when Persephone was restored, spring bloomed. In gratitude for the hospitality of the Eleusinians, Demeter taught them the arts of agriculture and based her rites there.

At Demeter's eight-day festival, the *mystai* imitated the goddess as she sought her daughter. They became Demeter Erinyes ("angry"), furious at her loss; then they acted the happy role of Demeter Lousia ("kindly one"), the mother transformed by reunion. The festival was celebrated annually from approximately 760 BCE until suppressed by the Christian emperor Theodosius in 389 CE, but the site may have been used as early as 1450 BCE for rituals of harvest. During the classical period, Eleusis was a vast temple complex where thousands attended the Mysteries. Men and women participated as equals. Slaves were welcomed, as were children.

The rites were held every Boedromion (late September/early October); every fourth year they were especially lavish. The public participated in processions and sacrifices on the first five days: Aghyrmos, when the Mysteries were called to order; Elasis, when initiates purified themselves in the ocean; a third day of sacrifices; Epidauria, the day of purification; and Pompe, the day of the procession to Eleusis from Athens, with celebrants bearing images of Demeter and Persephone.

From nightfall on the fifth day, only initiates could participate in the Teletai ("completion"). Over many centuries, only a few people ever broke the rule of secrecy. The soldier Alkibiades did imitations of the rituals while drunk, with the result that his property was confiscated. Diagoras the Melian and Andokides were condemned to death for talking about the rituals but escaped. Two youths who wandered into the ceremonies were put to death. Pausanias planned to write about the Mysteries but was warned by a dream not to do so; he paid attention and wrote instead about what could be "lawfully told." Theories abound about what happened at Eleusis (pig sacrifice, the revelation of a stalk of wheat, ceremonial drinking). The secrets of Demeter's rituals died with her initiates.

Other rituals to Demeter were similarly secret, although, unlike the Eleusinian Mysteries, they were limited to women. The Lesser Mysteries were held in springtime on a riverbank in Athens. These were sometimes called "Persephone's Mysteries," as compared to the Greater Mysteries, which were dedicated to Demeter. Women may have danced in the goddess's honor; a pageant embodying the myth of Persephone may have been performed.

Thesmophoria, the annual autumn ceremony in honor of Demeter Thesmophoros ("law giver"), was dedicated to the public good. The rites, believed to

date to pre-Olympian times, were celebrated when wheat was planted to overwinter. The festival had three parts. On the first day, women climbed to the shrine of Demeter. Building a small village of huts, they spent the night in ritual abuse and joking. On the second day, the women purified themselves; they may have eaten pomegranates, sacred to Persephone. After a torch-lit procession on the third day, priestesses descended into a snake-filled cave where offerings had been left. Decayed pig meat, pinecones and phallus-shaped cakes were brought to the surface, possibly to be used as fertilizer. Aristophanes described how a man spied upon the Thesmophoria, where he discovered that the women spent all their time talking about men.

These festivals of Demeter emphasize her connection with the earth's vegetative cycle as well as her relationship with her daughter. Although usually her maternal aspect was foregrounded, Demeter was occasionally described as sexually active; she had intercourse in the fields with her consort Iasion to bless Harmonia's marriage. Demeter's connection to plants is made clear in the tale of cruel Prince Erysichthon, who decided to build a banquet hall on the site of the goddess's sacred grove. When he sent men to kill her trees, Demeter appeared in the form of her priestess, Nicippe, warning of danger. Erysichthon scorned her, whereupon she cursed him with insatiable hunger.

Demeter's name is often translated as "earth mother." The second part of the word unarguably means "mother." The first part, however, translates into "cereal" as well as "earth." If her name was originally "Damater," deriving from words for "earth mother," the goddess would be another form of **Gaia**, also called Ge. As such, she appears mated to Poseidon, "the husband of Da." The possible identity of Demeter and Medusa, Poseidon's usual mate, is supported by the worship, in Arcadia, of Demeter Hippia, "horse-headed" Demeter. There, pursued by Poseidon, Demeter changed shape. When she became a mare, and he a stallion, Poseidon caught Demeter, engendering the marvelous horse Arion and the young goddess Despoina, "mistress," sometimes called **Artemis**. Yet Hesiod claims that the father of Persephone was Poseidon's brother, the sky father Zeus, and there is as well some question as to the name and parentage of Demeter's daughter.

Folklore is replete with survivals of Demeter, who was converted into the male Saint Demetrius, patron of agriculture and marriage. At Eleusis, she remained until 1801 as Saint Demetra, unknown elsewhere. An ancient statue of Demeter was decked in flowers, with prayers for a good harvest. Two Englishmen stole the statue, which now rests in mutilated form at Cambridge. (Aristophanes *Thesmophoriazusae*; Athanassakis; Brumfield; Callimachus; Dexter 1990; Farnell; Gimbutas 1982; Friedrich; Hesiod; Keller; Keuls; Lawson; Lubell; Meyer; Motz; Mylonas; Nilsson 1961; Hawley and Levick; O'Flaherty; Richardson; Schieffer; Suter; Versnel; Willetts; White)

Dike Personification of justice, Dike was the sister of the goddesses of peace (Eirene) and good order (Eunomia). One of the Horae, Dike encouraged rewarding good and punishing evil. She screamed in pain if a judge violated the law. Dike was depicted bearing a sword she used to cut through injustice and untruth. Her assistant was Poena, goddess of retribution; her opposite was Adicia, injustice; Hesychia, tranquility, was her daughter. (Athanassakis; Sanford; Smith)

Dione Dione's name means "bright sky," suggesting an early goddess of light, despite her classical connotations of fecundating moisture. She was either a Titan, daughter of the sea goddess Tethys (thus a **Nymph**), or a child of the primal couple, Gaia and Uranus. Impregnated by Zeus, Dione gave birth to Aphrodite, otherwise described as the child of the amputated phallus of Uranus. As Aphrodite is an imported divinity, this parentage was forged in order to connect the arriving goddess with the existing pantheon.

As divinity of moisture and fertility, Dione was associated with childbirth. She assisted in the difficult birth of Artemis and Apollo from their mother, Leto. She was oracular, original owner of the famous oracle at Dodona. There, the rustling of a beech tree answered questions on personal matters; three aged priestesses interpreted the tree's words. (Aeschylus *Oresteia*; Hadzsits; Hesiod; Homer *Iliad*; Smith)

Dryope Several minor goddesses bore this name. One was a water **Nymph** who, infatuated with a mortal man, lured him into her embrace and drowned him. Another was a Nymph from wild Arcadia who gave birth to that late addition to the Greek pantheon, lascivious Pan. An unfortunate Nymph named Dryope was raped by the sun god and turned into a poplar tree. Finally, Princess Dryope was the playmate of the Hamadryads, tree Nymphs who were her religious instructors. As she played with them, Apollo transformed himself into a turtle to gain access to her body. Charmed by the turtle, Dryope took it onto her lap, where it changed into a snake and raped her. She survived the attack and married a human, but the Hamadryads took her away to become one of them. No man was permitted to enter the woodland temple devoted to her. Dryope may have been originally more than a Nymph, possibly a water divinity or tree goddess. (Graves; Smith)

Ececheira The Greek personification of armistice or truce, this goddess appeared at the shrine of Zeus in Olympia because all hostilities were forbidden during the Olympic games. (Smith)

Echidna This monstrous serpent mated with her brother Typhon to produce the raging Nemean lion, the dangerous **Scylla**, the many-headed **Hydra**, the ferocious Chimera, and the **Sphinx**. Hesiod suggests that Echidna's mother was snake-haired **Medusa**, whose children were presumably conceived with Poseidon. A final option was that she was the daughter of **Styx**. Like many monsters, she may be a demonized form of an early goddess whose worship was suppressed. She has been connected to **Hera**, sometimes described as Typhon's mother. (Hesiod; O'Brien 1993; Smith)

Echo A **Nymph**, Echo became an attendant to **Hera**, but Zeus liked to tell Echo tales of his philandering. To prevent her strained marriage from becoming the laughingstock of heaven, Hera struck Echo mute. Then Zeus restored her speech, but she could only repeat what she heard. She became the lover of the wilderness god Pan, by whom she had two daughters, Iambe and Iynx. She fell in love with the mortal Narcissus, but the vain young man would not sleep with her. In retribution, Narcissus was condemned to fall in love with his image in a forest pool. He pined away, becoming a flower. There is no evidence of religious rituals attending upon Echo, although Porticoes of Echo were found in Greek buildings, where sound echoed as many as seven times. (Borgeaud 1988; Ovid *Met*; Smith)

Eileithyia This virginal Cretan birth goddess was later assimilated to **Artemis**. Eileithyia could curse a birthing mother by crossing her knees; until she unfolded her body, the woman's child remained unborn. Dogs and horses were her symbols; the sacrifice of a dog assured that Eileithyia would sit with uncrossed knees during birth. Occasionally there were said to be multiple birth goddesses, the Eileithyiae, daughters of **Hera** in her role as protector of marriage. (Athanassakis; Downing; Friedrich; Motz; Willetts)

Eireisone The female personification of a Greek ritual object, Eireisone was a branch of olive wood, twined with wool and hung with fruits, carried in festivals by children with two living parents. Goddesses can be created in many ways: Occasionally, as in the case of Eireisone, an object of ritual becomes imbued with feminine force and identity, but there is often no myth attached to the name. (Larson 1995)

Eirene The Greek goddess of peace, Eirene was worshipped with bloodless sacrifices at Athens, where the god of wealth shared an altar with her. This connection of peace with prosperity is also indicated by Greek coins that show Eirene as crowned with ears of corn. Other coins show her engaged in the unsurprising activity of destroying armaments. One of Eirene's shrines stood near the temple of **Hestia**, goddess of the hearth, connecting peace and the comforts of home. Other symbols of Eirene were the cornucopia and the olive branch. Some sources named Eirene as one of the **Horae**. When the Romans adopted her, they called her Pax. (Smith)

Electra The daughter of **Clytemnestra** plotted revenge for her mother's murder of her father, Agamemnon, which in turn was inspired by Agamemnon's murder of Electra's sister, **Iphigenia**. This character was most likely a literary contrivance, a mouthpiece for authors who wished to support the diminishment of women's power. No rituals or prayers were connected with her. (Aeschylus *Oresteia*; Euripides *Electra*; Sophocles *Electra*; Smith)

Eleos The goddess of mercy (also translated as "pity" and "clemency") had only one altar, in the marketplace in the center of Athens. There anyone who wished to gain the assistance of the city-state had to worship before requesting an alliance. Like **Dike**, Eleos was a personification rather than an actual goddess. She was recognized only in Athens, where she was honored with cut hair and cast-off garments. (Thompson; Smith)

Eos Winged Eos, the dawn goddess, drove a chariot hitched to four swift steeds; she changed at midday into Hemera, and later into the sunset goddess Hesperide. Eos had many lovers, often kidnapping men she fancied. One was Orion, who, because of his constant mistreatment of his wife Merope, was blinded by Merope's father and the wine god Dionysus. To restore his sight, Orion had to bathe his face in Eos's rays. She restored Orion's sight, then stole him away. Orion did not remedy his violent ways and was removed to the stars for an offense against **Artemis**. Another mortal lover was Tithonus, for whom Eos begged immortality, forgetting to request eternal youth. As Tithonus wizened, Eos fled his bed, then turned Tithonus into a cricket. Among

Eos's children were the strong west wind, Zepheros, the bracing north wind, Boreas, the rain-bringing south wind, Notos, and Eurus, the east wind. Her other children were stars that illuminate the earth in her absence. (Athanassakis; Boedeker; Friedrich; Hesiod)

Erigone The usual story of the Greek queen **Clytemnestra** says she lost one daughter, **Iphigenia**, to her husband's callous plotting, while the other, **Electra**, turned against her mother and plotted her murder. But other versions of the story exist in which Clytemnestra had another daughter, this one with her lover Aegisthus. Named Erigone, she remained faithful to the queen, her mother. In this version of the story, it was Erigone who brought her half brother Orestes to trial for Clytemnestra's murder. When he was acquitted, Erigone hanged herself, rather than live in a world that forgave matricide. She may have had a child by her half brother; she may also have been threatened with death at his hands, after which her goddess, **Artemis**, took her to a temple, where she served as priestess. Like that of **Jocasta** and her son, Oedipus, this entire story is replete with relationships that suggest an early matrilineal society giving way to a patrilineal one. (Graves; Smith)

Erinyes Embodiments of vengeance, the Erinyes were three immortal black maidens with serpent hair and eyes from which poisonous blood dripped. Clad in gray, bearing brass-studded whips, baying and barking, they roamed the world in pursuit of those who broke the laws of kinship. Untiring, they flew without wings and dropped without warning upon guilty people. Their breath could kill, but they also dismembered people with their claws. Born from the blood of Uranus where it touched **Gaia**, the goddesses could not be stayed by sacrifice or tears when blood of kin was shed, especially kin on the maternal side. Those hoping to avert their gaze from minor misdeeds would offer black sheep and honeyed water, white doves and narcissus flowers. There were three Erinyes: Alecto ("unresting"), Tisiphone ("avenger"), and Megaera

("grudge"). As a trinity, they were the Semnae ("kindly ones"), although they were just rather than gentle; as the Dirae, they were "curses" personified. As Maniae or Furiae, they were the "mad ones." Most often they were Erinyes, "strong ones."

The playwright Aeschylus removed their special concern for maternal kinship. At the end of his trilogy on the family of **Clytemnestra**, the first trial by jury was held with **Athena** presiding. At stake was whether the Erinyes should punish Orestes for killing his mother. Athena cast the deciding vote, letting Orestes go free because mothers served only as incubators for male-deposited offspring. The Erinyes threatened to ravage the land in retaliation, but Athena consoled them with promises of sacrifices. Finally, reconciled to the new order and renamed Eumenides, the goddesses agreed to exercise their calling only at the behest of Olympian divinities.

The helpful Eumenides were originally distinct. The "kindly ones" were goddesses of the underworld who pushed edible plants through the ground. By extension, the Eumenides ruled human reproduction. Their sacred cave on the Acropolis ultimately became the preserve of the Erinyes. There, a court met in darkness to discuss matters of state. In darkness, too, the rituals of these goddesses were held, celebrated by worshippers bearing torches. (Aeschylus *Oresteia*; Athanassakis; Farnell; Hesiod; Sanford)

Eris The embodiment of folly and mischief, Eris was the mother of **Ate**, whose apple of discord was the cause of the Trojan War. Although in classical literature the golden apple belongs to Eris's daughter, it has become associated with Eris as a force of disorder and sexual pandemonium. Eris was daughter of **Nyx**, mate of the war god Ares, and mother of a horde of woes named Pontus (sorrow), Lethe (forgetfulness), Limus (hunger), Algaea (pain), and **Ate**. The Romans adopted Eris and called her Discordia. (Hall; Sanford)

Europa The "wide-eyed one" after whom the subcontinent of Europe is named was originally Cretan.

Europa owned a magic spear that never missed its target and a monstrous brass warrior that protected her island while she rode the sky on the lunar bull. The Greeks rewrote Europa's legend, so that she became a Phoenician princess; the bull was Zeus, who spied the lovely woman bathing with her handmaids. Aroused, he transformed himself into a bull whose unusual tameness lured Europa into climbing onto his back. Then he leaped into the water and carried her to Crete to rape her. Abandoned there, she bore three kings: Minos, Sarpedon, and Rhadamanthus.

Some scholars suggest a Near Eastern origin for Cretan culture and religion, pointing out that Europa resembles **Asherah** and her bull consort El (see Eastern Mediterranean). The connection of Europa and the bull recalls the myth of **Pasiphae**, so some scholars argue they are the same. Others point out that there was a cult of **Demeter** Europa near Thebes, thus connecting these two goddesses of fertility. (Andrews; Ovid *Met*; Willetts)

Eurydice Many Greek heroines bear this name. One was a husband-killing Danaid (see **Danae**), another the historical mother of Philip of Macedon. The most famous Eurydice was spouse of the singer Orpheus, son of one of the **Musae**. When she died, he followed her to the kingdom of **Persephone**, begging for Eurydice's release in a song that moved the heart of the queen of death. Granted his wish, Orpheus was instructed not to look behind as he led his lover to the light. But he could not restrain himself and, looking back, saw the shade of Eurydice disappearing forever. A final Eurydice was an underworld serpent goddess to whom human males were sacrificed; whether this goddess and Orpheus's were connected is unclear. (Ovid *Met*)

Eurynome The most ancient Greek goddess rose naked from primordial chaos and danced to divide light from darkness, sea from sky. Whirling Eurynome created a wind that grew lustful toward her. Turning to face it, she grasped the wind in her hands, rolled it into a serpent, and named it Ophion. Eurynome had intercourse with the serpent and, transforming herself into a dove, laid the universal egg from which creation hatched. Installing herself on Mount Olympus, Eurynome looked down upon the earth. But Ophion bragged that he had been responsible for everything. Eurynome kicked out his teeth and threw him into an underworld dungeon.

A later goddess of this name was ruler of the sea, part of a trinity with **Tethys** and **Thetis**, and mother of the **Charites**. Her name was a title of **Artemis** at her temple in Arcadian Phigalea, difficult to reach and open only once a year. If pilgrims reached the sanctuary, they found a statue of a snake-tailed woman tied with golden chains. (Homer *Iliad*; Smith)

Gaia Her name means "earth"; from her alternative name, Ge, we derive "geology" and "geography." Gaia was first to emerge from formless chaos, a primordial soup that was neither hot nor cold, dark nor light, hard nor soft. After an immeasurable span, chaos settled into the form of Gaia. The goddess had parthenogenetic powers, able to produce life without a mate. She gave birth to mountains, seas, rivers, living beings. Then Gaia felt desire. To satisfy it, she bore Uranus, the heavens. Their nightly mating caused Gaia to bear beings both marvelous and monstrous, including the Titans, three of whom were **Themis**, **Mnemosyne**, and Chronos (time).

Gaia hid these new children from jealous Uranus, in the folds of mountains and the depths of oceans. When Gaia could bear her burden no longer, she created a new element: hard adamant. From it she fashioned a jagged-toothed sickle, which she gave to Chronos, who hid himself as night approached.

Out of darkness Chronos sprang. He grasped Uranus's genitals and sawed them off. Blood rained onto the fertile earth, so fertile that children sprang up instantly: the **Erinyes**, the giants, and the Meliae (see **Nymphs**). The genitals, thrown out to sea, created the goddess of love, **Aphrodite**. Even after Uranus was killed, Gaia continued to have children. Orion was born when the ocean god Poseidon, in company with the thunder god Zeus and the messenger Hermes, masturbated on an ox hide and buried it in the soil, thus impregnating the goddess with their mingled seed. Gaia gave birth after nine months, and the boy's foster father pretended it had been through urination that the gods had conceived him.

Many scholars describe her as a pre-Olympian divinity minimally absorbed into later pantheons. Little is known of Gaia's rituals. Barley and honey cakes were placed at sacred caves at ritual times. At such fissures, gifted people read Gaia's will, for she inspired oracles at Delphi, Dodona, and elsewhere. Her rulership of fertility may have forged this connection, for farmers always wish to know the future of their crops. (Athanassakis; Farnell; Hesiod; Thompson; Motz)

Galatea There are three figures by this name, one of whom was a water **Nymph** possibly invented by Ovid, who said Galatea's lover was crushed by a rock; she transformed his body into a stream. A second Galatea was a human woman whose husband demanded that she kill any infant girls. She could not and raised her daughter as a boy named Leucippus. When the girl had grown, the desperate mother feared for her life. Galatea took her daughter to a temple of **Leto**, where she begged for permanent transformation. Leto granted the prayer, the girl was turned into a boy, and a festival was established in celebration.

The most familiar Galatea was created by Pygmalion, who carved an ivory statue of **Aphrodite**, with which he used to sleep. Such unnatural love was distasteful to the goddess, so Aphrodite cursed Pygmalion by constantly increasing his desire for the statue until, driven to despair, Pygmalion threw himself upon Aphrodite's mercy. The goddess breathed life into the statue, which came alive as Galatea. The lovers produced a child, a daughter whom they named Paphos after one of Aphrodite's shrines. (Ovid *Met*)

Glauce Glauce, princess of Corinth, wed the unreliable Jason. But Jason already had a wife, **Medea**, who vengefully bewitched a wedding garment, which, when Glauce tried it on, burned her to death. The fountain into which she threw herself, seeking to dowse the flames, was visible in classical Corinth.

A secondary name given to Glauce is Kreusa, also the name of the daughter of **Athena**'s serpent son, King Erectheus (see **Aglauros**). With Apollo, Kreusa bore a son, Ion, but, ashamed that she was unwed, exposed the child. Apollo took him to the oracle at Delphi (see **Pythia**), and when Kreusa came years later to plead for children, Apollo had the oracle tell the king a lie: that Ion was his child by a **Maenad** in a forgotten night of pleasure. Thus Ion attained the throne of Athens, which Apollo revealed was his by matrilineal right, as Kreusa's son. (Euripides *Medea*, *Ion*; Clauss and Johnston; Winkler and Zeitli; Reeder)

Gorgons These three sisters had golden wings and lovely faces. But their skin was lizard-like, and their hair was hissing serpents. The Gorgons had boar's tusks and brass fingers, and their gaze was so powerful that a single glance petrified the onlooker. They existed from earliest times, beyond the sea, at the end of night. Their triplet sisters, the **Graeae**, guarded the path to them. All were children of the fish goddess **Ceto**.

Although usually Gorgons were depicted as multiple, occasionally a single monster appeared, named Gorgo. When there were three Gorgons, two were described as immortal: Sthenno and Euryale. They were less prominent in Greek legend than their mortal sister **Medusa** but as a group continued to appear in Greek folklore until recent times as half-fish women who haunted Black Sea resorts on Saturday nights. If a man wished to gain a Gorgon's affection, he would wait until she asked, "Is King Alexander living?" which he answered in the affirmative, whereupon the Gorgon would become human. (Garber and Vickers; Homer *Iliad*; Lawson; Lubell)

Graeae The three sisters of the **Gorgons** lived at the world's edge, guarding the path to their sisters' sanctuary. The Graeae were beautiful although gray haired from birth. They were also deformed, having only one eye and one tooth among them. Their names were Pemphredo, the beautifully clothed one; Enyo, who always dressed in yellow; and Deino the terrible. (Hesiod)

Hagne The obscure goddess Hagne ("pure one") is known from few ancient sources. The traveler to sacred sites Pausanius described an ancient sanctuary in Messenia, in the southwestern Peloponnesus, that was the center of a mystery religion almost as revered as that of **Demeter** at Eleusis. At a tree-shaded spring, the goddess Hagne was honored with other goddesses and with the gods Apollo and Hermes. He interpreted the goddess to be a form of **Persephone**, but as the sacred spring also bore the name of Hagne, this goddess may have originally been a **Nymph** of the pure spring water. In Syria, the name Hagne was used of **Atargatis** (see Eastern Mediterranean).

The religion is also described in the Andanian Rule, a record of regulations regarding rituals that have been dated to 92/91 BCE. Although the rule does not describe any of the secret rituals, instead focusing on financial accountability for the expensive public events, the rituals are hinted at in regulations that cover tents, a sacred meal, processions, and sacrifices. Women were required to wear a white felt cap and Egyptian-style tunic with strips not more than a half finger in width; "first initiates" were required to wear a tiara. Regulations regarding "women who must be dressed in the manner of the gods" suggest that selected women enacted the roles of divinities in the ritual. The procession included musicians and "chests containing the sacred things" used for the mysteries. The fountain named Hagne appears to have been the site of the sacrifice, which included animals and other offerings. (Meyer; Pausanius)

Hairo On the island of Chios, Orion desired the maiden Hairo, but before she could wed, her father, Oinopion, required the hero to rid the land of wild beasts. Growing impatient, Orion raped Hairo. In retaliation Oinopion blinded him. A similar story is told of the **Nymph** Merope. (Argenti)

Halcyone Daughter of the wind god Aeolus, Halcyone married Ceyx, song of the morning star. Because they were so happy, Halcyone recklessly asked her husband to call her **Hera**, while she referred to him as Zeus. This raised the ire of the real Hera and Zeus, who brought about a storm while Ceyx was at sea. Halcyone, warned by a dream, stood watch by the seashore and caught Ceyx's body. In grief, Halcyone drowned herself, but then she and her mate magically revived, transformed into kingfishers. So kindly did the Greek divinities look on this loyal love that they blessed the couple. Now, when the kingfisher is ready to lay its eggs near the winter solstice, a calm descends on the sea until they hatch, called by the ancient name of the loving mortals—the "halcyon days." (Ovid, *Met*)

Harmonia The "uniter" was the daughter of love (**Aphrodite**) and war (Ares), and from her the legendary **Amazons** claimed descent. Harmonia was also said to have founded the dynasty of Thebes and to have borne famous Dionysian women: **Semele**, mother of the god; and the **Maenads** Agave and Autonoe, as well as their sister Ino. At Harmonia's marriage to King Cadmus, all the Olympians bore gifts, including a famous necklace bestowed by Aphrodite that gave irresistible sexuality to its wearer. **Athena** gave Harmonia a golden robe that endowed the wearer with dignity; during the ceremony, **Demeter** made love with her consort Iasion in her fields, to assure their productivity. (Graves 1)

Harpies Originally they were death goddesses who snatched away the living as seabirds or whirlwinds. Later they became three fair-haired winged maidens, daughters of **Gaia**. They had the pale faces of beautiful starving women, the bodies of vultures, sharp claws, and bear's ears. Many names were given them, most commonly Aello, Celaeno, and Ocypete.

They captured murderers, who were punished by the **Erinyes**. (Harrison 1955; Hesiod)

Hebe Under the name Ganymeda, this maiden goddess refreshed the divinities with the ambrosia and nectar of immortal youth. The incarnation of all that is fresh, she could renew youth. The spring goddess, the image of her mother, **Hera**, was married to Hera's champion, Heracles, and bore him two sons.

The goddess later split in two, her name and position applied to Ganymede, a mortal boy elevated to heaven to replace her, while her other attributes remained in Greek mythology as Hebe. Greek legend recorded an excuse for replacing the goddess with a deified mortal: clumsy Hebe had embarrassed the divine assembly by exposing her genitals during a fall. The Romans called Hebe Juventas, "youth." (O'Brien 1993)

Hecate When the moon was new, Hecate walked the roads carrying a blazing torch and accompanied by sacred dogs. She gathered offerings left by her devotees wherever three roads crossed. Hecate could look three ways because she had three heads: a serpent, a horse, and a dog. Fearsome as she might appear, Hecate was also beloved, dressed in a golden cloak and frolicking with deer.

Hecate's origins are unclear. She may have been Thracian (possibly once named Enodia) and moved south with other gods, or she may have emerged from east-central Asia. Her family heritage was never described, nor did she have any children. Hecate was the most solitary of Greek divinities.

Whatever Hecate's origin, her myth soon joined that of **Demeter**, for she appears at significant points in the story of the abduction of **Persephone**. She was even evoked as Persephone, perhaps because ghosts accompanied Hecate, and Persephone was goddess of the dead. Hecate was also called **Baubo**, the bawdy joker who plays an important role in Demeter's myth. Connections among these goddesses are not fully understood.

The antiquity of Hecate's worship was recognized by the Greeks, who granted to Hecate a power shared with Zeus: giving or withholding anything she wished. Hecate's worship continued into classical times. While Hecate walked the night, her worshippers gathered to eat "Hecate suppers," at which secrets of sorcery were shared. The leftovers were placed outdoors as offerings to Hecate and her hounds.

Public sacrifices offered the goddess honey, black female lambs, dogs, and sometimes slaves. As queen of night and the dark moon, Hecate controlled hordes of ghosts. Greek women evoked Hecate for protection from her hosts whenever they left the house and put her threefold image at their doors. (Athanassakis; Dexter 1990; Farnell; Hesiod; Motz; Rabinowitz; Hawley and Levick)

Hegemone An ancient goddess of the soil whose name survives in a word for sovereignty, Hegemone disappeared so early that there is no record of her independent worship. Her name became attached to **Artemis**, the horse goddess Despoina, and the **Charites**. In this last identity, she was honored with her sister Auxo, their names signifying "increase" and "mastery." Her ancient importance survived in the Athenian ritual whereby new citizens took oaths of citizenship in her name. (Kerényi 1979)

Helen Before Dorians invaded the Peloponnesus, the goddess Helen bore the title of Dendritis ("she of the trees"). A vegetation deity, she was depicted with two husbands, the Dioscuri, later her brothers Castor and Pollux. All were born of an egg laid by the goddess **Leda**.

Helen had several famous sanctuaries. In Rhamnus she was worshipped as daughter of **Nemesis**; at Argos, in the temple of **Eileithyia**. In Sparta, young women were dedicated to her upon reaching the age of matrimony. Helen was honored in a shrine of trees, where figurines of her hung; the same tradition was found on Rhodes. Finally, at Helen's temple at Therapnai, figurines tie Helen to Spartan **Artemis** Orthia, a title also borne by Aphrodite.

The most familiar Helen figured in the epic struggle of Greeks against Trojans. There are several stories of her birth. Her mother, **Leto**, attracted the eye of lustful Zeus in the shape of a swan, who raped her. (When Helen was described as the daughter of **Nemesis**, her conception also followed rape by Zeus.) Leto slept with her mortal husband shortly before or after this assault, conceiving again and giving birth to twin boys, as well to Helen's mortal sister, **Clytemnestra**.

Like her mother, Helen was raped. She was a girl when the elderly Athenian king Theseus assaulted her. Later Helen took Menelaus as spouse, granting him the right to her city's throne. They had one daughter, Hermione, about whom little legend accrues. When Helen left Menelaus for the Trojan Paris, Menelaus lost his throne as well as his wife. He chased Helen to Troy and fought for ten years to win her back. But she outlived him, acquiring two more husbands, Deïphobos and the hero of the Trojan War, Achilles.

A persistent tradition says that Helen could not be removed from her land. Only a ghost accompanied Paris to Troy, and the famous war was fought over a specter. Another story says that Paris managed to steal Helen, but he was shipwrecked in Egypt, where the pharaoh detained Helen. The Greeks waged their war only to find out that Helen had never been in the city. (Aeschylus *Oresteia*; Euripides *Helen, Orestes*; Butterworth; Friedrich; Homer *Iliad*; Lyons; Meagher; Plutarch *Lives*)

Heliades Daughters of the sun god and the goddess **Rhode** (or of the otherwise unknown goddess Neaira), these goddesses cried amber tears at the death of their brother Phaethon, who stole their father's chariot and drove it too close to the sun. They were transformed into poplar trees, notable for the way their leaves glimmer in sunlight. Yet they also continued to serve their sun father, harnessing his horses every morning and guarding his cattle. Thus they may be related to such Indo-European dawn maidens

as **Eos**, Roman **Aurora**, and Baltic **Saulės Meita**. Homer thought there were only two daughters of Helios and Rhode, Lampetia (Lampetie), and Phatusa or Phaethusa (the feminine form of the name of her famous brother, Phaeton). As both names mean "illuminator," they may have originally been solar divinities rather than simply descendants of the sun. Other sources offer the names Aegilae (Aigle or Aegle, "light") and Lamethusa. Some names of the Heliades overlap with those given the star goddesses called the **Hesperides**, which suggests confusion of these collective goddesses. (Kerényi 1979; Ovid *Met*)

Helle King Athamas of Boeotia and the cloud queen **Nephele** had two children, Phrixus and Helle. But the king turned his attentions to **Ino**, who conspired against Nephele's children by urging the women of the kingdom to induce a famine. Someone had to be sacrificed to restore the earth's fertility, and Ino bribed an oracle to demand Nephele's children. But a winged ram took the children away. Helle grew dizzy and fell into the narrow strait that separates Europe and Asia, called the Hellespont in her honor. Her brother arrived safely in Colchis and sacrificed the ram, whose golden fleece figured in the legend of the sorceress **Medea**. (Smith)

Hera The name of cow-eyed sky queen Hera, which means "Our Lady" and may have been a title, is connected to the name of the seasonal goddesses, the **Horae**. Whether the Greek goddess descended from the Mycenaean figure called "Hera" by archaeologists is unclear, although many trace the Greek goddess to that source.

Magnificent of form and feature, Hera passed through three life stages. First, she was **Hebe** or Parthenia, symbol of the budding earth and maidenhood. Next, she was revealed as the mature woman, Nymphenomene or Teleia; she was the earth in summer, the woman in the prime of life. Finally she grew into Theira, the dying autumn earth and the mature solitary woman. As goddess of birth and death, of spring and autumn, Hera held the emblems, respectively, of a cuckoo and a pomegranate.

In honor of Hera's three phases, the Greeks celebrated an athletic festival. Every four years, women came to Hera's town of Argos for 160-yard races, running in three age groups to honor the three stages. Three winners each received olive crowns and a share of a sacrificed cow, as well as gaining the right to leave a statuette of herself in Hera's shrine.

Another festival marked Hera's annual revival. Celebrants carried the goddess's statue to the spring of Kanathes, to cleanse the winter from her. A pool fed by the sacred spring can still be visited. Her primary festival, the Hekatombaia, was a new-year celebration that included rituals similar to those found on the island of Samos, where the goddess's statue was tied to a sacred tree. The "roping" ritual, indicating the transference of the goddess's power to the tree, became a symbol of her "binding" in marriage to Zeus.

Originally Hera had no consort. When the Indo-European tribes arrived, Hera's religion was too strong to destroy, so a marriage was forged between the two predominant divinities. Even as late as Homer, Zeus was called "Hera's spouse." From this marriage, classical Hera emerged, a jealous wife who hounded the unfaithful husband whom she never wanted to marry. She was last in a line of paramours of Zeus, who previously had children with **Metis**, **Eurynome**, **Demeter**, **Mnemosyne**, and **Leto**. To gain access to her, Zeus transformed himself into a cuckoo and flew into her lap. Taking pity on the bird, Hera was astonished when it turned into Zeus, who raped her.

Shamed by the violation, the goddess agreed to restore her dignity through marriage. Two daughters were born, Hebe and Eileithuia, and a son, the war god Ares. When Zeus had children without mothers (see **Athena**), Hera gave birth parthenogenetically to the smith god Hephaestus. Then Hera wearied of her husband's pursuit of other goddesses and organized a heavenly revolt. The Olympians tied Zeus to his bed and mocked him. Zeus took his revenge by stringing Hera from the sky, her wrists tied to golden bracelets, her ankles weighted by anvils.

Despite the misery of her own marriage, Hera was honored as patron of marriage and the birth of children. The latter role echoes her original position as goddess of fertility, Hera Lecherna, goddess of childbed. Figures of nursing women were offered to her, and her milk, sprayed across the sky, formed the Milky Way. Anyone who drank Hera's milk was endowed with superhuman strength. As milk giver, Hera was connected with the cow. She was called Boôpis Potnia Hêrê, "ox-eyed Lady Hera," and she frequently turned those she persecuted into cows (see **Io**).

Several legends describe Hera's priestesses, who bore the title of Callirrhoe at the Heraion in Argos. Each priestess had to memorize the names of all her forebears. Some lists still exist, and the stories of some individuals are recorded. Cydippe had two sons to whom she was devoted. She prayed to Hera to grant them what was best for mortals. That night, they died in their sleep. In Corinth, **Medea** was priestess of Hera under her title of Akraia; an initiatory ritual for adolescents may have been centered there. (Athanassakis; Avagianou; Blundell and Williamson; Dexter 1990; Friedrich; Gimbutas 1989; Harrison 1962; Hesiod; Clauss and Johnston; Kerényi 1975; Keuls; Pantel; Motz; O'Brien 1993; Watson)

Hero A priestess of **Aphrodite** at Sestos, Hero took Leander as a lover. Each night he swam across water that separated them, guided by the lighthouse on her shore. Then he swam back at dawn. One night, Leander dove into stormy waters and was lost when the storm blew out the lighthouse flame. Hero joined him in death. (Smith)

Hesperides At the edge of night lived the evening stars, daughters of **Nyx** or of **Ceto**. Occasionally they were said to be children of the mountain god Atlas, from which they draw their alternative name of Atlantides. They guarded a golden-fruited apple tree that **Gaia** gave to **Hera** as a wedding gift. Some sources describe three Hesperides named Aegle, Hespere, and Erytheis; sometimes there were four, named Aegle, Erytheia, Hestia, and Arethusa. Rarely, there's reference to seven Hesperides. Sometimes these guardian goddesses were said to be winged demons like **Harpies**, at other times beautiful singers like **Sirens**. Most commonly, they were called **Nymphs**. (Larson 2001; Smith)

Hestia Hestia took no human form; only two statues existed, both lost, and no coins show her image. But she was ever present, for Hestia was the hearth's fire. She symbolized family unity and, by extension, she embodied the social contract. At the ever-burning public hearth, Hestia was called Prytantis. First fruits, water, oil, wine, and year-old cows were sacrificed to her. She also received the first part of sacrifices offered to other gods, for as purifying fire, she could not be ignored. Daily sacrifices to Hestia were offered in homes, for the hearth was not only a place for cooking and a source of heat but a religious center as well.

Hestia was first of the Olympians, born from **Rhea** and her consort Chronos. Her antiquity is attested by the Greek proverb "Start with Hestia," meaning "Begin things at the beginning." In all her shrines, Hestia offered sanctuary to anyone needing protection; her temples were locations for the reception of foreign dignitaries.

Hestia invented architecture and built the first house. A home was not considered established until a woman brought fire from her mother's. In the same way, Greek colonists brought fire from the mother city's public hearth to assure the cohesion of their new communities. Should a hearth fire go out, it could not be relit from earthly fire but had to be ignited from the sun. (Athanassakis; Farnell; Nilsson 1961; Smith)

Hippodameia A number of minor characters in Greek mythology bear this name ("horse tamer"), which has been connected with a goddess of pre-Olympian times honored in secret rites by women. The various Hippodameias included the daughter of the Pleiade Sterope (see **Nymphs**); the sister of the man-woman **Caenis**; and the woman Briseis, slave concubine to Achilles.

The most prominent Hippodameia was ancestral mother of the fated house of Atreus (see **Dione**), the daughter of King Oenomaus, who kept her unwed by engaging in a horse race with each suitor. Because the king's horses were mares sired by the wind, he always won. But when Pelops fell in love with Hippodameia, the young man borrowed a chariot with powerful horses from the ocean god Poseidon. To assure his victory, he bribed Oenomaus's charioteer, offering him a night with Hippodameia to throw the race, but then killed him when he came to claim his prize.

After Pelops's death, Hippodameia married Autonous, bearing four sons and one daughter. When her sons were devoured by wild mares, despite Hippodameia's attempt to stop the assault, the gods turned the grieving mother into a crested lark, because she had defended her children. (O'Flaherty; Smith)

Hipta Once a widely known goddess of Asian origin, Hipta is now obscure except for reference in the Orphic Hymns, dating to an indeterminate period between 600 BCE and 400 CE. In these sources, Hipta is called the nurse of the wine god Dionysos, taking part in his rituals as a **Maenad**. (Athanassakis)

Horae Also called the "hours" or the "seasons," this collective of goddesses appeared in various groupings. Sometimes there were two: Thallo (spring) and Carpo (autumn). Sometimes there were three: Eunomia (lawful order), **Dike** (justice), and Eirene (peace). A few authors provide lists of ten or eleven Horae. Whatever their number, they were goddesses of natural order and the seasons. By extrapolation they ruled the order of human society. Few legends were told of them, although they made appearances in myths of other goddesses. Thallo was **Persephone**'s companion. The Horae brought clothing to **Aphrodite** and a garland to **Pandora**. They danced with the **Charites**; annually, they opened heaven's gates so **Hera** could escape to solitude. They appeared more often in visual than in narrative art; the image of three dancing maidens has remained common in sculpture for more than 2,000 years. (Athanassakis; Smith)

Hydra This monster guarded the entrance to the underworld at Lerna, her many heads hissing at any mortal who tried to enter. If one head were chopped off, another took its place. The swamp of Lerna was also a sanctuary where murderers could purify themselves of spilled blood, giving rise to the Greek phrase "a Lerna of evils." Hydra's blood was so poisonous that, touched by it, the immortal centaur Chiron begged to die to escape its torture. (Graves; Harrison; Hesiod)

Hygieia Goddess of health, Hygieia was either the wife or daughter of the god of healing, Asclepius; her mother was Peitho, goddess of persuasive speech, suggesting the Greeks saw a connection between love and health, for Peitho served **Aphrodite**. Her sister was a little-known goddess of healing, Iaso; her relationship to Panacea ("all-healing") is unclear. Statuary shows Hygieia as a mild-looking young woman feeding a snake from a cup. Her worship dates to the seventh century BCE, with her great center at Epidaurus dating to 300 years later. There, the goddess appeared in dreams, wearing the guise of a snake. (Athanassakis; Smith)

Hypermnestra Oldest of the Danaid sisters (see **Danae**), she was worshipped in Argos as the founder of its royal dynasty. It is theorized that she was originally not a Danaid but a water goddess. She did not join her husband-murdering sisters but spared her mate, which was used as evidence of divine sanction for the Argive monarchy. The love goddess Aphrodite offered her support for Hypermnestra, saying her actions proved the centrality of love in human life. Some sources call Hypermnestra a priestess of **Hera**, the most important goddess of Argos. (Aeschylus *The Suppliants*; O'Brien)

Idothea A minor Greek sea goddess, she was daughter of the sea god Proteus. A favorite of sailors, she was so disrespectful of her father that she revealed Proteus's weather tricks to humans. She played an important part in the story of the Trojan War, for she provided information to the victorious Menelaus, abandoned husband of **Helen**, about how to trap her father and learn the best sea route home. (Smith)

Ino Daughter of the goddess of gentility, **Harmonia**, Ino was an early goddess of agricultural rites to whom sacrifices were offered in a magical attempt to make rain fall as freely as blood. When later tribes brought their own divinities to Ino's realm, the religious conflict was recorded in the legend that Ino was a rival of the king's wife, **Nephele**. Ino brought on a famine to show her strength, then bribed messengers to bring back a false oracle demanding the sacrifice of Nephele's children (see **Helle**). **Hera** then cursed Ino, who was transformed into Leucothea ("white goddess").

Although the king fled with Ino's remaining children and remarried a woman named Themisto, his love for Ino did not die. Some myths say that she did not die, either. Her husband, hearing she lived, set off in pursuit. Themisto planned to kill Ino's children, but the slave assigned to do the deed (Ino in disguise) substituted Themisto's children. When Themisto realized she had slaughtered her own children rather than her rival's, she hanged herself. (Farnell 1916; Lyons; Ovid *Met*)

Io The first king of Argos was a river god who voted against Poseidon and for **Hera** when the two divinities contested ownership of the city. To punish the Argives for refusing him, Poseidon cursed Argos with dry summer streams. But the Argives were unconcerned. The king's daughter led them in rainmaking dances, in which priestesses mimicked cattle driven mad by gadflies in the scorching heat. Early tablets from Argos show that a princess named Io, also called Callirhoe or Callithyia, headed the college of Hera's priestesses there.

Then came the Zeus-worshipping tribes. The indigenous cow goddess found her legend grafted onto that of the sky god: Hera, jealous of Zeus's love for her priestess Io, accused him of infidelity. To hide his transgression, Zeus transformed Io into a heifer, but Hera was not fooled. She asked for the cow, and Zeus could not refuse. Hera tied Io to a tree, setting the 100-eyed Argos to guard her. On Zeus's orders, Hermes freed the heifer and killed the Argos, whose eyes Hera placed into the tail of the peacock; she then sent a gadfly to torment Io. Io wandered the world until she found rest in Egypt.

Given that Hera originated in Argos, where she was called the "cow eyed," this myth doubles the cow imagery, suggesting that Io was an aspect of Hera, not merely her priestess. Hera's worship spread through the Peloponnesus, while Io's remained isolated in Argos. (Aeschylus *The Suppliants*; Dowden; O'Brien 1993; Ovid *Met*)

Iphigenia Daughter of **Clytemnestra**, she was sacrificed by her father to bring favorable winds for the voyage to Troy in pursuit of her aunt, **Helen**. Some sources say **Artemis** saved the girl from sacrifice, replacing Iphigenia with a stag and wafting the girl off to Asia Minor to become her priestess. There, after his trial for matricide, Iphigenia's brother, Orestes, came to steal the goddess's statue, which an oracle said would relieve his tortured conscience. Iphigenia discovered her brother and assisted him in moving the statue.

Some sources say Iphigenia was transformed into a goddess called Orthia or Brauronia, both titles of Artemis. Others claim she became **Hecate**. Finally, there is evidence that Iphigenia was originally an independent goddess demoted to a heroine; she is known in some texts as Artemis Iphigenia. (Dowden; Euripides *Electra*, *Iphigenia in Taurus*, *Iphigenia at Aulis*; Manning)

Ipsia Who was the mother of the great witch **Medea**? Although she plays little role in the tragic story of the woman who risks all for love, ancient authors give several names for Medea's mother, Ipsia and Idyia. Most commonly Medea's mother was said to be a human

queen, but in some cases, the goddess **Hecate** was said to have given birth to Medea, whom she trained in the magical arts. (Kerényi 1979)

Iris The winged rainbow goddess slept under **Hera**'s bed when not delivering messages. It was Iris who, when Hera slept with Zeus, prepared their bed. She was one of the few Olympians who could journey to the underworld, where she fetched water for oaths; for this reason, she was called a form of **Hecate**. (Aristophanes *The Birds*)

Jocasta When seers predicted the child of Laius and Jocasta would kill his father and marry his mother, the horrified parents exposed him on a mountainside. But the boy was found, saved, and brought up by another royal family. When he learned of the prediction, he ran away to spare his imagined father and mother. Meeting a man at a crossroads, he killed him, not knowing it was Laius, his real father.

Near Thebes, he vanquished the monstrous **Sphinx**, who held the region hostage. Hailed as a hero, Oedipus married the queen, again without knowing she had given him birth. But the land was struck by a blight caused by the incestuous conception of children, including noble **Antigone**. When she discovered the truth, Jocasta killed herself, whereupon Oedipus blinded himself and left the city. Jocasta's brother, Creon, then took the throne. In some variants, Jocasta does not kill herself but divides the throne between her two sons by Oedipus, suggestive of matrilineal inheritance. (Euripides *The Phoenician Women*; Sophocles *Oedipus the King*)

Ker This goddess of death, daughter of **Nyx** and sister of the **Moirae**, appeared as a black carrion bird hovering over corpses. The name was also used of any malevolent ghost. In the plural, Keres, she symbolized the many forms death can take. No one can escape Ker, but gods sometimes hid favorites from her. Occasionally Ker was called a goddess of vengeance. (Smith)

Koronides Two sisters, Metioche and Menippe, were born to the hunter Orion, who was killed by the virgin goddess **Artemis** for attempting to rape her. They lived in Boeotia, where **Athena** trained them in weaving and **Aphrodite** gave them beautiful manners. But then a plague threatened, and oracles proclaimed all would die unless two maidens offered themselves as a sacrifice. The girls did so, killing themselves with their shuttles. As they died, the gods raised them into the heavens as comets. (Fontenrose A)

Lamia Children were frightened with stories about Lamia, a mortal woman who bore Zeus several children. When jealous **Hera** destroyed all her offspring except **Scylla**, Lamia went crazy with grief and began stealing other women's children to suck their blood. Originally this half-snake figure may have been a form of the Cretan snake goddess, honored at rituals similar to those of **Demeter** at Eleusis. Lamia existed in Greek folklore until recent times, continuing her career as a frightening specter. (Argenti; Lawson)

Lampetia The sun's daughter was his chief herdswoman as well, guarding his fabulous cattle. The *Odyssey* tells how the Greeks arrived on the island of Trinacria (modern Sicily), where this goddess and her sister Phathusa lived. King Odysseus warned his men not to touch the sacred cattle, but a few disobeyed. The cattle suffered greatly: hides walked around by themselves; spitted flesh groaned over the fires. Lampetia reported the sacrilege to her father, who sent a storm to destroy the Greek boats. Only Odysseus was saved from the sun god's anger; he washed ashore on the island of **Calypso**. (Homer *Od*; Ovid *Met*)

Leda Originally she may have been Lada ("woman"); she may be connected to the similarly named **Leto**. Zeus, in the form of a swan, raped Leda. The same night, Leda slept with her husband, and later she laid an egg. Out hatched two sets of twins, male and female, mortal and immortal, the mortal children fathered by her husband, the immortal ones by Zeus.

The mortal twins were **Clytemnestra** and Pollux; the immortal ones, **Helen** and Castor. Leda was then raised to heaven, where she became known as **Nemesis**.

Variants say Zeus raped Nemesis herself. She fled from him, changing shape as she ran, but, finally overpowered in the body of a bird, Nemesis laid an egg that the woman Leda found and cared for. Another tale says Zeus tricked Nemesis by disguising himself as a swan, then raping her. The egg that resulted was laid between Leda's legs, so she was the foster mother of the four children. (Smith)

Lemna The island of Lemnos is in the far north of the Aegean Sea, near the mythic land of the **Amazons**. The people of Lemnos had direct connections to those women warriors, for they claimed descent from Myrine, one of the greatest Amazon queens. Their own goddess bore the name of their island: Lemna.

The women of Lemnos were so confident of their beauty that they neglected proper sacrifices to the goddess of desire, **Aphrodite**. In punishment, she put a curse on them appropriate to their neglect. They were stricken with a terrible odor that made them sexually repulsive. The men of the island began consorting with slave women, conceiving children upon their concubines. In revenge, the Lemnian women killed the men. They also killed the slave women and the children born of the illicit unions.

Only their queen, Hypsipyle, broke the women's covenant, by hiding her father from death. Later, the Greek hero Jason and his Argonaut companions stopped at the island. To repopulate their land, the women had intercourse with the strangers, Hypsipyle choosing Jason himself. It was said that the women, realizing the murders had changed their society utterly, thereafter called the children by their fathers' names, rather than by their own. The story offers a strong warning against women asserting rights of matrilineal succession. (Cantarella; Friedrich)

Lethe The Greek goddess of oblivion was the daughter of the matron of disorder, **Eris**. The underworld river through which the dead pass, and which causes them to forget their lives on this earth, is named for her. Some myths call Lethe the mother of Dionysus—the god of wine, whose heritage would explain the reason for drunken forgetfulness. (Hesiod; Smith)

Leto Classical myth said she was a paramour of Zeus who bore Apollo and **Artemis**, despite the persecutions of **Hera**. But she existed before Zeus appeared. Leto may have been part of the substratum of Greek religion shared with Hera; she was known in Crete, under the name of Phytia. She has been connected to **Leda** and to the goddess of vengeance, **Nemesis**. Or Leto may have been an imported goddess, perhaps **Al-Lat** (see Eastern Mediterranean).

She was the daughter of the moon goddess **Selene** and sister of **Asteria**, who saved her by becoming the sunken island Delos, on which Leto safely gave birth. Leto was called "gentlest of all Olympus," but her gentleness did not protect Leto from rape, for the mortal Tityus assaulted her and was executed for the crime by Apollo. (Homer *Iliad*; Hesiod; Keuls; Lyons; Meagher; Motz; Willetts)

Leucothea "White goddess" is a term given to several goddesses and heroines, including the cow goddess **Ino**, who was honored by seagoing people as an indicator of the sea's fertility, but also as an oracular being. Under the name Leucothea, she was honored as a primary divinity in the oracular shrine of Didyma. On Rhodes, she was originally Halia ("sea woman"), nurse to the baby ocean god Poseidon together with the heroine Kapheira. On Tedenos, she was called Hemithea, while in other areas that name was jointly held by a group of goddesses. (Lyons)

Lindia The goddess of the city of Lindos was worshipped from 1500 BCE until she became assimilated to **Athena**. Lindia embodied the abundance of harvest, as well as the culture a stable food supply sustains. An uncut plank represented Lindia's torso and limbs; a sculpted head rose above, crowned with the walls of her city, while garlands were strung across her unshaped breast. Lindia is a form of the goddess Karpophoros, "lady of the beasts," a goddess identified with wild places and animals. (Friedrich; Zuntz)

Litae Innumerable sweet-natured goddesses, they represented penitential prayers that, light as the Litae's frail bodies, wafted to Olympus to be answered. These goddesses accompanied **Ate**, goddess of discord, as she created difficulties on earth, offering to help those whose minds she confused. The word "litigate"—to plead one's case—is derived from their name, as well as the religious term "litany." (Sanford)

Lycippe With her sisters, Iphinoë and Iphianassa, she was a daughter of the early hero Proitos (from which they are called the Proitids), who, because she made fun of a statue of the goddess **Hera**, was stricken with an itching disease that caused her to go mad and wander, mooing like a cow. The name of the third sister is also used for the sacrificed heroine **Iphigenia**. (Dowden)

Macaria The "blessed one" was the only daughter of the champion Heracles and the warrior woman **Dejanira**. During a siege of Athens, an oracle announced the city would be overrun by its enemies unless a child of Heracles died. To save her home, Macaria committed suicide. A spring was named in Macaria's honor. (Euripides *The Heracleidae*; Graves 2; Smith)

Maenads A religion of ecstatic worship overtook Greece in the eighth century BCE, peaking in the fifth century BCE.

Myth says the Maenads ("mad ones"), or Bacchantes ("followers of Bacchus"), worshipped the wine god Dionysus, also called Bacchus, or "rowdy one." A latecomer to the Olympian pantheon, he was born of Zeus and **Semele**. (Alternate stories say he was conceived by **Demeter**, **Persephone**, **Iris**, **Io**, Lethe, or **Dione**, or by a human woman, either **Amalthea** or Arge.) When **Hera** made Semele doubt her lover's identity, the woman asked to see Zeus in all his brilliance. She was blasted apart by his power, but the divine fetus was saved, and Dionysus was born from Zeus's thigh. Hidden from other gods, Dionysus grew to manhood nursed by **Nymphs**, princesses, or the goddess **Persephone** or **Rhea**. Some sources say he spent his childhood disguised as a girl, spoon-fed honey by Macris, daughter of his aunt Autonoe.

When grown, he drove women mad. Portraits of Dionysus's followers show them tattooed with a fawn on their upper arm, dressed in wild-animal skins and bearing ivy-wreathed staffs of fennel (*thrysos*). Hundreds of Greek paintings show Maenads running through wilderness, heads flung back and hair unbound. They killed with bare hands and drank warm blood. They set their hair afire and remained uninjured. Weapons did not harm them, nor could armies disperse them.

Only women participated in this religion. The Maenads included married and unmarried women of all ages past girlhood. Those who did not participate honored those who did. One group of Maenads, caught in a war and unable to return home, stumbled into the town of Amphisa and fell asleep. When they awoke, the town's matrons stood ringed about them, silently holding hands.

Because the Maenads never revealed their rites beyond their circles, there is no way to know what the Dionysian Mysteries entailed. From early times, ignorance did not discourage speculation. Most of what is reported about the Maenads is imagined. Some myths describe the dreadful results of opposing their religion. In Thrace, King Lycurgus captured and imprisoned some Maenads. Dionysus cursed him, causing Lycurgus to mistake his own son for a vine and prune him to death. When the king did not repent, the Maenads made the land barren until his people offered up Lycurgus to be torn apart.

Men were unwelcome at Maenad gatherings and were punished severely for intruding, as the story of Agave's son, King Pentheus of Thebes, reveals. Daughter of Harmonia, Agave—Semele's sister and Dionysus's aunt—joined the Bacchic women. But her son was repulsed by his mother's religion. Climbing a tall pine he tried to spy on them. The Maenads dragged him from the tree and tore him to shreds, with Agave leading the attack. Then the women carried his bloody remains back to Thebes, Agave bearing his severed head aloft.

Several tales describe Maenads who killed their children in a Dionysian frenzy. Aura, a maiden who followed **Artemis**, attracted the lust of Dionysus. True to her vow of chastity, she spurned him. So the god turned to **Aphrodite**, and it was not long before Aura became a Maenad and mother of Dionysus's twin sons. But Artemis had not forgotten Aura and, to punish her, drove her mad. In the intoxication of ritual, Aura killed and ate one of her children. Then, despairing, she drowned herself.

While in Aura's tale Artemis caused her madness, more commonly Dionysus himself drove women insane. Leucippe jeered at a group of Maenads, in punishment for which she was stricken mad and her sons ripped to pieces; her sisters Aristippe and Alkithoe suffered a similar fate when, refusing to leave their looms, they saw weavings come alive with vines and ivy, whereupon the women ran raving into the woodlands, killing children as they went and finally being transformed into birds.

Many names of Maenads are recorded. Thyia was the first Maenad; Charopeia and Phasyleia led the women in dance, as did Terpsichore (see **Musae**). Methe became so divinely inspired she was deified. Chalcomede was protected by Dionysus when a warrior attempted to rape her; when he could not protect Coronis, Dionysus drove her rapist mad until he committed suicide.

Although the religion of the Maenads died out in Greece before Euripides wrote about them in 400 BCE, there is evidence that Dionysian rituals were celebrated in Greek-influenced areas of Italy into the common era. From the third century BCE, annual women-only festivals called bacchanalia were held on the Aventine Hill on March 16 and 17. Later the rites were opened to men and held more frequently, until suppressed by the Senate in 186 BCE. Nonetheless, as the Villa of Mysteries at Pompeii suggests, the rites may have continued in secret. (Dodds; Euripides *Bacchae*; Evans; Farnell; Harrison 1962; Hedreen; Henrichs; Keuls; Kraemer; Lyons; Meyer; Ovid *Met*; Cameron and Kuhrt; Sanford; Sourvinou-Inwood 2005; Whallon; Young; Pantel)

Maia The name May for the month is derived from this goddess who appeared in both Greek and Roman legend. In Greece, she was "grandmother," "midwife," or "wise one" (variant meanings of her name). Originally goddess of the night sky, later the oldest of the **Pleiades**, Maia survives in name only; all of her myth is lost except for the mention of her as mother of the phallic god Hermes, after an assignation with Zeus. The Romans identified Greek Maia with their fire goddess of the same name, who, with **Flora** and **Feronia**, ruled the forces of growth and warmth, including sexual heat. (Graves 1; Smith)

Manto We call prophetic words *mantic* speech after the name of this Greek heroine, daughter of the seer Tiresias and herself a gifted prophet. A Theban woman, she was captured by the people of Argos, who, impressed with her gifts, carried her off to become oracle at Delphi. She may be the same figure as the priestess called **Daphne**. Several minor characters bear this name in Greek mythology, including a daughter of Heracles who gave her name to the Italian town of Mantua. All were said to be prophets. (Graves 1; Smith)

Marpessa When Apollo tried to rape her, Marpessa appealed to Zeus for aid. He gave her a choice of mates: god or man. Marpessa chose the mortal Idas rather than her assailant. In another version of the tale, her father, Euenus, in an attempt to keep the girl from marriage, required suitors to run a chariot race, with losers beheaded. Idas borrowed a winged chariot from his father, the ocean god Poseidon, and carried away Marpessa, only to find Apollo claiming the bride. But Marpessa, knowing the fickleness of gods in love with mortals, chose Idas as her groom. (O'Flaherty)

Medea Without the aid of the "cunning one," Jason would have been unable to obtain the golden fleece from the kingdom of Colchis. He exploited the knowledge of Princess Medea, who was adept in herbal lore and magic, trained by **Hecate** herself. Urged on by her sister Chalaiope, Medea led the Greeks to the well-guarded treasure. Then she sailed with Jason on the *Argo*, bringing her brother Absyrtus so that, when capture seemed likely, she could kill him and cast him piecemeal overboard. The people of Colchis stopped to catch body parts, letting the Greeks escape. Other versions of the story say Jason, not Medea, killed Absyrtus.

When the *Argo* reached Greece, Medea found she could not hold the wandering attentions of Jason. Although Medea had borne children, he married again, this time Princess **Glauce**. Medea killed Glauce with a poisoned gift, a robe dipped in dragon's blood. She then killed her children by Jason, mounted her serpent chariot, and flew away.

Jason wandered homeless through Greece until he slumped beneath his old ship, the *Argo*. A piece of rotting hulk detached itself and brained him. Medea did better. Flying to Athens, she married King Aegeus. But she grew jealous of the attention he lavished on his son Theseus. So Medea flew home to Asia, where the Persian people were called the Medes in her honor. She restored her father to the throne and lived happily, continuing her magical practices.

Zeus tried to seduce her, but she refused, knowing how great Hera's anger could be. Zeus raped other women, but Medea was too powerful, so he left her alone. So great a sorceress did not need to pass through death's portals; she went straight to the Elysian Fields, where she became a goddess, worshipped in Italy as the snake divinity **Angitia**. (Barber; Clauss and Johnston; Euripides *Medea*; Kerényi 1979; Ovid *Met*; Reeder; Watson)

Medusa Medusa was pre-Olympian, with most of her legend dating from the eighth–seventh centuries BCE. Her name means "queen," a title often used of the primary female divinity. By historical times, she had been converted into the daughter of **Ceto**, who took Poseidon as a lover. Once, the pair made love in a shrine of **Athena**. The goddess turned Medusa into a snake-haired **Gorgon**, later engineering Medusa's murder by sending Perseus to decapitate her. He had to be specially equipped, because Medusa's glance turned living beings to stone. So Perseus carried a mirror. Looking into it, he saw Medusa's reflection and struck off her head.

As she died, Medusa gave birth. From her neck sprang the winged horse Pegasus and the hero Chrysaor. Drops of blood fell on the desert, engendering snakes. The Gorgon's remaining blood was caught in vials. A single droplet from the left side raised the dead, and the same amount from the right killed instantly. A lock of her hair was given to Heracles; it caused armies to be seized with panic.

Behind this eerie figure is an early goddess, possibly similar to **Demeter**, who also mated with Poseidon. Her connection with Athena also bears consideration, for once Medusa's head left her winged shoulders, it was mounted on the virgin goddess's goatskin robe. The connection may be even stronger, for a *pithos* from 700 BCE shows a winged, enthroned goddess sitting calmly while another winged figure, helmeted and armed with a spear, leaps from her head. Medusa and Athena, far from being opposites, appear intertwined. (Apollodorus; Burkert; Fontenrose J; Frothingham; Garber and Vickers; Gimbutas 1989; Goodison; Howe; Kerenyi 1978; Nilsson 1932; Ovid *Met*; Persson; Siebers; Tyrell; Friedrich; Hesiod)

Megara The first wife of the hero Heracles was Megara, niece of Queen **Jocasta** of Thebes. She had been held captive by a usurper, Lycus, but was rescued by Heracles, who then unaccountably went mad and murdered her as well as their children. (Euripides, *Heracles*)

Melanippe Because she could accurately predict the future, the Greek gods hated this daughter of centaurs. So they sent the wind god Aeolus to rape her, then transformed her into a horse, the mare Ocyrrhoe. Another version of the story describes Melanippe as Aeolus's daughter, who, to hide her affair with Poseidon, exposed the twin sons she bore. But a wild cow raised them, and when the peasants mistook the children for miraculous cattle, they were delivered to the king. Melanippe was told to prepare them for sacrifice, for such a prodigy was certainly meant for the gods. She tried to save them, but only drew attention to herself. Her secret exposed, Melanippe was imprisoned and her children killed. See also **Amazons**. (Warmington)

Melissa Although several women in myth bear this name, which means "bee," it is best attested as the title of priestesses of the earth goddess **Demeter** in Eleusis and of the many-breasted **Artemis** of Ephesus. Originally referring to bee-**Nymphs**, the name was used of priestesses in general because they lived in female groups. The most significant figure of this name was a Cretan princess who learned to collect honey to feed the infant Zeus; when he grew into a supreme god, Zeus turned his nurse into a bee. Artemis bore this title when she served as a midwife. (Cook; Elderkin; Smith)

Mentha The spirit of the mint plant was the beloved of the Greek underworld ruler; she may have been an aspect of Hades's other wife, **Persephone**. (Friedrich)

Meta In Greek legend, she was the daughter of the mortal Erysichthon, whom **Demeter** afflicted with insatiable hunger. Poseidon, who desired Meta, offered her the power of metamorphosis in return for sexual favors. She concurred, and when her father discovered her new talent for shape-shifting, he sold her in animal form at market, spent the money for food, then sold her again when she returned. (Larson 1995)

Meter The name of this goddess ("mother") survives in that of **Demeter**. Statues of Meter were half-carved: on the top was a stately maternal figure, while the lower half remained uncut. Hers was a mystery religion, involving initiation, about which little is known. In the Metroon (mother temple), Meter was honored in rituals that employed percussive instruments to create ecstatic union with the divine. Meter was often conflated with **Rhea**. (Borgeaud 2004; Farnell; Pantel; Munn; Mylonas; Roller; Vassileva)

Metis "Prudent counsel" was a Titan, daughter of **Tethys**. When Zeus arrived in her territory, Metis became his first "wife." Afraid of being surpassed by his offspring, Zeus devoured his pregnant spouse and gave birth to her daughter **Athena** through his head. This legend is a pastiche consistent only in its attempt to disguise the early religion, for art that shows Athena being born from a goddess's head exists, calling into question the father-birth story. (Hesiod; Kerényi 1978)

Mnemosyne The daughter of earth and sky, she was "memory" personified. She was mother of the nine **Musae**, whom she conceived in nine days of continual intercourse with Zeus. Another similar figure named Mneme ("memory") was mother of the Musae and a member of the group. (Athanassakis)

Moirae In Homeric times, there was one "fate," Moira. Later there were Fates of birth and of death, or for good and evil fortunes. Finally we find three Fates: Clotho ("spinner"), who spun the thread of life; Lachesis ("measurer"), who allotted circumstances of each life; and Atropos ("inevitable"), who snipped life's thread. The Fates controlled all aspects of a person's inheritance, from birth order to health to talent.

Usually they were said to be daughters of **Nyx**, but some myths say they sprang from the womb of **Themis**. Among the most ancient goddesses, they never lost their authority, for even powerful Zeus could not countermand them. Only once were they gainsaid:

Apollo got them drunk, in an attempt to save a friend's life, and they agreed to cut another person's thread.

Superstitions about haunted locations where the Fates lived were found until the early twentieth century. Caves were believed to be their domains, and offerings of cake, herbs, and honey were left for them. The Fates would then permit the seeker foreknowledge of his or her future spouse or children. This connects them with **Aphrodite**, sometimes called the oldest of the Moirae. (Athanassakis; Barber; Dexter 1990; Lawson; Sanford; Motz)

Musae Daughters of Mnemosyne, the Muses were born near Mount Olympus in a place they made a dancing ground. They were raised by the hunter Crotus, who was transported after death into the sky as Sagittarius. Usually there were nine Musae: Clio, ruler of history, depicted with an open scroll or a chest of books; Euterpe, the flute-playing lyric Muse; festive Thalia, who wore the comic mask and wreaths of ivy; Melpomene, who wore vine leaves and the mask of tragedy; Terpsichore, who carried a lyre and ruled choral song as well as dance; Erato, ruler of erotic poetry and nurse of Pan; Polyhymnia, whose name means "many hymns" and who inspired them; Urania, globe-bearing Muse of astronomy; and Calliope, ruler of epic poetry, shown with tablet and pencil.

Sometimes there were fewer than nine Musae. Three were symbolic: Melete ("practicing"), Mneme ("remembering"), and Aoide ("singing"). When there was only one Muse, she could be called by any of the names of the nine. The group had many alternative names, derived from sacred places. They were called Castalides for a spring called Castilia on Mount Parnassus; a minor goddess lived there and endowed people with inspiration, from which Parnassus remains a symbol of achievement in the arts. (Apollonius of Rhodes; Athanassakis; Farnell; Hesiod; Ovid *Met*)

Myrmex The warrior **Athena** fell in love with this woman because of her skill with the loom, her hardworking nature, and her gracious piety. But then Myrmex began to boast that she had invented the plough, although Athena had been the real inventor. Athena, furious, turned the girl into an ant. The story was connected with the tribal group called the Myrmidons in Thessaly, north of Attica, where it was said that the people were all transmogrified ants. (Smith)

Myrrha The goddess of the myrtle tree (sacred to **Aphrodite**) lured her father into a secretive affair, by which she conceived the beautiful Adonis. Changed into a tree, Myrrha gave birth. The word for myrtle was a pun on female genitals, especially the clitoris, and this goddess's son was said to be skilled in giving his lover Aphrodite orgasms. (Keuls)

Nemesis In her earliest form, Nemesis was one of a pair of goddesses worshipped in the city of Rhamnus, the other being **Themis**. Winged Nemesis held images of prosperity: an apple tree, an offering plate, a crown. She tormented those who broke the social rules Themis represented. Although sometimes described as one of the **Erinyes**, Nemesis had broader powers as the force of justice. She was goddess of balance, meting out difficulties to those for whom life was too easy, but offering relief to those who suffered. She was served by Poine, goddess of punishment.

When Zeus arrived in Greece, he pursued Nemesis, intent on rape. The goddess changed shape, but the god transformed himself as well. He overpowered her in bird form, and she laid an egg that hatched into **Helen**. (Farnell; Lloyd-Morgan; Sanford; Smith)

Nephele Originally a Semitic goddess whose name means "cloud," she came into Greek mythology as wife of a Theban king and mother of **Helle**. Her celestial nature led to her identification with **Hera**. The arrogant Ixion mistook her for Hera; intent upon raping the sky queen, he raped Nephele instead. From that mating, the half-horse centaurs were born. (Plutarch *Sparta*)

Nike Daughter of **Styx** and sister of **Bia** ("strength"), Nike was honored throughout Greece, especially at Athens, where as a companion of **Athena**, Nike was "winged victory." (Athanassakis; Hesiod; Mark et al.)

Niobe Early myth called her the mother of humanity; her daughters, the Meliae, or ash-tree **Nymphs**, produced humanity. Some say Niobe's children were without number, while others say she had two daughters, Chloris and Cledoxa. Later Greek legend called her a queen who bragged of the number of her children and mocked **Leto** for having only two. **Artemis** and Apollo avenged their mother by slaughtering Niobe's children. Only her daughter survived, to become one of Greece's great beauties; originally called Meliboea, she was renamed Chloris because she grew pale at the tragedy she witnessed. Overcome, Niobe wept for so long that the gods transformed her into a stone from which a fountain sprang.

Although most authors describe her as a human queen, there is evidence that Niobe was an early goddess; anyone who looked upon her children's bodies was turned to stone, an image that connects her with the **Gorgon Medusa**. The image of Niobe in mourning resembles that of **Demeter** grieving the loss of her daughter, **Persephone**. (Friedrich; Homer *Iliad*; Kerényi 1979; Ovid *Met*)

Nymphs Nature spirits took the form of feminine groups representing the essential forces the Greeks perceived in rocks, trees, and streams. There are no parallel groups of male divine figures. All collective nature spirits were feminine to the Greeks. Though called Olympians, the Nymphs lived on earth as beautiful naked women with long green hair. Not officially recognized as goddesses, the Nymphs were nonetheless honored with sacrifices of meat, milk, and oil; wine was never offered them, although they raised the wine god, Dionysus, son of **Semele**. The Nymphs were attached to **Artemis**, sometimes considered the chief Nymph.

Their name has connotations of sexuality, for it

was used of nubile women as well as nature spirits. A woman was "nymph" as a bride, and occasionally human heroines are referred to with this term, when their sexual agency is emphasized. Most often, Nymphs were nonmortal women, though not necessarily immortal ones.

Nymphs fell into several categories. Most were connected with running water, either as daughters of water gods or as water divinities themselves. Nymph names often include the syllable *naïs* or *rhoê*, both referencing running water. As water divinities, the Nymphs were associated with healing rituals that took place around water sources.

Most numerous of the watery Nymphs were the Oceanids, the 3,000 daughters of Oceanus and **Tethys**; most other Nymphs were said to be daughters of the sky god Zeus. Early Nymphs, the Oceanids were later replaced by another group, the Nereids, but play an important role as companions of **Persephone**. Some have described the Nereids as divinities of the Mediterranean, while the Oceanids lived in the Atlantic. Others consider the Nereids river goddesses, who bore names for the rivers they occupied. The 50 daughters of the sea goddess Doris and the god Nereus, the Nereids were famous for their oracular powers; they predicted shipwrecks or averted them. The Nereid Panopea helped sailors in danger; if they prayed to her, she calmed the ocean. Clymene gave birth to the sun's children, the Heliades. Finally, the mother of the hero Achilles, **Thetis**, was a Nereid.

Ponds, lakes, and other still waters were homes to Naiads, another form of water Nymph. Naiads were not so long-lived as oceanic Nereids, but lived longer than tree women or Dryads. As long as streams and rivers embodying them did not go dry, freshwater Naiads lived. Among the Naiads were the **Musae**, who lived in flowing springs; they bestowed oracular powers and artistic eloquence. Some Naiads were healers, but the Limnades were dangerous, haunting lakes, marshes, and swamps. They sang to strangers, luring them to a watery death, or called out desperately as

though they were drowning, luring passersby into mire.

The water Nymph Telphusa had prophetic powers, but the water of her fountain was so cold it killed anyone who drank it. Some legends say the famous seer Tiresias died trying to sip Telphusa's water. When Apollo was seeking a place for his oracle, he first selected Telphusa's spring. But she persuaded him to look elsewhere, directing him to **Gaia**'s Delphi, where the Nymph knew Apollo would have to fight **Python** for control. Aganippe inspired those who drank of her well at the foot of Mount Helicon, for which reason the Musae were called the Aganippicles; they may be a multiplied form of her.

Although some scholars argue that the term "nymph" can only refer to elementals of water, other collective goddesses are called Nymphs. Star Nymphs were called Hyades or Pleiades. Unlike most groups of Nymphs, the Hyades were limited in number. Often these Nymphs are connected with the constellation of the "seven sisters."

On land, Nymphs embodied animate and inanimate nature. The Limoniades lived in open meadows and entertained themselves by dancing with flowers. Rocks and mountains were the domain of the Oreads, sweet-singing pale women whose thin robes were woven in caves on fine looms visible only to the second-sighted. To honor the Oreads, the Greeks anointed rocks, hung belts on rocks, and left offerings in caves.

Among the Nymphs of animate nature, the Dryads, or Hamadryads, were best known. Every tree had a Dryad, who lived as long as the tree that embodied her. Sometimes a Dryad punished a mortal for breaking branches. Accidental death in a forest was blamed on Dryad revenge. Dryads were especially active in early August, when trees could not be cut. Nymphs associated with vegetation include the reed Nymph Syrinx, the lily Leiriope, and Rhodos of the roses, as well as the groups Ionides (violets) and Pterides (ferns).

Gaia conceived the ash-tree nymphs called Meliae; they were mothers of humankind, for people rose from the earth at their roots. In the singular, Melia was daughter of the ocean god and mother of the half-horse centaurs. Bee-Nymphs were called Melissae, a word also used of colleges of priestesses. Because Nymphs were endowed with prophecy, the term Melissa was sometimes used to designate a soothsayer. The original Melissa was a Nymph who discovered the use of honey.

A final category of Nymph was the inhabitant of a specific important place, of which Amnisiades (of the river Amnistis), Nysiades (of Nysia), Dodonides (of Dodona), and Lemniae (of Lemna) are examples. Sometimes, rather than Nymphs being named for locations, the opposite occurred; Phigalia was a Dryad for whom a town was named. At the sanctuary of Elis, a group of Nymphs called the Acmenes were honored at an altar surrounded by shrines to other gods. They may have been the genii loci (spirits of place).

In addition to collective myths, there are myths that describe Nymphs individually. A predominant theme is attempted rape of a woman who turns into a Nymph. Such stories include that of **Daphne**, turned into a tree to escape Apollo. Lotis, in a similar tale, was pursued by Priapus. The Nymph called out to mother earth, who transformed her into the first lotus tree. The Nymph Syrinx escaped from the woodland god Pan by changing herself into a reedy marsh. Pan cut down the reeds and made himself a pipe, afterward called by the Nymph's name.

Pitys also inspired Pan's obsession. He pursued her until she changed into a pine, thereafter sacred to him. Another story says Pan was her lover, but the wind god Boreas desired her. When she rejected him, he blew her off a cliff. As she was hanging there, Gaia took pity on her and transformed her into a weathered pine tree that weeps sap when the wind touches it.

In some cases, a god's love was returned. Apollo loved Acantha, who loved him back. At her death, she was transformed into a sun-loving herb. Clytie, too, fell in love with the sun. Transformed into a sunflower, she follows his movement across the sky.

When Nymphs fell in love with humans, suffering usually resulted. Abrya fell in love with the shepherd Selemnus. She took on a human body to seduce him, then lost interest and returned to her spring. But Selemnus could not forget. He pined away until **Aphrodite** turned him into a river so he could share Abrya's element. He was still sorrowful, so Aphrodite endowed his waters with the power to remove the sting of failed love.

The Nymph Echenais fell in love with mortal Daphnis and made him promise sexual fidelity to her. But he got drunk with a priestess and made love to her. Echenais blinded him so he would never be tempted by another woman's beauty. Another Nymph, Salmachis, was so feminine that any male who drank her waters became female. One day the son of Hermes and Aphrodite chanced by Salmachis's fountain. The Nymph reached to embrace him, but he drowned in her waters. Salmachis pleaded with the Olympians to unite them forever; they became the first hermaphrodite.

Belief in the elemental powers of Nymphs remained common in Greece until recently, when mountain, river, woodland, and ocean nymphs were depicted as amoral and possibly threatening to humanity. Precautions were necessary to protect self and property against thefts caused by Nymphs. The Nymphs were referred to with the kind of circumlocutions also found in ancient times. Such terms as "the ladies," "the kindly ones," and "the maidens" were used to distract them from mischief. (Argenti; Athanassakis; Barrington; Borgeaud 1988; Friedrich; Larson 2001, 1997; Lawson; Kerényi 1979; Ovid *Met*; Smith; Sourvinou-Inwood 2005)

Nyx The pre-Olympian creation myth says Nyx ("night"), first daughter of unruly Chaos, gave birth to the first male, Erebus, and mated with him to produce the **Nymphs** called the Hesperides. But she did not stop there, spewing out dreadful creatures like Age and Death and Fate. Many demonic Greek characters, such as the infrequently mentioned spirit of madness, Lyssa, were described as "daughters of night."

One daughter was bright rather than dark.

Hemera shared a home with her mother beyond the horizon in Tartarus. Twice each day Hemera and Nyx passed at the brass gates of the other world, waving from their chariots as one went home and the other mounted the sky. (Athanassakis; Hesiod; Cameron and Kuhrt)

Oeno Oeno ("wine") was a granddaughter of Dionysus, sister of Spermo ("wheat") and Elias ("olive oil"). Their grandfather gave them power to change water into wine, grass into wheat, berries into olives. They lived peacefully until the Greeks arrived. Oeno and her sisters helped them with their special powers, but the Greeks fell upon the women to imprison them. Dionysus turned them into doves so they could escape. (Smith I)

Oreithyia The daughter of Erechtheus, snaky son of the otherwise-virgin goddess **Athena**, and the woman Praxithea, Oreithyia was dancing by the River Ilissus one day when the north wind, Boreas, snatched her up and carried her to Sarpedon's rock in Thrace. There he called up a dark cloud to hide his crime and raped her. From this crime, two daughters, Cleopatra and Chione, were conceived, as were the winged Argonauts, Calaïs and Zetes, who accompanied the hero Jason on his raid into the territory of **Medea**. (Apollonius of Rhodes)

Ossa Last-born daughter of **Gaia** or the minor goddess **Spes**, Ossa was feathered and fleet-footed. She ran through the earth bearing rumors, some of them disguised messages from the gods. (Smith)

Pallas This pre-Olympian goddess survived in a story that she was **Athena**'s friend. Wrestling with the goddess, Pallas almost bested her. Zeus could not bear to see his daughter defeated, so he tricked Pallas into looking away at a crucial instant, and Athena killed her, whereupon the goddess took her friend's name as her own. Pallas's name also became part of the word

"palladium," the image of Athena that kept the city safe.

Troy also had a statue of Pallas that Athena carved after killing her friend; thus she became the patron of sculptors and artisans. The statue stood in Olympus until, feeling it watch him while he raped a **Nymph**, Zeus threw it to earth. Troy would not have fallen to the Greeks had not Odysseus stolen the palladium, after which the city's defenses were insufficient. (Hall; Kerényi 1978)

Pandora Originally she was the earth, the "all-giver," ceaselessly producing food; the name may have been a title of **Gaia**. She was also called Anesidora ("sender forth of gifts"), a title she shared with **Demeter**; in this identity, Pandora was shown as a gigantic woman rising from the earth while little men opened her way with hammer blows.

Later, she became the one who brought sorrow to earth. Zeus formed her, and **Athena** taught her crafts. **Aphrodite** gave her beauty; the **Charites** decked her with beautiful jewelry. Gifted with all talents, Pandora was given a box and instructed never to open it. When she did so, the ills that afflict humanity escaped to run rampant through the world. Only the hope goddess **Spes** remained in the box to comfort us. (Friedrich; Hesiod; Lubell; Meagher; O'Brien 1983; Hawley and Levick; Reeder)

Pasiphae This Cretan goddess mated with a magical bull who rose from the sea. Later, the Greeks called her a queen, daughter of the goddess Creta. Her sister was **Circe**; her niece, **Medea**. Pasiphae, conceiving an unnatural passion for a bull, had the architect Dedalus build a wooden cow. Hidden within it, she conceived the bull man, the Minotaur; her other children were **Ariadne** and **Phaedra**. (Euripides *Hippolytus*; Ovid *Met*)

Peitho This minor goddess, whose name means "winning eloquence," ruled seduction and the persuasive tricks of love. Some sources call Peitho the daughter of lustful **Aphrodite** and tricky Hermes. She was also said to have met Aphrodite when the love goddess arrived from the sea. Other myths call her the daughter of **Ate**; with Eros (love), she gave birth to the health goddess **Hygieia**. In another myth, the Greeks said Penia, goddess of poverty was the daughter of Porus (expediency), who was conceived on the birthday of Aphrodite (sex). She may have originally been a demonic goddess whose "persuasion" included whips and goads. Yet other records use this name as a title of Aphrodite herself. The Romans called her Suada. (Sanford)

Penelope The most familiar female figure of the Trojan War other than **Helen** was Penelope, weaving by day and unwinding her work each night. Behind the faithful wife looms a goddess with the power of life and death. Spinning and weaving symbolize woman's power to create life, so Penelope's endless reweaving indicates her status as a creatrix. Stories claim that during Odysseus's absence his wife was far from faithful; Penelope brought forth the wild woodland god Pan, fathered by all her suitors at once. After the happy reunion, Odysseus was banished again and returned to be killed, unrecognized, by his son by **Circe**; Penelope married Circe's son, while her own married Circe. (Cohen; Arthur; Heitman; Homer *Od*, *Iliad*; Schein; Katz; Kerényi 1979; Winkler)

Pero She was the granddaughter of the weeping **Niobe**, daughter of her only surviving daughter, the pale grief-stricken beauty Chloris. A beauty of Greek legend, she bore a title of a pre-Olympian moon goddess, of whom Pero may be a vestigial form. Another Pero was a wife of the sea god Poseidon. (Smith)

Perse "Light bearer" or "destroyer," she was the early Greek moon goddess, wife of the sun and daughter of the ocean. Her daughters were the Cretan goddess **Pasiphae** and the famous witch **Circe**; she may have later developed into the death queen **Persephone**. Her name is connected to that of the solar hero, Perseus,

which suggests she may have had an original identity as a light goddess. (Kerényi 1979)

Persephone One day **Demeter**'s beloved daughter was picking flowers with her maiden companions when the underworld god Hades appeared. The god carried Persephone through a crack in the earth, which closed after them. Hearing her daughter's cries, Demeter sought her, but no trace remained. Demeter went into mourning, broken only when the gods demanded the return of Persephone on the condition that she had not eaten anything in Hades's realm. Hades quickly pressed a pomegranate seed into Persephone's mouth. So the goddess was condemned to spend one-third of the year belowground, while the rest of the time she enjoyed the company of her mother on earth.

While Persephone was with her, Demeter brought forth blossom and fruit. While Persephone was absent, the earth wilted and died. This annual cycle was celebrated at the town of Eleusis in solemn mysteries the Greeks said made humans ready to face death, revealing beautiful Persephone, who waited for them.

Some scholars suggest that Persephone was originally the queen of death, and Demeter's daughter was originally Kore ("maiden"). As Greek theology assimilated various figures to fewer but more complex ones, these two goddesses were joined in one occasionally self-contradicting narrative. Such a theory explains variants of Persephone's story, like one that shows the goddess sitting in a cave, guarded by snakes and weaving the world on a loom. Zeus came to her as a snake and had intercourse with her; she gave birth to the wine god Dionysus. The occasional connection of Persephone with Aphrodite suggests an association with women's affairs (marriage and family) rather than with death. As with other important Greek myths, multiple and sometimes contradictory interpretations are possible.

Persephone and her mother, Demeter, were honored in Greek colonies, especially those on Sicily, where major temples to the goddesses exist. The most sacred location is Lake Pergusa, where swans nested

amid ever-blooming flowers. There the maiden goddess first descended to Hades, and a major religious
center celebrated her in ancient times. (Athanassakis;
Evans; Hesiod; Nilsson 1961; Hawley and Levick;
Ovid *Met*; Sourvinou-Inwood 1978; Suter; Zuntz)

Phaedra After Theseus abandoned **Ariadne**, he married his deserted mistress's sister, Phaedra. She soon
became infatuated with Hippolytus, Theseus's son by
another abandoned mistress, the **Amazon** Hippolyta.
When her stepson refused her, Phaedra cursed him,
and he was dragged to death by sea-dwelling horses.
This Phaedra seems a literary creation based on a
Cretan goddess of whom only the name survives.
(Euripides *Hippolytus*; Watson)

Philomena Philomena's sister Procne was married
to King Tereus. He raped Philomena and, to keep
her from reporting the crime, cut out her tongue. But
Philomena wove a tapestry picturing the brutal act,
which she sent to her sister. The women cut up Tereus's
son and served the child for dinner. During the meal,
Philomena brought in the boy's head and flung it upon
the table. At that point they were all transformed into
birds: Philomena into the first nightingale; Procne,
into a swallow; King Tereus, into a hawk; and the boy
Itylus, into a sandpiper. (Ovid *Met*; Barber)

Physis Although more an allegorical figure than a
goddess, Physis ("nature" or "matter") appears in the
Orphic Hymns as a celestial maternal goddess who
was born without a father, although no mother is mentioned, either. She served as animator of the whole
world. (Athanassakis)

Pleiades The seven daughters of the **Nymph** Pleione,
the Pleiades were born in wild Arcadia and followed the
goddess **Artemis** until they were turned into stars that
bear their name, the "seven sisters." Individually, their
names were Alcyone, Calaeno, Electra, **Maia**, Merope,
Sterope (or Asterope), and Taygete—almost all names
also borne by early Greek goddesses, which suggests

that the legend linking them has been lost. One legend
says the hunter Orion, aroused by the sight of Pleione
and her daughters, pursued them, intent upon rape.
After five years of pursuit, the women were transformed into stars, as was Orion; they still chase each
other about the sky.

Another version of the story of how they came to
be stars said they were old women who took care of the
newly born wine god Dionysus (see **Maenads**), for
which they were rewarded by being made young again
and sent to the sky. The distinction between these star
sisters and the Nymphs called the Hyades is unclear.

The rising of the Pleiades in spring and their
disappearance in fall marked the beginning and end
of the sailing season, for the stars are seasonal in the
temperate zones. Of the seven starry sisters, one of
them is virtually invisible to the naked eye; she was
called the shy sister or lost Pleiad. Several reasons
were given for her near invisibility, and several different names applied to the star. Sometimes she was
Electra, shrouded as she wept for the loss of Troy. At
other times, she was Merope, wife of the criminal king
Sisyphus, who stewed his children and was sentenced
to eternal punishment; in embarrassment and shame,
his star wife faded from human sight. The name
Merope was also used of a victim of rape. Orion, her
assailant, was blinded by Merope's father in retaliation after he broke into Merope's bedroom, drunk, and
assaulted her. (Graves 1)

Polycaste The sister of the great Greek architect
Daedalus, she bore a son who, as he grew, was found
to be even more brilliantly inventive than his uncle.
Seeing the boy as a threat, Daedalus murdered him;
the grieving mother flew away, transformed by sorrow
into a bird. When Daedalus's son died by his own care-
lessness and pride, Polycaste was there, chattering in
derision as Daedalus dug the grave. This name is also
given to the mother of **Penelope**. (Smith)

Potnia The Cretan goddess Potnia ("lady") was
depicted as a winged woman with birds perched on

her hands, holding snakes in her outstretched hands, or standing between two horses or other heraldic beasts. She has been connected with the later goddesses **Demeter**, who took the form of a horse to mate with the sea god Poseidon, and **Medusa**, another partner of Poseidon, who gave birth to Pegasus. She ruled the cosmos, land, and oceans and symbolized the life force. As Potnia Theron, "lady of the beasts," she was parallel to such divinities as **Athena** and **Artemis**. (Cantarella; Schieffer)

Praxidice A three-faced bodiless head symbolized this goddess of vengeance and enterprise, who punished evil actions and rewarded the good. She was honored by Helen's husband Menelaus when he returned with her from Troy, not far from the sanctuary her lover Paris had dedicated to the love goddess Aphrodite. As a triple goddess, Praxidice was honored especially in northern Boeotia, where the three sisters were named Alalcomenia, Thelxinoea, and Aulis. While other goddesses received as sacrifice the bodies of animals, Praxidice was offered only the heads. Sometimes this name appears as a title of **Persephone**. (Smith)

Procris Princess of Athens, she married a man named Cephalus. But Procris's husband soon drew the eye of the lustful dawn goddess **Eos**, who spirited him away. But Cephalus, true to Procris, refused to sleep with the dawn maiden. Eos, disgusted, returned the man to earth, first changing his appearance completely. When Cephalus entered his home, he seemed a handsome stranger, and Procris, infatuated, welcomed him into her bed. When Cephalus resumed his own shape, Procris, horrified to be caught in infidelity, fled.

In the forest, she joined a band of women, servants of the virginal goddess **Artemis**. Later reconciled to her mate, Procris grew jealous and began to spy on Cephalus. Eos, to avenge Cephalus's rejection, had the man mistake Procris for an animal and kill her. (Graves 1)

Pyrrha Far back in time, the violence of Bronze Age people provoked Olympian divinities to drown the whole race, saving one honorable couple: Deucalion and Pyrrha, daughter of **Pandora**, who escaped death by floating nine days and nine nights in a wooden box. When the flood receded, the couple found themselves on the sacred mountain Parnassus, beside a temple of **Themis**. There they offered sacrifice for their salvation and, granted one boon, asked that the earth be repopulated.

They received an answer: As they descended to the flood-wet valley, they should cast the bones of their mother behind them. Pyrrha penetrated the riddle. Picking up stones, she walked downhill. Deucalion joined her, throwing stones over his shoulder. Behind them sprang up the "stone age" people, men from stones cast by Deucalion, women from Pyrrha's. Protagenia, "firstborn" daughter of Pyrrha, was the ancestor of many Greek tribes. (Ovid *Met*)

Pythia A woman had to live fifty years before she could be called by this name designating the Oracle of Delphi. Pythia had to be married, in deference to the shrine's original owner, **Gaia** or **Hera**, for only later was Delphi dedicated to Apollo. The destruction of the goddess cult at Delphi was described in the "Homeric Hymn to Pythian Apollo," in which the sun god battled a female monster (see **Python**) to establish his oracle at the sacred spot.

Pythia's duties were as follows: on the seventh of each moon, she underwent ritual purification. Then, seated on a three-legged stool, she chewed bay leaves and breathed in fumes that rose from a chasm. Finally she spoke complicated, often enigmatic, prophecies, which were interpreted by her male attendants. Seekers, who could ask questions only once each year, had to be purified beforehand. (Connelly; Sophocles *Oedipus Rex*; Young)

Python This great snake nested near the flower-filled spring of Delphi. Some legends said Apollo killed her when he took over the famous oracular spring. Others said Python was the name of the snake's dead mate, while she was called Delphyne ("womb"). They claimed Delphyne continued to live at Delphi, where women could prophesy (see **Pythia**). (O'Brien 1993; Smith; Young)

Rhea This Titan gave birth to the Olympian gods after being raped by her husband, Chronos, who had murdered his father, Uranus. With Chronos she had several children, including **Hestia**, **Demeter**, and **Hera**. Chronos ate his children as they were born, until Rhea offered him a stone wrapped in swaddling, pretending that it was the newborn Zeus. Chronos gobbled it up, but then felt severe pains. (The stone was kept in the oracular sanctuary of Delphi; see **Python**.) Chronos vomited his children, who made war on him. The war between the gods and the Titans led to the displacement of the latter, who disappear from mythology at this point.

Most scholars read the tale as one of religious change, with the gods of immigrants taking over from earlier divinities. It is thus not surprising to learn that Rhea is Cretan. In pre-Olympian times, Rhea was embodied in mountains. She was depicted as a stately woman surrounded by worshipful animals and small subservient human males. Her religion was celebrated in musical processions of pipes and cymbals. The blazing torch, brass drum, and double-ax were her symbols. (Athanassakis; Friedrich; Apollonius of Rhodes; Hesiod; Roller)

Rhode A vague figure in late Greek mythology, she was daughter of the sea queen **Amphitrite** or of the goddess of love, **Aphrodite**. She was the mother of the **Heliades**, who were turned into poplar trees for excessive mourning for their dead brother, Phaeton, who drove the sun chariot recklessly and fell to earth from it. A woman named Rhode was also one of the husband-killing Danaids (see **Danae**).

It is unclear whether Rhode is the same as the similarly named Rhodos, goddess of the island Rhodes. A sea **Nymph**, she became the consort of the sun god Apollo after he missed the meeting where the Olympian gods divided up the world's lands. But

Rhodes was underwater at the time, and it emerged just in time for the tardy Apollo to claim it. Because Rhode lived in the sea that had covered the island, she became Apollo's consort there. (Kerényi 1979; Smith)

Satyria A goddess known from the Greek colonial area of Italy, Magna Graecia, Satyria is associated with a promontory on the coast near Taranto, occupied in the Bronze Age, named Satyrion after her. Artifacts from the fourth century BCE honor Satyria, daughter of the Cretan king Minos and wife of Poseidon. Whether a sacred spring at the site was devoted to Satyria is unknown. (Edlund)

Scylla Once this legendary Greek monster, daughter of **Lamia** or **Echidna**, was so beautiful she roused the jealousy of **Amphitrite** (or **Circe**, or **Hecate**), who poisoned her bath with magic herbs. When Scylla rose from the water, she had twelve feet ending in dogs' heads with six mouths each, each mouth with three sets of teeth. The embittered Scylla stationed herself on the seacoast, where she ate sailors. But she hated her life so much that she flung herself into the sea between Italy and Sicily and was transformed into a rock that continued to devour sailors. No one could safely pass the petrified woman unless Hecate permitted it. Scylla's companion was the transformed bulimic **Charybdis**, who daily gulped the sea and vomited it out; she was the personification of a dangerous whirlpool. "To pass between Scylla and Charybdis" means to pass safely through between two treacherous enemies.

Another figure in Greek legend has the same name; some scholars believe them the same. She was the daughter of King Nisus, who had a magical golden hair in the middle of his head that protected him from harm. But his daughter, infatuated with King Minos, betrayed her father by pulling out the golden hair and presenting it to Minos. The Cretan king spurned Scylla, and she committed suicide. At death, she was transformed into a lark, and her father into a hawk. (Cohen; Homer *Od*; Ovid *Met*; Smith)

Selene This early moon goddess was the daughter of **Thea** and spouse or sister of the sun, Helios. Winged and crowned with a crescent, Selene drove the lunar chariot across the night sky, whose goddesses **Leto** and **Hecate** were her daughters. Two white horses drew her chariot, and she herself had long wings and wore a crown of light. When she was not visible, Selene was in Asia Minor, visiting her human lover Endymion, for whom she had won the prize of eternal life and youth. He slept perpetually, even when his eyes were open, but he did sire fifty daughters upon her. She also had three children by Zeus. The wilderness god Pan seduced Selene, using a white fleece to lure her to his home. (Hesiod; Smith)

Semele Daughter of Harmonia and granddaughter of **Aphrodite**, Semele was a mortal in late Greek legend, where she appears as the mother of the wine god Dionysus. But her name came from Asia Minor, where it meant "subterranean," and Dionysus's mother was in some myths called the queen of death. Semele had been worshipped as a goddess before the introduction of Dionysus to Greece; she may have represented the earth in its darkly fruitful form.

Dionysus, born first of **Persephone**, was killed in infancy. His father, Zeus, made a broth of the baby's heart and brought it to Semele, who became pregnant by drinking it. But Semele recklessly asked Zeus to appear before her in Olympian glory. When he appeared in a flash of lightning, she was burned to cinders. Zeus grabbed the fetus, sewed it into his thigh, and gave surgical birth to the child later. Other versions of the story say Dionysus was conceived normally, within the womb of Semele. But when **Hera** discovered her husband's dalliance, she disguised herself as an old woman and lured Semele into the incautious request that destroyed her.

Yet another version tells how Semele, pregnant and unwed, was cast out of her home by her father, Cadmus. Placed into a chest and thrown out to sea, the mother and child floated away until they reached the Laconian coast. When the chest was opened, Semele was found dead, but her son lived. Semele's sister **Ino** brought up Dionysus from that point. Their other sisters Agave and Autonoe (see **Maenads**) became among the first followers of the wine god.

The wine god never freed himself from the influence of his mother. He descended to death's realm to reclaim her, bringing her back to Olympus and installing her as the foremost of his Maenads, under the title Thyone. Thus Semele, who started as a goddess and was demoted to mortality, was restored to divinity. (Athanassakis; Evans; Larson 1995; Lyons; Ovid *Fasti*; Sanford; Smith; Ovid *Met*)

Sirens Today we picture these sweet singers as feminine, but in early Greece the Sirens were both male and female bird-bodied prophets. Above their egg-shaped bodies rose beautiful human heads; the breasts and faces of women were added only later to the Sirens' feathered bodies. They were variously said to be daughters of the Pleiad Sterope; of the Muse of dance, Terpsichore (see **Musae**); of the Muse of epic poetry, Calliope; or of **Gaia**.

The Sirens served **Persephone**, having earned their wings when they helped her mother search for her. But they lost their wings when **Hera** tricked them into challenging the Musae to a singing contest. Beautiful as the Sirens' song was, it was no match for the goddesses of art. As servants of Persephone, they brought her souls by singing sweetly to passing ships; the enchanted sailors were smashed on the rocks. They tried this on Odysseus, but he had, upon the advice of the magician **Circe**, stuffed the ears of his crew with wax, so they passed safely. He sang louder than they did and, ashamed, the Sirens killed themselves and were transformed into treacherous rocks.

The Sirens are easy to confuse with **Harpies**, but Sirens represent death's sweet call, while their vulture-like sisters signify terrifying death. A related collective, the Celedones, were magical singers, although there is no evidence that hearing them was fatal. (Cohen; Garber and Vickers; Homer *Od*; Schein; Smith)

Spes An early Cretan goddess called Elphis in Greece, she was the one force left in the box of **Pandora** after evil escaped into the world. Spes was ruler of the underworld and of death's cousin, sleep; her plant was the poppy; she represented hope. (Marshall)

Sphinx She started life in Egypt, where the lion-bodied monster with a bearded male head represented royalty. But in Greece, the figure became Phix, daughter of **Echidna**. She was a **Maenad** who grew so wild she became monstrous: snake, lion, and winged woman combined. She lay waste the region around Thebes, strangling travelers if they could not answer a riddle the **Musae** had taught her. What walked on four legs in the morning, two at noon, and three in the evening? Finally Oedipus answered: Human beings, who crawl as children, walk upright as adults, and rely upon canes in age. Her reason for existence destroyed, the Sphinx killed herself.

Some Greek myths suggest the Sphinx, like the **Gorgons**, may have been a collective of monstrous goddesses who lived throughout the Peloponnesus and Asia Minor as well as in Italy and Sicily. They appeared as guardian figures, in pairs at doorways and gates, so they may have had an apotropaic function similar to the head of **Medusa**. (Regier)

Styx Between the land of the living and that of the dead wound the seven tributaries of the River Styx, whose goddess bore the same name. Styx prevented the living from crossing into **Persephone**'s realm without undergoing death's torments. Eldest and strongest daughter of **Tethys**, Styx was sometimes counted among the **Nymphs**. She was the mother of **Nike** and **Bia**; some sources call her Persephone's mother. Even among the Olympians, an oath taken on her name was inviolable; anyone who broke such an oath was deprived of **Hebe**'s ambrosia. When an immortal caused strife in Olympus, Zeus sent **Iris** for water from Styx, which paralyzed the offender for a year. (Hesiod; Smith)

Tethys This ancient sea goddess was part of a trinity of world creators with **Nyx** and **Gaia**. In some sources, she is Gaia's mother, but the ages eroded Tethys's power, until classical Greek mythology contained little information about her. She ceased giving birth after having 6,000 children. Half were sons, half the **Nymphs** called Oceanids. (Hesiod; Homer *Iliad*)

Thalassa In one Greek account of creation, she was the mother of all, possibly the same goddess as **Tethys**. Later she was said to be the fish mother, creator of sea life. Some find in her a personification of the Mediterranean Sea, others an image of all the world's oceans. (Homer *Iliad*; Smith)

Thea The pre-Olympian goddess of light, mother of dawn and the luminaries, Thea bore a name that meant "goddess." Although this hints at earlier eminence, nothing is known of Thea but the list of her children: Helios, **Selene**, and Eos. (Hesiod; Kerényi 1979)

Themis The "steadfast one," daughter of **Gaia**, represented the social contract. A hallowed goddess in early times, Themis later became an abstract personality. Evidence of her precedence is clear; no Olympian gathering could take place unless she called it, and no divinity could lift the cup of nectar before she had drunk. In the language of her people, *themis* was a common as well as a proper noun, the former indicating the power of convention. As personification of social cohesion, Themis carried a pair of scales; as the fruitful earth, she held the cornucopia. She was mother of the **Horae** and the **Moirae**. Themis ruled prophecy, sharing with Gaia the famous Delphic Oracle. For her worship, she demanded group dancing. She was the first to whom temples were built, for before her there was no human community to offer worship. (Athanassakis; Harrison 1962; Hesiod; Ovid *Met*; Sanford)

Thetis In late Greek mythology this goddess seems merely the mother of the hero Achilles. But clues in her legend suggest she was originally much more important. Daughter of **Tethys** and sister to the sea **Nymphs**, Thetis was a goddess of womanhood, raised by **Hera**. Thetis nursed two gods associated with women's rites: the appealingly dissolute Dionysus and the crippled artisan Hephaestus.

Thetis was gifted with the oceanic power of shape changing. When the Olympians, fearing the prophecy that she would bear a son greater than his father, condemned Thetis to marry a mortal, she resisted by changing herself into monsters and microorganisms. But her husband-to-be held fast until she resumed human form. At her wedding **Ate** tossed her famous apple into the crowd, which resulted in the Trojan War and the death of Thetis's mortal son, Achilles. After Achilles's death, Thetis abandoned Peleus, who until that time had remained youthful through her powers; he immediately aged and died. (Hesiod; Ovid *Met*; Aeschylus *Prometheus Bound*)

Roman women did not enjoy significant political or cultural power. They were not permitted citizenship rights, and Roman literature includes notably misogynistic statements. Yet Roman citizens claimed to descend from a goddess, the city's divine trinity included two goddesses but only one god, and its symbol of cultural unity was an ever-burning flame in a goddess's temple. The power of Roman goddesses may derive from earlier cultures.

Prior to Rome's rise, Italy was home to the Rasenna, better known by their Latin name, Etrusci, whose culture may have been the source of Roman goddesses' power. Etruscan women had greater freedom than those elsewhere in the ancient Mediterranean, as evidenced by descriptions of ambitious Etruscan queens in the sixth century BCE. But after the beginning of the Roman Republic, Etruscan culture declined. A century later, emperor Claudius compiled an Etruscan dictionary, but it was lost and with it, a window into Etruscan life. The language has not yet been deciphered.

During the long period of the Roman Empire (23 BCE–476 CE), religion served important civic functions. Attendance at festivals, marking of lunar progressions, and participation in family cults were part of every citizen's life. The aim of Roman religion was communal bonding, not union with a divine force or salvation of one's soul. Within that framework, women were worshippers but not priests, except in a few all-women's rites and in the important religion of the hearth goddess Vesta.

In addition to Roman civic religion, non-Roman mystery cults were practiced openly, so those who sought personal satisfaction through religion could select such practices. As the empire expanded, it absorbed competing cultures by giving local divinities with Roman names. Many tribal divinities, including Scandinavian and Celtic, were hidden under the name of "Jupiter" or "Minerva." Other divinities were imported into Rome itself, with distinctive Roman forms emerging. Rome also adopted some Greek divinities so enthusiastically that their own indigenous deities were altered to fit the Greek model, an unusual development in an imperial culture.

Roman power declined from the second through the fourth centuries, as Celtic and Gothic armies attacked. When Rome fell, the church centered in the "eternal city" sustained the empire's centralizing and hierarchical ideology. Rome's deities also survived, hidden within festival dates and cult locations. The Wiccan path called Strega ("witchcraft") derives from Roman and other Italic traditions, often transmitted via Catholicism. Strega practitioners often claim an unbroken lineage of pagan worship. Such claims are difficult to prove, but as with other Catholic lands, female saints and the Virgin Mary took over shrines and iconography of earlier goddesses.

ROMAN AND ITALIC PANTHEON

Acca Larentia Because **Rhea Silvia** could not raise her twins Romulus and Remus, the boys were exposed to the elements. Faustulus, a shepherd, brought them to his wife Acca Larentia, who raised them. This legend does not contradict one in which the boys were reared by the wolf **Lupa**, for Acca Larentia worked as a prostitute, called in Roman slang a "wolf."

Another myth says Acca Larentia spent the night with Hercules when a client lost her in a wager. As she departed, the demigod told Acca Larentia that the first man she met would pay her. That man was wealthy Tarutilus, who lived with Acca Larentia until his death, when she inherited his property. Some legends say Acca Larentia provided for the citizens of Rome by giving her foster son, Romulus, enough wealth to make the city prosper. Others say she created an endowment for the people, who celebrated her generosity every December 23 in the Larentalia. Acca Larentia's position as the city's ancestral mother is further suggested by the similarity of her name to that of the Lares (see **Lara**). (Balsdon; Beard 1989; Edlund 1987; Krapp 1942; Staples; Warmington)

Aetna The largest volcano in Italy, three times the size of Vesuvius, Mount Etna bears the name of this goddess. But she figures more prominently in Greek than in Roman legend because Sicily, where the mountain is located, was one of Greece's most important colonies. Aetna was said to be a daughter of Greek **Gaia** and the heaven god Uranus, turned into a volcano after the fire-breathing god Typhon was buried under her. The mountain is significant in the story of **Ceres** and her daughter **Proserpina** (Greek **Demeter** and **Persephone**), for it was from Aetna that the maiden goddess was kidnapped. The goddess's consort, the smith god Vulcan, hid thunderbolts under Aetna, which caused a constant dull roaring, after Aetna arbitrated a dispute between him and corn mother Demeter. Alternative legends say an imprisoned giant caused the noises, warning residents of impending eruptions. (Ovid *Met*; Smith)

Albunea A prophetic fountain spirit (see **Camenae**, **Egeria**), Albunea was honored at a shrine near the Tiber River. Her temple can still be seen at Tivoli. Called the tenth **Sibyl**, she was depicted holding a book. (Smith)

Angerona On Angerona's winter solstice feast, sunlight began to increase after a six-month decline. Angerona's festival was held not within her temple but in the nearby temple of Voluptia ("pleasure"), where Angerona's statue stood, mouth bandaged and finger to lips. Because Angerona healed angina (pains in the heart) as well as sorrow, her association with Voluptia may indicate that the two were aspects of each other. Angerona was also connected with **Dea Dia**. (Altheim; Dumézil; Richardson)

Angitia The early Italian goddess Angitia ruled healing and witchcraft. Renowned for her verbal and herbal charms, Angitia had special power over snakebite; her name refers to killing snakes through enchantment. In her temples, live snakes were draped around the goddess's statue by worshippers in need of a remedy against snake poisoning. Angitia has been identified with Greek **Medea**, who fled to Italy in her dragon chariot, but the Romans also connected her with **Bona Dea**. A few ancient authors considered her the same as the Greek sorceress **Circe**. Angitia was particularly honored in the area around Lake Fucinus, still famous as the home of witches. In the village of Cucullo, residents collect snakes as they emerge from hibernation and use them in processions and dances during the Serpari Festival on the first Thursday in May. (Fourbister; Jayne)

Anna Perenna The origin of this goddess has long been a subject of conjecture. One myth says this sister of **Dido** (see Eastern Mediterranean) went to Rome to seek faithless Aeneas. When Aeneas's wife grew jealous, Anna Perenna ran away, transforming herself into a river. Another legend describes Anna as an old woman who, when Roman revolutionaries were besieged, conveyed enough food to them to survive the siege. Current scholarship suggests Anna Perenna descended from an Etruscan goddess of reproduction. The annual March 15 festival was rowdy and promiscuous. The spring date of the festival and its nature suggest Anna Perenna was goddess of the fruitful earth, who responded to the reproductive activities of human beings by bringing forth edibles. (Ovid *Fasti*; Hall)

Aradia In 1899, American occultist Charles G. Leland published *Gospel of the Witches*, purporting to describe the Tuscan goddess Aradia. Leland contended a woman, "Maddalena," gave him a handwritten book, then disappeared. From the start, many doubted the book's authenticity. Given Leland's research in Italic folklore, the gospel could be an accurate account of folk religion, but the likelihood of its being an ancient manual of worship seems slight.

Leland describes Aradia as the daughter of **Diana**, born of a liaison with her brother Lucifer, the Christian devil. (Such syncretic descent may indicate that story-tellers substituted Lucifer for an older divinity.) According to Leland, when war broke out on earth, Aradia was taught the secrets of witchcraft to bring order and peace. She then taught these secrets to her followers, the witches. (Hutton; Leland 1990)

Arethusa Arethusa lived with the retinue of **Diana** until one day when, hot from the hunt, she threw herself into a cool stream. That stream was the disguised god Alpheus, which Arethusa realized too late. The stream rose up behind her as she ran away. A fog melted Arethusa into a pool, into which the river god poured himself. Diana saved her, changing Arethusa into a waterfall so she could flow away from Alpheus. The Romans considered Arethusa the spirit of pastoral poetry. (Ovid *Met*)

Aurora The dawn goddess Aurora was a lusty lover who enjoyed the favors of many men. Her legend duplicates that of Greek **Eos**, after whom she was patterned. (Ovid *Met*)

Befana A figure of Italian seasonal legend, Befana was the "lady of twelfth night," when the solstice period ends and the sun resumes its movement toward spring. Her name is a contraction of the alternative name for this figure, Epiphiana ("epiphany"), the Christian name of the January 7 feast day. She is also called La Vecchia di Natali ("the Christmas Old Woman") and Strina ("witch"). In Italy, an image of an old woman was constructed of old clothes stuffed with food and hung outside or burned ceremonially on Befana's day. (Miles)

Bellona Bellona ruled conflict, diplomatic as well as military, and the Latin word for war (*bellum*) derives

from her name. War was declared when a priest hurled Bellona's ceremonial spear. To ritually conclude war, the Senate met in the temple of this serpent-haired goddess. As Roman divinities assimilated those of conquered lands, Bellona combined with **Ninmah** (see Eastern Mediterranean) to symbolize territorial sovereignty and armed conflict. Several shrines in Rome were dedicated to her, including a grove where priests called *fanatici* conducted self-mutilating rituals. (Lloyd-Morgan; Ogilvie; Ovid *Fasti*; Richardson; Vermaseren)

Bona Dea Every December, women met at the home of a prominent woman for the rites of Bona Dea ("good goddess"). Slave women celebrated with their mistresses, prostitutes with matrons, for all women were equal in the goddess's eyes. The rituals were secret, but it appears that the women drank wine and offered sacrifice under the guidance of the Vestals (see **Vesta**). Texts suggest music and dancing were part of the celebration. This led to accusations of debauchery, which seem unsupported.

Myth says that after a battle with a giant, Hercules wandered, desperately thirsty. Stumbling into a band of women praying to Bona Dea, Hercules demanded water. But they refused because of a ritual requirement. Infuriated, Hercules banished women from his rituals, while Bona Dea's rites were barred to men. Another legend claims Bona Dea's father, Faunus, attempted to rape her. When she resisted, he beat her, then tried to get her drunk. Finally he transformed himself into a snake and raped her, whereupon Bona Dea withdrew from male company forever. One of Rome's greatest scandals occurred in 63 BCE, when Publius Clodius, disguised in women's clothing, invaded the rites. He was discovered and prosecuted, the crime causing political upheaval. The invader kept the rites he had witnessed secret, as did Bona Dea's rightful worshippers. Although Bona Dea's primary rituals were held in private homes, she also had temples, most prominently on the Aventine Hill. There a priestess called by the Damiatrix celebrated rituals and tended snakes. Healers administered herbal remedies; men were permitted to receive ministrations but could not enter the temple. (Beard et al. 1998; Berry; Brouwer; Cantarella; Richardson; Staples; Versnel; Woodard)

Camenae Goddesses of springs and rivers, the Camenae ("foretellers") were prophets and forces of inspiration. Their festival, the Fontinalia, was celebrated on October 13 by the tossing of wreaths into wells. A spring of especially clear water rose in a wooded area on the Caelian Hill, reputedly the home of these goddesses. Later the spring came under the control of the Vestals (see **Vesta**), who drew water from it each day.

Several Camenae had individual identities. Expectant mothers invoked Antevorta ("forward looking") to learn the outcome of their pregnancies. During labor, they called out to Postvorta ("backward looking") to remove the dangers of breech birth. Finally, Carmenta had a temple at the Porta Carmentalis, where her festival was held January 11–15. Goddess of prophecy and midwifery, Carmenta may have been the original from whom the multiple goddesses derive, for she was an early divinity to whom a priestly brotherhood was dedicated. (Courtney; Edlund 1987; Perowne; Richardson; Ovid *Fasti*)

Carna On June 1 (the Calends of June), Rome celebrated the feast of Calendae Fabrariae, offering the goddess Carna a soup of beans and bacon in gratitude for good health. Sometimes described as a goddess of food assimilation, Carna can be more accurately called a personification of the physical processes of survival. Her simple shrine, the Sacrum Dea Carna, was on the Caelian Hill. That she was not known outside Rome suggests a local indigenous goddess. (Richardson; Smith)

Ceres The Greek myth of **Demeter** influenced that of Ceres, an early goddess whose power was not limited to the "cereal" plants that carry her name. She was

celebrated each April 19 in the Cerealia, when foxes with burning sticks tied to their tails were set loose. Some scholars believe the ritual protected growing crops from disease, others that it assured bountiful harvests by increasing sunshine. Her second festival was in August, when women celebrated secret rituals in honor of Ceres's funereal aspect.

Ceres was one of the two ultimate sources of human society, the other being **Tellus**, the earth. Ceres shared a temple with **Flora**, although the two were opposed because married women honored Ceres, who blessed their wedding ceremonies, while Flora was goddess of prostitutes. Ceres was also associated with the goddess of sexuality, **Libera**. (Berger; Berry 1994; Dumézil; Ogilvie; Ovid *Met*, *Fasti*; Scheid; Spaeth)

Concordia Her name, the basis of the word "concord," conveys the harmony she embodied. Roman art showed Concordia as a heavyset matron, holding a cornucopia and an olive branch. Concordia's feast was April 30, when Salus, goddess of health, was also honored. (Axtell; Galinsky; Richardson; Smith)

Dea Dia One of Rome's great religious fraternities, the 180-member Arval Brotherhood, served this goddess of light, of whom little is known despite extensive documentation of her cult. Her four-day spring festival involved feasting and anointing of the goddess's image, after which pigs and a cow were sacrificed in her sacred grove. Libations of wine were poured and chariot races held. An Etruscan origin for the goddess has been suggested by identification of this goddess with **Acca Larentia**. (Feeney; Scheid; Woodard)

Dea Syria Lucian parodied a religious cult devoted to an imported goddess, **Atargatis** (see Eastern Mediterranean). Like many such imported religions, the rites that arrived with the Syrian goddess were different from Rome's civic rituals and in some cases distasteful to Romans. Nonetheless, such cults expanded in influence during imperial times. (Benko; Lucian)

Diana Diana's original identity has been all but lost in her identification with Greek **Artemis**. Queen of the sky, Diana was worshipped outdoors. She ruled the moment of birth, connected with the ladybug goddess **Lucina** (a name that, like Diana's, refers to "light"). Clay figures shaped like women in a birth-giving squat were offered to her as "opener of wombs." Few native myths describe Diana. The story of Athamas, who killed his son while in a fit of madness brought on by Diana, was transposed from Greek to Roman. To understand Diana requires a look at ritual.

Her most significant temple was on the lake of Nemi, where she was worshipped with **Egeria** and the woodland god Virbius. There, in the forest of Aricia, runaway slaves competed for mistletoe, the "golden bough" that gave them a chance to become king of the wood. As Diana's priest, this king ultimately died at a successful rival's hands—one of the few roles men could play in Diana's worship.

On Diana's festival, August 15, Roman women journeyed by torchlight to Aricia to offer thanks for Diana's help and to implore her continuing aid. Their companion hunting dogs were leashed so as not to disturb wild creatures. Later, Diana's worship moved to the Aventine Hill, where women flocked for ritual hair washing and invocations for safe childbirth. Another sanctuary of Diana was on Tifanta, whose temple dates to the sixth century BCE; there Diana Tifantina was honored as a solitary spirit of woodlands and springs. Finally, as Diana Trivia, Diana ruled crossroads, especially where three roads met.

The connection of Diana with her supposed daughter **Aradia** is unclear. Victorian folklorist Charles Leland named Diana as mother of this otherwise unknown goddess of witchcraft. From this source and from the image of the goddess and her companion nymphs, contemporary all-women's Wiccan groups label themselves Dianic. (Courtney; Dexter 1990; Blagg; Edlund 1987; Frazer; Horace; Ovid *Met*; Richardson)

Dido Although a Carthaginian goddess or ancestral heroine (see Eastern Mediterranean), Dido makes a significant appearance in Roman legend as the lover of Aeneas, the refugee from the Trojan War who settled in Italy and became an ancestral figure to the Romans. Dido found the god-like Aeneas irresistible and killed herself when he betrayed her. (Feeney; Virgil)

Egeria Goddess of wisdom, Egeria shared a shrine with Diana at Nemi, and with **Vesta**, whose priestesses drew ritual water from her spring; she is one of the **Camenae**. Roman myth shows Egeria as a semi-divine water nymph enamored of a king to whom she taught earth-worshipping rites; she pronounced the first laws of Rome. Later, pregnant women prayed to Egeria for easy delivery; she foretold newborns' futures. (Beard 1989; Blagg; Smith)

Febris Febris ("fever") represented malaria, with its recurrent and often lifelong chills and fever. Two associated goddesses ruled this recurrence: Dea Tertiana, goddess of fever that returns every third day; and Dea Quartana, of fever that returns every fourth day. Amulets against malaria were manufactured in Febris's temples. (Fox; Richardson)

Feronia This solitary goddess made her simple home in woodlands. She may be a vestigial Etruscan goddess who maintained her identity after Roman conquest; her major sanctuaries were in Etruscan territory. At her festivals on the Ides of November, agricultural fairs were held and first fruits offered, freedom was bestowed on any slave who sat on a stone in her temple, and men walked barefoot across coals to cheering crowds. In Tuscan folklore, Feronia appeared as a "strega-foletta," a witch spirit who begged alms of passersby. If given insufficient offering, she leveled curses. (Altheim; Edlund 1987; Leland 1963; Smith)

Fides Once dismissed as an abstraction, "good faith" was an ancient divinity who personified the basis of human community. She guarded integrity in dealings between individuals and groups. Depicted as an old woman wearing an olive wreath and carrying a basket of fruit, Fides brought peace and prosperity. Each October 1, Rome's three major priests sacrificed at her sanctuary, their right hands wrapped in white cloth. (Axtell; Dumézil; Richardson; Smith; Woodard)

Flora Goddess of flowers and prostitutes, Flora was linked with **Ceres**. Despite the valorization of the matron, who offered the only way Roman men could have citizen children, and of **Vesta**'s virgins, upon whose propriety the state depended, prostitutes played an important role in the city's mythology (see **Acca Larentia**, **Lupa**). Such women offered sacrifice in the Floralia from April 28 to May 3, when beans, lupines, and obscene medallions were scattered through the street, and celebrants enacted skits full of references to sexual activity. (Berger; Ogilvie; Ovid *Fasti*; Richardson; Showerman; Staples)

Fortuna The goddess of destiny was depicted as a blind woman holding a rudder (because she blindly steered a course for each life) and a cornucopia (because she could bring wealth). No mere "Lady Luck," she was the energy that drove men and women to reproduce themselves, an irresistible Fors ("force," her later Latin name). Fortuna was the deity who permitted fertilization. Thus she was worshipped by women desiring pregnancy and farmers seeking bumper crops.

Later, she grew into the monumental figure of Tyche, who ruled community destiny. But Fortuna retained her earlier function as Fortuna Virilis, the goddess who made women irresistible to men, celebrated in a regular invasion of men's public baths by luck-seeking women. She was also invoked by newly married women, who dedicated their virgin garments to her. She was served by Spes ("hope") and **Fides** ("faithfulness"). Fortuna ultimately became a power of chance and was honored by soldiers preoccupied with the fortunes of war. She was divided into Bona Fortuna ("good luck") and Mala Fortuna ("bad luck"). (Axtell; Billington; Dexter 1990; Feeney; Harrison; Horace; Lazarus; Ovid *Fasti*; Patch; Richardson; Woodard)

Furrina The prominence of this Italian (possibly Etruscan) goddess is obvious from the fact that, although by Cicero's time no one knew what Furrina represented, one of the twelve Roman priesthoods (*flamines*) was dedicated to her. Her feast, the Furrinalia or Fornalia, was celebrated July 25 at her sacred grove on the Tiber's southern bank. She may have originally been a multiple goddess, attested by dedications at her shrine. (Altheim; Perowne; Richardson)

Hybla The name of the early earth goddess of Sicily is not recorded, but given the number of places called Hybla, this has been interpreted as her name. Hybla has been connected with the gigantic goddess of the neighboring islands Malta and Gozo, whose name similarly has been lost. (Zuntz)

Isis Of Rome's imported goddesses, Egyptian **Isis** was the most widely celebrated, although she never joined the official pantheon. In Egypt she was connected with rivers and seas, but in Rome Isis became a goddess of land and grain, like **Ceres**.

Isis was not welcomed in early years. In 59 BCE, her temples were destroyed during political turmoil; in 53 BCE, the Senate ordered any remaining or rebuilt temples destroyed. A few years later the religion was attacked again, but when in 48–47 BCE Julius Caesar made an alliance with Cleopatra, the incarnation of Isis changed the tides of her religion.

Unlike native Roman religion, the Isis cult gave women the opportunity to serve as ritual celebrants; Isis as *panthea pantocrator* ("all goddess all ruler") provided an image of female equality. Isis's most important appearance in Roman literature was in Lucius Apuleius *The Golden Ass*, wherein she was adored as "mother of all living nature, mistress of all the elements." Her iconography was later transferred to the Christian **Mary** (see Eastern Mediterranean). (Apuleius; Dexter 1990; Donalson; Richardson; Scheid; Tyldesley; Young; Witt)

Juno A temple devoted to Juno on the Mons Cispius, whose sacred trees were planted before Rome was built, suggests Juno was older than the city. Similarly, the cult of Juno on the Capitoline Hill appears to antedate Rome. What Juno represented to her original worshippers is difficult to determine. Attempts to translate her name's meaning have been inconclusive, but it appears related to "light," an interpretation supported by the titles **Lucina** ("light") and Caelistis ("sky"). For this reason, and because she was honored on new moons, Juno has been interpreted as a moon goddess. But Juno has also been connected with the gate god Janus, both representing passage from one state to another; she may have originally been called Jana.

To the Romans, each man had a "genius," the spirit that made him alive and sexually active. Similarly, each woman had her "juno," an enlivening force of femaleness. Her many feast days included each woman's birthday and the birthday of every moon. Juno's most significant festivals were the Lupercalia on February 15, the Matronalia on March 1, the feast of Juno Meta on June 1, the Nonae Caprotinae on July 7, and the feast of Juno Regina on September 1. At Matronalia, married women demanded money from their husbands to offer to Juno, while at the unrestrained Nonae Caprotinae, girls staged mock fights. Most important was Lupercalia, when nearly naked young men ran around the Palatine Hill, bearing goatskin flails with which they struck passing women. This ritual served two purposes: to keep away wolves (*lupi*) and to ensure fertility.

Juno may have descended from an Etruscan original (see **Uni**). Like Greek **Hera**, Juno represented the phases of a woman's life. When the Greek and Roman sky goddesses merged, Juno's consort Jove became a philanderer, while Juno was transformed into a jealous wife. Juno's separate mythology was lost, except for the tale that, impregnated by a flower, she bore the war god Mars. While Hera's most famous child was the champion who bore her name, Heracles, Juno's was said to be the evil stepmother of the parallel Roman figure, Hercules.

But in civic cult, Juno appeared as the city's savior. Her major shrine was shared with Minerva and Jupiter, on the Capitoline Hill. She had other temples, including that of Juno Moneta, "the Warner." There, in 390 BCE, her sacred geese warned the city of invading Gauls. Another time, when an earthquake threatened, Juno's voice alerted the city. In that temple the mint cast the empire's coinage, so this title forms the base of the English word "money."

A vestige of Juno's worship remains: Brides still marry in the month that bears her name. As mother of the city, Juno concerned herself with the welfare of the entire "family" of Rome as Martialis, the warrior; Regina, the queen; Caelistis, sky queen; Caprotina, fertility goddess; and Saturnia, goddess of winter celebrations. Some of these names were titles of Juno that later became separate goddesses; some were minor goddesses absorbed into the great Juno. (Bremmer and Horsfall; Dexter 1990; Dumézil; Horace; Meadows and Williams; Nash; Ovid *Met*; Perowne; Rabinowitz; Richardson; Shields; Staples; Virgil; Watson; Ziolkowski; Warmington)

Lara Roman sources mention this goddess as "mother of the dead," sometimes identified with **Acca Larentia**. Alternatively, she may be the personified leader of the ancestral spirits called the Lares (the plural of her name), or a form of **Mania**. She was called Tacita or Muta after philandering Jupiter stopped her mouth so she could not reveal his escapades to **Juno**. She was invoked in magic to stop detractors, in which women tied shut mouths of dead fish so gossips would suffer the same fate. (Ovid *Fasti*; Taylor; Smith)

Libera With **Ceres** and the god Liber, this goddess made up a triad of agricultural divinities worshipped at the Liberalia on March 17. To celebrate the return of vegetation, Libera's ivy-decked elderly priestesses served fried honey pancakes. Romans offered a bit to the goddess and devoured the rest. Libera, with Liber, represented the female and male seed, respectively. (Dumézil; Fantham; Staples)

Libertas This goddess of liberty, depicted as a matron wearing a laurel wreath, was worshipped in three temples in Rome. In one, criminal records were kept, hostages were held, and censors did their deeds; later it was used as a public archive. (Smith)

Libitina Whenever a Roman died, the bereaved went to the temple of Libitina, from which all the necessities for a funeral could be purchased or rented. Lists of the dead were kept within the temple, where offerings in their honor were accepted by *libitinarri* (undertakers). An ancient divinity of the region, Libitina may have originally been a queen of the dead whose cult slowly withered while her necessary functions remained active. (Richardson; Smith)

Lucina The ladybug was the emblem of this goddess, later merged with **Juno** and **Diana**, and even later converted to Christianity as St. Lucy. The early Italic Lucina was a goddess of light and therefore of childbirth. She was celebrated in September and December, when her holidays were enforced by the superstition that any work done on those days would be undone before the next dawn. Although her name is used of other goddesses, Lucina's antiquity is evidenced by the legend that she was worshipped before the city was founded. (Shields)

Luna It is unclear whether Luna was originally divine or whether she was a poetic personification elevated to divinity. **Diana** was often described as riding in the lunar chariot, especially after her assimilation to Greek **Artemis**, but Luna and her companion Sol, the sun god, appear in literature and epigrams. They were, however, not revered in cult and had no festival dedicated to them. Luna was more honored than Sol, for while they shared a temple, she had three others. (Smith)

Lupa Although Rome officially honored wives and virgins, Roman myth is filled with laudable figures of sexually active unmarried women. One was the foster mother of Rome's founders, Romulus and Remus. The wolf Lupa nursed them at a fig tree sacred to an otherwise unknown goddess, Rumina. Because "lupa" was slang for "prostitute," and other legends name **Acca Larentia** as the twins' foster mother, these figures are difficult to distinguish from each other. The Lupercalia, on February 15, was named for the cave beneath the Palatine in which Lupa lived (after which she is sometimes called Luperca), but that festival is dedicated to **Juno**; the connection between the goddesses in unclear. (Balsdon; Ovid *Fasti*; Smith; Staples)

Magna Mater In 204 BCE, Rome was at war with Carthage, whose general Hannibal was advancing. The possibility of defeat led to an increase in fearful religiosity, with sacrifices and auguries offered. Rituals from other lands, previously considered impious and fiercely suppressed, became acceptable. Because some Roman nobility claimed descent from Trojans, adoption of a goddess from that area was considered as a way of reversing the tides of fortune. An obscure prophecy in the Books of the **Sibyl** suggested that if the Magna Mater ("great mother," the Roman term for **Cybele**; see Southeast European) moved from her home in Phrygia, Rome would be spared.

A delegation traveled to King Attalus, who was hesitant to let the goddess go, but she shook the ground until the king agreed. So the meteorite in which Magna Mater descended to earth was loaded onto a ship. In Rome, the boat stalled, and a diviner announced that only a pure noblewoman could move it. Claudia Quinta, wrongly accused of adultery, cleared her name by pulling the boat into the city.

Magna Mater lived in the temple of Victoria while her own temple was built on Palatine Hill. She kept her promise: Hannibal was turned away. And she showered greater benefits on her adopted city, for farmers saw their yields increase tenfold in the next harvest. Despite their salvation, Rome never entirely embraced the rites of Magna Mater, although individual Romans became passionate devotees. Her ceremonies focused on springtime, beginning with the entry of the goddess's young lover Attis, symbolized by a pine tree, into the city; a day of mourning for his death followed; finally, a festival celebrated the new growing season. Roman authorities sporadically banned another Cybeline ritual, the self-castration of the *galli*, priests of Magna Mater. This practice horrified the Romans, who killed slaves for participating. Less-mutilating rituals also existed. In the Taurobolium, the devotee stood in a pit beneath a bull whose slaughter drenched the worshipper with blood.

With the rise of Christianity, some rites and symbols of Magna Mater were transferred to the figure of **Mary** (see Eastern Mediterranean); Cybele's main temple became the still-used Basilica di Santa Maria Maggiore. Magna Mater worship was especially persecuted after Constantine, together with the rites of **Isis** and **Tanit** (see Eastern Mediterranean). With the burning in the late fourth century of the Sybiline books, the history of the Magna Mater in Rome ended. (Benko; Berger; Bremmer and Horsfall; Courtney; Dexter 1990; Godwen; Meyer; Moore; Näsström; Ovid *Fasti*; Roscoe; Richardson; Rives; Roller; Showerman; Vermaseren; Young)

Maia The Romans identified Greek Maia with an Italic fire goddess who, with **Flora** and **Feronia**, ruled growth and warmth, including sexual heat; she has been connected with **Mania**, who was similarly honored at crossroads. Maia's festival was held on the first of May. (Ogilvie; Taylor)

Mania Her name survives as a word used to describe an obsession, a reminder of how her children, ghostly Lares or Manes, returned after death to drive the living insane. Mania's children were penned in Rome's center, in a stone-capped well uncovered several times annually. On those nights, woolen effigies known as Manias were hung on doorposts in hopes ghosts would be fooled into leaving the living alone. At festivals of the obscure **Dea Dia**, Mania was honored with the sacrifice of two sheep; after a ritual dinner, the dishes were never used again. Mania may have been Etruscan in origin; she has been connected variously with **Maia**, **Lara**, and **Acca Larentia**. (Altheim; Ovid *Fasti*; Taylor; Woodard)

Marica This obscure goddess was honored at a sacred grove, any object taken into which could never be removed. Various Roman authors speculated that she was a form of **Diana** or **Venus**; as wife of the nature god Faunus, she was called Fauna. Her name has been connected to the ocean, although the word has also been linked with "marsh." Her shrine was on an island, where it is believed the earliest worshippers (seventh century BCE) honored the goddess at a simple altar. Later a temple was built of brick and timber. It was still in use in 207 BCE, when it was struck by lightning. The temple apparently survived, although its prestige declined until it was reconsecrated to **Isis**. (Salyer)

Mater Matuta Although Rome had a dawn goddess, **Aurora**, similar to the lustful figure found in other Indo-European cultures, there also was a more matronly goddess of dawn. Mater Matuta, "mother dawn," was worshipped in a touching ceremony on July 11, when women held their sisters' children in their arms and begged the goddess's blessings on them. At the same rite, the Matralia, the women drove a slave woman who symbolized night from the temple. Mater Matuta shared her temple at the foot of the Capitoline Hill with **Fortuna**, goddess of good fortune. Her name is sometimes used as a title of **Juno**, but it is not clear whether she was originally the same goddess. As she was associated with the summer solstice, she may be seen as the opposite of **Angerona**, goddess of the winter solstice. (Lucretius; Dumézil; Fox; Puhvel; Smith; Richardson)

Mens This figure was a personification of "mind," the meaning of her name. She was honored in a temple on Capitoline Hill, where people prayed they would act justly. Another important temple was found in southern Italy, in Paestum. Her festival was June 8. (Axtell)

Minerva As with many Roman divinities, Minerva's original identity became submerged when Rome adapted Greek myths. Minerva was subsumed under the aegis of the goddess of Athens, whose colonies in Sicily included Syracuse. Minerva became, like **Athena**, a goddess of handicrafts, intellect, and war. Her name derives from a root meaning "mind," so Minerva can be described as the intellect incarnate in female form.

Where she began is a matter of conjecture. Etruscan and Italic deities of handicrafts and war, respectively, may have merged. Minerva was ancient, dated to the reign of Numa (715–673 BCE), an Etruscan. Her worship was significant enough that she became part of the city's major trinity, the Capitoline Triad, with **Juno** and Jupiter, with a temple near the Forum.

Although in early days Minerva had no festival, later Romans celebrated her from March 19 to 23 during the Quinquatrus, the artisans' holiday, which was also a festival of purification. The "goddess of a thousand works" was pleased to see scholars and schoolmasters join those who labored with their hands. In the provinces, she became Minerva Medici when Celtic and Germanic goddesses were assimilated to Roman ones; ethnic "Minervas" were typically water goddesses connected with healing. (Dumézil; Perowne; Ovid *Met*, *Fasti*; Richardson)

Ops An ancient goddess, Ops bore several titles: Consivia, sower; Patella, stimulator of wheat; Rucina, promoter of harvest; Tutilina, protector of harvests. Her name survives in "opulent." Worshipped at harvest festivals on August 25 (the Ops Consiva) and December 19 (the Ops Opalia, when she was honored as consort of Saturn, god of the winter solstice), she protected newborn children and shoots of springtime plants. Ops had a temple on Capitoline Hill, but she was also honored by large straw-covered flat stones displayed as part of harvest celebrations. She was conflated with **Rhea** (see Greece). **Vesta** (usually a celibate goddess) was called Ops's mother, and **Ceres** her

sister. (Axtell; Fox; Gimbutas 1989; Richardson; Smith; Warmington)

Orbona This goddess had a poignant function: Parents offered sacrifice to her if a child died. These sacrifices were intended not for the soul of the deceased but for the safety of remaining children or for the conception of additional ones. Parents of ill children also prayed to Orbona. (Richardson; Smith)

Pales For many years, scholars called Pales a god, but recent scholarship confirms this deity of cattle was a goddess. She may have been not one goddess but two, respectively controlling small and large cattle. At the Parilia on April 21, stock-keeping farmers purified animals by driving them between fires; they asked Pales to forgive unintended slights against nature, such as burning the wrong dead tree. The apologetic ceremony ensured that animals would bear healthy offspring. Pales was an ancient divinity whose name was given to one of Rome's most important hills, the Palatine. (Ovid *Fasti*; Perowne; Richardson; Smith)

Patana A Tuscan folktale centers on a maiden of this name, who may derive from the Roman agricultural goddess of the same name. That goddess also appears in diminutive form as Patelena (the seed opener) and Patellana (the sprouter). Patana's story begins when she was held captive in a tower by her witch stepmother. A prince accidentally broke the stepmother's pitcher, and she cursed him so that he would never find love until he found Patana. The girl was hidden away, so despite traveling the world, the prince could find no rest. When the prince offered food to a starving old man, the man rewarded him with the information of Patana's location.

The prince and Patana fell in love instantly. They escaped, Patana bringing only a comb, knife, and fork, each of which she used when the pursuing witch threatened them. The fork became a church, and Patana pretended to be the sacristan; the comb became a garden, and Patana pretended to be the gardener;

and finally the knife became a shining lake, and Patana and the prince, fish within it. Though the witch was thwarted in recapturing Patana, she put a curse on the prince that, should his mother ever kiss him, he would instantly forget Patana.

When he returned home for their wedding, he avoided his mother's eager embrace, but she came to him while he slept and kissed him. The witch's curse came true. The prince forgot Patana and arranged to marry another. Patana sent two fish as a wedding gift, and with his memory restored, the prince married Patana. (Leland 1963)

Pomona Every spring, the Romans honored **Flora**; every fall, they honored the goddess of fruit, Pomona. Although she had no festival, Pomona was endowed with one of the twelve *flamines*, or high priests, and with a shrine called the Pomonal. Courted by several male fertility gods, including wild Pan, ever-erect Priapus, and debauched Silenus, Pomona refused them all. Then the agricultural god Vertumnus came courting, disguised as an old woman. He won Pomona's confidence and her love before revealing his true sex. (Johnson; Ogilvie; Ovid *Met*; Perowne)

Proserpina The Greek myth of **Demeter** and **Persephone** was so popular in Sicily that several nearby sites were claimed as locations of the tragic story of rape and loss. Over time, **Ceres** was conflated with Demeter, and although originally the Roman goddess had no daughter, one was found. Proserpina was originally unconnected to Ceres, whose companions were **Libera** and her consort Liber, but she was a maiden goddess of agriculture and fit into the imported narrative.

Rome's agricultural goddesses each ruled a moment in plant life, Proserpina serving as nursemaid to tender shoots. Whether she was originally goddess of death is unclear, but by classical times she bore the titles Averna (from the river of the underworld) and Inferna (for the underworld). Sicilians called her "The Savior" and used statues of Proserpina with Ceres

for many centuries in place of those of Jesus with Mary. Bouquets of wildflowers and sheaves of grain were placed before their altar according to the season. (Beard et al.; Ovid *Met*, *Fasti*; Nash)

Psyche Although her name is Greek, the literary allegory about this heroine was Roman. Psyche ("soul") was a beautiful princess, so beautiful that **Venus** grew envious of her. The goddess instructed Amor ("love," also called Cupid) to punish Psyche by making her fall in love with someone inappropriate, but Amor stole Psyche to be his secret bride. Psyche spent her days alone, making love each night in darkness with a husband she was forbidden to see. For a while she lived happily enough. But fearful curiosity drove Psyche to bring a lamp into the bedroom. Hardly had Psyche seen the winged body of her lover than oil fell from her lamp, awakening him. Amor, angry at her defiance, flew away.

Psyche set out to find her beloved. This brought her to a temple of Venus, who charged the girl with near-impossible tasks: sorting overnight a roomful of seeds; catching the sun sheep's fleece; traveling to the underworld to ask **Proserpina** for magical beauty ointment. Intent on regaining Amor, Psyche overcame these obstacles. But as Psyche returned with Proserpina's ointment, vanity overcame her. When she opened the box, Psyche fell into a swoon and might have died, but Amor persuaded the Olympian divinities that she had struggled enough. She ascended to heaven and was reunited with her lover, bearing two children, named Love and Delight. (Apuleius)

Ques The goddess of quiet (a word derived from her name) was honored by the people of pre-Roman Latium and, later, in Rome as well, although the cult was unofficial. She is sometimes paired with the goddess Murcia, who ruled inactivity. (Allen; Axtel)

Rehtia At a temple near Padua, a temple to this birth goddess has been dated to the sixth to fourth centuries BCE. Votive offerings included incantations for safe delivery and pleas for healing, presumably from childbirth illnesses. Rehtia was invoked as *vrota* ("turner") in instances where a child was positioned for breech birth. In Rehtia's temple, nails have been unearthed, which has suggested a tie to Etruscan **Nortia**. (Gimbutas 2001; Whatmough)

Rhea Silvia Princess Rhea Silvia was kidnapped by an uncle and dedicated to **Vesta** to ensure that her royal line would not survive. Any Vestal who broke her vows was buried alive, but Rhea Silvia became pregnant, through dream intercourse with Mars, by secretly sleeping with or being raped by the god, or by being impregnated by fire while she slept.

Given the circumstances, Rhea Silvia was not punished. Her children were not so fortunate, for Rhea Silvia was commanded by her uncle to drown them. Instead, she made an alliance with Tiberinus, god of the Tiber River, who carried the children downstream to safety. Upon landing, the babies were nursed by a she-wolf whom some say was Rhea Silvia herself. Others call her **Acca Larentia**, whose other name was **Lupa**, "wolf," an animal sacred to Mars. Some argue that all names refer to the same divinity or ancestral mother. (Balsdon; Bremmer and Horsfall; Warmington; Harrison; Krapp 1942; Ovid *Fasti*; Staples)

Roma Roma was born after the rise of the empire, less a goddess than an image of Roman power. She was honored in a huge temple, designed by the emperor Hadrian, that she shared with **Venus**, alleged ancestor of the land's rulers. She had little myth but was called the daughter of Mars, god of war. The earliest version of the goddess appears in the story that Rhome, a Trojan refugee, convinced women with her to burn their men's ships, forcing them to settle on the Tiber. She married Latinus, a man descended from **Circe** (see Greece) and Odysseus; other versions of the story say she wed Aeneas, Romulus, or Remus, each an important figure in the city's history. (Beard et al.; Mellor; Richardson)

Salacia The word "salacious" derives from her name, although there was nothing particularly lurid about Salacia. She ruled deep salt waters of the sea, while the goddess Venilia was in charge of the shallow coastal waters. (Smith)

Salus This goddess of "health" (the meaning of her name) was a deified abstraction in Roman times, but Salus may have originally been a goddess of the Italic people. She was frequently invoked in prayer and ritual, often with the goddess of harmony, **Concordia**. In rural areas, she was connected with **Spes** and **Diana**. (Axtell)

Sibyl From the sixth century BCE onward, a cave at Cumae was a site of prophecy where an old woman called the Sibyl received divine inspiration. She wrote her prophecies on leaves and put them at the cave's mouth. The enigmatic verses of the "Sibylline Leaves" were then bound into books. The Sibyl brought nine volumes to the Etruscan king Tarquin II, offering them at an outrageous price. He scoffed, so she burned three volumes, offering the remaining six at a higher price. Again he refused. Again she burned three volumes, again raising the price. Finally he purchased the Sibylline prophecies.

On momentous occasions, the Senate consulted the Sibylline volumes. Some were destroyed by fire in 83 BCE, but the rest survived until 405 CE, when they disappeared in another fire. The people of Rome searched the world unsuccessfully for replacement prophecies. The Sibyl herself had vanished, making way for production of pseudo-Sibylline prophecies, composed from fragments found at various sites. The safety of these new Sibylline books was supposed to ensure the safety of Rome; when the rebel Stilicho destroyed them in the early fifth century, riots broke out as fearful people imagined the end of their world.

The Sibyl originally gained her powers by attracting the attention of Apollo, who offered her anything if she would spend a night with him. She asked for as many years of life as grains of sand she could squeeze into her hand. The sun god granted her wish, but Sibyl still refused his advances. She slowly shriveled into a frail undying body, so tiny she fit into a jar. Her container was hung from a tree, where she croaked occasional oracles, while children stood beneath her urn and teased, "Sibyl, Sibyl, what do you wish?" To which she would faintly reply, "I wish to die." (Feeney; Showerman; Virgil; Young)

Silvanae Like the Greek **Nymphs**, these semidivine maidens frolicked in woodland and other natural areas, usually accompanied by their father, the nature god Silvanus. Iconographically, they are depicted in a line, bearing tree branches, shells, wreaths, or other natural objects. They have been linked to the Scandinavian multiple goddesses the **Matronen**. (Dorcey)

Tellus "Mother Earth" was honored each April 15 at the Fordicidia, when a pregnant cow was sacrificed and its unborn calf burned. The Romans felt the earth, pregnant in spring with sprouting plants, appreciated such sacrifice. Tellus's companion was **Ceres**; both controlled vegetative reproduction and humanity's increase, so were invoked at weddings. One swore oaths upon this goddess, for the all-seeing earth witnessed anyone who broke a promise. To swear by Tellus, one pointed fingers downward while speaking. Finally, Tellus, to whom bodies were returned at death, was associated with the underworld. Due to her connection to the soil of Italy, this goddess was sometimes called Italia. (Berger; Dumézil; Fox; Galinsky; Ovid *Fasti*; Richardson; Strong)

Venus We use her name in "vain" and "veneration" and "venereal." But familiar as her name might be, few today could distinguish the Roman goddess of strawberries and kitchen gardens from Greek **Aphrodite**. With the assimilation of Roman to Greek divinities, the identity of this goddess was lost. The original Venus ruled charm and beauty, herbs and cypress trees. Wherever a large stone rested near a tall tree, virgin priests and priestesses erected an altar to Venus for bloodless sacrifices. In her early Italic form, when she may have been called Herentas, Venus was goddess of youthful love, whose name derives from a root for "loveliness" and "intercourse."

In late classical times, the name Venus was given to a figure otherwise called Barbata, "The Bearded," a divinity in female attire with obvious facial hair. The statues may represent festivals in which cross-dressing was required or an androgynous deity; they do not seem connected to the ancient Italic divinity. Some scholars have interpreted the "beard" as rays descending from the star Venus, but others have pointed out that androgynous divinities appear in many cultures. Finally, the figure may represent women of ethnic groups that have facial hair.

Another title, Calva ("bald"), was given to Venus in memory of selfless action of Roman women during a siege. When the soldiers began to fail, matrons cut their hair and wove it into bowstrings. In their honor, women cut a lock of hair on their wedding day and sacrificed it at the temple of Venus Calva. An alternative story says an epidemic struck Rome, causing women's hair to fall out. When the epidemic passed and their locks grew back, Rome's women offered thanks to Venus. She is associated with peacefulness under the name of Pax or **Concordia**. (Dexter 1990; Feeney; Galinsky; Horace; Ovid *Fasti*; Richardson; Staples; Warmington)

Vesta An early Italic version of this goddess may have been Vesuna Erinia, a motherly hearth goddess. But the classical figure of Vesta, whose fire was tended by a college of six virgin priestesses, derives from the pan-Indo-European hearth goddess who represented the social bond. Vesta was fire, and fire was Vesta. In later days, when she was pictured on coins, her form was veiled.

Vesta was honored in Rome's only circular temple, where her sacred fire burned and, every March 1, was doused and then relit. The goddess's other sacred day was June 9, when barefoot Roman matrons offered food baked on their hearths, and the Vestals sacrificed salt cakes baked on Vesta's fire. After eight days, the Vestals closed the temple, cleaned it thoroughly and reopened it for the year. The Vestals consecrated and blessed new buildings within the city. They were present at every sacrifice offered, for only they could prepare the *mola salsa*, "salted flour," used to mark victims.

Chastity was demanded of the Vestals, for their purity magically protected the city. In Rome's earliest years, the Vestals were probably of royal lineage, and their dedication controlled their reproductive lives. Later, Vestals could be drawn from any noble family, but they had to serve their fertile years in the temple. Despite their virginity, the Vestals dressed as matrons and performed for the city the same rituals that a *materfamilias* ("mother of the family") performed for individual households. In return for chastity and ritual obligations, a Vestal had more rights than typical Roman women.

Unlike her virgin priestesses, Vesta was honored as a mother, and a phallus-shaped effigy was reverenced in her temple into imperial times. That and the tradition of rekindling the Vestal fires by rubbing wood together indicate that Vesta was a goddess of generation, symbol of the continual renewal of family and state. While Vesta was the only Roman goddess to lack a consort, she was linked to the ever-tumescent god Priapus. The connection between Vesta and the ever-virgin, ever-fertile earth was emphasized by the alternative name for her priestesses: **Tellus** Mater, "mother earth."

It was an ill omen for the public fire to go out. Similarly, it was a fearful omen if a Vestal was discovered to have a lover. Such a spoiled virgin was killed in a ritual. Although there were laws against executing anyone within the city's walls, the Vestal was provided with a small amount of food and water, then entombed alive. Priests celebrated sacrifice upon an altar quickly erected above the dying Vestal's tomb, eradicating evidence of her punishment.

On at least two occasions, Vestals seem to have been sacrificed for political reasons, when matters of state were blamed on their misconduct. Yet the foundation of Rome itself could be traced to the pregnancy of a Vestal, for **Rhea Silvia** was impregnated against her will and conceived the twin boys who founded Rome. This myth reinforces the tension between Rome's denial of the Vestals' sexuality and reliance upon it for the city's existence.

Interpretations of the roles and significance of the Vestals reveal as much about the interpreters as about the Vestals themselves. At various times, they have been seen as an intellectual elite, as self-denying nuns, and most recently as paradoxically primitive yet cultivated priestesses. The power of the Vestals' image is perhaps most clearly seen in the multiplicity of interpretations offered. (Beard 1980; Beard et al.; Cantarella; Dumézil; Feeney; Goux; Nash; Ovid *Fasti*; Perowne; Richardson; Pantel; Staples; Wildfang; Young)

Victoria The great stone of **Cybele** rested at Victoria's temple on Palatine Hill until a new temple was built to house it. Except for mentions of her temple as the location for celebrations of successfully concluded wars, there is little evidence Victoria was honored through cult or ritual. Thus she may have been more a deified abstraction than a goddess, although she may derive from the early Sabine agricultural goddess Vacuna. (Axtell; Grant; Richardson)

ETRUSCAN PANTHEON

Acca Larentia A figure of this name appears in Etruscan and Roman mythology (see above); her survival into Roman times suggests a significant deity whose worship was not easily eliminated. Her title of "Lady Mother" may indicate a maternal or ancestral goddess. (Staples)

Artume Goddess of night, the moon, and death, of nature, forests, and fertility, Artume appears to be an adoption of the Greek figure **Artemis**. (Pallottino)

Feronia This goddess's worship lasted into Roman times, suggesting a deity with a cult following who was absorbed rather than being eliminated. Her sanctuary north of Rome dates to the sixth century BCE. Merchants spread Feronia's cult; trading may have been part of her temple's activity. A statue of a striding woman may represent the goddess. (Edlund 1987)

Impusa della Morte The mythical Tuscan sorceress of this name may derive from the Greek Empusa. She was a witch so evil that she refused to share her massive wealth even with relatives. She hid everything so that, when she died, her secrets and her gold died with her. (Leland 1963)

Lasa This word may be the name of a specific divinity, a title, or a generic word for "goddess." Lasa may have been multiple, for we find references to "the Lasas." Lasa comforted worshippers in time of need; she may have been goddess of death and the underworld. She may have also been connected with love, for the love goddess called Alpan was invoked as Lasa; she appears in Tuscan folklore as a flying woman who loved flowers. (Leland 1963)

Menrva Counterpart to Greek **Athena** and Roman **Minerva**, Menrva ruled wisdom and war, art and commerce, and educational endeavors. Menrva was said to have been born from the head of her father, Tinia. With him and the important goddess **Uni**, Menrva formed a divine trinity. (Dumézil)

Nortia To the Etruscans, who believed in preordained life spans, Nortia was the force of destiny. In her temple, a nail was pounded into the wall at the close of each year. The figure called Norcia in Tuscan folklore may derive from Nortia, who protected truffles by hiding them from hunters. In that region, truffles are called "nails," which may connect the witch with the ancient goddess. (Leland 1963; von Vacano)

Phersipnai Queen of the dead, this goddess was depicted on sarcophagi with her husband Aita, king of the underworld. Her name appears to derive from Greek **Persephone**, suggesting influence from that culture. (Zuntz)

Turan Although Etruscans spoke a non-Indo-European language, one of their primary goddesses bore a name related to Greek *tyrannos*, "ruler." Turan was a divinity of sex and dominance depicted as a young girl with wings. The **Lasas** served her; she may have been the same goddess as Lasa. She survived into Italian folklore as Turanna, the "good fairy" of peace and love and beauty. (Leland 1963; von Vacano)

Uni Uni was the supreme Etruscan goddess, hurling thunderbolts when angered and, when happy, making childbirth easy. Her major sanctuaries were at the port city of Pyrgi, where she was offered silver and gold by her worshippers, and at Perugia. She may have been the basis of **Juno**. (Dumézil; Edlund 1987; Pallottino)

Vanths The most famous of the Vanths was Culsu, serpent goddess of the underworld. The Etruscans pictured death spirits as numberless hunters in short skirts and high boots, carrying torches or snakes, waiting to accompany the dead past the grave. As a single divinity, Culsu (or Vanth) alerted humans to death's arrival, for her eye-covered wings saw everything that happened in this world or the underworld. (Briquel)

SCANDINAVIA

From the Rhineland to the North Sea, from sub-arctic peninsulas to coastal lowlands, a culture called "Norse" (a language term), "Scandinavian" (a regional reference), or "Germanic/Teutonic" (an ethnic identity) held sway. Powerful goddesses existed in the region from earliest times. In the prehistoric era, petroglyphs showed chariots and sun wheels, later associated with goddesses. With the arrival of Indo-European tribes, around 2000 BCE, new divinities took precedence, with tales of wars between frost giants and gods expressing conflict between worshippers of different divinities.

The result of the collision of cultures was a double pantheon. Ancient divinities survived as the shamanic Vanir, while the new gods appeared as power-hungry Æsir. In addition to these two divine clans, there were adopted gods. The Scandinavian and Germanic peoples lived in close association with Celts, Finno-Ugrians, and Balts, whose myths and rituals had influence. Vikings brought back Irish motifs; classical figures resulted from trade with Mediterranean peoples. Thus the figures in this section show evidence of continual connection and conflict.

Scandinavian myths were conveyed orally, so written records must be weighed against possible biases. The earliest writer, Tacitus, wrote to enlighten invading generals; later, Christian writers recorded myths, possibly distorting them. Despite such challenges, Scandinavian mythology offers memorable goddess figures whose stories appear in Scandinavia's mythico-historical literature. The Poetic Edda dates from approximately the tenth century; Icelandic scholar Snorri Sturluson compiled a prose version in the twelfth century. Both were transcribed after Christianization. The original Norse word for "god" was neuter but under Christian influence was changed to masculine. Thus it is difficult to know how true these texts were to original oral sources.

Besides the Eddas, another important written source was the *Historica Danica* ("History of the Danes") by Saxo Grammaticus, written in Latin in approximately 1100 CE. Although colored by myth, Saxo's work was accepted as historically accurate for many centuries. Several quasimythic women figures in Saxo's work may derive from ancient goddesses.

In addition to transcribed poetry and epics, Germanic and Scandinavian myth survived as folktales. In the nineteenth century, folklorists Wilhelm and Jakob Grimm wrote down stories from family and friends of Wilhelm's wife, Dortchen, especially the brilliant young Maria Hassenpflug. Retold for a hundred generations, often by women, the stories included suppressed goddess material that can be compared with written records, folk tradition, and archaeological findings.

Although traditional Norse religion was extirpated with the coming of Christianity, some rituals and beliefs remained, occasionally disguised as Christian rites. Since the nineteenth century, reconstructed Norse paganism has gone by the name of Asatru. Norse reconstructionism began in the nineteenth century under the influence of romantic nationalism. Asatru had significant impact in Europe, especially through Nazis, who used images from Norse tradition; this version of Asatru has continuing influence among some white-supremacy groups in the United States. A more liberal form of Asatru was publicly recognized as a religion in Iceland in 1973, but other Scandinavian heathen reconstruction movements lack official recognition. Adherents in the United States may practice the *seidr* ritual, which sustains the tradition of women's prophecy.

SCANDINAVIAN PANTHEON

Alaisiagae Two goddesses of war were known from an inscription on Hadrian's Wall in England: "the two Alaisiagae, Bede and Fimmilene." They may be the same as those known elsewhere as Baudihillie and Friagabi, which may mean "ruler of battle" and "giver of freedom," respectively. They may have been local versions of the more widely known **Valkyries** or separate deities whose myths and rituals have been lost. (Davidson 1964)

Alfhild Alfhild dressed as a man to avoid being married to King Alf. Her father attempted to help, putting Alfhild in a room surrounded by snakes, but Alf fought through them. Alfhild then considered marrying him, but her mother taunted her for her sudden reversal until the girl became a pirate. She was notorious for her courage. When Alfhild attacked Alf's ship, they fought nearly to the death before she agreed to mate with him. (Jesch; Hollander; Larrington)

Angrboda The "one who bodes harm" was a giant mother of fearsome children: Jormungander, the Midgard Serpent who surrounded the earth; Fenrisulfr, the Fenris Wolf who would eat the world; and **Hel**, queen of the otherworld. Angrboda may be the same as troll wife Iárnvidia, "ironwood woman." She has also been identified as **Gollveig**. (Hollander; Saxo; Thorpe)

Audhumbla In primeval times, frost spread across the north, while the south was a land of constant fire. Between them stretched chaos. The interaction of heat and cold gave birth to the cow Audhumbla and the man Ymr. Audhumbla was sustained by the ice, which she converted into milk, on which Ymr fed. One day, a hard spot appeared in the ice. Audhumbla licked the ice, freeing Bur, grandfather of the god Odin. (Davidson 1998; Larrington; Saxo)

Bestla The primordial creatures of this earth were, according to Snorri Sturluson, both female. First came the cow **Audhumbla**. The frost giant Bestla followed, her name indicating she was created from a linden tree. She was mother of the god Odin but otherwise little legend described her. Her relation to Embla, the elm-tree woman also named as earth's primordial mother, is unclear. (Dumézil; *Poetic Edda*; *Prose Edda*)

Beyla This minor goddess had domain over the fermentation of alcoholic beverages. She is called "the one who kneads," so she may be connected as well with the action of yeast in bread; that term has, however, also been understood as describing the action of milking cows. She is connected with bees and, thus, with the intoxicating beverage made from it, mead. Indeed, her name may be a diminutive formed from the Old Icelandic word for "bee," pronounced much as the English word is today. (Dumézil)

Bil One morning, Bil was sent to fetch mead with her brother Hjuki. When the moon man saw them, he enslaved them. Today their pail and pole are visible on the moon's face. This legend may have given rise to the children's chant "Jack and Jill." (Saxo)

Böovildr In the Eddic poem Völundarkvioa and the Old English poem Deor, this maiden was raped by the prince of the elves. Völundr lost his wife Alvítr ("the all-wise," see **Shield Maidens**) when she left him to resume life as a swan. Pining for her, he began to make golden jewelry, intending the pieces as gifts in case she returned. But an evil human king captured Völundr and, crippling him so he could not escape, imprisoned him with a forge on an island. When the king's sons came to jeer, Völundr killed them and used their carcasses for ornaments.

Not knowing of the elf's murderous anger, Böovildr brought him a broken ring to mend. He did so, then plied her with beer until she passed out, after which he raped her. This empowered him to escape, although he was kind enough to his victim to demand that her father promise not to kill her because she had been violated. (Larrington)

Brimwylf Beowulf came to the Danish court, where Brimwylf's son Grendel besieged the people. Killing the son and then the grieving mother, Beowulf was hailed as a hero but met a woeful end. Grendel's mother bore many names: Brimwylf, "lake wolf"; Merewif Mihtig, "mighty mere woman"; Grundwyrgen, "ocean monster"; Algæc-wif, "woman monster"; Ides, "lady." Brimwylf's original stature as goddess of the hunt can be detected in her ability to give birth parthenogenetically, in her association with the wilderness, and in her superhuman strength. (Davidson 1998; Heaney)

Brynhild Odin cursed Brynhild to sleep behind a ring of fire. The hero Sigurd penetrated the ring, pledging himself in return for Brynhild's magical secrets. Then Sigurd wandered south, into the realm of the sorceress Grimhild. Foreseeing Sigurd's heroic future, Grimhild wanted him for her daughter Gudrun, so she drugged Sigurd to make him forget his promise. Sigurd and Gudrun were wed, after which Grimhild set herself to acquire Brynhild for her son, Gunnar. But Gunnar could not cross the fiery barrier to the Valkyrie. So Sigurd exchanged identities with Gunnar and passed safely through. There he slept three nights with Brynhild, marrying her in Gunnar's body. Sigurd resumed his usual appearance, but the interlude restored his memory, leaving him miserable with Gudrun.

When jealous Gudrun told Brynhild the truth about her marriage, Brynhild grew embittered. Gudrun urged Gunnar to kill Sigurd. Out of love for Sigurd, Brynhild stabbed herself in the heart. The lovers were burned on the same pyre. Married by force to Atli, who lusted for Sigurd's wealth, Gudrun killed their children and him, then burned their castle.

In Germanic tales, virtually the same story is told of Kriemhild. Recited orally since before the medieval period, the tale was lost for centuries until found in manuscript in 1755, after which it became popular with Romantic nationalists, including Richard Wagner. The connection of the story with Norse mythology is unsettled. Kriemhild's story parallels that of Gudrun, with a few differences: her mother, Uta, was not evil; her husband was Siegfried and her brother, Gunther; Siegfried assisted Gunther in winning Brynhild by invisibly aiding him in battle with her; Siegfried helped Gunther rape Brynhild (and possibly raped her himself); and Kriemhild provided information leading to Siegfried's death. (*Kudrun*; *Nibelungenlied*; Anderson and Swenson; Gildersleeve; Hollander; Anderson and Swenson; Saxo)

Buschfrauen Germany's forest women lived alone in the woods, seeking human mates but disappearing after lovemaking, never sharing their magical knowledge. These "bush women" were short, golden haired, and shaggy skinned, with pendant breasts and hollow backs. They lived in hollow trees, where they enforced three rules: never use caraway in baking bread (spirits cannot eat it), never peel bark off trees (it hurts the tree), and never tell your dreams. They also preferred that dumplings not be counted while cooking.

The Buschfrauen's queen, the Buschgrossmutter, was a white-haired elf with mossy feet attended by Moosfräulein ("moss maidens"). She was pursued by a hunter who left her alone if she sat on a fallen tree marked with three crosses; those who wished her aid blazed trees with that mark. When the Buschfrauen were pleased, they revealed secrets of herbal healing, made plants grow with their dancing, and gave away endless balls of yarn.

In Scandinavia, this figure appeared as Skogsrå, an old woman who gave luck to hunters or led them astray. The Skogsfruen (plural) were sweet-voiced creatures who herded woodland animals and knit socks. Before any animal was hunted, the Skogsfruen had to be contacted for assurance that the prey was not their pet. If well treated, the Skogsfruen directed hunters to available animals. If treated badly, they were dangerous. Until the seventeenth century, warrants listed "involvement with Skognufva" as a cause of death. Occasionally called Trollkaringen ("troll hag"), the Skogsrå sometimes had a personal name, such as Sigrid or Talle-Maja ("pine Mary"). (Davidson 1998; Kvideland and Sehmsdorf; Lofstedt; Lindow; Thorpe)

Cinderella The Grimm brothers collected a story about an orphaned girl enslaved by an evil step-mother and stepsisters, a story also told by French writer Charles Perrault. This does not mean the story does not derive from mythic sources, but it is unclear whether the figure ("cinder elf") was originally Germanic or Slavic. In variant versions of the story, Cinderella lived naked in a cave or at the bottom of a well, she wore a coat of cat's skins or golden chimes, or she wore shoes of the sun. The tale has been connected to that of orphaned **Vasilisa** (see Slavic), whose mother helped her from the spirit realm. Or Cinderella may have been a **Shield Maiden**, her feather cloak transformed into a glass slipper. (Bottigheimer; Grimm and Grimm 1987)

Dís Originally designating a deified woman ancestor, this term came to mean any Scandinavian goddess. The Dísir were fate goddesses worshipped in midwinter services called *dísablót*. With drinking and storytelling, a family honored these goddesses of heredity. The Dísir have been linked to fertility goddesses (**Matronen**) as well as with **Freyja**, known as Vanadís ("goddess of the Vanir"). (Jochens; Hollander; Näsström 1995)

Edda Her name ("great-grandmother") describes the compilations of Scandinavian mythology. Edda was the first woman to produce offspring; she gave birth to the race of Thralls, "enthralled" to service as food producers. Next came Amma ("grandmother"), who gave birth to the Churls, who conducted business and trades. Finally came Mothir, who gave birth to Jarls, who hunted, fought, and attended school. (*Poetic Edda*)

Elliser The "elf wife" left a circle of dew on the grass where she danced. Usually invisible to human eyes, she could be seen on sunny days. She is distinct from other Scandinavian fairy folk, who were killed by sunlight. Tiny and pretty, with a musical voice, she occasionally fell in love with human men and, to meet them, traveled on a sunbeam. She may be the same as the Skogsrå (see **Buschfrauen**). (Thorpe)

Embla The world's first woman was created from the wood of the elm tree. Her consort was the first man, Ask, created from the ash, after the god Odin found two logs on a beach and breathed life into them. The pair have been called the "Adam and **Eve**" (see Eastern Mediterranean) of the Norse. Some argue that their tale suggests an ancient totemic relationship between humans and trees. How this figure connects with the linden-tree primal woman named **Bestla** is unclear. (Dumézil; *Poetic Edda*)

Erce Mentions of this Anglo-Saxon goddess are few but significant. The second Merseberg Charm invokes her as "Mother of Earth…mother of men." Erce has been connected with the plow and oxen found in Scandinavian rock art. (Davidson 1998; Näsström 1995)

Fengi Once, in the days of King Frodi, Fengi and her sister Mengi turned a giant millstone that magically produced peace and plenty. The greedy king let them rest only as long as it took for them to sing a song. One night, exhausted, they sang a charm that caused Frodi's death at the hand of the sea king, Mysing. But Mysing set the giants to work again, this time grinding salt. They ground so much that the sea filled up with it. (Anderson and Swenson; Hollander; Saxo)

Freyja Beautiful Freyja wore a feathered cloak and a magical amber necklace (Brísingamen) as she rode through the sky in a cat-drawn chariot. Or she rode on the back of the huge gold-bristled boar Hildisvín, who may have been her brother, the fertility god Freyr.

Freyja's home in Asgard was located on Fólkvangar ("people's plain"). Her palace was called Sessrúmnir ("rich in seats"). She needed a huge palace to hold hordes of dead warriors, for as leader of the **Valkyries**, she had first choice of souls on every battlefield.

Freyja was also goddess of love and sexuality, taking lovers among the gods, including trickster Loki, who mated with her in the form of a flea. She spent a night with each of four dwarves to convince them to make her the most beautiful necklace ever seen. Yet she was not available to everyone; when giants courted her, she spurned them.

Although Freyja's favorite lover was Frey, she had a husband named Odr with whom she had a daughter, Hnossa or Gersemi, youthful goddess of infatuation. When Odr left home, Freyja shed tears of amber. Then she followed, assuming various names as she sought him: Mardol, Horn, and Gefn. But always she was "lady ruler," the meaning of her primary name, after which we call the sixth day of the week and to which the German word "frau" is related.

As she followed Odr, Freyja caused leaves to fall. She was thus connected with human sexuality but also with reproductive powers of plants and animals, for which she was called Sessrymner, "large wombed." She may be related to the goddess whom Tacitus called **Nerthus**, for she was honored with a ritual procession through the land in a wagon.

Freyja introduced the trance ritual called *seidr* to the divinities. Shamanism was the religion of early Scandinavians, but Freyja was a newcomer, so her trance magic connects the cultures. As leader of the Vanir, Freyja was called Vanabruder ("lover of the Vanir") and Vanadis ("goddess of the Vanir"). The similarity between Freyja and **Anat** (see Eastern Mediterranean) may be a result of her religion moving north with her worshippers.

Many goddesses associated with Freyja may have originally been separate. **Gefjion** led unmarried dead girls to Freyja's hall. The **Shield Maiden** Gondul retrieved kings from the battlefield. Golden-haired Syr was a minor divinity of love whose name means "sow"

or "protectress." **Fulla** had long unbound hair, symbol of sexuality and of wheat.

Freyja survived in folklore as Waldmichen, "Wood nymph," living in a grotto where visitors could see the souls of unborn babies. She owned a mill where she ground old men and young women. Her servants were rabbits, two of whom held the train of her cloak while others lit her way with candles. (Berger; Davidson 1998; Dumézil; Enright; Grundy; Hollander; Jesch; Larrington; Mundal; Näsström 1996, 1995; Saxo)

Frigg The White Lady of Midsummer, Frigg ruled heavenly Asgard, home of the Æsir. A quiet, wise goddess, dressed in the plumage of raptors, Frigg lived in Fensalir ("sea hall"), surrounded by goddesses who represented aspects of femininity: healing Eir, wise Saga, virginal Gefjion, and secretive **Fulla** (also associated with **Freyja**). A favored servant was Sjöfn, who stirred infatuation in human hearts. Frigg's messenger was fleet Gná, whose magical horse traversed the world in a flash; Hlin defended Frigg's favorite humans. As a goddess of the domestic arts who also ruled the celestial sphere, Frigg sat in the sky spinning. Her spinning wheel Friggerock is the constellation Orion's Belt.

Frigg loved her son Baldr so much that she made all earthly creatures promise they would never harm him. But she neglected to ask the apparently harmless mistletoe, which proved fatal to her son. Because he was protected, the gods used to throw darts at Baldr, laughing as their weapons glanced off. But envious Loki, disguised as an old woman, asked Frigg if anything could hurt Baldr. Frigg admitted she had not bothered with the mistletoe deep in the woods.

Loki took off like a shot. He cut the mistletoe and formed a sharp arrow, which he placed in the hand of the blind god Hoder. With Hoder's arm guided by Loki, the arrow found its way, and Baldr dropped dead. He went to the realm of **Hel**, accompanied by his wife Nanâ, who died of heartbreak. Frigg convinced every creature on earth to weep for Baldr's return. All did, save a female giant—Loki in disguise. Thus Frigg lost Baldr, who could not be freed from death's grip until a son of **Rind** matured into a hero.

Because of the similarity of this story to tales from the eastern Mediterranean, scholars propose that the story migrated from its original home. Baldr may derive from the dying-and-reviving god Attis, son of **Cybele** (see Southeastern Europe). His marriage to Nanâ (an otherwise unknown goddess whose name is identical to that of Attis's mother) suggests a non-Norse origin.

Sometimes Frigg was confused with **Freyja**; they may be descended from the same figure. But there are differences. Freyja was primary among the Vanir, while Frigg was queen over the Æsir. While Freyja had many lovers, Frigg was loyal to her consort Odin. And while Freyja's mother was not known, Frigg's was the earth goddess Fjörgynn, whose name was sometimes used as a title for Frigg. Despite these differences, abundant similarities suggest that the relationship between the goddesses has yet to be clarified.

The folkloric character Frau Fricke (Frick or Freen) is a late form of this goddess, a spinner who demands that women cease spinning whenever she travels through the land during the winter solstice. This figure is more commonly known as Frau **Holle**. (Enright; Grundy; Davidson 1969; Hollander; Jesch; Näsström 1995; Saxo)

Fulla Fulla, symbol of earth's abundance, was associated with both **Freyja** and **Frigg**. She was adopted under a Romanized version of her name (Abundia or Habondia) into medieval literature as a symbol of residual paganism. Her spirit women brought good luck. An associated minor goddess, Satia ("satiation") or Bensozia, may have been an invention of churchmen. (Hollander; Näsström 1995; Thorpe)

Fylgja In Iceland, a family's guardian spirit was called by this name, sometimes translated as "fetch." Unlike the **Dísir**, whom they otherwise resemble, the Fylgjakona (plural) were never worshipped. The Fylgjakona rarely appeared to human sight, but when they did, misfortune followed. The word *fylgia* means "caul," and a child born with a caul on the head was considered lucky and second sighted. After Christianization, the Fylgja was depicted as an angel. (Ellis 1968; Jochens; Kvideland and Sehmsdorf; Larrington; Simpson; Strömbäck)

Gefjion It is difficult to know whether two Gefjions were originally the same. One, a giant trickster, was promised as much land as four oxen could plow in a day, so she conceived four ox-shaped sons. When they had grown, Gefjion brought them to Sweden, plowed off part, and dragged it south, forming Denmark. The other Gefjion sold her hymen for a jewel but retained her virginity. All women who died maidens passed into Gefjion's possession to live thereafter with **Freyja** or **Frigg**; she has been called an aspect of both. Although she knew the fates of all humans, she kept silent. Gefjion may have been a Danish earth goddess, her name detectable in the English word "gift." (*Poetic Edda*; Battaglia; Davidson 1998; Mundal; Saxo; Thorpe; *Heimskringla*)

Gerd A goddess of light, Gerd lived in a house ringed by fire. Daughter of a frost giant and a human male, Gerd attracted the fertility god Freyr. He wooed her first with golden apples, then with threats. A runic spell finally won Gerd, who traveled to Asgard to live with Freyr. Some interpreters, tracing Gerd's name to a word for "field," see an allegory of the springtime earth ready to produce fruit under the god of fertility's influence, but still living in the grip of winter. (*Poetic Edda*; Davidson 1969, 1998; Larrington; Saxo; Motz 1981)

Gná Riding her horse Hofvarpnir ("hoof tosser"), this wind deity was the messenger of heaven and especially of Asgard's Queen **Frigg**. Gná's name was used as a synonym for "woman" in Scandinavian poetry. She was also goddess of abundance (see also **Fulla**). (Näsström; *Prose Edda*)

Gollveig Scholars have attempted to explain why this mighty witch entered Asgard demanding vengeance, why she was killed three times but lived, and why she possessed the power of the Vanir. Some see her as a symbol of the corruption of wealth, interpreting her name as "drunkenness of gold." Others say Gollveig embodied a historical combat. Among the latter are those who see Gollveig as a disguise for **Freyja**, who also possessed a golden necklace and the power of prophecy. (*Poetic Edda*; DuBois; Dumézil)

Gunnlod Ruler of poetry, Gunnlod was the owner of a cauldron of mead that endowed anyone who drank it with eloquence. The god Odin attempted to gain poetic power through trickery, coming to the hall of Gunnlod's father, the giant Suttungr, in disguise because the Norse gods were bitter enemies of giants. Gunnlod sat on a throne of gold, from which she dispensed mead to Odin. He seduced her and, while she was sleeping, drank all three vats of mead and shapeshifted into a bird to escape. Gunnlod's father pursued Odin back to the land of the gods, changing himself into an eagle, but the gods saw him coming and lit fires that killed him. (Larrington)

Hedrun This magical goat lived in Valhalla, the hall of heroes where the **Valkyries** brought those slain in battle. Every day Hedrun nibbled needles from a pine tree, possibly the tree that held up the world. She gave intoxicating mead so copiously that the heroes spent every day drinking. Odin, Valhalla's owner, lived solely on Hedrun's mead. (Ellis; Hollander; Saxo)

Hel The goddess who gave her name to the Christian place of eternal punishment ruled an underworld of miserable dullness. Her name means the "one who covers up" because she hid those who died of disease or old age in her nine-circled home, while the **Valkyries** carried off those who died heroically to the heavenly halls of **Freyja** or Odin. Black-and-white Hel, daughter of **Angrboda**, rode to earth to fold the dying in her horrible arms. Then they traveled past the guardian maiden, Modgud. In Helheim, Hel's palace had walls of worms and human bones. She ate with

utensils called Famine from the plate Hunger, while her slaves Gagnläti and Ganglöt ("senility" and "dotage") served her. (Ellis; Hollander; Saxo; Thorpe)

Hertha No legends survive of the Germanic goddess from whom we get our words for "earth" and "hearth." She was worshipped into historic times, when Christians carried plows in processions in her honor. Medieval witches invoked Hertha as their patron, as they did **Fulla** under her name Habundia. It is unclear whether Hlodyn was a title of Hertha or a distinct goddess. (Thorpe)

Hervor One of the few Scandinavian heroines to whom a saga—the *Hervarar Saga*—was devoted, Hervor ("Warder of Hosts") was a **Shield Maiden**. Needing a magical sword for her campaigns, Hervor dared to enter the rocky grave of her father and uncles. There, battling their violent spirits, she claimed her prize. Her name is also used for one of the **Valkyries**. (Durrenberger and Durrenberger)

Hilde When her father declared war on her lover, the **Shield Maiden** Hilde fought on the latter's side. Every night she performed magic to raise dead warriors, so her fight would go on until Ragnarök. Hilde also appears in the cycle of tales devoted to her daughter Gudrun. Her name appears on lists of **Valkyries**. (*Kudrun*)

Holle In German, Austrian, and Swiss folktales, she appears as a witch, but like her sister **Perchta**, Holle was originally a weather goddess. Sunshine streamed when she combed her hair, snow covered the earth when she shook a feather comforter, and rain fell when she threw away laundry water. She appeared each noon to bathe in a fountain from which children were born. She lived in a cave in the mountain or, disguised as a frog, in a well. When she left home, she rode the wind in a wagon. Once, when she broke a linchpin, a man helped her, later finding that wood shavings from the repairs had turned to gold.

Holle was associated with textile crafts. On the winter solstice, she checked the quality of each woman's work and offered rewards or punishment. A good spinner woke to find a single priceless golden thread, but sloppy ones found their work tangled, their spinning wheels shattered or burned. Between December 25 and January 6, the "twelve days of Christmas," Holle traveled the world in her wagon. No rotary actions were allowed; sleighs were used instead of wagons; all meal grinding had to cease.

As Frau Gôde, the goddess rode in a wagon drawn by dogs, looking for open doors and sending a dog inside when she found one. This dog barked for a year and could not be driven away; if killed, it turned into a stone that became a whining dog every night. The next year, the beleaguered residents could relieve themselves of the unwanted pet by firmly closing the door as Frau Gôde drove by.

Some church fathers called Holle the goddess of witches, to whose rituals women flew on animals. This belief was, however, not generally borne out by folklore, which considered Holle a goddess of weather. But as witches were believed to work weather magic, the connection may have been forged in monks' minds. A version of this figure related to **Frigg** appears as Frau Fricke or Freen. (Davidson 1998; Gimbutas; Grimm; List; Motz 1984; Thorpe)

Huldra Queen of the Germanic fairies, Huldra looked like a beautiful woman from the front, but from the back, she was hollow and long tailed. She lived with her people, the Huldrafolk, in remote mountains, where they danced and made mournful music. One hunter overheard girls saying he would never kill an animal because he was unclean, so he washed his face and brought down an elk. Other stories say Huldrafolk helped hunters by telling them what rituals they needed. (Davidson 1998; Kvideland and Sehmsdorf; Simpson)

Hyrrokin The death ship of Baldr, beloved son of the earth goddess **Frigg**, could not travel to the underworld because it was so weighted with the goddess's grief. So the giant woman Hyrrokin ("withered by fire"), strongest of a mighty race, was brought to heaven to throw her weight against the ship. She arrived riding a wolf, using snakes for a bridle, and performed the task of launching Balder into the afterlife. (Davidson 1998)

Idunn The Norse divinities were not immortal; they relied on Idunn's apples to survive. But once the trickster Loki let Idunn fall into the hands of the gods' enemies, the giants of Jotunheim. When the divinities began to age, they demanded that Loki return Idunn to them. Loki flew to Jotunheim, turned Idunn into a walnut, and carried her safely home. Idunn's consort was Bragi, god of poets. (Davidson 1969; Hollander; Saxo)

Jord Goddess of the primordial world, daughter of **Nótt**, the earth goddess Jord was worshipped on mountains, where she mated with the sky. It is sometimes difficult to know when this goddess is intended and when the referent is the planet Earth. (Hollander; Saxo)

Kriemhild The mythic heroine Gudrun in Norse legend bears this name in the Germanic versions of the story of the Nibelungen. Recited orally since before the medieval period, the tale was lost for centuries until found in manuscript in 1755, after which it became popular with Romantic nationalists, including Richard Wagner. The connection of the story with Norse mythology has been argued positively and negatively.

Although most of Kriemhild's story parallels that of Gudrun, there are a few mostly insignificant differences: Her mother Uta was not as evil as Grimhild; her husband was Siegfried rather than Sigurd; Kriemhild's brother was Gunther rather than Gunnar; Siegfried assisted Gunther in winning Brynhild by invisibly aiding him in battle with her; Siegfried helped Gunther to rape Brynhild (and possibly raped her himself, while invisible); and Kriemhild provided information that led to Siegfried's death, either treacherously or ignorantly. The battle and rape motifs make the Germanic version considerably more misogynistic than the Norse. (*Nibelungenlied*; *Poetic Edda*)

Matronen Throughout Romanized Germany, images of "the Mothers" have been found, usually depicted as a trinity. They are typically interpreted as goddesses of earth's abundance (see **Nerthus**, **Fulla**). Some scholars argue that they were Celtic or Italian, imported during Roman occupation; most images have been found in the Rhineland, where legions were stationed. These goddesses may have been honored in celebrations called Modranight, "mothers' night." Vestiges of this trinity can be found in saints ("Jungfrauen," or "young women") who appear in groupings of three. (Davidson 1964)

Menglod The "sun-bright maiden" Menglod appears in legend surrounded by a wall of flame from which a hero must rescue her. This peculiar entrapment was a frequent hazard to ancient Norse heroines, suggesting a connection between women and fire, also found in the story of **Brynhild**. Menglod's serving women were Bjort, Hlif, and Hlifthrasa. She may be a form of the goddess **Freyja**, one of her many names. (Näsström)

Modgud This maiden, whose name means "fierce battle," guarded the path to the underworld realm of the death goddess **Hel**. To reach her, the newly dead had to cross Hell-Ways, the caverns surrounding the World Tree, Yggdrasil, at whose roots Hel lived. Spanning the abysses where the roaring River Göll (Gjoll) flowed was a gold-paved bridge. There, with her maidservant Frith, Modgud stood watch, challenging all who came her way. (Davidson 1998)

Mrizala Heroine of a German folktale, Mrizala was lovely but very fussy. She refused young men in her village until she had no one left to refuse. When her mother said she was fated to die a spinster, Mrizala said, "I wish Death would come and marry me!" Immediately, a young man knocked at the door. He seemed pleasant, so Mrizala did not believe he was

Death. As she spent time in the man's company, she grew to regret her impulsive wish. But suddenly he left, and she cautiously followed him to the church, where she saw him roast and eat a baby. She knew then that Death had, indeed, come for her.

The next day her suitor asked her what she had seen in the church and she denied seeing anything. That day, her father died. He asked again; again she denied seeing him. Her mother died, and he asked again, and she denied again. Then Mrizala herself died, taken by her bridegroom.

From her grave, a rose grew. One day, a passing prince ordered it plucked for his hat. Thereafter, he had no appetite for food or drink, and each night he dreamed of a lovely young woman. A scholar was called, who told the family that the curse could only be broken if the prince could capture Mrizala at midnight and keep her in his arms. That night, the prince kept watch as the rose, promptly at midnight, turned into Mrizala. He captured her, held her tight, and won her back from Death.

Her first husband did not let go easily, for as she was nursing her first baby, he reappeared with the same question. She gave the same answer, so he strangled her newborn. Then he said he would take her princely husband, and Mrizala screamed out the truth, that she had seen Death roasting and eating children. Satisfied, Death gave her a golden ring as a memento and left her until her full life's span had been completed. (Ranke)

Nana This goddess plays little part in Germanic mythology except to grieve the needless death of her husband, the god Baldr. In this, she strongly resembles Sumerian **Inanna** (see Eastern Mediterranean), who similarly mourned a lost love, as did neighboring Egyptian **Isis** (see Africa). Such parallels have led scholars to suggest connections between Scandinavian and Mediterranean myths, probably brought about through trade. (*Poetic Edda*; *Prose Edda*)

Nerthus Tacitus said the Germanic tribes' primary divinity was the earth goddess Nerthus, honored in an island sanctuary where her image sat until her priest divined her desire to move among her people. She then began a solemn procession, drawn by oxen. Weapons were locked away until the journey was completed. Festivities accompanied her, and doors opened in hospitality. Finally, when the priest discerned that the goddess was tired of human company, the procession started back to Nerthus's island. In a hidden lake, slaves bathed the goddess and her chariot, then were offered to her in death. Some argue that Nerthus was a god, but the ritual of carrying a deity around the fields was more typically associated with goddesses. Others say Nerthus was another Scandinavian goddess, possibly **Freyja**. While the ritual was clearly described, scholars debate its ultimate cultural source. (Berger; Hollander; Tacitus)

Nixies Germanic and Swedish folklore describe prophetic water spirits. Like the rivers they inhabited, the Nixies were changeable in nature: sometimes charming and peaceful, sitting in the sun to comb their hair; sometimes fierce and hungry, drowning people for food. They assumed human form to go to market, appearing as long-breasted women who looked human but who, beneath their dresses, had fish tails.

Mortal men fell in love with Nixies, wasting away because of their beauty. Sometimes a Nixie agreed to marry a human, always making him vow never to ask her origin. Excellent dancers, they danced with human men, but should one steal her glove it meant the Nixie's death. The next day her river would run red with her blood. If they appeared at a wedding it was good luck. If they appeared at a birth, they could either aid or thwart the process. (Thorpe)

Norns The vast tree Yggdrasil rose from the world of **Hel** to pass through Midgard (Middle Earth), where humans lived, as well as the giants' land of Jotunheim and the dwarves' home Nidavellir, finally reaching the heavenly worlds of Asgard (home of the Æsir), Álfheim (home of the elves), and Vanaheim (home of the Vanir). At Yggdrasil's foot lived three sisters, the Norns. Each day they drew water and, mixing it with gravel, sprinkled Yggdrasil. From their privileged position, the Norns saw the future. Not even gods could undo what they predicted.

Sometimes there was one all-powerful Norn; sometimes there were two; occasionally the Norns were innumerable, one for each person. But the most common depiction was of three sisters. Oldest was Urd, whose name becomes "weird," derived from a word meaning "to become." Norn of the past, Urd gave her name to the well (Urtharbrunnr) from which her sisters drew water. Verdandi ("becoming") was Norn of the present, and the youngest sister, Skuld (from *skula*, "shall"), ruled the future. A powerful sorceress and queen of the elves, Skuld carried scrolls of fortune. (Kernshaw; *Poetic* II; Bauschatz; Davidson 1998; Jochens; Saxo)

Nótt The primeval goddess Nótt ("night") gave birth to earth (**Jord**) and light. She was dark skinned and born of the race of giants. Her family consisted of her father, her consort, and her son Aud. She also took a second consort by whom she conceived Jord. She rode forth each evening in a chariot drawn by her horse Hrimfaxi ("frosty mane"), from whose mouth dew fell. (Hollander; Saxo; Thorpe)

Ostara The Germanic spring's goddess was celebrated in the fourth month of the year, called Eostremonat or Ostaramonath after her. In Anglo-Saxon, her name became Estre or Eastre. She was honored among the Germanic people with painted eggs. Some scholars believe Ostara is a back-formation from the month's name rather than an actual goddess. (Bede)

Perchta An "elf woman" of folklore hides an old goddess of weather and the winter solstice. She was generally described in negative terms, unlike her beloved sister **Holle**. Perchta could not tolerate laziness. She inspected distaffs and spinning wheels, looking for wasted bits of wool. If she found them, she tore open the spinner's stomach and stuffed the remnants into the cavity. But Perchta herself was sloppy, with long, matted hair and tattered clothes. Her face was wrinkled, her eyes lively. Her favorite time of year was the twelve days of Christmas, which culminated in Perchta's Day, when everyone ate pancakes of meal and milk in her honor. Bits were left for Perchta, who came secretly to enjoy them; if anyone spied her, he was blinded for the year.

Despite her untidy appearance, Perchta seduced young men and carried them off to the mountains (especially the Venusberg, named for Roman **Venus**); they were never heard from again. The distinction between Perchta and Holle is unclear, for Holle was also described as a seductress. (Davidson 1998; Grimm; Gimbutas; List; Motz 1984; Rumpf et al.; Thorpe)

Ran Sea goddess and queen of the drowned, Ran could hold a ship steady with one hand while she netted sailors with the other. Because Ran permitted the drowned to attend their funerals, anyone seen at his own wake was assumed to be in Ran's keeping. Because Ran loved gold, Scandinavian sailors kept gold coins in their pockets, in case they went "faring to Ran."

The waves ("claws of Ran" or "wave maidens") were Ran's daughters and, like their mother, mermaids. These girls could help or hinder a sailor, pushing a ship faster or slowing passage. With her daughters, Ran made herself visible during the winter, when she splashed close to her worshippers' campfires. She may derive from the mythology of the nearby Finns. (Kernshaw; Hollander; Thorpe; Turville-Petre; Guerber)

Rapunzel "Rapunzel, Rapunzel, let down your hair!" the prince called from beneath the tower where this maiden was held prisoner by the witch Mother Gothel. Then he climbed to her bed on the plaits of her long hair. Like other Germanic fairy tales, this story probably derives from ancient myth. (Grimm)

Rheda The Venerable Bede, writing of the Anglo-Saxons, mentions Rheda as one of their goddesses, but no trace of her name is found among their Germanic cousins on the Continent. Little is known of her except that the month of March, Hrethmonath (Rhedmonath), bore her name in that land. Presumably she was a spring goddess, to whom sacrifices were offered during March. (Bede)

Rind Only a child of Rind could avenge the death of the god Baldr (see **Frigg**). Odin traveled to her court disguised as a soldier to convince her to help, but Rind rebuffed him. The next year, Odin came disguised as a smith, with the same result. A third time Odin came, in disguise as a young courtier. Rind again refused his advances. Finally Odin disguised himself as a maiden healer and drew Rind's eye. When she fell sick, Odin cured her, and when they slept together, Rind conceived the hero Vali. (Davidson 1969; Hollander; Larrington)

Rotkäppchen Like many Germanic folk tales, the story of the little girl who went to grandmother's house, wearing her red cape and cap, only to get eaten by a wolf is replete with archetypal feminine imagery. Although collected by the Grimm brothers, the story appears in the collection of French folklore by Charles Perrault. While it is commonly described as Germanic, its source is unknown. (Grimm)

Saga In the Scandinavian pantheon, all-knowing Saga came second, after Frigg, in order of precedence. Saga lived at Sökkvabekk ("sinking beach"), a waterfall of cool waves where she offered her guests drinks in golden cups. Her name was applied to the epic tales of her people; words related to her name mean "narrative." (Hollander; Saxo; Thorpe)

Shield Maidens Scandinavian warrior women could be either divine (see **Brynhild**, **Norns**, **Valkyries**) or human (**Alfhild**, **Hilde**). Typically their stories and images concentrate on their prowess in battle, but they also showed a softer side. Sometimes they shed their cloaks to dance. Human men could capture such women by stealing a feather cloak and keeping it hidden. No matter how happily she lived with the man or how many children they had, a Shield Maiden who found her cloak flew away. Sometimes, these women wore their souls on chains around their necks that, if removed, meant their death. (*Poetic Edda*; Davidson 1998)

Sif The grain goddess, renowned for her golden hair, lived with thunder-wielding Thor. When trickster Loki cut Sif's hair, Thor made him travel to the lands of the dwarfs to bring back those master artisans. The dwarfs made hair of spun gold that, attached to Sif's head, grew like the original. (Davidson 1969; Hollander)

Sigrdrífa Wisest of the **Valkyries**, Sigrdrífa once stole from battle a hero to whom Odin had promised victory. In punishment Odin stung her with sleep thorns, after which Sigrdrífa sank into a trance, not to awaken until a fearless man claimed her. When the hero Sigurd found a mountain lit by fire, he saw in the center Sigrdrífa. Riding into the flames, he cut her armor from her, for it had grown into her flesh as she slept. Then he awakened the **Shield Maiden** and asked her to teach him wisdom. Sigrdrífa spoke at length with the hero, telling him magic runes and the ways of sorcery. Finally, she sank back into sleep. She is often conflated with the **Valkyrie Brynhild**. (*Poetic Edda*)

Sjörå Although sometimes found in male form, this sea spirit was typically female. Left alone or offered gifts, the Sjörå was helpful, warning of storms and pointing out fishing areas. If angered, she caused death by drowning. The Sjörå could be magically "bound" by circling her pond with consecrated soil. This imprisoned her and, desperate, she offered fish in return for freedom. (Lindow)

Skadi The goddess for whom Scandinavia was named lived on snow-covered mountains, where her favorite occupations were skiing and snowshoeing. But when the gods caused her father's death, Skadi traveled to Asgard, intent upon vengeance. Even alone, she was more than a match for the gods, and they were forced to sue for peace. Skadi demanded that they make her laugh, and that she be allowed to choose a mate from among them. Trickster Loki met the first condition by tying his testicles to a goat. It was a contest of screeching, until the rope snapped and Loki landed on Skadi's knee. She laughed.

Next, the gods lined up. Skadi's eyes were masked, for she intended to select her mate by feeling his legs. When she'd found the strongest—thinking them the legs of beautiful Baldr—she flung off her mask and was disappointed to discover she had picked the sea god Njord. She moved to the god's ocean home, where she was miserable. The couple moved to Skadi's mountain palace, but the water god was as unhappy there as Skadi had been in the water. They agreed to separate, and Skadi took up with Ullr, god of skis.

Honored especially in Norway, Skadi may have derived from the pantheon of the Saami people there. Her appearance as a hunter connects her with the woodland women called **Buschfrauen** in German. (Davidson 1998; Hollander; Saxo; *Heimskringla*)

Sneewitcchen Two German folktales collected by the Grimm brothers include characters named Snow White. One, Sneewitcchen ("snow witch"), with her sister Rose Red, saved a bear from freezing and later helped a dwarf whose beard was frozen into a lake. When the bear later met the dwarf, he killed the dwarf and was transformed into a prince. The other Snow White was condemned to death by her evil stepmother but survived with the assistance of a group of dwarves. The presence in the tales of dwarves suggests a descent from Scandinavian mythology. (Grimm)

Sól The Scandinavians saw the sun as a spinning girl who lived on earth, where she was so beautiful her father, Mundilfari, named her after the sun. Such presumption annoyed the gods. They took Sól to heaven, where she rode the chariot of day. Divine horses, Árvak ("early waker") and Alsvid ("all-strong") pulled her; under their harnesses were bags of cooling winds. Sól also carried the shield Svalin ("cool"), which protected the earth. Her consort was a human, Glen.

Sól was not immortal, for like other Scandinavian gods, she was doomed to die at Ragnarök. She was chased through the sky by the Fenriswolf, offspring of **Angrboda**, who on the last day would catch her and devour her. Before her another wolf, Hati, chased her brother, the moon. Just before being swallowed up, Sól would give birth, and this daughter would take her mother's place in the new sky. (*Poetic Edda*; Saxo)

Syn The goddess gatekeeper of heaven was named Syn ("denial") because she denied entry to anyone she judged unworthy. Because she was all-seeing and perfectly just, Syn was the goddess on whom oaths were sworn. She was also invoked in lawsuits so that justice would prevail. (*Prose Edda*; Thorpe)

Thorgerd Originally a human woman, Thorgerd Holgabrud was deified because of her skill in divination and sorcery. She and her sister Irpa were the special goddesses of Icelandic nobleman Jarl Haakon, who built them a temple and became king of Norway with Thorgerd's help.

Thorgerd was a mighty warrior, charged with protecting Haakon's people. If they were attacked, she sprang to life, arrows flying from each finger, each arrow killing a man. Because she had power over natural forces necessary for her people's happiness, she was invoked for luck in fishing and farming. Her worship was among the last vestiges of the ancient religion, remaining vital into Christian times. The Christians, denouncing her, called her Thorgerd Holga-Troll, although she had no troll blood. She may be a form of the goddess **Gerd**. (*Poetic Edda*; Davidson 1969, 1998)

Ursula The Germanic moon goddess was honored on her feast day, October 21. Later, Christians in the same area adopted her as a saint, calling the old lunar feast St. Ursula's day and describing her as the chief among 11,000 murdered virgins. She was reputedly a woman of Cornwall who, betrothed against her will to a German prince, assembled thousands of companions in maidenhood but, traveling to her marriage, encountered Huns who killed them all. The date of this event is set in legend as October 31, 237, or perhaps 451. But lists of martyrs through the tenth century do not mention Ursula, although the virgin sacrifice crops up now and again, with as many as a dozen given credit for martyrdom. By the eleventh century, the number of virgins takes a staggering leap upward, with a text in 1112 giving Ursula's story complete with vows of celibacy and demands for thousands of handmaidens. The excavation of an ancient, crowded cemetery in Cologne at the time may have given rise to the story.

Ursula's name suggests a connection with the bear (Latin, *ursus*). Despite the Roman background to her name, the goddess may derive from a Finno-Ugric source. Or she may be connected with the weather-witching Germanic **Holle**. (Baring-Gould)

Valkyries The helmeted battle maid who flew her supernatural horse over war's carnage is a familiar Scandinavian image. These maidens were also forces of fate. Before battles started, the Valkyries wove webs of war, raising a warp of spears and weighting it with human heads, running a red weft through the spears, using arrows as shuttles. In this tapestry, they read the fates of warriors. When they had determined the battle's outcome, the Valkyries flew to take the slain. Many writers describe the Valkyries as servants of Odin, retrieving his selected heroes. Some tales showed Valkyries opposing Odin's will, selecting their own favorites and teaching magic to heroes they intended to save. The question of whom the Valkyries served is made more complex when the goddess **Freyja** is called their chief.

The Valkyries did not always ride horses. Sometimes they appeared on wolves or disguised themselves as ravens. At times the Valkyries appear like **Shield Maidens** in swan disguise, in which form they occasionally mated with human men. Several stories describe Valkyries who married the same hero lifetime after lifetime. Such was the case with Svava, reborn as the princess Sigrun, who married a man named Helgi in several incarnations.

There were two kinds of Valkyries: divine ones, of whom there were nine, or nine times nine; and the half-mortal Vaetter maidens, visible as humans to the second sighted, while the average eye saw only the aurora borealis illuminating the field of battle. Among the Valkyries, some had individual names and stories. Battle maiden names include Helde ("brilliant"), Hlathguth ("necklace-adorned warrior maiden"), Olrun ("rune reader"), Skeyh ("axe time"), Baudihillie ("rule of battle"), Friagabi ("offering freedom"), Gunnr ("battle"), and Göndul ("handling the magic wand"); others are Guth, Geirskögul, Hlathguth, Hjörðprimul, Ljod, Olrun, Rota, Svipul, Snngriðr, and Valkyrjr.

Of the Valkyries with specific duties and stories, eleven carried the magical mead of the nanny goat Hedrun to the heroes in Välholl: Göll, Hildr ("combat"), Skeggjöld, and Trúðr, as well as Geirönul (Geirronul, "spear bearer"), Herfjötur (Herfjoter,"panic terror"), Hlökk (Hlok, "shrieker"), Rangild ("shield bearer"), Rathgild ("plan destroyer"), Reginleif ("companion of gods"), and Skögul ("raging one"). Two more, Hrist ("shaker") and Mist ("torpor"), bore the mead to Odin, who lived solely upon it.

Hervor and **Hilde** both appear in sagas as warrior women with powers over the world of death. Skuld, otherwise known as one of the **Norns**, is sometimes named as a member of the Valkyries. **Brynhild** (also called Sigrdrífa) is the most famous of the Valkyries, appearing as she does in literature, art, and music, surrounded by a flaming circle, asleep in her armor because she opposed Odin's will.

Kara, called a Valkyrie although apparently mortal, accompanied her lover Helgi to battle, swooping above him in swan plumage and singing such a sweet song that his enemies laid down their arms to listen. But one day Helgi raised his sword too high, too abruptly, and stabbed Kara to death, then lived in misery and guilt until he joined her. Finally, Svava appears in a romantic tale of the warrior Helgi. She was reborn as the human woman Sigrún and wed a later incarnation of Helgi. (Kernshaw; *Poetic Edda*; Davidson 1969, 1964; Ellis; Enright 1990; Jochens)

Vár This Scandinavian love goddess dealt with promises lovers made to each other outside wedlock, called *várar* after her, and took vengeance on anyone who broke such vows. An aspect of the all-knowing earth, Vár saw and heard everything. Nothing could be hidden from her, so when a lover complained of wrongdoing by a love partner, Vár knew instantly if the accusation was correct. (*Prose Edda*)

Voluspa Born before this world began, Voluspa was asked to tell the history of the world. Once begun, she did not stop, even though the gods did not wish to hear of their deaths at Ragnarök. Other women seers were Heith, whose witchcraft included casting spells, and Oddibjord, who traveled telling stories and fortunes. (*Poetic Edda*; Hollander; Jochens; McKinnell)

Since prehistory, a number of cultures have made southeastern Europe home. Archaeology has unearthed many early artifacts that appear to depict goddesses in this region, which stretches from the Caucasus Mountains to the Caspian and Black Seas. But little narrative explains the sculptures, bas-reliefs, and jewelry found there. Scanty information comes from Greeks like Herodotus, who visited in the fifth century BCE, but such writings may be distorted versions of actual religious traditions or invented images of a frightening enemy.

Transcription of oral stories has therefore been important in reconstruction of the region's early religion. Until a century ago, scholars assumed oral literature was less reliable than written, until Milman Parry showed how storytellers could memorize epic-length poems. It is now established that the oral tradition was accurate in conveying lengthy narratives and that such narratives were the basis for later written work.

Southeastern Europe has seen millennia of migration and invasion, making it difficult to know the genesis of a figure or a story. Celtic influence has been detected from 279 BCE through the establishment of the kingdom of Galatia. The Roman Empire extended to Thrace, whose religion influenced Rome and which received Rome's influence. After the fall of Rome, parts of the region fell under Persian and Turkish control. With the arrival of Christianity and Islam, goddess worship was suppressed or disguised. Thus, in addition to indigenous beliefs, we find a multiplicity of imported religious ideas, symbols, and figures.

Of the region's many cultures, the Indo-European Thracian may have been the richest. Of obscure origin, renowned for beautiful goldwork, Thrace occupied northern Greece, Macedonia, Bulgaria, Albania, and parts of Turkey. Even after the area came under Greek rule, the inhabitants held to their ancient ways, some mythic figures becoming incorporated into the conqueror's religion. Thracian imagery and mythic narrative may also have influenced Slavic mythology.

From 7000 to 200 BCE, while Thrace was thriving, nomadic Scythians and Sarmatians lived on the Russian steppes. Although patrilineal, the Scythians had a tradition of divine ancestral mothers. The Sarmatians claimed they were the descendants of Scythians and Amazon women. Little remains of Sarmatian culture, although some legends may be based upon their myths.

Finally, in Caucasian Georgia, we find a culture where archaic material has been sustained to the present. Although patriarchal and hierarchical, the culture features vivid female divinities that suggest that the feminine was once valued. Incestuous brother/sister divinities are a special feature of the Georgian culture, a pairing that elsewhere indicates a primeval creation.

From this area, once known as Phrygia, come the impressive sagas of the Narts. Although Islamic today, the region sustained pagan beliefs through its bardic tradition. Both men and women sang long sagas about the heroic Narts, ninety-nine descendants of a single miraculous woman. These tales, only recently available in English, reveal powerful feminine characters, some of whom have been connected to the religion of the Scythians and Sarmatians.

SOUTHEASTERN EUROPEAN PANTHEON

Adif The Nart heroine Adif lived in a tower surrounded by darkness. When she opened its windows and revealed her beautiful elbow, night was dispelled. Her home was above a gorge, over which she built a bridge of hand-woven linen. Every morning her husband, Psapeta, drove horses across the bridge to plunder the countryside.

One morning, Psapeta spoke harshly to Adif. The next time he attempted to cross the linen bridge, Adif pulled her elbow inside the tower. In the darkness, he fell to his death. Although she had been angry at his disrespect, Adif mourned the loss of her husband. She sat by his grave and cut herself until she bled.

After a year, the hero Sawseruquo saw Adif mourning in the rain. Opening his cloak, he begged her to take shelter and warmed her cold bleeding hands with his breath. Adif pulled away and went to Psapeta's grave, where she began to dig, intending to pull her husband's corpse out to feed to wild animals. After three shovelfuls, Sawseruquo begged her not to hold on to miserable memories. The couple left the unhappy home and lived happily thereafter. (In some versions of this story, the woman in question is **Setenaya**.) See also **Qaydukh**. (Colarusso)

Apia According to Herodotus, this Scythian earth goddess was the wife of Papaeus, or "great father," a storm or sky god. No images were made of Apia, and no altars were built to her. Herodotus also mentions the hearth goddess Tabiti and Argimpassa, the latter of whom he calls the Scythian version of "heavenly Aphrodite." (Herodotus)

Bendis A Thracian goddess whose worship traveled to Greece, Bendis was depicted holding a twig that granted passage to the underworld. Her name ("to bind") indicated her oversight of marriage, although she was worshiped in orgiastic rituals. A midnight horse race, with riders bearing torches, was part of the Bendideia; a spring month was named for her, Bendideios. The distinction between Bendis and **Kotys** is not clearly established. (Hoddinott; Macurdy; Planeaux; Smith W, 1)

Conkiajgharuna The Georgian **Cinderella** (see Scandinavia) was a mistreated orphan called Conkiajgharuna ("ragamuffin"). Her stepsister always got whatever she wanted, but Conkiajgharuna got nothing but chores. One task was tending the cow,

which the girl did carefully, though weeping from loneliness and hunger. The cow told Conkiajgharuna that one of her horns was made of honey, the other of butter. After that, Conkiajgharuna was always well fed, which angered her stepmother.

When the cow wandered onto the sod roof of a buried house, Conkiajgharuna scrambled behind her. The girl dropped her spindle, which fell down the chimney. Inside, Conkiajgharuna met an old woman whose head was crawling with worms. Although disgusted, the girl flattered the old woman with comments about her admirable cleanliness. In return, the old woman told Conkiajgharuna of a magical spring that would turn her hair golden. Following the hag's directions, the girl came to a stream, where, when she washed her hair, it turned gold. When Conkiajgharuna returned home, her stepmother grew enraged. She refused to let Conkiajgharuna tend the cow after that, sending her own daughter instead.

That girl did exactly as Conkiajgharuna had done, except that when she met the old woman, she could not control her disgust. The woman told her of a special stream with magical powers. When the girl followed the woman's directions, she bathed and turned entirely black. After that, persecution of Conkiajgharuna grew worse, until she thought she could endure no more. Then the cow died, whispering a promise to be always available.

The stepmother gave Conkiajgharuna even more work. But whenever the stepmother went away, the cow provided Conkiajgharuna with robes and a horse. In that garb she dropped a silver slipper, which was found by the king, who demanded its owner be found. He searched without success, finally coming to Conkiajgharuna's house. There the stepsister was seated on a throne-like chair, while Conkiajgharuna was hidden beneath a basket. When the king sat on the basket, Conkiajgharuna poked him with a needle until he leaped up and pulled the basket away, revealing the girl. She claimed the slipper, which fit her perfectly, and she and the king lived happily ever after. (Wardrop)

Cybele This important goddess may descend from Anatolian **Kubaba** (see Eastern Mediterranean), who was associated with mountains and wild cats. A similar goddess, known in Crete as **Rhea**, was associated with Cybele in classical times, as were **Meter** and **Niobe** (see Greek). In Rome, this goddess became known as **Magna Mater**.

Greeks and Romans claimed that self-castration was part of Cybele's worship, yet there is no evidence of the ritual in Cybele's homeland until the Romans. Cybele's reputation as a goddess of emotional excess is also not upheld by her early form. She was depicted as a stout, strong woman of indeterminate age and great serenity. She received the reverence of animals as she strode through the woods. Trees showered fruit, and beneath her feet the earth blossomed. Rivers ran free and clear; birds whirled about her head.

When Cybele appeared as a boulder, she was called Agdos. Greek Zeus attempted to rape her but, unable to penetrate the rock, ejaculated on the ground. Because the soil was Cybele, she conceived a child, the violent hermaphrodite Agdistis. Dionysus drugged him with alcohol and tied him to a tree so that, on awakening, he pulled off his testicles. Agdistis died of the wound, and from his blood sprang up a beautiful tree.

From this tree, the **Nymph** (see Greeks) Nanâ picked a fruit that impregnated her with a son, Attis. When he grew into a man, Attis aroused Cybele's passion. She took him as her lover, bearing him through the world in her lion-drawn chariot. The goddess's love was not enough for Attis, who turned to another woman. So Cybele drove him mad. Attis castrated himself and bled to death beneath a pine tree.

A variant story says Cybele was exposed in infancy but nursed by wild animals. In adulthood, she fell in love with Attis. Reunited with her parents, Cybele went mad with grief when they murdered Attis, wandering until both lovers were deified. Another variant says Agdistis fell in love with Attis, tearing off his genitals to seduce him. Yet another source calls Attis a priest of Cybele who expanded her cult before being killed by a wild boar.

Similar confusion arises from the name Agdistis, sometimes used of a separate character in Cybele's story and sometimes of Cybele herself. Agdistis may have been another goddess absorbed into Cybele; or the name, derived from Mount Agdos, may have been a title of Cybele's. (Borgeaud; Crowfoot; Meyer; Munn; Näsström; Roller; Showerman; Tacheva-Hitova; Vassileva; Vermaseren)

Dali The Ossete had two hunting divinities, Æfsati and his sister Dali. When Æfsati was on duty, hunters made easy kills, but Dali protected the wild herds, especially horned beasts such as sheep, deer, and chamois. If humans came near, she disguised herself as an animal with some unusual feature: a golden horn, a white hide, a huge or tiny size. Hunters made offerings to Dali before a hunt, and afterward when successful.

Sometimes Dali appeared as a captivating woman with gold braids. When a man became Dali's lover, she gave him an arrow tip or ring that brought hunting luck. But the price of Dali's affection was high, for her chosen hunter could never sleep with a human woman again.

One such mate bedded down with a girl. The next night, he saw a huge white deer that led him into high peaks. When he found himself balanced on a rock outcropping above an abyss, the rock crumbled beneath him. He fell but, at the last moment, his foot caught on a branch. There he hung for days. Every time someone tried to rescue him, the mountain grew taller. Finally, realizing he had wronged the goddess, the hunter let himself drop to his death. Some versions of the tale say the hunter's sister was **Tamar**, who let him go to hunt without ritual purification. (Chaudhri; Charachidze; Davidson and Chaudhri)

Falvara The Osset people honored this "saint" whose name combines the names of Flora and Laura—patrons, respectively, of vegetation and of sheep—thus creating a figure of prosperity who was loved for her kindness and patience. As the Ossetes considered themselves descendants of the Scythians, Falvara may encompass their ancient fertility goddess. Her feast day was in August, when each family offered Falvara a sheep. During the rest of the year she was content with a paste of flour, butter, and milk. (Charachidze)

Gundra This Nart woman refused any man unable to win a wrestling match with her; those who lost had their ears cut off and were branded with a hot iron. She had bested ninety-nine young men when Khozhorpas arrived. Because he was handsome, Gundra tried to discourage him from fighting, but he was eager to test himself against her. The earth shook with their strength. After a long match, Khozhorpas slammed Gundra to the ground. At that, **Setenaya** rejoiced, for her daughter had found a husband worthy of her strength. (Colarusso)

Kotys Greeks claimed the Thracians revered a goddess whom they called "patron of debauchery." Kotys's servants celebrated secret festivals called Kotyttia. Kotys has been associated with the best-known goddess of the region, **Cybele**, because of the reputed licentiousness of her festivals. She has also been compared to **Bendis** and **Tabiti**. (Smith W, 1)

Meghazash Daughter of the Nart ocean goddess Psethe Gase, Meghazash flew each night with her two sisters to a golden tree. The tree bore half-red, half-white fruit. A woman who bit the white side bore a daughter, while those who bit the red side had sons. But every time a fruit ripened, Meghazash and her sisters stole it, so the Narts were in danger of dying out. Finally, brave Pizighash shot Meghazash. He followed her to the ocean, where her trail disappeared. So he entered the water, finding himself in the banquet hall of the deep, where Meghazash lay bleeding. She could only be cured by her own shed blood, which Pizighash caught on a handkerchief. He cured her, so she married him. She bore three sons and three daughters.

Years later, dying, she made a prophecy. Seven months later a man would arrive for the first daughter;

after three months, another horseman would come for the second daughter; finally another man would come for the third. The children agreed to follow their mother's wishes.

When the time came, only the youngest son, Warzameg, was willing to let his sisters go away. The older sons made life miserable for Warzameg, especially after he announced that he would marry the most beautiful Nart, **Psatina**. For the rest of the tale, see **Psatina**. (Colarusso)

Mezytkha The Circassian people of the Caucasus saw this divinity sometimes as male, sometimes as female. A hunting goddess, she also controlled the fecundity of humans; women prayed to her when unable to conceive. (Chaudhri)

Mitra Herodotus mentions a sky goddess with this name, which seems to be a feminine form of Mithras, the name of a more familiar Persian divinity. In that language, *mihr* meant "sun," so Mitra may have been an ancient sun goddess who was the twin or double of Mithras, or the goddess may have undergone a redefinition into a male god. Herodotus connected this goddess with Greek **Aphrodite** and Arabic **Al-Lat** (see Eastern Mediterranean). (Herodotus)

Psatina Part of **Meghazash**'s legacy to Warzameg was a horse on which he rode to find a bride. He soon encountered his oldest sister, whom he had helped find a husband by following his mother's peculiar instructions. Her marriage was happy, but her husband was away, attending the wedding of the maiden Psatina. He returned with the shocking news that a mysterious rider had abducted the bride. Warzameg rescued Psatina from a giant, who wounded Warzameg. Psatina married him and bore hero sons. The heroine bears a name that reveals her early identity as a goddess of abundance, for she is "life-giving mother." One of her "sisters" was **Setenaya**; Psatina may be a title of that goddess, as both are described as Warzameg's spouse. (Colarusso)

Qaydukh Qaydukh lived with her husband Psabida, a cattle rustler. Every day he crossed a linen bridge across a river, rolling up the bridge as he crossed. Every night, in order to return, he relied upon Qaydukh to put her diamond ring out the window to lighten the sky.

One day they argued, and he claimed he could find his way without her help. That night he set out, riding Qaydukh's horse on a saddle Qaydukh had made, wearing clothing Qaydukh had sewn. The horse, knowing Psabida had argued with Qaydukh, went the wrong way. Soon Psabida was in a cold land where Qaydukh's cloak offered no protection. He rode until he reached some unprotected cattle. Rounding them up, he ran for home.

It was late when he returned, but because Qaydukh had second sight, she knew he was coming. She put her finger out the window. But when he was halfway across, she remembered his arrogance and withdrew her finger. Psabida fell to his death in the darkness. Qaydukh buried and mourned him as required. The hero Sosruquo saw her grief and swam the river on his horse to offer his sympathy.

Qaydukh was amazed, for her husband could not have swum the river. After Sosruquo rode away, Qaydukh prayed to Gwasha, goddess of waters, to bring a storm. Sosruquo returned and became her husband. See also **Adif**. (Colarusso)

Samdzimari Sister of heroic Giorgi, the Georgian heroine Samdzimari was held captive by evil blacksmiths called Kadzhi. Giorgi, sewn into the skin of a horse, was smuggled into their hideout and killed them. Then he freed Samdzimari and captured a cow with one horn and the secret Kadzhi tools. The metal objects became sacred. The cow's horn became the official measure of a glass of beer, and Samdzimari was promoted to goddess. But later she became demonized as a force of wild sexuality. She took the forms of other women to make love to their mates, transforming herself into a demon when semen was released. Or she disappeared as the man climaxed, leaving terrified sexual partners about whom she sang derisive ballads. Samdzimari was the goddess of marriage, which she invented in order to keep her hero brother close. She also cared for women in childbed and animals as they bore their young. (Charachidze)

Sana The beautiful Nart lady Sana was a warrior when women's hearts were full of war and love. She loved a beautiful boy but killed him in battle. When she realized what she'd done, she killed herself with the same weapon. Their blood flowed together until they became the healing spring Nart Sana, which brought strength and courage to any who drank there. Lady Sana also went by the name of Amazan; she may be a form of **Setenaya**. (Colarusso)

Setenaya The primary Nart goddess Setenaya lived in a labyrinthine city until Warzameg came to court her. Warzameg was old and ugly, while Setenaya was young and fair. When she refused him, he raised an army to abduct her. His strongest, ugliest soldier was the swineherd Argwana, who held Setenaya captive while Warzameg taunted her, threatening to give her away as war booty. Desperate, Setenaya agreed to marry Warzameg. But while she was preparing for the wedding, Argwana raped her. Setenaya said nothing. But that night, her husband saw her bruises and pledged to protect her. He sent two men to Argwana's home. After eight nights of fighting, they killed the rapist and brought his head to Setenaya.

When her husband was away, Setenaya gave birth to the son conceived of rape and gave it to the hunter Shebatin's wife. When Warzameg returned, she made sure he saw her in the yard digging. In response to his questions, she said the child had been stillborn. But she knew the child would live to save her husband when, late in life, he was threatened with poisoning.

Setenaya bore many children. Once she attracted the lust of a herdsman, who saw her bathing and ejaculated in excitement. His sperm shot like an arrow over the water, but missed Setenaya and struck a rock, impregnating it. She picked it up and took it home. She kept it on her stove for nine months, then took it to a blacksmith, who broke the stone and revealed the baby within.

Setenaya took many lovers. Once a man seduced her by crafting two small daggers that could transform themselves into slaves. Desiring the knives, Setenaya slept with their creator. But her husband came home and Setenaya escaped, dressed as a man. Still disguised, she met her husband and showed him the knives, which he immediately coveted. He offered them in exchange for a woman. He replied that he would gladly sleep with her, were he a woman. She revealed her identity then, showing her husband that they were equally likely to be unfaithful.

Setenaya domesticated the rose tree and invented intoxicating beverages; she made the sun stand still in the sky so she could finish weaving; she foresaw the future of newborn children. She had an apple tree with which she healed the sick and old. But when an evil spirit came disguised as a cripple in need of healing, she saw the truth and refused him an apple. In anger, he cut the tree down, so people now age and die. Setenaya appears in various Nart legends, sometimes as an old woman who lusts after men, sometimes as a single woman who gives birth, sometimes as the Amazonian warrior maiden **Sana**. She is an ancestral figure, almost unquestionably a folkloric memory of a major goddess. (Colarusso)

Tabiti The primary Scythian goddess ruled fire and animals. She may have been worshipped in southern Russia before the Scythians. Pottery statues found there show an upright goddess bearing a child. The Scythians showed her as half serpent, often seated between a raven and a dog. She may have been the same as the otherwise-unnamed "Mistress of the Woodlands," ancestral mother of the Scythians. (Herodotus; Hubbs; Jettmar)

Tamar Georgian Tamar rode through the air on a golden-bridled serpent. In her mountain palace, built by storks and nightingales, Tamar kept as a slave the morning star, master of winter. Whenever he escaped, snow fell, but when she captured him again, summer came to the land. While a virgin, Tamar was impregnated by a beam of light that penetrated her castle's walls. After a year, she bore a son, but she abandoned him in the woods, where he was raised by deer and became an angel. A sky goddess who ruled weather and seasons, Tamar also controlled the sea by covering it with straw or by setting it alight. (Charachidze)

SLAVIC PEOPLES

Slavic Europe reaches from the Baltic to the Aegean, from the eastern steppes across the Carpathian Mountains. Archaeology shows that a Neolithic agricultural people dominated the region in approximately 5500–3500 BCE. Numerous sites attest to the high level of this culture, whose substantial villages often centered on areas where copper was mined and worked.

Then the region saw an influx of Indo-European speakers, with both Celtic and Germanic tribes attested by 1000 BCE. The Slavs come into written history in the second century CE, then disappear to reemerge in the sixth century. These scanty records suggest speakers of a proto-Slavic tongue settled in central Europe sometime in the early part of the common era. Proto-Slavs left their unknown homelands, driven by invasions of central Asian peoples including the Huns and Magyars. Within a few hundred years, these migrants had divided into west Slavs (Polish, Czech, Slovak, and Wendish); southern Slavs (Slovenian, Serbo-Croatian, Macedonian, and Bulgarian); and east Slavs (Russian and Ukrainian).

We do not know who the proto-Slavs were, for "Slavic" describes a linguistic identity. Speakers of Slavic languages may be ethnically Slav, mixed, or not of Slavic descent, for Turks and others intermarried with ethnic Slavs and began to employ their language. Slavic mythology absorbed figures, narratives, and themes from non-Slavic religions. Goddesses of the new arrivals were accorded a high status denied to indigenous goddesses, who were demoted to spirits or even demons. Some mythic figures were adopted into Christianity as saints, maintaining symbols, rites, seasonal holidays, and sacred sites. Others continued to exist as officially unacknowledged powers, so some Slavs have a "double faith" (*duoeveri*) in which conflicting worldviews are held simultaneously.

Written sources are meager compared to the richness of Slavic oral lore. In Russia, professional storytellers kept mythic tales alive. After the eighteenth century, the practice ceased to be supported by the wealthy, but peasants still sustained ancient traditions. Among the renowned storytellers were women who preserved important goddess myths and folklore. Then, in the nineteenth century, a folkloric revival led to recording and publishing many tales. This movement intersected with Slavophilism, which embraced folklore as a means of promoting ethnic identity.

Finally, mythic material was conveyed in crafts and in ritual. Embroidery is especially important to Slavic goddess studies, for goddess images are still worked on household items and apparel. Slavic rituals included honoring natural places such as mountains, rivers, and boulders. Trees were especially important, whether in the form of significant isolated oaks, elders, and walnuts, or as sacred forests to which entry was forbidden.

For nearly a century Slavic research was rarely published outside the Soviet Union. That, plus active discouragement of religion in the secular Soviet state, meant some ancient practices were lost or suppressed. However, with the dissolution of the USSR, reclamation of religious heritage has emerged. This has led to political tensions in some areas but a greater openness to alternative viewpoints. Interest in Slavic paganism has led to the establishment of the Slaviantso movement, predominantly outside the region, which promotes a religious worldview centered on the feminine earth. Some contemporary practitioners propound a form of revived Slavic religion that posits the "earth" not as the planet but as a homeland for the Slavic people, which can be construed in nationalistic terms.

SLAVIC PANTHEON

Avdotya One of the few Slavic goddesses referenced by classical authors, who called her after Greek

Artemis, Avdotya also appears in Russian heroic songs and epics. She had a somewhat treacherous character, perhaps reflecting her origin as a guardian of the woodland animals. Her legend tells how she was sought by a prince, Ivan Godinovich, although she was only the daughter of a merchant. She was beautiful and exotic, with a swan-like white complexion and white swan wings. After becoming engaged to Ivan, Avodtya conspired with his rival, despite which Ivan was victorious in battle against him. In retaliation, Ivan cut off Avdotya's arms, lips, and feet, claiming they had led her astray from her duty. Then, excited by his power, he cut off her head.

In another legend, Avdotya appears as a resplendent white swan with golden skin who floated on the water wearing a pearl-and-gold crown. Despite her beauty, the hunter Mikailo aimed to kill her, until she threatened him with limitless bad luck. Then she turned into a lovely woman, with whom Mikailo fell in love. The couple vowed that if one were to die before they wed, the other would go to the otherworld and stay there three months. Avdotya (here called Marya) died, and Mikailo went to the otherworld. Once on the earth again, the girl ran off with the tsar, and when Mikailo caught up with his escaped bride, he beheaded her. Behind the violence of the folktales, scholars have detected a lost bird goddess of the region, perhaps originally called Obida ("insult") or Dyevitsa ("maiden"), who lives on the river Don. She may be related to the Tatar swan maiden Tjektschäkäi, who could only be killed if an enemy found her external soul and destroyed it. She may have been absorbed into Greek mythology as **Iphigenia**. (Manning)

Baba Yaga This powerful Russian seasonal goddess survived as a folkloric witch who flies through the air in a mortar, rowing with a pestle, sweeping the air with a broom. A shape-shifter, Baba Yaga appeared as a snake, a bird, or a pincushion, but most typically as a bony, big-toothed, iron-nosed, blue-skinned hag. She lived in the last sheaf of grain, which concentrated the force of fertility; the woman who bound it bore a child that winter.

Except during harvest, Baba Yaga lived in the forest, in a rotating hut mounted on chickens' legs. She liked to scare people to death, then make a meal out of them. When she lay on her cottage floor, she stretched from one end to the other, her nose sticking through the ceiling. When she went out, the winds roared and the earth shook.

Baba Yaga gave her name to "woman's summer" or Bab'e Lyeto, when spiderwebs predict the winter's length. In the Carpathian Mountains, the season is called Bab'in Moroz, "woman's frost," because of a legend that winter's sudden arrival left a witch exposed on the road, where she froze into stone. (Alexander; Gimbutas 1989; Hubbs; Ivanits; Johns; Matossian 1973; Simonov; Ralson; Warner)

Berehinia Each spring, a girl dressed in red scarves and crowned with flowers represented this Russian goddess who awakened seeds with gentle moisture. Berehinia's name may derive from a term for "protection." It may also mean "riverbank," for Berehinia is often depicted as a mermaid, in which form she was sometimes conflated with the **Rusálki**. Rituals to her involved hanging distaffs or spindles in trees near rivers, which pleased Berehinia because she was a spinner.

Berehinia was also a goddess of air. Embroideries show her accompanied by the magical Firebird, which sheltered her beneath its wings. Other embroideries depict Berehinia holding birds, perhaps indicating a ritual in which girls offered dough bird sculptures to the sun. In her solar and her watery manifestations, Berehinia produced healthy crops. She may descend from an early goddess of abundance. (Ivanits; Kelly 1984, 1989; Welters)

Boginka The Polish water nymph appeared in many forms: as an old woman with long breasts that she threw over her shoulder; as a naked laundress with pig teeth; as a beautiful woman who lured away pregnant women, then stole their babies. The Boginka was usually cruel, although she could appear as a collective of kindly fate goddesses who brought good luck to the newborn. (Kmeietowicz)

Bogoroditsa This term, meaning "Mother of God," was used of the Virgin **Mary** (see Eastern Mediterranean). This apparently orthodox devotion hides the traditional reverence Slavic people felt for the fruitful earth (see **Mokosh, Zemyna**). Such icons as the Black Madonna of Czestochawa derive from ancient images of the goddess, whose black skin represented the moist earth of spring. Reverence for Mary far outstrips that offered her son in Slavic lands, suggesting continuing influence of the ancient divine mother. (Ivanits)

Colleda The Serbian goddess of the winter solstice was honored with the ceremonial log burned as sunlight drained away. When daylight was reborn, sweet cakes were served to children who begged favors for the "sweet maiden goddess," who promised the revival of growth. In northern Russia, this goddess appears as Koliada, a woman who recreated the world each winter solstice by embroidering a new one. In Slavic parts of the former Yugoslavia, the goddess of time was Koleda, in whose honor groups sang songs on New Year's Day. (Ivanits; Mihanovich)

Dolya The Russian fate goddess lived behind the stove. When she was in a fine mood, she was Dolya, the old lady who brought good luck. When annoyed, she was Nedolya or Licho, the hag of bad fortune who dreamed up misfortunes. Occasionally she appeared as a young woman; she presided over birth, when her prophetic powers were invoked. She controlled health and wealth, but not inner happiness. (Dexter 1990; Gimbutas 2003; Machal)

Dziwozony Throughout the Slavic lands, legends abound of wild women who lived in woodlands and who knew nature's secrets, especially those of herbal medicine. They were of unusual appearance, although the details differed according to region. In Poland, the Dziwozony had large heads, long fingers, chicken feet, and red bodies; they lived in underground burrows and emerged to tend their productive farms. The Dziwozony made excellent hardworking and sensual wives with a passion for motherhood, but if one grew bored with a human husband, she tickled him to death. The Bulgarian Divi-te Ženi was notable for her poor pronunciation and the size of her breasts. She lived on licorice root and stolen corn, and when she baked bread, the forest smelled of it. She could be wooed, but she disappeared at the words "wild woman." (Gimbutas 2003; Machal)

Elena A Russian folktale begins when a young man was ordered to find a magical Firebird. A friendly wolf helped him find the bird, but the owner awakened during the theft and demanded a horse in recompense. The young man found the horse, but the owner awakened as he was stealing it and demanded the beautiful Elena. When the hero met Elena, he fell in love with her. The wolf, a shape-shifter, stood in for the horse and the Firebird. This allowed the youth to return home with Elena, mounted on the real horse and carrying the real Firebird. But his brothers set upon him and killed him, stealing Elena and the other treasures. The wolf magically revived him in time to prevent Elena's marriage to one of the murderous brothers. (Yovino-Young)

Grozdanka A Bulgarian story tells how the sun fell in love with this young woman. Her mother called her Grozdanka, "ill featured," in hopes the sun would never notice her. But one summer day the sun dropped a golden swing from the sky. When Grozdanka took her turn, she swung until she reached the sky, where the sun won her heart. (Georgieva; Ralson)

Kamennye Baby "Stone Woman" took the form of a rough-hewn stone whose base was sunk into the ground and whose upper section showed a featureless woman. No myths describe the statues, which appear to be early goddess figures. (Kmeietowicz)

Kostrubonko This Russian goddess was impersonated each spring by a young woman who would lie on the earth as though dead. People of her village would form a ring around the girl, singing mournfully "Kostrubonko is dead, our loved one is dead." Then the girl leapt up, accompanied by the songs of her friends and family, who rejoiced, "Come to life has our Kostrubonko!" This figure may be related to the similar one of **Kupala**, despite the difference in seasons. (Frazer)

Kupala The Slavic goddess of summer solstice took her name from a word that means "to bathe," for her worshippers bathed in rivers and in dew gathered on June mornings. Water healed as well as purified; to gain relief from illness, one tossed bread into a stream while praying for health. The name is also given to a squatting goddess on Slavic embroideries.

In Russia and the Ukraine, Kupala was honored in a summer ritual in which young men and women leaped over a bonfire, dragging a straw maiden. The next day, everyone bathed the figure, which was released to drift downstream, removing evil from the village. Such images were also constructed in Serbia and other Slavic countries. Dressed in a fine gown and decked with garlands, the Kupala image was hung from a tree in which all but the upper branches were trimmed, so the tree formed a green-haired woman. Only women performed these rituals.

Kupala ruled herbs. Purple loosestrife was her favorite; its roots had the power to banish demons if gathered at dawn on the summer solstice. The flowering fern granted its possessor the power to understand the language of trees, which on the night before solstice wandered rootless through the world.

This divinity has been described as a god named Ivan Kupalo, a derivation that appears to come from

association of the goddess's feast with that of St. John (Ivan) the Baptist on June 24. (Hubbs)

Lada A daughter of the sea, Lada drew the attention of the sun god while she was rowing a golden boat with silver oars. He wanted to marry Lada, but her father refused. So the sun spread gorgeous clothes along the riverbanks to attract Lada's attention, then kidnapped her. Her father raised storms, to no avail. Lada became the sun's wife and the mother of the god of springtime, Iarilo. Like him, she represented the forces of emerging vegetation. She was honored with tinsel-decked clay larks, smeared with honey, carried in procession by celebrants. (Dexter 1990; Ralson; Simonov)

Lisunki The Lisunki was a hairy, big-breasted woman who lived in the woods. Folklore tells of naked babies left behind by forgetful Lisunki mothers. If a passerby covered the infant with a cloth until the errant mother returned, the Lisunki offered a generous reward. Similarly, if a traveler found a hairy woman giving birth in the woods, he should cover the child as it emerged, being careful not to pray or make Christian gestures. (Ivanits; Ralson)

Maslenitsa As spring approached, Russian people dressed a straw maiden in rags, carried her out to the fields, and burned her with much singing and dancing. Pancakes were prepared, representing the strengthening sun. Eating and drinking in excess was believed to encourage the earth to produce abundantly. This figure may be connected to a winter goddess, Marena, and the burning may represent the banishing of winter from the land. In Poland, Marzana, "Old Woman Winter," was embodied in an effigy carried through town and destroyed to represent the end of winter's hunger. (Alexander; Hatto; Ivanits)

Mokosh When the Rus emperor Vladimir I erected statues of the Slavic pantheon in 980 CE, only one goddess was honored. She was Mokosh, "moistness," the earth mother. Although Vladimir converted to

Christianity and destroyed the idols, this did not deter his subjects from continuing to offer Mokosh reverence. As late as the sixteenth century, Christian chronicles complained that Slavic women still "went to Mokosh," for she was preeminently a woman's divinity. Her image remains strong in Slavic lands, now disguised as the Christian **Mary** (see Eastern Mediterranean) or as **Paraskeva**. Because Mokosh was a spinner, ceremonial cloths bore her embroidered image: a woman with a large head, bearing a spindle. Her worshippers envisioned her spinning the threads of life. She was also the ruler of death, as the dark earth into which the dead are placed.

Although little is known of her worship, Mokosh has been interpreted as a force of fertility. In addition to being envisioned as a strong matron, she was represented by stones, particularly breast-shaped boulders. People prayed to these stones for health and prosperity. The stones had power over the land as well as people: In the nineteenth century in the Ukraine, archaeologists moved some Mokosh stones and, when a drought ensued, were blamed for it. The stones were restored, and fertility returned.

Rain was Mokosh's milk, so the Czech people invoked her in times of drought. This connection of earth and water was emphasized in myths connecting Mokosh with the flowering spring, when she was discovered sleeping in a cave by the spring god, Iarilo (see **Lada**), with whom she conceived the fruits of the earth. Another myth tells how, in the first springtime, she conceived a child by a human man. The boy became Mokosh's first priest and offered sacrifices of sheep, which she rewarded with dreams of how to shear and weave. He established the format of sacrifice, with the first offering made to Mokosh and the fertility goddess Pripelaga.

The source of this goddess has not been established. Some argue she was originally Finno-Ugric (see **Jumala**). Others believe Mokosh was an aboriginal goddess from the area where she was first recorded, the region of Kiev. The difference between her and the other Russian earth goddess, **Zemyna**, is not clearly established. (Gimbutas 1971; Ivanits; Hubbs; Simonov; Znayenko; Warner)

Mora In Serbian belief, stray pieces of straw were Mora in disguise. The Polish version of her name, Mara ("demon"), lives on in our language as "nightmare," for she was the night-riding witch who strangled victims and sucked their blood. Although some legends say Mora only had power during the winter solstice, most myths show her active throughout the year.

The Russians called her Kikimora, a tiny woman who lived behind the stove. The family knew she was present in case of danger or threat, when she would make strange thumping sounds. Otherwise, she was an invisible pest who tormented women by snarling yarn if they did not pray before laying down the spindle.

Mora could turn herself into a butterfly and hang over the lips of sleeping people, bringing bad dreams. She could become a hank of horsehair or a horse. A Serbian folktale tells of a man who kept running from a frightening Mora. Finally, almost dead from exhaustion, he collapsed in the home of a man who, awakened by his guest's calls, found a horse's tail suffocating the sleeper. The host cut the tail, and the next day the two found the corpse of the horse on which the traveler had arrived—the Mora in disguise.

Behind this witch figure is a fate goddess; the thread she used to strangle her victims was the thread of life, which she had earlier spun and cut. Anyone who saw Mora took it as an omen of death. It is unclear whether the goddess Smert, who has many of the same attributes, was a separate goddess. (Dexter 1990; Ivanits; Gimbutas 1989; Machal; Ralson)

Navky In Slavic lands, children who drowned or babies who died in infancy haunted their parents for seven years. Then they were transformed into water-dwelling women who called out to passing travelers. When the passerby approached, the Navky leaped on him and tickled him to death. (Machal)

Orisnitsi The Bulgarian fate goddesses, often considered sisters, appeared as three white-cloaked women ranging from twenty to thirty-five years old. They lived at the end of the world but every time a child was born appeared to predict its fate. Once a king, learning his daughter would be killed by a snakebite, had her shut up in a tower where no snakes could reach her. After she was married, her husband brought her grapes. A snake hidden among them killed her. (Georgieva)

Paraskeva After Christianization, **Mokosh** was transformed into Saint Paraskeva, a Roman virgin put to death during the reign of the emperor Diocletian. Because her name means "Friday" in Greek, she became "Mother Friday" in eastern Slavic lands, where her rituals and feasts were identical to those of Mokosh. Because Paraskeva was a spinner, she demanded that no one spin, weave, or mend on her feast day, October 28. Offenders were blinded by dust or had itchy hemp thrown into their eyes. Tales abound of punishments she meted out to those who refused to honor her: a woman was turned into a frog, another's fingers became blistered, yet another's eyes failed.

Just as women were the main worshippers of Mokosh, so Paraskeva was a women's saint. Her feast day coincided with the beginning of the marriage season in Russia. Thus, despite being a virgin, she was invoked as patron of fertile marriages. Paraskeva was honored at wells and springs, where miracle-working icons appeared spontaneously. In addition to her feast day, Paraskeva was invoked during agricultural stress, such as drought and insect invasions. (Hubbs; Ivanits; Matossian 1973)

Percunatele This Polish figure probably derives from the thunder goddess of neighboring Balts (see **Saulė**). The name was adopted as an epithet of the Virgin **Mary** (see Eastern Mediterranean), who was called Maria Percunatele. Because many Slavic goddesses were conflated with the Christian madonna, it can be difficult to distinguish the goddesses she absorbed. (Ralson)

Pizamar This Slavic goddess was originally a woman beloved of the god Svarozhich. Because the gods ruled against marriage between gods and mortals, their love was doomed. She attempted suicide, walking to a cliff every night intending to throw herself off. But the fairy Nochnitsa put her to sleep every night, so she was never able to take her life. The goddesses Chors and **Lada** took pity on Pizamar and decided to steal the mead of immortality from Podaga, its guardian goddess. Feeding it to Pizamar as she slept, the goddesses made her a divinity who entertained other gods so joyously with music and dance that she became goddess of all the arts. (Hudec)

Poldunica In eastern Europe, the goddess of midday was a white lady who floated about the fields on gusts of wind, killing people with a touch. Each region offered slight variations in her legend. In Moravia, she was a white-gowned old woman with horse hoofs, staring eyes, and wild hair, although sometimes she appeared as a twelve-year-old girl who carried a whip and killed anyone she encountered. In Poland, the extraordinarily tall Poldunica carried a sickle, asking riddles of those abroad at midday, then reaping those who could not answer. In Russia, she was beautiful, something her victims noticed just before she twisted their heads, bringing intense pain or death. In Serbia, she guarded crops, staying in the fields while everyone else went to lunch; if one went to find out what she was doing, she talked relentlessly and, if the visitor turned away, killed him. She descends from an ancient protective spirit of vegetation. (Gimbutas 2003; Ivanits; Machal; Ralson)

Pszeniczna Matka The "wheat mother" of Poland was a vegetation goddess who also appeared as Owsiana Matka ("oat mother") or Żytnia Matka ("rye mother"), depending on the grain in which she was embodied. She was honored with a wreath made from the last harvested stalks, worn by a maiden during harvest season and kept safe until spring, when the wreath was crumbled and used for planting. In the area of Gdansk, the person who cut the last sheaf made it into a doll that was kept through the year. An alternative name for this figure was Baba ("old woman"), a term used in Czechoslovakia as well as Poland. (Kmeietowicz)

Rozanica Early Slavic Christian texts warn against offering bread, mead, and cottage cheese to Rozanica and her consort, Rod. The pair represented forces of human incarnation: Rod, the generic power of life and sexual reproduction; Rozanica, the individualization of that power. In the singular, Rozanica was an ancestral mother, her name meaning "mother," "heritage," and "destiny." In the plural, she becomes Rozanicy, all deified ancestral mothers. The winter solstice and the day of an infant's birth are her feast days. Some researchers believe this figure to be identical to **Sudice**.

Russian researchers propose the name Rozhanitza for the Paleolithic divinity of the steppes, a goddess of deer and the hunt, a horned goddess of successful childbirth. Her image appears in Russian folk art as a woman with spread legs in what is called the "**Kupala** position," after the midsummer goddess. Some depictions show daughters hiding in Rozhanitza's skirt. Others show the goddess giving birth to deer as she reaches upward, her body forming an X shape. (Gimbutas 2003; Hubbs; Ivanits; Kelly 1989; Machal; Rybakov)

Rusálki These Russian water spirits began their existence as women who drowned or committed suicide. Thereafter, they haunted the land, rising from streams each spring naked and wild haired to beg bits of white linen. After cleaning the land, the Rusálki performed dances, wearing white tunics or robes of green leaves, their green-haired heads decked with crowns. A man could lose his soul witnessing the dances of the Rusálki, or they might tickle him to death.

The Rusálki had the power to grant or withhold fertility, for they poured spring rains from their magical horns. Water was important to the Rusálki, for if their hair dried out, they died. After the end of June, the Rusálki were dangerous, for if one trod on their linens then, death or illness resulted. When summer was over, the Rusálki retreated to nests, where they hibernated.

On Rusal'naia Week in early summer, rural Russians decked their houses with garlands and left offerings of omelets. Young girls threw garlands into rivers to detect future husbands' identities. Then straw figures in the form of Rusálki were ceremonially dismembered. Such rituals indicate the power the Rusálki once had, as does the probability that their name gave rise to the name of their land, Russia. (Agapkina; Welters; Hubbs; Ivanits; Kelly 1989; Machal; Netting; Ralson; Rybakov; Sokolov; Warner)

Sirin This minor goddess was shown in Russian embroideries with the tail and body of a bird, but breasts and head of a woman. Often confused with the Vila, she was associated with luck as the "Bird of Joy." A similar figure, Alconest, was the "Bird of Sorrow." (Kelly 1989)

Snegurochka The heroine of a Russian fairy tale often known as "The Snow Maiden," Snegurochka was a little girl found one winter by a childless couple. She filled their lives with happiness and warmth. But human warmth was the only kind the girl could tolerate, for when spring came she melted away. Behind this folkloric figure hides an ancient winter goddess who changed form with the passing of her season (see **Maslenitsa**). Seasonal celebrations ritually reenacted the struggle between winter and spring, with associations of a struggle between death and life. (Hatto)

Solntse The Slavic sun goddess lived with the moon in a three-bedroom house in the sky. One room was hers, one his, and the children—all the stars in the sky— bunked in the last. (Dexter)

Sreca In Serbia, the fate goddess Sreca appeared as a maiden spinning golden thread; this vision meant good fortune. Nesreca, the same goddess appearing as a sleepy old woman with bloodshot eyes, brought bad luck. Sreca is probably the same divinity found in Russia as **Dolya**. (Machal)

Sudice The goddesses of fate were beautiful old women with white skin and white clothes, who wore white kerchiefs and necklaces of gold and silver. They glistened as they walked, sometimes decking themselves with garlands or carrying lit candles. Sudice, who could appear as a single or multiple goddess, was most active at birth, when a newborn's destiny was sealed. For that reason, gifts of candles, bread, and salt were offered. Sometimes there are said to be three sisters named Sudice, each of whom spoke a fortune as the child was born. The oldest spoke last, and her words could never be countermanded. (Machal)

Treska The Bulgarians saw disease as a feminine force with this name. Ogneya ("fiery"), Ledeya ("icy cold), and Glouheya ("deaf") were sisters who rose from the sea at time's beginning, intent upon wreaking havoc on humankind. They tormented women in childbed, when newborns could be killed easily, but they also afflicted those who neglected seasonal rituals. (Georgieva)

Vasilisa Vasilisa was born to a loving mother who died when the girl was eight. On her deathbed, the mother gave Vasilisa a doll, warning her to keep it secret. If the girl were in trouble, the mother whispered, she should ask the doll for advice. After her mother's death, Vasilisa's father married a widow with two children who tormented Vasilisa, so she turned to the doll for advice.

One day, the stepmother sent Vasilisa to get a candle from the fierce **Baba Yaga**. When Vasilisa consulted her doll, she was told to obey, but to take the doll with her. The girl walked all night, passing a rider dressed in white riding a white horse at the moment dawn broke; then a red-dressed rider riding a red-saddled horse as the sun rose; and finally a rider on a black horse who brought night. Baba Yaga's home was frightening, bolted with skeleton arms and locked with a skull. But Baba Yaga took pity on the girl and offered help, if Vasilisa would become a servant for a few days.

Baba Yaga gave impossible orders. Vasilisa consulted her doll, which told her to go to sleep. The girl obeyed and, when she awoke, all the assigned work was completed. The same happened for several nights, until Baba Yaga grew suspicious and, giving her a flaming skull, sent Vasilisa away.

When she got home, Vasilisa gave the stepmother the candle. The skull flamed up, killing the stepmother and her children. Then Vasilisa found a home with a woman who sewed shirts for the king. The king fell in love with Vasilisa, and she ended her life in the palace, her doll with her. This Russian figure may be a goddess who survived in folkloric form. (Alexander; Haney; Hubbs; Ralson; Warner)

Ved'ma The term "Vyed'ma" formerly described a prophet whose image degenerated into a scary witch who rode a rake through the sky after sprinkling herself with magical water. A shape-shifter, Ved'ma could appear young and beautiful, or old and fierce. In either form she was said to know healing properties of plants, which she would share with those who pleased her. (Ralson)

Vesna Every spring, Vesna seduced the lightning god, Perun, and their mating brought an end to winter. Her twin was Morena, the winter goddess who was barren except for one son, Triglav, god of war, whose father was dark Chernobog. The final Slavic seasonal goddess was Zhiva, the summer goddess who ruled over crops. There was no goddess of autumn, for the one who would have become its ruler, the unnamed daughter of the moon goddess Chors, was bewitched at birth and disappeared. Vesna and Morena compete for control of autumn weather. (Hudec)

Vila This woodland spirit was a fair-skinned, winged woman with golden hair that fell to her feet. She lived in the woods, where she guarded animals and plants; she also cleaned streams of rubble and assured sufficient rainfall. Hunters had to be wary of women who spoke the languages of animals, for the Vila was possessive of her wild herds. Should an animal be injured or killed, the Vila mutilated the offender or danced him to death. Alternatively, the Vila might bury him in rocks by starting an avalanche or cause him to keel over with a heart attack.

There were three categories of Vila: cloud, mountain, and water. Most legendary was the cloud Vila. Born on a day of misty rain, she knew secrets of healing and herbcraft. Should a human wish to learn her skills, the applicant appeared before sunrise on a Sunday of the full moon. Drawing a circle with a birch twig, she placed several horsehairs, a hoof, and some manure inside the circle, then stood with her right foot on the hoof calling the Vila. Should the spirit be greeted as a sister, the Vila would grant any wish.

Mountain Vile assisted with the care of orphans and needy children. Water Vile, who had power over free-flowing streams, could make water sweet or poisonous at will. Some legends say the Vile were originally human and either died tragically or were punished in the afterlife for bad behavior. But more likely, the Vile were powers of nature in feminine form. (Agapkina; Barber; Dexter 1990; Georgieva; Gimbutas 1971, 2003; Hubbs; Machal; Pocs)

Vodni Panny These Slavic water goddesses were beautiful, sad, huge-breasted women dressed in translucent robes. They lived under the rivers in crystal castles surrounded by silver paths; they may be **Rusálki**. (Machal)

Yevdokia The Russian spirit of spring, this figure was especially connected with the date of March 14, the feast of Yevdokia the whistler, because marmots waken from hibernation and make whistling sounds. The day was considered the first day of spring, when ritual pastries called larks were made with cranberries pressed into dough to represent birds' eyes marking the return of migrating birds. Women would dress in their best clothes but tuck in their hems, to represent holding the grief of the winter. Then they walked from the house to the gate, where they opened their hems and shook

out their troubles. Charms were placed on the front door to avert gossip and envy; women desirous of children went to the hillsides and placed garlands there, praying for offspring. (Rozhnova)

Zemyna It was a sin to strike the earth with iron implements before March 25, for the earth was pregnant, and one does not strike a pregnant woman. Her name was Mati Syra Zemyna ("moist Mother Earth"), and she was the source of power and strength. When the Russians swore oaths, they did so by eating soil or placing lumps of dirt on their heads; when they married, each party swallowed a bit of earth.

The Russians also cared for the earth's honor by demanding that anyone who spit on her apologize. They acknowledged Zemyna's prophetic powers; to know how the harvest would turn out, one dug a hole in the ground and placed an ear to it. The sound of a full sleigh meant a good harvest; the tinkling of an empty one meant trouble.

Zemyna's greatest festival was held at the summer solstice, when families bathed in streams in celebration of the moisture that had fructified the earth. Zemyna was also invoked when poor weather threatened the harvest. The celebrant turned in the four directions and poured libations on the earth, then prayed to be purified by earth's flames, to be protected from bad weather, and to be shielded against unseasonable cold. Singing Zemyna's praises, one poured oil on the earth, then smashed the oil container.

Zemyna appeared as an ancestral mother in the story of a farmer who, hearing a snake hiss, tried to kill it. But the snakeskin fell off like a multicolored dress, revealing a naked woman named Zemyna. She lived with him and bore his children. But then Zemyna found the dress the farmer had hidden. Putting it on, she bit her husband and children to death, then escaped into the wild. This goddess may be the same as the Baltic goddess with an identical name, **Žemyna**, as the territories of the goddesses are nearby; the distinction between Zemyna and the other Slavic earth goddess,

Mokosh, is also not clear. (Gimbutas 1989; Hubbs; Robbins 1980; Simonov)

Zorya There were three Slavic dawn goddesses: Zorya ("light") Utrennyaya, the morning star; Zorya Vechernyaya, the evening star; and the midnight Zorya. All had the same job: to guard a chained dog that tried to eat the constellation Ursa Minor. If the chain broke and the dog got loose, the universe would end. The Zoryas also guarded warriors, appearing as maidens with veils who shielded their favorites in battle. When described as a single goddess, Zorya lived on an island just east of sunrise. In Serbia, as Zvezda Dennitsa, she was the moon's wife and the morning star. (Ralson)

THE AMERICAS

NORTH AMERICA

North America's eight ecological regions serve as useful divisions in discussing more than 500 Native American cultures. In this section, we consider myths from people of the northeastern woodlands, the Southeast's forested mountains, the forests and savannahs of the Great Lakes, the buffalo-rich Great Plains, the southwestern deserts, the mountainous central West, coastal California, and the northwestern Pacific coast.

The continent's northern portion was covered by glaciers until approximately 14,000 BCE, and a landmass connected it to Asia. Humans may have traveled from Asia prior to glaciation, to populate Central and South America. The evidence is far from clear, but scholars agree that as glaciers melted, people in Alaska and Canada migrated southward. When Christopher Columbus arrived in 1492 CE, tens of millions of people occupied the continent. We know little of these prehistoric people's languages, myths, or customs, although historical cultures probably inherited from them.

Each region's environmental and geographical features affected myths. Corn-raising southeastern farmers envisioned different goddesses than salmon fishers in the Pacific Northwest. In addition, social and familial structures varied widely, from matrilineal clans in the Northwest to patriarchal groups on the Plains, with attendant mythic differences. Even within regions, there was as much diversity as commonality, so each nation's myths should be examined individually.

In the northeastern woodlands, which extended from Québec to coastal Virginia, we find agriculturalists of two major language groups. The first, the Algonquian of New England and Canada, was the language of the Micmac, Passamaquoddy, Penobscott, Malecites, Mohicans, and Delaware. The second, the Iroquoian group, included the five nations that formed the Haudenosaunee Confederacy: the Seneca, Cayuga, Onandaga, Oneida, and Mohawk. Later the Tuscarora, driven north by British settlement, joined the confederacy, as did the Susquehanna. These cultures are of special interest because each matrilineally organized clan had its own longhouse, owned by women and shared by related families. The culture's mythology, with its prominent creatrix, reflects the high social status of women.

Another significant area for the study of goddess mythology stretches from the Atlantic to the Mississippi River, and from the Ohio River valley to the Gulf of Mexico. The fertile region was inhabited by important cultures, including the Mississippian, whose ancient monuments still stand; the matrilineal Natchez appear to descend from them. The region's rich land attracted Europeans, resulting in early destruction of some groups, while others maintained control of traditional lands until the 1800s. Among the latter were the "Five Civilized Tribes" (Cherokee, Chickasaw, Chocktaw, Creek, and Seminoles), whose confederacy promoted shared interests. They attempted to assimilate to European culture while retaining Native values but were finally driven westward in the infamous "Trail of Tears."

To the north, a different scenario played out along the Great Lakes, whose nations were pressured by migrants fleeing the European invasion. Oneida from New York moved into the territory of the Wisconsin Ho-Chunk, while Plains Sioux were driven northward into regions previously inhabited by the Ojibway/Anishinaubae. Although some of these nations had come into contact with French priests and voyageurs early in the seventeenth century, only in the early 1800s did large numbers of European settlers move in.

The most widespread Great Lakes culture was the Algonquin. A large and linguistically related group, the Algonquins of the Great Plains include the Anishinaubae, Algonquin, Menominee, and Ho-Chunk (Winnebago) nations. Prairie Algonquins include the Kickapoo and Shawnee. They lived in houses built by women, supporting themselves through a mixture of hunting (typically men's work) and agriculture (typically women's). Many "traditional American" foods were discovered and refined by Algonquin women, including hominy, maple syrup, and the "three sisters" of corn, beans, and squash.

Southward ranged the Great Plains people who followed buffalo, carrying teepees on travois behind sturdy Indian ponies. Of the region's nations, the best known is the Sioux, who struggled to preserve their lands under such leaders as Sitting Bull. Similarly well known because of their fierce defense of their lands were the Apache and the Comanche. Other Plains groups include Arikara, Mandan, Pawnee, Blackfoot, Cree, Crow, and Kiowa. In these societies, women made buffalo-skin covers for the teepees, meticulously joining between three and thirty hides to make a single home. In religion, women's contributions are emphasized in myths of the goddess who brought culture and religion.

To the southwest, goddess scholars find a wealth of important myths. Although dry and rugged, the region has been home to nations that cultivated corn, introduced from Mexico, as well as beans and squash. The low rainfall in the area required the use of irrigation, ingeniously designed to take advantage of recurrent floods. Around 1400 CE, the Anasazi ("ancient ones" in Navajo), a highly refined urban culture, became the dominant force. Then, possibly because of drought, their place was taken by modern groups, including the Hopi, Zuñi, Yavapai, and Mojave. Athabaskan people moved from the north to settle in the region; these include Navajo and Mescalero (Apache). Together, these people are known as "Pueblo Indians" after the region's cliff dwellings.

West of the Pueblo people stretched the culturally dense region of California, where over 100 nations lived when Europeans first made contact. Some estimate that 15 percent of all Native Americans lived in California, despite the fact that it is only 5 percent of the continent's landmass. Most central Californian groups descend from people who moved to the area in approximately 5000 BCE, creating various cultures: Karok and Shasta in east-central California; Miwok, Maidu, Yokut, and Wintun near the Pacific coast; and the "mission Indians" (so-called by Spanish missionaries) to the south, including the Cahuila, Luiseno, and Serrano. Although religion varied widely in the area, a common experience among women was seclusion during the menses, a time of power and danger.

North and east of California, the continent opens out into high mountains and broad river valleys. In the arid Great Basin, centered around the Great Salt Lake, lived Shoshone, Northern Paiute, and Ute. To the north, between the Rocky Mountains and the Cascades, great rivers brought shoals of salmon inland, providing a strong economic base. Elk and moose ranged the forests, and vegetable foods are plentiful. Nations of the region include the Penutians (Klamath, Modoc) and the Salish (Kalispel, Spokane, Coeur d'Alene). Because these people did not encounter Europeans until late in the eighteenth century, their traditions were sustained until relatively recent times. Women held prestige as leaders, as can be seen from the lives of Sacajawea, the Shoshone woman who guided the Lewis and Clark expedition (1804–1806), and Sarah Winnemucca, a Paiute and the first Native American woman author.

A land of even greater abundance was the Pacific Northwest, home to many groups whose cultures still flourish. In villages surrounded by forests of huge cedar lived people including the Haida, Tlingit, Chinook, Tsimshian, Bella Coola, Bella Bella, and Kwakiutl. Some nations organized themselves matrilineally; most had clear gender roles, with women's economic importance evident.

A complete listing of the female powers and divinities of native North America would be longer than what follows, which is limited due to two historical factors. The first is that many of the cultures were exterminated or suppressed by warfare intended to take their lands. In addition, researchers often failed to record names of goddesses. Many sources refer to female figures by status names like "Old Mother" or "Young Girl," or by translations of Indian names, such as "Slender Reed." This section includes only figures whose original names are recorded.

Native American religion is still practiced, sometimes combined with Christianity, sometimes kept as a separate spiritual path by people who are otherwise Christianized, sometimes serving as an individual's primary or sole religion. Some Indian people actively discourage interest in Native American religions by

non-Natives, connecting participation (especially unauthorized or uninvited) of non-Natives in Native ceremonials with spiritual colonialism. Pseudo-Native "traditions" have been propounded by non-Native authors, some claiming to honor indigenous goddesses. Occasionally Native or part-Native individuals offer allegedly traditional knowledge for a fee, a practice controversial among Native people. Given the diversity of Native traditions in the Americas, it is impossible to make categorical statements about them all. However, it is generally true that traditional Native Americans do not see spiritual knowledge as a commercial product.

NORTH AMERICAN PANTHEON

Agischanak Among the Tlingit, this mountain goddess held the pillar that supports the earth. It could collapse, but Agischanak holds fast because people honor her with fires. Once a year, her brother brings greetings of thunder, his eyes darting like lightning. Another visitor is Raven, who tries to trick Agischanak into abandoning her post. She refuses, so he shoves her, causing earthquakes.

The nearby Chilkat say a dog tricked Agischanak's mother into mating, which resulted in the birth of seven boys and Agischanak. The mother was happy, but her rejecting family left mother and infants to starve. Convincing the children to take off their fur coats, Agischanak's mother made them human. When the youngest boy fell in love with Agischanak, he transformed himself into a thunderbird, while she became a deep crevice. (Krause)

Ailsie This Cherokee heroine was a tall woman beloved of both the crane and the hummingbird. Her father wished her to marry the powerful crane, but she preferred the hummingbird. So Ailsie set her suitors a challenge: The one who could fly fastest would win her. She trusted in the hummingbird's speed, but after five circuits around the racecourse the hummingbird tired, and the crane won. Furious at her loss, Ailsie vowed never to marry rather than wed a crane. But her father pledged to kill her unless she married. Ailsie asked for a reprieve of seven days. During that time she wept so much she turned into a deep pool in the Etowah River. (Kilpatrick and Kilpatrick)

Aliquipiso The Oneida of the northern woodlands tell of this warrior girl who endured torments to save her people. The Oneida were besieged by their enemies, the Mingoes (Iroquois who had moved to Pennsylvania and Ohio). Trapped on a plateau, the Oneida would have starved but for the bravery of Aliquipiso, whose dream led them out of their predicament. In her dream, the girl saw a space below where the Mingoes could be killed by rocks thrown down upon them. She convinced the chiefs to let her lead the Mingoes into a trap.

Aliquipiso went to the Mingo camp and pretended to be lost. Captured, she endured torture but refused to reveal her people's hiding place. Finally appearing to give in under the pain, she led the Mingoes to the designated spot. There, she called out for the attack to begin, dying at her enemies' hands just before they were killed. From her hair sprang the plant called woodbine, a form of honeysuckle that twines itself around supports with hair-like tendrils. From her body grew shrubby honeysuckle, which her people called by a term that means "blood of brave women." (Long)

Ataensic The Iroquoian ancestral mother lived when there was no land, only a vast blue lake filled with birds, otters, and turtles. In heaven, Ataensic was pregnant with a daughter, Enedeka Dakwa, when she was thrown down to the earth lake. Waterbirds saw Ataensic falling. To save her, the birds and animals decided to build land from the lake mud. Many animals tried until Ketq Skwayne ("Grandmother Toad") dove deep and returned with dirt that, landing on turtle's back, began to grow. By the time Ataensic reached the water, there was enough land for her to give birth.

Enedeka Dakwa became pregnant by the West Wind with twins, Good Mind and Flint, the latter of whom burst from her side, killing her. Grieving Ataensic fashioned the sun and moon from Enedeka Dakwa's body. She blamed Flint for her daughter's death, so she always sided with his brother, Good Mind. (In some variants, Ataensic herself gave birth to the twins.)

Only once did Ataensic agree with Flint. She had placed her daughter's head in the sky, and Good Mind wanted it to shine. Flint objected, because he did not want sunlight to nurture plants. To settle their dispute, Good Mind and Ataensic played a game. Good Mind won, so his mother's face began to shine as the sun. Furious at losing, Ataensic hid Enedeka Dakwa's head. For three days, the earth was plunged into darkness. Traveling with animal friends, Good Mind stole back the sun. Throwing it back and forth like a ball, they brought back the sun, and the earth bloomed. (Barbeau 1915; Beauchamp 1922; Bruchac 1989; Converse; Elm and Antone; Hale; Hewitt; Leland; Parker)

Atatalia The giant cannibal woman of the Wasco, who lived along the salmon-rich Columbia River, captured a boy and a girl for dinner. But when the clever girl told Atatalia her children were burning, the cannibal ran home, dropping her prey. Discovering she had been tricked, Atatalia returned to find her prisoners fleeing. She chased them until they reached the river. There the children leaped into a canoe and raced away, calling to the fish and the rocks to help them escape. The giant waded into the water but was attacked by nibbling fish and falling rocks. (Lowenstein)

Atira To the Pawnee, the earth fed the living and embraced the dead. She brought food and culture through her daughter, **Uti Hiata**, who taught people how to raise food and make tools. A ceremony called Hako called on the goddess to sustain human life. Symbols used in the ceremonial included white feathers, representing sky, and an ear of corn, representing earth. (Dorsey 1997; Grinnell)

Atse Estsan The primal woman of Navajo religion was born in the darkness of the First World and gradually rose to the surface of our Fifth World. To do so, she joined first man and trickster Coyote as they passed through the Second World, where a man assaulted her. Coyote called the other dwellers in the Second World, and all decided to climb to the Third World.

There, in a lake-filled mountain land, they met a water monster whose children Coyote stole. The monster began to raise the water's level. The people piled the world's four mountains so they almost reached the sky. Still the waters rose until they reached the feet of the people who, climbing up a water weed that punctured the sky, gained the Fourth World.

There an argument arose between men and women. The women claimed social precedence because they were the fire makers, the child bearers, and the planters. The men contended that because they hunted and danced, they were more important. The alienated sexes went their separate ways. But within four years, weary of isolation, they reunited.

The water monster's lake seeped into their land, turning soil to mud. Finally the lake rose about them again. Piercing the sky with a long reed, everyone climbed to the Fifth World. But, instead of peace and safety, they found themselves on the bottom of another lake, with the monster in hot pursuit. Discovering Coyote had hidden the monster babies in his pack, the people forced him to toss them back, and the waters retreated. Then Atse Estsan and her people built this earth.

But humans grew selfish, so Atse Estsan created more monsters to plague them. When they had been punished enough, she brought forth **Estsánatlehi** and retreated to the eastern sky. (Levy; Matthews; Moon 1970)

Atsintma Canadian Athabascans say Atsintma opened her eyes to an empty world. Building a loom, she wove fireweed-blossom cloth, which she spread across the land, anchoring it with sacred mountains. Then she began to sing. Soon the earth gave birth to animals. As each was born, Atsintma lifted it from beneath earth's blanket. Some stories say Atsintma gave birth to the animals, beginning with mouse and continuing to ever-larger offspring until moose was born. Then Atsintma stretched a blanket between mountains and bounced her children on it, throwing each into a suitable habitat. Afterward, Atsintma punished hunters who did not perform rituals to honor animals they killed.

The neighboring Tahlian said Raven wanted to see how fast animals could run. He convinced Atsintma to call them, then watched as they raced to her. They were all too fast for humans to catch, so he convinced Atsintma to let him make changes. On the caribou, Raven placed extra lower-leg flesh, slowing them; he shortened the bears' legs. The animals could still get home to Atsintma, but sometimes people could catch them for food. (Teit 1919)

Awasiûkiu The Menominee bear woman attracted a man with whom she had a child who, like his mother, looked human. Her man noticed that although Awasiûkiu never cooked, food appeared. He did not know sacrifices from Indian people to the bear people provided their meals. When the husband's relatives visited, they saw Awasiûkiu as a bear and tried to kill her. She escaped, badly wounded. Afterward, Awasiûkiu decided to remain constantly disguised. She and her husband moved in with his family. Not long after, Awasiûkiu appeared naked to the waist, a scar running across her shoulders. When the brothers who had wounded her expressed disgust, she revealed the truth. After that, she was called Mat'citiniu ("scar-shoulder woman"), and the Menominee realized animals could take human shape and live among them. (Skinner and Satterlee)

Awitelin Tsita The Zuñi earth mother lay in intercourse with the sky until her four wombs were filled with his seed. She gave birth to the human race, then made mountains, so the land's divisions would be clear, and clouds filled with rain, so the earth's surface might bloom. (Thompson; Wherry)

Baachini Two Navajo star goddesses bear this name, thought to indicate two stars in the constellation called the Hyades, near the Pleiades. They are said to be identical twins called Hard Flint Women, daughters of an arguing couple, Dilyéhé (the Pleiades) and Coyote Man. Or the daughters themselves are argumentative, always fighting over who won the latest gambling match. (Miller)

Baculbotet The grain goddess Baculbotet provided all the Pomo people needed. When a monster threatened to destroy this abundance, Baculbotet wove a basket, covered with images of food that changed with the seasons. Through this artistry, Baculbotet restored earth's abundance. But the monster still threatened. Using her hair and sticks painted with her blood, Baculbotet wove a snare and caught the monster, so people could again gather food. But while they feasted, the monster crushed Baculbotet with a snap of his tail. She turned into a white fawn and escaped, never to be seen again in human form. (Berlo; Clark and Williams)

Ca-the-ña The Mojave describe Ca-the-ña as ruler of the sky, although whether she is embodied in the sky itself, or one of the luminaries, is unclear. The first woman, she invented sexual intercourse by inviting all animals to make love to her. The last was gopher, who lived far away. By the time he arrived she was menstruating, so their twin sons were born spotted. The boys grew into hunters, for whom their mother invented the reed flute so they could lure women. No sooner had the boys found sisters to wed than Ca-the-ña grew jealous. She moved the men around while they were sleeping, so the women unwittingly had intercourse with both. When her sons were killed, the goddess disappeared into the west. (Bourke)

Cenakatla'x Cenakatla'x lived near a stream filled annually with spawning salmon that provided all the food they needed. But once when Cenakatla'x was hungry, her parents gave her a moldy piece of fish. Soon after, she disappeared. She found her way to the salmon people, who showed her their ways, including swimming upstream to Cenakatla'x's village. There Cenakatla'x, seeing her people armed with spears, grew frightened. The salmon chief told her that when she was speared she should pull her soul into her tail. The salmon people did this every year, being reborn as other salmon.

Her father speared Cenakatla'x, and her mother decided to cook the fish. As she was cleaning it, she discovered the necklace Cenakatla'x had been wearing when she disappeared. Knowing this was their daughter, her parents wrapped the fish in feathers and fasted beside it. For eight days nothing happened, but on the ninth day, the fish turned back into Cenakatla'x. She told her parents to honor the salmon, which provided food for the people. (Teit 1921)

C-ga The Ho-Chunk people of the upper Midwest say C-ga was born with shiny white hair. When she reached puberty, she was sought after by men fascinated by her exotic hair. She grew vain and refused all suitors, preferring instead to sit near a pond rubbing her skin with flowers. When an especially homely man came in hopes of gaining her hand, she laughed at him. He was the trickster Turtle, who changed her into the first skunk in punishment. (Smith)

Chehiayam The Luiseño people of California describe the spring-rising stars, the Pleiades, as seven sisters called the Chehiayam, who climbed up into the sky in hopes of escaping death. Coyote, the trickster divinity, tried to follow them, but they cut the rope so he fell to earth. (Miller)

Chietsum According to the Chehalis in the Pacific Northwest, this woman was the daughter of the wisest chief, Seloyum. She was a happy girl who loved gathering berries and digging root vegetables. But she was always in danger of capture by the witch Tatlashea, who wandered the forests looking for children to eat. One day, lured from the village by a chipmunk,

Chietsum was snared by the cannibal woman, who shoved her into a basket.

As she traveled, Tatlashea captured another child, the boy Pauk, who whispered to Chietsum who their captor was. Chietsum called out to her guardian spirit, the eagle. He came, shoving a stone knife through the basket canes so Chietsum could cut the ropes that held them captive. Once escaped, the children found themselves confronted by the Skookumchuck River. On its banks, a lovely supernatural woman named Cloque sat carving a canoe. Begging her for help, Chietsum softened Cloque's heart, and she took the children to safety even though she knew Tatlashea would soon be at the river's other shore.

As soon as Cloque returned, Tatlashea approached and demanded a ride across the river, claiming her own children were there. Cloque knew better. She convinced Tatlashea that the boat was unsteady and that to stabilize it, the cannibal would have to tie rocks into her long hair. Tatlashea did so, but when they reached the center of the river Cloque upended the boat, tossing Tatlashea into the waves. Even today, there are rapids that result from Tatlashea trying to rise from the depths. Back in the village, Chietsum's father sponsored a potlatch to celebrate his daughter's return from the wilderness and the end of Tatlashea, a scourge to his people. (Griffin)

Clem Among the people of Thomson River, this woman ("pelican") lived in an area overrun with rushes. One of these plants became human and made love with Clem, who gave birth to the original people of the land. (Boas 2002)

Cowgan The Haida said the forests are filled with Cowgans, transformed mice who look like lovely women. The Cowgans could be helpful if a person showed kindness, but they could also be spiteful, seducing men and turning them into stumps. (Deans 1892)

Dagwanoe^{n}yent "Whirlwind old woman" lived in the forest, say the Seneca people, with her two grandchildren, a boy and a girl. When Dagwanoe^{n}yent went to dig roots, a frost woman named Geno^{n}skwa came into the cabin, ate the girl, then kidnapped the boy. Dragged along behind his captor, the boy cried. His grandmother heard and followed, turning into a whirlwind. Geno^{n}skwa hid the boy in a hole in the ground, but his grandmother heard and rescued him. Then she burned tobacco and made medicine to reclaim her granddaughter. But the girl did not come forth from the frost woman's belly, so Dagwanoe^{n}yent called her relatives and they, too, made offerings of tobacco while calling for the girl's return. The girl emerged from the body of the frost woman. When the frost people appeared to avenge the death, Dagwanoe^{n}yent and her relatives successfully fought them off. (Curtin)

Dayunisi To the Cherokee, the tiny water beetle is the beaver's granddaughter. She helped create the world, for at the beginning, all animals lived in the sky, which became too crowded for them. They went prospecting for a new place, and when the council of beings was held, it was Dayunisi whose voice was heard, for she spoke of a land below the great sea. Convinced she saw the best homeland for them, the animals approved of her descent into the waters. From below, she drew up mud, a bit at a time, until it formed the earth. (Caduto)

Deohako The Iroquoian people told of three sisters who thrived when they were together but wilted when separated. The oldest towered over the others in her long green shawl. The second wore a yellow dress and loved running in the sunshine. The youngest sister wore green and crawled after the others. The sisters were never separated until a young man met them in a forest late one summer. Shortly after, the youngest sister disappeared. The young man returned, and the second sister disappeared. The oldest made sorrowful sounds until the young man came back. He carried her to his parents' home, where she found her younger sisters living happily. The "sisters" were corn, beans, and squash, primary foods of several American peoples. (Beauchamp 1898; Hardin)

Djigonasee A heroine of the northern woodlands, Djigonasee, the "mother of nations," was a lineal descendant of the first woman and leader of her people. Her longhouse stood between warring groups. But Djigonasee's son would change all that, for he was the peace bringer Deganiwada, who united the Six Nations (Seneca, Cayuga, Onondaga, Oneida, Mohawk, and Tuscarora) into the Iroquois.

Like many mothers of heroes, Djigonasee was a virgin when her son was born. A herald from beyond this world announced he would be born to bring peace, and Djigonasee accepted his announcement. Whether this theme was influenced by the Christian story of the annunciation of the angel to the Virgin Mary is unclear. When Djigonasee's son was grown, she conveyed messages and treaties among the nations. In this role, she began the woodland traditions whereby leaders were chosen by wise women, who also removed leaders who acted selfishly or foolishly. (Bruchac)

Djīyi'n This Tlingit orphan lived in an impoverished village. When the villagers moved to find food, Djīyi'n was left behind. But she found a boat filled with food, on which she lived while she transformed into a shaman. When her people returned, they found Djīyi'n living with wood ducks. Thereafter, she served as a powerful healer. (Swanton 1909)

Djū When the Haida ruler of the northeast wind raised her dress, fair winds blew softly, but when she brought it up to her knees, the winds grew strong. (Swanton 1905)

Duskeah Like many North Americans, the Quileute, a Chimakuan-speaking people of western Washington, envision the wilderness as the home of a cannibal woman. Duskeah feasted on children, whom she kept in captivity until she had enough to make stew. She covered their eyes with gum so they could not see her

build a fire to roast them. One girl, feeling heat, figured out what was about to happen. She held her hands close enough to the fire to get them very warm, then used the warmth to melt the gum from her eyes. When Duskeah, dancing around the flames, drew near, the girl pushed the cannibal into her own fire, freeing the other children. (Farrand and Mayer; Mayer)

Dzelarhons Once the volcano goddess Dzelarhons was a mortal woman who migrated into Haida country with her uncle, Gitrhawn. Her people came in six canoes across the western sea, seeking a warmer climate and a richer land. Dzelarhons fell in love with a Haida man and had her uncle arrange a marriage. Decked in sea otter furs and shell-trimmed leather, Dzelarhons was escorted to the village of her chosen mate. Splendid ceremonies marked the wedding, but Dzelarhons soon found she had mistaken her husband's character. He demanded she spend their first night holding a lighted torch above his head. As the torch shrank, the woman protected her arms with her garments, which were burned.

The next morning the Haida, shocked at the young man's behavior, warned him about Gitrhawn's vengeance. But the bridegroom continued to demand that Dzelarhons hold his torch until her garments were burned and she was naked. Gitrhawn's people came to her rescue. They burned the Haida village but did not find Dzelarhons, only a stone statue holding a burning staff topped by a copper frog, between whose legs a stream flowed.

Thereafter Dzelarhons was a powerful divinity who judged people's actions toward animals. In one village, people grew accustomed to the wealth the sea provided and began to kill animals needlessly. They caught spawning salmon, slit their backs, and inserted pitch-soaked branches, then lit the torches and laughed as the fish, crazed with pain, swam about lighting the sea. Soon the people heard terrible rumblings. Fright ran through the village, but it was too late for repentance as Dzelarhons poured forth fiery wrath. Few escaped, for even the rivers ran hot with the goddess's fury. (Barbeau 1953; Bierhorst 1985; Wherry)

E'lg'Eldokwila The Kwakiutl of the Pacific coast call medicinal plants by this name, which means "Long-Life-Maker Woman." The goddess of the same name was the special guardian of berry bushes, which the Kwakiutl burned in order to make them bear more heavily. When they did so, they prayed to E'lg'Eldokwila to forgive them, explaining that the tradition dated to ancestral times. They also prayed in gratitude to this goddess when gathering food. (Boas 1966)

Enamtues On the Washington-Canada border stood a human-sized boulder at which the Okanogon people stopped to make wishes for good fortune. It became sacred when a girl, Enamtues, became infatuated with the reputation of a young man in a neighboring village. Traveling to see if what she had heard was correct, she stopped on a mountain summit to twine flowers into her hair. The lad and his brothers, hearing a girl was coming to visit, started up the mountain. When they met Enamtues, her intended and a brother began to fight over her, for all three brothers found her irresistible. The trickster Coyote, annoyed at the noise, cast a spell on Enamtues so her lower body turned to stone, while the young men turned into mountains. Seeing her lover was no longer in human form, Enamtues raised her own power and turned herself entirely into stone so she could forever look at him. This sacred stone was smashed to bits by a white man whose Indian neighbors had warned him of its powers. Within a year, he was dead, dragged to death by his own horses. (Clark 1953)

Estsánatlehi The Navajo sky goddess, wife of the sun, lived in a turquoise palace at the western horizon. Sister of **Yolkai Estsan**, Estsánatlehi was called Changing Woman because when her age began to show, she walked east until she met herself walking westward. She kept walking until her young

self merged with her aging self and then, renewed, returned home.

Atse Estsan, discovering Estsánatlehi beneath a mountain, reared her to be the savior of earth's people. When she was grown, Estsánatlehi met a young man with whom she went into the woods to make love. When her parents saw only one set of footprints on the ground, they knew their daughter had taken the sun as a lover. Delighted at the honor, they were delighted again when Estsánatlehi gave birth to twins who grew so fast that eight days after birth they were men, ready to seek their father. They won magical weapons from him, which they used to clear the earth of monsters. Then the twins built Estsánatlehi a magnificent home at the sky's end, so the sun could visit her again.

Because the twins' wars with the monsters had depopulated the earth, Estsánatlehi brushed dust from her breasts. White flour fell from her right breast and yellow meal from her left, with which she made a paste from which she molded a man and a woman. The next morning they were alive and breathing; their children became the four great Navajo clans. But the creative urge of Estsánatlehi was not fulfilled. She made four more groups of people, this time from the dust of her nipples, for which reason the women of these clans were famous for their nipples. Estsánatlehi continued to bestow blessings: seasons, plants and food, and the tender sprouts of spring. Only four monsters survived: age, winter, poverty, and famine, which she allowed to live so her people would treasure her gifts. (Allen 1991; Bierhorst 1985; Levy; Matthews; Newcomb; Reichard; Stephen; Wherry)

Gâus! tukoba'nî The "fair girls of the sky" are among many Tlingit feminine sky spirits. The moon was inhabited by two girls who had been walking when one looked up and said, uncourteously, "that moon looks just like my grandmother's labret (mouth ornament)," whereupon they were transported to the moon, the speaker being crushed against it, the other visible, still holding her berry bucket. When a lunar eclipse occurred, the Tlingit people blew toward the moon, to drive away sickness from the girls. (Swanton 1908)

Gawaunduk "The Guardianess," heroine of an Anishinaubae (Ojibway or Chippewa) legend, was a young woman given in marriage to a distinguished elder. She went obediently but without joy, feeling her life would be more satisfying if she had a love mate her own age. As the years passed and she bore children to the old man, her heart softened. When, in his eighty-fifth year, he grew sick, Gawaunduk was frantic for his survival. He recovered and lived another fifteen years. Then, a century old, he died in his sleep. She mourned so wildly at his grave that she died of grief and they were buried together. Mists in spruce forests are her tears as she mourns her beloved. (Johnston)

Geezhigo-Quae To the Anishinaubae, Geezhigo-Quae dwelt in the heavens and watched over her people. She created the earth, descending into the primal soup to find land under the waves. She brought it forth and fashioned it into hills and mountain ranges. (Johnston 2001)

Gendenwitha The great hunter Sosondowah, stalking a supernatural elk, wandered too close to heaven and was captured by the jealous dawn, who used Sosondowah as her doorkeeper. But on earth he saw Gendenwitha and left his duties to court her. While dawn colored the sky, the hunter sang to his beloved: in spring as a bluebird; in summer, a blackbird; in autumn, a hawk. As a hawk, he tried to carry Gendenwitha to heaven. But dawn, angry at his disappearance, turned the woman into a star and set Gendenwitha out of reach. There is evidence Gendenwitha was once widely revered, but her worship died away in historic times. (Converse; Parker)

Genetaska "Maiden peace queen" of the Iroquois was a woman so wise that disputes were brought to her for settlement. She lived alone in the forest and spent her days in tranquil contemplation. Genetaska was renowned for her impartiality, but she once found balance hard to achieve.

Two arguing men came to her door with a problem. They both claimed the carcass of a deer, for both had shot it, although only one's arrow was fatal. She suggested each take half of the meat. One man refused, offending Genetaska with suggestive comments. The other respectfully asked the peace queen to marry him. She refused both, but she found she could not forget the quiet young man who had offered to share his life with her. When he returned that winter to repeat his offer, she left her post and went with him. After her abdication, the Five Nations abolished the office of peace queen, with resulting warfare. (Beauchamp 1922; Spence)

Glispa The Navajo heroine who brought the healing beauty chant to her people may have been a form of **Estsánatlehi**. With her sister, she was lured from their village by young men. But when dawn came, the men were withered and old. Although her sister was too terrified to escape, Glispa fought her way to freedom. At the center of the world, Glispa stopped to drink. Snake people lifted the water so Glispa could travel beneath it. There she met her lover, again firm and handsome, who told Glispa he was a shaman of the snake people and taught her healing chants and rituals. They settled down happily together. After many years, Glispa grew homesick, and the snake husband taught her how to return. On earth, she taught the healing chant to her brother, then returned to her home below the waters. (Allen)

Godasiyo The Tuscarora said that when people all spoke the same language, Godasiyo was the leader of the biggest human village. One day, Godasiyo's dog gave birth to puppies, one completely white with little dark markings over each eye. It was so sweet everyone wanted to pet it. People to began fight over possession of the dog. Frightened, Godasiyo tried to keep the warring parties apart, but the threats continued.

So Godasiyo decided to establish a new village where everyone could live in peace with the puppy.

She loaded her people into canoes. But arguments began about which canoe the puppy would ride in. Godasiyo invented an outrigger so she could ride between several canoes, but even this was not enough. The migrating people reached a fork in the river and argued about which way to go. During the argument, the leader and her dog were thrown into the water and drowned. Immediately they were reborn, she as a sturgeon, the puppy as a whitefish. When the people tried to comment on this miracle, they found they could no longer understand each other, and thus human languages were born. (Bruchac 1989)

Gonoñk'goes "The Big Breast," the Seneca say, was a giant woman with enormous pillow-like breasts who roamed about searching for sweethearts who were inappropriately intimate. If she found such miscreants, she used her huge breasts to suffocate them. Then she tossed them off a cliff and went off looking for others. (Parker)

Gyihldepkis Gyihldepkis was a kindly forest spirit of the Tlingit and Haida, who envisioned her in mossy branches of great cedars. A protective spirit, Gyihldepkis was disturbed by a whirlpool that devoured ships. To break its power, Gyihldepkis invited ice, forest fire, wind, and other powers to a feast in her underwater home, where she convinced them that human beings needed protection from the whirlpool. The powers rearranged the coast, smoothing the whirlpool into a gentle river. (Barbeau 1953)

Haka Lasi The California Yana tell of this young woman who fell in love with her brother Hitchinna. She lived with her father, Juka, and many siblings, including her sister Tsore Jowa. One day, after dreaming of Hitchinna, Haka Lasi dressed as a bride and demanded a husband. One after another of the brothers was sent to her, but she turned all away until Hitchinna came. Together, they ran away.

That night they slept together but he, growing frightened, left a piece of wood in her arms as he stole away to return home. Haka Lasi woke enraged. Returning home, she set the house on fire and killed everyone except Tsore Jowa and Juka, who escaped. She burned their bodies and made a necklace out of their burned-up hearts. But Tsore Jowa killed her, took her heart out, and made magic with all the hearts, bringing her siblings back to life—even Haka Lasi, whose heart was pure after she had passed through death and regeneration. (Curtin 2004)

Hanwi The moon goddess of the Ogalala and Lakota lived with Wi the sun god, with whom she had one daughter, **Wohpe**. Coming late to a banquet, Hanwi saw another woman, Ite, sitting in her place. Ite's mother, Wakanka, had tried to raise her daughter's status by arranging an assignation between Ite and the sun god, even though Ite was married to the wind. Because the sun god had allowed this substitution, Hanwi left Wi's residence. To compensate for her humiliation, she was given rulership over dawn and twilight, but she always hid her face near the sun.

In punishment for her actions, the high god gave Ite two faces, for which she was thereafter known as Anukite ("two-faced Ite"). The offspring of Ite and the sun was the destructive tornado. But some good came of the deceit. Bored with life after her affair, Ite convinced the trickster spider to bring fire and human settlement to earth. When women dreamed of Anukite, they became very seductive to men. (Bierhorst 1985; Dooling; Powers; Sullivan; Walker)

Hawelakok According to the Wishram people, the female swan named Hawelakok lived in a vast lake that once stretched beneath the Cascade Mountains in the Pacific Northwest. She hated humans. Whenever they came near, she drowned them, making water rise around them faster than they could run. But people continued to try, because the lake's water made those who bathed in it long-lived and wealthy. Once a young woman risked the swan's wrath by diving into the lake.

When she feared the swan would find her, she climbed onto the limbs of a huge spreading tree. She did not know she was crawling onto the antlers of a huge elk, who bore her away and impregnated her. When the half-elk child was born, the girl killed it. In retaliation, the elk people withdrew from the lake, and the lake itself dried up, so now it is only a marsh. (Clark 1953)

Hé-é-e This Hopi woman was having her hair done by her mother, in the traditional double-whorled fashion that showed she was of marriageable age. When her mother had half finished, the pair heard enemies sneaking into the village. Hé-é-e grabbed a bow and arrows and ran outdoors. Rushing into the face of the enemy, she led her people to victory in defense of their village. She was thereafter depicted as a **Kachina** with her hair whorled on one side, loose on the other. (Neithammer)

Hekoolas The body of this Miwok sun goddess was covered with abalone shells. In primeval times, she lived on the other side of the sky, so the earth was dark and cold. Coyote sent men to invite the sun closer, but she refused. Then Coyote sent men to tie her up and drag her to this side of the sky, where she lit the earth.

In another Miwok tale, the sun woman Heima shut herself up in her stone house. The sky grew dark, and Hawk Chief demanded Coyote bring back daylight. Coyote went to the doves who knew the way to the sun's house. When they got there, they sat and waited. Nothing happened, so they decided to shoot stones. The younger dove's stone went through the wall of the sun's house. The frightened sun rose from her smoke-hole, but when she found everything undamaged, she went back in. The older dove whirled the slingshot. When he let the stone fly, it sailed through the air so fast it smashed into the sun's house, right in the center. The sun rose straight into the air and stood overhead, returning light to earth. (Gifford and Block; Merriam)

Hulluk Miyumko The Miwok star chiefs were beautiful women who lived beneath a whistling elderberry tree, which kept them awake so they could work all the time. (Merriam)

Huruing Wuhti This goddess of rock and clay was, to the Hopi, the primordial being. Around her circular underwater home, the universe accumulated; thus she was called Hard Surfaces Woman. She was connected with jewels and shells, coral and stone.

In the west lived her twin, also named Huruing Wuhti. The sisters shared a husband, the sun, who wore the eastern goddess's colored fox skins as he traveled across the sky and then sounded the western sister's rattle as he set. Noticing the earth lacked creatures, the two goddesses created birds, then animals, and finally people. The first woman was Tuwu'boñtumsi (Sand Altar Woman or Childbirth Water Woman, although the latter is sometimes a separate goddess called Tih'kuyi), mother of the **Kachinas** and ruler of human fecundity.

In another part of the world, **Kókyangwúti** was inspired by the twin goddesses' activity to create humans herself. Because she was less talented, she sometimes left people without mates or in mismatched pairs. Thus people made by the twin sisters are happy in marriage, while those made by Kókyangwúti are not. (Erdoes and Ortiz; Tyler)

Ioi The Chinook people of the northwest coast tell how the Ghost-people stole Ioi from her village. She had begged her brother Blue Jay to take a wife from Ghost-land to help her with housework. Blue Jay found a chief's daughter, recently dead, and married her. Then, through trickery, he restored her to life. When her relatives came to ask for the now-living girl's bride-price, Blue Jay changed into bird form and attacked them. His new wife died from the fright and could not be revived.

In retaliation, the Ghost-people stole Ioi. Blue Jay went to find her in Ghost-land. There she was living among heaps of bones she believed were her relatives by marriage. He teased the bones and made fun of them, but very soon Blue Jay himself died and became a heap of bones. Even in that condition, he was mischievous and teased his sister, but she loved him enough that she went with him to play tricks on the world's animals. (Spence)

'Isánáklésh The Mescalero Apache goddess of creation appeared as a woman with her face half painted with white clay and her body yellow with cattail pollen. She emerged from primal water when the land was still beneath the waves. At first she was not visible, but Holy People sang to her as she revealed herself. Songs offered today in ceremonies of 'Isánáklésh re-create those songs. (Sullivan)

Kachinas Appearing in dances, embodied in human followers or in carved representations, the Kachinas are powerful spirits of plants and planets, animals and ancestors, even stars whose light we cannot see. There are between 220 and 335 Kachinas, among whom are many important female figures. There is old Warrior Mother Héhewúti, who appears half-dressed with messy hair, in memory of the time she helped defend her people against an attack without pausing to dress fully. There is Whipper Mother Angwushahai'í, who whips boys and girls with yucca strips in initiation ceremonies, and Butterfly Maidens who represent spring's energy. Beautiful Crow Mother Angwúsnasomtaqa dresses in bridal attire and a magnificent headdress, in honor of the time when she left her wedding to aid her Hopi children. Dolls representing Kachinas are sacred objects, not playthings. (Capps; Neithammer; Waters; Wherry)

Kanene Ski Amai Yehi The Cherokee primal being, Grandmother Water Spider, brought the sun to the world. Trying to light the sky, Possum burned off his tail and Buzzard, his claw feathers. So Kanene Ski Amai Yehi wove herself a basket and, spinning out a web, traveled across the world. Then she reached out arms and grabbed the sun. Popping it into her basket, she fled back across the web to light the world. (Hudson; Davis)

Kókyangwúti The Hopi and Zuñi earth goddess possessed a sacred hoop that allowed passage to the otherworld. The Hopi say Kókyangwúti came to earth early in creation, sent by the sun to lead people up from the First World. She led them to the Second World, where they fought among themselves. So Kókyangwúti led them into the Third World, where she taught them to live harmoniously and express themselves through weaving and pottery. Because the world was cold, she and a hummingbird taught people to make fire. After that, people could cook food, and life seemed good.

But there were challenges. Evil ones caused people to grow greedy, so the earth began to withhold its gifts. Starvation threatened, but Kókyangwúti planted a tree that grew to puncture the sky. Then, drawing a line over which the evil ones could not cross, she led the people to the Upper World, where we live today. (Erdoes and Ortiz; Hausman; Leeming and Page; Matthews; Moon; Mullett; Stephen 1930, 1929; Tyler; Waters; Wherry)

Kotchpih'lah Once when six sisters, say the Yokut, were gathering seeds for food, they decided they were too cold to work and would try to get closer to the sun. So they made tea from hallucinogenic datura and soon were flying around like condors. But they still could not reach the sun, so they invoked the whirlwind and managed to fly there. Back on earth, the women's husbands, following their footsteps, discovered the remainder of their drug. They took it and flew to the sun, where they joined their wives as the Pleiades, Kotchpih'lah. When they try to return to earth every spring, their wings bring thunder and rain. (Miller)

Kuchininako At the pueblo of Laguna in New Mexico, this girl lived alone with no brothers to hunt for her. So Kuchininako ("Yellow Woman") went out to hunt for herself. She did well, catching two rabbits and building a fire to cook them. But the dangerous wildwoman Shkuyo smelled the cooking meat and came to Kuchininako's campfire. There she demanded one rabbit, then the other, then Kuchininako's headdress, then her moccasins, finally her dress. The frightened girl gave up each thing asked of her, until finally Shkuyo said she would eat Kuchininako.

At this Kuchininako began to scream, drawing the attention of two young men who were hunting nearby. They arrived just in time to save Kuchininako and then cut open the cannibal and took out Kuchininako's clothing so she no longer stood naked before them. Kuchininako returned home, while the dismembered parts of the cannibal woman became features of the landscape. (Parsons 1931)

Kusi'tawa'qari A widespread North American myth says the sky in primeval time was empty of stars. When Coyote, the trickster, tried to force his daughters to have intercourse with him, the girls ran away to the sky and became stars, called Izá'a padimi, "Coyote's Daughters" by the Paiute. Most often, these stars were the spring-rising Pleiades that in many lands are seen as "seven sisters." Among the Shoshone of the great basin, the same stars were called Kusi'tawa'qari, "women fighting," and were said to have been sisters who fought with each other over an attractive man and were transferred to the sky, still fighting. (Miller)

Kųtsæbukwi oyikaga According to the Tewa pueblo people, "ice mother" or "winter mother" is one of the primal beings from the time before the emergence of humanity. She was born in a lake where her people lived underwater. Accompanied by other female beings who became the Corn Mothers of the people—most prominent among them was her twin, the summer mother—she helped them into the upper world. As the people emerged, Kųtsæbukwi oyikaga was given the eastern hills, where she can always be seen, while the summer goddess was given the western hills, where she is always accompanied by cloud people. (Parsons 1994)

Kuwánlelenta "To make beautiful surroundings" is the meaning of this Hopi goddess's name. As guardian of the sunflower plant, she was ancestral mother to the sunflower clan. In Owaqlt ("melons on vine" or "rocks in the field"), a women's ceremony, Kuwánlelenta appears in double form, represented by two girls whose faces are painted with ground sunflower petals. Like all plants, sunflowers are seen as living beings worthy of respect and honor. Owaqlt, a harvest ceremony, is based in the redistribution of food by the Hopi women. (Waters)

Ku'yapalitsa The Zuni and Hopi goddess of childbirth and the hunt is a virgin warrior woman. Her virginity expressed her desire to keep everything to herself, including animals she controlled. She was called "Yellow Woman" by the Keres and was said to have been tricked into marriage and into releasing animals to be hunted. (Tyler)

Látkakáwas The Modoc primal woman looked like an old woman, but she had only to shake herself to become bright blue and beautiful. She lived with five brothers on Klamath Lake, where she gathered food while they hunted. People noticed Látkakáwas was sometimes young and sometimes old. Some men set out to capture her, to torment her for her odd ways, but they could not move fast enough. One young man did not make fun of her, so she grew fond of him.

Her brothers decided to take her away from the cruel people, but the young man followed them as a salmon. To her horror, one of her brothers speared the fish. When they learned it was Látkakáwas's lover, the brothers held a funeral ceremony. As soon as the young man's body was consumed by flame, it turned into a metal disc that Látkakáwas took to the magician Kumash. Although Kumash could revive the dead, he found Látkakáwas attractive and so did not perform his magic but, instead, burned the disc. But Látkakáwas leaped into the fire and burned together with her lover. (Curtin 1971)

Lê'nXAĄĪ'dAq The Tlingit wilderness spirit was a curly-haired woman with long fingernails, who ran through the woods carrying a baby on her back. Lê'nAXAẠĪ'dAq could bring wealth, but first she had to be caught, so she could scratch the pursuer with her long fingernails. As the scratches healed, they brought good luck. Bits of scab could be shared with friends, providing wealth. (Swanton 1908)

Loha The beautiful daughter of a Klamath leader, Loha had the misfortune of attracting the lust of the chief of the underworld, who lived under a volcano near Mount Shasta. When she refused to become his bride, he erupted in flames. Lava and ash descended upon the people, who were nearly destroyed. But the rage of the underworld chief caused his mountain to collapse upon him, locking him beneath the earth. The lake that fills the cavern where he once came forth is known as Crater Lake. (Clark 1953)

Lok Snewédjas This Modoc woman was a bear every night but transformed herself into a beautiful woman in daylight. She lived in wealth and comfort on a mountain, but she was lonely until she saw a handsome hunter. She made herself visible, so he fell in love with her, but at night he discovered she turned into a bear. Fearful of being rejected, she suggested he return to his human family, but he refused, saying they had been abusive to him. So they lived together until their son was born, at which point the man felt he should visit his family and introduce the child. Lok Snewédjas warned him he should never leave the child with other children. But Lok Snewédjas's husband failed to notice his son turning into a bear while playing with other children. Terrified, they killed the boy.

Away on her mountain, Lok Snewédjas knew her child had died and roared into the village. Hunters brought her down, whereupon she turned back into a beautiful woman. Her husband was distraught with grief, but a young girl who understood magic revivified Lok Snewédjas and her son. The family returned to the mountain and were never seen by humans again, although sometimes their voices are heard on the wind. (Curtin 1971)

Loo-Wit The Multnomah and Klickitat said the goddess of Mount Saint Helens was an old woman who, because of her generosity, was granted a boon by the sky spirit. She wished for eternal youth and beauty. The sky father told Loo-Wit to build a fire on the bridge separating the Multnomah and the Klickitat, whose greed had set them at odds. When beautiful Loo-Wit appeared on the bridge, they made peace.

But trouble soon started. Chiefs of both people courted Loo-Wit, and she could not choose between them. The men started a war, breaking the bridge in the battle. The sky father intervened, turning the chiefs into Mount Hood and Mount Adams (the latter sometimes said to be **Pahto**) and Loo-Wit into Mount Saint Helens. Afterward the chiefs continued to make war, shooting fire at each other and spilling rocks (the Columbia Cascades) into the space where the bridge once stood. (Clark 1953)

Luhdee The Pomo panther goddess came from the east at the beginning of time, bearing the laws of right living: do not kill any fellow being; do not be dishonest or deceitful; be courteous to all, even to enemies, and especially to elders; be loyal and kind to your marriage partner. She is the symbol of everything connected with women. (Clark and Williams)

Mahohrah At the age of eight, this Huron girl showed she was both wise and beloved of all creatures; snakes came when she called them, trees bowed their heads so she could talk to their leaves, and fish splashed up from the water when she passed. But she became inexplicably ill and could not be cured; her father traveled to the great goddess **Ataensic** to beg for his daughter's life. But it was too late, for he saw Mahohrah passing along the skyway of death, bearing torches in her hands. Overcome with grief, the father flew into the sky to try to turn her back. But she did not alter her course. Out of sympathy for the father's loss, Ataensic turned Mahohrah and her father into the stars that form the belt of the constellation Orion. (Barbeau 1915)

Máidikdak When the two daughters of the Modoc snowbird woman were to be married, they set off to meet the sons of a nearby chief. Their mother, Máidikdak, warned them not to take a path that would take them past the home of the fox, Wus. But the older daughter thought that way was shorter, so despite the younger daughter's objections, the girls embarked upon the dangerous route.

As predicted, they encountered Wus, who attempted to get them to stay with him. When they refused, he turned them into old women dressed in rags, who disappointed the chief's sons when they arrived at their destination. But the youngest son followed them at night, when they turned back into lovely young women, and when the girls went home, he followed and married both. (Curtin 1971)

Maka The Lakota earth mother Maka could not see herself in the primal darkness, so the sky god created light. Disturbed by how bare she seemed, Maka divided the waters into rivers and streams, braiding them into fanciful designs. Because she was cold, the sky god made the sun to warm her. Then Maka created living beings. (Dooling; Powers 1986)

Mem Loimis Among the Wintun, this underworld goddess controlled earth's water. When the world caught fire, Mem Loimis doused the flames, but her waters reached the heavens, where the frog woman Yoholmit Pokaila lived. She got into a floating basket, but the water continued to rise. So the gods drove Mem Loimis back to a hole in the earth, and the waters receded with her.

Later she returned to marry the creator god Olelbis, by whom she had two sons. Then she left him for another man. Because Mem Loimis was the essence of water, Olelbis and his sons became very thirsty. A shaman danced for five nights but was unable to discern where Mem Loimis had gone.

Olelbis sent for a stronger shaman. After sixty pipes of tobacco, he could not gain a vision of Mem Loimis, so he danced for sixty nights. Finally he saw Mem Loimis far to the east. Her sons set off to plead for water. Mem Loimis held a basket to her breast and filled it. Carrying it back, the boys let some fall. Everywhere the drops fell, water became abundant. Elsewhere, the land remained desert. (Curtin 2004)

Menil This moon goddess was the heroine of the Cahuilla people. Because the primal universe was dark, twin gods created Menil to light the sky. One twin did not like the beings made by the other, who created women with breasts front and back, men with webbed toes, and other monsters. The twins also disagreed about how to launch the seasons, how to create plants, and virtually everything else. To settle matters, Menil established rules of culture and human interaction. She divided humans into clans and designed religious rituals. She invented singing so people could entertain their children while teaching them. As long as she lived among the people, everyone was happy. Women were especially happy, because they were free.

Then one of the twin gods invented death. He helped Menil invent bows and arrows, then told her to teach people how to make sharp-pointed arrowheads. Finally he asked her to have people hit each other with the arrows, assuring Menil no one would be hurt. But people fell down dead. The remaining people went into mourning, alleviated only by the presence of the moon. But the twin god drove her into the sky, and life has never been as pleasant as when Menil lived on earth. (Williamson and Farrar)

Moasäm Beps When people starved during winter, this Modoc south wind spirit brought minnows and pine nuts to sustain them. She married a human chief, telling him she would protect him as long as he wore moccasins she made. He did so, until a long hunting trip when he got wet. He took off the shoes and perished in sudden snow. (Curtin 1971)

Momoy The Chumash said datura could be made into a hallucinogenic drug. The essence of the plant was Momoy, who washed her hands in a basin of water, impregnating it with visionary power. Momoy's daughter became pregnant by a bear who disguised himself as human and then ate the girl. Momoy found a bit of her daughter's blood on an alder leaf. Her magic congealed the blood into a fetus, which she nurtured into a hero. Guided by his grandmother's visionary ability, the boy rid the land of monsters and made it fit for human habitation. (Bierhorst 1985; Blackburn)

Mooinaarkw "Mama Bear" or "Grandmother Bear" of the Algonquins was tormented by a trickster named Lox, the wolverine, who blinded her by kicking ashes from her fire. Unable to hunt or fish and thus reliant upon the meals her family could provide, Mooinaarkw cut holes into her head that would serve as eyes. The experiment worked, but she discovered that her family had been feasting lavishly while offering her only bones and gristle. She waited until she had been presented with a plateful of bones before remarking on the juicy meat on the others' plates. Shamed, the others switched plates, claiming they had always served her the best because she was blind. After that, Mooinaarkw always kept her eyes open, even if the others did not realize she could see. (Leland)

Muzzu-Kummik-Quae The Anishinaubae hero Nana'b'oozo found himself floating on a raft in a flood. Wild creatures swam around him, calling for help. Nana'b'oozo remembered an earlier flood, when **Geezhigo-Quae** dived to the bottom of the sea and brought back mud from which she created the world. Animals attempted the feat, descending but always coming back with nothing. Finally the muskrat brought back a bit of soil into which Nana'b'oozo breathed in imitation of Geezhigo-Quae. The soil grew until it became the earth.

Muzzu-Kummi-Quae appeared to a group of hunters who were unable to find water or food. When they came upon her, disguised as an old woman, they stopped to help her. To reward them, Muzzu-Kummik-Quae gave them medicine bundles, warning them not to open the package until they got home, then to

make tea from it. The men did so and soon died. From their graves grew wonders: from the first, a pine tree whose seeds grew into forests where deer and moose appeared. From the second grew a birch, from which canoes could be made. From the third, flint grew so people could make cooking fires. The last grave offered the sacred plant tobacco. (Johnston 2001)

Nahkeeta The goddess of Lake Sutherland in the Olympic Mountains was originally a delicate maiden, gentle as a water bird. She was beloved of her people, and she herself loved the dense forests where they lived. One day while Nahkeeta was gathering wild plants, she lost her way in the rain forest. As the light dimmed beneath the trees, she wandered until exhausted, then fell asleep beside a fallen tree. There, the next day, her family found her bloodied body, marked with the claws of a wild beast. They had loved her so much that sorrow was unceasing—until the day she reincarnated herself in a soft blue lake, a lake filled with waterbirds and the slow sound of wind on her surface. (Clark 1953)

Náhookoz Ba'áadii To the Navajo, the constellation Cassiopeia is Náhookoz Ba'áadii, "whirling woman" or "she who carries the fire in her basket." She may have been the ancestral first mother of the Navajo people; she was envisioned as married to the Big Dipper, with whom she forms a couple in the sky. (Miller)

Nalq The Tshimshian ancestral mother was the only human left after the sky divinity, irritated by how noisy people were, sent a beautiful magic plume that, when touched, stuck like glue. One after another of the people were captured and carried away, but Nalq was indoors giving birth to many children, whom she warned against the magic plume. But Nalq's children were magical, and when the plume presented itself, they grabbed hold and were taken to the heavens, where they married spirits, tamed the winds, and then settled on earth. (Lévi-Strauss)

Ne Hwas A Passamaquoddy family lived by the side of a blue lake, about which the mother always warned her daughters. But they sneaked away from her to swim there, until one day they did not come home. Their father found them unable to leave the water, for their lower extremities had become snakes. But their torsos and faces had grown incomparably beautiful, and they sang melodically. The girls had become Ne Hwas, mermaids, and remained in the lake. (Leland)

Nemissa The Algonikan people of Lake Huron tell of the star maiden Nemissa, who descended to earth to seduce a hunter. Carrying him to her heavenly home, Nemissa showed him their magnificent lodge but, when she heard her brother coming home, demanded Cloud Carrier hide under a pile of her clothes. But the brother smelled the presence of human blood. Although she had been forbidden to speak with the people of earth, Nemissa's family agreed to let Cloud Carrier remain. But Nemissa's lover grew homesick. Once on earth, heaven seemed like only a dream, so he settled down and married an earthly woman. But she died immediately. He married again, and the same thing happened. Undeterred, he married a third time, and a third woman died. After that Nemissa came to get Cloud Carrier, who disappeared from his village and was never seen again. (Spence)

Netami-gho The primal mother of the Lenni Lenape (Delaware) created the turtles, beasts, and birds that inhabit the earth, while monsters and snakes were created by a bad spirit who also made flies and mosquitoes. (McCutchen)

Netche'nsta The Tahlian said this goddess was like a post and the soil was like a tent. When Netche'nsta grew tired and shifted, earthquakes shook the land. The goddess grew slowly weaker, so someday the earth would disappear beneath heavenly waters. Netche'nsta was the mother of all beings, both human and animal, for whom she provided food. (Teit 1919)

Nokomis Nokomis is the Algonquin name for the goddess called Eithinoha by the Iroquois. She ruled the earth and its produce, and she created food for people and animals. She had a daughter, Oniata, the corn maiden. When Oniata was wandering through the land, looking for dew, an evil spirit abducted her and held her under the earth, but the sun found her and led her back to the surface. Another legend says men, attracted by Oniata's loveliness, fought over her. When the Iroquois women complained, Oniata explained that she never wished for the men's attentions. To ensure that men would return to their families, she left the earth, leaving behind only spring wildflowers.

The Menominee described Nokomis, also known as Masâkamek'okiu, as grandmother of the trickster rabbit Mánabus. A number of variants of her story were told, with the daughter typically dying while birthing twins or triplets, only one of whom survived. Overwhelmed by grief, Nokomis put the surviving baby under a bowl, later finding a rabbit that she raised as her grandchild. In one story, Nokomis's daughter became pregnant by the wind while gathering wild potatoes, after which she gave birth to Mánabus, a wolf named Múhwase, and a sharp flint stone that cut the girl in two. Nokomis punished the flint by throwing it away but raised the other children. Another version said the goddess found under her food dish a daughter, Pikâkamik'okiu, who grew into a woman instantly. Impregnated by four invisible beings, Pikâkamik'okiu died, ripped apart during delivery. Nokomis found no solace from her grief until she laid down her food dish, from which the trickster rabbit was born.

Among the Penobscot, Nok-a-mi was the primal woman, who appeared at time's beginning, already bowed with age. The next woman to appear was Nee-gar-oose, who brought love and color to the universe and who became the mother of all people. After a time, she became downcast because her children were hungry. So she asked her husband to kill her and bury her with a certain ritual. The man did as he was told. Seven days later, he returned to find that, from his wife's body, the first corn and tobacco had grown. (Bierhorst

1976; Converse; Johnston 1995; Judson; Nicolar; Skinner and Satterlee)

Nomhewena Pokaila A California Wintun myth begins in the home of this old woman who lived by digging roots, her only food. After ten years, she had used up all the root vegetables in her area, except for one small portion that, when she started to dig it, began crying like a child. She dug deeper until she found a baby, whom she brought home. There she raised the child, who grew fast. Within a few weeks, he was old enough to talk and to run around, so she warned him he must never approach the east. He was curious but obeyed. A few weeks later, when he was fully grown, Nomhewena Pokaila told him her people had all been devoured by a cannibal who lived in the direction of sunrise. The boy, Tulchuherris, determined to kill them. Although Nomhewena Pokaila feared for her child, she sent along her own wisdom in the form of a dwarfish being who hid in Tulchuherris's hair and warned him against difficulties. With that help, the boy tricked the cannibal so that he split in half and was thrown into the sky, becoming the sun and moon. (Curtin 2004)

Nonō'osqua The Bella Coola "mother of flowers" lives in the House of Myths, from which she brings forth all the plants every spring, when two old women call forth her power in ritual. (Boas 1898)

Norwan This Wintun goddess brought food to earth. Daughter of earth and sun, Norwan danced above growing plants each day until sunset. Bearing a flowering staff and with flowers in her hair, she rubbed acorns between her hands, creating forests. Feathers from behind her ears formed flocks of birds.

She had many suitors. But she rejected them: this one smelled bad, that one had a crooked mouth, another had a hot temper. Then came Norbis Kiemila, a wild-looking man. Despite his peculiar appearance, Norwan could not keep her eyes off him. The next night he slept with her but slipped away before daybreak.

Norwan created a magical outfit of flowers and went off to a dance attended by all beings, including divinities of light and beauty. Two of them, twin brothers, seduced Norwan with erotic dancing. Although she had created a bond with Norbis Kiemila, Norwan was unable to resist the twins, with whom she left the dance.

At this moment Norbis Kiemila arrived, beautifully attired. He sought Norwan, but she could not be found. He roused a group of fighters to help him reclaim Norwan, but the twins refused to give her up. So the world's first war was launched. While it went on, the twins kept Norwan tied up. Escaping, she regretted her attraction to the twins, although she also regretted meeting Norbis Kiemila, whom she liked less than the twins. To her horror, the wars continued, with allies gathering warriors and many battles. To end it all, Norwan's brother Olelbis turned people into animals. No longer able to recognize their enemies, they ceased their warfare. (Curtin 2004)

Nunnehi Gourd-headed, hairless, and tall, these Cherokee spirits liked to attend funerals, for they knew dancing would follow. Enamored men followed them home, only to see the Nunnehi walk into a lake or through a rock. Benevolent nature spirits, they worried about the difficulties Cherokee people face. Once, they tried to move all the Cherokee to their own world, so people would be free of suffering and pain. They visited each village in turn, telling its residents to fast for seven days and seven nights. That was too much for many people, who ate morsels of food during the preparatory week. When the Nunnehi led the people through a mountain, those who had kept faith disappeared, while the rest remained. (Uguwiyuak)

Núwakanda This was the name taken after her transformation into a spirit woman by an Iowa girl originally named Thiógrita'mi. Her original name meant "born from a foot," because the youngest of her brothers got a splinter in his foot that, when removed, turned into a baby girl with magical powers. When her four brothers were killed by a cannibal spirit, the girl went after the cannibal's brothers, killing them all and carrying their heads around until the cannibal found her. Then she challenged the cannibal, infuriating the spirit sufficiently that it threw the heads of her brothers at the girl. She then did magic over them, so they re-formed into living beings and awoke, believing they had only slept a long time. She then told them she was transforming herself into a spirit and disappeared from sight. (Skinner)

Omamama The Cree ancestral goddess, beautiful and old as the earth, was loving to her children, the spirits and the divinities. Her firstborn was the thunderbird; her second, the sorcerer frog; her third, the hero Weesakayjac; and finally the wolf and beaver. Rocks and plants fell from her womb until the earth was populated. (Waters)

Öng Wuhti Öng Wuhti appears in the mythology of the Hopi, Zuñi, Keres, and Acoma as a divinity connected with the earth. To encourage abundance and fertility, a ritual simulated intercourse, after which the participants offered each other bowls of seeds and of salt. The Zuñi said Öng Wuhti originally lived in the ocean, but feeling crowded by people living on the shores, she moved to the mountains, turning interior pools and basins salty when she sat beside them. In Zuñi territory she met the god of turquoise, with whom she lived until people discovered her home, whereupon she hid within the mountains. Her lover followed, leaving footprints of blue stone. (Hardin; Tyler)

Oochigeaskw' This Micmac girl was regularly tormented by her two older sisters, who burned her with coals until she was covered with scars (hence her name, "rough-faced girl") and claimed she caused her own injuries by playing with fire. But she found a way to escape. In the village was an invisible man who walked out each night accompanied by his sister. Any girl who could see him would become his wife, but none managed to see the invisible one. Because no one would give her decent attire, Oochigeaskw' made her own from rags and birch bark and went to the home of the invisible one. There she was welcomed kindly by the sister, who asked if she could see the man. And indeed she could. The sister magically transformed Oochigeaskw' into a beautiful bride and she married the invisible man and moved to his lodge.

Another version of the story has more supernatural overtones, with the main character being Noomeegal, the rain woman who arrived with her brother, the invisible thunder man, at a Micmac village, where she set up her camp and announced that any girl who could see her brother would become his wife. Because Noomeegal had plenty of fresh meat, it was clear her brother was an excellent hunter and therefore a great catch as a husband. They did not want to let his invisibility put them off, so they began to lie to Noomeegal when she asked the girls, one at a time, to describe her brother's appearance. Each time, it was clear that the girl could not see him.

Among the girls was Oojeegwee-esgay, "covered with scars," a girl beaten regularly by her older sisters, hence her unfortunate name. Both of the sisters had tried and failed to gain Noomeegal's brother, but dreams introduced Oojeegwee-esgay to the young man, so when she went to try her luck, she was able to describe accurately the hunter brother to Noomeegal. But when she gained a husband, Oojeegwee-esgay began to weep, afraid her scarred face would make her unlovable. Noomeegal turned the girl's skin smooth and unmarked, then gave her fabulous bridal garments. After she had dressed herself, a handsome young man appeared and begged her to become his wife. When Oojeegwee-esgay shyly agreed, Noomeegal caused a heavy rain to fall, which erased any sign of the camp she shared with her brother. None were ever seen in human form again. The story may be a local version of the famous story of **Cinderella** (see Scandinavia), brought to the area by French settlers. (Leland; Melançon)

Oo-kwa-we O-ne-ha-tah, primal mother of the Onondaga, gave birth to three children: bear, wolf, and deer. When a lost human baby came upon the trio, all offered to care for him, but O-ne-ha-tah pointed out that the wolf would find the baby a tempting morsel, and the deer would run away. So she gave the baby to bear mother Oo-kwa-we. The boy grew up as a bear, eating berries and salmon. His human scent scared other bears away, so Oo-kwa-we's family always had the best pickings in the berry patches.

But one day Oo-kwa-we had a dream and warned her children they were about to die. She packed sacred bundles for the bears but gave nothing to her human son. One at a time, the bears walked up to the humans and were shot, but the boy could see their spirits, escaped on the contents of their sacred bundles. When his bear family was dead, the boy discovered the hunter was his lost father. Brought back to humanity, the boy never forgot his animal relatives. (Beauchamp 1893)

Pahalali This little girl cried so much, said the Serrano Indians of California's San Bernardino County, that her mother threw her away. A rock spirit adopted her. When the girl was old enough to ask questions, she asked a gopher who lived with them whether the spirit was her mother. The gopher told Pahalali she had a human mother in the nearby village. With gopher's help, Pahalali escaped from the rock cave and returned to her human home, where her mother was delighted to see her. But all did not end well, because the rock spirit came after his adopted daughter and, although she used courage and trickery to try to save the village, both the spirit and the villagers died, fighting over the rejected daughter. (Gifford and Block)

P'áh-hlee-oh The Tigua say the moon woman P'áh-hlee-oh gave birth to plants, animals, and people. There was no darkness, for when the moon rose, the earth was as bright as during the day. Everyone on earth grew exhausted, so P'áh-hlee-oh voluntarily gave up one of her eyes. Her light diminished, and the earth rested.

Despite being blind in one eye, P'áh-hlee-oh made her husband, the dawn, supremely happy. But two sisters (the Yellow Corn Maidens, Ee-eh-ch-chó-ri-ch'áhm-nin) who envied P'áh-hlee-oh lured her into a trap and drowned her. Her husband withdrew, plunging the world into darkness. No one could locate the missing P'áh-hlee-oh. Finally a turkey buzzard came back with news that he had found a mound of extraordinarily beautiful white flowers. The dawn man found it and revived P'áh-hlee-oh. Once home, she cast a spell on her rivals, who turned into rattlesnakes. (Erdoes and Ortiz)

Pahto A mountain goddess of the Yakima and Klickitat, she was embodied in Mount Adams. Once, she was a wife of the sun, who had four other mountain wives, and two of them stood in the way of the sun's rays each morning. Plash-Plash and Wahkshum received sunshine long before the god even noticed Pahto. So Pahto killed the other wives. She dashed off their heads so she could feel the sun's first rays.

Then she grew greedy. She stole berries and trees, salmon and trout, from other mountains. Klah Klahnee demanded the gods do something. First a truce was proposed, with the return of half the stolen goods. When Pahto refused, her head was blown off, leaving a pile of rocks. What had been stolen was returned, leaving only a few berry bushes and some elk and fish. The sky spirit, seeing how Pahto had been humbled, offered her a new head: a cap of snow that shined in the sunlight. (Clark 1953)

Pakchuso Pokaila The Wintuns said the creator god Olelbis lived with two women who had this name and who were his grandmothers. They lived in the world before our world. People lived there too, different from today's humans. When those people set the world afire, the grandmothers built a new world. They instructed

Olelbis to provide white oak for the lodgepole, with black and western oak for the wall supports. But there was no roof until one grandmother waved her hands and a blooming plant grew from it. She wove it into a mat and gave it to her grandson to form the roof. The two then wove mats for walls from blooming plants they created. (Curtin 2004)

Panyoka The people of the Tewa pueblo in San Juan, New Mexico, were divided into halves, or moities, that represented summer and winter. The goddess of summer was Panyoka, who was honored with a small stone figure, while the winter goddess was Oyika. Ceremonies in the appropriate season honored the two divinities. (Kurath)

Pavinmana From the Hopi settlement of Oraibi comes the story of "water girl," a heroine who went with her sister to draw water from a sacred well at Lenva ("flute spring") and saw an insect singing a **Kachina** song while skating on the water. She caught the cute bug and brought it home, providing it with water on which it skated and sang, delighting the people of Oraibi. But not long afterward, Pavinmana's house was flooded by rain, and the insect was carried out the door on the flood. Pavinmana ran after the insect as it was swept along until it reached land at Duwanasavi, another sacred place and the home of the god of seed germination.

There she met a handsome man. "I am looking for my pet," she said, to which he responded, "I am your pet. My name is Hicanavaiya." The young man explained that he had come to take Pavinmana home to his family, and she readily agreed to go. As they were traveling, she felt the need to urinate. When she stepped off the path to do so, she heard a voice beneath her asking her to hold her water. When she looked, there was Spider Woman, **Kókyangwúti**, who told her she had come to prepare Pavinmana for the challenges that lay before her.

After receiving six magical turkey feathers from Kókyangwúti, Pavinmana went back to her

companion, who flew them to the ice mountains. There she met Angwushahai'í, mother of the Kachinas, who put her into a bedroom of ice, where she was warned she might freeze to death. But following Kókyangwúti's instructions, Pavinmana put a magical turkey feather beneath her and another over her, and so she slept comfortably. The next day Angwushahai'í was surprised to find Pavinmana alive and so set another test for her: to grind ice like corn. She left the girl alone, and Kókyangwúti appeared to help her out. Pavinmana ground the ice and, under Kókyangwúti's instructions, treated all around her with kindness.

Because of this kindness, as well as her powers of survival, the Kachina mother decided Pavinmana could become the bride of her nephew. So Angwushahai'í instructed the people to make a bridal costume for Pavinmana in preparation for her return to Oraibi. The girl and her new husband returned, to discover their happiness roused envy in the hearts of other men, and so Hicanavaiya assumed again the form of an insect and escaped, leaving Pavinmana behind but promising to watch over her from the ice mountains. A similar story tells of the girl Pasiyaunim, who was courted by the germination god Muyingwa; the tales may have originally been the same story. (Titiev)

Pêp'äkijisê "Panther Woman" appeared to the midwestern Menominee as a powerful being who lived under the water, a theme that also appears in the ancient effigy mounds of the "underwater panther" found in the region. She drew a warrior to herself through her magical powers, even though he was already living with a powerful woman magician. But when he brought her from beneath the waves to witness a ball game, she saw the other team wearing the skins of her massacred panther relatives. Distraught with grief, she begged to be taken away from the ball ground, but her husband played another game and defeated the thunderbirds who had destroyed Pêp'äkijisê's relations, thus avenging his wife. Such wars between the underwater people and the sky people are a common feature of Menominee mythology. (Skinner and Satterlee)

Pohaha This Tewa heroine refused to learn women's skills, preferring to hunt and raid. Although she was mocked for this choice, the raillery ended when she became leader of the men's war party. Lest anyone question that this redoubtable warrior was female, she raised her skirts as she approached enemies. She wore a mask with one side blue and the other yellow to terrify her opponents. Named Chief Defender of the Clan, Pohaha held that title throughout her life. After her death, her mask became an honored relic. A similar story is told of the girl warrior Chakwena, whose face turned into a mask while she was fighting. (Elledge; Neithammer; Parsons 1994)

Pook-jin-skwess This Algonquin witch was a shapeshifter who could appear as a woman, as a group of women, or as an old man. Her antagonist was the adventuring hero Gloosap. Once he stuck her to a tree in the shape of an old man, but she found a hatchet and cut herself free. Wood stuck to her, for which she was relentlessly teased. In disgust, she ran away in the shape of a wolf, then turned into a mosquito to torment humans. Other versions of the story say Pook-jin-skwess was a voluptuous woman who, when she was ready to die, transformed herself into a mosquito so she might continue to enjoy the flesh of young men. (Elledge; Leland; Speck 1935)

Puchi Yushuba It is difficult to know what impact Christianization had upon the recorded "great flood" story of the Choctaws, in which this mysterious bird woman appears. A prophet forecast doom: first impenetrable darkness, then a vast flood. The flood swept away everyone but the prophet, who rested upon a raft of sassafras logs. As he drifted on the floodwaters, a black bird flew over, cawed, and disappeared. Not long after, a blue bird appeared, who flew around the prophet's head and into the west. This turned the prophet's boat in that direction, and he came to an island filled with animals of all sorts—except mammoths, which had been killed in the flood. There were, however, no women with whom he might repopulate the earth, until

the blue bird came back and transformed herself into a woman, who became the mother of all people. She bore the name Puchi Yushuba ("lost pigeon" or "turtledove") in memory of her original identity. (Swanton 2001)

Qamā'its Among the Bella Coola, Qamā'its was a warrior who lived in the east. Although she created the earth, she also brought death, famine, and disease. Better for all the people, the Bella Coola say, when Qamā'its stays in her sea home or in the treeless prairie behind the sky. Her myths say the mountains were once much larger, but Qamā'its brought them to their current size by breaking their noses. Researchers in the early part of the twentieth century found evidence that she had once been the most important Bella Coola divinity. (Boas 1898; Judson; Wherry)

Qeuxu This Snuqualmi ancestral mother brought food to this world. Qeuxu ("steelhead") and her four sisters (each of whom represented a different kind of salmon) stole a baby and raised it to become their shared husband. By him they had so many children that, when he returned to humanity, he brought the abundant salmon with him. (Haeberlin and Boas)

Rhpisunt The Haida tell of Rhpisunt, daughter of the Wolf clan's chief, who was insensitive to the feelings of bears, chatting with friends in the forest instead of singing to warn bears of her presence. The bear people felt her behavior mocked them. One day, she stepped into droppings and cursed the bears. Then the strap on her pack broke and, while she was mending it, her friends left her. Two handsome men came out of the brush and spoke to her courteously, offering to help.

The men, wearing bear robes, led her to their village. One introduced Rhpisunt to the chief, his father, a huge man who sat in a log house lined with bearskin cloaks. Suddenly, at Rhpisunt's side, a fat lady named Tsects appeared. She whispered to Rhpisunt that she should never relieve herself without breaking off a piece of copper and placing it on the ground above the buried excrement.

Rhpisunt did as she was told. Soon she saw why: the Bear People, finding copper left behind after the woman's trip to the bushes, judged her complaints about the bear's leavings justifiable, as she herself passed shiny metal. Rhpisunt married the Bear Prince, and Tsects provided a huge feast.

But the woman's family had found her footprints with those of bears. The Haida raged through the forest killing bears, and in the village of the Bear People there was mourning. Finally, led by Rhpisunt's dog, one of the woman's brothers found her, together with her Bear Prince and their twin sons, in a cave. The visionary prince knew he would die, so he shared magical formulas with his wife before he was speared. Rhpisunt was brought back to the Haida village, where she grew to a great and revered age. Her sons, taking off their bear jackets while in human company, returned at her death to their father's people, but the Wolf clan always recognized bears as relatives.

Raven clan members tell a similar story about Bear Mother Kind-a-wuss. Because she loved a man of her own clan whom she could not marry, Kind-a-wuss refused to marry anyone. She and her lover eloped and lived for a time in happiness. When he wished to go home, Kind-a-wuss refused, saying she did not wish to face the approbation. When the young man returned, he could not find Kind-a-wuss, who had been stolen by a bear. Many years later, the man consulted a shaman, who revealed that Kind-a-wuss could be found in a huge cedar, from the top of which a ladder hung. Once at home, she pined for her half-bear children, whom her lover had kidnapped. In consideration of the years they had lost, the families of the lovers agreed to let them marry. (Barbeau 1946, 1953; Bierhorst 1985; Deans 1889; Erdoes and Ortiz; Krause)

Sanyu.xáv Among the Yuma people of California (also known as the Quechan or Kwtsaan), Sanyu.xáv was a mythic figure, possibly the sun, because her name means "to set in the west." The mother of twins, Sanyu.xáv conceived miraculously by making two flutes from willow that grew in water where she was swimming. Despite being past menopause, she gave birth to two boys who could become birds or lizards at will. She tried to bring them up well, but they were forever changing into another form and escaping her watchful eye. Finally the boys settled into human form and grew into handsome lads.

When they were grown, they picked up the flutes that Sanyu.xáv had made and began to play them to attract women. It worked: soon twin girls arrived, perfect mates for the men. Although Sanyu.xáv set magical barriers against the girls, they found their way to the boys. Sanyu.xáv was furious but wily. She announced a wedding dance and, while the girls enjoyed themselves, bewitched one so that she fell over dead. Out of sorrow, her intended mate died too. Sanyu.xáv was not done: she turned the other girl into a buzzard. But the people, angry at Sanyu.xáv's abuse of her magical power, drove her from their village and banished her. (Swann)

Scomalt The Okanogan and Salish say Scomalt ruled a primordial titanic race. Her people, the white giants, lived on an island in midocean, where they were constantly at war. Scomalt separated the most warlike and set them adrift, where they died of exposure, except for one man and one woman. This couple discovered a rich land and settled. Although they had once been white giants, their time at sea had burned them brown and shrunk them, so their children were all bronze and the size of humans today. If rivers begin to grow, the continents will shrink to islands, and the end of the world will be near. (Allen 1991; Clark 1953, 1966)

Selmayi Peyote Woman of the Kiowa makes her presence known when one eats a female peyote button, which permits the worshipper to hear her high-pitched voice as she sings with the leader, who holds the rattle and staff. (LaBarre)

Sélu The Cherokee vegetation goddess Sélu lived alone, an old woman full of wisdom but set in her ways. One day, she saw blood on the ground and covered it with a jar. A few days later, she picked up the jar and found an infant boy, whom she raised to be a hunter. Sélu taught him nothing of plants, for she provided all the maize and beans they could eat. She cautioned him never to look at her when she was making dinner.

The boy became curious. One day, peering into Sélu's window, he saw her disrobe and scratch herself over a pot. Cornmeal and beans ran into the pot, for she herself was food. When he refused dinner, Sélu knew he had spied upon her. She sent him away with instructions that he should set fire to her house. He did so and followed her dying instructions by seeking a wife from a distant group. When he brought his bride back to Sélu's land, he found enough food growing to feed their descendants. (Allen 1991; Awaikta; Kilpatrick and Kilpatrick; Leeming and Page; Mooney 1888; Swanton 1931, 1929)

Sintesepela win This Lakota enchantress lured men into sexual relationships when they were hunting, causing them to become mute or die. Sometimes she appeared to women in dreams as Winyan Nunpapika ("double woman"); after their encounter endowed them with spiritual power, such women were alluring to men and took many lovers. They sometimes became doctors or renowned artists. Sintesepela win was sometimes conflated with Ite (see **Hanwi**). However, they appear to have originally been distinct figures. (Berlo)

Sit! tu kohan'nî The Tlingit "fair girls of the glaciers" lived on the ice and came to shamans to inspire them. When traversing glaciers, the Tlingit people talked to these spirit women, asking that they not sit on travelers, apparently a reference to the threat of avalanche. (Swanton 1908)

Skwákowtemus The Penobscot Skwákowtemus (or Pskégdemusaz) went half-naked, wearing only bits of moss. She haunted the woods, looking for children to kidnap. If one wandered into the forest beyond the campfire, Skwákowtemus snatched him or her. Even to think of her attracted her; men who thought about her found they could never marry human women.

Even nastier was the smelly, seductive Maskíkcwsu, who wore strips of bark and a mossy headdress as she rambled about the forest looking for men. She was a bereaved human mother killed by a man because her attentions to his child made him anxious. Afterward, she took revenge on humanity by stealing men and children. (Speck 1935)

Snēnē'ik This Bella Coola cannibal woman stole children and robbed graves, throwing bodies into a woven basket. She owned a home, where she offered visitors food that paralyzed them. She had many children, all wolves. In this world, she appeared as a black-faced hag with sleepy eyes who emitted low whistles. Despite her appearance and demeanor, Snēnē'ik was also the bestower of copper and food. (Boas 1898, 2002; Wherry)

Snîtsma'na With her sister AiaLilā'axa, this Bella Coola goddess helped humans wake from sleep. A protector, Snîtsma'na assisted anyone threatened with sickness or death. AiaLilā'axa protected the moon goddess En-kla-loi'-killa, washing her dirty face after eclipses and restoring her each month at the full moon. (Boas 1898)

Soi'ka Gäa'kwa The Seneca moon goddess is called "our grandmother" but represents all stages of woman's life. Each stage of her lunar cycle has a different name, and each moon within the year has a name of its own. No celestial body had more power, for this goddess brought luck in hunting. (Parker)

S'ts'tsi'naku Among the Keres, S'ts'tsi'naku created the earth by thinking. Whatever she visualized came to be, including the sacred beings who helped her create. By singing, she made the sacred sisters **Utset and Nowutset** from her medicine pouch. Her name means "thought woman," but she is also called Spider

Woman or Grandmother Spider; she is a form of the spider-creator found in other pueblo cultures under the name **Kókyangwúti**. Her sister was Shro-tu-na-ko, "Memory Woman."

Among the Acoma pueblo people, a similar goddess named Tsitctinako helped the sacred sisters create the world. Once they arrived in the surface world, she taught them how to prepare corn, how to make mountains by throwing stones, how to create living things, including humans. When the girls became envious of each other and fought, Tsitctinako was banished from this world. (Allen 1991; Erdoes and Ortiz; Leeming and Page; Tyler; Weigle 1987, 1989)

Tacoma The earth goddess of the Salish, Nisqualli, Puyallup, and Yakima was embodied in the snowy peak of Mount Rainier. Tacoma, protector of fresh waters and spawning salmon, was a hugely fat woman who shared a man with two other wives. The man, angered at their constant quarreling, set two on one side of Puget Sound, and Tacoma on the opposite shore. But this did not deter her from shooting insults at her co-wives. One legend says her husband and a co-wife kept Tacoma constantly on the move until, exhausted, she refused to go farther. But she continued to hate the other wife, at whose head she threw hot coals, so Mount Constance today is bald.

Another story says that when Tacoma was a young mountain, she married a mountain prince. Though not yet full grown, she soon outstripped her husband in size. To make room for her husband and his people, she moved across Puget Sound, taking berries and salmon with her. Tacoma grew so huge that she ate anything that set foot on her slopes, people as well as animals. Finally a god dared Tacoma to swallow him, after he'd pinned himself to another mountain. Tacoma engorged vast quantities of rock and water, but the god could not be moved. She burst open and died, and today's mountain is her corpse. (Clark 1953)

Tahc-i The kingfisher courted the Tunica sun goddess in human disguise. He took Tahc-i home in the dark, telling her he lived in an upstairs room. When the girl woke up, she was out on the limb of a hackberry tree. She was perplexed, ashamed, and hungry and was not satisfied when the kingfisher brought her minnows for breakfast. She began to sing mournfully and rose into the sky, radiating light. (Haas)

Tetogolee A geographical story told by the Loucheaux, a people from near the Mackenzie River in Canada, begins at the start of time, when the world was filled with giants. A widow named Tetogolee lived with three sons. She was a sorcerer, and when game grew scarce one year she made magic and sent her sons to hunt. She told them they should be careful never to look back once they had started home. All went well until they were nearly home, when one of the boys looked over his shoulder to see how long it was until sunset. At that moment he and his brothers were turned to stone and his mother into a sandstone bluff that bears her name. (Carnsell and Barbeau)

Tlitcaplitana The Bella Coola heavenly woman descended from her home to heal the sick, granting them secret knowledge and chants. Sometimes contact with her power killed the patient. But that is not because of any ill will on the Tlitcaplitana's part, for she is the most generous of heavenly spirits, though ugly in the extreme, with a big snout and ropelike breasts. Her singing was as beautiful as she was not. (McIlwraith)

Tomaiyovit The Luiseño people said Tomaiyovit gave birth to the landscape by copulating with her brother, the sky god Tukmit. But she made the sun too bright and the earth was scorched. Tomaiyovit took the sun away until the earth recovered, then brought it out again. The people raised it high into the sky so it did not burn them anymore. (Gifford and Block; Leeming and Page)

Totolmatha The morning star goddess of the Pomo people lived on Clear Lake, where she sang every morning in a beautiful high voice, so high that people could barely hear her. Every morning she swam in the lake while her hawk husband flew above her. But one morning they were playing together in the lake when the sky began to brighten. When she returned to the village, she was teased by those who had seen her at play. This made her sad and angry, especially when she realized she would never be happy among people because she was from the sky land, from which the eagle god Gulluk descended to prey upon them. Totolmatha decided to deal with Gulluk.

Tata, her husband, wanted to go along. When the pair reached the heavens, they found pools of blood and mountains of bleached bones, the work of Gulluk. Shrinking Tata into a speck and hiding him, Totolmatha hid herself in Gulluk's house and, as soon as he returned sated with eating human flesh, cut him so deeply with her fingernail that he bled to death. Packing all the riches she could carry, Totolmatha set fire to Gulluk's house and ran from the flames down the long path to earth. Behind them, the flames filled the sky, lighting their way to home and a victory celebration. (Clark and Williams)

Tsagigla'lal On the Columbia River, this Wishram woman was a culture heroine and chief. When Coyote decreed that women could no longer be chiefs, she refused to give up responsibility for her people. Instead, she turned herself into stone so she could forever protect them. A petroglyph depicts her watchful eyes. (Clark 1953)

Tsihooskwallaa The most brilliant weaver of her people, the Chilkat heroine Tsihooskwallaa lived as a recluse near the mountains, where she gathered wild sheep's wool for her blankets. She had no interest in marrying but made her solitary home in the woods beside a great river. There the salmon people noticed her and, despite her request that they keep her whereabouts secret, gossiped about her and revealed her location. This attracted the attention of a man named Num-Kil-slas, who traveled upriver to find her and

proposed that she marry his son, Gunnuckets. She agreed but soon regretted it, for these were not people but animals, a raven and a martin, respectively, who stole all her blankets and left her cold and destitute. In despair, she wandered about the woods until she died of exposure. The blankets became the treasures of the Chilkat people, who brought them out for ceremonies and who learned the craft of weaving by studying them. (Taylor)

Tso The Yucchi creation myth begins with a water-covered earth, a few creatures, and the sun goddess Tso. The creatures decided to find earth on which to live, by diving under the water. Beaver and otter were defeated, but crawfish managed to bring back a clawful of soil. From it, animals and birds built the earth. But the earth was not fertile, for the sun lived on it, making it too hot. Out of love for the other creatures, she leaped into the sky. From that height she dropped blood as she was menstruating. Where it fell, a baby grew. Tso raised him and made him a warrior. From him all the Yucchi descended, and because of his relationship to Tso, they considered themselves descendants of the sun. (Speck 1909; Swanton 1929)

Tukwishhemish Once there were three little girls named Moki, Kopi, and Tewe, say the Cahuilla people of southern California. They were plain-looking children but charming because they laughed often. In their village a very beautiful woman named Tukwishhemish giggled sometimes but never laughed, because she would not open her mouth very wide. This made the girls curious, so they tried to make Tukwishhemish laugh. Their success revealed her secret: she had two rows of teeth in her upper jaw. Humiliated at having her deformity revealed, Tukwishhemish rose into the sky to become the North Star, and the girls, ashamed for having tormented her, also rose into the sky, where they became three of the Pleiades, the other four being formed from ornaments the girls were wearing when they were transformed. The Cahuilla call this constellation Chehaum (see also **Chehiayam** above). (Gifford and Block)

Uncegila Southwestern and lower midwestern people say this earth-shaking serpent was a transformed witch. Her body was covered with mica, her head crowned with a red crystal. She was always ravenously hungry. She was so terrifying that looking at her blinded onlookers, who went mad and died. The red heart of Uncegila gave the power to see into the future, but only medicine arrows of a magical woman could kill the monster.

Two boys, one of them blind, went to find that woman. When she demanded that a boy sleep with her to gain the medicine arrows, the blind one volunteered. As soon as he touched her, the old woman turned into a beautiful maiden who gave the boys the powerful arrows and the secret ways to kill Uncegila. When the boys returned, they found nothing but a rock face where the crone's cave had been.

The Lakota described Unktehi as the enemy of Thunderbird, one of their culture heroes. She lived in the Missouri River, which she filled with her snaky body; her children were streams running into the river. Because she disdained humanity, she flooded the land. Thunderbird came to the rescue, launching a battle against Unktehi and her children. When the storms subsided, Unktehi's skeleton stretched across the land, forming the Badlands. (Erdoes and Ortiz; Swann 2004; Walker)

Unelanuhi Early in creation, the Cherokee sun goddess lived on the other side of the world. At a council of the animals, fox announced where light could be found. Possum tried to bring it to this side but burned off his tail. Buzzard tried but burned off the feathers on his claws. Then Grandmother Spider, **Kanene Ski Amai Yehi**, spun a web on which she traveled across the sky. She grabbed the sun, roped it into her basket, and brought it to this world.

But the new sun sat too low in the sky. People were dying from its heat. So, handbreadth by handbreadth,

the animal elders moved the sun upward. At seven hands high, the sun was just right, and there she has stayed to this day.

Unelanuhi slept with a young man once a month who refused to tell his name. So she dipped her hands in ashes and rubbed his face in the dark. When daylight came, her brother met her at breakfast with ash on his face. He ran in shame and stayed as far away in the sky as he could. Once a month, however, he could not resist visiting her in the new moon's darkness.

Unelanuhi had a daughter, whom she visited every day in her house on the point of noon. Every day, she saw people squint at her. This made her think them ugly, so she decided to kill them with heat. The spirit people told their human kin that, to survive, they had to kill the sun. They transformed two people into a copperhead snake and a spreading adder, who traveled to heaven and awaited Unelanuhi.

As she stopped, the sun's brilliance blinded the adder, so he spit yellow slime, and the snakes slunk off in disgrace. The spirits transformed two more people into a rattlesnake and the monstrous Uktena, who traveled to the sky. But the rattlesnake rushed at the sun's daughter rather than wait for the sun. He killed her, then ran away with Uktena back to earth.

The sun mother shut herself up in grief. Darkness descended, and people began to freeze. The spirits told the humans to bring back the sun's daughter. Seven men were outfitted with a box to carry the sun daughter's soul. In the land of ghosts, the travelers trapped her in the box, which they had been warned to keep tightly closed. But the girl pleaded to be let out. Her captors took pity and pushed back the lid. Something flew past. Then a cardinal called out. When they returned to the land of life, the box was empty, for the bird was the sun's daughter. Since then, no one can come back from the land of ghosts.

The sun's tears threatened to flood the world. Young people tried to help by dancing and singing, but the sun never glanced up. When the drummer changed the beat, Unelanuhi looked up in surprise and smiled. Her light returned to earth. (Allen 1991; Erdoes and

Ortiz; Hardin; Payne Manuscripts; Mooney 1900; Uguwiyuak; Hudson; Davis; Thompson)

Unk She was created by the earth-mother **Maka**, say the Lakota people of the plains, to be the most beautiful woman on earth and to be the earth woman's companion. But Unk was so beautiful that Maka became jealous of her. They quarreled, and Maka threw Unk into the water and remained alone.

Unk, desiring revenge, took waters as her domain and mated with a male god to conceive Iya the whirlwind, who frightened everyone but his mother. She took him as her lover and conceived the spirit of deceit and flattery, the trickster Gnaski. Then she grew aroused by the ugliness of a reptile named Unhcegi, whom she took as her mate and produced the monster race called the Unktehi as well as the germ-like beings called Mini Watu. Finally she gave birth to Keya, the turtle, who became her servant. Angry that the other divinities would not offer her partner a place among them, she withdrew to cause trouble for people and gods. (Dooling)

U'thu Uta This Cherokee giantess could change shape at will. But her natural form was a rock-skinned woman with a bony forefinger. She could lift boulders, cement rocks together by touching them, and build mountains from pebbles. Always hungry, she lured children from their play and stole their livers. She caused no pain, left no wound, but the afflicted died. Anyone who met an old woman singing about eating livers ran away.

A council determined that a trap would be the best way to rid the earth of U'thu Uta, so a pit was dug and a bonfire lit. Soon she came down the path, looking like an ordinary woman. She was not shot immediately, because the men felt kinship with her. But when she fell into the hole and turned into a monster, they lost sympathy.

The hunters emptied their quivers. Nothing could penetrate U'thu Uta's skin. She was immensely strong,

and it seemed as though she would climb out and kill them. A titmouse sang "un, un, un," which the hunters thought meant "unahu," or heart. So they shot at U'thu Uta's heart, but the arrows glanced off. Then a chickadee bravely landed on U'thu Uta's right hand. The hunters shot there, and the old woman fell dead, for her heart was hidden in her wrist. Thereafter the chickadee was honored for bravery, and the earth was freed from U'thu Uta. (Mooney 2006)

Uti Hiata "Mother Corn" was a significant Pawnee and Arikara divinity, born in primeval times after ducks brought silt from the bottom of the cosmic lake to build prairies and foothills. The sky father, seeing giants populating the earth, sent a flood to destroy them. After he replanted the earth with maize seeds that sprouted into human beings, he sent Uti Hiata to assist at their birth.

Finding no one on earth, Uti Hiata walked about. Thunder kidnapped her and hid her beneath the earth. There, she was helped by mole, mouse, and badger to dig through the ground. As she emerged, so did people, to whom she taught secrets of life, methods of agriculture, and religious rituals. (Dorsey 1997)

Utset and Nowutset The first mothers of humanity are, to the pueblo dwellers of the Southwest, two sisters created by **Kókyangwúti**. They were sung into being, then they created earth, sky, people, plants, language, and gods through song.

The Acoma say these goddesses, born in the underworld, grew impatient to move, but a spirit counseled them to wait. Eons passed, and baskets appeared, full of seeds to plant. The land above was soon filled with life. Finally a tree pulled them along toward the surface. With the help of a badger, they reached the upper world.

The sisters lived in peace until a rivalry began. Stories said they started a riddle contest, and Nowutset, the duller sister, lost to Utset, who killed her. Another narrative says the sisters argued and decided that whoever the sun touched first in the morning would be the winner. Nowutset was taller, but Utset cheated and won. The contest was restaged, and a fight began. The sisters, unable to live with each other, separated. Utset became the mother of pueblo-dwelling people, and Nowutset, of all others. (Allen 1991; Erdoes and Ortiz; Tyler; Weigle 1989)

Wah-Kah-Nee The Chinook were struck with an endless winter. The ice never moved, and people began to fear for their survival. A council was called, and the elders recalled that such winters resulted from murdering birds. Each person was asked about such a crime. The children pointed to Wah-Kah-Nee, who confessed she had struck a bird with a stone, and it had died.

The Chinook dressed the girl in fine garments and exposed her on a block of ice. Instantly the ice crashed from the river, and summer came like a flood. A year later, when the ice was moving, they saw a block of ice containing the girl's body and fetched it to shore. The girl revived and lived among them a sacred being, able to walk unprotected through the winter and to communicate with its spirits. (Clark 1953)

Wah Sil This sun goddess was the ancestor of all chiefs, for the matrilineal Natchez traced descent through the mother, and the chief was of the sun's family. In Wah Sil's honor, the Natchez kept a perpetual fire burning on the hearth of the solar temple, with three logs alight. (Berthoud; Swanton 1928)

Wäh-trōhn-yŏ-nōh'-nĕh According to the Wyandots, relatives of the Huron who in historical times moved to Kansas, this name ("keeper of the heavens") was borne by Little Turtle Woman, also called "Grandmother." She lived at the dawn of time, when there was no sun, no moon, no stars. Little Turtle was carried on a river of darkness, until she grabbed lightning and set a flame in the sky. But that first attempt baked the earth, so the council of beings told mud turtle to fix the problem. She made a hole in the sky where the sun went every night, but that left the earth dark again. So Little Turtle made the moon,

who married the sun, and they had the stars for children. When the sun grew jealous of his moon wife, he maimed her by taking some of her heat and imprisoned her. Little Turtle cured the moon woman so she grew back to her earlier size, but she grew sick with longing for her husband, shrinking back to a shadow. Women of the Wyandot were named in her honor into historical times. (Connelley)

Warharmi The Yuma said the creator sent the ambiguously gendered Warharmi to bring seeds and techniques of agriculture. Warharmi also brought the tradition of painting one's face and body for war, because she arrived war painted, frightening the people. The nearby Mohave honored a similar goddess, the primal woman warrior Nyohaiva, who brought war paint and feathers to earth. (Roscoe)

Waslaag This chipmunk heroine of the Klamath people of the Pacific Northwest and her companion Chihlas were kidnapped, to become wives of stars. Above the earth, Waslaag found her husband, a stellar rabbit, likable, but the husband of Chihlas would not let her see his face. When, encouraged by Waslaag, she managed to do so, Chihlas was horrified to discover he was all bloody. So the two girls plotted to escape. Although they were watched carefully, they managed to plait ropes out of weeds and to lower themselves from the heavens. But the husbands saw them and pursued. Quick-thinking Waslaag bit the rope of descent, and the girls fell safely back to earth. (Stern)

Weshellequa The primary Shawnee divinity was called "our grandmother" (Kohkomh∂ena), although she also had a personal name, possibly Weshellequa ("great spirit") or Paapood∂kwaki ("cloud"). Her name may be in a non-Shawnee language thought to have been spoken only by children. Weshellequa was huge and gray haired, with bad teeth. She lived in a bark house, where she wove and cooked like any other woman. No dish she cooked could ever be emptied, except by Weshellequa herself. Some myths suggest that her home was in the sky, where the dead went after passing over. Weshellequa gave them a sweat bath, then brought them to their final abode. Their activities depended upon their earthly lives. Warriors spent eternity dancing, while others had less exciting afterlives.

This goddess controlled all earthly elements. She specifically instructed winds not to blow women's clothing about immodestly. Women who wished to bring the sun on a cloudy day lifted their skirts to their waists, frightening the winds, who would blow the clouds away. Weshellequa set standards for human behavior and threatened doom if those standards were not upheld. Although turned into a male god in historical times, evidence is clear that the Shawnee supreme deity was originally female. (Schutz; Voegelin)

Winonah In Anishinaubae mythology, Winonah was a virgin mother raped four times, over many generations, by the same spirit. She was in the forest picking berries and, overtaken with a need to urinate, forgot the warning that women should never face west while making water. When the spirit saw her vagina, he had intercourse with her immediately. Through this spirit union, she acquired magical powers of fertility and longevity and four heroic sons. (Hardin; Johnston 2001)

Witsduk The family members of the California Modoc nature spirit Witsduk were made of light snow that drifts easily. They terrified the people until the shaman Tcutûk told them she would destroy them. But Tcutûk was frightened that she would meet the wily fox, Wus, while trying to destroy Witsduk and her family, so the people promised they would protect her. Fright got the better of them, however, and they ran away when Tcutûk was climbing a mountain, intent upon burying Witsduk and her family under a rock there. Sure enough, Tcutûk encountered Wus, who tore from her the bag that held the Witsduks. They all flew about and, although Wus could eat anything, he could not devour enough of them to save the people,

who were eaten by the Witsduks. Tcutûk turned into a squirrel, and Witsduk herself still haunts the place where the shaman tried to bury her. (Curtin 1971)

Wohpe This sacred woman brought secret knowledge to the Lakota and Ogallala. She appeared to two young men as a white-clad woman in clothing lavishly embroidered with porcupine quills. One young man was overtaken by lust, but the second recognized that she was no earthly woman. The first could not contain himself. He rushed open armed toward the woman. Wohpe smiled, and a cloud descended to cover their embrace.

When it passed, the woman stood alone with a skeleton at her feet. She told the second man to return to his village and build a sacred tent. When she entered the village, the people were enraptured. Walking seven times around the central fire, she gave them a sacred pipe and taught them ceremonies. Then she reminded them of the mysteries of their mother earth. Urging them always to honor her, she disappeared as a white buffalo.

Wohpe, the force of order and goddess of birds, appears as the source of all flowers, for she blew upon dust at the dawn of time until her breath enlivened them into bloom. She was the pattern of beauty for the divinities who made Hunku, the first woman and ancestor of all people who followed the buffalo. Wohpe offered rules of culture to people as they emerged. (Bierhorst 1985; Dooling; Erdoes and Ortiz; Powers; Vecsey; Sullivan; Steltenkamp; Walker)

Xa'a da The California Pomo described the morning star as "Day Woman" (or "morning eye fire"); her younger sister was Duwe da ("night woman"). Xa'a da lived originally on earth, where she saw people commit incest and other objectionable acts. So she fled to the sky to become the star of morning. Xa'a da traveled beyond the earth to kill a monstrous eagle that threatened humankind, for which she and her hawk husband were honored daily by the Pomo. (Miller)

Xa txaná At the beginning of time, said the Tshimshian, everything was flat, the land and the weather. Because the endless sunlight was tiring, the animals decided to go through the sky. Once above the earth, the animals found the sky stretched tight as a drumskin. It took the sharp teeth of ermines to gnaw a hole big enough for the animals to crawl through to a green and fertile land. There lived Xa txaná, in a house filled with pillows that contained the winds and snow. She told them to open the pillows, which they did, bringing seasons and growth to the earth. (Boas 1896)

Yaulilik The Modoc woman named "snowbird" had two daughters and a son, but she was old and poor, with no hunter to help provide for the children. So she sent her two daughters to look for the man whose singing they had heard. She believed he would be a good hunter. She warned them only to enter a house where fresh deer meat was hanging outside, for old men could masquerade as young hunters, dressed in finery and playing music. When they found the home of Isis, the great hunter, his father, Kumash, was sitting indoors, playing a pipe. The older sister believed Kumash was a good hunter, but the younger sister was not fooled. Nonetheless ,she agreed to accompany her sister indoors. When Isis came home and found his father entertaining two nubile women, he sent them all outdoors, where the girls scratched Kumash to death in annoyance. They ran away, but Isis found them and beheaded them.

Their heads and bodies floated back down the river to their mother's home, where their brother snared them in a net. Yaulilik restored them to life, then sent them to pick seeds for their food. While they were harvesting, the younger sister found the skeleton of Isis, which she restored to life. In gratitude, Isis married both sisters and impregnated them. But when the younger sister went to gather food, leaving her son to die from a fall, Isis turned the girls and their mother into snowbirds and departed from the world for good. (Curtin 1971)

Yeselbc The Snuqualmi tell of this woman who, with her elder sister Tapaltx, complained that there were no men nearby. They were overheard by star men, who became the girls' husbands. The sisters soon tired of living in the sky, so when a stranger told them they could dig down to earth, they made a hole. Yeselbc was pregnant and the girls did not want to be trapped in the sky with a baby, so they dropped to earth on a rope. On earth's surface, they surprised their family and friends, who used the rope ladder as a swing. Gulches formed wherever people dragged their feet as they swung. (Haeberlin and Boas)

Yolkai Estsan Sister of **Estsánatlehi**, called "white shell woman" because she was made from abalone, Yolkai Estsan ruled dawn and ocean. She also created fire and maize and taught women's crafts, including weaving and grinding corn.

Some legends said she was an aspect of Estsánatlehi rather than her sister. When her sister mated with the sun's light, Yolkai Estsan sat with her legs open over a waterfall, so she could conceive. After four days she felt movement. Four days later, the child was born, and with Estsánatlehi's son, he soon set out to eliminate humanity's problems. When they had killed everything but old age, cold, poverty, and hunger, Estsánatlehi told him to stop, for without old age, life would lose its savor; without cold, the sun would scorch the earth; without poverty, people would not work hard; and without hunger, there would be no reason to cook and eat together. (Allen 1991; Leeming and Page; Matthews; Moon; Neithammer; Wherry)

Yomumuli "Enchanted bee" is a culture heroine of the Pascua Yacqui of the southwestern desert. She was a wild woman who lived with an old woman named Yo'o Sea Hamut ("Elder Flower Woman") far from other humans. Yomumuli hunted for food, but she also understood the languages of all beings. So when the Yacqui, who at that time were only two feet tall, found a tree that seemed to be singing, they asked Yomumuli to interpret. She listened to the tree, then revealed that the tree knew change was coming in the form of tall people who would bring fire-shooting metal snakes. She said the people could disappear into earth or sea, or they could grow larger and interact with the new-comers, hoping to salvage what they could of the true ways. Some people leapt into the sea, where they can still be heard by those with the gift to hear them; others descended into the earth and became ants, which to this day understand the Yacqui language. Those who chose to become big people asked the deer to sacrifice himself for them so they could keep their land. The deer agreed, and a purple flower bloomed from the dying breath of the deer. Then the Yacqui danced the first Deer Dance. As it concluded, red roses (sacred to deer) suddenly burst out in blooms around the talking tree. (Giddings 1993; Royals)

Yonot The Wintu said that in primeval time this goddess always stayed indoors with her son Pohila ("fire child"). But after her husband helped steal flint from her brother, Yonot brought her son into the village center, where he started fires whenever anything flammable came near him. Everything would have burned had not Yonot brought her child back indoors. The world continued to blaze, requiring **Mem Loimis** to drench it. (Curtin 2004)

Mesoamerica's mythology has drawn little attention from scholars of women's spirituality. A possible reason is human sacrifice offered to goddesses as well as gods, a practice that runs counter to essentialist gender presumptions. This was not the predominant form of worship but was practiced in urban cultures. Elsewhere, decentralized cultures survived until modern times despite colonization, first by regional cultures, then by European invaders. Myths of interest to scholars of women's spirituality can be found in these cultures and among the Maya and Aztec. Mesoamerican religion presents multiplicity rather than uniformity throughout its development.

The centralized and literate cultures of central Mexico are the best known. The Maya thrived for hundreds of years, then declined, possibly because of drought. Much of what's known of Mayan religion derives from a document called the Popol Vuh, in which the Maya described the world as moving through various stages ("suns"), each ending with a cataclysmic event, hence the Mayan attention to eclipses, comets, and other celestial events over sometimes thousands of years.

In the twelfth century CE, the Huaxtec were dominant in central Mexico. The names of a few of their goddesses remain, usually due to conflation with later divinities. Then came the Aztecs, who were flourishing when the Spanish arrived in the early sixteenth century. In 1299, the Aztecs had settled in Toltec territory, but when, in 1323, the Aztecs sacrificed the Toltec king's daughter, the group was expelled. They drained swamps to create their city of Tenochtitlán. In 1426 the Aztec empire began, controlling much of Mexico for a century until Cortés arrived. Two generations of war led to the control of the region by Spain.

Epidemics of diseases brought by the conquerors and previously unknown in Mesoamerica killed as much as 50 percent of the population. Some survivors adapted to the new regime and left invaluable records. Christian missionaries recorded information about the Aztec religion, although generally with the aim of destroying rather than preserving it.

Beyond the literate centralized societies, ethnographers and anthropologists have recorded myths from oral sources, which represent a fraction of what were rich traditions. Indigenous religious revivals have not been widespread in Central America, in part because some religious ways were absorbed into Catholic rituals and in part because of the extirpation of tribal people. North Americans' interest in the region often focuses on shamanic aspects, an interest not entirely welcomed by native Central Americans. Revival of ritualized goddess religion has not been prominent, although feminists have recently worked to claim the image of Guadalupe as a symbol of indigenous feminine power.

MESOAMERICAN PANTHEON

Chalchihuitlicue This jade-skirted goddess ruled streams and rain. Lake waters were also under her command, for her people lived in flood areas. Chalchihuitlicue ruled salt water, controlling the sea and those who traveled on it. In her honor, the Aztecs called the Gulf of Mexico Chalchiuhcueyécat, "water of Chalchihuitlicue."

Chalchihuitlicue was depicted in a jade necklace, turquoise earrings, a crown of iridescent blue feathers, and a skirt trimmed with lilies. Her headdress featured large tassels that hung on each side of her face. She may have been honored at Teotihuacán in the cave under the Pyramid of the Sun, where a statue of her was found. After Christianization, Chalchihuitlicue appeared as Doña María Matlacoya, invoked in prayers for rain. (Alarcón; Caso; Clendinnen; Durán; Heyden; Kellogg; Nash 1978, 1997; Sahagún; Schwerin; Weigle)

Chicomecóatl "Seven Serpent," an Aztec agricultural goddess who promoted human as well as vegetative reproduction, had many forms: a maiden decked with water flowers, a young woman whose embrace brought death, a mother carrying the sun as a shield. Chicomecóatl had several festivals. On April 5, homes were decorated with herbs sprinkled with blood. Everyone marched to the fields, where they offered corn sprouts decked with flowers and bundles of the previous year's harvest, with petitions for abundance. Every family offered a basket of food, topped with a cooked frog to remind the goddess of her need to work with **Chalchihuitlicue** to produce a good crop.

Another festival lasted from late-June to mid-July, when wind pollinated corn. Women wore their hair loose to encourage corn silk to gather pollen. Corn pudding was eaten; people made merry. In the goddess's temple, a slave danced, adorned with face paint. On the final night of the festival, the woman danced all night, meeting her death at daybreak, when she was sacrificed. It was important that her heart be beating when it was offered to Chicomecóatl with prayers for an abundant harvest. (Caso; Clendinnen; Durán; Léon-Portilla; Sahagún; Weigle)

Cihuacóatl The Aztec goddess of life's trials has been considered a form of **Coatlicue**. Her alternative names include Quauhciuatl ("eagle woman"), Yoaciuatl ("warrior woman"), and Tzitziminciuatl ("devil woman"), perhaps each a separate aspect of the goddess.

Cihuacóatl wandered decked in jewels, moaning about coming disasters. In Tenochtitlán, she had a temple before which a perpetual fire burned. Within it, effigies of captured gods were imprisoned. She was depicted with an open mouth, eager for victims, wearing obsidian earplugs but otherwise dressed in white. More human sacrifices were offered to her than to any other divinity.

In her pre-Aztec identity, she was a goddess of wilderness, but by Aztec times she was a divinity of war and sacrifice. She retained her identity as a goddess of creation, for she received the bones of the dead and ground them into paste, from which she created humans. She was served by the **Cihuateteo**. (Brundage; Clendinnen; Durán; Josserand and Dakin; Sahagún; Weigle)

Cihuateteo Women who died in childbirth were envisioned by Aztecs as roaming the world weeping. They haunted crossroads, where they captured children. The Cihuateteo ("goddess women") were also called Ciuapipiltin ("honored women") because the deaths of women in childbirth equaled heroic deaths in war.

The innumerable Cihuateteo lived in a western paradise called Cincalco, "house of corn." When they appeared every fifty-two days, they stood out from living women by their golden eyebrows and stark white complexions. Sometimes they were fearsome, with claws for hands and a skull instead of a head. Temples were erected at crossroads, and cakes offered to keep them from stealing children.

In contemporary folklore, they have been transformed into La Llorona, who carries a dead child through the streets. This "weeping woman" appears as a seducer of men, who die violently, as a kidnapper of children, or as a grieving mother. New Mexican legend claims she was never heard weeping until Cortés invaded Mexico, after which she drowned her children and roamed moonlit streets. She has been identified as Cortés's interpreter, La Malinche, described as a traitor for collaborating with the invader and cursed to wander after death. (Barakat; Caso; Sahagún; Weigle; Weigle and White)

Cipactónal Before creation, the Aztec goddess Cipactónal was a monstrous alligator who contained all potential life, which appeared as eyes all over her body. But this life could not be freed until Cipactónal offered her body. Two gods tore her apart. Her lower body formed the earth, her upper body the heavens. Her coat became the mountains; her eyes and mouth turned into caves; grasses and flowers came from her skin.

Another legend, in which the goddess was called Tlaltecuhtli or Tlalteotl, says this goddess had eyes and teeth at every joint so she could look everywhere and protect herself. (Bierhorst 1992, 1976; Carrasco; Graulich; Léon-Portilla; Weigle)

Coatlicue The earth was a fivefold goddess to the Aztecs, who counted four directions and a central point, which extended up and down, on their compasses. The earth goddess sometimes appeared to them as a woman with four sisters who gathered to work magic. (Some, Christianized, texts say the sisters prayed together.)

Coatlicue gathered white feathers to adorn her breasts. Becoming pregnant, she gave birth to Huitzilopochtli, who was born fully armed to defend his mother against her earlier children, who planned to kill her (see **Coyolxauhqui**). In other legends, she was impregnated by emeralds and gave birth to the god Quetzalcóatl.

Coatlicue was a creatrix who floated in a misty world. Even the sun and his magicians did not realize her potential. Once they did, they brought her love charms, causing her to flower. But when she was not tended, the earth turned into wilderness, as the emperor Montezuma discovered when he sent a delegation to the land of his ancestors. There they found a deformed Coatlicue, surrounded by thistles and cacti, sorrowing for her abandonment.

Coatlicue's most famous images show her garlanded with hearts and hands, wearing a skirt of serpents, hung with skulls, vested in a flayed human skin. The distinction between Coatlicue and the goddesses **Tonan** and **Toci** is unclear. Similarly, Coatlicue has been connected with **Cihuacóatl** and **Tlazoltéotl**. (Alarcón; Brundage; Caso; Clendinnen; Elzey; Gingerich; Kelly; Nash 1997; Weigle)

Coyolxauhqui The Aztec moon goddess named "golden bells" was among **Coatlicue**'s children, who tried to kill their mother rather than let her bear rivals to them. Coyolxauhqui tried to warn her mother, so her siblings decapitated her and threw her head into the sky. A grieving Coatlicue placed Coyolxauhqui's shining head in the night sky. Coyolxauhqui may have descended from the older moon goddess Metztli, who had two phases: one that promoted growth, another that discouraged it. She was associated with midwives and sweat baths. (Brundage; Caso; Clendinnen; Elzey; Gingerich; Josserand and Dakin; Weigle)

Huixtocihuatl One day, the sister of the Aztec rain gods quarreled with them and left home to live in the ocean, where she became ruler. Her ten-day June festival celebrated the invention of salt extraction by Huixtocihuatl; patron of salt makers, she was depicted wearing a fishnet skirt. A woman who embodied Huixtocihuatl during her festival was sacrificed. (Alarcón; Caso; Driver and Massey)

Itzpapalotl Once the Aztec goddess of the soul Itzpapalotl came to earth to pick roses. Pricking her finger angered her. Ever afterward, she made sure humanity paid for its pleasures, as she had to pay for her rose with blood. In human form, Itzpapalotl ("obsidian butterfly") had jaguar claws and a face tattooed with the symbols for death. Itzpapalotl derived from the Chichimec, indigenous peoples subjugated by the Aztec. (Bierhorst 1992; Brundage; Gingerich; Josserand and Dakin; Léon-Portilla; Weigle)

Ix Chel Among the Yucatán Maya, Ix Chel was the snake goddess of water and the moon, childbirth and weaving; she may also have controlled maize. She took the sun as her lover, but her grandfather jealously killed her. Grieving dragonflies sang over Ix Chel for thirteen days, at the end of which she emerged and followed her lover to his palace. But the sun also grew jealous, accusing Ix Chel of loving his brother, the morning star. The sun threw Ix Chel from heaven, and she found sanctuary with the vulture divinity. The sun pursued her and lured her home, growing jealous again. A weary Ix Chel left the sun's bed, making her-self invisible whenever he came near. Hiding in the rainbow, she nursed women through pregnancy and labor, taking care of those who visited her sacred island of Cozumel. In the Yucatán into historical times, heal-ers used stone images of Ix Chel. She has been con-nected with Ix Azal Uok, goddess of weaving. She has also been identified as Ix U Sihnal, "lady moon birth." (Brady and Prufer; Paxton)

Kacíwali Born of the sea, the Huichol corn god-dess Kacíwali was carried to a mountain lake, where she lived underwater as a snake. An ant man asked if his people could live on the shore. Finding them hardworking, Kacíwali agreed. So ant people moved in around Kacíwali's lake. They planted, the corn grew, the ant people prospered. But when harvest came, things became difficult. Because the singer who offered songs of gratitude could barely carry a melody, gods never heard their prayers. Neglecting to invite Kacíwali, the ants drank corn beer and started dancing.

Kacíwali dressed in rags and went to the party but was turned away because of her poverty. Kacíwali went to her mother, **Nakawé**, who agreed to punish the ant people. The next time they planted, rain fell when they needed sun; the sky was cloudless when rain was needed. Only when the ant people held ceremonials to the goddesses did rain fall at necessary times and the corn revive. (Zingg)

Mayauel This 400-breasted Aztec goddess ruled earth and sky, hallucinations and drunkenness. She nursed the stars, who were fish in the oceanic heaven; her chil-dren were Centzon Totochtin, the 400 gods of drunk-enness. In sculpture, Mayauel sat naked on a throne of tortoises and snakes, offering a dish of pulque to her worshippers.

One legend says Mayauel, a peasant woman, passed a mouse who danced about under her gaze. Mayauel noticed the rodent had been nibbling maguey plant, so she caught some of the sap in a pot. Thus she discovered the basis of intoxication, which she

introduced to the gods. Her gift was so popular that they welcomed her and her earthly husband as the god of gambling and flowers. (Caso; Clendinnen; Weigle)

Mictecacíhuatl This Aztec goddess ruled the nine rivers of the afterlife to which evil souls were con-demned. There, they suffered boredom and monotony, while better souls enjoyed heaven's existence. She was depicted with no face, only the bones of a skull. (Caso; Carrasco)

Nakawé When, at the beginning of time, the earth was threatened by the fire god, the Huichol prayed to the rain goddess Nakawé to save them. Loosening her hairnet, she created rain that fell for five days and five nights, dowsing the fire god and leaving only an oven fire. Later, she showed people how to create rituals to encourage conception.

At creation, when serpents attacked people try-ing to draw water, Nakawé called to the stars, who fell upon them. Nakawé spared a pregnant snake, mother of the gods. At first, only female snake divinities were born, but later Nakawé permitted some male divinities. Nakawé was identified with the Virgin of Guadalupe (see **Tonan**). (Zingg)

Omecíhauatl This Aztec goddess was the female half of the androgynous divinity Ometéotl. One day, she gave birth to an obsidian knife, which she threw down on the empty earth; it shattered into 1,600 heroes. The heroes could have become gods in heaven. But, lazy and ambitious, they wished to remain on earth and be served.

There were, however, no humans in existence. Turning to Omecíhauatl, "Lady of Duality," they asked her to create some. She suggested they seek re-union with her. Instead, the heroes sent to the under-world for ashes and bones, which they formed into the bodies of the first man and woman. This goddess has been identified with **Tonan** and **Chalchihuitlicue**. Among the Maya of the Yucatán peninsula, she was known as Ix Chebel Yax. In the Popol Vuh, she was called Alom and Xmucane. (Alarcón; Brundage; Caso; Christenson; Haly; Graulich; Léon-Portilla; Weigle)

Tlazoltéotl "Dirty lady" was Aztec goddess of the moon and of sexuality, who ruled gambling and black magic. She was also the source of purification, for only her priests could hear confessions of guilt. Depictions of Tlazoltéotl show her wearing the flayed skin of a sacrificial victim, her head decked with spindles, her hands carrying a broom. Because of her power over childbirth, she was a goddess of divination. (Klein; Sahagún; Boone)

Toci Goddess of healers and midwives, "Our Grandmother" was also goddess of abortionists and fortune-tellers. In her shrine, a straw image showed the goddess holding spinner's equipment, revealing her control over life and death. She has been associated with **Tlazoltéotl**, who controlled divination by midwives.

Toci's late-summer festival was one of the most important in the year. During Ochpaniztli, a woman representing the goddess was feted for days. A priest accompanied her at the ritual's end and, taking the goddess's mask from the woman, flayed her and placed her bleeding skin on priests who represented her son and the goddess herself. A battle then ensued among the partisans of the two deities, after which vegetable seeds were distributed for planting.

Toci, under the name Teteo Innan, appears as "Mother of the Gods," companion of the primary god. She is associated with the obscure goddesses Tlalli iyollo and Temazcalteci. (Clendinnen; Couch; Durán; Gingerich; Léon-Portilla; Nash 1997; Sahagún; Weigle)

Tonan This Aztec goddess, who watched over birthing mothers, was honored in a winter solstice festival at which a woman dressed in white and covered with shells and eagle feathers danced. The next day, men struck women with little bags full of paper, to which older women responded with catcalls, while younger women endured the abuse, weeping.

At Tonan's shrine, the Virgin of Guadalupe manifested herself. On December 9, 1531, Cuautlatóhuac (Juan Diego) was climbing the hill of Tepeyacac, sacred to Tonan, where he met a woman. Speaking Nahuatl, she commanded him to build a church where the shrine to Tonan had stood. Juan Diego went to the Spanish bishop of the area, who refused to honor the command. Juan returned to the spot, and the woman told him to gather roses for the bishop. The roses, which do not normally bloom in December, convinced the bishop. The image of the lady herself appeared on Juan Diego's cloak.

The bishop said she was the Virgin **Mary** (see Eastern Mediterranean) and provided the Spanish place-name of Guadalupe. Guadalupe was recognized as a female power who interceded for the Mexican people, as she did during the Mexican war of independence, when her image was a revolutionary symbol. Her image is the national symbol of Mexico, and pilgrimages to Tepeyacac honor her.

Tonan is honored in a feast on December 20–24 that includes music and the placement of marigold garlands on statues of the goddess or her substitute, Guadalupe. The titles Morena ("dark one") and Morenita ("little dark one") recall her origin as a goddess of the soil. (Brundage; Castillo; Harrington; Sahagún; Taylor; Weigle; Wolf)

Xochiquetzal The goddess of flowers, this Aztec divinity was also a deity of sexual license. Her name means "Precious Feather Flower," and she brought menstruation into the world when, after a bat bit her vulva, she bled flowers. At that moment, orgasm was created.

Marigolds were her favorites, but she loved every plant and every creature. In some legends, she was the only female survivor of the flood that destroyed the world (see **Chalchihuitlicue**). With a man, she escaped the torrent in a small boat. Faced with the prospect of repopulating the world, they set to work.

But all of their children were born without speech. Finally a pigeon endowed them with language, but every child received a different tongue, so they could not communicate.

As goddess of femininity, Xochiquetzal ruled the arts, including music, textile crafts, and dance; she was the goddess of prostitutes. Women who made their living as embroiderers celebrated her feast day.

She also was connected to anyone who loved flowers, including the Xochimilcans, who created the floating gardens still seen in Mexico today. Much loved by Aztec women, she was honored with pottery figurines that showed her with feathers in her hair. (Caso; Clendinnen; Durán; Graulich; Josserand and Dakin; Pohl; Tedlock; Weigle)

SOUTH AMERICA *and the* CARIBBEAN

Europeans, imagining South America controlled by women, named its major river after mythic Greek warrior women. But far from being an Amazonian paradise, South America is home to myths describing the destruction of woman-centered religion. Whether those myths recall actual social change or express tension between the sexes is impossible to know, but native South American mythology bears consideration by those interested in women's religious status.

South America has been settled for some 30,000 years, although the southern tip was settled only about 7,000 years ago. The continent's written history began in the fifteenth century CE, when South America supported between 8 and 30 million people. More than 3 million were under the rule of the Inca Empire, while smaller societies spread through the Amazon basin, the valleys of the Andes, and the southern plateaus. Such diverse geography encouraged development of some 3,000 cultures, ranging from small village groups to fairly large states.

The earliest known South American civilization was the Chavín of coastal Peru (900–200 BCE). Because the culture ended in prehistory, the names of its divinities are unknown, although some later figures may descend from them. Following the Chavín, the Chibcha (400–300 BCE) developed a corn-based economy, with salt and emerald mining providing goods for trade. Later, Arawak- and Carib-speaking people forced the Chibcha from their fertile valleys. Descendants of the Chibcha still occupy parts of Colombia; Bogotá was one of their ancient strongholds. As with many South American cultures, the Chibcha declined after assault by the Spanish.

Much literature about South American religion centers on the Inca, whose civilization held sway from 1438 to 1533. Patriarchal theocrats, the Inca oppressed the region's tribal people, including the Quichua-Aymara, who domesticated the llama and alpaca. The Inca are of relatively little interest to goddess scholars, having few known female divinities.

Beyond the Andes, people of the tropical forests were agriculturalists whose religion centered on a shamanic worldview. Hundreds of cultures existed (some still) in the watersheds of the Amazon and Orinoco. Elsewhere, southern Andean people relied upon river trade and agriculture, although they also were pastoralists with herds of llamas. Religion was shamanic, and belief in witchcraft common. Finally, those in economically marginal areas relied upon shamanic practices to sustain their hunting economy.

After the arrival of the Spanish *conquistadores*, the region's history was written from a European perspective. In terms of religion, with the exception of documents describing indigenous divinities as devilish, the region was generally ignored. Many cultures were destroyed or assimilated, leaving no record of their goddesses. In the late nineteenth century, anthropologists began recording myths and legends. Although collection of myths and folklore continues, most collectors are men, who often pay greater attention to male than to female motifs.

South America attracts scholarly and popular interest because of its continuing shamanic cultures. Although South American shamans were typically male, the role was also open to women, and men often wore female ritual clothing. Some legends suggest shamanism was originally a women's role, later taken over by men.

Central to most South American cultures was a feminine divinity, most often an earth goddess or ancestral mother. Several myths suggest an ancient cultural primacy of women, describing how men claimed power by killing women and girls, keeping only female infants to reproduce the tribe. Despite this, concern for the earth as a maternal being who, in turn, must be cared for by her children, was widespread in South America.

After the European invasion, a Christian veneer covered some native traditions. In addition, the arrival of enslaved Africans led to the development of syncretic religions: Macumba in Brazil, Santeria in Puerto Rico, and Voudoun in Haiti. As in other areas where literacy and Christianity arrived together, written documents that describe pre-contact South American and Caribbean religion are of questionable reliability. Most South American and Caribbean cultures relied upon oral transmission of myths and history, so massacres and persecution destroyed some mythologies when the culture bearers were killed, as was the case in Uruguay, where no native cultures survive. (Afro-Brazilian and Afro-Caribbean religions are discussed on pp. 2–3.)

In the past fifty years, the establishment of coffee plantations and cattle ranches has significantly endangered the survival of ethnic cultures in Amazonia. In other parts of South America, natural resources similarly put other indigenous cultures at risk. Recently, spiritual tourism has flourished, with pilgrims traveling to famous sites such as Machu Picchu. As most of the visitors are from wealthy countries and many indigenous people live in poverty, concern has been raised about the ethics of such exchanges. Although some tourism opportunities are offered under government sponsorship, and many purveyors of spiritual tourism are of indigenous origin, some native South Americans object to the commodification of their spirituality and resist sharing.

SOUTH AMERICAN AND CARIBBEAN PANTHEON

Abé mangó The sun's daughter among the Amazonian Tukano peoples, Abé mangó taught humanity weaving, cooking, pottery, and herbal medicine. Raped by her father before she descended to live among humans, she taught women to wear clothing to avoid men's lustful gaze. When the first death occurred, Abé mangó invented funeral rites. (Reichel-Dolmantoff)

Aiakélem The Yamana people of Tierra del Fuego, on the southern tip of South America, describe Aiakélem as a whale woman. When her husband's village did not provide her with sufficient food, she returned to her own for supplies. There she met a man with extremely long fingers. On her first night home, he sat next to her, putting his fingers into her vagina so deeply that she grew faint. Aiakélem returned to her husband, but only to retrieve her children, then moved in with the man with the pleasingly long fingers. (Wilbert 1977)

Akewa The solar myth of the matrilineal Toba of Argentina described a primeval land in the sky filled with beautiful sun women, while earth was full of hairy men. One day the sun women descended to the surface, leaving Akewa behind. On earth, the sun maidens were trapped when the hairy men ate their rope ladder. After that, the sun women's descendants lived among men, looking up at Akewa, a fat smiling woman who walked the sky. She grew older as the year aged, walking more slowly and lengthening days in summer, but she grew younger in winter, and her speedy stride made days shorter. (Karsten; Metraux)

Alamigi In central Brazil, the Kalapalo people live in the national park of Xingu, where they support themselves in traditional fashion from their fields of manioc. They tell the cautionary story of Alamigi, one of the Dawn People who lived on the primordial earth. Every night Alamigi teased the gray birds called nightjars for their ugly song. But the birds, angry at her disrespect, punished Alamigi.

First they sent a bird, disguised as a human, into Alamigi's house while the girl was away and tricked a woman into revealing the girl's name. Then they put a spell on the whole village, so everyone fell into a profound sleep. The birds slipped into Alamigi's house

351

and tied the girl up in her hammock. By the time she woke up, she was in the middle of a lake.

Frightened, she called for help. A bird, the banded tinamous, called loud enough to guide Alamigi from the lake. But then the bird flew away, leaving Alamigi frightened and alone. Then she heard the sound of a tiger heron and, following its call, got lost in the forest. The bird took pity on the girl and, after extracting a promise from her that she would never deride birds again, led her home. (Basso)

Amao A fish impregnated this Amazonian ancestral mother by entering her vulva, but her infant died. She wept desperately until the child awakened and revealed that he had been frightened to death by animals. In grief, she turned the animals to stones near her child's grave, then invented the arts of civilization that she taught people before disappearing. (Lévi-Strauss)

Amáru The ancestral mother of the Amazonian Baniwa and Wakuén was one of three beings breathed into existence at the beginning of time. All-powerful Amáru made herself pregnant with a hairy child born without a mouth. Another primal being blew smoke on the boy, who began eating people until he was killed; his body grew into a poisonous plant from which mosquitoes and snakes were born. But the plant had its uses, for it formed the first flutes, which Amáru claimed on behalf of all women.

The men denied the women's claim to the instruments, so they suggested a race to settle the question. But Amáru stole back the flutes and ran away with them, inventing music as she ran. Her brother then killed all women except Amáru with a thunderbolt. Afterward, the men used the flutes in magical ceremonies. (Bierhorst 1988)

Amusha According to the Yupa of Venezuela, this baby girl grew up to be a deer. She never was happy indoors, crying incessantly until her mother left her alone in the house. When she returned, Amusha was gone. She was found nestled in the roots of a huge

old tree. After that point, the girl would eat nothing but leaves. White spots and fur began to appear on her body. Finally she ran on four legs into the woods, where she was transformed into a deer. (Wilbert 1974)

Auchimalgen This kindly moon goddess was a primary divinity of the Araucanians of Chile. Auchimalgen was a seer, foretelling great events by changing the color of her face. Her servants were nymphs called Amchimalghen. (Alexander)

Anuanaitu Just after creation, said the Caribbean peoples, men were ugly and women beautiful. But there was one handsome man, Maconaura, who lived with his mother in the jungle of primordial time, when there was no evil and no fear.

One day Maconaura found someone had been raiding his fishnet. The thief also had ripped the nets. Maconaura set a woodpecker to guard the nets and soon heard the bird's cry. Running to the pond, the man saw a water monster and shot it. Then he discovered on the shore a girl, Anuanaitu, whom he took home for his mother to raise.

When she grew up, Anuanaitu was Maconaura's choice for a wife. She demurred at first, for she could not marry without her parents' consent and she refused to reveal their identity. Finally she gave way and married Maconaura. The pair decided it would be best to travel to the woman's village and seek the blessing of her parents. Anuanaitu's mother quickly agreed to the match, but her father subjected Maconaura to near-impossible tests of skill and courage, on which the young man performed well.

One day Maconaura decided to visit his own family. On his return to Anuanaitu's village, her father shot him dead. War broke out between the families, with Anuanaitu's kin destroyed in the battles. She lived but became entranced with the spirits of the dead. Traveling in rattlesnake form to her husband's village, she determined to take revenge. She struck a poisonous blow, revealing that the water monster slain by Maconaura had been her brother.

Then Anuanaitu ran through the world, which turned dark and fearsome as she crossed it, until she reached the ocean. She threw herself into the water and drowned where today a dangerous whirlpool sucks. There she was reunited with her lover, and she reigns there now as the Soul of the Ocean. (Bierhorst 1988)

Anuntero The Tapirapé people, who once inhabited lands along the Brazilian river that bears their name, have almost disappeared. They considered themselves aboriginal to the area, for when their culture hero Apuwenonu descended from the sky, he took a wife from the Tapirapé. She was Anuntero, the first woman to learn to make useful objects (hammocks, body ornaments) from cotton. (Wagley)

Atabei The primary being of the pre-Hispanic people of the Antilles was called by many names: Attabeira, Momona, Guabancex, Guacarapita, Iella, Guimazoa, Iermaoguacar, Apito, Zuimaco. Little is known of her rites, although she was recognized as an earth goddess by the Antillean people, whose language included a vocabulary known only to women. Atabei was served by a messenger goddess, Guatauva, and by the hurricane goddess Coatrischie. Some sources suggest that Haitian Guabancex was a separate spirit, able to raise storms when angry. (Alexander; Roth)

Aturuaródo The Bororo Indians of Bolivia describe this woman, who helped domesticate plants, as the unwitting mother of a monster child. When a hero avenged the death of his mother by killing a snaky monster, he brought pieces of his prey back to the village, where the women celebrated with a victory dance. One woman, Aturuaródo, failed to cover herself with leaves to protect herself from the monster's dripping blood and found herself pregnant. Stricken with the food cravings of pregnancy, she found herself staring at some ripe fruit and, to her surprise, heard a voice from her belly. It was her unborn son, who climbed out and got the fruit for his mother. Aturuaródo was distressed to see the child was a monster like his father. She told

the other villages, and they returned to the tree with her and saw how the unborn child emerged. So they killed it, to Aturuaródo's relief and grief. Later, when she returned to where they had burned the body of her son, she found that his ashes had turned into seeds of useful plants. (Wilbert and Simoneau 1983)

Bachúe The ancestor goddess of Colombia's Chibcha, Bachúe lived beneath lake waters but, deciding to live on land, rose from the waves with her son. When he had grown, Bachúe mated with him to produce the human race. Teaching her offspring suitable religious rites, Bachúe transformed herself and her son-husband into snakes. Thereafter, Bachúe served humankind as a protector of fields and crops. (Bierhorst 1988; Alexander; Osbourne)

Ceiuci One of the stars of the Pleiades lived on earth as Ceiuci, said the Amazonian Anambé. One day, the shadow of a young man fell across the pond where she was fishing. Ceiuci ordered him to dive into the pool. The man refused, but when the goddess sent stinging red ants, he obeyed.

Once she had him in the water, Ceiuci snagged the man with her fishing line. At home, while the goddess was gathering wood to cook her catch, Ceiuci's daughter hid him. When Ceiuci demanded her prey, the girl and the boy ran away, dropping palm branches as they went. These became animals, which Ceiuci gobbled up. Even when all species had been created, Ceiuci pursued the runaways. The girl stopped, but the young man continued until he reached his home.

In other tales, this goddess appears as a star woman who dances in the Pleiades. A similarly named goddess, Ceucy, was believed by the Tupi to have been impregnated by tree sap; she gave birth to a boy who stole women's religious powers and forbade them to witness rituals. When Ceucy tried to attend one, her son put her to death. (Bierhorst 1976; Jones)

Chaupi Ñamca Born before time began, the Inca's principal goddess Chaupi Ñamca created women, while her consort created men. She loved sex and turned herself into a human woman in order to seduce men. But after she met a man named Rucancota, she turned herself to stone to remain with him forever. She was honored at the winter solstice, when her priests performed erotic dances. Her five-armed stone image was hidden from Spanish invaders, and her festival was converted to the Christian one of Corpus Christi. (Steele)

Chuquillanto An Incan romance begins with Chuquillanto, daughter of the sun, falling in love with a llama herder who wore a silver locket that showed a heart being eaten by lice. Chuquillanto felt her heart eaten away after meeting the young man, Acoynapa. She returned to the palace where she lived with other sun women who were pledged to a life without men and who tended four fountains named pebble (northwest), frog (southwest), water weed (northeast), and algae (southeast). There she dreamed of a little bird who listened to her tale of thwarted love and advised her to sit at the center of the four fountains and sing of her love. When the fountains sang back to her, she knew she had to follow her heart.

But she was pledged to her duties as priestess of the sun, so she did not know how she might find her way to Acoynapa's bed. His mother, however, dreamed of her son and, climbing the mountains to him, found him almost sick with love of Chuquillanto. Employing magic, she turned him into a carved stick, which, when Chuquillanto came to visit, she gave to the maiden. Thus was Chuquillanto able to bring her lover right into the sun palace and to sleep with him there. But one day, when she took the staff out to a mountain ravine and Acoynapa emerged from it, they were observed by palace guards. As they tried to escape, the pair of lovers were turned to stone, which can still be seen today as the crags of Pitusiray. (Bierhorst 1976)

Cïki This helpful child of the vegetation goddess **Nugkui** could simply say "let there be manioc,"

and the house would fill with manioc. Bullying children demanded Cïki produce various foods, which she obligingly did. But when the children demanded demons, and Cïki brought them forth, the children beat her. Cïki disappeared. When the parents came home and found the magical child missing, they searched everywhere. When they found her, her powers were gone. (Harner)

Coadidop Among the Amazonian Jauareté, the creatrix Coadidop grew bored with her solitude and invented smoking. Using two of her own bones to create a cigar holder, she squeezed tobacco from her body. Then she created and smoked the coca plant. She began to see beings. In claps of thunder and bursts of lightning, men came into being but disappeared. It took Coadidop three tries before she created a man who remained in existence. Then she set about creating women. Her son made three brothers, while Coadidop made two sisters. She measured her head with a cord, laid the cord in a circle, then squeezed her breast. Milk filled the circle and formed the earth, which she gave to the women. But men wrested away control, refusing women access to religious rituals. (Bierhorst 1988)

Cocomama The coca goddess was cut in half by jealous lovers. Her dismembered body grew into the first coca bush, whose leaves men could not chew until they had satisfied a woman's sexual needs. Since Incan times, coca leaves have been used in ceremonies honoring **Pachamama**, who demanded it in exchange for good crops. (Alexander; Arriaga; Osbourne)

Gasogonaga This Toba weather goddess appeared to shamans in visions induced by psychotropic plants. The Toba's nomadic existence ended with Spanish colonization; they now live as agriculturalists, their traditional religion mostly lost to Pentecostal Christianity. Nonetheless, some practitioners still encounter Gasogonaga, who looks like a vast multicolored animal from whose mouth comes lightning. (Langdon and Baer)

Gaulchováng "Song Woman" was the primary divinity of the Kogi of Colombia. A beautiful, fat, black-haired woman who sat on a stone in the lowest of nine worlds, she gave birth to all beings and actions. Gaulchováng pulled from herself maleness and created a child, then a jaguar. She created humans, then ancestors and culture heroes. Finally Gaulchováng gave birth to nine daughters, each a different kind of soil (Black Earth, Red Earth, and so forth). She swallowed half the ocean, so land appeared.

At this point Sintána, one of the ancestors, demanded a wife, so Gaulchováng offered him the eight less powerful daughters, trying to keep Black Earth for herself. But Sintána stole the maiden and ran across the earth with her; wherever Black Earth set foot, soil good for raising crops appeared. Gaulchováng sent lizards in pursuit of the eloping couple, but Sintána and Black Earth evaded them to become ancestors of the Kogi people. (Bierhorst 1988)

Gauteovan The ancestral mother of the people of the Sierra Nevada in Colombia created the sun from her menstrual blood. She created the visible and the invisible worlds, including demons that cause illness. She was the region's most significant deity. (Steward 2)

Hálpen This powerful goddess of the Argentinean Selknam and Alacaluf lived in the sky, from which she descended to eat humans. Her sister was Tanu, who lived inside the earth. Looking for Tanu, women dug holes, forming lakes and mountains. When they could not find her, they impersonated her in rituals. When religious power was taken from women, men continued to invoke Hálpen and Tanu. (Bierhorst 1988; Koppers)

Húanaxu A myth of the Yamana of Tierra del Fuego concerned this spirit of the moon. At a time when women ruled, she brought her people from the east to a land called Yáiasaága, where the men did housework and raised children. A few talented male hunters pro-vided women with meat, while the latter concentrated on ritual.

The men felt oppressed by work, but the powerful spirits the women invoked frightened them. Then Húanaxu's brother-in-law overheard girls discussing impersonating spirits. In punishment, the girls were transformed into quacking ducks. The men plotted to grab power, which Téšurkipa learned. She tried to warn her sisters. Furious at being tricked, the men broke into the ritual area and killed all the women except the very old and very young. After that, men took over the rituals and made the women do housework. If the women were ever to find the secret of their lost power, the power would pass again to them.

Húanaxu survived the massacre and rose into the sky, causing a flood that wiped out many of the Yamana people. She still bears the scars from the great battle of men against women, visible on the moon's face. (Wilbert 1977)

Huitaca The Chibcha moon goddess of intoxication, Huitaca was the rival of a male preacher, Bochica, who taught crafts along with a puritanical attitude toward life. Continually undoing his efforts was the owl woman Huitaca, sometimes said to be his wife. Once, Huitaca became so angry she raised a flood, drowning Bochica's followers. So her husband threw her to the sky, where she became the moon. (Steward 2; Osbourne)

Itiba Cahubaba Among the Taíno, a pre-Hispanic people of Cuba and other Caribbean islands, this woman ("bloodied mother hag") was the great ancestor. She died attempting to bear quadruplet sons, so the boys were torn from her corpse. The creator god had killed his only son and put his bones in a gourd hung in the rafters. The bones turned to fish, on which the god lived. But the newborn boys wanted to eat too, so they climbed up and knocked the gourd down. It fell and broke, and its water created oceans. (Arrom)

Kasoronara' The Toba goddess of lighting disliked spirits, so she threw herself on their homes whenever a rainstorm gave her the chance. Once on the surface, she hid, calling out to passersby to help build a fire. Those who answered gained the ability to call forth rain when needed. On the smoke of the fires, Kasoronara' wafted back into the sky. (Metraux)

Kopecho The Yupa said two suns once parched the earth. So Kopecho invited both suns to a feast, where she danced suggestively. One sun grasped at her and fell into a pit of coals. He was accustomed to heat, so nothing happened except that his light dimmed, turning him into the moon. He threw Kopecho into water, where she transformed into the first frog. (Wilbert 1974)

Korobōna With her sister Korobonáko, this Warrau divinity lived beside a lake the girls were forbidden to enter. Rebellious Korobōna went swimming and accidentally released a captive divinity, who had intercourse with her. Korobōna gave birth to a human child, then visited the water deity again, returning pregnant with a half-serpent baby her brothers killed. When Korobōna offered the dead babe her breasts, it revived. Korobōna's brothers discovered the baby and dismembered it. The grieving mother gathered the pieces, planted them in the earth, and watched a Carib warrior spring forth and drive the brothers away. Scholars believe Korobōna was a local name for the creator goddess Kururumany, sometimes described as a god who created men while a goddess, Kulimina, created women. (Alexander; Brett; Bierhorst 1976; Jones)

Kuma Among the Yaruro people of western Venezuela, the creator goddess Kuma dressed as a shaman with gold jewelry. She was the first living being on earth, for which reason the people said, "Everybody sprang from Kuma." She created land and then asked the god Puana to have intercourse with her thumb, but instead he impregnated her womb. After Kuma gave birth to sun, moon, snake, and jaguar, she sent her children looking for people, who were found in a hole.

Kuma gave the gods a rope and hook, with which they pulled up human life.

In the cold, dark world to which they had been brought, the people shivered. But a divine toad woman, Kibero, held fire in her breast and gave it to the people. Kuma taught the women pottery skills and basket weaving, then created society. She remained accessible to shamans who painted her on their drums. (Bierhorst 1988; Lyon)

Léxuwa The sensitive ibis woman lived in the Yamana primeval time, when women controlled everything. She grew angry because, when she brought springtime, people screamed with delight, hurting her sensitive ears, so she dropped unseasonable snow on them. To avoid late snows, people were silent when they saw an ibis fly in spring. Once, Léxuwa brought a huge storm. Snow fell until glaciers covered the earth. When the glaciers began to melt, the seas rose. Some peoples ran for five tall mountains and survived, but most people died. Léxuwa intended to kill humanity, because men were warring against women for control of ritual and religion. After the flood, the men remained in control. (Wilbert 1977)

Mama Cocha The eldest Peruvian divinity was "Mother Sea," worshipped along South America's Pacific coast. As fish provider and whale goddess, Mama Cocha was the source of food. She also ruled fresh water as goddess of rain. Her image was shaped in blue-green stone and stood on the shore of Lake Titicaca, where Peruvians believed creation occurred. (Arriaga; Steward 2)

Mama Ocllo When the Spanish invaded South America, they found many names for the foremothers of the Inca: Mama Ocllo or Mama Ocllo Huaca ("fat woman"), Mama Huaco/Wako ("great-grandmother," "tooth woman"), Mama Coya/Cura ("aunt," "daughter-in-law"), and Mama Rahua ("burning woman"). Alternatively, the names of the quartet of goddesses were Topa Huaco, Mama Coya, Cori Ocllo, and Ipa Huaco.

Mama Ocllo, the most intelligent, found habitable land. She killed a Poque Indian and removed his lungs. Carrying the bloody organs, Mama Ocllo entered the towns, where residents fled, leaving the region to the people of Mama Ocllo. (This may be a folk memory of Incan massacres of indigenous people.)

Mama Coya was the daughter of the sun and sister-wife of the original Incan leader. Born from the waters of Lake Titicaca, the pair traveled to Cuzco, stopping along the way to puncture the earth with a golden spike. Where it entered the ground easily, they stopped and gathered people. Mama Coya and her brother founded cities over which Mama Coya and her brother ruled, she over women, he over men. The same story is told of Mama Ocllo, so the distinction between the ancestral mothers was not sharp. (Bandelier; Bierhorst 1976; Lamadrid; Osbourne; Steele)

Mama Quilla Among the Inca, this was "Mother Moon," honored at calendar-fixed rituals and during eclipses, when it was believed that a supernatural jaguar attempted to devour her. The Inca made noise with weapons to threaten the intruder, a custom that has not died in Cuzco. (Arriaga; Steward 2)

Nugkui At the beginning of time, the Aguaruna people lived on mashed balsa wood cooked in their armpits. A woman saw peeled manioc floating downstream and followed the trail upriver to Nugkui, who was washing her dinner in the river. The woman begged Nugkui to go with her, but Nugkui sent her daughter **Ciki** to the humans to teach cooking and gardening. Although Ciki was mistreated by human children, Nugkui decided to help the humans. She came into a woman's dreams and taught her where to find seeds of good-tasting plants. She taught her how to make pottery and how to bake it in the sun.

Nugkui lives in good garden soil, where she nurtures plants. She also is found in caves, from which

she sends forth animals for hunters. Her companions were goddesses of plants found in association with the important food plant manioc: Chiki (arrowroot), who provides water to Nugkui; Sagku (cocoyam), a big-leaved plant that also brings water; and Tuju (ahicra), a plant with twisted leaves that grows with manioc. Nugkui may be the same as the figure as Mama Dukuji, who lives in the biggest manioc plant in the garden; she was never to be looked at directly, or she would defecate weeds.

Among the Jívaro of eastern Ecuador, the goddess Nunuí provides food by pushing plants up through the soil. Attracting Nunuí means placing three jasper rocks around the garden and leaving enough open space that fat Nunuí can dance. Dressed in black, she comes out at night and spins among the plants, dancing with each in turn.

Letting weeds grow among the manioc plants drove Nunuí from the garden, for if she felt crowded, she retreated underground, taking the manioc with her. Heat also caused Nunuí to move underground, which is why women gathered crops early in the day. (Bierhorst 1988; Brown; Brown and Van Bolt; Harner; Paper; Von Hagen)

Orchu The Arawak say the divine Orchu rose from a stream bearing a branch, which bore the first gourds. She taught humanity how to put stones in the dried gourds to make rattles, as well as how to use the instruments in ritual. (Brett)

Pachamama Among the Chibcha of Colombia, the earth was a dragon who lived beneath the mountains. Occasionally she quivered, causing earthquakes. All beings on earth were children of voluptuous Pachamama, the preeminent deity of agriculture. During planting and harvest, women talked softly to Pachamama, sometimes pouring an offering of cornmeal on her surface. As agricultural rituals were the domain of women, Pachamama was especially important to them; she was honored at weddings to encourage fertility.

Other South Americans honored her at all their ceremonies. Coca and beer were offered to her, and balls of grease decorated with silver paper. Kissing the earth honored Pachamama. Among the Tacana, Pachamama survives as the "old woman of the forest," who taught humans the art of making beer and who created night and day. This earth mother is distinguished from the fat dwarf mother of vegetation, called Chagra Mama by the neighboring Canelos Quechua. (Arriaga; Bierhorst 1988; Lyon; Salles-Reese; Steward 2)

Petá To the Yanomamö people of Brazil and Venezuela, this was the name of the first woman, born from the leg of a bird. She married four brothers, with whom she lived happily. But trouble arose when the men argued over which of them should have sex with Petá. So she tied their penises up while they slept, attaching them with strings to their waistbands. Only when she untied them could they have intercourse with her.

Because women had stronger children if they had intercourse with many men during pregnancy, Petá enjoyed all four husbands while carrying her son, who shot an arrow at the moon that caused an eclipse, which in turn caused the earth to be flooded with blood. From this blood, the Yanomamö were born, and Petá remained their chief.

One night while the village slept, a jaguar dragged Petá away into his cave den, where she found two jaguar cubs beside their dead mother. She offered her breasts to the cubs, who grew overnight into full-sized jaguars. At that moment, Petá's husbands arrived to save her. Miraculously, the jaguar mother recovered and came between the men and the jaguars. Thanking Petá for saving her children, she turned into a woman, Perimbó, and the cubs turned into her daughters. The girls returned home with Petá, while the jaguar couple disappeared. (Becher; Wilbert and Simoneau)

Pulówi The Guajiro honored the underworld mother Pulówi. She resented hunters, so she seduced them to keep animals safe. One hunter wounded a doe and, following her, found himself under the earth, where only women lived. Pulówi appeared wearing golden bands around her ankles and wrists. The man spit on the ground, turning the women into animals. Impressed with his power, Pulówi entreated him to remove his arrow from the doe. He did so and found himself on the surface world again. Shortly afterward he and his family disappeared. (Bierhorst 1988)

Sicasica A mountain goddess of the Aymara of Bolivia, Sicasica seduced men by luring them into glaciers. Anyone found dead was believed to have refused to honor Sicasica. (Osbourne)

Táita This Selknan woman controlled the world's water, which she covered with fur. Desperate people tried to steal water, but Táita killed them. So the hero Táiyin killed her, then began throwing stones around, forming the mountains. (Wilbert 1975)

Takasa To the Yamana, the animals and birds on which they depended each had a special divinity. Takasa and her associate Wémarkipa were spirits of the seagull; other similar feminine spirits included Wíyen (sea duck), Kimoa (goose), Wípatux (duck), Cilawáiakip (fox), and Wesána (rat). (Wilbert 1977)

Tamparawa Among the Amazonian Tapirapé people, this moon goddess was ancestor of all. Assaulted by her brother, the sun, who slapped her and caused marks on the moon's face, Tamparawa married a man of the Tapirapé. But he found it difficult to have intercourse because he feared her strong vagina would cut off his penis. So she bathed in fish poison and had intercourse with a piranha, making her husband safe. (Wagley)

Tséhmataki The Chorote people believed in a cannibal woman with a long tail who hunted people, knocking down houses to get to them. She controlled the earth, which shook at her voice. The ground turned soggy when she wished to capture humans, who found themselves trapped in quicksand. But a shaman killed her. He burned her body, from which emerged vampire bats, owls, and cuckoos. Monkeys and other helpers of shamans also came forth. Finally a plant grew where she had fallen: tobacco. (Bierhorst 1988)

Tsugki The central Andean spirit Tsugki lived in the bottom of a whirlpool, above which she appeared as a rainbow. Once she lured a handsome man home. But an anaconda lived with her, and the man could not abide the serpent. So the couple moved onto land, but the man's mother saw Tsugki in snake shape and drove her from the village. Insulted, Tsugki caused a flood and attacked with an army of dolphins and anacondas, killing everyone except her husband. She became the first shaman and was invoked for love magic. (Bierhorst 1988; Brown)

Uretane This primeval woman knew she was a man despite her woman's body. The more she wished it, the more she found her body changing. She grew breasts but also a penis, so she would not bathe with others. One day she noticed a woman she desired, so she asked the girl to bathe with her. The girl was delighted to discover Uretane had both breasts and penis. There was no objection when she decided to marry Uretane, who did men's work while the girl performed women's duties. (Wilbert 1974)

Usirumani At the beginning of time, according to the Warao, there was only a colorless void. A male shaman owned darkness but kept it wrapped up in a basket. When another male shaman released it, the world grew so dark people could not see to hunt or gather. To bring back light, the offending shaman carved a woman from plum-tree wood. She had no vagina, so the woodpecker dug one, in the process staining his beak red. As the woman's blood flowed, other animals painted themselves; vultures are dark black, for they came late, when the blood had coagulated.

Among the nearby Waroa, a similar story

described Usi-diu, whom a childless shaman created by carving her from plum wood. Usi-diu was incomplete, for she was missing a vagina. This was not obvious until Yar, the sun god, married her. A bird pecked out a vagina, and Usi-diu was soon pregnant. Abandoned by her husband, she got lost trying to find him. Wandering, she found the home of Nanyobo, the frog woman, who sheltered her in return for cleaning the lice from her hair, warning her not to eat the insects. But the nervous Usi-diu forgot the rule and put the lice in her mouth. They poisoned her, and she fell dead. Nanyobo cut out the twins Usi-diu was carrying and raised them. When they were old enough to notice, they grew frightened because every night, Nanyobo made fire by vomiting. They killed the frog woman, and the fire in her body passed into wood. (Wilbert 1970)

Wekatánaxipa This Yamana fisherwoman invented the sinker, which made her lucky at fishing. But she kept her catch for herself, feeding her grandson only tiny fish. He was always half-starving but thought they were poor, until he discovered his grandmother's store of fish. Feeling rejected, he painted himself red and flew into the air, becoming a bird. The grandmother, overcome with tears of sorrow, became a cold stream. (Wilbert 1977)

Wowtā The frog goddess of the Warao could change shape. She used this power when, enamored of the boy Aboré, she transformed herself into a nursemaid. She did magic, stretching him into unrecognizable shape. When the family returned, they thought Aboré had disappeared. Wowtā intended to keep Aboré for her own until he was mature enough to marry. But he figured out her intention. He tried to kill Wowtā, but she escaped. Aboré tried to flee across the water, but Wowtā's powers extended to the wood of his canoe, which refused to carry him. So he fashioned a canoe out of wax, hoping it would be outside her magic. She almost caught him but liked honey so much that she stopped to eat his boat, permitting his escape. She resumed her frog shape and can be heard in spring, lamenting her loss. (Brett; Wilbert 1970)

Yampan This goddess of abundance produced gardens full of tasty foods, but no one seemed able to learn her magic, according to the Aguaruna. So she gave up on humanity and moved to the sky, where she lived with the sun. She taught her daughters the power of singing to the garden, and her descendants know secret gardening songs. Her songs were also helpful in brewing beer. (Brown)

Yamuricumá According to the Kamayurá, the Yamuricumá were women whose husbands were transformed into animals. Left without men, the Yamuricumá women dressed as warriors and began dancing. For days they danced, covering themselves with herbs that transformed them into powerful spirits. Then they found an old man, whom they turned into an armadillo and pressed into service as their herald. Thereafter they wandered the world, calling women away from their homes to join them as warriors. (Bierhorst 1988)

Yanyonböri The Mundurucú of Brazil said the sacred trumpet was once owned by women but was taken over by men. Three women, Yanyonböri and her companions Tuembirü and Parawarö, discovered a magic lake. Knowledge of the lake led the women to useful inventions, including nets for capturing fish. Once three fish turned into three hollow cylinders, with which the women made music. The three women loved the music so much they forgot their housework. Upset at the mess in which they were forced to live, the men convinced Yanyonböri to bring the trumpets into the village.

Possession of the magical instruments gave the women power, which the men envied. The men had to cook, tend babies, and have sex with the women whenever the women wished. And they had to hunt as well, because the trumpets demanded offerings of meat. The men went on strike, refusing to hunt until they were given the trumpets. Yanyonböri agreed they would share. But the men took the trumpets and refused to let women have access to them. Women since that time have been forced to perform housework and have been refused access to spiritual secrets. (Murphy and Murphy)

Yoálox-tárnuxipa The most intelligent being of primeval time, said the Yamana, was this woman, sister to two men named Yoálox. She invented the harpoon so they could kill sea animals and created human culture. When Yoálox-tárnuxipa's brothers wanted to marry, they were too lazy to figure out how. So she invited all the birds to find the best mates for them, and they came back with Mákuxipa, who was already married to a wren. Despite this, the boys settled down to share their wife. All went well until the older brother overheard Mákuxipa telling the younger brother she preferred him sexually because his penis was large. In retaliation, the older brother raped Mákuxipa, who bled from her wounds in the first menstruation. After this, the older brother would have nothing to do with Mákuxipa, who bore a son to the younger brother. Unfortunately, the child was so noisy that the energy of his screams split him in two. Mákuxipa died, leaving her identical sons with their father, who shortly afterward took up with the fox woman, Cilawáiakipa. She dug up and ate Mákuxipa's body, and she yearned to eat the children, but the boys discovered her intention, and their father killed his new wife. (Koppers; Wilbert 1977)

BIBLIOGRAPHY

AFRICA

Primary Sources in Translation

Abrahams, Roger D. *African Folktales: Traditional Stories from the Black World.* Pantheon Books, 1983.

Bartels, Lambert. "Birth Customs and Birth Songs of the Macha Galla." *Etymology,* Vol. 8, No. 4.

Beier, Ulli, ed. *The Origin of Life and Death: African Creation Myths.* Heinemann International, 1966.

———. *Yoruba Myths.* Cambridge University Press, 1980.

———, ed. *Yoruba Poetry: An Anthology of Traditional Poems.* Cambridge University Press, 1970.

Courlander, Harold. *Tales of Yoruba Gods and Heroes.* Crown Publishers, 1973.

Faulkner, R. O. *The Ancient Egyptian Book of the Dead.* University of Texas Press, 1990.

———. "The Pregnancy of Isis." *Journal of Egyptian Archaeology,* Vol. 54.

Herskovits, Melville J., and Frances S. Herskovits. *Dahomean Narrative.* Northwestern University Press, 1958.

Lichtheim, Miriam. *Ancient Egyptian Literature: A Book of Readings.* Vol. 2: *The New Kingdom.* University of California Press, 1976.

———. *Ancient Egyptian Literature: A Book of Readings.* Vol. 3: *The Late Period.* University of California Press, 1980.

Matateyou, Emmanuel. *An Anthology of Myths, Legends and Folktales from Cameroon: Storytelling in Africa.* Edwin Mellon Press, 1997.

Meyer, Marvin W., ed. *The Ancient Mysteries: A Sourcebook of Sacred Texts.* Princeton University Press, 1999.

Nassau, R. H. "Batanga Tales." *Journal of American Folklore,* Vol. 28, No. 107.

Parkinson, R. B. *Voices from Ancient Egypt: An Anthology of Middle Kingdom Writings.* University of Oklahoma Press, 1991.

Osoba, Funmi. *Benin Folklore.* Hadada Books, 1993.

Radin, Paul, ed. *African Folktales.* Schocken Books, 1983.

Silbree, James. "The Oratory, Songs, Legends and Folk-Tales of the Malagasy (Concluded)." *The Folk-Lore Journal,* Vol. 1, No. 11.

Wilson, Epiphanius, ed. *Egyptian Literature.* Colonial Press, 1901.

Žabkar, Louis V. *Hymns to Isis in Her Temple at Philae.* University Press of New England, 1988.

Other Sources

Abiodum, Rowland. "Woman in Yoruba Religious Images." *African Languages and Culture,* Vol. 2, No. 1.

Amadiume, Ifi. *Afrikan Matriarchal Foundations: The Igbo Case.* Karnak House, 1987.

Bádejo, Diedre L. "African Feminism: Mythical and Social Power of Women of African Descent." *Research in African Literatures,* Vol. 29, No. 2.

———. *Òṣun Ṣè, è gèsí: The Elegant Deity of Wealth, Power and Femininity.* Africa World Press, 1996.

Barnet, Miguel. *Afro-Cuban Religions.* Translated by Christine Renata Ayorinde. Markus Wiener Publishers, 2001.

Bascomb, William. "Ọba's Ear: A Yoruba Myth in Cuba and Brazil." *Research in African Literatures,* Vol. 7, No. 2.

Bastide, Roger. *The African Religions of Brazil: Towards a*

361

Sociology of the Interpenetration of Civilizations. Translated by Helen Sebba. Johns Hopkins University Press, 1978.

Bellegarde-Smith, Patrick, ed. *Fragments of Bone: Neo-African Religions in a New World.* University of Illinois Press, 2005.

Bleeker, C. J. *Hathor and Thoth: Two Key Figures in the Ancient Egyptian Religion.* E. J. Brill, 1973.

———. "Isis as Savior Goddess." In Brandon, S. G. F., ed. *The Saviour God.* Barnes & Noble, 1963.

Boddy, Janice. *Wombs and Alien Spirits: Women, Men and the Zār Cult in Northern Sudan.* University of Wisconsin Press, 1989.

Bonnefoy, Yves, ed. *Mythologies.* Vol. I. University of Chicago Press, 1991.

Booth, Newell S. "God and the Gods in West Africa." In Booth, Newell S., ed. *African Religions: A Symposium.* NOK Publishers, 1977.

Bosse-Griffiths, Kate. "The Great Enchantress in the Little Golden Shrine of Tut'ankhamūn." *Journal of Egyptian Archaeology,* Vol. 59.

Brandon, S. G. F. *Creation Legends of the Ancient Near East.* Hodder and Stoughton, 1963.

Brown, Karen McCarthy. *Mama Lola: A Vodou Priestess in Brooklyn.* University of California Press, 2001.

Buhl, Marie-Louise. "The Goddesses of the Egyptian Tree Cult." *Journal of Near Eastern Studies,* Vol. 6, No. 2.

Burton, John W. *God's Ants: A Study of Atuot Religion.* Studia Instituti Anthropos. Anthropos Institute, 1981.

———. "Lateral Symbolism and Atuot Cosmology." *Africa: Journal of the International African Institute,* Vol. 52, No. 1.

———. "'The Moon Is a Sheep': A Feminine Principle in Atuot Cosmology." *Man,* New Series, Vol. 16, No. 3.

———. "Nilotic Women: A Diachronic Perspective." *Journal of Modern African Studies,* Vol. 20, No. 3.

Cole, Herbert M. "The Survival and Impact of Igbo Mbari." *African Arts,* Vol. 21, No. 2.

Cott, Jonathan. *Isis and Osiris: Exploring the Goddess Myth.* Doubleday, 1994.

Courlander, Harold. "Gods of the Haitian Mountains." *Journal of Negro History,* Vol. 29, No. 3.

Cummings, S. L. "Sub-tribes of the Bahr-El-Ghazal Dinkas." *Journal of the Anthropological Institute of Great Britain and Ireland,* Vol. 34.

Dieterlen, Germaine. "Masks and Mythology among the Dogon." *African Arts,* Vol. 22, No. 3.

De La Torre, Miguel. *Santería: The Beliefs and Rituals of a Growing Religion in America.* William E. Eerdmans, 2004.

Dunham, Katherine. "Excerpts from the Dances of Haiti: Function." *Journal of Black Studies,* Vol. 15, No. 4.

Ellis, Normandi. *Feasts of Light.* Quest Books, 1999.

Ephirim-Donkor, Anthony. *African Spirituality: On Becoming Ancestors.* Africa World Press, 1997.

Evans-Pritchard, E. E. *Nuer Religion.* Clarendon Press, 1956.

Feldmann, Susan. *African Myths and Tales.* Dell Publishing, 1963.

Ford, Clyde. *The Hero with an African Face: Mythic Wisdom of Traditional Africa.* Bantam Books, 1999.

Frankfurter, David. *Religion in Roman Egypt: Assimilation and Resistance.* Princeton University Press, 1998.

Gates, Brian, ed. *Afro-Caribbean Religions.* Ward Lock Educational, 1980.

Gleason, Judith. *Orisha: The Gods of Yorubaland.* Athenaeum, 1971.

———. *Oya: In Praise of the Goddess.* Shambhala, 1987.

Gordon, Jacob. "Yoruba Cosmology and Culture in Brazil: A Study of African Survivals in the New World." *Journal of Black Studies,* Vol. 10, No. 2.

Graeber, David. "Painful Memories." *Journal of Religion in Africa,* Vol. 27, Fasc. 4.

Herskovits, Melville J. "African Gods and Catholic Saints in New World Negro Belief." *American Anthropologist,* New Series, Vol. 39, No. 4, Part 1.

Houlberg, Marilyn. "Sirens and Snakes: Water Spirits in the Arts of Haitian Vodou." *African Arts,* Vol. 29, No. 2.

Iloanusi, Obiakoizu A. *Myths of the Creation of Man and the Origin of Death in Africa.* Peter Lang, 1984.

Jaenen, Cornelius J. "The Galla or Oromo of East Africa." *Southwestern Journal of Anthropology,* Vol. 12, No. 2.

Jell-Bahlsen, Sabine. *The Water Goddess in Igbo Cosmology: Ogbuide of Oguta Lake.* Africa World Press, 2008.

Johnson, Sally B. *The Cobra Goddess of Ancient Egypt.* Kegan Paul, 1990.

Jones, G. Howard. *The Earth Goddess: A Study of Native Farming on the West African Coast.* Longmans, Green, 1936.

Kaplan, Flora Edouwaye S., ed. *Queens, Queen Mothers, Priestesses, and Power: Case Studies in African Gender.* New York Academy of Sciences, 1997.

Kiddy, Elizabeth W. "Congados, Calunga, Candombe: Our Lady of the Rosary in Minas Gerais, Brazil." *Luso-Brazilian Review,* Vol. 37, No. 1.

Knappert, Jan. *Kings, Gods and Spirits from African Mythology.* Peter Bendrick Books, 1986.

Koech, Kipng'eno. "African Mythology: A Key to Understanding African Religion." In Booth, Newell S., ed. *African Religions: A Symposium.* NOK Publishers, 1977.

Lachantañeré, Rómulo. *Afro-Cuban Myths: Yemayá and Other Orishas.* Translated by Christine Ayorinde. Markus Wiener Publishers, 2005.

Landes, Ruth. "Fetish Worship in Brazil." *Journal of American Folklore*, Vol. 53, No. 210.

Lawal, Babtunde. "New Light on Gelede." *African Arts*, Vol. 11, No. 2.

Leibovitch, Joseph. "Gods of Agriculture and Welfare in Ancient Egypt." *Journal of Near Eastern Studies*, Vol. 12, No. 2.

Lesko, Barbara S. *The Great Goddesses of Egypt*. University of Oklahoma Press, 1999.

Lienhardt, Godfrey. *Divinity and Experience: The Religion of the Dinka*. Clarendon Press, 1961.

Magness, Jodi. "The Cults of Isis and Kore at Samaria-Sebaste in the Hellenistic and Roman Periods." *Harvard Theological Review*, Vol. 94, No. 2.

Manyoni, Joseph R. "The Ubiquity of the Mother Goddess: Some African Manifestations." In Subramaniam, V., ed. *Mother Goddesses and Other Goddesses*. Ajanta Books, 1993.

Mbon, Friday M. "Women in African Traditional Religion." In King, Ursula. *Women in the World's Religions, Past and Present*. Paragon House, 1987.

McCall, Daniel F. "Mother Earth: The Great Goddess of West Africa." In Preston, James J., ed. *Mother Worship: Theme and Variations*. University of North Carolina Press, 1982.

McClelland, E. M. *The Cult of Ifá among the Yoruba*. Vol. 1: *Folk Practice and the Arts*. Ethnographica, 1982.

Mettraux, Alfred. *Voodoo in Haiti*. Schocken Books, 1972.

Mischel, Frances. "African 'Powers' in Trinidad: The Shango Cult." *Anthropological Quarterly*, Vol. 30, No. 2.

Müller, W. Max. *Egyptian Mythology*. Vol. 12 of *The Mythology of All Races*. Marshall Jones Company, 1918.

Murphy, Joseph M., and Mei-Mei Sandford, eds. *Osun across the Waters: A Yoruba Goddess in Africa and the Americas*. Indiana University Press, 2001.

Ngubane, Harriet. *Body and Mind in Zulu Medicine*. Academic Press, 1977.

Olupona, Jacob K., ed. *African Spirituality: Forms, Meanings and Expressions*. Crossroad, 2000.

Ogunwale, Titus A. "Oshun Festival." *African Arts*, Vol. 4, No. 4.

Okpewho, Isidore. "Poetry and Pattern: Structural Analysis of an Ijo Creation Myth." *Journal of American Folklore*, Vol. 92, No. 365.

Olmos, Margarie, and Lizabeth Paravisini-Gebert. *Sacred Possessions: Vodou, Santería, Obeah, and the Caribbean*. Rutgers University Press, 1997.

Omari, Mikelle Smith. *From the Inside to the Outside: The Art and Ritual of Bahian Candomblé*. Museum of Cultural History, UCLA, Monograph Series, No. 24, 1987.

Osoba, Funmi. *Benin Folklore*. Hadada Books, 1993.

Ottino, Paul. "Myth and History: The Malagasy 'Andriambahoaka' and the Indonesian Legacy." *History in Africa*, Vol. 9.

Parringer, (Edward) Geoffrey. *African Mythology*. Paul Hamlyn, 1967.

———. *African Traditional Religion*. Greenwood Press, 1970.

———. "Ibadan Annual Festival." *Africa: Journal of the International African Institute*, Vol. 21, No. 1.

Piankoff, Alexander. "The Sky-Goddess Nut and the Night Journey of the Sun." *Journal of Egyptian Archaeology*, Vol. 20, No. 1/2.

Pinch, Geraldine. "Offerings to Hathor." *Folklore*, Vol. 93, No. 2.

———. *Votive Offerings to Hathor*. Griffith Institute, Ashmolean Museum, 1993.

Pobee, John. "Aspects of African Traditional Religion." *Sociological Analysis*, Vol. 37, No. 1.

Radimilahy, Chantal. "Sacred Sites in Madagascar." In Carmichael, David, et al. *Sacred Sites, Sacred Places*. Routledge, 1994.

Ray, Benjamin C. *African Religions: Symbol, Ritual and Community*. Prentice Hall, 2000.

———. *Myth, Ritual and Kingship in Buganda*. Oxford University Press, 1991.

Rosenberg, Donna. *Folklore, Myths and Legends: A World Perspective*. NTC Publishing Group, 1997.

Scott, Nora E. "The Cat of Bastet." *Metropolitan Museum of Art Bulletin*, New Series, Vol. 17, No. 1.

Sekoni, Ropo. "Yoruba Market Dynamics and the Aesthetics of Negotiation in Female Precolonial Narrative Tradition." *Research in African Languages*, Vol. 25, No. 3.

Shafer, Byron E., ed. *Religion in Ancient Egypt: Gods, Myths and Personal Practice*. Cornell University Press, 1991.

Simpson, George Eaton. "The Vodun Service in Northern Haiti." *American Anthropologist*, New Series, Vol. 42, No. 2, Part 1.

Springborg, Patricia. *Royal Persons: Patriarchal Monarchy and the Feminine Principle*. Unwin Hyman, 1990.

Tacheva-Hitova, Margarita. *Eastern Cults in Moesia Inferior and Thracia*. E. J. Brill, 1983.

Traunecker, Claude. *The Gods of Egypt*. Cornell University Press, 2001.

Troy, Lana. "Engendering Creation in Ancient Egypt: Still and Flowing Waters." In Brenner, Athalya, and Carole Fontaine, eds. *A Feminist Companion to Reading the Bible: Approaches, Methods and Strategies*. Sheffield Academic Press, 1997.

Wiedemann, Alfred. *Religion of the Ancient Egyptians*. Dover Publications, 2003.

Wilkinson, Richard H. *The Complete Gods and Goddesses of Ancient Egypt.* Thames and Hudson, 2003.

EASTERN MEDITERRANEAN

Primary Sources in Translation

The Bible (Ben Sirach, 2 Chronicles, Dan, Deuteronomy, Enoch, Esther, Exodus, Genesis, Hosea, Jeremiah, John, Judges, 1 Kings, 2 Kings, Luke, Mark, Matthew, Micah, Numbers, Proverbs, Revelation, 2 Samuel, Tobit, Wisdom of Solomon).

The Oxford Annotated Apocrypha. Revised Standard Edition. Edited by Bruce M. Metzger. Oxford University Press, 1965.

The Qur'an.

al-Kalbi, Hishām Ibn. *The Book of Idols.* Translated by Nabih Amin Faris. Princeton University Press, 1952.

Barton, George. *The Royal Inscriptions of Sumer and Akkad.* Yale University Press, 1929.

Cassuto, U. *The Goddess Anath: Canaanite Epics of the Patriarchal Age.* The Magnes Press, 1951.

Craig, James A. "The Babylonian Ištar-Epic." *The Hebrew Bible Student,* Vol. 8, No. 7.

Dexter, Miriam Robbins. *Whence the Goddesses: A Sourcebook.* Pergamon Press, 1990.

Enheduanna. *Inanna: Lady of Largest Heart: Poems of the Sumerian High Priestess Enheduanna.* Translated by Betty De Shong Meador. University of Texas Press, 2000.

Gibson, J. C. L. *Canaanite Myths and Legends.* T&T Clark, 1977.

Hallo, William W., and J. J. A. Van Dijk. *The Exaltation of Inanna.* Yale University Press, 1968.

Hoffman, Harry A. *Hittite Myths.* Society of Biblical Literature Writings from the Ancient World Series. Scholars Press, 1990.

Livingstone, Alasdair. *Mystical and Mythological Explanatory Works of Assyrian and Babylonian Scholars.* Clarendon Press, 1986.

Lucian (attr.). *De Dea Syria/The Syrian Goddess.* Translated by Harrold W. Attridge and Robert A. Oden. Scholars Press, 1976.

Malandra, William W. *An Introduction to Ancient Iranian Religion: Readings from the Avesta and Archaemenid Inscriptions.* University of Minnesota Press, 1983.

Meyer, Marvin, with Esther A. De Boer. *The Gospels of Mary.* HarperSanFrancisco, 2004.

Prince, J. Dyneley. "A Hymn to the Goddess Kir-g'i-lu (Cuneiform Texts from the British Museum, 15, Plate 23) with Translation and Commentary." *Journal of the American Oriental Society,* Vol. 30, No. 4.

Pritchard, James B. *Ancient Near Eastern Texts Relating to the Old Testament.* Princeton University Press, 1969.

Sandars, N. K., trans. *Poems of Heaven and Hell from Ancient Mesopotamia.* Penguin Books, 1971.

Temple, Robert. *He Who Saw Everything: A Verse Translation of the Epic of Gilgamesh.* Rider, 1991.

Virgil (P. Virgilius Maro). *The Aeneid.* Translated by Rolfe Humphries and edited by Brian Wilke. Macmillan Publishing, 1987.

Young, Serinity, ed. *An Anthology of Sacred Texts by and about Women.* Crossroad, 1993.

Wolkstein, Diane, and Samuel Noah Kramer. *Inanna: Queen of Heaven and Earth, Her Stories and Hymns from Sumer.* Harper and Row, 1983.

Other Sources

Ackerman, Susan. *Under Every Green Tree: Popular Religion in Sixth-Century Judah.* Scholars Press, 1992.

———. "The Queen Mother and the Cult in Ancient Israel." *Journal of Biblical Literature,* Vol. 112, No. 3.

Ackroyd, Peter R. "Goddesses, Women and Jezebel." In Cameron, Averil, and Amelie Kuhrt. *Images of Women in Antiquity.* Routledge, 1993.

Albright, W. F. "Anath and the Dragon." *Bulletin of the American Schools of Oriental Research,* No. 84.

———. "The Goddess of Life and Wisdom." *American Journal of Semitic Languages and Literatures,* Vol. 36, No. 4.

———. *Yahweh and the Gods of Canaan: A Historical Analysis of Two Contrasting Faiths.* Doubleday, 1968.

Ananikian, Mardiros H. *Armenian Mythology.* Vol. 7 of *The Mythology of All Races.* Marshall Jones Company, 1931.

Arthur, Rose Horman. "The Wisdom Goddess and the Masculinization of Western Religion." In King, Ursula. *Women in the World's Religions, Past and Present.* Paragon House, 1987.

Azarpay, G. "Nanâ, the Sumero-Akkadian Goddess of Transoxiana." *Journal of the American Oriental Society,* Vol. 96, No. 4.

Bal, Mieke. *Lethal Love: Feminist Literary Readings of Biblical Love Stories.* Indiana University Press, 1987.

Becking, Bob, Meindert Dijkstra, Marjo C. A. Korpel, and Karel J. H. Vriezen. *Only One God? Monotheism in Ancient Israel and the Veneration of the Goddess Asherah.* Sheffield Academic Press, 2001.

Bikerman, E. "Anonymous Gods." *Journal of the Warberg Institute*, Vol. 1, No. 3.

Binger, Tilde. *Asherah: Goddesses in Ugarit, Israel and the Hebrew Bible. Journal for the Study of the Hebrew Bible.* Supplement Series 232. Sheffield Academic Press, 1997.

Bird, Phyllis. *Missing Persons and Mistaken Identities: Women and Gender in Ancient Israel.* Fortress Press, 1997.

Bodington, Alice. "Legends of the Sumiro-Accadians of Chaldea (Continued)." *American Naturalist*, Vol. 27, No. 314.

Boyce, Mary. "Some Reflections on Zurvanism." *Bulletin of the School of Oriental and African Studies*, University of London, Vol. 19, No. 2.

Brandon, S. G. F. *Creation Legends of the Ancient Near East.* Hodder and Stoughton, 1963.

Brenner, Athalya, ed. *The Feminist Companion to Samuel and Kings.* Sheffield Academic Press, 1994.

———. *The Feminist Companion to the Later Prophets.* T&T Clark International, 1995.

Brenner, Athalya, and Carole Fontaine, eds. *A Feminist Companion to Reading the Bible: Approaches, Methods and Strategies.* Sheffield Academic Press, 1997.

Bronner, Leah. *The Stories of Elijah and Elisha as Polemics against Baal Worship.* E. J. Brill, 1968.

Bryce, T. R. "Disciplinary Agents in the Sepulchral Inscriptions of Lycia." *Anatolian Studies*, Vol. 31.

Camp, Claudia V. *Wisdom and the Feminine in the Book of Proverbs.* Almond/JSOT Press, 1985.

Camp, Claudia, and Carole R. Fontaine. "Women, War and Metaphor: Language and Society in the Study of the Hebrew Bible." *Semeia*, Vol. 61, 1993.

Carnoy, Albert J. *Iranian Mythology.* Vol. 6 of *The Mythology of All Races.* Marshall Jones Company, 1931.

———. "Iranian Views of Origins in Connection with Similar Babylonian Beliefs." *Journal of the American Oriental Society*, Vol. 36.

Clay, A. T. "The Origin and Real Name of NIN-IB." *Journal of the American Oriental Society*, Vol. 28.

Cornelius, Izak. *The Many Faces of the Goddess: The Iconography of the Syro-Palestinian Goddesses Anat, Astarte, Qedeshet, and Asherah c. 1500–1000 BCE.* Orbis Biblicus et Orientalis, 204. Academic Press, 2004.

Corrington, Gail Patterson. "The Milk of Salvation: Redemption by the Mother in Late Antiquity and Early Christianity." *Harvard Theological Review*, Vol. 82, No. 4.

Cross, Frank Moore. *Canaanite Myth and Hebrew Epic.* Harvard University Press, 1973.

Dalley, Stephanie. *Myths from Mesopotamia: Creation, The Flood, Gilgamesh and Others.* Oxford University Press, 1991.

———. "Semiramis in History and Legend." In Gruen, Erich S., ed. *Cultural Borrowings and Ethnic Appropriations in Antiquity.* Franz Steiner Verlag, 2005.

Dan, Joseph. "Samael, Lilith and the Concept of Evil in Early Kabbalah." *Association for Jewish Studies Review*, Vol. 5.

Day, John. "Asherah in the Hebrew Bible and Northwest Semitic Literature." *Journal of Biblical Literature*, Vol. 105, No. 3.

———. *Yahweh and the Gods and Goddesses of Canaan. Journal for the Study of the Old Testament.* Supplement Series 265. Sheffield Academic Press, 2000.

Day, Peggy, ed. "Anat: Ugarit's 'Mistress of Animals.'" *Journal of Near Eastern Studies*, Vol. 51, No. 3.

———. *Gender and Difference in Ancient Israel.* Fortress Press, 1989.

Deighton, Hilary J. *The Weather-God in Hittite Anatolia: An Examination of the Archaeological and Textual Sources.* BAR International Series, No. 143, 1982.

Dever, William G. "Asherah, Consort of YHWH?" *Bulletin of the American Schools of Oriental Research*, No. 255.

———. *Did God Have a Wife? Archaeology and Folk Religion in Ancient Israel.* William B. Eerdmans Publishing, 2005.

Fernea, Robert A., and James M. Malarkey. "Anthropology of the Middle East and North Africa: A Critical Assessment." *Annual Review of Anthropology*, Vol. 4.

Freedman, David Noel. "YHWH of Samaria and His Asherah." *Biblical Archaeologist*, Vol. 50, No. 4.

Frothingham, A. L., Jr. "The Meaning of Baalim and Ashtaroth in the Old Testament." *American Journal of Philology*, Vol. 5, No. 3.

Frymer-Kensey, Tikva. *In the Wake of the Goddesses: Women, Culture and the Biblical Transformation of Pagan Myth.* Fawcett Columbine, 1992.

Fuchs, Esther. "Marginalization, Ambiguity, Silencing: The Story of Jephthah's Daughter." *Journal of Feminist Studies in Religion*, Vol. 5, No. 1.

Garstang, Theodore. *Thespis: Ritual, Myth and Drama in the Ancient Near East.* Anchor Books, 1961.

Ginsberg, Louis. *Legends of the Jews.* 7 vols. Translated by Henrietta Szold. Jewish Publication Society of America, 1968.

Graves, Robert, and Raphael Patai. *Hebrew Myths: The Book of Genesis.* Greenwich House, 1983.

Gurney, O. R. *Some Aspects of Hittite Religion.* Oxford University Press, 1977.

Hadley, Judith M. *The Cult of Asherah in Ancient Israel and Judah.* Cambridge University Press, 2000.

Hanaway, William R., Jr. "Anāhitā and Alexander." *Journal of the American Oriental Society*, Vol. 102, No. 2.

Harrington, Patricia. "Mother of Death, Mother of Rebirth: The Mexican Virgin of Guadalupe." *Journal of the American Academy of Religion*, Vol. 56, No. 1.

Harris, Rivkah. *Gender and Aging in Mesopotamia: The Gilgamesh Epic and Other Ancient Literature.* University of Oklahoma Press, 2000.

———. "Inanna-Ishtar as Paradox and a Coincidence of Opposites." *History of Religions*, Vol. 30, No. 3.

Heimpel, Wolfgang. "A Catalog of Near Eastern Venus Deities." *Syro-Mesopotamian Studies*, Vol. 4, No. 3.

Hinnells, John R. *Persian Mythology.* Hamlyn Publishing, 1973.

Honeyman, A. M. "Varia Punica." *American Journal of Philology*, Vol. 68, No. 1.

Hooke, S. H. *Middle Eastern Mythology.* Penguin Books, 1975.

Horowitz, Wayne. *Mesopotamian Cosmic Geography.* Eisenbrauns, 1998.

Jacobsen, Thorkild. "The Battle between Marduk and Ti'âmat." *Journal of the American Oriental Society*, Vol. 88, No. 1.

———. *The Treasures of Darkness: A History of Mesopotamian Religion.* Yale University Press, 1976.

Jobling, W. J. "Desert Deities: Some New Epigraphic Evidence for the Deities Dushares and Al-Lat from the Aqaba-Ma'an Area of Southern Jordan." *Religious Traditions*, Vols. 7–9.

Kapelru, Arvid S. *The Violent Goddess: Anat in the Ras Shamra Texts.* Universitets-Forlaget, 1969.

Kirsch, Jonathan. *The Harlot by the Side of the Road: Forbidden Tales of the Bible.* Ballantine Books, 1997.

Kletter, Raz. *The Judean Pillar-Figurines and the Archaeology of Asherah.* BAR International Series, 1976.

Kraft, John. *The Goddess in the Labyrinth.* Religionsvetenskapliga Skrifter No. 11. Abo Akademi, 1985.

Kramer, Samuel Noah. *From the Poetry of Sumer: Creation, Glorification, Adoration.* University of California Press, 1979.

———. *The Sacred Marriage Rite: Aspects of Faith, Myth and Ritual in Ancient Sumer.* Indiana University Press, 1969.

———. *Sumerian Mythology: A Study of Spiritual and Literary Achievement in the Third Millennium B.C.* Harper and Row, 1961.

Langdon, Stephen Herbert. *Semitic Mythology.* Vol. 5 of *The Mythology of All Races.* Marshall Jones Company, 1931.

———. *Tammuz and Ishtar.* Clarendon Press, 1914.

Laroche, Emmanuel. "Tesup and Hebat: The Great Hurrian God and His Consort." In Bonnefoy, Yves, ed. *Mythologies*, Vol. 1. University of Chicago Press, 1991.

Lerner, Gerda. *The Creation of Patriarchy.* Oxford University Press, 1986.

Levi Della Vida, G. "A Hurrian Goddess at Carthage?" *Journal of the American Oriental Society*, Vol. 68, No. 3.

Lichtenstadter, Ilse. "A Note on the Gharaniq and Related Qur'anic Problems." *Israel Oriental Studies*, Vol. 5.

Lipinsky, Edward. "The Goddess Ātirat." *Orientalia Lovensia Periodica*, Vol. 3.

Lutzky, Harriet. "Shadday as a Goddess Epithet." *Vetus Testamentum*, Vol. 48, Fasc. 1.

Macqueen, J. G. "Hattian Mythology and Hittite Monarchy." *Anatolian Studies*, Vol. 9.

Maier, Walter A. *'Aserah: Extrabiblical Evidence.* Harvard Semitic Monographs, No. 37. Scholars Press, 1986.

Margalit, Baruch. "The Meaning and Significance of Asherah." *Vetus Testamentum*, Vol. 40, Fasc. 3.

Mastin, B. A. "YHWH's Asherah, Inclusive Monotheism and the Question of Dating." In Day, John. *In Search of Pre-exilic Israel.* T&T Clark International, 2004.

McCall, Henrietta. *Mesopotamian Myths.* Austin: University of Texas Press, 1990.

Mellaart, James. *The Goddess from Anatolia.* 4 vols. Eskenazi, 1989.

Meyers, Carol. *Discovering Eve: Ancient Israelite Women in Context.* Oxford University Press, 1988.

Milik, J. T., and J. Teixidor. "New Evidence on the North-Arabic Deity Aktab-Kutbâ." *Bulletin of the American Schools of Oriental Research*, No. 163.

O'Brien, Joan. "Nammu, Mami, Eve and Pandora: 'What's in a Name?'" *Classical Journal*, Vol. 79, No. 1.

Oden, R. A., Jr. "The Persistence of Canaanite Religion." *Biblical Archaeologist*, Vol. 39, No. 1.

———. *Studies in Lucian's 'De Syria Dea.'* Scholars Press, 1977.

Olyan, Saul M. *Asherah and the Cult of YHWH in Israel.* Society of Biblical Literature Monograph Series No. 34. Scholars Press, 1988.

Otwell, John H. *And Sarah Laughed: The Status of Women in the Old Testament.* Westminster Press, 1977.

Pagels, Elaine. "What Became of God the Mother? Conflicting Images of God in Early Christianity." *Signs*, Vol. 2, No. 2.

Patai, Raphael. "The Goddess Asherah." *Journal of Near Eastern Studies*, Vol. 24, No. 1/2.

———. *The Hebrew Goddess* (Third Enlarged Edition). Wayne State University Press, 1990.

———. "Lilith." *Journal of American Folklore*, Vol. 77, No. 306.

———. "Matronit: The Goddess of the Kabbala." *History of Religions*, Vol. 4, No. 1.

Petty, Richard J. *Asherah: Goddess of Israel.* New York: Peter Lang, 1990.

Prince, J. Dyneley. "A Hymn to the Goddess Bau." *American Journal of Semitic Languages and Literatures*, Vol. 24, No. 1.

Pritchard, James Bennett. *Palestinian Figures in Relation to Certain Goddesses Known through Literature.* University of Pennsylvania, 1943.

Qualls-Corbetter, Nancy. *The Sacred Prostitute: Eternal Aspect of the Feminine.* Inner City Books, 1982.

Roberts, J. J. M. *The Earliest Semitic Pantheon.* Johns Hopkins University Press, 1972.

Rodney, Nanette B. "Ishtar, the Lady of Battle." *Metropolitan Museum of Art Bulletin*, New Series, Vol. 10, No. 7.

Rubin, Uri. "Abū Lahab and Sūra CXI." *Bulletin of the School of Oriental and African Studies*, University of London, 1979.

Sayce, A. H. "The Legend of Semiramis." *English Historical Review*, Vol. 3, No. 9.

Septimus, Bernard. "Petrus Alfonsi on the Cult at Mecca." *Speculum*, Vol. 56, No. 3.

Sered, Susan. "Rachel, Mary and Fatima." *Cultural Anthropology*, Vol. 6, No. 2.

———. "Rachel's Tomb and the Milk Grotto of the Virgin Mary: Two Women's Shrines in Bethlehem." *Journal of Feminist Studies in Religion*, Vol. 2, No. 2.

Shearman, Susan Lee, and John Briggs Curtis. "Divine-Human Conflicts in the Hebrew Bible." *Journal of Near Eastern Studies*, Vol. 28, No. 4.

Sheres, Ita. *Dinah's Rebellion: A Biblical Parable for Our Time.* Crossroad, 1990.

Skipwith, Grey Hubert. "Asthtoreth, the Goddess of the Zidonians." *Jewish Quarterly Review*, Vol. 18, No. 4.

Smith, W. Robertson. "Ctesias and the Semiramis Legend." *English Historical Review*, Vol. 2, No. 6.

Stowasser, Barbara Freyer. *Women in the Qur'an, Traditions, and Interpretation.* Oxford University Press, 1994.

Strugnell, John. "The Nabatean Goddess Al-Kutba' and Her Sanctuaries." *Bulletin of the American Schools of Oriental Research*, No. 156.

Stuckey, Johanna. *Feminist Spirituality: An Introduction to Feminist Theology in Judaism, Christianity, Islam and Feminist Goddess Worship.* Toronto: Centre for Feminist Research, 1998.

——— "'Inanna and the Huluppu Tree': An Ancient Mesopotamian Narrative of Goddess Demotion." In Devlin-Glass, Frances, and Lyn McCredden. *Feminist Poetics of the Sacred: Creative Suspicions.* Oxford University Press, 2001.

———. "The Shift to Male Dominance in the Religion in Ancient Syria and Canaan: Mother Goddess Asherah and Her Relationship to Anath and Astarte." In

Subramaniam, V., ed. *Mother Goddesses and Other Goddesses.* Ajanta Books, 1993.

Taylor, William B. "The Virgin of Guadalupe in New Spain: An Inquiry into the Social History of Marian Devotion." *American Ethnologist*, Vol. 14, No. 1.

Teubal, Savina. *Sarah the Priestess: The First Matriarch of Genesis.* Swallow Press, 1984.

Toy, C. H. "The Queen of Sheba." *Journal of American Folklore*, Vol. 20, No. 78.

Van der Toorn, Karel. "Anat-Yahu, Some Other Deities, and the Jews of Elephantine." *Numen*, Vol. 39, Fasc. 1.

———. *From Her Cradle to Her Grave: The Role of Religion in the Life of the Israelite and the Babylonian Woman.* JSOT Press, 1994.

Vieyra, Maurice. *Hittite Art.* Alex Tiranti, 1955.

Walls, Neal. *Desire, Discord and Death: Approaches to Near Eastern Myth.* American Schools of Oriental Research, 2001.

Ward, Willliam Hayes. "Bel and the Dragon." *American Journal of Semitic Languages and Literatures*, Vol. 14, No. 2.

Warner, Marina. *Alone of All Her Sex: The Myth and the Cult of the Virgin Mary.* Alfred A. Knopf, 1976.

Weems, Renita. *Battered Love: Marriage, Sex and Violence in the Hebrew Prophets.* Fortress Press, 1995.

Yamauchi, Edwin M. "Tammuz and the Bible." *Journal of Biblical Literature*, Vol. 84, No. 3.

ASIA AND OCEANIA
CHINA

Primary Sources in Translation

Birrell, Anne, trans. *The Classic of Mountains and Seas.* Penguin Books, 1999.

Rachewiltz, Igor de, trans. *Secret History of the Mongols: A Mongolian Epic Chronicle of the Thirteenth Century.* Brill Inner Asian Library, 2004.

Sommer, Deborah. *Chinese Religion: An Anthology of Sources.* Oxford University Press, 1995.

Walls, Jan, and Yvonne Walls, ed. and trans. *Classical Chinese Myths.* Joint Publishing Company, 1984.

Wu Cheng'en (attributed). *Journey to the West.* Translated by W. J. F. Jenner. Foreign Languages Press, 2000.

Other Sources

Birrell, Anne. *Chinese Mythology: An Introduction.* Johns Hopkins University Press, 1993.

———. *Chinese Myths.* University of Texas Press, 2000.

Blofeld, John. *Bodhisattva of Compassion: The Mystical Tradition of Kuan Yin.* Shambhala, 1978.

Boltz, Judith Magee. "In Homage to T'ien-fei." *Journal of the American Oriental Society,* Vol. 106, No. 1.

Bonnefoy, Yves, ed. *Asian Mythologies.* University of Chicago Press, 1993.

Cahill, Suzanne E. "Performers and Female Taoist Adepts: Hsi Wang Mu as the Patron Deity of Women in Medieval China." *Journal of the American Oriental Society,* Vol. 106, No. 1.

———. "Sex and the Supernatural in Medieval China: Cantos on the Transcendent Who Presides over the River." *Journal of the American Oriental Society,* Vol. 105, No. 2.

———. *Transcendence and Divine Passion: The Queen Mother of the West in Medieval China.* Stanford University Press, 1993.

Chamberlayne, John H. "The Development of Kuan Yin: Chinese Goddess of Mercy." *Numen,* Vol. 9, Fasc. 1.

Chin, Y-Lien C., Yetta S. Center, and Mildred Ross. *Traditional Chinese Folktales.* M. E. Sharp, 1989.

Ching, Julia, and R. W. L. Guisso. *Sages and Filial Sons: Mythology and Archaeology in Ancient China.* Chinese University Press, 1991.

Colegrave, Sukie. *The Spirit of the Valley: The Masculine and Feminine in Human Consciousness.* J. P. Tarcher, 1979.

Curtin, Jeremiah. *A Journey in Southern Siberia.* Arno Press, 1971.

Dudbridge, Glen. *The Legend of Miaoshan.* Oxford University Press, 2004.

Ferguson, John C. *The Mythology of All Races.* Vol. 7. Marshall Jones Company, 1966.

Graham, David C. *The Tribal Songs and Tales of the Ch'uan Miao.* Asian Folklore and Social Life Monographs, Vol. 102. Chinese Association of Folklore, 1978.

Heissig, Walther. *The Religions of Mongolia.* University of California Press, 1980.

He Liyi, trans. *The Spring of Butterflies and Other Folktales from China's Minority Peoples.* Lothrop, Lee & Shepard Books, 1985.

Irwin, Lee. "Divinity and Salvation: The Great Goddesses of China." *Asian Folklore Studies,* Vol. 49, No. 1.

Jungsheng, Cai. "The Projection of Gender Relations in Prehistoric China." In Biaggi, Cristina. *The Rule of Mars: Reflections on the Origins, History and Impact of Patriarchy.* Knowledge, Ideas and Trends, 2005.

Katz, Brian. *Deities and Demons of the Far East.* Metro Books, 1995.

Liu, Tao Tao. "Chinese Myths and Legends." In Larrington, Carolyne. *The Feminist Companion to Mythology.* Pandora, 1992.

Mackenzie, Donald Alexander. *China and Japan.* Avenel Books, 1986.

Miller, Alan L. "The Woman Who Married a Horse: Five Ways of Looking at a Chinese Folktale." *Asian Folklore Studies,* Vol. 54, No. 2.

Overmyer, Daniel. *Folk Buddhist Religion: Dissenting Sects in Late Traditional China.* Harvard University Press, 1976.

———. "Kuan-Yin: The Development and Transformation of a Chinese Goddess." *Journal of Religion,* Vol. 82, No. 3.

Palmer, Martin, and Jay Ramsay. *Kuan Yin: Myths and Prophecies of the Chinese Goddess of Compassion.* Thorsons, 1995.

Paper, Jordan. "The Persistence of Female Deities in Patriarchal China." *Feminist Studies in Religion,* Vol. 6, No. 1.

Pomeranz, Kenneth. "Power, Gender and Pluralism in the Cult of the Goddess of Taishan." In Huters, Theodore, R. Bin Wong, and Pauline Yu, eds. *Culture and State in Chinese History: Conventions, Accommodations and Critiques.* Stanford University Press, 1997.

Ruitenbeek, Klaas. "Mazu, the Patroness of Sailors, in Chinese Pictorial Art." *Artibus Asiae,* Vol. 58, No. 3/4.

Sagren, P. Steven. "Power and Transcendence in the Ma Tsu Pilgrimages of Taiwan." *American Ethnologist,* Vol. 20, No. 3.

Sanders, Tao Tao Liu. *Dragons, Gods & Spirits from Chinese Mythology.* Schocken Books, 1983.

Saso, Michael. "Taiwanese Feasts and Customs." In *Folk Cultures of Japan and East Asia.* Monumenta Nipponica Monographs, No. 25. Sophia University Press, 1966.

Schafer, Edward H. *The Divine Woman: Dragon Ladies and Rain Maidens in T'ang Literature.* University of California Press, 1973.

Shahar, Meir, and Robert P. Weller. *Unruly Gods: Divinity and Society in China.* University of Hawai'i Press, 1996.

Strassberg, Richard E. *A Chinese Bestiary.* University of California Press, 2002.

Tay, C. N. "Kuan-Yin: The Cult of Half Asia." *History of Religions,* Vol. 16, No. 2.

Thompson, Stuart E. "Death, Food and Fertility." In Watson, James E., and Evelyn S. Rawski, eds. *Death Ritual in Late Imperial and Modern China.* University of California Press, 1988.

Van Deusen, Kira. *Woman of Steel: A Tuvan Epic.* Udagan Books, 2000.

Visser, Marinus Willem de. *The Dragon in China and Japan.* Verhandelingen der Koninklijke Akademie van Wetenschappen te Amsterdam, 1969.

Waley, Arthur. "Avalokitésvara and the Legend of Miao-Shan." *Artibus Asiae*, Vol. 1, No. 2.

Werner, E. T. C. *Ancient Tales and Folklore of China*. Bracken, 1986.

Wong, Eva. *Tales of the Taoist Immortals*. Shambhala, 2001.

Yüan, Ke. *Dragons and Dynasties: An Introduction to Chinese Mythology*. Selected and translated by Kim Echlin and Nie Zhixiong. Penguin Books, 1993.

KOREA

Primary Sources in Translation

Allen, Horace Newton. *Korean Tales: Being a Collection of Stories Translated from the Korean Folk Lore, Together with Introductory Chapters Descriptive of Korea*. Putnams, 1889.

Carpenter, Frances. *Tales of a Korean Grandmother*. Doubleday, 1947.

Grayson, James Huntley. "Female Mountain Spirits in Korea: A Neglected Tradition." *Asian Folklore Studies*, Vol. 55, No. 1.

———. *Myths and Legends from Korea: An Annotated Compendium of Ancient and Modern Materials*. Curzon, 2001.

Kim Yol-gyn. *Korean Folk Tales*. Korean Culture Series 7. International Cultural Foundation, 1979.

Korean Folklore. Korean National Commission for UNESCO. Si-sa-yong-o-sa Pub, 1983.

Olmstead, D. L. *Korean Folklore Reader*. Indiana University, 1963.

Tae-Hung Ha. *Folk Tales of Old Korea*. Yonsei University Press, 1958.

Yun, Ch`i-won (Thomas Yoon). *The BuDoZhi: The Genesis of MaGo (Mother Earth) and History of the City of Heaven's Ordinance*. Cross Cultural Publications, 2003.

Zong In-Sob. *Folk Tales from Korea*. Grove Press, 1953.

Other Sources

Covell, Alan Carter. *Ecstasy: Shamanism in Japan*. Hollym International Corporation, 1983.

———. *Shamanist Folk Paintings: Korea's Eternal Spirits*. Hollym International Corporation, 1984.

Lee, Tai-Dong. "Princess Pari." *Korea Journal*, June 1978.

CIRCUMPOLAR NORTH

Primary Oral and Textual Sources in Translation

Chapman, John W. *Ten'a Texts and Tales from Anvik, Alaska*. Vol. 6. Publications of the American Ethnological Society. E. J. Brill, 1914.

Holtved, Erik. *The Polar Eskimos: Language and Folklore*. Vol. 1: *Texts*. C. A. Reitzels Forlag, 1951.

Jochelson, W., with I. Surovov and A. Yachmeneff. *Aleut Traditions*. Alaska Native Language Center, 1977.

Kazachinova, Galina, and Kira Van Deusen. *Khakass Stories*. Udagan Books, 2003.

Rink, Johannes. *Tales and Traditions of the Eskimo*. W. Blackwood and Sons, 1875.

Swann, Brian, ed. *Voices from Four Directions: Contemporary Translations of the Native Literatures of North America*. University of Nebraska Press, 2004.

Thompson, Stith. *Tales of the North American Indians*. Indiana University Press, 1966.

Other Sources

Boas, Franz. "Notes on the Eskimo of Port Clarence, Alaska." *Journal of American Folklore*, Vol. 7, No. 26.

———. "A Year among the Eskimo." *Journal of the American Geographical Society of New York*, Vol. 19.

Bonnefoy, Yves. *Mythologies*. University of Chicago Press, 1991.

Dioszegi, V., ed. *Popular Beliefs and Folklore Traditions in Siberia*. Indiana University Press, 1968.

Dioszegi, V., and M. Hoppal, eds. *Shamanism in Siberia*. Akademiai Kaido, 1978.

Giddings, J. L. *Kobuk River People*. University of Alaska Department of Anthropology and Geography, Studies of Northern People No. 1, 1961.

Holtved, Erik. *The Polar Eskimos: Language and Folklore*. Vol. 1: *Texts*. C. A. Reitzels Forlag, 1951.

Hultkrantz, Äke. "Water Sprites: The Elders of the Fish in Aboriginal North America." *American Indian Quarterly*, Vol. 7, No. 3.

Irimoto, Takashi, and Takado Yamada, eds. *Circumpolar Religion and Ecology: An Anthropology of the North*. University of Tokyo Press, 1994.

Kroeber, A. L. "Tales of the Smith South Eskimo." *Journal of American Folklore*, Vol. 12, No. 46.

Lantis, Margaret. "The Mythology of Kodiak Island." *Journal of American Folklore*, Vol. 51, No. 200.

Levin, M. G., and L. P. Potapov. *The Peoples of Siberia*. University of Chicago Press, 1956.

Merkur, Daniel. "Breath-Soul and Wind Owner: The Many and the One in Inuit Religion." *American Indian Quarterly*, Vol. 7, No. 3.

Michael, Henry N., ed. *Studies in Siberian Shamanism*. University of Toronto Press, 1963.

Motz, Lotte. *The Faces of the Goddess.* Oxford University Press, 1997.

Osterman, H., ed. *Knud Rasmussen's Posthumous Notes on the Life and Doings of the East Greenlanders in Olden Times.* C. A. Reitzels Forlag, 1938.

Paper, Jordan. *Through the Earth Darkly: Female Spirituality in Comparative Perspective.* Continuum, 1997.

Porterfield, Amanda. "Shamanism: A Psychosocial Definition." *Journal of the American Academy of Religion,* LV-4.

Rasmussen, Knud. *Eskimo Folk-Tales.* Translated by W. Worster. Gyldendal, 1921.

———. *Intellectual Culture of the Hudson Bay Eskimos.* Gyldendalske Boghandel Nordisk Forlag, 1930.

Riordan, James. *The Songs My Paddle Sings: Native American Legends.* Pavilion Books, 1997.

Smith, Harlan. "Notes on Eskimo Traditions." *Journal of American Folklore,* Vol. 7, No. 26.

Sonne, Birgitte. "Mythology of the Eskimos." In Larrington, Carolyne, ed. *The Feminist Companion to Mythology.* Pandora, 1992.

Van Deusen, Kira. *Raven and the Rock: Storytelling in Chukotka.* University of Washington Press, 1999.

———. *Singing Story, Healing Drum: Shamans and Storytellers of Turkic Siberia.* University of Washington Press, 2004.

Wardle, H. Newell. "The Sedna Cycle: A Study in Myth Evolution." *American Anthropologist,* New Series, Vol. 2, No. 3.

Weyer, Edward Moffat. *The Eskimos, Their Environment and Folkways.* Yale University Press, 1932.

INDIA AND SOUTHEAST ASIA

Primary Textual Sources in Translation

Brown, W. Norman. *The Saundaryalaharī or Flood of Beauty.* Harvard University Press, 1958.

Dexter, Miriam Robbins. *Whence the Goddesses: A Sourcebook.* Pergamon Press, 1990.

Dimmitt, Cornelia, and J. A. B. van Buitenen, eds. and trans. *Classical Hindu Mythology: A Reader in the Sanskrit Purāṇas.* Temple University Press, 1978.

Gupta, Sanjukta. *Lakṣmī Tantra: A Pāñcarātra Text.* E. J. Brill, 1972.

Hixon, Lex. *Mother of the Universe: Visions of the Goddess and Tantric Hymns of Enlightenment.* Quest Books, 1994.

Narasimhan, Chakravarthi V. *The Mahābhārata.* Columbia University Press, 1965.

Narayan, R. K. *The Ramayana.* Penguin Books, 1972.

O'Flaherty, Wendy Doniger, ed. *Hindu Myths: A Sourcebook Translated from the Sanskrit.* Penguin Books, 1975.

Parthasarathy, R., trans. *The Cilappatikāram of Iḷaṅkō Aṭikaḷ.* Columbia University Press, 1993.

Sen, Rāmprasād. *Grace and Mercy in Her Wild Hair: Selected Poems to the Mother Goddess.* Great Easter, 1982.

Warrier, A. G. Krishna. *The Sākta Upaniṣads.* Adyar Library and Research Center, 1967.

Young, Serinity, ed. *An Anthology of Sacred Texts by and about Women.* Crossroad, 1994.

Primary Oral Sources in Translation

Beck, Brenda E. F., Peter J. Claus, Praphulladatta Goswami, and Jawaharlal Handoo, eds. *Folktales of India.* University of Chicago Press, 1987.

Benedict, Laura Watson. "Bagobo Myths." *Journal of American Folklore,* Vol. 26, No. 99.

Bhattacharya, Tarun. *The Myths of the Shimongs of the Upper Siang.* North-East Frontier Agency, 1965.

Dange, Sadashiv Ambadas. *Legends in the Mahabharata: With a Brief Survey of Folk-Tales.* Motilal Banarsidass, 1969.

Do Vang Ly. *The Stork and the Shrimp: The Claw of the Golden Turtle and Other Vietnamese Tales.* Siddhartha Publications, 1959.

Elwin, Verrier. *Folk-Tales of Mahakoshal.* Arno Press, 1980.

———. *Myths of Middle India.* Oxford University Press, 1949.

———. *Myths of the North-East Frontier of India.* North-East Frontier Agency, 1958.

———. *Studies in N.E.F.A. Folk-Lore.* Vol. 1. Privately published, 1955.

———. *Tribal Myths of Orissa.* Oxford University Press, 1954.

Ghosh, G. K., and Shukla Ghosh. *Fables and Folk-Tales of Assam.* Firma KLM Private Limited, 1998.

Ghosh, Oroon. *The Dance of Shiva and Other Tales from India.* New American Library, 1965.

Hart, Donn, and Harriet Hart. "Maka-andog: A Reconstructed Myth from East Samar, Philippines." *Journal of American Folklore,* Vol. 79, No. 311.

Livo, Norma J., and Dia Cha. *Folk Stories of the Hmong.* Libraries Unlimited, 1991.

Nguyen Ngoc Bich. *The Original Myths of Vietnam.* Indochina Institute, 1985.

Pakrasi, Mira. *Folk-Tales of Assam.* Sterling Publishers, 1969.

Paul, Diana Y. *Women in Buddhism: Images of the Feminine in the Mahāyāna Tradition.* University of California Press, 1985.

Rafy, K. U. *Folk Tales of the Khasis*. Macmillan and Company, 1920.

Other Sources

Aiyappan, A. "Myth of the Origin of Smallpox." *Folklore*, Vol. 42, No. 3.

Allen, Michael. *The Cult of Kumari: Virgin Worship in Nepal*. Institute of Nepal and Asian Studies, 1975.

———. "Kumari or 'Virgin' Worship in the Kathmandu Valley." *Contributions to Indian Sociology*, Vol. 10, No. 2.

Atkinson, Clarissa, Constance H. Buchanan, and Margaret R. Miles, eds. *Immaculate and Powerful: The Female in Sacred Image and Social Reality*. Beacon Press, 1985.

Babb, Lawrence A. *The Divine Hierarchy: Popular Hinduism in Central India*. Columbia University Press, 1975.

Beane, Wendell. "The Cosmological Structure of Mythical Time: Kālī Śakti." *History of Religions*, Vol. 13, No. 1.

Bennett, Lynn. *Dangerous Wives and Sacred Sisters: Social and Symbolic Roles of High-Caste Women in Nepal*. New York: Columbia University Press, 1983.

Berkson, Carmel. *The Divine and Demonic: Mahisa's Heroic Struggle with Durgā*. Oxford University Press, 1995.

Bernbaum, Edwin. *Sacred Mountains of the World*. Sierra Club Books, 1990.

Beyer, Stephan. *The Cult of Tārā: Magic and Ritual in Tibet*. University of California Press, 1973.

Beswick, Ethel. *The Hindu Gods*. Crest Publishing House, 1993.

Bhardwaj, Surinder Mohan. *Hindu Places of Pilgrimage in India: A Study in Cultural Geography*. University of California Press, 1973.

Blackburn, Stuart H., Peter J. Claus, Joyce B. Flueckiger, and Susan S. Wadley. *Oral Epics in India*. University of California Press, 1989.

Bonnefoy, Yves, ed. *Asian Mythologies*. University of Chicago Press, 1993.

Brakel, Clara. "Sandhang-pangan for the Goddess: Offerings to Sang Hyang Bathari Durga and Nyai Lara Kidul." *Asian Folklore Studies*, Vol. 56, No. 2.

Brinkgreve, Francine. "Offerings to Durga and Pretiwi in Bali." *Asian Folklore Studies*, Vol. 56, No. 2.

Brooks, Douglas Renfrew. *The Secret of the Three Cities: An Introduction to Hindu Śākta Tantrism*. University of Chicago Press, 1990.

Bühnemann, Gudrun. "The Goddess Mahācīnakrama-Tārā (Ugra-Tārā) in Buddhist and Hindu Tantrism." *Bulletin of the School of Oriental and African Studies*, Vol. 59, No. 3.

Caldwell, Sarah. *Oh Terrifying Mother: Sexuality, Violence and the Worship of the Goddess Kāli*. Oxford University Press, 1999.

Campbell, June. *Traveler in Space: In Search of Female Identity in Tibetan Buddhism*. Athlone Press, 1996.

Caughran, Neema. "Shiva and Pārvatī: Public and Private Reflections in Stories in North India." *Journal of American Folklore*, Vol. 112, No. 446.

Chandola, Sudha. "Some Goddess Rituals in Non-narrative Folk Song of India." *Asian Folklore Studies*, Vol. 36, No. 1.

Cormack, Margaret, ed. *Sacrificing the Self: Perspectives on Martyrdom and Religion*. Oxford University Press, 2002.

Cort, John. "Medieval Jaina Goddess Traditions." *Numen*, Vol. 34, Fasc. 2.

Crooke, W. "The Cults of the Mother Goddesses in India." *Folklore*, Vol. 30, No. 4.

Dang Nghiem Van. "The Flood Myth and the Origins of Ethnic Groups in Southeast Asia." *Journal of American Folklore*, Vol. 106, No. 421.

Daniélou, Alain. *Hindu Polytheism*. Pantheon Books, 1964.

Dehejia, Vidya. *Devī: The Great Goddess; Female Divinity in South Asian Art*. Smithsonian Institution, 1999.

Demetrio, Francisco. "Creation Myths among the Early Filipinos." *Asian Folklore Studies*, Vol. 27, No. 1.

Elwin, Verrier. *The Religion of an Indian Tribe*. Oxford University Press, 1955.

Foulston, Lynn. *At the Feet of the Goddess: The Divine Feminine in Local Hindu Religion*. Sussex Academic Press, 2002.

Frey, Katherine Stenger. *Journey to the Land of the Earth Goddess*. Gramedia Publishing Division, 1986.

Fuller, C. J. "The Divine Couple's Relationship in a South Indian Temple: Mīnāṣī and Sundareśvara at Madurai." *History of Religions*, Vol. 19, No. 4.

———. *Servants of the Goddess: The Priests of a South Indian Temple*. Cambridge University Press, 1984.

Galland, China. *Longing for Darkness: Tārā and the Black Madonna, a Ten-Year Journey*. Viking Press, 1990.

Gatwood, Lynn E. *Devi and the Spouse Goddess: Women, Sexuality and Marriages in India*. Riverdale Company, 1985.

Gentes, M. J. "Scandalizing the Goddess at Kodungallur." *Asian Folklore Studies*, Vol. 51, No. 2.

Gombrich, R. "Food for Seven Grandmothers." *Man*, New Series, Vol. 6, No. 1.

Gombrich, Richard, and Gananath Obeyesekere. *Buddhism Transformed: Religious Change in Sri Lanka*. Princeton University Press, 1988.

Gupta, Lina. "Ganga: Purity, Pollution and Hinduism." In Adams, Carol J., ed. *Ecofeminism and the Sacred*. Continuum, 1993.

Gupta, Śakti M. *Festivals, Fairs and Fasts of India*. Clarion Books, 1991.

———. *Plant Myths and Traditions in India*. E. J. Brill, 1971.

Gupta, Sanjunkta, and Richard Gombrich. "Kings, Power and the Goddess." *South Asia Research*, Vol. 6, No. 2.

Hamilton, Roy W. *The Art of Rice: Spirit and Sustenance in Asia*. UCLA Fowler Museum of Cultural History, 2003.

Handelman, Don. "Myths of Murugan: Asymmetry and Hierarchy in a South Indian Puranic Cosmology." *History of Religions*, Vol. 27, No. 2.

Harle, James C. "Durgā, Goddess of Victory." *Artibus Asiae*, Vol. 26, No. 3/4.

Harman, William P. *The Sacred Marriage of a Hindu Goddess*. Indiana University Press, 1989.

Hawley, John Stratton. *Satī, the Blessing and the Curse: The Burning of Wives in India*. Oxford University Press, 1994.

Hawley, John Stratton, and Donna M. Wulff. *Devī: Goddesses of India*. University of California Press, 1996.

———. *The Divine Consort: Rādhā and the Goddesses of India*. Beacon Press, 1982.

Headley, Stephen C. *Durgā's Mosque: Cosmology, Conversion and Community in Central Javanese Islam*. Institute of Southeast Asian Studies, 2004.

Hiltebeitel, Alf. *The Cult of Draupadī*. University of Chicago Press, 1988.

———. *Rethinking India's Oral and Classical Epics: Draupadī among Rajputs, Muslims and Dalits*. University of Chicago Press, 1999.

Hiltebeitel, Alf, and Kathleen M. Erndl. *Is the Goddess a Feminist? The Politics of South Asian Goddesses*. New York University Press, 2000.

Ions, Veronica. *Indian Mythology*. Peter Bedrick Books, 1986.

Jamison, Stephanie J. *The Ravenous Hyenas and the Wounded Sun: Myth and Ritual in Ancient India*. Cornell University Press, 1991.

Jayakar, Pupul. *The Earth Mother: Legends, Goddess and Ritual Arts of India*. Harper and Row, 1990.

Jenson, Adolph. *Myth and Cult among Primitive People*. University of Chicago Press, 1951.

Jordaan, Roy E. "Tārā and Nyai Lara Kidul: Images of the Divine Feminine in Java." *Asian Folklore Studies*, Vol. 56, No. 2.

Kapadia, Karin. *Siva and Her Sisters: Gender, Caste and Class in Rural South India*. Westview Press, 1995.

King, Karen L., ed. *Women and Goddess Traditions in Antiquity and Today*. Fortress Press, 1997.

Kinsley, David R. "Freedom from Death in the Worship of Kālī." *Numen*, Vol. 22, Fasc. 3.

———. *The Goddesses' Mirror: Visions of the Divine from East and West*. State University of New York Press, 1989.

———. *Hindu Goddesses: Visions of the Divine Feminine in the Hindu Religious Tradition*. University of California Press, 1986.

———. *The Sword and the Flute: Kālī and Kṛṣna, Dark Visions of the Terrible and the Sublime in Hindu Mythology*. University of California Press, 1975.

———. *Tantric Visions of the Divine Feminine: The Ten Mahāvidyās*. University of California Press, 1997.

Koppers, Wilhelm. "On the Origins of the Mysteries." In Campbell, Joseph, ed. *The Mystic Vision: Papers from the Eranos Yearbooks*. Princeton University Press, 1968.

Kramrisch, Stella. "The Indian Great Goddess." *History of Religions*, Vol. 14, No. 4.

Kripal, Jeffrey J. *Kālī's Child: The Mystical and the Erotic in the Life and Teachings of Ramakrishna*. University of Chicago Press, 1995.

Kumar, P. Pratap. *The Goddess Lakṣmī: The Divine Consort in South Indian Vaiṣṇava Tradition*. Scholars Press, 1997.

Larson, Gerald James, Pratapaditya Pal, and Rebecca P. Gowen. *In Her Image: The Great Goddess in Indian Asia and the Madonna in Christian Culture*. UCSB Art Museum, 1980.

Leslie, Julie, ed. *Roles and Rituals for Hindu Women*. Fairleigh Dickinson University Press, 1991.

McDaniel, June. *The Madness of the Saints: Ecstatic Religion in Bengal*. University of Chicago Press, 1989.

———. *Making Virtuous Daughters and Wives: An Introduction to Women's Brata Rituals in Bengali Folk Religion*. State University of New York Press, 2003.

———. *Offering Flowers, Feeding Skulls: Popular Goddess Worship in West Bengal*. Oxford University Press, 2004.

McDermott, Rachel Fell. *Mother of My Heart, Daughter of My Dreams: Kālī and Umā in the Devotional Poetry of Bengal*. Oxford University Press, 2001.

Misra, Babagrahi. "'Sitala': The Small-Pox Goddess of India." *Asian Folklore Studies*, Vol. 28, No. 2.

Mookerjee, Ajit. *Kālī: The Feminine Force*. Destiny Books, 1988.

Ngaranjan, Vijaya Rettakuda. "Soil as the Goddess Bhudevi in a Tamil Women's Ritual: The Kolam in India." In Low, Alaine, and Soraya Tremayne. *Sacred Custodians of the Earth? Women, Spirituality and the Environment*. Berghan Books, 2001.

Obeyesekere, Gananath. *The Cult of the Goddess Pattini*. University of Chicago Press, 1984.

———. *Medusa's Hair: An Essay on Personal Symbols and Religious Experience*. University of Chicago Press, 1981.

O'Flaherty, Wendy Doniger. "Sacred Cows and Profane Mares in Indian Mythology." *History of Religions*, Vol. 19, No. 1.

———. *Tales of Sex and Violence: Folklore, Sacrifice and Danger in the Jaiminīya Brāhmaṇa*. University of Chicago Press, 1985.

———. *Women, Androgynes, and Other Mythical Beasts*. University of Chicago Press, 1980.

Overmyer, Daniel. *Folk Buddhist Religion*. Harvard University Press, 1976.

Pattanaik, Devdutt. *The Goddess in India: The Five Faces of the Eternal Feminine*. Inner Traditions, 2000.

Pintchman, Tracy, ed. *The Rise of the Goddess in the Hindu Tradition*. State University of New York Press, 1994.

———. *Seeking Mahādevī: Constructing the Identities of the Hindu Great Goddess*. State University of New York Press, 2001.

Preston, James. *Mother Worship: Theme and Variations*. University of North Carolina Press, 1982.

Ramaswamy, Sumathi. "Maps and Mother Goddesses in Modern India." *Imago Mundi*, Vol. 53.

Resink, G. J. "Kanjeng Ratu Kidul: The Second Divine Spouse of the Sultans of Ngayogyakarta." *Asian Folklore Studies*, Vol. 56, No. 2.

Rodrigues, Hillary Peter. *Ritual Worship of the Great Goddess: The Liturgy of the Durgā Pūga with Interpretations*. State University of New York Press, 2003.

Santiko, Hariani. "The Goddess Durgā in the East-Javanese Period." *Asian Folklore Studies*, Vol. 56, No. 2.

Sax, William S. *Mountain Goddess: Gender and Politics in a Himalayan Pilgrimage*. Oxford University Press, 1991.

Schnepel, Burkhard. "Durgā and the King: Ethnohistorical Aspects of Politico-Ritual Life in a South Orissan Jungle Kingdom." *Journal of the Royal Anthropological Institute*, Vol. 1, No. 1.

Scott, James George. *Indo-Chinese Mythology: Mythology of All Races*. Marshall Jones Company, 1931.

Sen, Mala. *Death by Fire: Satī, Dowry Death, and Female Infanticide in Modern India*. Rutgers University Press, 2002.

Sharma, Bublul. *The Book of Devī*. Viking Press, 2001.

Shaw, Miranda. *Buddhist Goddesses of India*. Princeton University Press, 2006.

———. *Passionate Enlightenment: Women in Tantric Buddhism*. Princeton University Press, 1994.

Shulman, David Dean. *Tamil Temple Myths*. Princeton University Press, 1980.

Spiro, Melford E. "Some Ifaluk Myths and Folk Tales." *Journal of American Folklore*, Vol. 64, No. 253.

Spivak, Gayatri Chakravorty. "Moving Devi." *Cultural Critique*, No. 47.

Stoddard, Heather. "Dynamic Structures in Buddhist Mandalas: Apradaksina and Mystic Heat in the Mother Tantra Section of the Anuttarayoga Tantras." *Artibus Asiae*, Vol. 58, No. 3/4.

Subramaniam, V., ed. *Mother Goddesses and Other Goddesses*. Ajanta Books, 1993.

Thadani, Giti. *Sakhiyani: Lesbian Desire in Ancient and Modern India*. Cassell, 1996.

Vetschera, Traude. "The Potaraja and Their Goddess." *Asian Folklore Studies*, Vol. 37, No. 2.

Wessing, Robert. "A Princess from Sunda: Some Aspects of Nyai Roro Kidul." *Asian Folklore Studies*, Vol. 56, No. 2.

———. "Spirits of the Earth and Spirits of the Water: Chthonic Forces in the Mountains of West Java." *Asian Folklore Studies*, Vol. 47, No. 1.

———. "Sri and Sedana and Sītā and Rama: Myths of Fertility and Generation." *Asian Folklore Studies*, Vol. 49, No. 2.

Whitehead, Henry. *The Village Gods of South India*. Association Press, 1916.

Winslow, Deborah. "Rituals of First Menstruation in Sri Lanka." *Man*, New Series, Vol. 15, No. 4.

Young, Serinity. *Courtesans and Tantric Consorts: Sexualities in Buddhist Narrative, Iconography, and Ritual*. Routledge, 2004.

Younger, Paul. "A Temple Festival of Mariyanman." *Journal of the American Academy of Religion*, Vol. 48, No. 4.

Zimmer, Heinrich. *The Art of Indian Asia: Its Mythology and Transformations*. Vol. 1: *Text*. Edited by Joseph Campbell. Princeton University Press, 1955.

———. *Myths and Symbols in Indian Arts and Civilization*. Edited by Joseph Campbell. Bollingen Series. Pantheon Books, 1946.

JAPAN

Primary Sources in Translation

Aston, W. G. *Nihongi: Chronicles of Japan from the Earliest Times to A.D. 697*. Allen & Unwin, 1956.

Chamberlain, Basil Hall. *Ainu Folktales*. Publication of the Folk-Lore Society, Vol. 22, 1888.

Phillipi, Donald, trans. *Kojiki*. University of Tokyo Press, 1968.

Wheeler, Post, trans. and ed. *The Sacred Scriptures of the Japanese*. H. Schuman, 1952.

Other Sources

Averbuch, Irit. "Shamanic Dance in Japan: The Choreography of Possession in Kagura Performance." *Asian Folklore Studies*, Vol. 57, No. 2.

Baba, Moses Osamu. "Iku-Nishi of the Saghalien Ainu." *Journal of the Royal Anthropological Institute of Great Britain and Ireland*, Vol. 79, No. 1/2.

Batchelor, John. *Ainu Life and Lore: Echoes of a Departing Race.* Johnson Reprint Corporation, 1971.

———. *The Ainu of Japan.* The Religious Tract Society, 1892.

———. "Items of Ainu Folk-Lore." *Journal of American Folklore*, Vol. 7, No. 24.

Blacker, Carmen. *The Catalpa Bow: A Study of Shamanistic Practices in Japan.* George Allen & Unwin, 1982.

———. "The Mistress of Animals in Japan: Yamanokami." In Billington, Sandra, and Miranda Green, eds. *The Concept of the Goddess.* Routledge, 1996.

Bonnefoy, Yves. *Asian Mythologies.* University of Chicago Press, 1993.

Fairchild, William P. "'Mika'-Jar Deities in Japanese Mythology." *Asian Folklore Studies*, Vol. 24, No. 1.

Hori, Ichiro. "Mountains and Their Importance for the Idea of the Other World in Japanese Folk Religion." *History of Religions*, Vol. 6, No. 1.

Katz, Brian. *Deities and Demons of the Far East.* Metro Books, 1995.

Kawai, Hayao. *The Japanese Psyche: Major Motifs in the Fairy Tales of Japan.* Spring Publications, 1988.

Kirkland, Russell. "The Sun and the Throne: The Origins of the Royal Descent Myth in Ancient Japan." *Numen*, Vol. 44, No. 2.

Kuzono, Tatsujiro. "Ainu Gods and Beliefs." In Irimoto, Takashi, and Takado Yamada, eds. *Circumpolar Religion and Ecology: An Anthropology of the North.* University of Tokyo Press, 1994.

Littleton, C. Scott. *Shinto.* Oxford University Press, 2002.

Matsumae, Takeshi. "The Heavenly Rock-Grotto Myth and the Chinkon Ceremony." *Asian Folklore Studies*, Vol. 39, No. 2.

———. "Origin and Growth of the Worship of Amaterasu." *Asian Folklore Studies*, Vol. 37, No. 1.

McAlpine, Helen, and William McAlpine. *Japanese Tales and Legends.* Henry Walck, 1959.

Miller, Alan L. "Ame No Miso-Ori Me (The Heavenly Weaving Maiden): The Cosmic Weaver in Early Shinto Myth and Ritual." *History of Religions*, Vol. 14, No. 1.

———. "Myth and Gender in Japanese Shamanism: The 'Itako' of Tohoku." *History of Religions*, Vol. 32, No. 4.

———. "Of Weavers and Birds: Structure and Symbol in Japanese Myth and Folktale." *History of Religions*, Vol. 26, No. 3.

Monaghan, Patricia. *O Mother Sun: A New View of the Cosmic Feminine.* Crossing Press, 1994.

Munro, Neil. *Ainu: Creed and Cult.* Columbia University Press, 1965.

Murakami, Fuminobu. "Incest and Rebirth in Kojiki." *Monumenta Nipponica*, Vol. 43, No. 4.

Opler, Morris E., and Robert Seido Hashima. "The Rice Goddess and the Fox in Japanese Religion and Folk Practice." *American Anthropologist*, New Series, Vol. 48, No. 1.

Piggot, Joan R. *The Emergence of Japanese Kingship.* Stanford University Press, 1997.

Ross, Floyd Hiatt. *Shinto: The Way of Japan.* Beacon Press, 1965.

Schattschneider, Ellen. "My Mother's Garden: Transitional Phenomena on a Japanese Sacred Mountain." *Ethos*, Vol. 28, No. 2.

Shillony, Ben-Ami. "The Princess of the Dragon Palace. A New Shinto Sect is Born." *Monumenta Nipponica*, Vol. 39, No. 2.

Tyler, Royall. *Japanese Tales.* Pantheon, 1987.

PACIFIC ISLANDS AND AUSTRALIA

Primary Oral and Textual Sources

Alpers, Antony. *Maori Myths and Tribal Legends.* John Murray, 1964.

Anderson, Johannes C. *Myths and Legends of the Polynesians.* Dover Publications, 1995.

Beckwith, Martha. *Hawaiian Mythology.* University of Hawaii Press, 1970.

Collocott, E. E. "Tongan Myths and Legends, III." *Folklore*, Vol. 35, No. 3.

Ellis, Jean A. *From the Dreamtime: Australian Aboriginal Legends.* Collins Dove, 1991.

Emerson, Nathaniel B. *Pele and Hi'iaka: A Myth from Hawaii.* Charles Tuttle, 1978.

Flood, Bo. *Marianas Island Legends: Myth and Magic.* Bess Press, 2001.

Flood, Bo, Beret Strong, and William Flood. *Pacific Island Legends: Tales from Micronesia, Melanesia, Polynesia, and Australia.* Bess Press, 1999.

Hopkins, Charles G. "Native Hawaiian Creation Story: Excerpts from a Voyage of Rediscovery." *First Peoples Theology Journal*, Sept. 2001.

Kame'eleihiwa, Lilikala K. *A Legendary Tradition of Kamapua'a: The Hawaiian Pig-God.* Bishop Museum, 1996.

"Laieikawai: A Legend of the Hawaiian Islands." *Journal of American Folklore*, Vol. 13, No. 51.

Luomala, Katharine. *Voices on the Wind: Polynesia Myths and Chants.* Bishop Museum, 1955.

MacKenzie, Donald. *South Seas: Myths and Legends*. Random House, 1996.

McLeod, Pauline, Francis Firebrace Jones, and June Barker. *Gadi Mirrabooka: Australian Aboriginal Tales from the Dreaming*. Edited by Helen McKay. Libraries Unlimited, 2001.

Parker, K. Langleoh. *More Australian Legendary Tales*. David Nutt, 1898.

———. *Wise Women of the Dreamtime: Aboriginal Tales of the Ancestral Powers*. Edited by Johanna Lambert. Inner Traditions, 1993.

Reed, A. W. *Aboriginal Myths, Legends and Fables*. Reed New Holland, 1993.

———. *Treasury of Maori Folklore*. A. H. & A. W. Reed, 1963.

Wohlers, J. F. H. "New Zealand Heaven and Earth Myth." *Journal of the Anthropological Institute of Great Britain and Ireland*, Vol. 6.

Other Sources

Allen, Louis A. *Time before Morning: Art and Myth of the Australian Aborigines*. Thomas Y. Crowell, 1975.

Beaglehold, Ernest, and Pearl Beaglehold. *Ethnology of Pukapuka*. Bernice P. Bishop Museum Bulletin 150, 1938.

Berndt, Catherine H. "The Ghost Husband: Society and the Individual in New Guinea Myth." *Journal of American Folklore*, Vol. 79, No. 311.

Berndt, Ronald. *Australian Aboriginal Religion*. E. J. Brill, 1974.

———. *Djanggawul: An Aboriginal Religious Cult of North-Eastern Arnhem Land*. Routledge and Kegan Paul, 1952.

———. *Kunapipi: A Study of an Australian Aboriginal Religious Cult*. International Universities Press, 1951.

———. "The Wuradilagu Song Cycle of Northeastern Arnhem Land: Content and Style." *Journal of American Folklore*, Vol. 79, No. 311.

Berndt, Ronald M., and Catherine H. Berndt. *The World of the First Australians*. University of Chicago Press, 1969.

Best, Elsdon. *The Astronomical Knowledge of the Maori*. Dominion Museum Monograph No. 1, 1955.

Bozic, Sreten, with Alan Marshall. *Aboriginal Myths*. Gold Star Publications, 1972.

Buck, Peter Henry (Te Rangi Hiroa). *Anthropology and Religion*. Yale University Press, 1939.

Caruana, Wally, and Nigel Lendon, eds. *The Painters of the Wagilag Sisters Story 1937–1997*. National Gallery of Australia, 1997.

Chadwick, Nora K. "Notes on Polynesian Mythology." *Journal of the Royal Anthropological Institute of Great Britain and Ireland*, Vol. 60.

Charlesworth, Max, Howard Morphy, Diane Bell, and Kenneth Maddock. *Religion in Ancient Australia*. University of Queensland Press, 1984.

Chaseling, Wilber S. *Yulegor: Nomads of Arnhem Land*. Epworth Press, 1957.

Codrington, Robert Henry. *The Melanesians: Studies in Their Anthropology and Folk Lore*. Dover Publications, 1972.

———. "Religious Beliefs and Practices in Melanesia." *Journal of the Anthropological Institute of Great Britain and Ireland*, Vol. 10.

Diab, Elizabeth. "Hawaii." In Larrington, Carolyne, ed. *The Feminist Companion to Mythology*. Pandora, 1992.

Dixon, Roland B. *The Mythology of All Races*. Vol. 9: *Oceanic*. Marshall Jones Company, 1967.

Eliade, Mircea. *Australian Religions: An Introduction*. Cornell University Press, 1973.

Emerson, Nathaniel B. "Unwritten Literature of Hawaii." *American Anthropologist*, New Series, Vol. 8, No. 2.

———. "Australian Religions. Part III: Initiation Rites and Secret Cults." *History of Religions*, Vol. 7, No. 1.

———. "Australian Religions. Part V: Death, Eschatology, and Some Conclusions." *History of Religions*, Vol. 7, No. 3.

Emory, Kenneth P. "The Tuamotuan Tale of the Female Spirit Who Assumed the Form of Tu's Wife." *Journal of American Folklore*, Vol. 62, No. 245.

Fox, C. E., and F. H. Drew. "Beliefs and Tales of San Cristoval (Solomon Islands)." *Journal of the Royal Anthropological Institute of Great Britain and Ireland*, Vol. 45.

Gill, W. Wyatt. "On the Origin of the South Sea Islanders, and on Some Traditions of the Hervey Islands." *Journal of the Anthropological Institute of Great Britain and Ireland*, Vol. 6.

Grace, Patricia. *Wahine Toa: Women of Maori Myth*. Collins, 1984.

Handy, E. S. Craighill. *Polynesian Religion*. Bernice P. Bishop Museum Bulletin 34, 1927.

Herda, Phillis, Michael Reilly, and David Hilliard, eds. *Vision and Reality in Pacific Religion*. MacMillan Brown Centre for Pacific Studies, 2005.

Hogbin, Ian. *The Island of Menstruating Men: Religion in Wogeo, New Guinea*. Chandler Publishing Company, 1970.

Holms, Sandra Le Brun. *The Goddess and the Moon Man: The Sacred Art of the Tiwi Aborigines*. Craftsman House, 1995.

Kalahaua, King David. *The Legends and Myths of Hawaii*. Charles E. Tuttle, 1972.

Lawrence, P., and M. J. Meggitt. *Gods, Ghosts and Men in Melanesia: Some Religions of Australian New Guinea and the New Hebrides*. Oxford University Press, 1965.

Lawrie, Margaret. *Myths and Legends of Torres Strait*. Taplinger Publishing Company, 1971.

Massola, Aldo. *Bunjil's Cave: Myths, Legends and Superstitions of the Aborigines of South-East Australia*, 1968.

Mountford, Charles P., and Ainslie Roberts. *The Dawn of Time*. Taplinger Publishing Company, 1972.

———. *The Dreamtime*. Rigby Limited, 1965.

Orbell, Margaret. "Maori Mythology." In Larrington, Carolyne, ed. *The Feminist Companion to Mythology*. Pandora, 1992.

Poignant, Roslyn. *Oceanic Mythology: The Myths of Polynesia, Micronesia, Melanesia, Australia*. Paul Hamlyn, 1967.

Powdermaker, Hortense. "Leadership in Central and Southern Australia." *Economica*, No. 23.

Robertson, Carole. "The Māhū of Hawai'i." *Feminist Studies*, Vol. 15, No. 2.

Skinner, Margo. "Pele's Habitat and Smoking Habits." *Western Folklore*, Vol. 12, No. 1.

Somerville, Boyle T. "Ethnological Notes on New Hebrides." *Journal of the Anthropological Institute of Great Britain and Ireland*, Vol. 23.

Swain, Tony, and Garry Trompf. *The Religions of Oceania*. Routledge, 1995.

Te Awekotuku, Ngahuia. *Ruahine: Mythic Women*. Huia, 2003.

White, Isobel. "Australian Aboriginal Myth." In Larrington, Carolyne, ed. *The Feminist Companion to Mythology*. Pandora, 1992.

Williamson, Robert W. *Religious and Cosmic Beliefs of Central Polynesia*. Vol. 1. Cambridge University Press, 1933.

Wirz, P. "Legend of the Dauan Islanders (Torres Straits)." *Folklore*, Vol. 43, No. 3.

EUROPE
THE BALTIC

Primary Oral and Textual Sources in Translation

Balys, Jonas. *Lithuanian Narrative Folksongs*. Draugas Press, 1954.

Beliajus, Vytautas. *Evening Song (Vakarine Daina)*. Privately printed, 1954.

Benjamins, Eso. *Dearest Goddess*. Current Nine Publications, 1985.

Dexter, Miriam Robbins. *Whence the Goddesses: A Sourcebook*. Pergamon Press, 1990.

Katzenelenbogen, Uriah. *The Daina: An Anthology of Lithuanian and Latvian Folksongs*. Latvian News Publishing Company, 1935.

Kiskytė, Birurė, trans. *Lithuanian Mythological Tales*. VAGA Publishers, 2002.

Landsbergis, Algiris, and Clark Mills. *The Green Linden: Selected Lithuanian Folksongs*. Voyages Press, 1964.

Paterson, Adrian, trans. *Old Lithuanian Songs*. Pribacis Kaunas, n.d.

Rubulis, Aleksis. *Latvian Folktales*. AKA Publishing, 1982.

Tacitus. *Dialogus, Agricola, Germania*. The Loeb Classical Library. Harvard University Press, 1914.

Zobarskas, Stevas. *Lithuanian Folk Tales*. Gerald Rickard, 1958.

Other Sources

Bojtár, Endre. *Foreword to the Past: A Cultural History of the Baltic People*. Central European University Press, 1999.

Bradunas, Elena. "If You Kill a Snake, the Sun Will Cry." *Lituanis*, Vol. 21.

Chase, George Davis. "Sun Myths in Lithuanian Folksongs." *Transactions and Proceedings of the American Philological Association*, Vol. 31.

Dexter, Miriam Robbins. "Dawn-Maid and Sun-Maid: Celestial Goddesses among the Proto-Indo-Europeans." In Jones-Bley, Karlene, and Martin Huld, eds. *The Indo-Europeanization of Northern Europe*. Journal of Indo-European Studies Monograph No. 17. Institute for the Study of Man, 1996.

Gimbutas, Marija. *Ancient Symbolism in Lithuanian Folk Art*. Memoirs of the American Folklore Society, Vol. 49.

———. *The Balts*. Ancient People and Places Series. Frederick A. Praeger, 1963.

———. *The Language of the Goddess*. Thames and Hudson, 1989.

———. *The Living Goddesses*. Edited and supplemented by Miriam Robbins Dexter. University of California Press, 1999.

———. *The Prehistory of Eastern Europe*. Peabody Museum, 1956.

———. "Religion and Mythology of the Balts." In Trinkūnas, Jonas, ed. *Of Gods and Holidays: The Baltic Heritage*. Tverme, 1999.

Greimas, Algirdas J. *Of Gods and Men: Studies in Lithuanian Mythology*. Translated by Milda Newman. Indiana University Press, 1992.

Jaskievicz, Walter C. "A Study in Lithuanian Mythology: Jan Lasicki's Samogitian Gods." *Studi Baltici*, Vol. 9.

Jurgines, J. M. "Relics of Paganism among the Baltic Peoples after the Introduction of Christianity." In Bharati, Agehananda, ed. *The Realm of the Extra-Human: Ideas and Actions*. Mouton Publishers, 1976.

Machal, Jan. *Celtic, Slavic, Baltic*. Vol. 3 of *The Mythology of All Races*. Cooper Square, 1964.

Motz, Lotte. *The Faces of the Goddess*. Oxford University Press, 1997.

Neuland, Lena. *Motif-Index of Latvian Folktales and Legends*. Academeia Scientarium Finnica, 1981.

Rubulis, Aleksis. *Baltic Literature: A Survey of Finnish, Estonian, Latvian and Lithuanian Literatures*. University of Notre Dame Press, 1970.

Trinkūnas, Jonas, ed. *Of Gods and Holidays: The Baltic Heritage*. Tverme, 1999.

Ward, Donald. "Solar Mythology and Baltic Folksongs." In Wilgus, D. K., and Carol Sommer, eds. *Folklore International*. Folklore Associates, 1967.

THE CELTIC WORLD

Primary Textual Sources in Translation

Bedier, Joseph. *The Romance of Tristan and Iseult*. Translated by Hilaire Belloc. Vintage Books, 1965.

Bourke, Angela, ed. *The Field Day Anthology of Irish Writing*. Vol. 4: *Irish Women's Writing and Traditions*. New York University Press, 2002.

Cambrensis, Geraldis (Gerald of Wales). *The History and Topography of Ireland*. Penguin Books, 1982.

Cross, Tom Peete, and Clark Harris Slover, eds. *Ancient Irish Tales*. Henry Holt and Company, 1936.

Deane, Seamus, ed. *The Field Day Anthology of Irish Writing*, Vol. 1. Field Day Publications, 1991.

Dexter, Miriam Robbins. *Whence the Goddesses: A Sourcebook*. Pergamon Press, 1990.

Dillon, Myles. *The Cycles of the Kings*. Four Courts Press, 1994.

———. *Early Irish Literature*. Four Courts Press, 1994.

———, ed. *Irish Sagas*. Mercier Press, 1968.

Gantz, Jeffrey, ed. and trans. *Early Irish Myths and Sagas*. Penguin Books, 1984.

———. *The Mabinogion*. Barnes and Noble Books, 1976.

Guyot, Charles. *The Legend of the City of Ys*. Translated and illustrated by Deirdre Cavanagh. University of Massachusetts Press, 1979.

Gwynn, Edward. *The Metrical Dindshenchas*. 5 vols. Royal Irish Academy, Todd Lecture Series. Hodges, Figgis, and Company, 1906–1924. Reprinted, Dublin Institute for Advanced Studies, School of Celtic Studies, 1991.

Hull, Eleanor. *The Cuchullin Saga in Irish Literature*. David Nutt, 1898.

———. *The Poem-Book of the Gael*. Chatto & Windus, 1913.

Jackson, Kenneth Hurlstone. *A Celtic Miscellany: Translations from the Celtic Literatures*. Penguin Books, 1971.

Jones, Gwyn, trans. *The Mabinogion*. Dutton, 1963.

Joyce, P. W. *Ancient Celtic Romances*. Parkgate Books, 1997.

Kinsella, Thomas, trans. *The Táin*. The Dolmen Press, 1969.

Koch, John T., ed., with John Carey. *The Celtic Heroic Age: Literary Sources for Ancient Celtic Europe and Early Ireland and Wales*. Celtic Studies Publications, 2000.

MacAlister, R. A. Stewart. *Lebor Gabála Érenn: The Book of the Taking of Ireland, Parts 1–4*. Irish Texts Society, 1941.

———. *Lebor Gabála Érenn: The Book of the Taking of Ireland, Part 5*. Irish Texts Society, 1956.

Merriman, Brian. *The Midnight Court*. Translated by Frank O'Connor. O'Brien Press, 1989.

O'Faoláin, Sean, ed. *The Silver Branch: A Collection of the Best Old Irish Lyrics*. Viking Press, 1937.

Skeat, Walter W., trans. *The Romans of Partenay or of Lusignen, Otherwise Known as the Tale of Melusine*. Kegan Paul, Trench, Trübner and Company, 1866.

Tacitus. *The Agricola and the Germania*. Translated by H. Mattingly. Penguin Books, 1948.

Primary Oral Sources

Campbell, J. F. *Popular Tales of the West Highlands*. Vol. 3. Edmonston and Douglas, 1862.

Carmichael, Alexander. *Carmina Gadelica: Hymns and Incantations*. Lindisfarne Press, 1992.

Clarke, David. *Ghosts and Legends of the Peak District*. Jarrold Publishing, n.d.

Croker, T. Crofton. *Fairy Legends and Traditions of the South of Ireland*. William Tegg, 1862.

Crossley-Holland, Kevin. *Folk-Tales of the British Isles*. Pantheon Books, 1985.

Curtin, Jeremiah. *Hero-Tales of Ireland*. Benjamin Blom, 1894.

Danaher, Kevin. *Folktales from the Irish Countryside*. Mercier Press, 1967.

Gregory, Lady Augusta. *Cuchulain of Muirthemne: The Story of the Men of the Red Branch of Ulster*. In Gregory, Lady. *A Treasury of Irish Myth, Legend and Folklore*. Gramercy Books, 1986.

———. *Gods and Fighting Men: The Story of the Tuatha De Danaan and of the Fianna of Ireland*. John Murray, 1905.

———. *Visions and Beliefs in the West of Ireland*. Colin Smythe, 1970.

Hull, Eleanor. *Folklore of the British Isles*. Methuen & Company, 1928.

Hunt, Robert. *Cornish Customs and Superstitions*. Tor Mark Press, n.d.

———. *Cornish Folk-Lore*. Tor Mark Press, n.d.

Hyde, Douglas. *Beside the Fire: A Collection of Irish Gaelic Folk Stories*. David Nutt, 1890.

Kiernan, Thomas J. *The White Hound on the Mountain and Other Irish Folk Tales.* Devin-Adair, 1962.

Kraft, John. *The Goddess in the Labyrinth.* Religionsvetenskapliga Skrifter No. 11. Abo Akademi, 1985.

MacDougall, James. *Folk Tales and Fairy Lore in Gaelic and English.* John Grant, 1910.

MacGregor, Alasdair Alpin. *The Peat-Fire Flame: Folk-Tales and Traditions of the Highlands & Islands.* Moray Press, 1937.

MacKenzie, Donald A. *Scottish Folk-Lore and Folk Life: Studies in Race, Culture and Tradition.* Blackie & Sons, 1935.

MacNeill, Máire. *The Festival of Lughnasa, Parts I and II.* Comhairle Bhéaloideas Éireann, 1982.

McKay, John G. *More West Highland Tales.* Vol. 2. Scottish Anthropological and Folklore Society. Oliver and Boyd, 1969.

Meuss, Ruth E. K., trans. *Breton Folktales.* G. Bell & Sons, 1971.

Paton, C. I. *Manx Calendar Customs.* Publications of the Folklore Society. Reprinted, Kraus Reprint Limited, 1968.

Trevelyan, Marie. *Folklore and Folk-Stories of Wales.* Elliot Stock, 1909.

Wavle, Ardra Soule, and Jeremiah Edmund Burke. *The Stories of the Emerald Isle.* D. C. Heath and Company, 1923.

Westropp, T. J. *Folklore of Clare: A Folklore Survey of County Clare and County Clare Folk-Tale and Myths.* Clasp Press, 2000.

Wilde, Lady. *Ancient Legends, Mystic Charms and Superstitions of Ireland.* Chatto and Windus, 1902.

Yeats, W. B. *Fairy and Folk Tales of Ireland.* Simon and Schuster, 1973.

Other Sources

Almqvist, Bo, Séamus Ó Catháin, and Páidaig ó Héalaí. *The Heroic Process: Form, Function and Fantasy in Folk Epic.* The Glendale Press, 1987.

Anderson, Jorgen. *The Witch on the Wall: Medieval Erotic Sculpture in the British Islands.* George Allen & Unwin, 1977.

Beck, Jane C. "The White Lady of Great Britain and Ireland." *Folklore,* Vol. 81, No. 4.

Benigni, Helen, Barbara Carter, and Éadhmonn Ua Cuinn. *The Myth of the Year.* University Press of America, 2003.

Billington, Sandra, and Miranda Green, eds. *The Concept of the Goddess.* Routledge, 1996.

Bonnefoy, Ives, ed. *Mythologies.* University of Chicago Press, 1991.

Bord, Janet, and Colin Bord. *The Secret Country: An Interpretation of the Folklore of Ancient Sites in the British Isles.* Walker and Company, 1976.

Brenneman, Walter, and Mary Brenneman. *Crossing the Circle at the Holy Wells of Ireland.* University of Virginia Press, 1995.

Brenneman, Walter L. "Serpents, Cows, and Ladies: Contrasting Symbolism in Irish and Indo-European Cattle-Raiding Myths." *History of Religions,* Vol. 28, No. 4.

Briggs, K. M. *The Anatomy of Puck: An Examination of Fairy Beliefs among Shakespeare's Contemporaries and Successors.* Routledge and Kegan Paul, 1959.

———. *The Fairies in Tradition and Literature.* Routledge and Kegan Paul, 1967.

Brown, Theo. "Tertullian and Horse-Cults in Britain." *Folklore,* Vol. 61, No. 1.

Buchholtz, Peter. "Religious Sculpture in Roman Germania and Adjacent Regions." *Journal of Indo-European Studies,* Vol. 12.

Clark, Rosalind. *The Great Queens: Irish Goddesses from the Morrígan to Cathleen ní Houlihan.* Irish Literary Studies 34. Colin Smythe, 1991.

Colum, Padraic, ed. *A Treasury of Irish Folklore.* Wings Books, 1967.

Concannon, Maureen. *The Sacred Whore: Sheela, Goddess of the Celts.* Collins Press, 2004.

Condren, Mary. *The Serpent and the Goddess: Women, Religion and Power in Ancient Ireland.* Harper and Row, 1989.

Cooney, Gabriel. *Landscapes of Neolithic Ireland.* Routledge, 2000.

Dames, Michael. *The Avebury Cycle.* Thames and Hudson, 1976.

———. *Mythic Ireland.* Thames and Hudson, 1992.

Danaher, Kevin. *The Year in Ireland: Irish Calendar Customs.* Mercier Press, 1922.

Davidson, Hilda Ellis. "The Legend of Lady Godiva." In *Patterns of Folklore.* Rowman & Littlefield, 1978.

Davidson, Hilda Ellis, and Anna Chaudhri. "The Hair and the Dog." *Folklore,* Vol. 104, No. 1/2.

Delaney, Mary Murray. *Of Irish Ways.* Harper and Row, 1973.

Dexter, Miriam Robbins. "Assimilation of Pre-Indo-European Goddesses into Indo-European Society." *Journal of Indo-European Studies,* Vol. 8.

———. "Queen Medb, Female Autonomy in Ancient Ireland, and Irish Matrilineal Traditions." In Jones-Bley, Karlene, Angela Della Volpe, Miriam Robbins Dexter, and Martin E. Huld, eds. *Proceedings of the Ninth Annual UCLA Indo-European Conference.* Institute for the Study of Man, 1998.

———. "Reflections on the Goddess *Donu." *Mankind Quarterly,* Vol. 31, Nos. 1 and 2.

Dorcey, Peter F. *The Cult of Silvanus: A Study in Roman Folk Religion.* E. J. Brill, 1992.

Ellis, P. Berresford. *Celtic Women: Women in Celtic Society and Literature.* William B. Eerdmans Publishing, 1995.

———. *The Druids.* Constable, 1988.

Evans-Wentz, W. Y. *The Fairy-Faith in Celtic Countries*. Colin Smythe Humanities Press, 1911.

Geddes, Arthur. "Some Gaelic Tales of Herding Deer or Reindeer." *Folklore*, Vol. 62, No. 2.

Gilroy, John. *Tlachtga: Celtic Fire Festival*. Pikefield Publications, 2000.

Graves, Robert. *The White Goddess: A Historical Grammar of Poetic Myth*. Farrar, Straus and Giroux, 1948.

Green, Miranda. *Celtic Goddesses: Warriors, Virgins and Mothers*. British Museum Press, 1995.

———. *Celtic Myths*. University of Texas Press, 1993.

———. *The Gods of Roman Britain*. Shire Publications, 1983.

———. *The Gods of the Celts*. Alan Sutton, 1986.

———. *Symbol and Image in Celtic Religious Art*. Routledge, 1989.

Hemming, Jessica. "Reflections on Rhiannon and the Horse Episodes in 'Pwyll.'" *Western Folklore*, Vol. 57, No. 1.

Henig, Martin, and Anthony King, eds. *Pagan Gods and Shrines of the Roman Empire*. Oxford University Committee for Archaeology, 1986.

Herm, Gerhard. *The Celts: The People Who Came out of the Darkness*. St. Martin's Press, 1975.

Hondius-Crone, A. *The Temple of Nehalennia at Domberg*. J. M. Menlenhoff, 1995.

Hull, Eleanor. *A Text Book of Irish Literature*. David Nutt, 1906.

Kelly, Eamonn. *Sheela-na-Gigs: Origins and Functions*. Country House, 1996.

Kennedy, Patrick. *Legendary Fictions of the Irish Celts*. Benjamin Blom, 1969.

Lenihan, Edmund. *Defiant Irish Women*. Mercier Press, 1991.

———. *In Search of Biddy Early*. Mercier Press, 1987.

Löffler, Christa Maria. *The Voyage to the Otherworld Island in Early Irish Literature*. Institut für Anglistik und Amerikanistik, 1983.

Logan, Patrick. *The Holy Wells of Ireland*. Colin Smyth, 1980.

———. *The Old Gods: The Facts about Irish Fairies*. Appletree Press, 1981.

Long, George. *The Folklore Calendar*. Senate, 1930.

Loomis, Roger S. "Morgain La Fee and the Celtic Goddesses." *Speculum*, Vol. 20, No. 2.

———. *Wales and the Arthurian Legend*. University of Wales Press, 1956.

MacAnna, Proinsias. *Celtic Mythology*. Newnes Books, 1987.

MacCulloch, J. A. *Celtic Mythology*. Academy Publishers, 1996.

———. *The Religion of the Ancient Celts*. Constable, 1911.

MacKinlay, James M. *Folklore of Scottish Lochs and Springs*. William Hodge and Company, 1893.

Mahon, Bríd. *Land of Milk and Honey: The Story of Traditional Irish Food and Drink*. Mercier Press, 1991.

Markale, Jean. *Courtly Love: The Path of Sexual Initiation*. Inner Traditions, 2000.

———. *The Epics of Celtic Ireland*. Inner Traditions, 2000.

———. *The Pagan Mysteries of Halloween: Celebrating the Dark Half of the Year*. Traditions, 2000.

———. *Women of the Celts*. Inner Traditions, 1986.

Marples, Morris. *White Horses and Other Hill Figures*. Alan Sutton, 1981.

Matthews, John. *The Song of Taliesin: Tales from King Arthur's Bard*. Quest Books, 2001.

McCrickard, Janet. *Eclipse of the Sun*. Gothic Image, 1994.

McKay, J. G. "The Deer-Cult and Deer-Goddess Cult of the Ancient Caledonians." *Folklore*, Vol. 43, No. 2.

McMahon, Joanne, and Jack Roberts. *The Sheela-na-Gigs of Ireland and Britain: The Divine Hag of the Christian Celts*. Mercier Press, 2001.

McNeill, F. Marian. *The Silver Bough*. Vol. 1. Canongate Classics, 1989.

Monaghan, Patricia. *O Mother Sun: A New View of the Cosmic Feminine*. The Crossing Press, 1994.

Ó hÓgáin, Dáithí. *The Hero in Irish Folk History*. Gill and Macmillan, 1985.

———. *Myth, Legend and Romance: An Encyclopedia of the Irish Folk Tradition*. Prentice Hall, 1991.

———. *The Sacred Isle: Belief and Religion in Pre-Christian Ireland*. The Collins Press, 1999.

O'Kelly, M. J., and C. O'Kelly. *Illustrated Guide to Lough Gur*. O'Kelly, 1997.

O'Rahilly, Thomas. *Early Irish History and Mythology*. The Dublin Institute for Advanced Studies, 1946.

Pennick, Nigel. *Celtic Sacred Landscapes*. Thames and Hudson, 2000.

Raftery, Brian. *Pagan Celtic Ireland: The Enigma of the Irish Iron Age*. Thames and Hudson, 1994.

Rees, Alwyn, and Brinley Rees. *Celtic Heritage: Ancient Tradition in Ireland and Wales*. Thames and Hudson, 1998.

Rhŷs, John. *Celtic Folklore: Welsh and Manx*. Clarendon Press, 1941.

———. *The Welsh People*. T. Fisher Unwin, 1906.

Rolleston, T. W. *Myths and Legends of the Celtic Race*. David D. Nickerson and Company, 1923. Republished as *Celtic Myths and Legends*. Dover Publications, 1990.

Ross, Anne. "The Divine Hag of the Pagan Celts." In Newall, Venetia, ed. *The Witch Figures*. Routledge and Kegan Paul, 1973.

———. *Pagan Celtic Britain: Studies in Iconography and Tradition*. Routledge and Kegan Paul, 1967.

Ross, Anne, and Michael Cyprien. *A Traveler's Guide to Celtic Britain*. Historical Times, 1985.

Sax, Boria. *The Serpent and the Swan: The Animal Bride in Folklore and Literature*. McDonald and Woodward, 1998.

Sharkey, John. *Celtic Mysteries: The Ancient Religion*. Crossroad, 1975.

Sheehan, Jeremiah, ed. *Beneath the Shadow of Uisneach: Ballymore and Boher, County Westmeath*. Ballymore-Boher History Project, 1996.

Sjoestedt, Marie-Louise. *Celtic Gods and Heroes*. Translated by Myles Dillon. Four Courts Press, 1994.

Slavin, Michael. *The Book of Tara*. Wolfhound Press, 1996.

Spence, Lewis. *The Minor Traditions of British Mythology*. Benjamin Blom, 1972.

Squire, Charles. *Mythology of the Celtic People*. Bracken Books, 1996.

Stephens, G. Arbour. "Was Dozmare Pool a Celtic Lake of the Underworld?" *Folklore*, Vol. 46, No. 2.

Straffon, Cheryl. *The Earth Goddess: Celtic and Pagan Legacy of the Landscape*. Blandford, 1997.

Wallace, Cathryn. *Folk-Lore of Ireland: Legends, Myths and Fairy Tales*. J. S. Hyland and Company, 1910.

Webster, G. *The British Celts and Their Gods under Rome*. Batsford, 1986.

Westropp, T. J. *Archaeology of the Burren: Prehistoric Forts and Dolmens in North Clare*. Clasp Press, 1999.

Williams, Mary. "Folklore and Placenames." *Folklore*, Vol. 74, No. 2.

Zucchelli, Christine. *Stones of Adoration: Sacred Stones and Mystic Megaliths of Ireland*. The Collins Press, 2007.

FINNO-UGRIC CULTURES

Primary Textual Sources in Translation

Abercromby, John. *The Pre- and Proto-historic Finns, Both Eastern and Western, with the Magic Songs of the West Finns*, Vol. II. David Nutt, 1898.

Comparetti, Domenico. *The Traditional Poetry of the Finns*. Longmans, Green, 1898.

Honko, Lauir, Senni Timonsen, and Michael Branch, eds. *The Great Bear: A Thematic Anthology of Oral Poetry in the Finno-Ugrian Languages*. Oxford University Press, Finnish Literature Society, 1994.

Kruetzwald, R. *Kalevipoeg: An Ancient Estonian Tale*. Symposia Press, 1982.

Lönnrot, Elias. *The Kalevala: Epic of the Finnish People*. Translated by Eino Friberg. Otava Publishing, 1988.

————. *The Old Kalevala and Certain Antecedents*. Prose translations with foreword and appendices by Francis Peabody Magoun, Jr. Harvard University Press, 1969.

Sadovszky, Otto J. von, and Mihály Hoppál. *Vogul Folklore*. Académiai Kiadó, 1995.

Other Sources

Abercromby, John. *The Pre- and Proto-historic Finns, Both Eastern and Western, with the Magic Songs of the West Finns*, Vol. I. David Nutt, 1898.

Alhbäck, Tore, ed. *Saami Religion*. Donner Institute for Research in Religious and Cultural History, 1987.

Bäckman, Louise. "The Akkas: A Study of Four Goddesses in the Religion of the Saamis (Lapps). In *Current Progress in the Methodology of the Science of Religions*. Tyloch Witold, ed. Polish Scientific Publishers, 1984.

Bäckman, Louise, and Ake Hultkrantz. *Studies in Lapp Shamanism*. Stockholm Studies in Comparative Religion 16. Almqvist & Wiksell, 1978.

Billson, William. "Some Mythical Tales of the Lapps." *Folklore*, Vol. 29, No. 3.

Bonser, Wilfrid. "The Mythology of the Kalevala, with Notes on Bear-Worship among the Finns.'" *Folklore*, Vol. 39, No. 4.

Buday, Korélia. *The Earth Has Given Birth to the Sky: Female Spirituality in the Hungarian Folk Religion*. Académiai Kiadó, 2004.

Dioszegi, Vilmos, ed. *Popular Beliefs and Folklore Traditions in Siberia*. Indiana University Press, 1968.

Dömötör, Tekla. *Hungarian Folk Beliefs*. Indiana University Press, 1982.

Holmberg, Uno. *Finno-Ugric Mythology*. In *Mythology of All Races*. Cooper Square, 1964.

Hoppál, Mihály. *Studies on Mythology and Uralic Shamanism*. Académiai Kiadó, 2000.

————. "Traces of Shamanism in Hungarian Folk Beliefs." In *Shamanism in Eurasia*, part 2. Edition Herodot, 1984.

Hoppál, Mihály, and Juha Pentikäinen, ed. *Northern Religions and Shamanism*. Académiai Kiadó, 1992.

Hubbs, Joanna. *Mother Russia: The Feminine Myth in Russian Culture*. Indiana University Press, 1993.

Itkonen, T. I. "The Lapps of Finland." *Southwestern Journal of Anthropology*, Vol. 7, No. 1.

Jones, W. Henry, and Lewis L. Kropf. *The Folk-Tales of the Magyars*. Folk-Lore Society, Elliot Stock, 1889.

Karsten, Rafael. *The Religion of the Sameks*. E. J. Brill, 1955.

Lundmark, Bo. "They Consider Sun to Be a Mother to All Living Creatures: The Sun Cult of the Saamis."

In Bäckman, Louise, and Ake Hultkrantz, eds. *Saami Pre-Christian Religion*, 1985.

March, H. Colley. "The Mythology of Wise Birds." *Journal of the Anthropological Institute of Great Britain and Ireland*, Vol. 27.

Michael, Henry N., ed. *Studies in Siberian Shamanism*. University of Toronto Press, 1963.

Paulson, Ivar. *The Old Estonian Folk Religion*. Translated by J. K. Kitching and H. Kõvamees. Indiana University Press, 1971.

————. "Outline of Permian Folk Religion." *Journal of the Folklore Institute*, Vol. 2, No. 2.

Pocs, Eva. *Fairies and Witches at the Boundary of South-Eastern and Central Europe*. Academia Scientiarum Finnica, 1989.

Ränk, Gustav. "The Symbolic Bow in the Birth Rites of North Eurasian Peoples." *History of Religions*, Vol. 1, No. 2.

Riordan, James. *The Sun Maiden and the Crescent Moon: Siberian Folk Tales*. Interlink Books, 1989.

Róheim, Géza. *Hungarian and Vogul Mythology*. University of Washington Press, 1954.

Sebeok, Thomas A., and Frances J. Ingemann. *Studies in Cheremis: The Supernatural*. Viking Fund Publications in Anthropology, No. 22, 1956.

GREECE

Dramatic Literature

Aeschylus: *Oresteia, Prometheus Bound, The Suppliants*
Aristophanes: *Thesmophoriazusae*
Euripides: *Alcestis, Andromache, Bacchae, Electra, Hecuba, Helen, The Heracleidae, Hippolytus, Ion, Iphigenia at Aulis, Iphigenia in Tauris, Medea, Orestes, The Phoenician Women, The Trojan Women*
Sophocles: *Antigone, Electra, Oedipus at Colonus, Oedipus the King, The Trachiniae*

Primary Sources in Translation

Apollodorus. *The Library*. Translated by Sir James George Frazer. Vol. 1. Harvard University Press, 1959.

Apollonius of Rhodes. *The Voyage of Argo: The Argonautica*. Translated by E. V. Rieu. Penguin Books, 1967.

Athanassakis, Apostolos N., trans. *The Orphic Hymns: Text, Translation, and Notes*. Society of Biblical Literature: Texts and Translations, Graeco-Roman Religion Series. Scholars Press, 1988.

Boer, Charles, trans. *The Homeric Hymns*. Swallow Press, 1970.

Callimachus. *Hymn to Demeter*. Edited by N. Hopkinson. Cambridge University Press, 1984.

Dexter, Miriam Robbins. *Whence the Goddesses: A Sourcebook*. Pergamon Press, 1990.

Herodotus. *The Histories of Herodotus of Helicarnassus*. Translated by Henry Carter. Heritage Press, 1959.

Hesiod. *Theogany, Works and Days*. Translated by Dorothea Wender. Penguin Books, 1973.

Homer. *The Iliad*. Translated by Richard Lattimore. University of Chicago Press, 1951.

————. *The Odyssey*. Translated by Robert Fagles. Penguin Books, 1996.

Knox, Bernard, ed. *The Norton Book of Classical Literature*. W. W. Norton, 1993.

Lefkowitz, Mary R., and Maureen B. Fant. *Women's Life in Greece and Rome*. Duckworth, 1982.

Lind, L. R., ed. *Ten Greek Plays in Contemporary Translations*. Houghton Mifflin, 1957.

Meyer, Marvin W., ed. *The Ancient Mysteries: A Sourcebook, Sacred Texts of the Mystery Religions of the Ancient Mediterranean World*. University of Pennsylvania Press, 1999.

Ovid. *Fasti: Roman Holidays*. Translated by Betty Rose Nagle. Indiana University Press, 1995.

————. *The Metamorphoses. A Complete New Version*. Translated by Horace Gregory. New American Library, Viking Press, 1958.

Pausanias. *Description of Greece*. Translated by W. H. S. Jones. 5 vols. Harvard University Press, 1965.

Plutarch. *Plutarch on Sparta*. Translated by Richard J. A. Talbert. Penguin Books, 1988.

————. *The Rise and Fall of Athens: Nine Greek Lives by Plutarch*. Translated by Ian Scott-Kivert. Penguin Books, 1960.

Richardson, N. J., trans. *The Homeric Hymn to Demeter*. Clarendon Press, 1974.

Sargent, Thelma, trans. *The Homeric Hymns*. Norton, 1975.

Warmington, E. H., ed. and trans. *Remains of Old Latin: Ennius and Caecilius*. Harvard University Press, 1935.

Other Sources

Argenti, Philip. *The Folk-Lore of Chios*. Cambridge University Press, 1949.

Arthur, Marilyn. "The Origins of the Western Attitude towards Women." In Perandotto, John, and J. P. Sullivan, eds. *Women in the Ancient World: The Arethusa Papers*. State University of New York Press, 1984.

Avagianou, Aphrodite. *Sacred Marriage in the Rituals of Greek Religion*. Peter Lang, 1991.

Barber, Elizabeth Wayland. *Women's Work: The First 20,000*

Years. Women, Cloth and Society in Early Times. W. W. Norton, 1994.

Bennet, Florence Mary. *Religious Cults Associated with the Amazons.* AMS Press, 1967.

Bernal, Martin. *Black Athena: The Afroasiatic Roots of Classical Civilization.* Rutgers University Press, 1987.

Blundell, Sue, and Margaret Williamson. *The Sacred and the Feminine in Ancient Greece.* Routledge, 1998.

Boedeker, Deborah Dickmann. *Aphrodite's Entry into Greek Epic.* E. J. Brill, 1974.

Bonnefoy, Ives, ed. *Mythologies.* University of Chicago Press, 1991.

Borgeaud, Philippe. *The Cult of Pan in Ancient Greece.* University of Chicago Press, 1988.

———. *Mother of the Gods: From Cybele to the Virgin Mary.* Translated by Lysa Hochroth. Johns Hopkins University Press, 2004.

Burkert, Walter. *Structure and History in Greek Mythology and Ritual.* University of California Press, 1979.

Butterworth, E. A. S. *The Tree at the Navel of the Earth.* Walter De Gruter, 1970.

Cameron, Averil, and Amelie Kuhrt, eds. *Images of Women in Antiquity.* Routledge, 1993.

Cantarella, Eva. *Pandora's Daughters: The Role and Status of Women in Greek and Roman Antiquity.* Johns Hopkins University Press, 1987.

Clauss, James J., and Sarah Iles Johnston, eds. *Medea: Essays on Medea in Myth, Literature, Philosophy and Art.* Princeton University Press, 1997.

Cohen, Beth, ed. *The Distaff Side: Representing the Female in Homer's Odyssey.* Oxford University Press, 1995.

Connelly, Joan Breton. *Portrait of a Priestess: Women and Ritual in Ancient Greece.* Princeton University Press, 2007.

Cook, Arthur Bernard. "The Bee in Greek Mythology." *Journal of Hellenic Studies,* Vol. 15.

Davis-Kimball, Jeannine, with Mona Behan. *Warrior Women: An Archaeologist's Search for History's Hidden Heroines.* Warner Books, 2002.

Dodds, E. R. "Maenadism in the Bacchae." *Harvard Theological Review,* Vol. 3, No. 3.

Dowden, Ken. *Death and the Maiden: Girls' Initiation Rites in Greek Mythology.* Routledge, 1989.

Downing, Marymay. "Prehistoric Goddesses: The Cretan Challenge." *Journal of Feminist Studies in Religion,* Vol. 1, No. 1.

Edlund, I. E. M. *The Gods and the Place: Location and Function of Sanctuaries in the Countryside of Etruria and Magna Graecia.* Skrifter Utgivna av Svenska Institutet I Rom, Acta Instituti Romani Regni Sueciae, 4:43, 1987.

Elderkin, G. W. "The Bee of Artemis." *American Journal of Philology,* Vol. 60, No. 2.

Evans, Arthur. *The God of Ecstasy: Sex-Roles and the Madness of Dionysos.* St. Martin's Press, 1988.

Farnell, Lewis Richard. *The Cults of the Greek States.* Clarendon Press, 1909.

———. "Ino-Luekothea." *Journal of Hellenic Studies,* Vol. 36.

Flemberg, Johan. "Aphrodite and Old Age." In *Opus Mixtum: Essays in Ancient Art and Society.* Skrifter Utgivna av Svenska Institutet I Rom, Acta Institui Romani Regni Sueciae, 8:21, 1994.

Fontenrose, A. *Orion: The Myth of the Hunter and the Huntress.* Publications in Classical Studies 23, University of California, 1981.

Fontenrose, Joseph. *Python: A Study of Delphic Myth and Its Origins.* University of California Press, 1959.

Friedrich, Paul. *The Meaning of Aphrodite.* University of Chicago Press, 1978.

Frothingham, A. "Medusa, Apollo and the Great Mother." *American Journal of Archaeology: The Journal of the Archaeological Institute of America,* Vol. 15, No. 3.

Garber, Marjorie, and Nancy J. Vickers, ed. *The Medusa Reader.* Routledge, 2003.

Gimbutas, Marija. *The Goddess and Gods of Old Europe.* University of California Press, 1982.

———. *The Language of the Goddess.* Harper and Row, 1989.

Goodison, Lucy. *Women, Death and the Sun: Symbolism of Regeneration in Early Aegean Religion.* University of London Institute of Classical Studies. Bulletin Supplement 53, 1989.

Graves, Robert. *The Greek Myths.* 2 vols. Penguin Books, 1990.

Grigson, Geoffrey. *The Goddess of Love: The Birth, Triumph, Death and Return of Aphrodite.* Stein and Day, 1977.

Hadzsits, George Depue. "Aphrodite and the Dione Myth." *American Journal of Philology,* Vol. 30, No. 1.

Hall, Lee. *Athena: A Biography.* Addison-Wesley, 1997.

Harrison, Jane Ellen. *Prolegomena to the Study of Greek Religion.* 1903 reprint. Meridian Books, 1955.

———. *Themis: A Study of the Social Origins of Greek Religion.* University Books, 1962.

Hawley, Richard, and Barbara Levick, eds. *Women in Antiquity: New Assessments.* Routledge, 1995.

Hedreen, Guy. "Silens, Nymphs and Maenads." *Journal of Hellenic Studies,* Vol. 114.

Heitman, Richard. *Taking Her Seriously: Penelope and the Plot of Homer's Odyssey.* University of Michigan Press, 2005.

Henrichs, Albert. "Greek Maenadism from Olympias to Messalina." *Harvard Studies in Classical Philology,* Vol. 82.

Holland, Leicester B. "The Danaoi." *Harvard Studies in Classical Philology,* Vol. 39.

Howe, Thalia. "The Origin and Function of the Gorgon-Head." *American Journal of Archaeology*, Vol. 58, No. 5.

Johnson, W. R. "The Rapes of Callisto." *Classical Journal*, Vol. 92, No. 1.

Katz, Marylin. *Penelope's Renown: Meaning and Indeterminacy in the Odyssey*. Princeton University Press, 1991.

Keller, Mara Lynn. "The Eleusinian Mysteries of Demeter and Persephone: Fertility, Sexuality and Rebirth." *Journal of Feminist Studies in Religion*, Vol. 3, No. 1.

Kerényi, Karl. *Athene: Virgin and Mother in Greek Religion*. Translated by Murray Stein. Spring Publications, 1978.

———. *Goddesses of Sun and Moon*. Spring Publications, 1979.

———. *Zeus and Hera*. Bollingen Series. Princeton University Press, 1975.

Keuls, Eva C. *The Reign of the Phallus: Sexual Politics in Ancient Athens*. University of California Press, 1985.

Kraemer, Ross S. "Ecstasy and Possession: The Attraction of Women to the Cult of Dionysus." *Harvard Theological Review*, Vol. 72, No. 1/2.

Larson, Jennifer. *Greek Heroine Cults*. University of Wisconsin Press, 1995.

———. *Greek Nymphs: Myth, Cult, Lore*. Oxford University Press, 2001.

———. "Handmaidens of Artemis?" *Classical Journal*, Vol. 92, No. 3.

Lawson, John Cuthbert. *Modern Greek Folklore and Ancient Greek Religion: A Study in Survivals*. Cambridge University Press, 1910.

Lefkowitz, Mary R. *Women in Greek Myth*. Johns Hopkins University Press, 1986.

Lonsdale, Steven. *Dance and Ritual Play in Greek Religion*. Johns Hopkins University Press, 1993.

Loraux, Nicole. *The Children of Athena: Athenian Ideas about Citizenship and the Division between the Sexes*. Princeton University Press, 1993.

Lubell, Winifred Milius. *The Metamorphosis of Baubo: Myths of Woman's Sexual Energy*. Vanderbilt University Press, 1994.

Lyons, Deborah. *Gender and Immortality: Heroines in Ancient Greek Myth and Cult*. Princeton University Press, 1997.

Macurdy, Grace Harriet. "The Origin of a Herodotean Tale in Connection with the Cult of the Spinning Goddess." *Transactions and Proceedings of the American Philological Association*, Vol. 43.

Manning, Clarence Augustus. "The Tauric Maiden and Allied Cults." *Transactions and Proceedings of the American Philological Association*, Vol. 51.

Marinatos, Nannó. *The Goddess and the Warrior: The Naked Goddess and Mistress of Animals in Early Greek Religion*. Routledge, 2000.

Mark, Ira S., Machteld J. Mellink, and James R. McCredie.

"The Sanctuary of Athena Nike in Athens." *Hesperia Supplement*, Vol. 26.

Marshall, F. H. "Elpis-Nemisis." *Journal of Hellenistic Studies*, Vol. 33.

Meagher, Robert Emmet. *Helen: Myth, Legend and the Culture of Misogyny*. Continuum, 1995.

Motz, Lotte. *The Faces of the Goddess*. Oxford University Press, 1997.

Munn, Mark. *The Mother of the Gods, Athens, and the Tyranny of Asia: A Study of Sovereignty in Ancient Religion*. University of California Press, 2006.

Mylonas, George E. *Eleusis and the Eleusinian Mysteries*. Princeton University Press, 1969.

Nilsson, Martin P. *Greek Folk Religion*. Harper Torchbooks, 1961.

———. *The Mycenaean Origin of Greek Mythology*. University of California Press, 1932.

O'Brien, Joan V. "Namu, Mami, Eve and Pandora: What's in a Name?" *Classical Journal*, Vol. 79, No. 1.

———. *The Transformation of Hera: A Study of Ritual, Eros and the Goddess in the Iliad*. Rowman & Littlefield, 1993.

O'Flaherty, Wendy Doniger. *Women, Androgynes, and Other Mythical Beasts*. University of Chicago Press, 1980.

Olender, Maurice. "Aspects of Baubo: Ancient Texts and Contexts." In Halperin, David M., John J. Winkler, and Froma I. Zeitlin, eds. *Before Sexuality: The Construction of Erotic Experience in the Ancient Greek World*. Princeton University Press, 1990.

Pantel, Pauline Schmitt, ed. *A History of Women in the West, Volume 1: From Ancient Goddesses to Christian Saints*. Cambridge, MA: The Belknap Press of Harvard University, 1992.

Perandotto, John, and J. P. Sullivan, eds. *Women in the Ancient World: The Arethusa Papers*. State University of New York Press, 1984.

Persson, Axel W. *The Religion of Greece in Prehistoric Times*. University of California Press, 1971.

Pomeroy, Sarah, ed. *Women's History and Ancient History*. University of North Carolina Press, 1991.

Rabinowitz, Jacob. *The Rotting Goddess: The Origin of the Witch in Classical Antiquity*. Autonomedia, 1998.

Reeder, Ellen, ed. *Pandora: Women in Classical Greece*. Princeton University Press, 1995.

Regier, Willis Goth. *Book of the Sphinx*. University of Nebraska Press, 2004.

Roller, Lynn. *In Search of God the Mother: The Cult of Anatolian Cybele*. University of California Press, 1999.

Säflund, Gösta. *Aphrodite Kallipygos*. Acta Universitatis Stockholmiensis: Stockholm Studies in Classical Archaeology. Almqvist & Wiksell, 1963.

Sanford, John A. *Fate, Love and Ecstasy: Wisdom from the Lesser-Known Goddesses of the Greeks.* Chiron Publications, 1995.

Schein, Seth L., ed. *Reading the Odyssey: Selected Interpretive Essays.* Princeton University Press, 1996.

Schieffer, Charlotte. "Female Deities, Horses and Death(?) in Archaic Greek Religion." In *Opus Mixtum: Essays in Ancient Art and Society.* Skrifter Utgivna av Svenska Institutet I Rom, Acta Institui Romani Regni Sueciae, 8:21, 1994.

Siebers, Tobin. *The Mirror of Medusa.* University of California Press, 1983.

Smith, William, ed. *Dictionary of Greek and Roman Biography and Mythology.* 1870.

Sobol, Donald. *The Amazons of Greek Myth.* A. S. Barnes, 1972.

Sourvinou-Inwood, Christiane. *Hylas, the Nymphs, Dionysos and Others: Myth, Ritual, Ethnicity.* Skrifter Utgivna av Svenska Institutet I Athen, Acta Instituiti Atheniensis Regni Suecia, 2005.

———. "Persephone and Aphrodite at Locri: A Model for Personality Definitions in Greek Religion." *Journal of Hellenic Studies,* Vol. 98.

———. *Studies in Girls' Transitions: Aspects of the Arteia and Age Representation in Attic Iconography.* Kardamitsa, 1988.

Suhr, Elmer George. "Herakles and Omphale." *American Journal of Archaeology,* Vol. 57, No. 4.

———. *The Spinning Aphrodite: The Evolution of the Goddess from Earliest Pre-Hellenic Symbolism through Late Classical Times.* Helios Books, 1969.

Suter, Ann. *The Narcissus and the Pomegranate: An Archaeology of the Homeric Hymn to Demeter.* University of Michigan Press, 2002.

Thompson, Homer. "The Altar of Pity in the Athenian Agora." *Hesperia,* Vol. 21, No. 1.

Tyrrell, William Blake. *Amazons: A Study in Athenian Mythmaking.* Johns Hopkins University Press, 1984.

Varmaseren, Maarten S. *Cybele and Attis.* Thames & Hudson, 1977.

Vassileva, Maya. "Further Considerations on the Cult of Kybele." *Anatolian Studies,* Vol. 51.

Versnel, H. S. "The Festival for Bona Dea and the Thesmophoria." *Greece & Rome,* 2nd Series, Vol. 39, No. 1.

Walbank, Michael B. "Artemis Bear-Leader." *Classical Quarterly,* New Series, Vol. 31, No. 2.

Whallon, William. "Maenadism in the Oresteia." *Harvard Studies in Classical Philology,* Vol. 68.

White, Donald. "The Post-Classical Cult of Malophoros at Selinus." *American Journal of Archaeology,* Vol. 71, No. 4.

Willetts, R. F. *Cretan Cults and Festivals.* Routledge and Kegan Paul, 1962.

Winkler, John J. *The Constraints of Desire: The Anthropology of Sex and Gender in Ancient Greece.* Routledge, 1990.

Winkler, John J., and Froma I. Zeitlin, eds. *Nothing to Do with Dionysos? Athenian Drama in Its Social Context.* Princeton University Press, 1990.

Zuntz, Günther. *Persephone: Three Essays on Religion and Thought in Magna Graecia.* Clarendon Press, 1971.

ROME

Primary Sources in Translation

Apuleius, Lucius. *The Transformations of Lucius, or the Golden Ass.*

Courtney, E. *The Fragmentary Latin Poets.* Clarendon Press, 1993.

Dexter, Miriam Robbins. *Whence the Goddesses: A Sourcebook.* Pergamon, 1990.

Horace. *The Odes and Epodes of Horace.* Translated by Joseph P. Clancy. University of Chicago Press, 1962.

Lucian. *De Dea Syria: On the Syrian Goddess.* Translated by J. L. Lightfoot. Oxford University Press, 2003.

Meyer, Marvin W., ed. *The Ancient Mysteries: A Sourcebook, Sacred Texts of the Mystery Religions of the Ancient Mediterranean World.* University of Pennsylvania Press, 1999.

Ovid. *Fasti: Roman Holidays.* Translated by Betty Rose Nagle. Indiana University Press, 1995.

———. *The Metamorphoses.* Translated by Horace Gregory. Viking Press, 1958.

Virgil (P. Virgilius Maro). *The Aeneid.* Translated by Rolfe Humphries and edited by Brian Wilke. Macmillan Publishing, 1987.

Warmington, E. H., ed. and trans. *Remains of Old Latin: Ennius and Caecilius.* Harvard University Press, 1935.

Young, Serinity. *An Anthology of Sacred Texts by and about Women.* Crossroad, 1994.

Other Sources

Allen, Archibald. "A Goddess in Catullus (25.5)." *Classical Philology,* Vol. 69, No. 3.

Altheim, Franz. *A History of Roman Religion.* Methuen and Company, 1938.

Axtell, Harold L. *The Deification of Abstract Ideas in Roman Literature and Inscriptions.* University of Chicago Press, 1907.

Balsdon, J. P. *Roman Women: Their History and Habits.* John Day, 1963.

Beard, Mary. "Acca Larentia Gains a Son: Myths and

Priesthoods at Rome." In Mackenzie, M. M., and C. Roueché, eds. *Images of Authority: Papers Presented to Joyce Reynolds on the Occasion of Her 70th Birthday.* Cambridge University Press, 1989.

———. "Re-reading (Vestal) Virginity." In Hawley, Richard, and Barbara Levick, eds. *Women in Antiquity: New Assessments.* Routledge, 1995.

———. "The Sexual Status of Vestal Virgins." *Journal of Roman Studies,* Vol. 70.

Benko, S. *The Virgin Goddess: Studies in the Pagan and Christian Roots of Mariology.* Brill, 2004.

Berger, Pamela. *The Goddess Obscured: Transformation of the Grain Protectress from Goddess to Saint.* Beacon Press, 1985.

Berry, Ingrid Edlund. "Whether Goddess, Priestess or Worshiper: Considerations of Female Deities and Cults in Roman Religion." In *Opus Mixtum: Essays in Ancient Art and Society.* Skrifter Utgivna av Svenska Institutet I Rom, Acta Institui Romani Regni Sueciae, 8:21, 1994.

Billington, Sandra. "Fors Fortuna in Ancient Rome." In Billington, Sandra, and Miranda Green, eds. *The Concept of the Goddess.* Routledge, 1996.

Blagg, T. F. C. "The Cult and Sanctuary of Diana Nemorensis." In Henig, Martin, and Anthony King, eds. *Pagan Gods and Shrines of the Roman Empire.* Oxford University Committee for Archaeology.

Bremmer, J. N., and N. M. Horsfall. *Roman Myth and Mythography.* Institute of Classical Studies, Bulletin Supplements 52, 1987.

Briquel, Dominique. "Etruscan Religion." In Jones, Lindsay, ed. *The Encyclopedia of Religion,* 2nd ed., Vol. 5. Thomson Gale, 2005.

Brouwer, H. H. J. *Bona Dea: The Sources and a Description of the Cult.* E. J. Brill, 1991.

Donalson, Malcolm Drew. *The Cult of Isis in the Roman Empire: Isis Invicta.* Edwin Mellen Press, 2003.

Dorsey, Peter. *The Cult of Silvanus: A Study in Roman Folk Religion.* E. J. Brill, 1992.

Dumézil, Georges. *Archaic Roman Religion.* University of Chicago Press, 1966.

Edlund, I. E. M. "Etruscan and Roman Religion." In Young, Serinity, ed. *Encyclopedia of Women and Religion.* Macmillan and Company, 1999.

———. *The Gods and the Place: Location and Function of Sanctuaries in the Countryside of Etruria and Magna Graecia.* Skrifter Utgivna av Svenska Institutet I Rom, Acta Institui Romani Regni Sueciae, 4:43, 1987.

Fantham, E. "Ceres, Liber and Flora: Georgic and Anti-Georgic Elements in Ovid's *Fasti.*" *Proceedings of the Cambridge Philological Society,* Vol. 28.

Feeney, Denis. *Literature and Religion at Rome: Cultures, Context, and Beliefs.* Cambridge University Press, 1998.

Fourbister, Linda. *Goddess in the Grass: Serpentine Mythology and the Great Goddess.* EcceNova Editions, 2003.

Fox, William Sherwood. *Myths of All Races.* Vol. 1: *Greek and Roman.* Cooper Square, 1964.

Galinsky, Karl. "Venus, Polysemy and the Ara Pacis Augustae." *American Journal of Archaeology,* Vol. 93, No. 3.

Godwen, Joscelyn. *Mystery Religions in the Ancient World.* Thames and Hudson, 1981.

Goux, Jean-Joseph. "Vesta, or the Place of Being." *Representations,* No. 1.

Grant, Mary A. "The Location of a Shrine of Vacuna." *Classical Journal,* Vol. 4.

Hall, John Franklin. "Mars and Anna Perenna: March Gods and the Etruscan New Year in Archaic Rome." In Lundquist, John M., and Stephen D. Ricks, eds. *By Study and By Faith: Essays in Honor of Hugh W. Nibley on the Occasion of His 80th Birthday,* Vol. 1. Deseret Book Company, 1990.

Harrison, Jane Ellen. *Themis: A Study of the Social Origins of Greek Religion.* University Books, 1962.

Hutton, Ronald. *The Triumph of the Moon.* Oxford University Press, 1999.

Jayne, J. *The Healing Gods of Ancient Civilizations.* University Books, 1971.

Johnson, W. R. "Vertumnus in Love." *Classical Philology,* Vol. 92.

Krapp, Alexander H. "Acca Larentia." *American Journal of Archaeology,* Vol. 46, No. 4.

———. "The Bearded Venus." *Folklore,* Vol. 56, No. 4.

Lazarus, Francis M. "On the Meaning of Fors Fortuna: A Hint from Terence." *American Journal of Philology,* Vol. 106, No. 3.

Leland, Charles. *Etruscan Magic and Occult Remedies.* University Books, 1963.

———. *The Gospel of the Witches.* Phoenix Publishing, 1990.

Lloyd-Morgan, Glenys. "Nemesis and Bellona: A Preliminary Study of Two Neglected Goddesses." In Billington, Sandra, and Miranda Green, eds. *The Concept of the Goddess.* Routledge, 1996.

Meadows, Andrew, and Jonathan Williams. "Moneta and the Monuments: Coinage and Politics in Republican Rome." *Journal of Roman Studies,* Vol. 91.

Mellor, Ronald. *Dea Roma: The Worship of the Goddess Roma in the Greek World.* Vandenhoeck & Ruprecht, 1975.

Miles, Clement A. *Christmas in Ritual and Tradition, Christian and Pagan.* T. Fisher Unwin, 1912. Republished as *Christmas*

Customs and Traditions: Their History and Significance. Dover, 1976.

Moore, Clifford Herschel. "On the Origin of the Taurobolium." *Harvard Studies in Classical Philology*, Vol. 17.

Nash, E. *Pictorial Dictionary of Ancient Rome.* Rev. ed. 2 vols. Thames & Hudson, 1968.

Näsström, Britt-Marie. *O Mother of the Gods and Men.* Plus Ultra, 1990.

Ogilvie, R. M. *The Romans and Their Gods in the Age of Augustus.* W. W. Norton, 1969.

Pallottino, M. *The Etruscans.* Translated by J. Cremona. Penguin Books, 1955.

Patch, Howard Rollin. *The Tradition of the Goddess Fortuna in Roman Literature and in the Transitional Period.* Folcroft Library Editions, 1976.

Perowne, Stewart. *Roman Mythology.* Paul Hamlyn, 1969.

Puhvel, Jaan. *Comparative Mythology.* Johns Hopkins University Press, 1987.

Rabinowitz, Jacob. *The Rotting Goddess: The Origin of the Witch in Classical Antiquity's Demonization of Fertility Religion.* Autonomedia, 1998.

Richardson, L. *A New Topographical Dictionary of Ancient Rome.* Johns Hopkins University Press, 1992.

Rives, J. B. *Religion and Authority in Roman Carthage from Augustus to Constantine.* Clarendon Press, 1955.

Robbins, Miriam. "The Assimilation of Pre-Indo-European Goddesses into Indo-European Society." *Journal of Indo-European Studies*, Vol. 8, Nos. 1 and 2.

Roller, Lynn E. *In Search of God the Mother: The Cult of Anatolian Cybele.* University of California Press, 1999.

Roscoe, Will. "Priests of the Goddess: Gender Transgression in Ancient Religion." *History of Religions*, Vol. 35.

Salyer, William Clark. "Swamp Goddess." *Classical Journal*, Vol. 42, No. 7.

Scheid, John. *An Introduction to Roman Religion.* Edinburgh University Press, 2003.

Shields, Emily Ledyard. *Juno: A Study in Early Roman Religion.* Smith College Classical Studies, No. 7.

Showerman, Grant. *The Great Mother of the Gods.* Bulletin of the University of Wisconsin, Philology and Literature Series, Vol. 1, No. 3.

Smith, William. *Dictionary of Greek and Roman Biography and Mythology.* C. C. Little and J. Brown, 1870.

Spaeth, Barbette Stanley. *The Roman Goddess Ceres.* University of Texas Press, 1996.

Staples, Ariadne. *From Good Goddess to Vestal Virgins: Sex and Category in Roman Religion.* Routledge, 1998.

Strong, E. "Terra Mater or Italia?" *Journal of Roman Studies*, Vol. 27, Part 1.

Taylor, Lily. "The Mother of the Lares." *American Journal of Archaeology*, Vol. 29, No. 3.

Tyldesley, Joyce. *Daughters of Isis: Women of Ancient Egypt.* Penguin Books, 1994.

Vermaseren, Maarten J. *Cybele and Attis: The Myth and the Cult.* Translated by A. M. H. Lemmers. Thames and Hudson, 1977.

Versnel, H. S. "The Festival for Bona Dea and the Thesmophoria." *Greece & Rome*, 2nd Series, Vol. 39, No. 1.

Von Vacano, Otto-Wilhelm. *The Etruscans in the Ancient World.* St. Martin's Press, 1960.

Whatmough, Joshua. "Rehtia, the Venetic Goddess of Healing." *Journal of the Royal Anthropological Institute of Great Britain and Ireland*, Vol. 52.

Wildfang, Robin Lorsch. *Rome's Vestal Virgins.* Routledge, 2006.

Witt, R. E. *Isis in the Graeco-Roman World.* Cornell University Press, 1971.

Woodard, Roger D. *Indo-European Sacred Space: Vedic and Roman Cult.* University of Illinois Press, 2006.

Ziolkowski, Adam. "Between Geese and the Auguraculum: The Origin of the Cult of Juno on the Arx." *Classical Philology*, Vol. 88, No. 3.

Zuntz, Günther. *Persephone: Three Essays on Religion and Thought in Magna Graecia.* Clarendon Press, 1971.

SCANDINAVIA

Primary Textual Sources in Translation

Bede, The Venerable. *The Reckoning of Time.* Translated by Faith Wallis. Liverpool University Press, 1999.

Dronke, Ursula, trans. *The Poetic Edda I* (Heroic Poems). Clarendon Press, 1969.

———. *The Poetic Edda II* (Mythological Poems). Clarendon Press, 1997.

Durrenberger, Paul, and Dorothy Durrenberger. *The Saga of Hávarur of Ísafjörður, with an Essay on the Political, Economic and Cultural Background of the Saga.* Hisarlik Press, 1996.

Gibbs, Marion E., and Sidney M. Johnson, trans. *Kudrun.* Vol. 79, Series B, Garland Library of Medieval Literature. Garland Publishing, 1992.

Heaney, Seamus. *Beowulf: A New Verse Translation.* W. W. Norton, 2000.

Hollander, Lee M., trans. *The Poetic Edda.* 2nd ed., revised. University of Texas Press, 1988.

Kernshaw, N., ed. and trans. *Anglo-Saxon and Norse Poems.* University Press, 1922.

Saxo (Grammaticus, Saxo). *The History of the Danes,* Books

I–IX. Translated by Hilda Ellis Davidson and Peter Fisher. D. S. Brewer, 2002.

Shumway, Daniel Bussie, trans. *Nibelungenlied*. Houghton Mifflin, 1909.

Sturluson, Snorri. *Heimskringla, or the Lives of the Norse Kings*. Edited by Erling Monson. Dover Publications, 1990.

———. *The Prose Edda*. Translated by Arthur Gilchrist Brodeur. American-Scandinavian Foundation, 1929.

Tacitus. *Dialogus, Agricola, Germania*. The Loeb Classical Library. Harvard University Press, 1914.

Primary Oral Sources in Translation

Grimm, Jacob. *Teutonic Mythology*. Translated by James Steven Stallybrass. G. Bell Sons, 1883.

Grimm, Jacob, and Wilhelm Grimm. *The Complete Fairy Tales of the Brothers Grimm*. Translated by Jack Zipes. Bantam Books, 1987.

———. *The Complete Grimm's Fairy Tales*. Introduction by Padraic Colum. Commentary by Joseph Campbell. Pantheon Books, 1972.

Kvideland, Reimund, and H. K. Sehmsdorf. *Scandinavian Folk Belief and Legend*. Minnesota University Press, 1988.

Lindow, John. *Swedish Legend and Folktales*. University of California Press, 1978.

Rumpf, Marianne, Anthony Hellenberg, and Elizabeth Tucker. "The Legends of Bertha in Switzerland." *Journal of the Folklore Institute*, Vol. 14, No. 3.

Simpson, Jacqueline, trans. and ed. *Scandinavian Folktales*. Penguin Books, 1988.

Other Sources

Anderson, Sarah M., with Karen Swenson. *Cold Counsel: Women in Old Norse Literature and Mythology*. Routledge, 2002.

Baring-Gould, Sabine. *Curious Myths of the Middle Ages*. Longmans, Green, and Company, 1901.

Battaglia, F. "The Germanic Earth Goddess in *Beowulf*." *Mankind Quarterly*, Vol. 35, No. 1/2.

Bauschatz, Paul C. *The Well and the Tree: World and Time in Early Germanic Culture*. University of Massachusetts Press, 1982.

Berger, Pamela. *The Goddess Obscured: Transformation of the Grain Protectress from Goddess to Saint*. Beacon Press, 1985.

Bottigheimer, Ruth B. *Grimms' Bad Girls and Bold Boys: The Moral and Social Vision of the Tales*. Yale University Press, 1987.

Davidson, H. R. Ellis. *Gods and Myths of Northern Europe*. Penguin Books, 1964.

———. *The Road to Hel: A Study of the Conception of the Dead in Old Norse Literature*. Greenwood Press, 1968.

———. *Roles of the Northern Goddess*. Routledge, 1998.

———. *Scandinavian Mythology*. Hamlyn Publishing, 1969.

———. "The Smith and the Goddess: Two Figures on the Franks Casket from Auzon." *Frühmittelalterliche Studien*, Vol. 3.

Dumézil, Georges. *Gods of the Ancient Northmen*. Edited by Enar Haugen. University of California Press, 1973.

Enright, M. "The Goddess Who Weaves," *Frühmittelalterliche Studien*, Vol. 24.

Gildersleeve, Virginia C. "Brynhild in Legend and Literature." *Modern Philology*, Vol. 6, No. 3.

Gimbutas, Marija. *The Language of the Goddess*. Thames and Hudson, 1989.

Grundy, Stephan. "Freyja and Frigg." In Billington, Sandra, and Miranda Green, eds. *The Concept of the Goddess*. Routledge, 1996.

Guerber, H. A. *Myths of Northern Lands*. Singing Tree Press, 1970.

Jesch, Judith. *Women in the Viking Age*. Boydell, 1991.

Jochens, Jenny. *Old Norse Images of Women*. University of Pennsylvania Press, 1996.

Larrington, Carolyne. "Scandinavia." In Larrington, Carolyne, ed. *The Feminist Companion to Mythology*. HarperCollins, 1992.

List, Edgar A. "Holda and the Venusberg." *Journal of American Folklore*, Vol. 73, No. 290.

Lofstedt, Torsten Martin Gustaf. *Russian Legends about Forest Spirits in the Context of Northern European Mythology*. Unpublished dissertation in Slavic languages and literature. University of California, Berkeley, 1993.

McKinnell, John. *Both One and Many: Essays on Change and Variety in Late Norse Heathenism*. Philologia, 1994.

Motz, Lotte. "Gerd: A New Interpretation of the Lay of Skírnir." *Maal og mine*, 1981.

———. "Sister in the Cave: The Stature and the Function of the Female Figures in the Eddas." *Arkiv för nordisk filologi*, Vol. 95.

———. "The Winter Goddess: Percht, Holda, and Related Figures." *Folklore*, Vol. 95, No. 2.

Mundal, Else. "The Position of the Individual Gods and Goddesses in Various Types of Sources—with Special Reference to the Female Divinities." In Albäck, Tore, ed. *Old Norse and Finnish Religions and Cultic Place-Names*. Donne Institute for Research in Religious and Cultural History, 1990.

Näsström, Britt-Mari. "Freyja: A Goddess with Many Names." In Billington, Sandra, and Miranda Green, eds. *The Concept of the Goddess*. Routledge, 1996.

———. *Freyja: The Great Goddess of the North*. Lund Studies in the History of Religions 5. Lund University, 1995.

Ranke, Kurt. *Folktales of Germany*. Translated by Lotte Baumann. University of Chicago Press, 1966.

Raudvere, Catharina. "Now You See Her, Now You Don't: Some Notes on the Conception of Female Shape-Shifters in Scandinavian Tradition." In Billington, Sandra, and Miranda Green, eds. *The Concept of the Goddess*. Routledge, 1996.

Strömbäck, Dag. "The Concept of the Soul in Nordic Tradition." *Arkiv för nordisk filologi*, Vol. 31.

Thorpe, Benjamin. *Northern Mythology*. Vol. 1. Edward Lumley, 1851.

Turville-Petre, O. G. *Myth and Religion of the North: Religion of Ancient Scandinavia*. Holt, Reinhart & Winston, 1964.

SOUTHEASTERN EUROPE

Primary Oral and Textual Sources

Colarusso, John. *Nart Sagas from the Caucasus*. Princeton University Press, 2002.

Herodotus. *The Histories of Herodotus of Halicarnassus*. Translated by David Grene. University of Chicago Press, 1987.

Meyer, Marvin W., ed. *The Ancient Mysteries: A Sourcebook, Sacred Texts of the Mystery Religions of the Ancient Mediterranean World*. University of Pennsylvania Press, 1999.

Wardrop, Marjory, trans. *Georgian Folk Tales*. David Nutt, 1894.

Other Sources

Borgeaud, Philippe. *Mother of the Gods: From Cybele to the Virgin Mary*. Johns Hopkins University Press, 2004.

Charachidze, Georges. "The Religion and Myths of the Georgians of the Mountains." In Bonnefoy, Yves. *Mythologies*. University of Chicago Press, 1991.

Chaudhri, Anna. "The Caucasian Hunting-Divinity, Male and Female: Traces of the Hunting Goddess in Ossetic Folklore." In Billington, Sandra, and Miranda Green, eds. *The Concept of the Goddess*. Routledge, 1996.

Crowfoot, J. W. "The Lions of Kybele." *Journal of Hellenic Studies*, Vol. 20.

Davidson, Hilda Ellis, and Anna Chaudhri. "The Hair and the Dog." *Folklore*, Vol. 104, No. 1/2.

Hoddinott, R. F. *The Thracians*. Thames & Hudson, 1981.

Hubbs, Joanna. *Mother Russia: The Feminine Myth in Russian Culture*. Indiana University Press, 1993.

Jettmar, Karl. *Art of the Steppes*. Crown Publishers, 1964.

Macurdy, Grace Harriet. "The Origin of a Herodotean Tale in Connection with the Cult of the Spinning Goddess." *Transactions and Proceedings of the American Philological Association*, Vol. 43.

Munn, Mark. *The Mother of the Gods, Athens, and the Tyranny of Asia: A Study of Sovereignty in Ancient Religion*. University of California Press, 2006.

Näsström, Britt-Mari. *O Mother of the Gods and Men*. Plus Ultra, 1990.

Planeaux, Christopher. "The Date of Bendis' Entry into Attica." *Classical Journal*, Vol. 96, No. 2.

Roller, Lynn E. *In Search of God the Mother: The Cult of Anatolian Cybele*. University of California Press, 1999.

Showerman, Grant. *The Great Mother of the Gods*. Bulletin of the University of Wisconsin, Philology and Literature Series, Vol. 1, No. 3.

Smith, Cecil. "The Torch Race of Bendis." *Classical Review*, Vol. 13, No. 4.

Smith, William, ed. *Dictionary of Greek and Roman Biography and Mythology*. 2 vols. Harper & Brothers, 1893.

Tacheva-Hitova, Margarita. *Eastern Cults in Moesia Inferior and Thracia*. E. J. Brill, 1983.

Vassileva, Maya. "Further Considerations on the Cult of Kybele." *Anatolian Studies*, Vol. 51.

Vermaseren, Maarten J. *Cybele and Attis: The Myth and the Cult*. Thames and Hudson, 1977.

SLAVIC PEOPLES

Primary Oral Sources in Translation

Alexander, Alex E. *Russian Folklore: An Anthology in English Translation*. Nordland Publishing Company, 1975.

Dexter, Miriam Robbins. *Whence the Goddesses: A Sourcebook*. Pergamon Press, 1990.

Haney, Jack V., ed. and trans. *Russian Legends*. M. E. Sharpe, 2003.

Ralson, W. R. S. *The Songs of the Russian People: As Illustrative of Slavonic Mythology and Russian Social Life*. Haskell House, 1970.

Other Sources

Agapkina, Tatíana A. "On 'Todortsi,' 'Rusalki' and Other 'Navi'." *Studia Mythologica Slavica*, Vol. 2.

Barber, E. J. W. "On the Origins of the Vily/Rusalki." In

Dexter, Miriam Robbins, and Edgar C. Polomé. *Varia on the Indo-European Past: Papers in Memory of Marija Gimbutas.* Journal of Indo-European Studies. Monograph Number 19.

Frazer, James George. *The Golden Bough: A Study in Magic and Religion.* Abridged ed. Macmillan, 1922.

Georgieva, Ivanichka. *Bulgarian Mythology.* Svyat Publishers, 1985.

Gimbutas, Marija. *The Language of the Goddess.* Thames and Hudson, 1989.

———. "Slavic Religion." In Jones, Lindsay, ed. *Encyclopedia of Religion.* 2nd ed. Macmillan Reference, 2003.

———. *The Slavs.* New York, 1971.

Hatto, A. T. "Folk Ritual and the Minnesang." *Modern Language Review,* Vol. 58, No. 2.

Hubbs, Joanna. *Mother Russia: The Feminine Myth in Russian Culture.* Indiana University Press, 1993.

Hudec, Ivan. *Tales from Slavic Myths.* Bolchazy-Carducci Publishers, 2001.

Ivanits, Linda J. *Russian Folk Belief.* M. E. Sharpe, 1989.

Johns, Andreas. "Baba Iaga and the Russian Mother." *Slavic and East European Journal,* Vol. 42, No. 1.

Kelly, Mary B. *Goddess Embroideries of Eastern Europe.* Northland Press, 1989.

———. "Goddess Embroideries of Russia and the Ukraine." *Woman's Art Journal,* Vol. 4, No. 2.

Kmeietowicz, Frank. *Slavic Mythical Beliefs.* Frank Kmeietowicz, 1982.

Machal, J. *The Mythology of All Races,* Vol. 2: *Slavic Mythology.* Marshall Jones Company, 1918.

Manning, Clarence Augustus. "The Tauric Maiden and Allied Cults." *Transactions and Proceedings of the American Philological Association,* Vol. 51.

Matossian, Mary. "In the Beginning, God Was a Woman." *Journal of Social History,* Vol. 6, No. 3.

Mihanovich, Clement Simon. "Religious Folklore of the Poljica Region of Dalmatia." *Journal of American Folklore,* Vol. 61, No. 241.

Netting, Anthony. "Images and Ideas in Russian Peasant Art." *Slavic Review,* Vol. 35, No. 1.

Pocs, Eva. *Fairies and Witches at the Boundary of South-Eastern and Central Europe.* Academia Scientiarum Finnica, 1989.

Robbins, Miriam. "The Assimilation of Pre-Indo-European Goddesses into Indo-European Society." *Journal of Indo-European Studies,* Vol. 8, No. 1 & 2.

Rozhnova, Polina. *A Russian Folk Calendar.* Novosti, 1992.

Rybakov, B. A. *Old Slavic Paganism.* Izdatelstvo Nauka, 1981.

Simonov, Pyotr. *Essential Russian Mythology.* Thorsons, 1997.

Sokolov, Y. M. *Russian Folklore.* Folklore Associates, 1966.

Warner, Elizabeth. *Russian Myths.* University of Texas Press, 2002.

Welters, Linda, ed. *Folk Dress in Europe and Anatolia: Beliefs about Protection and Fertility.* Berg, 1999.

Yovino-Young, Marjorie. *Pagan Ritual and Myth in Russian Magic Tales: A Study of Patterns.* Edwin Mellen Press, 1993.

Znayenko, Myroslava T. *The Gods of the Ancient Slavs: Tatishchev and the Beginnings of Slavic Mythology.* Slavica, 1980.

THE AMERICAS
NORTH AMERICA
Primary Oral and Textual Sources

Barbeau, Charles M. *Huron and Wyandot Mythology.* Anthropological Series No. 11. Government Printing Bureau, 1915.

Barbeau, Marius. "Bear Mother." *Journal of American Folklore,* Vol. 59, No. 231.

———. *Haida Myths.* Bulletin No. 127, Anthropological Series No. 32. National Museum of Canada, 1953.

Beauchamp, William M. *Iroquois Folk Lore: Gathered from the Six Nations of New York.* Ira J. Friedman, 1922.

———. "Onondaga Tales." *Journal of American Folklore,* Vol. 6, No. 22.

Bierhorst, John. *The Mythology of North America.* William M. Morrow, 1985.

———. *Mythology of the Lenape: Guide and Texts.* University of Arizona Press, 1995.

———, ed. *The Red Swan: Myths and Tales of the American Indians.* Farrar, Straus and Giroux, 1976.

Blackburn, Thomas C. *December's Child: A Book of Chumash Oral Narratives.* University of California Press, 1975.

Boas, Franz. *Indian Myths and Legends from the North Pacific Coast of America.* Translated by Dietrich Bertz and edited by Randy Bouchard and Dorothy Kennedy. Talon Books, 2002.

———. *Kwakiutl Ethnography.* Edited by Helen Codere. University of Chicago Press, 1966.

———. *The Mythology of the Bella Coola Indians: The Jesup North Pacific Expedition.* Anthropology I. Memoirs of the American Museum of Natural History, Vol. 2, 1901.

———. "Traditions of the Ts'ets'a'ut I." *Journal of American Folklore,* Vol. 9, No. 35.

Bruchac, Joseph. *Iroquois Stories: Heroes and Heroines, Monsters and Magic.* Crossing Press, 1985.

———. *Return of the Sun: Native American Tales from the Northeast Woodlands.* Crossing Press, 1989.

Carnsell, Charles, and C. M. Barbeau. "Loucheux Myths." *Journal of American Folklore*, Vol. 28, No. 109.

Clark, Cora, and Texa Bowen Williams. *Pomo Indian Myths*. Vantage Press, 1954.

Clark, Ella. *Indian Legends from the Northern Rockies*. University of Oklahoma Press, 1966.

———. *Indian Legends of the Pacific Northwest*. University of California Press, 1953.

Connelley, William Elsey. *Wyandot Folk-Lore*. Crane and Company, 1899.

Converse, Harriet Maxwell. *Myths and Legends of the New York Iroquois*. Ira J. Friedman, 1962.

Curtin, Jeremiah. *Myths of the Modocs: Indian Legends of the Northwest*. Benjamin Blom, 1971.

———. *Native American Creation Myths*. Reprint of *Creation Myths of Primitive America in Relation to the Religious History and Mental Development of Mankind*. Dover Publications, 2004.

———. *Seneca Indian Myths*. E. P. Dutton, 1923.

Deans, James. "Legend of the Fin-Back Whale Crest of the Haidas, Queen Charlotte Island, B.C." *Journal of American Folklore*, Vol. 5, No. 16.

———. "The Story of the Bear and His Indian Wife: A Legend of the Haidas of Queen Charlotte Island, B.C." *Journal of American Folklore*, Vol. 2, No. 7.

Dooling, D. M., ed. *The Sons of the Wind: The Sacred Stories of the Lakota*. University of Oklahoma Press, 2000.

Dorsey, George. *The Pawnee Mythology*. University of Nebraska Press, 1997.

———. *Traditions of the Arikara*. Carnegie Institution, 1904.

Elm, Demus, and Harvey Antone. *The Oneida Creation Story*. University of Nebraska Press, 2000.

Erdoes, Richard, and Alfonso Ortiz, eds. *American Indian Myths and Legends*. Pantheon Books, 1984.

Farrand, Livingston, and Theresa Mayer. "Quileute Tales." *Journal of American Folklore*, Vol. 32, No. 124.

Giddings, Ruth Warner, ed. *Yaqui Myths and Legends*. University of Arizona Press, 1993.

Gifford, Edward, and Gwendolyn Block. *A California Indian Night's Entertainment*. Arthur Clark Company, 1930.

Griffin, Arthur. *More Ah Mo: Indian Legends from the Northwest*. Hancock House, 1993.

Grinnell, George Bird. "Pawnee Mythology." *Journal of American Folklore*, Vol. 6, No. 21.

Haeberlin, Hermann, and Franz Boas. "Mythology of Puget Sound." *Journal of American Folklore*, Vol. 37, No. 145/146.

Hardin, Terri, ed. *Legends and Lore of the American Indians*. Barnes and Noble, 1993.

Hausman, Gerald. *The Gift of the Gila Monster: Navaho Ceremonial Tales*. Simon and Schuster, 1993.

Hewitt, J. N. B. *Iroquoian Cosmology*. AMS Press, 1974.

Johnston, Basil. *The Manitous: The Spiritual World of the Ojibway*. Minnesota Historical Society Press, 2001.

Judson, Katharine Berry, ed. *Myths and Legends of British North America*. A. C. McClurg, 1917.

Kilpatrick, Jack F., and Anna G. Kilpatrick. *Friends of Thunder: Folktales of the Oklahoma Cherokees*. Southern Methodist University Press, 1964.

Kurath, Gertrude Prokosch, with Antonio Garcia. *Music and Dance of the Tewa Pueblos*. Museum of New Mexico Press, 1970.

Leeming, David, and Jake Page. *The Mythology of North America*. University of Oklahoma Press, 1998.

Leland, Charles. *Algonquin Legends of New England*. Houghton Mifflin, 1884. Reprint, Dover Publications, 1962.

Lévi-Strauss, Claude. *The Raw and the Cooked*. Translated by John and Doreen Weightman. Harper and Row, 1969.

Levy, Jerrold E. *In the Beginning: The Navaho Genesis*. University of California Press, 1998.

Long, John. *Pale Moon: Tales of the American Indian*. ICS Books, 1995.

Lowenstein, Tom. *Mother Earth, Father Sky: Native American Myth*. Buncan Baird Publishers, 1997.

Mayer, Therese. "Quileute Tales." *Journal of American Folklore*, Vol. 32, No. 124.

McCutchen, David, trans. *The Red Record/The Wallam Olum*. Avery Publishing, 1993.

McIlwraith, T. F. *The Bella Coola Indians*. University of Toronto Press, 1948.

Melançon, Claude. *Indian Legends of Canada*. Gage Publishing, 1974.

Merriam, C. Hart. *The Dawn of the World: Myths and Weird Tales Told by the Mewuk Indians of California*. Arthur H. Clark Company, 1910.

Mooney, James. "Myths of the Cherokees." *Journal of American Folklore*, Vol. 1, No. 2.

Mullett, G. M. *Spider Woman Stories: Legends of the Hopi Indians*. University of Arizona Press, 1979.

Newcomb, Franc J. "Origin Legend of the Navaho Eagle Chant." *Journal of American Folklore*, Vol. 53, No. 207.

Nicolar, Joseph. *The Life and Traditions of the Red Man*. Edited by Annette Kolodny. Duke University Press, 2007.

Parker, Arthur C. *Seneca Myths and Folk Tales*. University of Nebraska Press, 1989.

Parsons, Elsie Clews. "Laguna Tales." *Journal of American Folklore*, Vol. 44, No. 172.

———. *Tewa Tales*. University of Arizona Press, 1994.

Skinner, Alanson. "Traditions of the Iowa Indians." *Journal of American Folklore*, Vol. 38, No. 150.

Skinner, Alanson, and John V. Satterlee. *Folklore of the Menomini Indians*. Anthropological Papers of the American Museum of Natural History. Vol. 13, Part 3, 1915.

Smith, David Lee. *Folklore of the Winnebago Tribe*. University of Oklahoma Press, 1997.

Speck, Frank G. *Ethnology of the Yucchi Indians*. University Museum, 1909.

———. "Montagnais and Naskapi Tales from the Labrador Peninsula." *Journal of American Folklore*, Vol. 28, No. 147.

———. "Penobscot Tales and Religious Beliefs." *Journal of American Folklore*, Vol. 48, No. 187.

Stephen, Alexander. "Hopi Tales." *Journal of American Folklore*, Vol. 42, No. 163.

———. "Navaho Origin Myth." *Journal of American Folklore*, Vol. 43, No. 167.

Stern, Theodore. "Klamath Myth Abstracts." *Journal of American Folklore*, Vol. 76, No. 299.

Swann, Brian. *Voices from Four Directions: Contemporary Translations of the Native Literatures of North America*. University of Nebraska Press, 2004.

Swanton, John R. *Haida Texts and Myths*. Smithsonian Institution Bureau of Ethnology, Bulletin 29, 1905.

———. *Myths and Tales of the Southeastern Indians*. University of Oklahoma Press, 1929.

———. *Social Condition, Beliefs, and Linguistic Relationship of the Tlingit Indians*. Extract from 26th Annual Report of the Bureau of American Ethnology. Government Printing Office, 1908.

———. *Source Material for the Social and Ceremonial Life of the Choctaw Indians*. University of Alabama Press, 2001.

———. *Tlingit Myths and Texts*. Smithsonian Institution Bureau of Ethnology, Bulletin 39, 1909.

Teit, James A. "Tahltan Tales." *Journal of American Folklore*, Vol. 32, No. 124.

———. "Tahltan Tales (Continued)." *Journal of American Folklore*, Vol. 34, No. 134.

Thompson, Stith. *Tales of the North American Indians*. Indiana University Press, 1972.

Titiev, Mischa. "Two Hopi Myths and Rites." *Journal of American Folklore*, Vol. 61, No. 239.

Uguwiyuak. *Journey to Sunrise: Myths and Legends of the Cherokee*. Egi Press, 1977.

Other Sources

Allen, Paula Gunn. *Grandmothers of the Light: A Medicine Woman's Sourcebook*. Beacon Press, 1991.

———. *The Sacred Hoop: Recovering the Feminine in American Indian Traditions*. Beacon Press, 1986.

Awaikta, Marilou. *Selu: Seeking the Corn-Mother's Wisdom*. Fulcrum Publishing, 1993.

Beauchamp, W. M. "Indian Corn Stories and Customs." *Journal of American Folklore*, Vol. 11, No. 41.

Berlo, Janet. "Dreaming of Double Woman: The Ambivalent Role of the Female Artist in North American Indian Myth." *American Indian Quarterly*, Vol. 17, No. 1.

Caduto, Michael J. *Earth Tales from around the World*. Fulcrum Publishing, 1997.

Capps, Walter Holden, ed. *Seeing with a Native Eye: Essays on Native American Religion*. Harper and Row, 1976.

Elledge, Jim. *Gay, Lesbian, Bisexual and Transgender Myths from the Arapaho to the Zuñi: An Anthology*. Peter Lang, 2002.

Hale, Horatio. "Huron Folk-Lore. I. Cosmogonic Myths. The Good and Evil Minds." *Journal of American Folklore*, Vol. 1, No. 3.

Johnston, Basil. *The Manitous: The Spiritual World of the Ojibway*. Minnesota Historical Society Press, 2001.

Judson, Katharine B., ed. *Native American Legends of the Great Lakes and the Mississippi River*. Northern Illinois University Press, 2000.

Krause, Aurel. *The Tlingit Indians: Results of a Trip to the Northwest Coast of America and the Bering Straits*. University of Washington Press, 1970.

LaBarre, Weston. "Kiowa Folk Sciences." *Journal of American Folklore*, Vol. 60, No. 263.

Matthews, Washington. *Navaho Legends*. University of Utah Press, 1994.

Miller, Dorcas. *Stars of the First People: Native American Star Myths and Constellations*. Pruett Publishing, 1997.

Moon, Sheila. *A Magic Dwells: A Poetic and Psychological Study of the Navaho Emergence Myth*. Wesleyan University Press, 1970.

Mooney, James. "The Cherokee River Cult." *Journal of American Folklore*, Vol. 13, No. 48.

Neithammer, Carolyn. *Daughters of the Earth: The Lives and Legends of American Indian Women*. Macmillan, 1977.

Powers, Marla N. *Oglala Women: Myth, Ritual and Reality*. University of Chicago Press, 1986.

Reichard, Gladys. *Navaho Religion: A Study of Symbolism*. Bollingen Series. Princeton University Press, 1970.

Roscoe, Will. *Changing Ones: Third and Fourth Genders in Native North America*. St. Martin's Press, 1998.

Royals, Debbie. "Creation: The Talking Tree." *First Peoples Theology Journal*, September 2001.

Schutz, Noel William. *The Study of Shawnee Myth in an*

Ethnographic and Ethnohistorical Perspective. PhD dissertation, Department of Anthropology, Indiana University, 1975.

Spence, Lewis. *Myths and Legends of the North American Indians*. Senate, 1994.

Steltenkamp, Michael F. *The Sacred Vision: Native American Religion and Its Practice Today*. Paulist Press, 1982.

Sullivan, Lawrence E., ed. *Native Religions and Cultures of North America*. Continuum, 2000.

Swanton, John. *Social Condition, Beliefs, and Linguistic Relationship of the Tlingit Indians*. Extract from 26th Annual Report of the Bureau of American Ethnology. Government Printing Office, 1908.

Taylor, Colin F. *Myths of the North American Indians*. Laurence King, 1995.

Tyler, Hamilton A. *Pueblo Gods and Myths*. University of Oklahoma Press, 1964.

Vecsey, Christopher, ed. *Religion in Native North America*. University of Idaho Press, 1990.

Voegelin, C. F. "The Shawnee Female Deity." Yale University Publications in Anthropology No. 10. Reprinted, Human Relations Area Files, 1970.

Walker, James R. *Lakota Belief and Ritual*. Edited by Raymond J. DeMallie and Elaine A. Jahner. University of Nebraska Press, 1980.

Waters, Frank. *The Book of the Hopi*. Drawings and source material recorded by Oswald White Bear Fredericks. Penguin Books, 1977.

Weigle, Marta. "Creation and Procreation, Cosmology and Childbirth: Reflections on Ex Nihilo, Earth Diver, and Emergence Mythology." *Journal of American Folklore*, Vol. 100, No. 398.

———. *Creation and Procreation: Feminist Reflections on Mythologies of Cosmogony and Parturition*. University of Pennsylvania Press, 1989.

———. *Spiders and Spinsters*. University of New Mexico Press, 1985.

Wherry, Joseph H. *Indian Masks and Myths of the West*. Funk & Wagnall's, 1969.

MESOAMERICA

Primary Oral and Textual Sources

Alarcón, Hernando Ruiz de. *Treatise on the Heathen Superstitions*. Translated and edited by J. Richard Andrews and Ross Hassig. University of Oklahoma Press, 1984.

Bierhorst, John, trans. and ed. *History and Mythology of the Aztecs: The Codex Chimalpopoca*. University of Arizona Press, 1992.

Christenson, A. *Popol Vuh: The Sacred Book of the Maya*. O Books, 2003.

Durán, Fray Diego. *Book of the Gods and Rites and the Ancient Calendar*. University of Oklahoma Press, 1971.

Graulich, Michel. *Myths of Ancient Mexico*. Translated by Bernard R. and Thelma Ortiz de Montellano. University of Oklahoma Press, 1997.

Léon-Portilla, Miguel, ed. *Native Mesoamerican Spirituality: Ancient Hymns, Discourses, Stories, Doctrines, Hymns, Poems from the Aztec, Yucatec, Quiche-Maya and Other Sacred Traditions*. Paulist Press, 1980.

Sahagún, Fr. Bernardino de, Arthur J. O. Anderson, and Charles E. Dibble, eds. *The Florentine Codex: General History of the Things of New Spain*. School of American Research and the University of Utah Press, 1982.

Other Sources

Barakat, Robert. "Wailing Women of Folklore." *Journal of American Folklore*, Vol. 82, No. 325.

Bierhorst, John, ed. *The Red Swan: Myths and Tales of the American Indians*. Farrar, Straus and Giroux, 1976.

Boone, Elizabeth Hill, ed. *The Art and Iconography of Late Post-Classic Central Mexico*. Dumbarton Oaks, 1977.

Brady, James E., and Keith M. Prufer. "Caves and Crystal-mancy: Evidence for the Use of Crystals in Ancient Maya Religion." *Journal of Anthropological Research*, Vol. 55, No. 1.

Brundage, Burr Cartwright. *The Fifth Sun: Aztec Gods, Aztec Worlds*. University of Texas Press, 1979.

Carrasco, Davíd. "Cosmic Jaws: We Eat the Gods and the Gods Eat Us." *Journal of the American Academy of Religion*, Vol. 63, No. 3.

Caso, Alfonso. *The Aztecs: People of the Sun*. University of Oklahoma Press, 1958.

Castillo, Ana. *Goddess of the Americas/La Diosa de las Américas: Writings on the Virgin of Guadalupe*. Riverhead Books, 1996.

Clendinnen, Inga. *Aztecs: An Interpretation*. Cambridge University Press, 1991.

Couch, N. C. Christopher. *The Festival Cycle of the Aztec Codex Borbonicus*. BAR International Series 270, 1985.

Driver, Harold E., and William C. Massey. "Comparative Studies of North American Indians." *Transactions of the American Philosophical Society*, New Series, Vol. 47, No. 2.

Elzey, Wayne. "A Hill on a Land Surrounded by Water: An Aztec Story of Origin and Destiny." *History of Religions*, Vol. 31, No. 2.

Gingerich, Willard. "Three Nahuatl Hymns on the Mother

Archetype: An Interpretive Commentary." *Mexican Studies/Estudios Mexicanos*, Vol. 4, No. 2.

Haly, Richard. "Bare Bones: Rethinking Mesoamerican Divinity." *History of Religions*, Vol. 31, No. 3.

Harrington, Patricia. "Mother of Death, Mother of Rebirth: The Mexican Virgin of Guadalupe." *Journal of the American Academy of Religion*, Vol. 56, No. 1.

Heyden, Doris. "An Interpretation of the Cave underneath the Pyramid of the Sun in Teotihuacan, Mexico." *American Antiquity*, Vol. 40, No. 2.

Josserand, J. Kathryn, and Karen Dakin, eds. *Smoke and Mist: Mesoamerican Studies in Memory of Thelma D. Sullivan.* Part I. BAR, 1988.

Kellogg, Susan. "The Woman's Room: Some Aspects of Gender Relations in Tenochtitlan in the Late Pre-Hispanic Period." *Ethnohistory*, Vol. 42, No. 4, Women, Power, and Resistance in Colonial Mesoamerica.

Kelly, Patricia Fernandez. "Death in Mexican Folk Culture." *American Quarterly*, Vol. 26, No. 5, Special Issue: Death in America.

Klein, Cecelia F. "Teocuitlatl, 'Divine Excrement': The Significance of 'Holy Shit' in Ancient Mexico." *Art Journal*, Vol. 52, No. 3, Scatological Art.

Motz, Lotte. *The Faces of the Goddess.* Oxford University Press, 1997.

Nash, June. "The Aztecs and the Ideology of Male Dominance." *Signs*, Vol. 4, No. 2.

———. "Gendered Deities and the Survival of Culture." *History of Religions*, Vol. 36, No. 4.

Paxton, Merideth. *The Cosmos of the Yucatec Maya: Cycles and Steps from the Madrid Codex.* University of New Mexico Press, 2001.

Pohl, John M. D. "Nahua Drinking Bowl with an Image of Xochiquetzal." *Record of the Art Museum*, Princeton University, Vol. 63.

Schwerin, Karl H. "Ceremonies Concerned with Hail and Rain in Tlaxcala." *Journal of American Folklore*, Vol. 76, No. 301.

Taylor, William B. "The Virgin of Guadalupe in New Spain: An Inquiry into the Social History of Marian Devotion." *American Ethnologist*, Vol. 14, No. 1.

Tedlock, Barbara. *The Woman in the Shaman's Body: Reclaiming the Feminine in Religion and Medicine.* Bantam Books, 2005.

Weigle, Marta. "Mexican Mythology: Divine Androgyny but 'His' Story: The Female in Aztec Mythology." In Larrington, Carolyne, ed. *The Feminist Companion to Mythology.* HarperCollins, 1992.

Weigle, Marta, and Peter White. *The Lore of New Mexico.* University of New Mexico Press, 1988.

Wolf, Eric R. "The Virgin of Guadalupe: A Mexican National Symbol." *Journal of American Folklore*, Vol. 71, No. 279.

Zingg, Robert M. *Huichol Mythology.* University of Arizona Press, 2004.

SOUTH AMERICA AND THE CARIBBEAN

Primary Oral and Textual Sources

Arriaga, Pablo Joseph de. *The Extirpation of Idolatry in Peru.* Translated and edited by L. Clark Keating. University of Kentucky Press, 1968.

Wilbert, Johannes, ed. *Folk Literature of the Selknam Indians: Martin Gusinde's Collection of Selknam Narratives.* University of California Press, 1975.

———. *Folk Literature of the Yamana Indians: Martin Gusinde's Collection of Yamana Narratives.* University of California Press, 1977.

———. *Yupa Folktales.* University of California Latin American Center, 1974.

Wilbert, Johannes, and Karin Simoneau, eds. *Folk Literature of the Bororo Indians.* UCLA Latin American Center Publications, 1983.

———. *Folk Literature of the Yanomani Indians.* UCLA Latin American Center Publications, 1990.

Other Sources

Alexander, Hartley Burr. *Mythology of All Races.* Vol. 11: *Latin America.* Cooper Square, 1964.

Arrom, José Juan. "The Creation Myths of the Taíno." In Bercht, Fatima, Estrellita Brodsky, John Farmer, and Dicey Taylor, eds. *Taíno: Pre-Columbian Art and Culture from the Caribbean.* Monacelli Press, 1997.

Bandelier, Adolph F. "Aboriginal Myths and Traditions Concerning the Island of Titicaca, Bolivia." *American Anthropologist*, New Series, Vol. 6, No. 2.

Basso, Ellen. *A Musical View of the Universe: Kalapalo Myth and Ritual Performances.* University of Pennsylvania Press, 1985.

Becher, Hans. "Moon and Reincarnation: Anthropogenesis as Imagined by the Sunára and Pakidái Indians of Northwestern Brazil." In Bharti, Agehananda, ed. *Realm of the Extra-Human: Agents and Audiences.* Mouton, 1976.

Bierhorst, John. *Black Rainbow: Legends of the Incas and Myths of Ancient Peru.* Farrar, Straus and Giroux, 1976.

———. *The Mythology of South America.* William Morrow, 1988.

Brett, W. H. *The Indian Tribes of Guiana: Their Condition and Habits.* Bell and Daldy, 1968.

Brown, Michael. *Tsewa's Gift: Magic and Meaning in an Amazonian Society.* Smithsonian Institution Press, 1985.

Brown, Michael F., and Margaret L. Van Bolt. "Aguaruna Jivaro Gardening Magic in the Alto Rio Mayo, Peru." *Ethnology*, Vol. 19, No. 2.

Harner, Michael. *The Jívaro: People of the Sacred Waterfalls.* Doubleday, Natural History Press, 1972.

Jones, David. *Mythology of the Incas.* Southwater, 2003.

Karsten, Rafael. *The Toba Indians of the Bolivian Gran Chaco.* Acta Academiae Aboensis, Humaniora IV. Anthropological Publications, 1967.

Koppers, Wilhelm. "On the Origins of the Mysteries." In Campbell, Joseph, ed. *The Mystic Vision: Papers from the Eranos Yearbooks.* Princeton University Press, 1968.

Lamadrid, Enrique R. "Treasures of the Mama Huaca: Oral Tradition and Ecological Consciousness in Chinchaysuyu." *Journal of Folklore Research*, Vol. 29, No. 3.

Langdon, E. Jean Matteson, and Gerhard Baer. *Portals of Power: Shamanism in South America.* University of New Mexico Press, 1992.

Lyon, Patricia J., ed. *Native South Americans: Ethnology of the Least Known Continent.* Waveland Press, 1974.

Metraux, Alfred. *Myths of the Toba and Pilagá Indians of the Gran Chaco.* American Folklore Society, 1946.

Murphy, Yoland, and Robert M. Murphy. *Women of the Forest.* Columbia University Press, 1974.

Osbourne, Harold. *South American Mythology.* Paul Hamlyn, 1968.

Paper, Jordan. "Through the Earth Darkly: The Female Spirit in Native American Religions." In Vecsey, Christopher, ed. *Religion in Native North America.* University of Idaho Press, 1990.

Reichel-Dolmantoff, Geraldo. *Amazonian Cosmos: The Sexual and Religious Symbolism of the Tukano Indians.* University of Chicago Press, 1971.

Roth, H. Ling. "The Aborigines of Hispaniola." *Journal of the Anthropological Institute of Great Britain and Ireland*, Vol. 16.

Salles-Reese, Verónica. *From Viracocha to the Virgin of Copacabana: Representation of the Sacred at Lake Titicaca.* University of Texas Press, 1997.

Steele, Paul R. *Handbook of Inca Mythology.* ABC-CLIO, 2004.

Steward, Julian. *Handbook of South American Indians.* 2 vols. Cooper Square, 1963.

Von Hagen, V. Wolfgang. *The Tsátchela Indians of Western Ecuador.* Museum of the American Indian, 1939.

Wagley, Charles. *Welcome of Tears: The Tapirapé Indians of Central Brazil.* Oxford University Press, 1977.

Wilbert, Johannes. *Folk Literature of the Warao Indians: Narrative Material and Motif Content.* University of California Latin American Center, 1970.

INDEX

ABOUT THE AUTHOR

Photo by Linda Schwartz

Patricia Monaghan (1946–2012) was a pathbreaker and leader in the contemporary women's spirituality movement as well as an award-winning poet, scholar, activist, and mentor. Born in Brooklyn, New York, to Irish American parents, Patricia spent her early years in Queens surrounded by a large extended family. Her family moved to Colorado following the transfer of her father, an Air Force officer, and then to Alaska.

Patricia earned her undergraduate and first graduate degrees at the University of Minnesota, where she studied English and French literature. She worked as a journalist in both Minnesota and Alaska, writing about culture, nature, and the intersection of the two. She later earned an MFA in creative writing (poetry) from the University of Alaska and a doctorate in interdisciplinary studies (science and literature) from the Union Institute in Cincinnati. In 1995, she joined the faculty of the School for New Learning at DePaul University, where she was a professor in arts and environmental sciences.

In 1979, she published the first encyclopedia of female divinities, a book that has remained in print since then in various formats and that she later expanded into the current volume. She also published *The Encyclopedia of Celtic Mythology and Folklore* and edited a three-volume collection of essays titled *Goddesses in World Culture*. Patricia brought her life-long interest in Ireland together with her commitment to women's spirituality in *The Red-Haired Girl from the Bog: The Landscape of Celtic Myth and Spirit*, a travelogue of Irish heritage sites and their relation to goddess figures. Her other books on goddesses include *The Goddess Path* and *The Goddess Companion*, both introductory books on the subject; *Wild Girls: The Path of the Young Goddess*, a collection of stories for girls about

431

youthful goddesses; and *Magical Gardens*. She was awarded the Pushcart Prize in literature and the Paul Gruchow Award for Nature Writing. She also wrote five books of poetry, each centered on a specific theme. *Seasons of the Witch* won the Friends of Literature Award for poetry and the COVR award for best multimedia work. Her most recent, *Sanctuary*, drew from two areas dear to her, Ireland's West and Wisconsin's Driftless Area, where she made her home.

A longtime member of the Society of Friends (Quakers), Patricia was also a companion of the Fourth Order of Francis and Clare, an interfaith religious organization, as well as a member of SIEF, the European folklore society. She painted a picture of a different—and, she thought, better—world in her art, and at the same time tried to bring a better world to life with her teaching, mentoring, activism, and organizational talents. She was a founder of and senior fellow at the Black Earth Institute (Wisconsin), dedicated to having art serve spirit, earth, and society, and a leader in the founding and development of the Association for the Study of Women and Mythology.